A Companion
to Heidegger

Blackwell Companions to Philosophy

This outstanding student reference series offers a comprehensive and authoritative survey of philosophy as a whole. Written by today's leading philosophers, each volume provides lucid and engaging coverage of the key figures, terms, topics, and problems of the field. Taken together, the volumes provide the ideal basis for course use, representing an unparalleled work of reference for students and specialists alike.

A Companion to Heidegger

Edited by

Hubert L. Dreyfus

and

Mark A. Wrathall

Blackwell
Publishing

BLACKWELL PUBLISHING
350 Main Street, Malden, MA 02148-5020, USA
108 Cowley Road, Oxford OX4 1JF, UK
550 Swanston Street, Carlton, Victoria 3053, Australia

First published 2005 by Blackwell Publishing Ltd

Library of Congress Cataloging-in-Publication Data

A companion to Heidegger / edited by Hubert L. Dreyfus and Mark A. Wrathall.
    p. cm.—(Blackwell companions to philosophy)
  Includes bibliographical references and index.
  ISBN 1-4051-1092-9 (hardcover : alk. paper)
  1. Heidegger, Martin, 1889–1976. I. Dreyfus, Hubert L. II. Wrathall, Mark A. III. Title. IV. Series.

B3279.H49C64 2004
193—dc22

2004019151

A catalogue record for this title is available from the British Library.

Set in 10/12.5 Photina
by SNP Best-set Typesetter Ltd, Hong Kong
Printed and bound in the United Kingdom
by MPG Books Ltd, Bodmin, Cornwall

The publisher's policy is to use permanent paper from mills that operate a sustainable forestry policy, and which has been manufactured from pulp processed using acid-free and elementary chlorine-free practices. Furthermore, the publisher ensures that the text paper and cover board used have met acceptable environmental accreditation standards.

For further information on
Blackwell Publishing, visit our website:
www.blackwellpublishing.com

Contents

Notes on Contributors

William Blattner is Associate Professor of Philosophy at Georgetown University and the author of *Heidegger's Temporal Idealism* (1999).

Edgar C. Boedeker Jr received his PhD from Northwestern University. During his graduate studies, he spent three semesters studying Heidegger at the University of Freiburg, Germany, with a fellowship from the German Academic Exchange Service (DAAD). He also conducted postdoctoral research at the Edmund-Husserl-Achiv in Leuven, Belgium. He is currently an Assistant Professor of Philosophy at the University of Northern Iowa, where he teaches phenomenology, philosophy of language, history of philosophy, and logic. His publications include "Individual and community in early Heidegger: situating *das Man*, the *Man*-self, and self-ownership in Dasein's ontological structure" (*Inquiry*, 44, 2001) and "A road more or less taken" (*Inquiry*, forthcoming). He is currently working on a book on Wittgenstein's *Tractatus*.

Albert Borgmann has taught philosophy at the University of Montana, Missoula since 1970. His special area is the philosophy of society and culture, with particular emphasis on technology. Among his publications are *Technology and the Character of Contemporary Life* (1984), *Crossing the Postmodern Divide* (1992), *Holding on to Reality: The Nature of Information at the Turn of the Millennium* (1999), and *Power Failure: Christianity in the Culture of Technology* (2003).

Robert Brandom is Distinguished Service Professor of Philosophy at the University of Pittsburgh, a fellow of the Center for the Philosophy of Science, and a Fellow of the American Academy of Arts and Sciences. His interests center on the philosophy of language, the philosophy of mind, and the philosophy of logic. He has published more than 50 articles on these and related areas.

Taylor Carman is Associate Professor of Philosophy at Barnard College, Columbia University. He is the author of *Heidegger's Analytic: Interpretation, Discourse and Authenticity in "Being and Time"* (2003) and co-editor of *The Cambridge Companion to Merleau-Ponty* (2005), and has written articles on various topics in phenomenology. He is currently writing a book on Merleau-Ponty.

David R. Cerbone is Associate Professor of Philosophy at West Virginia University. He has published articles on Heidegger, Wittgenstein, and the continental and analytic traditions more generally. His work has appeared in such journals as *Inquiry*, *Philosophical Topics*, *International Journal of Philosophical Studies*, and *The New Yearbook for Phenomenology and Phenomenological Philosophy*, and in such books as *The New Wittgenstein* (2000), *The Grammar of Politics: Wittgenstein and Political Philosophy* (2003), *A House Divided: Comparing Analytic and Continental Philosophy* (2003), and *Heidegger, Authenticity, and Modernity: Essays in Honor of Hubert Dreyfus, Volume 1* (2000). He is currently writing an introductory-level book on phenomenology.

Steven Crowell is Mullen Professor of Philosophy and Professor of German Studies at Rice University. He is the author of *Husserl, Heidegger, and the Space of Meaning: Paths toward Transcendental Phenomenology* (2001), editor of *The Prism of the Self: Philosophical Essays in Honor of Maurice Natanson* (1995), and editor of the "Series in Continental Thought" at Ohio University Press.

Daniel O. Dahlstrom is Professor of Philosophy at Boston University, author of *Das logische Vorurteil* (1994) and *Heidegger's Concept of Truth* (2001), editor of *Nature and Scientific Method, Philosophy and Art* (1991), and *Husserl's Logical Investigations* (2003), and translator of Schiller's *Aesthetic Essays* (1993), Moses Mendelssohn's *Philosophical Writings* (1997), and Heidegger's *Introduction to Philosophical Research* (2005).

Hubert L. Dreyfus is Professor of Philosophy in the Graduate School at the University of California at Berkeley. His publications include *What Computers (Still) Can't Do* (3rd edn 1993), *Being-in-the-World: A Commentary on Division I of Heidegger's Being and Time* (1991), *Mind over Machine: The Power of Human Intuition and Expertise in the Era of the Computer* (with Stuart Dreyfus, 1987), and *On the Internet* (2001).

James C. Edwards is Professor of Philosophy at Furman University, where he has taught since 1970. His books include *Ethics without Philosophy: Wittgenstein and the Moral Life* (1982), *The Authority of Language: Heidegger, Wittgenstein, and the Threat of Philosophical Nihilism* (1990), and *The Plain Sense of Things: The Fate of Religion in an Age of Normal Nihilism* (1997).

Charles Guignon, Professor of Philosophy at the University of South Florida, is the author of *Heidegger and the Problem of Knowledge* (1983), editor of *The Cambridge Companion to Heidegger* (1993) and *The Existentialists* (2003), and co-editor of *Existentialism: Basic Writings* (2nd edn 2001). His most recent book is *On Being Authentic* (2004).

Béatrice Han-Pile, former pupil of the Ecole Normale Superieure, Paris, is Reader in Philosophy at the University of Essex. She is the author of *Foucault's Critical Project: Between the Transcendental and the Historical* (2002) and of various articles (mostly on Foucault, Heidegger, and Nietzsche). She is currently working on a book entitled *Transcendence without Religion*.

Piotr Hoffman studied philosophy in Poland and in France. He taught philosophy at the University of California, Berkeley, and is now Professor of Philosophy at the University of Nevada, Reno. His most recent book is *Freedom, Equality, Power: The Ontological Consequences of the Political Philosophies of Hobbes, Locke and Rousseau*.

Stephan Käufer is Assistant Professor of Philosophy at Franklin and Marshall College.

Cristina Lafont is Associate Professor of Philosophy at Northwestern University. She is the author of *The Linguistic Turn in Hermeneutic Philosophy* (1999) and *Heidegger, Language, and World-disclosure* (2000). Some of her recent articles include: "Heidegger and the synthetic apriori", in J. Malpas and S. Crowell (eds), *Heidegger and Transcendental Philosophy* (forthcoming), "Précis of *Heidegger, Language, and World-disclosure*" and "Replies," *Inquiry,* 45 (2002), "The role of language in *Being and Time*," in H. Dreyfus and M. Wrathall (eds), *Heidegger Reexamined: Heidegger and Contemporary Philosophy* (2002), and "Continental philosophy of language," *International Encyclopedia of Social and Behavioral Sciences, volume 3, Philosophy* (2002).

Stephen Mulhall is Fellow and Tutor in Philosophy at New College, Oxford. He is the author of *On Being in the World: Wittgenstein and Heidegger on Seeing Aspects* (1990), *Heidegger and "Being and Time"* (2nd edn 2005), and *Inheritance and Originality: Wittgenstein, Heidegger, Kierkegaard* (2001).

Mark Okrent is Professor of Philosophy at Bates College and the author of *Heidegger's Pragmatism* (1988).

Richard Polt is Professor of Philosophy at Xavier University in Cincinnati, author of *Heidegger: An Introduction* (1999) and *The Emergency of Being: On Heidegger's "Contributions to Philosophy"* (2005), co-translator and co-editor with Gregory Fried of *Heidegger's Introduction to Metaphysics* (2000) and *A Companion to Heidegger's "Introduction to Metaphysics"* (2001), and editor of *Critical Essays on Heidegger's "Being and Time"* (2005).

Richard Rorty is Professor of Comparative Literature at Stanford University. He is the author of *Philosophy and the Mirror of Nature* (1979), *Contingency, Irony, and Solidarity* (1987), and *Achieving our Country* (1998), as well as of several volumes of philosophical papers.

Joseph Rouse is the Hedding Professor of Moral Science and Chair of the Science in Society Program at Wesleyan University, and the author of *How Scientific Practices Matter: Reclaiming Philosophical Naturalism* (2002), *Engaging Science: How Its Practices Matter Philosophically* (1996), and *Knowledge and Power: Toward a Political Philosophy of Science* (1987).

Hans Ruin is Professor in Philosophy at Södertörns Högskola, Stockholm, Sweden, author of *Enigmatic Origins: Tracing the Theme of Historicity through Heidegger's Works* (1994), editor (with Aleksander Orlowski) of *Fenomenologiska perspektiv. Studier i Husserls och Heideggers filosofi* (1997), translator (with Hækan Rehnberg) and author of *Herakleitos Fragment* (a complete annotated edition of the fragments in Swedish, 1997), editor (with Dan Zahavi and Sara Heinämaa) of *Metaphysics, Interpretation, Facticity. Phenomenology in the Nordic Countries* (2003), translator into Swedish of Derrida, *Origine de la Géometrie* and (with Aris Fioretos) of Derrida, *Schibboleth*, and co-editor of the Swedish edition of *Nietzsche's Collected Writings*.

Theodore R. Schatzki is Professor and Chair of Philosophy at the University of Kentucky. He is author of a book on Heidegger as a theorist of space (forthcoming), of *The Site of the Social: A Philosophical Exploration of the Constitution of Social Life and*

Change (2002), and of *Social Practices: A Wittgensteinian Approach to Human Activity and the Social* (1996). Among the books he has co-edited is *The Practice Turn in Contemporary Theory* (2001).

Thomas Sheehan is Professor of Religious Studies at Stanford University.

Hans Sluga is Professor of Philosophy at the University of California at Berkeley and author of *Gottlob Frege* (1980) and of *Heidegger's Crisis* (1993). He has also edited (with David Stern) *The Cambridge Companion to Wittgenstein* (1998) and has written numerous essays on Frege, Wittgenstein, Heidegger, and Foucault. He is currently finishing a book on political philosophy with the title *The Care of the Common*.

Charles Spinosa is currently a Group Director specializing in strategy at VISION Consulting. He is co-author of *Disclosing New Worlds* (1997) and has published on Heidegger and Derrida in *The Practice Turn of Contemporary Theory* (ed. Theodore Schatzki), on Heidegger and Greek gods in *Heidegger, Coping, and Cognitive Science* (ed. Jeff Malpas and Mark Wrathall), with Hubert Dreyfus on Heidegger and Modernity in "Further reflections on Heidegger, technology, and the everyday" in the *Bulletin of Science, Technology, and Society* (2003), and with Hubert Dreyfus on Heidegger and Realism in "Coping with things-in-themselves," *Inquiry* (1999).

Charles Taylor is Emeritus Professor of Philosophy and Political Science at McGill University. His books include *Sources of the Self, The Ethics of Authenticity*, and *Modern Social Imaginaries*.

Iain Thomson is Assistant Professor of Philosophy at the University of New Mexico. His work on Heidegger has appeared in such journals as *Inquiry, International Journal of Philosophical Studies, Journal of the British Society for Phenomenology*, and *Journal of the History of Philosophy*.

John van Buren is Professor of Philosophy and Director of Environmental Studies at Fordham University, author of *The Young Heidegger: Rumor of the Hidden King* (1994), editor of *Reading Heidegger from the Start: Essays in His Earliest Thought* (1994), translator of and commentator on Heidegger's 1923 lecture course *Ontology – The Hermeneutics of Facticity* (1999), editor and translator of *Supplements: From the Earliest Essays to Being and Time and Beyond* (2002), and editor of the series *Environmental Philosophy and Ethics* at the State University of New York Press.

Carol J. White was Associate Professor of Philosophy at Santa Clara University. Her book *Time and Death: Heidegger's Analysis of Finitude* is being published posthumously.

Mark A. Wrathall is Associate Professor of Philosophy at Brigham Young University. He has published articles on topics in the history of philosophy and philosophy of language and mind, drawing on both the analytic and continental traditions in philosophy. He has edited *Religion after Metaphysics* (2003), and co-edited *Heidegger Re-examined* (2002), *Heidegger, Authenticity, and Modernity* (2000), *Heidegger, Coping, and Cognitive Science* (2000), and *Appropriating Heidegger* (2000).

Acknowledgments

The editor and publisher gratefully acknowledge the permission granted to reproduce the copyright material in this book:

Brandom, Robert, "Heidegger's Categories in *Being and Time*" from *The Monist* 66, no 3 (1983): 387–409. © 1983 *The Monist: An International Quarterly Journal of General Philosophical Inquiry*, Peru, Illinois, USA 61354. Reprinted with permission.

Okrent, Mark, "Truth of Being and History of Philosophy" from *Heidegger: A Critical Reader*, edited by Hubert L. Dreyfus and Harrison Hall. Oxford: Blackwell, 1992. Reprinted with permission.

Rorty, Richard, "Heidegger, Contingency, and Pragmatism" from *Heidegger: A Critical Reader*, edited by Hubert L. Dreyfus and Harrison Hall. Oxford: Blackwell, 1992. Reprinted with permission.

Spinosa, Charles, "Derrida and Heidegger: Iterability and *Ereignis*" from *Heidegger: A Critical Reader*, edited by Hubert L. Dreyfus and Harrison Hall. Oxford: Blackwell, 1992. Reprinted with permission.

Taylor, Charles, "Heidegger, Language, and Ecology" from *Heidegger: A Critical Reader*, edited by Hubert L. Dreyfus and Harrison Hall. Oxford: Blackwell, 1992. Reprinted with permission.

Every effort has been made to trace copyright holders and to obtain their permission for the use of copyright material. The publisher apologizes for any errors or omissions in the above list and would be grateful if notified of any corrections that should be incorporated in future reprints or editions of this book.

References

Explanatory Note

With the publication of Heidegger's collected works in the *Gesamtausgabe* (*Complete Edition*) (Frankfurt am Main: Vittorio Klostermann), a more or less standard system of reference is finally possible. Most English translations of Heidegger's works now include references to the pagination of the *Gesamtausgabe* volume in the header, footer, or body of the translated work. Thus, for many of Heidegger's writings, a reference to the *Gesamtausgabe* page number suffices to find readily the page in translation. The *Gesamtausgabe* also includes marginal references to the pagination of the original German edition of Heidegger's work, so that it is possible with the reference to the *Gesamtausgabe* to find the reference to other German versions.

For this reason, we have elected to list only references to the *Gesamtausgabe* pagination except in those cases where the author is using an English translation that does not list the *Gesamtausgabe* page numbers. For those volumes, we list the *Gesamtausgabe* page number followed by the page number in translation. For example, (GA 9: 330/252) refers to page 330 in *Wegmarken* and its translation on page 252 in *Pathmarks* (for bibliographic information on the translations used, please refer to the list of works cited section below).

In two cases – *Being and Time* (*Sein und Zeit*, *Gesamtausgabe* volume 2), and *Introduction to Metaphysics* (*Einführung in die Metaphysik*, *Gesamtausgabe* volume 40) – the English translations include no references to the *Gesamtausgabe* pagination, but they do list marginal references to prior German language editions. The *Gesamtausgabe* editions of those volumes also include this marginal reference. Thus, references to *Being and Time* (SZ) and *Introduction to Metaphysics* (EM) list only the marginal numbers.

Several of Heidegger's collections of essays – most prominently GA 7 and GA 12 – have not been translated as a collection, although the essays are available in other collections of essays. In those cases, or when the author of a particular chapter has preferred not to refer to the translations listed in the *Works Cited* section, we list the *Gesamtausgabe* reference followed by a separate reference to the translated source. In those cases, bibliographic information to the translation will be found in the chapter-specific *References and further reading* section. For example, (GA 12: 7/Heidegger 1971:

189) refers to page 7 of *Unterwegs zur Sprache* and its translation on page 189 of *Poetry, Language and Thought* (trans. A. Hofstadter). New York: Harper and Row, 1971).

List of Works Cited

GA 1   *Frühe Schriften.* Frankfurt am Main: Klostermann, 1978.

GA 3   *Kant und das Problem der Metaphysik.* Frankfurt am Main: Klostermann, 1991. Translated as: *Kant and the Problem of Metaphysics* (trans. R. Taft). Bloomington: Indiana University Press, 1997.

GA 4   *Erläuterungen zu Hölderlins Dichtung.* Frankfurt am Main: Klostermann, 1981. Translated as: *Elucidations of Hölderlin's Poetry* (trans. K. Hoeller). Amherst, NY: Humanity Books, 2000.

GA 5   *Holzwege.* Frankfurt am Main: Klostermann, 1977. Translated as: *Off The Beaten Track* (trans. J. Young and K. Haynes). Cambridge: Cambridge University Press, 2002.

GA 6.1   *Nietzsche I.* Frankfurt am Main: Klostermann, 1996.

GA 6.2   *Nietzsche II.* Frankfurt am Main: Klostermann, 1997.

GA 7   *Vorträge und Aufsätze.* Frankfurt am Main: Klostermann, 2000.

GA 8   *Was heisst Denken?.* Frankfurt am Main: Klostermann, 2002. Translated as: *What Is Called Thinking?* (trans. J. G. Gray). New York: Harper & Row, 1968.

GA 9   *Wegmarken.* Frankfurt am Main: Klostermann, 1996. Translated as: *Pathmarks.* (ed. W. McNeill). Cambridge: Cambridge University Press, 1998.

GA 10   *Der Satz vom Grund.* Frankfurt am Main: Klostermann, 1997. Translated as: *The Principle of Reason* (trans. R. Lilly). Bloomington: Indiana University Press, 1991.

GA 12   *Unterwegs zur Sprache.* Frankfurt am Main: Klostermann, 1985.

GA 13   *Aus der Erfahrung des Denkens.* Frankfurt am Main: Klostermann, 1983.

GA 15   *Seminare.* Frankfurt am Main: Klostermann, 1986.

GA 16   *Reden und andere Zeugnisse eines Lebensweges, 1910–1976.* Frankfurt am Main: Klostermann, 2000.

GA 17   *Einführung in die phänomenologische Forschung.* Frankfurt am Main: Klostermann, 1994.

GA 18   *Grundbegriffe der Aristotelischen Philosophie.* Frankfurt am Main: Klostermann, 2002.

GA 19   *Platon, Sophistes.* Frankfurt am Main: Klostermann, 1992. Translated as: *Plato's Sophist* (trans. R. Rojcewicz and A. Schuwer). Bloomington: Indiana University Press, 1997.

GA 20   *Prolegomena zur Geschichte des Zeitbegriffs.* Frankfurt am Main: Klostermann, 1979. Translated as: *History of the Concept of Time* (trans. T. Kisiel). Bloomington: Indiana University Press, 1985.

GA 21   *Logik: Die Frage nach der Wahrheit.* Frankfurt am Main: Klostermann, 1976.

GA 22   *Die Grundbegriffe der antiken Philosophie.* Frankfurt am Main: Klostermann, 1993.

GA 24 *Die Grundprobleme der Phänomenologie.* Frankfurt am Main: Klostermann, 1975. Translated as: *Basic Problems of Phenomenology* (trans. A. Hofstadter). Bloomington: Indiana University Press, 1982.

GA 25 *Phänomenologische Interpretation von Kants Kritik der reinen Vernunft.* Frankfurt am Main: Klostermann, 1977. Translated as: *Phenomenological Interpretation of Kant's Critique of Pure Reason* (trans. P. Emad and K. Maly). Bloomington: Indiana University Press, 1997.

GA 26 *Metaphysische Anfangsgründe der Logik.* Frankfurt am Main: Klostermann, 1978. Translated as: *The Metaphysical Foundations of Logic* (trans. M. Heim). Bloomington: Indiana University Press, 1984.

GA 27 *Einleitung in die Philosophie.* Frankfurt am Main: Klostermann, 1996.

GA 28 *Der deutsche Idealismus. Fichte, Schelling, Hegel) und die philosophische Problemlage der Gegenwart.* Frankfurt am Main: Klostermann, 1997.

GA 29/30 *Die Grundbegriffe der Metaphysik: Welt, Endlichkeit, Einsamkeit.* Frankfurt am Main: Klostermann, 1983. Translated as: *The Fundamental Concepts of Metaphysics: World, Finitude, Solitude* (trans. W. McNeill and N. Walker). Bloomington: Indiana University Press, 1995.

GA 31 *Vom Wesen der menschlichen Freiheit: Einleitung in die Philosophie.* Frankfurt am Main: Klostermann, 1982. Translated as: *The Essence of Human Freedom* (trans. T. Sadler). London: Continuum, 2002.

GA 32 *Hegels Phänomenologie des Geistes.* Frankfurt am Main: Klostermann, 1980. Translated as: *Hegel's Phenomenology of Spirit* (trans. P. Emad and K. Maly). Bloomington: Indiana University Press, 1988.

GA 33 *Aristoteles, Metaphysik Θ 1–3.* Frankfurt am Main: Klostermann, 1981. Translated as: *Aristotle's Metaphysics Theta 1–3* (trans. W. Brogan and P. Warnek). Bloomington: Indiana University Press, 1995.

GA 34 *Vom Wesen der Wahrheit: zu Platons Höhlengleichnis und Theätet.* Frankfurt am Main: Klostermann, 1988. Translated as: *The Essence of Truth* (trans. T. Sadler). London: Continuum, 2002.

GA 36/37 *Sein und Wahrheit.* Frankfurt am Main: Klostermann, 2001.

GA 38 *Logik als die Frage nach dem Wesen der Sprache.* Frankfurt am Main: Klostermann, 1998.

GA 39 *Hölderlins Hymnen "Germanien" und "Der Rhein."* Frankfurt am Main: Klostermann, 1980.

GA 41 *Die Frage nach dem Ding: zu Kants Lehre von den transzendentalen Grundsätzen.* Frankfurt am Main: Klostermann, 1984. Translated as: *What Is a Thing?* (trans. W. B. Barton Jr and V. Deutsch). Chicago: Henry Regnery Company, 1967.

GA 42 *Schelling: vom Wesen der menschlichen Freiheit.* Frankfurt am Main: Klostermann, 1988. Translated as: *Schelling's Treatise on the Essence of Human Freedom* (trans. J. Stambaugh). Athens: Ohio University Press, 1984.

GA 43 *Nietzsche: der Wille zur Macht als Kunst.* Frankfurt am Main: Klostermann, 1985.

GA 44 *Nietzsches metaphysische Grundstellung im abendländischen Denken: die ewige Wiederkehr des Gleichen.* Frankfurt am Main: Klostermann, 1986.

GA 45   *Grundfragen der Philosophie: ausgewählte "Probleme" der "Logik."* Frankfurt am Main: Klostermann, 1984. Translated as: *Basic Questions of Philosophy. Selected "Problems" of "Logic"* (trans. R. Rojcewicz and A. Schuwer). Bloomington: Indiana University Press, 1994.

GA 46   *Zur Auslegung von Nietzsches II. Unzeitgemässer Betrachtung.* Frankfurt am Main: Klostermann, 2003.

GA 47   *Nietzsches Lehre vom Willen zur Macht als Erkenntnis.* Frankfurt am Main: Klostermann, 1989.

GA 48   *Nietzsche, der europäische Nihilismus.* Frankfurt am Main: Klostermann, 1986.

GA 49   *Die Metaphysik des deutschen Idealismus (Schelling).* Frankfurt am Main: Klostermann, 1991.

GA 50   *Nietzsches Metaphysik; Einleitung in die Philosophie, Denken und Dichten.* Frankfurt am Main: Klostermann, 1990.

GA 51   *Grundbegriffe.* Frankfurt am Main: Klostermann, 1981. Translated as: *Basic Concepts* (trans. G. Aylesworth). Bloomington: Indiana University Press, 1993.

GA 52   *Hölderlins Hymne "Andenken."* Frankfurt am Main: Klostermann, 1982.

GA 53   *Hölderlins Hymne "Der Ister."* Frankfurt am Main: Klostermann, 1984. Translated as: *Hölderlin's Hymn "The Ister"* (trans. W. McNeill and Julia Davis). Bloomington: Indiana University Press, 1996.

GA 54   *Parmenides.* Frankfurt am Main: Klostermann, 1982. Translated as: *Parmenides* (trans. A. Schuwer and R. Rojcewicz). Bloomington: Indiana University Press, 1992.

GA 55   *Heraklit.* Frankfurt am Main: Klostermann, 1979.

GA 56/57   *Zur Bestimmung der Philosophie.* Frankfurt am Main: Klostermann, 1987. Translated as: *Towards the Definition of Philosophy* (trans. T. Sadler). London: Continuum, 2002.

GA 58   *Grundprobleme der Phänomenologie.* Frankfurt am Main: Klostermann, 1993.

GA 59   *Phänomenologie der Anschauung und des Ausdrucks: Theorie der philosophischen Begriffsbildung.* Frankfurt am Main: Klostermann, 1993.

GA 60   *Phänomenologie des religiösen Lebens.* Frankfurt am Main: Klostermann, 1995. Translated as: *The Phenomenology of Religious Life* (trans. M. Fritsch and J. A. Gosetti). Bloomington: Indiana University Press, 2004

GA 61   *Phänomenologische Interpretationen zu Aristoteles/Einführung in die phänomenologische Forschung.* Frankfurt am Main: Klostermann, 1985. Translated as: *Phenomenological Interpretations of Aristotle* (trans. R. Rojcewicz). Bloomington: Indiana University Press, 2001.

GA 62   *Phänomenologische Interpretationen ausgewählter Abhandlungen des Aristoteles zu Ontologie und Logik.* Frankfurt: Klostermann, 2004.

GA 63   *Ontologie: Hermeneutik der Faktizität.* Frankfurt am Main: Klostermann, 1988. Translated as: *Ontology: The Hermeneutics of Facticity* (trans. J. van Buren). Bloomington: Indiana University Press, 1999.

GA 65   *Beiträge zur Philosophie (vom Ereignis).* Frankfurt am Main: Klostermann, 1989.

GA 66   *Besinnung*. Frankfurt am Main: Klostermann, 1997.

GA 67   *Metaphysik und Nihilismus*. Frankfurt am Main: Klostermann, 1999.

GA 68   *Hegel*. Frankfurt am Main: Klostermann, 1993.

GA 69   *Die Geschichte des Seyns*. Frankfurt am Main: Klostermann, 1998.

GA 75   *Zu Hölderlin/Griechenlandreisen*. Frankfurt am Main: Klostermann, 2000.

GA 77   *Feldweg-Gespräche 1944/45*. Frankfurt am Main: Klostermann, 1995.

GA 79   *Bremer und Freiburger Vorträge*. Frankfurt am Main: Klostermann, 1994.

GA 85   *Vom Wesen der Sprache*. Frankfurt am Main: Klostermann, 1999.

EM   *Einführung in die Metaphysik*. Frankfurt am Main: Klostermann, 1983. Translated as: *Introduction to Metaphysics* (trans. G. Fried and R. Polt). New Haven, CT: Yale University Press, 2000 (original work published 1953).

SZ   *Sein und Zeit*. Tübingen: Niemeyer, 1957. Translated as: *Being and Time* (trans. J. Macquarrie and E. Robinson). New York: Harper & Row, 1962.

1

Martin Heidegger: An Introduction to His Thought, Work, and Life

HUBERT DREYFUS AND MARK WRATHALL

Martin Heidegger is one of the most influential philosophers of the twentieth century. His work has been appropriated by scholars in fields as diverse as philosophy, classics, psychology, literature, history, sociology, anthropology, political science, religious studies, and cultural studies.

At the same time, he is a notoriously difficult philosopher to understand. The way he wrote was, in part, a result of the fact that he is deliberately trying to break with the philosophical tradition. One way of breaking with the tradition is to coin neologisms, that is, to invent words which will, in virtue of their originality, be free of any philosophical baggage. This is a method that Heidegger frequently employed, but at the cost of considerable intelligibility. In addition, Heidegger believed his task was to provoke his readers to thoughtfulness rather than provide them with a facile answer to a well defined problem. He thus wrote in ways that would challenge the reader to reflection.

Our hope is that this book will be of assistance in making Heidegger more accessible as a writer and thinker. The chapters in this volume review the main formative influences on and developments in his philosophy, tackle many of the central elements in Heidegger's thought, and address his relevance to ongoing issues and concerns in the field of philosophy, broadly construed. By way of introduction to the chapters that follow, we would like to offer here a brief overview of Heidegger's life, thought, and work.

Heidegger's Early Life and Early Work

For all Heidegger's emphasis on the history of philosophy, he had little interest in the historiographical details about the lives of the philosophers he studied. In his introduction to a lecture course on Schelling, for example, he claimed that " 'the life' of a philosopher remains unimportant," at least where we have access to his work, or even "pieces and traces of his work." This is because, he explained, "we never come to know the actuality of a philosophical existence through a biography" (GA 42: 7). For him, philosophers were of interest because of what they could contribute to our own efforts to grapple with philosophical problems. He thus refused "to fill the hours with stories of the lives and fortunes of the old thinkers," because that "does not add anything to the understanding of the problem" (GA 22: 12).

He did, however, occasionally offer "some rough indications of the external course of life" of the thinker (in the Schelling lecture course, for example), in order to "place this course of life more clearly into the known history of the time" (GA 42: 7). In a similar way, we think that Heidegger's notorious involvement in his historical time justifies some such indication of the "external course of his life."

Heidegger was born on September 26, 1889, in Meßkirch in Baden, a staunchly Catholic region of Germany. He always felt rooted in this region, and its native practices and modes of speech (see, for example, "Dank an die Heimatstadt Messkirch," in GA 16, and "Vom Geheimnis des Glockenturms," "Der Feldweg," "Schöpfersiche Landschaft: Warum bleiben wir in der Provinz?" and "Sprache und Heimat" in GA 13). He spent most of his career living and teaching in Freiburg, with as much time as possible in his ski hut in a rural mountain valley in Todtnauberg. Indeed, he went so far as to claim that his "whole work is supported and guided by the world of these mountains and their farmers" (GA 13: 11). Heidegger died on May 26, 1976 and was, according to his wishes, buried in Meßkirch on May 28.

His father, Friedrich Heidegger, was a craftsman – a master cooper – and a sexton. Religious and theological studies played a central role in his early education. He studied at Gymnasia in Constance (1903–6) and Freiburg (1906–9), and he entered the Jesuit Novitiate of Tisis, Austria, in the fall of 1909, before being dismissed on health grounds. He commenced theological studies at the University of Freiburg in 1909, but eventually left theology, briefly pursuing the study of mathematics and then philosophy. By 1919, Heidegger broke with "the *system* of Catholicism," which he now found "problematic and unacceptable." The rejection of the system did not, however, include a rejection of "Christianity and metaphysics" ("Letter to Father Engelbert Krebs," Heidegger 2002: 69), and Heidegger lectured often on the phenomenology of religion and metaphysics in the ensuing years (see, for example, "Einleitung in die Phänomenologie der Religion" (1920/1) and "Augustinus und der Neuplatonismus" (1921), both found in GA 60, as well as "Phänomenologie und Theologie" (1927) in GA 9). In later years, he returned often to the importance of fostering a sense for the sacred (see, for example, *Hölderlins Hymnen "Germanien" und "Der Rhein,"* GA 39; GA 4; *Hölderlins Hymne "Andenken,"* GA 52; "Wozu Dichter?," in GA 5; "Der Fehl heiliger Namen," in GA 13).

In the meantime, Heidegger had received his doctoral degree in philosophy (1913), from the University of Freiburg, with a dissertation on the "Theory of Judgment in Psychologism" (GA 1). He completed a habilitation dissertation on "The Theory of Categories and Meaning in Duns Scotus" (GA 1) in 1915, and began lecturing in Freiburg in Winter Semester 1915–16. His early interest in both logic and medieval thought continued in later years, and Heidegger lectured frequently on philosophical logic (for example, *Logik. Die Frage nach der Wahrheit,* GA 21; *Logik. Metaphysische Anfangsgründe der Logik im Ausgang von Leibniz,* GA 26; *Über Logik als Frage nach der Sprache,* GA 38; see Käufer, this volume, chapter 9) and medieval philosophy (GA 60).

Edmund Husserl's arrival at the University of Freiburg in 1916 allowed Heidegger, as he expressed it himself, "the occasion, which I had desired since my first semesters, to systematically work my way into phenomenological research" (GA 17: 42; see Crowell, this volume, chapter 4). Heidegger worked for a time as Husserl's assistant, but gradually made a break with Husserlian phenomenology as he began teaching his own courses on phenomenology at Freiburg and then at Marburg University following his appointment to a professorship in 1923. The break became public with the publication of *Being and Time* in 1927, although it was only recognized by Husserl himself following Heidegger's appointment to Husserl's chair at the University of Freiburg in 1928. For a more thorough account of Heidegger's thought leading up to the publication of *Being and Time*, see Van Buren (this volume, chapter 2).

Being and Time

In his *magnum opus*, *Being and Time*, Heidegger undertakes an ambitious ontological project – the central task of the book is to discover the meaning of being, i.e. that on the basis of which beings are understood (see SZ: 150). Although Heidegger never completed the project he had outlined for elucidating the meaning of being, he did manage to articulate a revolutionary approach to thinking about the problem in terms of time as the "horizon of all understanding of being" (see SZ: 17 and Blattner, this volume, chapter 19). Most of *Being and Time* itself is concerned with "preparing the ground" for understanding the meaning of being by carrying out a subtle and revolutionary phenomenology of the human mode of existence (see Sheehan, this volume, chapter 12).

When it comes to thinking about ontology, Heidegger argues that traditional treatments of being have failed to distinguish two different kinds of questions we can ask: the ontic question that asks about the properties of beings, and the ontological question that asks about ways or modes of being. *Being and Time* focuses on three ontological modes and three kinds of beings – Dasein, the available (or ready to hand), and the occurrent (or present at hand). If one investigates an item of equipment, say a pen, ontologically, then one asks about the structures in virtue of which it is available or ready to hand. These include, for example, its belonging to a context of equipment and referring or pointing to other items of equipment. In an ontic inquiry, on the other hand, one asks about the properties or the physical relations and structures peculiar to some entity – in the pen's case, for example, we might make the following ontic observations about it: it is black, full of blue ink, and sitting on top of my desk. Heidegger's critique of the tradition comes from the simple observation that the ontological mode of being cannot be reduced to what we discover in an ontic inquiry, no matter how exhaustively we describe the entity with its properties. This is because no listing of, for example, a pen's properties can tell me what it is to be available rather than occurrent.

An ontological inquiry into human being, then, will not look at the properties possessed by humans, but rather at the structures which make it possible to *be* human. One of Heidegger's most innovative and important insights is that the essence of the human mode of existence is found in our always already existing in a world. He thus named the human mode of existence "Dasein," literally, being-there. Dasein means existence in colloquial German, but Heidegger uses it as a term of art to refer to the peculiarly

3

human way of existing (without, of course, deciding in advance whether only humans exist in this way). Translators of Heidegger have elected to leave the term untranslated, and so it has now passed into common parlance among Heidegger scholars.

Using his account of what is involved in human existence so understood, Heidegger argues that the philosophical tradition has overlooked the character of the world, and the nature of our human existence in a world. Dasein, for instance, is not a subject, for a subject in the traditional sense has mental states and experiences which can be what they are independently of the state of the surrounding world. For Heidegger, our way of being is found not in our thinking nature, but in our existing in a world. And our being is intimately and inextricably bound up with the world that we find ourselves in. In the same way that the tradition has misunderstood human being by focusing on subjectivity, it also failed to understand the nature of the world, because it tended to focus exclusively on entities within the world, and understood the world as merely being a collection of inherently meaningless entities. But attention to the way entities actually show up for us in our everyday dealings teaches us that worldly things cannot be reduced to merely physical entities with causal properties. *Worldly* things, in other words, have a different mode of being than the causally delineated entities that make up the *universe* and which are the concern of the natural sciences. To understand worldly entities – entities, in other words, that are inherently meaningfully constituted – requires a hermeneutic approach (see Lafont, this volume, chapter 16).

We first encounter worldly things, Heidegger argued, as available rather than as causally delineated. Equipment is paradigmatic of the available. Something is available when (1) it is defined in terms of its place in a context of equipment, typical activities in which it is used, and typical purposes or goals for which it is used, and (2) it lends itself to such use readily and easily, without need for reflection. The core case of availableness is an item of equipment that we know how to use and that transparently lends itself to use.

The other primary mode of being is "occurrentness" or "presence-at-hand." This is the mode of being of things which are not given a worldly determination – that is, things constituted by properties they possess in themselves, rather than through their relations to uses and objects of use. Most available things can also be viewed as occurrent, and in breakdown situations (i.e. situations in which our easy fluid dealings with the environment encounter some sort of difficulty – a tool breaks, a new or unanticipated situation presents itself, etc.), the occurrentness of an available object will obtrude.

Once we free ourselves of the idea that everything is "really" occurrent, we are open to the phenomenon of the world as something other than a mere collection of entities. The world, properly understood, is that on the basis of which entities can be involved with one another. And it is our familiarity with the world so understood which makes it possible for us to act on, think about, experience, etc. things in the world. This idea, in turn, allows Heidegger to address skeptical worries about truth and the reality of the "external" world. Since we always already find ourselves involved with entities in a world, worries that there is no world are ungrounded and unmotivated.

Once we see that human beings are inherently and inextricably in a world within which entities and activities are disclosed as available to us, we are in a position to ask about what is involved in the structure of this world and its disclosure to us. In philosophical accounts of human beings, moods are often dismissed as merely subjective colorings of our experience of the world. But, Heidegger argues, moods actually reveal something important about the fundamental structure of the world and our way of being in it. First of all, Heidegger notes that "moods assail us." In other words, it is not wholly up to us how we will be affected by the situations we find ourselves in. This shows that we are delivered over to, or "thrown" into, a world not of our own making. Second, while it is clear that moods are not objective properties of entities within the world, it is also clear that moods in fact are not merely subjective either. A boring lecture really is boring, a violent person really is frightening. This shows that the subjective–objective distinction fails to capture the interdependence of our being with the world and the entities around us. In addition, moods in fact make it possible for us to encounter entities within the world by determining how those entities will matter to us. Finally, Heidegger argues that moods are not private, inner phenomena, but can be shared. We often speak, for example, of the mood of the party, or the mood of the nation.

So, being-in-the-world means that we always find ourselves in the world in a particular way – we have a "there," that is, a meaningfully structured situation in which to act and exist – and we are always disposed to things in a particular way, they always matter to us somehow or other. Our disposedness is revealed to us in the way our moods govern and structure our comportment by disposing us differentially to things in the world. So disposedness is an "attunement," a way of being tuned in to things in the world.

But this attunement necessarily goes with an understanding of what things are. Heidegger describes Dasein's understanding of the world as a kind of "projecting onto possibilities," rather than the cognitive and conceptual grasp of things that one normally thinks of as understanding. He argues, however, that a projective existential understanding of the world grounds our cognitive grasp of and explicit experiences of things. To see what Heidegger has in mind with the term "understanding," one needs to focus primarily on practical contexts and practical involvements with things in an organized and meaningful world. I am in the world understandingly when I am doing something purposively, for example, making an omelet in my kitchen. In doing so, I "let" the things in my kitchen be "involved with" each other – the eggs are involved with the mixing bowl, which is involved with the wire whisk and the frying pan and the spatula. As I heat the frying pan in order to melt the butter in order to fry up the omelet in order to feed my children, I am ultimately acting for the sake of some way of being a human being – for the sake of being a father, for example. All of these connections between activities and entities and ways of being are constitutive of the understanding of the world I possess. In the process of acting on the basis of that understanding, in turn, I allow things and activities to show up *as* the things and activities that they are (frying pans *as* frying pans, spatulas *as* spatulas, etc.) (see, for example, SZ: 86).

In acting in the world, then, I understand how things relate to each other – that is to say, I understand in the sense of "knowing how" everything in the world hangs together. Heidegger is clear that this understanding is not normally a cognitive mastery of roles and concepts – "grasping it in such a manner would take away from what is projected in its very character as a possibility, and would reduce it to the given contents which we have in mind" (SZ: 145). In other words, "understanding" as a cognitive state would prevent the understanding from doing its job. Why is this? Because the understanding, as Heidegger shows, works not simply by having an abstract idea of how things hang together, but rather in so far as we are "projecting" or "pressing" into the possibilities for action opened up by how they hang together.

Heidegger is using the term "possibility" here in a specific sense. Sometimes we use "possible" to mean "empty logical possibility" – that is, there is no contradiction in things being thus and so. But the possibilities for the world, in the logical sense, are much broader than what we ever know how to deal with. Sometimes we use "possible" to mean "the contingency of something occurrent" – that is, this is just one way it could be, but there are other ways too. But this also doesn't capture our understanding of the world – we understand our world not simply as one way the world can be, but as that way in which everything makes sense. A possibility in Heidegger's sense is a way of dealing with things that shows them as the things they are. For example, because I am able to deal with wire whisks and frying pans in an omelet-making way, they show up *as* wire whisks and frying pans. Being used in the making of omelets is a possibility for such things.

When Heidegger describes understanding as showing us the possible, then, what he means is that it shows us the available range of ways to be, it shows us our can-be or ability-to-be (*Seinkönnen*) (see, for example, SZ: 143–4). These possibilities are constrained, and not indifferent. It is not the case that anything goes, as we do indeed care about the fact that things are going or not going in a particular direction. So, for example, there are lots of possible ways for me to pursue being a professor. But I can't do just anything in the name of being a professor; I am constrained by the possible ways of professorial being available in my world. In being a professor, in other words, I *project* or *press into* the possibilities opened up by my world. Together, understanding and disposedness show us the possibilities available to us, and give them a way of mattering to us.

In summary, then, one of the distinguishing features of Heidegger's analysis of Dasein is the priority he accords to non-cognitive modes of being-in-the-world. The propositional intentional states that the philosophical tradition has seen as constitutive of Dasein are, on Heidegger's analysis, derivative phenomena. In understanding human comportment in the world, Heidegger argues that we need to focus first on skillful, practical coping.

But, as we have just noted, Heidegger's conception of the world accords a constitutive role to others as somehow determining what possibilities are available for me to pursue. Heidegger offers a trenchant analysis of the role that social relations play in constituting who we are (see Schatzki, this volume, chapter 14). It is a constitutive feature of our way of being that we take over our understanding of ourselves and the world around us from those others with whom we exist. This means that who I am cannot be understood in terms of a subject who could be constituted as he is, independently of any relationship to other human beings. Even seemingly contrary examples – human beings who are alone, or indifferent to their fellows, or misfits and outcasts – confirm this since they are *human beings* who are alone or indifferent or rejected by society. A chair can't be alone, or indifferent to other chairs, or a social outcast from the fellowship of chairs. In a similar way, the care we take for people is even manifest in deficient modes – when I am indifferent to another person, my indifference as an attitude is constituted in part by the fact that it is another person to whom I am indifferent. If I stand by and indifferently watch as you die, this has a very different character as an act than if I stand by, unconcerned that a pen has ceased functioning.

It is thus clear that we are (to a significant degree) constituted as the beings that we are by the fact that we always inhabit a shared world, and the way we exist in this world is always essentially structured by others. This has important consequences when we turn to the question "who am I," for it turns out that, at least in the everyday existence which immediately structures my world, my essence is not dictated by me, but by others.

Heidegger calls the fact that we are constantly concerned about and taking measure of how we differ from others or relate to them "distantiality." In our everyday existence, our distantiality takes the form of "standing in subjection to others" (SZ: 126). That is, we simply accept unthinkingly the ways in which one does things. But the "one" who decides how things ought to be done is no definite person or group: "the 'who' is not this one, not that one, not oneself, not some people, and not the sum of them all. The 'who' is the neuter, the 'one'" (SZ: 126).

A few tendencies result. First, there is a tendency toward levelling down to the lowest common denominator, or toward the average. The norms that govern things are the norms available to anyone – thus there is an inescapable public character to the intelligibility of the world. I understand what everybody else also understands. Next, there is a tendency toward "disburdening" – that is, by doing what *one* does, we free ourselves from the burden of responsibility for the decisions we make. This disburdening, and even the publicness and levelling, are not necessarily a bad thing. It would be a disaster if one constantly had to decide on every little thing to do (what to wear, what to eat, which side of the road to drive on, etc.). Conformity thus provides the ground – the organization of our common world – against which we are freed to make important decisions. But Heidegger does see these features of the one as tending to consequences that we might not wish to accept – namely, a conformism in which it is all too easy never to take a stand for oneself. Heidegger calls this sort of conformism "inauthenticity." In my ordinary, everyday being, I am not myself at all, I am the "one." It takes a great effort of "clearing-away concealments and obscurities" if I am to "discover the world in my own way" (SZ: 129).

This leaves open the question exactly *how* to be *my own* self in inhabiting the world. This is the problem of authenticity. The possibility of authentic self-determination arises from the fact that, unlike occurrent entities, the way that Dasein takes up its residence in the world is not fixed or necessitated. That is to say, the relationships that Dasein enjoys with other things, and the significance that other things hold for Dasein, are contingent, and it is always possible for us to change them. Heidegger makes this point by saying that for Dasein, "in its very being, that being is an issue for it" (SZ: 12).

A consequence of this is that any particular way of existing in the world is necessarily ungrounded – "Dasein is the null basis of its own nullity" (SZ: 306). This is a disquieting fact, and one that Dasein disguises from itself – primarily by taking up societal norms as if they somehow revealed the ultimate truth about how one should live. But anxiety in the face of death, Heidegger argues, if faced up to, can open the door to an authentic existence: "Anxiety," Heidegger explains, "liberates one from possibilities which 'count for nothing', and lets one become free-for those which are authentic" (SZ: 344).

In being toward death, we acknowledge that our way of being must inevitably come to an end, meaning that it will become impossible at some point to continue in our familiar kind of worldly existence. Death is the "the possibility of the impossibility of every way of comporting oneself towards anything, of every way of existing" (SZ: 262). To say it is a possibility, however, doesn't mean that it is not necessary, that is, that we might not die. Death is impending, and it can't be gotten around. It is rather a possibility in the sense that we have already discussed – the way we relate to death is a fundamental kind of dealing in the world, one that affects the character of the way things show up at a very basic level. Thus, it is not an empirical certainty, but instead certain because it is the basis for disclosing ourselves to us. That is, our experience of everything is an experience in the light of the fact that we are mortal and temporal beings (see Hoffman, this volume, chapter 20), and thus at some point we will no longer be able to be in the world.[1]

There are, of course, different ways of trying to deal with death. We can flee from it, distract ourselves by absorbing ourselves in the world of concern, submit ourselves to what are publicly taken as urgent, possible, necessary, and so on. Such are, of course, the responses of everydayness, and they tranquilize us to our death by giving us practices for dealing with it, thus offering us the illusion that we can cope with death after all. By contrast, an authentic being towards death means taking death as a possibility – that means, not thinking about it or dwelling on it, but rather taking it up in the way it shapes all our particular actions and relations. In fact, it requires anticipating it as a possibility. That is, we are ready for the world in light of the fact that each decision has consequences, and will someday culminate in our not being able to get by any longer. This, in turn, makes it possible for me to live my life as my own. Death shows me that all forms of concern and solicitude "will fail me" – common norms of intelligibility won't relieve me from the fact that my being will become impossible. That means that I must henceforth shoulder the responsibility for my decisions. This taking of responsibility is supported by my living anxiously, for in such a way of being disposed for the world, it is revealed as lacking any inherent, unchanging meaning or purpose[2] (for more on death, see Mulhall, this volume, chapter 18).

Because authenticity is a *way* of relating to our existence, there is no specific content to authenticity, nothing that every authentic Dasein does. But we can say some general things about it. First, it does not surrender itself to the interpretation of the "one," although it is dependent on it. Second, it discloses the specific situation rather than the general situation. Within the general situation, one sees the meaning things seem to have thanks to the public's banalized, levelled off understanding. Authentic Dasein, by contrast, is open to the particular needs of the situation. Having recognized the fact that its being is at issue, it responds appropriately to the particular situation before it. So, in authenticity, I take up the public understanding of my world, and I make it my own by projecting on my own possibilities. I do this through anxiously seeing the uncanniness of myself in my world (including the ungroundedness of this world) (for more on authenticity, see Carman, this volume, chapter 17).

Being and Time advanced no further than the preparatory temporal analysis of Dasein. In returning in the final section of the book to the question of the meaning of being, Heidegger could do no more than ask: "is there a way which leads from primordial time to the meaning of Being? Does time itself manifest itself as the horizon of Being?" (SZ: 488). In fact, in the years that followed its publication, Heidegger became convinced that there was no way to go on to answer these questions on the basis of the foundation he had laid through an analysis of Dasein. This conviction, in turn, produced fundamental changes in the aim, method, and style of his thought. As a consequence, his later works are in many respects different than *Being and Time*.

After *Being and Time*

In the past, it has been commonplace to subdivide Heidegger's work into two (early and late) or even three (early, middle, and late) periods. While there is something to be said for such divisions – there is an obvious sense in which *Being and Time* is thematically and stylistically unlike Heidegger's publications following the Second World War – it is also misleading to speak as if there were two or three different Heideggers. The bifurcation, as is well known, is something that Heidegger himself was uneasy about,[3] and scholars today are increasingly hesitant to draw too sharp a divide between the early and late.

Heidegger's phenomenological method provides an example of the complications involved in dividing his work into periods. Heidegger's early philosophy was profoundly shaped by his study of the phenomenological works of Husserl and, to a lesser degree, Scheler. But he broke very early on with any formal "phenomenological method" as such, and eventually largely dropped the term "phenomenology" as a self-description, worried that representing his thought as phenomenology would cause him to be associated with Husserl's substantive philosophical views. But despite his break with the phenomenological movement, Heidegger considered his work throughout his life to be "a more faithful adherence to the principle of phenomenology"[4] (in his own loose sense of the term; for more on Heidegger and phenomenology, see Boedeker, this volume, chapter 10). For Heidegger, phenomenology is an "attitude" or practice in "seeing" that takes its departure from lived experience. It aims at grasping the phenomena of lived involvement in the world, before our understanding of the world becomes determined and altered in "thematic" or reflective thought. In this respect, Heidegger's work is in marked contrast to the method of conceptual analysis that has come to dominate philosophy in the English-speaking world following the "linguistic turn" of the early twentieth century. For Heidegger, our concepts and language presuppose our unreflective involvement, and have a different structure than our pre-propositional way of comporting in the world. It is thus not possible to discover the most fundamental features of human existence through an analysis of language and concepts. Instead, a constant feature of his work is the effort to bring thought before the phenomena of existence – in this sense, his "method" is always that of phenomenology.

Another constant in Heidegger's thought is his notion of unconcealment. Heidegger first discusses unconcealment in his 1924 lectures on Plato (GA 19), and for the next

9

two decades nearly every book or essay Heidegger published, and nearly every lecture course he taught, includes a significant discussion of the essence of truth under the headings of "unconcealment" or "alêtheia" (the Greek word for truth). The later Heidegger continued his research into unconcealment through his writings on the clearing or opening of being – a topic that preoccupied Heidegger for the last three decades of his life. Thus, one could safely say that the problem of unconcealment was one of the central topics of Heidegger's life work. Throughout, Heidegger consistently insisted that many traditional philosophical problems need to be understood against the background of a more fundamental account of the way we are open to the world, the way in which the world opens itself and makes itself available for thought, and how we thoughtfully respond.

A prime case in point is the problem of truth. Heidegger recognized that any inquiry into propositional truth quickly leads to some of the most fundamental issues addressed in contemporary philosophy – issues such as the nature of language, and the reality or mind-independence of the world. He held that the philosophical discussion of truth can only be pursued against the background of assumptions about the nature of mind (in particular, how mental states and their derivatives like linguistic meaning can be so constituted as to be capable of being true or false), and the nature of the world (in particular, how the world can be so constituted as to make mental states and their derivatives true). Heidegger's focus on unconcealment in his discussions of the essence of truth is intended to bring such background assumptions to the foreground. The claim that unconcealment is the essence of truth, then, is motivated by the recognition that we have to see truth in the context of a more general opening up of the world, i.e. in the context of an involvement with and comportment toward things in the world that is more fundamental than thinking and speaking about them (see Wrathall, this volume, chapter 21).

In *Being and Time*, Heidegger analyzed the unconcealment that grounds truth in terms of the disclosedness of Dasein, that is, the fact that Dasein is always in a meaningful world. Heidegger did not shy away from the consequences of this: "Before there was any Dasein," he argued, "there was no truth; nor will there be any after Dasein is no more" (SZ: 226). He illustrated this claim with an example drawn from physics – the best candidate for discovering independent truths about the universe: "Before Newton's laws were discovered, they were not 'true'" (SZ: 226). The controversial nature of such a claim is a little diminished by the qualifications Heidegger immediately adds. To make it clear that he is not claiming that Newton's laws are somehow completely dependent for their truth merely on their being believed, he notes: "it does not follow that they were false, or even that they would become false if ontically no discoveredness were any longer possible" (SZ: 226). And he further explains, "to say that before Newton his laws were neither true nor false, cannot signify that before him there were no such entities as have been uncovered and pointed out by those laws. Through Newton the laws became true and with them, entities became accessible in themselves to Dasein. Once entities have been uncovered, they show themselves precisely as entities which beforehand already were" (SZ: 226).

In such passages, Heidegger is clearly trying to walk a fine line between realism and constructivism about truths, and the status of scientific entities. But where exactly that line falls has been subject to considerable debate (see Rouse, chapter 11, and Han, chapter 6, in this volume; for less constructivist readings of Heidegger, see Carman, chapter 17, Cerbone, chapter 15, and Dreyfus, chapter 25).

The historicism implicit in Heidegger's discussion of science was extended in Heidegger's subsequent work on the unconcealment of being. In later works, Heidegger came to argue that the philosophical history of the West consists of a series of "epochs," of different total understandings of being, and that the unconcealment of beings varies according to the background understanding of being. Heidegger's account of the history of philosophy was prefigured in *Being and Time*, which, as we have mentioned already, is only a fragment of the volume as Heidegger originally conceived it. In the second part of the volume, Heidegger intended to provide "a phenomenological destruction of the history of ontology, with the problematic of Temporality as our clue" (SZ: 39). Before abandoning the project of *Being and Time*, Heidegger conducted a sustained critique of the history of philosophy in the years following its publication. Heidegger's historical engagements during this period included readings of Kant (see GA 3, 25, 41, and Han-Pile, this volume, chapter 6), the German idealists (see GA 28 and Dahlstrom, this volume, chapter 5), and the Greeks (see GA 33, 34, 35, and White, this volume, chapter 8).

Momentous changes were occurring in Germany during this same period. In 1933, the year that saw Hitler rise to the chancellorship and the passage of the Enabling Act that allowed Hitler to seize absolute power in Germany, Heidegger was appointed rector of Freiburg University and joined the National Socialist Party. He resigned the rectorship one year later, but not before becoming intensely involved with the Nazi Party's program of university reform, and with trying to offer some philosophical guidance to the movement (see Thompson, this volume, chapter 3).

Philosophically, the 1930s were decisive years for Heidegger. In private notebooks (see Ruin, this volume, chapter 22), and in a series of lecture courses and public essays, he developed the themes that were to occupy his attention for decades to come. One of these themes was a radicalization of the project announced in *Being and Time*, and continued through the late 1920s and early 1930s, of uncovering the meaning of being (see, for example, "What is metaphysics?" in GA 9, and *Introduction to Metaphysics*, GA 40). As he came to realize the historical nature of understandings of being, Heidegger's attention turned to the problem of understanding how it is that a history of being can happen – that is, how it is that understandings of being are given to us. The rubric under which he now pursued this problem was *Ereignis*, the event by which entities and the world are brought into their own (see Polt, this volume, chapter 23, who explores the way this concept was used and developed over Heidegger's career, and Spinosa, this volume, chapter 30, who argues that *Ereignis* should be understood as the tendency in the practices of gathering).

Another focal point of Heidegger's work during this period was poetry and art. During winter semester 1934 to 1935, Heidegger offered his first lecture course devoted to the work of the poet Hölderlin (*Hölderlins Hymnen "Germanien" und "Der Rhein,"* GA 39). Over the next three decades, Heidegger taught several more courses devoted to Hölderlin and poetry, and presented a number of lectures on poetry and art. These lectures include "The Origin of the Work of Art" (GA 5), ". . . Poetically Man Dwells . . ." (GA 7), and "The Nature of Language" (GA 12), among many others.

Heidegger's interest in art and poetry is driven by the belief that they can play a privileged role in instituting and focusing changes in the prevailing unconcealment of being. As he noted in a 1935 lecture course, "Unconcealment occurs only when it is achieved by work: the work of the word in poetry, the work of stone in temple and statue, the work of the word in thought, the work of the *polis* as the historical place in which all this is grounded and preserved."[5] This view was later explained and explanded in "The Origin of the Work of Art": "The essence of art, on which both the artwork and the artist depend, is the setting-itself-into-work of truth. It is due to art's poetic essence that, in the midst of beings, art breaks open an open place, in whose openness everything is other than usual."[6] Works of art can show us a new way of understanding what is important and trivial, central and marginal, to be ignored or demanding of our attention and concern. They do this by giving us a work which can serve as a cultural paradigm. As such, the work shapes a culture's sensibilities by collecting the scattered practices of a people, unifying them into coherent and meaningful possibilities for action, and epitomizing this unified and coherent meaning in a visible fashion. The people, in turn, by getting in tune with the artwork, can then relate to each other in the shared light of the work. As we become attuned to the sense for the world embodied by a work of art, our ways of being disposed for everything else in the world can change also (see Dreyfus, this volume, chapter 25).

After his resignation from the rectorship, Heidegger also began an intensive engagement with Nietzsche's thought (see Sluga, this volume, chapter 7), offering lecture courses on Nietzsche in each year between 1936 and 1940 (see GA 43, 44, 45, 46, 47, 48; see also GA 6.1 and 6.2, and the essay "Nietzsches Wort: 'Gott ist Tot'" in GA 5). He later claimed of these courses that "anyone with ears to hear heard in these lectures a confrontation with National Socialism" (Heidegger 1993a: 101). Whatever political relevance these lectures had, they were philosophically decisive, as Heidegger further developed in them his account of the history of being, and the dangers of our contemporary understanding of being.

Following the war, Heidegger was banned from teaching by the Denazification Commission. The ban was lifted in 1949, but Heidegger immediately took emeritus status at Freiburg University. He offered, after 1949, only occasional university or professional seminars (for example, *What is Called Thinking?* (1951/2) in GA 8, or the *Heraclitus Seminar* (1966/7) and the other seminars in GA 15). For the most part, Heidegger developed his later views on the history of being, the event of appropriation, unconcealment, language, the work of art, technology, and the need to foster poetical dwelling, etc., in the form of public lectures and essays.

For example, in his first publication after the war, "The Letter on Humanism," Heidegger argued that the history of being is not to be abstracted from historical events, but rather historical events need to be understood on the basis of history. "History comes to language in the words of essential thinkers" (GA 9: 335), and this history of being "sustains and defines every *condition et situation humaine*" (GA 9: 314). Thus, for Heidegger, the most fundamental historical events are changes in the basic ways that we understand things, changes brought about by a new unconcealment of being (see Guignon, chapter 24, and Okrent, chapter 29, in this volume).

"The Letter on Humanism" also launched a string of published essays and public lectures devoted to warning against the dangers of technology (see, for example, the lectures collected in GA 79). Heidegger had commented as early as 1934 on the rise of a technology which "is more than the domination of tools and machine," but "rather has its fundamental significance in man's changed position in the world" (GA 38: 143). In the years following the war, Heidegger came to see more clearly that the real meaning of technological devices is found in the way that they, like works of art, have come to embody a distinct way of making sense of the world (see Borgmann, this volume, chapter 26). As we become addicted to the ease and flexibility of technological devices, Heidegger argues, we start to experience everything in terms of its ease and flexibility (or lack thereof). The result is that everything is seen, ultimately and ideally, as lacking any fixed character, or determinate "nature." Thus, Heidegger claims, the nature of technology consists in its being a mode of revealing. To say that technology is a mode of revealing amounts to the claim that within the technological world, everything appears as what it is in a certain uniform way. In the Christian age, everything showed up as God's creation, and showed up in terms of its nearness or distance from God's own nature. In the modern age, everything showed up as either a subject with a deep essence, or an object with fixed properties. In the technological age, by contrast, everything shows up in light of what will allow us to put it to "the greatest possible use at the lowest expenditure" (GA 7: 19). That is, we want it to be as maximally usable as possible. As technology expands into new domains, the world is gradually becoming a place in which everything shows up more and more as lacking in any inherent significance, use, or purpose.

Heidegger's name for the way in which objects will come to appear and be experienced in a purely technological world is "resource" – by which he means entities that are removed from their natural conditions and contexts, and reorganized in such a way as to be completely available, flexible, interchangeable, and ready to be employed in an indefinite variety of manners. If all we encounter are resources, Heidegger worries, our lives and all the things with which we deal, will lose their weightiness or importance. All becomes equally trivial, equally lacking in goodness and rightness and worth. Thus, in the technological age, even people are reduced from modern subjects with fixed desires and a deep immanent truth, to "functionaries of enframing" (GA 79: 30). In such a world, nothing is encountered as really mattering, that is, as having a worth that exceeds its purely instrumental value for satisfying transitory urges. In such a world, we lose a sense that our understanding of that in virtue of which things used to matter – a shared vision of the good, or the correct way to live a life, or justice, etc. – is grounded in something more than our willing it to be so.

Heidegger initially hoped that art and poetry could play a role in resisting the transition to a technological world. But they can only do this if we have non-technological practices for experiencing art and language. This is because even art and poetry, in a technological age, are understood as resources for the production of mere aesthetic experiences. The result is that "the world age of technological-industrial civilization conceals within itself an increasing danger that is all-too-rarely considered in its foundations: the supporting enlivening of poetry, of the arts, of reflective thinking cannot be experienced any more in their self-speaking truth."[7]

Thus, a central theme of Heidegger's post-war lectures is the need to reconceive language in terms of world disclosure (see, for example, the essays collected in *Unterwegs zur Sprache*, GA 12; see also Taylor, this volume, chapter 27). Traditional accounts of language as a conventional means of designation assume that a world has already been disclosed, for it is on the background of shared way of being in the world that language can designate. But how is it that the world is opened up in the first place, and opened up in such a way that language can serve to designate or refer to objects in the world? Heidegger argues that human speech originates from something that is prior to human communicative activity. Heidegger names this something "originary language." This originary language is the "saying" that shows things – it is the articulation prior to any human speech which brings things into a certain structure, and makes salient particular features of the world. It is a kind of pointing out – a highlighting of some features of the world and not others. "We speak from out of" a language, and this language speaks to us "in everything that addresses us; in everything that awaits us as unspoken; but also in every speaking of *ours*" (GA 12: 246/Heidegger 1993b: 413). Human speaking is always a "hearing" – a responding to the articulation of the world worked by the originary language.

We can thus think of overcoming technology in terms of learning to hear a different language than that spoken by the technological world. We learn to hear and respond differently, Heidegger thought, by practicing dwelling with the fourfold of earth, sky, mortals, and divinities (see Edwards, this volume, chapter 28). The fourfold names the different regions of our existence which can contribute to giving us a particular, localized way of dwelling. As we learn to live in harmony with our particular world – our earth, our sky, our mortality, and our divinities – we can be pulled out of a technologically frenzied existence. This is because, in such being at home, we allow ourselves to be conditioned by *things*, understood as a special class of entities – namely, entities that are uniquely suited to our way of being in the world. As Heidegger noted in one of the very last things he wrote, "reflection is required on whether and how, in the age of the technologized uniform world civilization, there can still be a home" (GA 13: 243).

Notes

1 In this respect, an immortal would experience herself and the world differently than we do. For example, our decisions are inherently marked by the fact that we don't have endless opportunities to revisit them. Pursuing one way of being restricts the possibility of pursuing others, because every passing day brings us nearer to our death.

2 Of course, it doesn't follow that the world is revealed as lacking meaning. We always already encounter ourselves in a meaningful world. Anxiety shows us, however, that the world need not have the meaning that it does (even if we can't help but see it as having the meaning that it does).

3 Writing to Richardson, Heidegger noted: "The distinction you make between Heidegger I and II is justified only on the condition that this is kept constantly in mind: only by way of what [Heidegger] I has thought does one gain access to what is to-be-thought by [Heidegger] II. But the thought of [Heidegger] I becomes possible only if it is contained in [Heidegger] II" (Richardson 1974: 8).

4 Richardson (1974: 4). See also "My way to phenomenology," in Heidegger (1972: 74–82).

5 EM: 146/Heidegger (1959: 191).

6 GA 5: 59/Heidegger (1993b: 197).

7   "Ein Grusswort für das Symposion in Beirut, November 1974," in GA 16: 741, and
    "Grusswort anlässlich des Erscheinens von Nr. 500 der Zeitschrift Riso" (November 16,
    1974), GA 16: 743.

References and further reading

Heidegger, M. (1959) *An Introduction to Metaphysics* (trans. R. Manheim). New Haven, CT: Yale
    University Press.
Heidegger, M. (1972) *On Time and Being* (trans. J. Stambaugh). New York: Harper Torchbooks.
Heidegger, M. (1993a) "Only a God can save us": *Der Spiegel*'s interview with Martin Heidegger
    (1966). In R. Wolin (ed.), *The Heidegger Controversy*. Cambridge, MA: MIT Press.
Heidegger, M. (1993b) *Basic Writings* (ed. D. F. Krell). San Francisco: HarperSanFrancisco.
Heidegger, M. (2002) *Identity and Difference*. Chicago: University of Chicago Press (originally pub-
    lished 1957).
Richardson, W. (1974) *Heidegger: Through Phenomenology to Thought*. The Hague: Martinus
    Nijhoff.

Part I

EARLY HEIDEGGER: THEMES AND INFLUENCES

2

The Earliest Heidegger: A New Field of Research[1]

JOHN VAN BUREN

The rediscovery of the earliest Heidegger, made possible by the recent publication of his hitherto virtually forgotten writings before his 1927 *Being and Time*, has today led to a new field of Heidegger scholarship and changed the whole face of Heidegger studies. We now understand this thinker much differently than we did a decade ago. This chapter provides a general overview of the development of Heidegger's Early Freiburg Period (1915–23) leading up to *Being and Time* and its historical sources in neo-Scholasticism, phenomenology of religion, and Aristotle, and broaches some of its implications for rereading Heidegger today.

Much is known and made of the later Heidegger's "turn" (*Kehre*) in the years following the publication of his *Being and Time* in 1927. But an equally profound turn took place around 1917–18, when Heidegger underwent a difficult religious, philosophical turn from the Catholic faith and the neo-Scholastic philosophy of his student years (1909–15) to a novel phenomenology of religion and phenomenological ontology. This turn is documented in Heidegger's correspondence with his colleague and friend at the University of Freiburg, Father Engelbert Krebs, who on March 21, 1917 married Heidegger and his fiancée, Elfride Petri, a Lutheran who had attended the very first university course Heidegger taught in WS[2] 1915–16. Mrs Heidegger had consulted with Krebs before the wedding about her wish to convert to Catholicism, but when she visited him again shortly before Christmas of 1918, she brought with her some weighty news that he recorded in his journal: "My husband no longer has his faith in the Church, and I did not find it. His faith was already undermined by doubt at our wedding." "Both of us now think in a Protestant manner (i.e., without a fixed dogmatic tie), believe in the personal God, pray to him in the spirit of Christ, but without Protestant or Catholic orthodoxy" (Ott 1988: 99–108). On January 9, 1919 Heidegger himself wrote to Krebs, reminding him of his wife's visit and explaining that "epistemological insights extending to a theory of historical knowledge have made the *system* of Catholicism problematic and unacceptable to me, but not Christianity and metaphysics – these, though, in a new sense." He assures Krebs that he has lost neither his scholarly interest in "the Middle Ages," nor his "deep respect for the lifeworld of Catholicism," nor his Christian faith. He concludes with a statement that has the ring of Luther's "Here I stand." "I believe that I have the inner calling to philosophy and, through my research and teaching, to do what stands in my power for the sake of the eternal vocation of the inner man, and *to do it for this alone*, and so justify my existence and work ultimately before God" (Heidegger 2002: 69–70). With this remarkable letter, Heidegger's previously declared struggle to defend the "Catholic worldview" and his "career in the service of researching and teaching Christian-Scholastic philosophy" officially ends. The conservative Catholic has become a liberal Protestant and, given the continuation of his interests in medieval mysticism from his student days, the exponent of a kind of free Lutheran mysticism.

Heidegger's former neo-Scholasticism, which had been worked out in his 1915 post-doctoral dissertation (*Habilitationsschrift*) on Duns Scotus, but was now no longer "acceptable" to him in light of "theory of historical knowledge," consisted in an "onto-logic" (GA 1: 55) of the categories of being, which approached categories as a timeless ideal nexus by means of which intentional "judgments" gain access to real being and which is itself grounded in the absolute being of God. Philosophically, the former neo-Scholastic now becomes an anti-philosopher who begins to speak of the end of philoso-phy and a new beginning for both philosophy and theology – themes that until recently were thought to be found exclusively in the later Heidegger. In his first lecture course after the war in KNS 1919, he maintains that "phenomenological critique" leads to "the catastrophe of all (previous) philosophy" and "a completely new concept of phi-losophy" (GA 56/57: 11–12, 125–31). On August 19, 1921 he actually writes to his student Karl Löwith that "I am no philosopher. I do not presume even to do something comparable; it is not at all my intention" (Heidegger 1990: 28). Around 1921–2, he tells his students that post-metaphysical thinking is a kind of skepticism, and that "skep-ticism is a beginning, and as the genuine beginning it is also the end of philosophy." And for support he quotes Kierkegaard: " 'But what philosophy and the philosopher find difficult is stopping.' Kierkegaard, *Either/Or*, Vol. I. (Stopping at the genuine begin-ning!)" (GA 61: 35, 186, 182). Again on May 9, 1923 he told them "that as far as he was concerned, philosophy was over" (Sheehan 1979: 82). In the texts of Heidegger's Early Freiburg Period, we glimpse the daring, experimental, and anti-philosophical type of thinking that Heidegger was doing before *Sein und Zeit*. They remind one less of Kant or Heraclitus than of the ancient skeptics, the mystics, the young Luther, Kierkegaard, and even Derrida. Heidegger is at this time a great destroyer and demythologizer of Western metaphysics. The scope and passion of this criticism and innovation remain perhaps unmatched in his entire corpus. By the time *Being and Time* is published in 1927, his plans for the end of philosophy and a new beginning have already been modified and tamed under the influence of the transcendental thought of Husserl and Kant. The early Freiburg period gives us a good sense of how the earliest version of Heidegger's planned book about "being and time" that later became the plodding sci-entific treatise called *Being and Time* (an aberration in Heidegger's own eyes) originally read. And, just as importantly, this period allows one to understand how it could be that his "turn" around 1930 was in part made possible by a re-turn to and creative rep-etition of themes in his earliest thought (Heidegger 2002: 10–14).

The details of Heidegger's first "turn" in the late teens are becoming more known today, but are still shrouded in darkness, because his corpus from these years is rela-tively small and little of it is extant. He held lecture courses on "The Basic Outlines of Ancient and Scholastic Philosophy" in WS 1915–16, "German Idealism" in SS 1916, and "Basic Problems in Logic" in WS 1916–17. But neither his own manuscripts nor student transcripts for these courses have been found. The university course catalogues announced that he was giving courses on "Hegel" in SS 1917, on "Plato" in WS 1917–18, and on "Lotze and the Development of Modern Logic" in SS 1918. But he did not deliver them since he was actually away most of the time doing military service, which included a two-month sojourn at a meteorological station on the western front (Ott 1988: 104–5). But we do know that during these interim years he made a new and intensive turn to Husserl's phenomenology and to its application in a phenomenology of religion.

When Husserl arrived at the University of Freiburg in 1916 as Heinrich Rickert's successor, Heidegger began soliciting the established scholar's support of his studies and career, making visits, sending letters, and presenting Husserl with copies of his journal articles as well as his postdoctoral dissertation, which Husserl helped to get published. But during 1916 and early 1917 Husserl kept the young lecturer at arm's length, apologizing in a few postcards that his busy schedule did not allow him to do more. In the winter of 1917–18 Husserl suddenly becomes more enthusiastic and actively takes on the role of fatherly supporter, writing on March 28, 1918 to the "Home Guard Soldier Martin Heidegger" about his imminent return from "the field" to university life and how "I will sincerely and gladly do my part to put you back *in medias res* and familiarize you with this *res* in *symphilosophein*," co-philosophizing. Then comes a long and intimate letter on September 10, 1918 in which Husserl discusses in detail his recent work and plans for Heidegger's own work (Husserl 1994: 129–30, 135–6). When Heidegger was discharged from military service on November 16, 1918 and returned to Freiburg, he finally met Husserl in his workshop, writing to his friend Elisabeth Blochmann on January 14, 1919 about his "intensive work with Husserl" and again on May 1 about his "continual learning in the company of Husserl" (Heidegger and Blochmann 1989: 12, 16). The two were working together so well that Husserl submitted a request on January 7 to the Ministry of Education for Heidegger's promotion to the unprecedented position of assistant to his chair. Thanks to Husserl's persistence, the request was granted in the following year, but with the stipulation that the assistantship be restricted to the person of Heidegger (Ott 1988: 96–104, 114–15). He was now officially Husserl's assistant and remained such until his departure to Marburg in 1923. The neo-Scholastic had become a card-carrying phenomenologist.

Heidegger's phenomenological turn was bound up with a reformulation of the phenomenology of religion that he had already announced in his postdoctoral dissertation on Duns Scotus. It was supposed to entail "a phenomenological elaboration of mystical, moral-theological, and ascetic literature," including "Eckhartian mysticism" (GA 1: 205, 402). These plans were still alive when Heidegger wrote to the medievalist Martin Grabmann on January 7, 1917 about a possible review of his Scotus book and stressed that "your friendly postcard and a letter from Bäumker are for me the most valuable incentives for further works in the area of medieval Scholasticism and mysticism" (Köstler 1980: 104). In his letter of September 10, 1918 to Heidegger on the front, Husserl writes: "Thus each to his own as if the salvation of the world depended upon it alone, and so I in philosophy and you as weatherman and in the side job of phenomenologist of religion." During the preceding summer Heidegger and his friend Heinrich Ochsner had brought Rudolf Otto's book *The Holy* to the attention of Husserl, whose letter of September 10 suggests that Heidegger may have been thinking of doing a review of this work. "I am reading with great interest Otto's book *The Holy*, an attempt in fact at a phenomenology of the consciousness of God. . . . Too bad that you do not have time to write a (deeply penetrating) critical review" (Husserl 1994: 135–6). Then in his letter of January 9, 1919 to Krebs, Heidegger himself mentions "my investigations in the phenomenology of religion, which will draw heavily on the Middle Ages" (Heidegger 2002: 69).

The phenomenology of religion that Heidegger tentatively broached in his postdoctoral dissertation on Duns Scotus focused on a personalist and historically oriented mysticism. But he later came to see that it was permeated by problematic elements from the Aristotelian-Scholastic worldview of Catholicism, the speculative theological thinking of German Idealism, and the "onto-logic" of neo-Kantianism and Husserlian phenomenology. In his courses from KNS 1919 onwards, Heidegger now repeatedly expresses the view that the Aristotelian and neo-Platonic conceptuality of both Catholic and mainstream Protestant theology amounted to a foreign infiltration and distortion of the concrete historicity of the "primal Christianity" (*Urchristentum*) of the New Testament, which had nonetheless violently reasserted itself at key points in religious history, namely in Augustine, the medieval mystics, Pascal, Schleiermacher, Kierkegaard, and especially the young Luther. "The historical," Heidegger writes in KNS 1919, "is somehow co-given in the essence of Christianity itself . . . apart from a few imperfect attempts in the new Protestant theology, there is not even the slightest consciousness that a problem with the greatest consequences lies here" (GA 56/57: 26). This is the realization that he had come to in the interim war years of 1917–18, judging from his letter of 1919 to Krebs and from his counsel to Elisabeth Blochmann on November 7, 1918 that "what you search for you find in yourself – there is a path from primal religious experience to theology, but it *need not* lead from theology to religious consciousness and its vivacity" (Heidegger and Blochmann 1989: 10). Following in the footsteps of the key thinkers in whom he thought that primal New Testament Christianity had reasserted itself, Heidegger's newly conceived phenomenology of religion became the project of a "destruction" of the Greek conceptuality of traditional theological thought that would penetrate to the historicity of "the religious lifeworld" of primal Christianity and find a more adequate conceptuality for it with the help of Husserl's phenomenology and Dilthey's philosophy of life. The young Heidegger's idea of the end of philosophy also meant the end of theology and a new beginning for it. The Scholastic paradigm in which God appears as the presence of the *summum ens* given to contemplation was to be dismantled back to the more primal New Testament experience of God as the *deus absconditus* who is accessible only to an anxious and wakeful faith within kairological time.

Around 1917 Heidegger was especially attracted to the Protestant theologian and romantic philosopher Friedrich Schleiermacher, giving a talk on August 2, 1917 on Schleiermacher's *Discourses on Religion* (GA 60). Heidegger's enthusiasm must have been great because that Easter he had actually been giving away copies of Hermann Süskind's *Christianity and History in Schleiermacher* (Ochwadt and Tecklenborg 1981: 92). Then in 1918 and 1919, we find him discussing Schleiermacher at great length in his correspondence with his friend Elisabeth Blochmann (Heidegger and Blochmann 1989: 9–13). After having presented a reading of the development of Christianity in its relation to Greek philosophy in his first postwar course of KNS 1919, Heidegger's SS

1919 course states that "[Schleiermacher] discovered primal Christianity" through his regress to primal religious experience in the realm of "feeling." What specifically interested Heidegger was that Schleiermacher cut through the foreign infiltration of Greek philosophy into primal Christianity by distinguishing religion sharply from metaphysics and theological doctrine, arguing that it is founded autonomously on the immediate intuition of the historical manifestation of the infinite in the unique particularities of the world and, more specifically, on the personal self-consciousness of the "feeling of dependence" on the infinite (GA 56/57: 18, 134).

Medieval mysticism played the same critical "deconstructive" role for Heidegger's phenomenology of religion, as he saw it to be a fusion of the "religious lifeworld" of primal Christianity and the "researching lifeworld" of Scholasticism. "The original motives and tendencies of both lifeworlds enter into and flow together in mysticism" (GA 56/57: 5, 18, 211). While doing military service in 1918, he had found time to study Adolf Deissmann's studies of Pauline mysticism and works by Bernard of Clairvaux and Theresa of Avila. He later scheduled a course titled "The Philosophical Foundations of Medieval Mysticism" for WS 1919–20, but canceled it apparently due to lack of time to prepare for both this and the other course he was planning. His notes for this course show that he was planning to deal with Meister Eckhart, Bernard of Clairvaux, Theresa of Avila, Francis of Assisi, and Thomas à Kempis (GA 60). Heidegger's WS 1921–2 course likewise pointed out the rediscovery of primal Christianity in the mystics. The late Scholasticism "consolidated through the reception of Aristotle" was, he wrote, "again loosened up in its vivacity of experience through the mysticism of Tauler" (GA 61: 7).

In Heidegger's course of KNS 1919 we read that after the flourishing of high-medieval mysticism "religious consciousness wins its new position with Luther" (GA 56/57: 18) All indications are that sometime shortly after the war Heidegger entered into an intensive study of Luther's writings, as he was drawn to Luther's ferocious critique of Greek and Medieval philosophy and his return to the original biblical sources of Christianity. Karl Jaspers recalls that during his visit with Heidegger in April 1920 "he sat alone with him in his den, watched him at his Luther studies, and saw the intensity of his work" (Jaspers 1977: 93). Julius Ebbinghaus remembers that after the war his friend Heidegger "had received the Erlangen edition of Luther's works as a prize or gift – and so we read Luther's reformatory writings for a while in the evenings we spent together [one per week]." Later in 1923 Heidegger and Ebbinghaus co-taught a seminar on "The Theological Foundations of Kant's *Religion within the Limits of Mere Reason*," which explored the influence of Luther on Kant and German Idealism (Pongratz 1977: 33). In 1922 Heidegger had actually planned to published a journal essay on "The Ontological Foundations of Late Medieval Anthropology and the Theology of the Young Luther," but like so many of his other early publication plans, it never appeared. Heidegger's preoccupation with Luther continued even after his move to the University of Marburg in 1923. For example, he attended Rudolf Bultmann's theology seminar on the ethics of Saint Paul, presenting a two-part lecture on "The Problem of Sin in Luther" (Heidegger 2002: 105–10). Though Luther was the main theological influence on Heidegger's phenomenology of religion and the new kind of ontology he was also developing, mention must also be made of his intense interest in Kierkegaard, which stretched back to around 1911. A decisive point came in 1919 with the appearance of Jaspers's book *Psychology of Worldviews*, which provided extensive treatment of Kierkegaard's concepts of "human existence," "death," "guilt," "the moment," "repetition," and "indirect communication." Heidegger was so interested in this work that between 1919 and 1921 he worked on a long review of it, though it was published only much later in his life (Heidegger 2002: 71–103).

Heidegger's concern was both a general phenomenological ontology of being and a regional phenomenological theology of primal Christianity, both a new ontological language and a new theological language. The phenomenologist of religion was also an ontologist, the ontologist also a theologian. In his philosophy courses he talked about theology, and in his religion courses he talked about philosophy. There is a peculiar back-and-forth movement in his youthful thought between religion and ontology, such that each was supposed to make the other possible. To begin with, the destruction of the Greek philosophical conceptuality of theology back to primal Christian sources that Heidegger found carried out in key religious thinkers like Luther became a model not only for his own *theological* deconstruction, but also for his wider project of the end of *philosophy* itself, that is, for his destruction of Greek, medieval, and modern metaphysics back to its concealed sources in the historicity of being. This is the philosophical way that he used Paul's attacks on the vanity of Greek philosophy, the mystics' *via negativa* to the efflux of the divine life, Luther's scathing critiques of the "theology of glory" of Aristotelian Scholasticism, Schleiermacher's anti-metaphysical regress to the feeling of absolute dependence, and Kierkegaard's parodies of modern speculative thought in the name of the earnestness of ethico-religious *Existenz*. Heidegger had become a philosophical rebel, and his first allies in this reawakened battle of Greek giants about being were neither Heraclitus nor Aristotle, but a band of anti-Greek and anti-philosophical Christian trouble-makers. Armed with the analogical model of the Biblical exhortation "Return you sons of men!" Heidegger was making his first decisive "turn" from being to his lifelong topic of the mysterious depth-dimension of the temporal giving of being, which he described as a "there is/it gives" (*Es gibt*), "worlding" (*Welten*), and "appropriating event" (*Ereignis*) (1919), as kairological time (1920–1), and as temporal motion (*kinesis*) (1921–2). Such were the earliest paths on which Heidegger searched for a new "genuine beginning" for ontology, paths that would again be taken up in his later thought after *Being and Time*. "One thing [is] certain," Heidegger wrote in WS 1921–2, "not at an end; therefore begin, *begin genuinely* . . . beginning has its 'time'. To begin for another time is senseless" (GA 61: 186).

Heidegger the ontologist was interested not only in the explosive force of his favourite religious thinkers, but also in their rich positive analyses of the historical nature of primal Christian experience. He took the Christian experience of such realities as mystery, the coming (parousia), the moment (*kairos*), wakefulness, and falling to be particular "ontic" models from which to read off and formalize general, ontically non-committal "ontological" categories that would make up his new beginning for ontology. He pursued an analogy between mystical experience and experience in general, between the hidden god of Pauline kairology and the non-objectifiable dimension of concealment that belongs to the historicity of being. Around 1921 he will start also using Aristotle's investigations of moral life as an ontic model, and in the 1930s he turns to the model of aesthetic and mythic experience in poetry. Referring to the fact that many of the major German philosophers had actually begun in Protestant theol-

24

ogy, he told his students bluntly in 1921 that "Fichte, Schelling, and Hegel were [Lutheran] theologians, and Kant is to be understood theologically, so long as one is not inclined to turn him into the rattling skeleton of a so-called epistemologist" (GA 61: 7). "Fichte, Schelling, and Hegel come out of *theology* and received from it the basic impulses of their speculative thought" (Heidegger 2002: 125). In teasing out the onto-logical significance of the experience of historicity in Christian experience, Heidegger knew that he was taking up the strategies of Kant, the German Idealists, Dilthey, Kierkegaard, Jaspers's *Psychology of Worldviews*, and Scheler, who all carried out a "for-malizing detheologization" of Christian experience (GA 63: 26–7). For example, in the correspondence between Dilthey and Count Yorck that Heidegger read with great inter-est in 1923, Count Yorck writes that "dogmatics was the attempt to formulate an ontol-ogy of the higher, the historical life." And Dilthey echoes him in maintaining that Christianity must be lifted up into something like a "transcendental theology." That is, "all dogmas must be brought to their universal value for all human life . . . they are the consciousness of the trans-sensual and trans-rational nature of historicity pure and simple." "If the dogmas . . . are untenable in their restriction to the facts of Christian history, then in their universal sense they express the highest living content of all history" (von Schulenburg 1923: 154–8). Bultmann went too far in stressing Heidegger's indebtedness to Christian sources when he said that his early thought was "no more than a secularized, philosophical version of the New Testament view of human life" (Bultmann 1953: 23). Heidegger had already in the late teens given up his previous equation of philosophy with the "true worldview," namely, the "Catholic worldview" of neo-Scholasticism. He now maintained a sharp separation of worldview and ontology, which as "primal science" can provide only a formal content that is reli-giously non-committal and therefore not restricted in its ontic application to the par-ticular positive domain of Christian experience (GA 56/57: 7–12). Philosophy, he insisted, must be "atheistic in principle," not because it holds that God does not exist, but because, first, access to God is based on faith and, second, the formal indications of ontology must be capable of being applied to non-religious experience as well (Heidegger 2002: 121).

Heidegger certainly thought that he could simultaneously be both an ontological and a theological thinker. "He saw himself – at that time – as a Christian theologian," writes Gadamer. "All his efforts to sort things out with himself and with his own ques-tions were provoked by the task of freeing himself from the prevailing theology in which he had been educated, in order that he could become a Christian" (Gadamer 1983: 142). Heidegger wanted to apply his new phenomenological ontology to the regional task of developing a new theological conceptuality in his phenomenology of religion. Since the conceptual basis of theology had after all been provided originally by Platonic and Aristotelian philosophy, theo*logical* reform presupposed philosophical reform. Only a new ontological language able to do justice to the historicity of being in general would be able to displace the static objectifying language of Aristotelian Scholasticism that underlay Christian theology. In KNS 1919 Heidegger explains that, after the synthesis effected in the age of mysticism at the end of the Middle Ages, Luther's reformation had the result that the *religious* lifeworld of New Testament Christianity and the *philosoph-ical* lifeworld of Aristotelian Scholasticism "split apart" (GA 56/57: 18). Neither Luther nor his followers succeeded in finding a new conceptuality for the rediscovery of primal religious consciousness; rather, everything fell back into a new "Protestant Scholasticism which through Melanchthon was immediately supplied with specifically interpreted Aristotelian motives. This dogmatic with its essential Aristotelian directions is the soil and root of German idealism." Reformation theology and the German philosophy built on it led to a "derailing of the new motifs of Lutheran theology" (GA 61: 7) and "succeeded only in very small measure in providing a genuine explication of Luther's new fundamental religious position and its immanent possibilities" (Heidegger 2002: 125). Heidegger likewise thought that due to his entanglement in Hegelian dialectics, Kierkegaard likewise failed to develop a conceptuality fully adequate to Luther's historical insights (GA 63: 41–2). That became the task of Heidegger's application of his new historically oriented phenomenological ontology to a phenomenology of religion.

In his letter of 1917 to Grabmann about "further works in the area of Scholasticism and mysticism," Heidegger adds the proviso: "But beforehand I want to acquire sufficient assurance about systematic problems, something that aims at an investigation of philosophy of value and phenomenology *from the inside out*" (Köstler 1980: 104). On May 1, 1919 he writes to Blochmann that "my own work is very concentrated, having to do with principles and the concrete: basic problems of phenomenological method . . . constantly penetrating anew into the genuine origins, preliminary work for a phenomenology of religious consciousness" (Heidegger and Blochmann 1989: 16). In 1921, he writes to his student Karl Löwith that "I am no philosopher." "I am a 'Christian theo*logian*'" (Heidegger 1990: 28–9). This meant both that his own way of doing philosophy (in contrast to Löwith) is to start from the historical *logos* of Christianity, and that he is also searching for a fitting *logos* with which one can speak about religious experience. In a theological discussion in which he participated in 1923, he threw out the challenge that "it is the true task of theology, which must be discovered again, to find the word that is able to call one to faith and preserve one in faith" (Gadamer 1983: 29). He repeated this challenge in his discussion of the relation between ontology and theology in his course of SS 1925 and in *Being and Time*: "Theology is seeking a more original interpretation of the being of the human being toward God, prescribed from the meaning of faith and remaining within it" (GA 20: 6). After centuries it is only now "slowly beginning to understand once more Luther's insight that its dogmatic system rests on a 'foundation' that has not arisen from a questioning in which faith is primary, and whose conceptuality is not only not adequate for the problematic of theology, but rather conceals and distorts it" (GA 1: 10).

This peculiar back-and-forth movement between religion and ontology shows up in the series of courses that Heidegger began in 1919 (Heidegger 2002: 25–30). His three courses of 1919 are titled "The Idea of Philosophy and the Problem of Worldviews," "Phenomenology and Transcendental Philosophy of Value," and "On the Essence of the University and Academic Studies" (GA 56/57). On November 7, 1918 he wrote to Blochmann that he had also scheduled "a seminar on the problem of the categories," which was the very title of the conclusion he wrote for the publication of his postdoctoral dissertation on Duns Scotus (Heidegger and Blochmann 1989: 12). In these courses he takes as his main theme phenomenological and neo-Kantian ontology, referring back to his earlier doctrine of categories in his postdoctoral dissertation and essays. Here he is moving from religion to ontology in order to rethink the latter historically with aid of the former. In WS 1919–20 he then plans to hold the course titled "The Philosophical Foundations of Medieval Mysticism," in which he goes in the opposite direction of applying his new ontology to a phenomenology of mysticism. This course was to have been taught alongside the other course he announced on "Selected Problems in Recent Phenomenology." But Heidegger replaced the course on mysticism with an expansion of the course on phenomenology, which was then retitled as "Basic Problems in Phenomenology" (GA 24). Heidegger may very well have replaced the course on mysticism not only because of the official reason given, namely lack of time, but also because he felt that he had still not adequately worked out the philosophical conceptuality and methodology needed for executing the concrete analyses of his phenomenology of religion. In SS 1920 he continued with a course on "Phenomenology of Intuition and Expression: Theory of Philosophical Concept-Formation" (GA 59). It was not only until WS 1920–1 that Heidegger ventured in the opposite direction of applying his developing ontology to a phenomenology of religion. In this semester he holds the course "Introduction to the Phenomenology of Religion," the first part of which dealt with general methodological and conceptual considerations in connection with contemporary philosophy of religion (GA 60). Once the students had gone to the dean to complain about the lack of religious content in the course, Heidegger now finally had no choice but to enter into interpretations of concrete religious phenomena, and so in the second part of the course he gave a powerful phenomenological analysis of kairological time and the non-objectifiability of God found in Paul's letters on the Second Coming. Then in SS 1921 he continued with a course on "Augustine and neo-Platonism" (GA 60), in which he investigated how Augustine's understanding of the historicity of New Testament Christianity was obscured through his adoption of neo-Platonic conceptuality. But it was not until 1927 that Heidegger delivered the final fruits of his phenomenology of religion in the lecture "Phenomenology and Theology," which was delivered in 1927 before the Protestant theological faculty at the Univerisity of Tübingen. Here he showed the theologians how ontological concepts such as history, guilt, falling, and conscience in *Being and Time* could make possible a new theological language that would finally be able to do justice to Luther's statement that "faith means surrendering oneself to matters that cannot be seen" (Heidegger 1976: 5–21). By this time, however, Heidegger's Christian faith and his interests in Christian theology had been on the wane for a number of years. If the development of Heidegger's religious interests can be broken down into three phases, namely, the anti-modernist neo-Scholastic phase (1909–13), the mystical neo-neo-Scholastic phase (1914–16), and the free Protestant mystical phase from 1917 into the early 1920s, then treatment of a fourth phase would have to show that sometime in the later 1920s he began to identify with the experience of the death of God in Nietzsche and Hölderlin, as well as with their aspirations toward the birth of a new and more Greek God, which became central themes in his later writings.

In 1921 a third major influence entered the horizon of Heidegger's thinking and teaching, namely Aristotle. From this point on, there is a more complicated three-way movement between Christianity, phenomenology, and Aristotle. Each of Heidegger's texts during this period is a highly creative, reproductive weaving of these and other sources into a *textum* that momentarily clothed his "darkly intimated" topic of the relation between "being and time," until it eventually came apart at the seams, and the remains were then rewoven into the next draft of a planned book about "being and time." In retrospectively describing this period, Heidegger later wrote: "I always followed only an unclear trace of the right path, but I followed. The trace was an almost imperceptible promise announcing a release into the open, now dark and confused, now lightning-sharp like a sudden insight, which then again for a long time withdrew from every attempt to say it" (Heidegger 1971: 121, 130). The trace he began to follow in 1921 involved attempting to decipher Aristotle's texts with the help of the conceptuality of phenomenology, but the way was cleared for this by his radicalization of Luther's "destruction" of Aristotelian Scholasticism and of Aristotle himself. Taking up the novel interpretations of Aristotle he found in Luther and Kierkegaard, Heidegger attempted to dismantle Aristotle's metaphysics of "substance" back to the more primal moments of "practical wisdom," "motion," and "the moment" in Aristotle's practical writings. In turn, he used Aristotle's analyses of moral life as an ontic model from which to read off general ontological categories that could help him work out his new phenomenological ontology.

Heidegger's teaching record betrays an intense engagement with Aristotle at this time. Already in SS 1921, while he was presenting his course on Augustine, he also gave the seminar "Phenomenological Exercises for Beginners in Connection with Aristotle's *De anima*." Then in WS 1921–2 he gave his first course on Aristotle which was titled "Phenomenological Interpretations in Connection with Aristotle: Introduction to Phenomenological Research," which he planned to revise and publish as a book about "being and time" (GA 61: 201). In it he never really did get around to dealing with Aristotle's texts, but rather went through the history of the interpretation of Aristotle (stressing Luther's attack), dealt with the question of what philosophy is, explored the formally indicative nature of philosophical conceptuality, and gave a long preparatory analysis of the categories of being as they show themselves within "factical life." This course was followed by another course on Aristotle in SS 1922 with the same major title, but the different subtitle "Ontology and Logic." It proceeded by way of translating key terms and phrases from Aristotle's *Metaphysics* and *Physics* (GA 62). Out of his two courses on Aristotle, Heidegger composed in October 1922 a long introduction to a massive projected work on Aristotle that had the same major title as his two Aristotle courses and was to have been published in the 1923 issue of Husserl's phenomenological journal (Heidegger 2002: 111–45). This introduction outlined both the history of the reception of Aristotle in Christian theology from Augustine to Luther and a preparatory phenomenological ontological analysis of the categories of being found in factical life, which was then applied to preliminary interpretations of Book One of *Metaphysics*, Book Six of *Nicomachean Ethics*, and Book One of *Physics*. The body of the work was to have provided expanded interpretations of Aristotle's texts, but it was never published even though Heidegger worked on it in the following years. In its place, the much different work titled *Being and Time* appeared in Husserl's journal four year later.

Due to the extra time needed for his book on Aristotle, WS 1922–3 saw Heidegger giving no lecture course, but only two seminars, one on Aristotle and the other on Husserl. Then in SS 1923 we find the last course of Heidegger's Early Freiburg Period, the course "Ontology – The Hermeneutics of Facticity" (GA 63), the crowning achievement of this period which presented the most masterful weaving together of phenomenology, primal Christianity, and Aristotle, as well as his first systematic, though succinct, expression of his new conception of ontology. He later said that this text constituted "the first notes for *Being and Time*" (Heidegger 1971: 9, 29), and rightly so since it presents the basic outlines of the later work, i.e. a hermeneutical and phenomenological approach to the question of being which precedes by way of an analysis of the "existentials" that structure human Dasein's encounter with its world and are ultimately based in temporality. However, unlike *Being and Time* and rather more like Heidegger's later poetic thinking, the investigation of being and Dasein's existentials was centered on the verb "to while" (*weilen*) and the neologism "awhileness" (*Jeweiligkeit*). Dasein's existentials such as "being in a world," "spatiality," "dealings," and "idle talk," and the ways in which it understands "being" within these existentials, were seen to be modes of "whiling" or "awhileness." Moreover, Heidegger centered all this also on a sustained analysis of his young family "whiling" at "the table" in their home, as they pursued activities from the children's play to the adults' research. Again, Heidegger seems to have worked unsuccessfully on this course manuscript with the plan of turning it into a book about "being and time" (GA 63: xi, 105). Instead, the work *Being and Time* was published in Husserl's journal three years later, though the terms "whiling" and "awhileness" had completely dropped out, only to resurface in his later writings, and there was little treatment of his earlier readings of Aristotle, primal Christianity, and phenomenology. What had happened in Heidegger's development in the first years of his Marburg Period (1923–8)?

When Heidegger moved to the University of Marburg in WS 1923–4, he did indeed for a while keep working on his book publication plan in the same vein as before, offering the course "Introduction to Phenomenological Research" on Aristotle and Husserl in his first semester (GA 17), the course "Basic Concepts in Aristotelian Philosophy" in SS 1924 (GA 18), and "Interpretations of Plato's Dialogues (*Sophist, Philebus*)" in WS 1924–5 (GA 19), which dealt equally with Plato's question of being and Aristotle's practical writings as the proper horizon to pursue this question. Then In SS 1925 he held the course "History of the Concept of Time: Prolegomena to a Phenomenology of History and Nature," which opened with a long reading of not just the method but more so the content of Husserl's transcendental phenomenology (GA 20). In WS 1925–6 he held the course "Logic," which began with an analysis of the concept of truth in Husserl and Aristotle, but then after the Christmas break dramatically turned to a discussion of Kant's transcendental idealism, including his Doctrine of Schematism (GA 21). These last two courses marked a decisive shift toward the model of Husserl's and Kant's transcendental thought at the very time that Heidegger was sitting down in 1926 to transform and weave the "traces" of his earlier course manuscripts and book plans into a more publishable text titled *Being and Time*, which was immediately hailed as a remarkable achievement presenting an existentialized version of transcendental phenomenology, and which henceforth became known as Heidegger's *magnum opus*, eclipsing and burying in obscurity the earlier, quite different, and less "transcendental" drafts of his planned book on "being and time," until they were rediscovered and began to be published in the 1980s and 1990s, leading to a new field of Heidegger studies.

By locating this *magnum opus* on the "path" of "traces" and drafts stretching back into the Early Freiburg Period and then forward into Heidegger's later post-turn writings after *Being and Time* when he re-turned for fresh takes on much earlier themes like "worlding," "appropriating event," and "whiling," we get a better sense of how it, too, for all its greatness, was itself but a "trace" on the path of differing drafts of a planned book about the "topic" of "being and time" that Heidegger kept trying to write and publish from the Early Freiburg Period to the end of his career in 1976, but never really did in anything like a final form.

Notes

1 Detailed discussion of the earliest Heidegger, on which the present chapter draws, can be found in van Buren (1994a, b), and my editorial introduction to Heidegger (2002: 1–15). The chronology of Heidegger's education, professional appointments, teaching, research, and publications to the composition of his *Being and Time* in 1926, on which this essay also draws, can be found in Heidegger (2002: 17–33).
2 The abbreviation "KNS" is employed for *Kriegsnotsemester* (Special Wartime Semester), "SS" for "Summer Semester," and "WS" for "Winter Semester."

References and further reading

Bultmann, R. (1953) New Testament and mythology. In *Kerygma and Myth* (trans. R. H. Fuller). London: SPCK.
Gadamer, H.-G. (1983) *Heideggers Wege*. Tübingen: Mohr.
Heidegger, M. (1971) *On the Way to Language* (trans. P. D. Hertz). New York: Harper & Row.
Heidegger, M. (1976) *The Piety of Thinking* (trans. J. G. Hart and J. C. Maraldo). Bloomington: Indiana University Press.
Heidegger, M. (1990) Drei Briefe Martin Heideggers an Karl Löwith. In D. Papenfuss and O. Pöggeler (eds), *Zur philosophischen Aktualität Heideggers*, volume 2: *Im Gespräch der Zeit*. Frankfurt: Klostermann.
Heidegger, M. (2002) *Supplements: From the Earliest Essays to Being and Time and Beyond* (trans. J. van Buren et al.). Albany: State University of New York Press.
Heidegger, M. and Blochmann, E. (1989) *Briefwechsel, 1918–1969*. Marbach am Neckar: Deutsche Schillergesellschaft.
Heidegger, M. and Jaspers, K. (1990) *Briefwechsel 1920–1963*. Frankfurt: Klostermann.
Husserl, E. (1994) *Briefwechsel*, volume IV. Dordrecht: Kluwer.
Jaspers, K. (1977) *Philosophische Autobiographie*. Munich: R. Piper.
Köstler, H. (1980) Heidegger schreibt an Grabmann. *Philosophisches Jahrbuch*, 87, 98–104.
Ochwadt, C. and Tecklenborg, E. (1981) *Das Mass des Verborgenen: Heinrich Ochsner (1891–1970) zum Gedächtnis*. Hannover: Charis-Verlag.
Ott, H. (1988) *Martin Heidegger: Unterwegs zu seiner Biographie*. Frankfurt: Campus Verlag.
Pongratz, L. J. (1977) *Philosophie in Selbstdarstellungen*, volume 3. Hamburg: Felix Meiner.
Sheehan, T. (1977) Heidegger's early years: fragments for a philosophical biography. *Listening*, 12, 3–20.
Sheehan, T. (1979) The "original form" of Sein und Zeit: Heidegger's Der Begriff der Zeit. *Journal of the British Society for Phenomenology*, 10, 78–83.

van Buren, J. (1994a) *The Young Heidegger: Rumor of the Hidden King*. Bloomington: Indiana University Press.

van Buren, J. (ed.) (1994b) *Reading Heidegger from the Start: Essays in His Earliest Thought*. Albany: State University of New York Press.

von Schulenburg, S. (ed.) (1923) *Briefwechsel zwischen Wilhelm Dilthey und dem Grafen Paul*. Halle: Niemeyer.

3

Heidegger and National Socialism

IAIN THOMSON

Introduction

It is unfortunate but in retrospect undeniable that Heidegger's brief but very public tenure as the first Nazi Rector of Freiburg University in 1933–4 helped to cast an early sheen of intellectual legitimacy over the brutal regime which, less than a decade later, earned everlasting historical infamy for Auschwitz and the other horrors of the Shoah. The question for many of us, then, is this: how do we come to terms with the fact that the man who was probably the greatest philosopher of the twentieth century threw the considerable weight of his thought behind what was certainly its most execrable political movement? This profoundly troubling juxtaposition has haunted intellectuals for nearly seventy years (Marcuse 1988), generating a secondary literature of singular immensity. Although the debates carried on in this literature are multifaceted and complex, a historical examination of this "Heidegger controversy" (Thomson 1999) shows that it has long had the character of a trial, both before it actually became one and after Heidegger himself was no longer alive to stand trial. Indeed, an "accuse or excuse" dichotomy still structures the field of competing interpretations, obliging scholars to take sides, as though with either the prosecution or the defense. Unfortunately, this adversarial logic increasingly dominates the public sphere in the West, its common spectacle of talking heads talking past one another working to obscure the fact that in complex matters the truth is usually located between the opposing extremes, unfit for the polemical purposes of demagogues on either side. Such a binary polarization has long diminished the signal-to-noise ratio of the so-called "Heidegger case" by putting the juridical imperative to either condemn or exonerate before the hermeneutic necessity first to understand.

The primary goal here, accordingly, is just to understand something of the relationship between Heidegger's philosophy and his politics. (Throughout, "politics" is a convenient shorthand for what Wolin characterizes less euphemistically as Heidegger's "short-lived, though concerted, partisanship for Hitler's regime" (in Löwith 1995: 7).) Recently scholars have done invaluable work situating Heidegger within the broader context of the many German intellectuals who implicitly contributed to or actively collaborated with the rise of the National Socialist Workers' Party (Zimmerman 1990; Sluga 1993; Losurdo 2001), but such approaches tend not to focus on what was philosophically unique about Heidegger's politics, which is what readers of this volume are likely to be most interested in. I will thus take a narrower approach, addressing the following two questions. Q1, *Did Heidegger's politics stem directly from his philosophy?* Q2, *Did Heidegger learn anything philosophically from his terrible political "mistake"?* In this limited space, we cannot investigate many of the proposed connections between Heidegger's philosophy and politics, nor the lessons he might have learned subsequently from those connections (see Derrida 1989; Dallmayr 1993; Young 1997; Thomson 1999; Rickey 2002; Bambach 2003). Nevertheless, I believe I can still say enough to answer "yes" to both questions. To whittle the topic down to a more manageable size, I will devote most of this chapter to setting out what I take to be the most convincing affirmative answer to Q1, to establishing, in other words, the most direct connection between Heidegger's philosophy and his politics.[1] This will then allow us to address Q2 within the purview of Q1, thereby showing as precisely as possible at least one lesson that Heidegger learned from this connection between his thought and National Socialism.

Because I seek to establish a direct relationship between Heidegger's philosophy and his politics, my interpretation is likely to run afoul of the aforementioned controversy – despite the fact that Heidegger himself affirmed just such a connection in no uncertain terms (Löwith 1994, discussed below). For, in order to deflect precipitous attempts to use Heidegger's politics simply to dismiss his thought outright (a move no serious critic makes today), Heideggerians have become accustomed to rigidly separating Heidegger's philosophy from his politics. Even such thinkers as Lyotard (1990), Pöggeler (in Neske and Kettering 1990), Schürmann (1990), Rorty (1999), and Olafson (2000) employ this strategy, seeking to insulate Heidegger's important philosophical achievements from what he later called his life's "greatest stupidity." Gadamer, however, rightly observes of the claim that Heidegger's "political errors have nothing to do with his philosophy," that: "Wholly unnoticed was how damaging such a 'defense' of so important a thinker really is" (Gadamer 1989: 428). As a defensive strategy, moreover, such a move is fatally flawed, for it accepts the major premise of the most devastating political criticisms of Heidegger. This idea that Heidegger's politics are unrelated to his thought forms the basis of the accusations that his politics represent arbitrary *decisionism* (Wolin 1990: 52), careerist *opportunism* (Bourdieu 1991: 70–3), and even the fundamental *betrayal* of his philosophy (Marcuse 1988: 41).[2] Here, however, both prosecution and defense fail to do justice to the philosophical integrity of Heidegger's work. The ongoing publication of his *Complete Works* makes it increasingly clear that Heidegger regularly invoked his own philosophical views as justifications for his political decisions. As a result, even long-embattled Heideggerians are beginning to realize that a firm separation of Heidegger's politics from his philosophy is no longer tenable. Thus Rorty supplemented his well known counterfactual argument that Heidegger's politics are philosophically irrelevant.[3] Tellingly, Rorty now judges that "Heidegger's books will be read for centuries to come, but the smell of smoke from the crematories – the 'grave in the air' – will linger on their pages" (Rorty 1998: 2).

As Rorty's quote from Celan suggests, another question haunts the two we will focus on in this chapter, and it is perhaps the most vexed. What was Heidegger's relationship to Nazi anti-Semitism? My first sentence expresses the general view I take on this disturbing issue. Many edifying details from the exculpatory narrative disseminated by

Heidegger and his most loyal followers – for example, that Heidegger became Rector of Freiburg reluctantly, and did so only in order to use his fame to protect his Jewish colleagues, students, and the academic freedom of the university (Neske and Kettering 1990: 15–22) – have been seriously compromised by the facts (Ott 1993; Safranski 1998). We now know, for instance, that Heidegger occasionally resorted to strategic uses of anti-Semitism in the service of his academic political goals, and that this led (after a letter from Heidegger containing a derogatory reference to "the Jew Fraenkel" was leaked to Jaspers) to Heidegger's indefinite loss of his teaching license and his subsequent hospitalization for depression (Ott 1993: 190; Lang 1996; Safranski 1998). At the same time, however, even Heidegger's critics acknowledge that he publicly condemned the "biologistic" racial metaphysics behind the Nazi "final solution" to Marx's "Jewish question" (Wolin 1990), and that he did help some Jewish colleagues and students (see Safranski 1998, which also shows the notorious rumor that Heidegger barred Husserl from Freiberg's library to be completely false). Moreover, although Heidegger never made the kind of public apology for which Marcuse and others long called (Thomson 2000b), he did not in fact remain "silent" on the Shoah. A 1949 lecture proclaimed "the manufacture of corpses in the gas chambers and the death camps" to be "essentially the same" as mechanized agribusiness (GA 79: 56), that is, symptomatic of our nihilistic, "technological" ontotheology (for the philosophical context of Heidegger's deliberately provocative remark, see Agamben 1999; Thomson 2000c).[4] Until the long-sealed archives all come to light, it is only reasonable to expect this troubling issue to continue to animate and inform the Heidegger controversy. For the current range of views, compare the important (but diametrically opposed) works by Wolin (1990) and Young (1997). Neither critic nor defender, however, maintains that Heidegger's decision to join the Nazis can be explained in terms of anti-Semitism.

To find such an explanation, we need to turn to what I take to be the most immediate connection between Heidegger's philosophy and politics, namely his long-developed philosophical vision for a radical reformation of the university. Put simply, Heidegger's philosophical views on higher education were largely responsible for his decision to become the first Nazi Rector of Freiburg University. In 1933, Heidegger seized upon the National Socialist "revolution" as an opportunity to enact the philosophical vision for a radical reformation of the university he had been developing since 1911 (Crowell 1997; Milchman and Rosenberg 1997; Thomson 2001, 2003). The full depth and significance of this fact only begins to become clear, however, when we understand the complexities of Heidegger's politically crucial view of the relationship between philosophy and the other academic disciplines or fields of science. ("Science" is the standard but notoriously misleading translation of the German *Wissenschaft*, which refers more broadly to the "knowledge" embodied in the humanities as well as the natural and social sciences.) That task will occupy most of this chapter.

From Historicality to Heidegger's University Politics: Restoring Philosophy to Her Throne

In 1936, at a time when Heidegger had no reason to try to cover his political tracks, he told Löwith that the conception of "historicality" presented in *Being and Time* (1927) provided the philosophical "basis" for his political "engagement" (Löwith 1994: 60). Still, scholars disagree about whether this formal framework did (Wolin 1990; Löwith 1994) or did not (Guignon 1983; Olafson 2000) give Heidegger reason to join the Nazis. Although there is certainly no necessary connection between the concept of historicality and Nazism (as Guignon and Olafson show), Heidegger's understanding of authentic historicality clearly did play a crucial role in "bridging" the divide between philosophy and politics (Wolin 1990; Sluga 1993; Thomson 1999) and so encouraging Heidegger's attempt to "seize the moment."[5] This is not primarily because *Being and Time*'s discussion of authentic historicality already philosophically appropriates concepts that would soon become highly charged National Socialist *philosophemes* – such as "struggle" (*Kampf*), "people" (*Volk*), "community," "fate," and "destiny" (SZ: 384). Such rhetorical and historical affinities, while striking in retrospect, are also potentially quite misleading (as in Fritsche 1999). More important here is the philosophical content such concepts helped to give to the notion of authentic historicality *as Heidegger himself understood it*. Put simply, but in the terms of authentic historicality, Heidegger chose Nietzsche as his "hero" and so sought a historically appropriate way to carry on Nietzsche's struggle against nihilism (Fynsk 1993; Thomson 1999). The eagerness with which Heidegger answered Spengler's Nietzschean call for radical university reform in 1933 followed from his sense that it was his philosophical "fate" – and so his role in focusing the "destiny" of his generation – to combat the growing problem of historical meaninglessness "by way of the university" (Heidegger 1991: 103).[6]

There can be little doubt that the concept of historicality presented in ¶¶72–7 of *Being and Time* provides the general philosophical framework in terms of which Heidegger understood his decision to join the National Socialist "revolution" in 1933. I submit, nonetheless, that if one is interested in the specific philosophical motives that justified, in Heidegger's mind at least, the actual political initiatives he attempted to enact in 1933 as the Rector of Freiburg University, then the philosophical rubber really hits the political road much earlier in *Being and Time*, in ¶3. For it is here, without naming Kant, that Heidegger follows Kant in rejecting advice that philosophy's relation to the other sciences should be that of a "train bearer" (who follows behind, straightening out the tangles), rather than a "torch bearer" (who goes first, lighting the way). Reversing that humble view, Heidegger instead maintains that philosophy "must run ahead of the positive sciences, and it *can*" do so (SZ: 10).

Despite its great political importance, Heidegger's attempt to fulfill Husserl's Kantian ambition to restore philosophy to her throne as the queen of the sciences has not received the attention it deserves in the context of the "Heidegger controversy." For, Husserl, in "Philosophy as Rigorous Science" (1910), presented phenomenology as a "revolution in philosophy" that will "prepare the ground for a future philosophical system" (Husserl 1965: 75). As Heidegger became Husserl's heir apparent during the 1920s, he increasingly saw it as his appointed task to develop – atop the ground cleared by Husserl's phenomenological revolution – that "systematic fundamental science of philosophy, the port of entry to a genuine metaphysics of nature, of spirit, of ideas" for which Husserl called. Unfortunately, in Heidegger's very fidelity to this incredibly ambitious Husserlian project, he would fail to take to heart Husserl's prophetic warning of a "great danger." Because the "spiritual need of our time has, in fact, become unbearable," Husserl cautioned, "even a theoretical nature will be capable of giving in to the force of the motive to influence practice more thoroughly than his theoretical vocation would permit" (Husserl 1965: 75, 116–17, 173). To understand how Heidegger fell prey to the danger Husserl discerned, and what Heidegger learned from this, let us examine the details of his view of the relationship between philosophy and the other sciences. (Understanding this view will also enable us to discern a further, heretofore unnoticed, connection between "authentic historicality" and Heidegger's politics.)

For Heidegger, every scientific discipline with a discrete subject matter is a "positive science." The term "positive science" conveys Heidegger's claim that each of the scientific disciplines rests on an ontological "posit," a presupposition about what the class of entities it studies *is*. Biology, for example, seeks to understand how living beings function. As biologists successfully accomplish this important task, they allow us to understand in ever greater detail the *logos* of the *bios*, the order and structure of living beings. Nevertheless, Heidegger asserts, biology proper cannot tell us what life *is*. Of course, the biologist must have some understanding of what "life" is, simply in order to be able to pick out the appropriate entities to study. Heidegger maintains, however, that this ontological understanding of "the kind of being which belongs to the living as such" is a presupposition rather than a result of the biologist's empirical investigations (SZ: 10). Heidegger makes the same point with respect to the social and human sciences. Psychology, for example, can tell us a great deal about the functioning of consciousness, the *psyche*, but, notoriously, it cannot tell us what consciousness *is*. Analogously, history greatly increases our understanding of historical events, yet historians cannot tell us what history *is*.

Heidegger is not claiming that biologists cannot distinguish organic from inorganic entities, that psychologists are unable to differentiate between conscious and non-conscious states, or that historians cannot tell historical from non-historical events. His point, rather, is that in making just such fundamental conceptual differentiations, biologists, psychologists, and historians are always already employing an ontological understanding of what the entities whose domain they study *are*. Indeed, no science could get along without at least an implicit ontological understanding of the beings it studies. Simply to *do* historiography, historians must be able to focus on the appropriate objects of study, which means they must already have some understanding of what makes an historical event "historical." To distinguish the entities from the past destined for museums from those headed for junk heaps, for example, historians rely on an ontological understanding of what makes an entity historical, a sense of what Heidegger calls the "historicality" of the historical (SZ: 10). Likewise, botany relies on an ontological understanding of "the vegetable character of plants," physics on "the corporeality of bodies," zoology on "the animality of animals," and anthropology on "the humanness of human beings" (GA 5: 78/59). Heidegger's list could be expanded indefinitely because he believes that *every* positive science presupposes such an ontological posit, a background understanding of the *being* of the class of entities it studies.

By thus extending Husserl's claim about the "naïveté" or "inadequacy" of the *natural* sciences to the *positive* sciences in general, Heidegger thinks he has found a way to fulfill Husserl's grand ambition to deliver "the systematic fundamental science of philosophy." How exactly does Heidegger propose to restore philosophy to her throne as the queen of the sciences? The core of his argument can be broken down into three steps, the first of which we have just reconstructed. Building on this first claim that all the positive sciences presuppose an ontological posit, Heidegger declares, second, that there is a basic difference between these positive sciences and the "science" of philosophy:

> Ontic sciences in each case thematize a given entity that in a certain manner is always already disclosed *prior* to scientific disclosure. We call the sciences of entities as given – of a *positum* – positive sciences. . . . Ontology, or the science of being, on the other hand, demands a fundamental shift of view: from entities to being. (GA 9: 48/41)

The positive sciences all study classes of entities, so Heidegger also refers to the positive sciences as "ontic sciences." Philosophy, on the other hand, studies the being of those classes of entities, making philosophy an "ontological science" or, more grandly, a "science of being." Heidegger's second claim, in other words, is that philosophy studies precisely that which the positive sciences take for granted: their ontological posits. The subject matters of the positive sciences and of philosophy are thus distinguished by what Heidegger famously calls "the ontological difference": the difference between "entities" (*Seienden*) and the "being of entities" (*Sein des Seienden*). Positive sciences study entities of various kinds, while philosophy studies the being of those kinds of entities (GA 27: 223). Here, then, we have the first two steps in Heidegger's argument: first, each positive science presupposes an understanding of the being of the class of entities it studies; second, the science of philosophy concerns itself with precisely these ontological posits.

The crucial third step in Heidegger's argument is his claim that the positive sciences' ontological posits *guide* the scientists' actual investigations. As he writes in 1927: "Philosophy . . . does of its essence have the task of directing all . . . the positive sciences with respect to their ontological foundations." These ontological "basic concepts determine the way in which we get an understanding beforehand of the area of subject-matter underlying all the objects a science takes as its theme, and all positive science is guided by this understanding" (GA 9: 65–6/53). Heidegger's point, I take it, is that a scientist's ontological understanding of what the class of entities she studies *is* impacts not only *what* she studies (which is fairly obvious) but also *how* she studies it (which is perhaps less so). When, for example, contemporary biologists proceed on the basis of an ontological understanding of life as a "self-replicating system," then the entities whose functioning they seek to understand will include not only those self-replicating beings now thought to populate the plant and animal kingdoms, but also such entities as computer viruses, nanotechnology, "electric fish," and other forms of so-called "artificial life" (Boden 1996). To study such artificial life will require, in turn, new modes and models of investigation, such as the observation of "living systems" entirely confined to complex computer simulations.

While this is not a fanciful example, it may seem slightly atypical in that here biology's guiding ontological "posit" (namely, that "life *is* a self-replicating system") has been rendered explicit, whereas Heidegger holds that normally such posits function only as presuppositions in the background of a science's investigations. Anticipating Thomas Kuhn, however, Heidegger recognizes that such ontological posits often enter into the foreground of scientific discussion during a crisis in the normal functioning of that science. Indeed, *Being and Time* contends that the "real 'movement' of the sciences" occurs when such crises lead the sciences to subject their guiding ontological understandings to "a revision which is more or less radical and lucid with regard to itself" (SZ: 9). During such a crisis, a science often throws its guiding ontological understanding of the being of the class of entities it studies into question, usually settling the crisis only by revising its previous ontological understanding. Those who explicitly recognize and take part in such ontological questioning and revision are doing *philosophy*, Heidegger says, whether or not they happen to be employed by a philosophy department. This, moreover, allows us to understand Heidegger's provocative but widely misunderstood (and so highly controversial) claim that science as such "does not think," a view he espoused throughout his life.

For Heidegger, philosophy is essentially an activity of ontological questioning (later he will usually call this activity "thinking" in order to distinguish it from the metaphysical tradition). In his 1928–9 lectures, *Introduction to Philosophy*, he says that "philosophy is not knowledge of wisdom. . . . Philosophy is philosophizing [*Philosophieren*]." In a twist on the standard etymology of the word "philosophy," Heidegger unpacks *philia* as "a genuine friendship which, in its essence, struggles [*kämpf*] for that which it loves" and *sophos* as "an instinct for the essential," and so defines *philosophizing*, the active practice of philosophy, as the struggle to employ one's sense for the essential (GA 27: 21–2). By "essence" Heidegger means the ontological presupposition or "posit" that guides a positive science. Heidegger can thus say that: "When we speak of the sciences, we shall be speaking not against them but for them, for clarity concerning their essence" (GA 8: 16/49). One is "philosophizing" whenever one explicitly examines and seeks to clarify the ontological understanding that normally guides a science implicitly but which can come into question during a period of scientific crisis. Thus biologists as well as philosophers of biology were philosophizing in so far as they explicitly questioned the ontological understanding of what life *is* during the recent debate over "artificial life." To say that the positive sciences, as such, do not "think" simply means that they do not, as positive sciences, question their guiding ontological presuppositions. As Heidegger puts it: "The researcher always operates on the foundation of what has already been decided: the fact that there are such things as nature, history, art, and that these things can be made the subject of consideration" (GA 6.1: 429/Heidegger 1987: 6).

Of course, scientists do occasionally engage in such potentially revolutionary ontological questioning, but when they do, they are (by Heidegger's definition) doing philosophy, not research. Because quantum mechanics engaged in such revolutionary questioning, Heidegger recognized that "the present leaders of atomic physics, Niels Bohr and [Werner] Heisenberg, think in a thoroughly philosophical way" (GA 41: 67/67). Philosophy, conversely, is "only alive and actual" when engaged in the ontological questioning at the center of such scientific crises. That is, philosophers (and others) *philosophize* only by doing the potentially revolutionary work of questioning the ontological presuppositions that guide the natural, social, and human sciences. Thus Heidegger proclaims in 1928 that the Husserlian concept of a "scientific philosophy" is like the concept of a "circular sphere," that is, not simply redundant, for as a sphere is more circular than any circle, so "philosophizing" is "more scientific than any possible science." Indeed, strictly speaking, "philosophy is *not* science, . . . but rather the origin [*Ursprung*] of science" (GA 27: 17–18, 221, 226). Science "springs from" philosophy in a way which resembles the emergence of normal science from revolutionary science, namely through an eventual routinization and procedural exploration of the ontological insights gained philosophically during a period of revolutionary science, a time of crisis and decision over the ontological posits that normally guide the positive sciences.

To practice philosophy so conceived, Heidegger explains in *Being and Time*, is "to interpret entities in terms of the basic constitution of their being" (SZ: 10). Focusing on a positive science's guiding ontological presuppositions, philosophy explicitly interprets the being of the domain of entities a positive science studies. In so doing, philosophy can clarify the ontological posits of the positive sciences and so transform and guide the course of their future development.[7] Thus Heidegger writes:

> Laying the foundations for the sciences in this way is different in principle from the kind of "logic" which limps along behind, investigating the status of some science as it chances to find it, in order to discover its "method." Laying the foundations . . . is rather a productive logic – in the sense that it *leaps ahead*, as it were, into a particular region of being, discloses it for the first time in its constitutive being, and makes the structures acquired thereby available to the positive sciences as lucid directives for their inquiry. (SZ: 10, emphasis added)

Here Heidegger is employing *Being and Time*'s well known distinction between "leaping ahead" and "leaping in," which for him marks the difference between the authentic and inauthentic methods of pedagogical "being-with" (*Mitsein*). The point of using this distinction here, I take it, is that philosophy guides the sciences not by imposing preexisting standards upon them from outside, but rather by anticipating the ontological understanding toward which the sciences themselves are heading and reflecting that understanding back to them in a perspicacious manner, thereby illuminating their developmental trajectory from within and so facilitating their continued progression. (Heidegger tried to do this himself for the positive science of "historiography," through close readings of Nietzsche, Dilthey, and other philosophers of history – as Guignon, chapter 24 in this volume, shows – and this reveals another important connection between Heidegger's conception of "historicality" and his politics.[8]) Philosophy so-conceived is no longer the Kantian "train-bearer," following behind the sciences, retroactively straightening out their methodological tangles. By clarifying the positive sciences' ontological posits, philosophy plays a guiding role with respect to the other sciences, proactively clarifying their development, even issuing "lucid directives for their inquiry." In this way, Heidegger believes philosophy can reclaim its historic role as the "torch-bearer" of the sciences. But toward what end will philosophy thus light the way? Does Heidegger know in which direction he seeks to guide the sciences, the university, Germany?

The Philosophical Lesson

As such questioning reminds us, Heidegger's attempted restoration of philosophy to her throne as the queen of the sciences can easily sound, under a less flattering description, like a kind of philosophical imperialism. Such an impression would seem to be reinforced by the idea that the positive sciences as such can neither account for nor supply their own guiding ontological posits, but must rather take these over from philosophy. Recall, however, that Heidegger's view does not entail a subordination of scientists to philosophers, since, as we have seen, he does not conceive of the philosophizing that guides science as the exclusive provenance of any particular academic department. Scientists too can philosophize; indeed, Heidegger strongly urges that they should. It is just that when scientists philosophize they are no longer doing positive science; they are doing philosophy. Exchanging one hat for another, they have, in Kuhnian terms, left behind the background ontological suppositions of their normal scientific paradigm in order to philosophize, entering, at least temporarily, into the uncharted waters of revolutionary science by throwing into question the basic ontological assumptions that normally guide their research. In fact, Heidegger's Rectoral Address lays great stress on the need for scientists to philosophize, since he thinks that when "the faculties and disciplines get the essential and simple questions of their science underway," this will bring "down disciplinary barriers" and "transform the faculties and the disciplines from within" (Neske and Kettering 1990: 36–7). Still, an underlying worry remains. Given Heidegger's strong emphasis on the importance of cross-disciplinary philosophical questioning and his assurance that such ontological questioning will transform the scientific disciplines from within by revitalizing and reunifying fragmented academic departments, how are we to explain the authoritarian character of some of the actual reforms he sought to impose during his brief tenure as the *Führer-Rektor* of Freiburg University – including, most notably, his proposal to abolish academic freedom and his seeming readiness to reorganize the departmental divisions of the university immediately, by philosophical fiat if necessary?

To begin to answer this question, we must understand several further aspects of Heidegger's view. At the time he wrote *Being and Time*, Heidegger believed that the various ontological presuppositions guiding the different positive sciences were not all distinct and irreducible. Instead he held, first, that the positive sciences' guiding understandings of the being of life, history, the psyche, and so on all reduce down to a small number of what he calls "regional ontologies," and, second, that these regional ontologies are all grounded in a single common foundation, what *Being and Time* calls a "fundamental ontology," that is, an understanding of "the meaning of being in general" (SZ: 183; Guignon 1983: 65–7). Taken together, these two claims entail that the different ontological posits implicitly guiding the various positive sciences all stem from a common ontological ground. An understanding of the meaning of being in general (a *fundamental ontology*) underlies the regional ontologies, which themselves underlie the positive sciences' various ontological posits. In 1927, Heidegger writes that "it is integral to the positive character of a science that its prescientific comportment toward whatever is given (nature, history, economy, space, number) is . . . already illuminated and guided by an understanding of being, even if this understanding of being is not conceptualized" explicitly (GA 9: 50/42). Hence, as *Being and Time* says:

> The question of being aims therefore at ascertaining the *a priori* conditions not only for the possibility of the sciences which examine entities as entities of such and such a type, and, in so doing, already operate with an understanding of being, but also for the possi-

bility of those [regional] ontologies themselves which are prior to the ontical sciences and which provide their foundations. (SZ: 11)

What, then, is this fundamental ontology which ultimately underlies and implicitly guides all the positive sciences? It takes Heidegger most of the decade after *Being and Time* to answer unequivocally this difficult but crucial question.

Being and Time famously calls for a "deconstruction" (*Destruktion*) of the history of ontology by which Heidegger believes he will be able to "recover" the fundamental understanding of being which has shaped every subsequent ontology in the history of the West (SZ: 22–3). This idea that a transhistorically binding ontology can be discovered "beneath" Western history helps explain the more authoritarian dimension of Heidegger's Rectoral Address. For, if a philosophical vision which recognized that and how all the different ontological posits fit together into a fundamental ontology could reunify the university (and, behind it, the nation), then Heidegger, as the unique possessor of just such a vision, would be the natural ("fated") spiritual leader of the university – and thus the nation (see Thomson 2003a). Clearly, Heidegger's neo-Husserlian ambition to restore philosophy to her throne as the queen of the sciences helped to fuel his political vision for the revitalization of the German university. Such political defects in Heidegger's Rectoral Address now seem glaringly obvious. The main *philosophical* problem, however, is that Heidegger got ahead of himself here. For he had not yet actually worked out *how* the ontological posits fit into the regional ontologies, or how the regional ontologies fit into an underlying fundamental ontology, *before* he assumed this mantle of political leadership. It is in this sense that despite Husserl's warning, Heidegger did indeed give "in to the force of the motive to influence practice more thoroughly than his theoretical vocation would permit." In 1933 Heidegger was still in the process of working out his view of the way in which an underlying ontology gave rise to the different ontological posits, and when he does, the details of the view undermine rather than support the authoritarian elements of his political project.

In *Being and Time* and in 1929's "What is Metaphysics?" Heidegger singles out the ontological classes of "nature" and "history" as "regional ontologies" (GA 9: 121/95). By 1935, he has traced the regional ontologies of nature and history back to the pre-Socratic conceptions of *phusis* and *alētheia*, respectively (EM: 77–8). By 1941, he will explicitly characterize this "*phusis-alētheia*" couple as "the inceptive essence of being," that is, as the first way Western thinkers conceptualized "being" (Heidegger 1973: 10). Already in 1937, however, he begins redescribing "being" as a never fully conceptualizable phenomenological "presencing" (*Anwesen*) that, owing to its non-static and non-substantive nature, cannot be the "meaning of being in general" (GA 65: 285; Thomson 2003b). Between 1929 and 1937, that is, during the period of intense philosophical tension and transformation popularly known as Heidegger's "turn" (or *Kehre*), one of the things he came to realize was that there was no *substantive* fundamental ontology waiting beneath history to be recovered. When Heidegger traces the regional ontologies of nature and history back to *phusis* and *alētheia*, then traces this *phusis–alētheia* couple back to a conceptually inexhaustible ontological "presencing," this is as close as he ever comes to actually "grounding" the regional ontologies in a fundamental ontology, and it is quite instructive. For it shows that the relations between the positive sciences, the regional ontologies, and fundamental ontology are too murky

41

and indirect to allow for a top-down hierarchical reorganization of the university in which the philosopher who has learned to be receptive to phenomenological presencing will be able first to carve the regional ontologies out of this basic fundamental ontological presencing and then to construct the new academic disciplines around these regional ontologies. In other words, had Heidegger succeeded in working out these views a few years earlier, in 1933 instead of 1937, they would have undermined some of the authoritarian policies of his Rectorate, such as his apparent readiness immediately to legislate new academic disciplines.[9] Ironically, Heidegger thus illustrates the real dangers he and Husserl had so presciently cautioned against, since he allowed "external entanglements" to interfere with his philosophical development and so gave in to the temptation to intercede politically before having worked out the philosophical views that would have legitimated or, more to the point, *undermined* such an engagement. What, then, did Heidegger learn from this mistake?

Heidegger drops the very notions of "fundamental ontology" and "regional ontologies" from his later work, and instead builds his mature understanding of university education around the idea that "ontotheologies," rather than regional ontologies, mediate between a basic ontological "presencing" and the guiding ontological presuppositions of the positive sciences. Whatever its political motivations, this was basically a *philosophical* lesson. For, when Heidegger actually carried out the deconstruction of the history of ontology called for in *Being and Time*, he discovered that a series of metaphysical "ontotheologies" have temporarily grounded and justified a succession of ontological "epochs," historical constellations of intelligibility. Every age in the West has been unified by such a basic metaphysical understanding of what and how beings are, he concludes (Thomson 2000a). It thus turns out that the ontological posits that guide each of *our* positive sciences come not from some fundamental ontology beneath Western history, but rather from our contemporary age's reigning ontotheology. The later Heidegger would thus hold that contemporary biology, for instance, takes over its implicit ontological understanding of what life *is* from the metaphysical understanding of the being of entities that governs our own Nietzschean epoch of "enframing." And, indeed, one has to admit that when contemporary philosophers of biology proclaim that life *is* a self-replicating system, it certainly appears that they have unknowingly adopted the basic ontotheological presuppositions of Nietzsche's metaphysics, according to which life *is* ultimately the eternal recurrence of will to power, that is, sheer will-to-will, unlimited self-augmentation. (It is alarming – if predictable, given Heidegger's critique of our historical reliance on this unnoticed ontotheology – to thus find philosophers of biology extending the logic of Nietzschean metaphysics in such a way as to grant "life" to the technological entity *par excellence*, the computer virus.) Because Heidegger comes to believe that all of the sciences' guiding ontological posits are implicitly taken over from this nihilistic Nietzschean ontotheology underlying our "atomic age," the first task of his mature understanding of *ontological education* involves making us reflective about the way in which our experience of what is commonly called "reality" has been shaped by the fundamental conceptual parameters and ultimate standards of legitimacy provided by Nietzsche's metaphysics. When we become aware of the way our age's reigning ontotheology shapes our understanding of ourselves and our worlds, and thereby come to recognize the subtle but pervasive influence of this ontological understanding of entities as mere resources to be optimized, we begin to open up the possibility of understanding ourselves otherwise than in these nihilistic, Nietzschean terms (Thomson 2000c; 2001).

In 1933, however, Heidegger was still "on the way" to clearly articulating these mature views and, not surprisingly, he had little success convincing audiences to follow a philosophical leadership they could barely understand. This lack of understanding was disastrous politically, for it allowed Heidegger to appear to be endorsing a regime he was in fact attempting philosophically to contest and redirect (Edler 1990). As we have seen, the views Heidegger worked out by 1937 would have undermined authoritarian aspects of his Rectoral Address (see also Dreyfus 1993). One crucial question, then, is: would Heidegger's later claim that the sciences take their ontological pre-understandings over from a subterranean ontotheology – one which they need to learn to use the methods of Heideggerian phenomenology in order to explicitly recognize and so contest in order to progress beyond – still have helped convince him to institute a philosophical version of the *Führer-Prinzip* at Freiburg University? Here we must tread carefully, acknowledging that Heidegger's later views could indeed have justified the core of the politico-philosophical program he advanced in the Rectoral Address. For if one examines "The Self-assertion of the German University" carefully, the role of the rector (as Heidegger presents it there) is to unify the university around the various disciplines' shared commitment to ontological questioning. I believe the later Heidegger would modify this program primarily by *refining* it, focusing such potentially revolutionary ontological questioning more precisely on the Nietzschean ontotheology that, he came to realize, the various university disciplines already implicitly shared. The goal would no longer be the Rectoral Address's neo-Nietzschean pursuit of ontological revolution simply for the sake of revitalization (by 1937–8 Heidegger will realize that this Nietzschean program of constant overcoming is part of the problem), but the basic strategy would likely remain the same: first, awaken the faculty to the way in which their research is grounded in unquestioned ontological presuppositions, then send them out to the ontological frontiers of knowledge, so to speak, in order that they might discover ways of understanding the being of the classes of entities they study otherwise than in terms of this underlying Nietzschean ontotheology, the nihilistic effects of which Heidegger is just beginning to recognize.[10] The core of the Rectoral Address would be preserved in such an attempt to enlist the entire academy in the philosophical struggle to transcend the nihilistic ontotheology of the age. Indeed, such a project is deeply consistent with Heidegger's lifelong philosophical goal, although it does not seem that one would need the full authority of a *Führer-Rektor* (rather than, say, a powerful university president or even an influential funding agency) in order to awaken the university community to their possible role in fomenting such an ontohistorical revolution. What this shows, then, is that it is not the core of the Rectoral Address that is objectionable.

I should thus add that the single most troublingly authoritarian aspect of the Rectoral Address – namely, Heidegger's infamous rejection of "academic freedom" – is not solely related to the underlying philosophical views we have been examining. Indeed, I believe we better understand Heidegger's enthusiastic institution of the "leadership principle" in 1933 as a result of the influence of Nietzsche, who argued in early lectures *On the Future of Our Educational Institutions* that the educational renaissance Germany needed would require a revolution, one which could be accomplished only by the great *leadership* of a philosophical genius (see Nietzsche 1909; Thomson 2003a). It seems likely that Nietzsche's virulent critique of academic freedom and his call for a "great *Führer*" to lead this revolution of the university exercised a strong and regrettable influence on the program for university reform Heidegger set forth in the Rectoral Address. Those seeking to understand Heidegger's famous later complaint that "Nietzsche ruined me! [*Nietzsche hat mich kaputt gemacht!*]" would thus do well to consider this political dimension of Nietzsche's influence on Heidegger.

In conclusion, let me try to forestall any unnecessary controversy by stating that the direct connection between Heidegger's philosophy and his politics I have argued for here will not enable anyone to dismiss Heidegger's philosophy, for at least two reasons. First, because, as we have seen, the excesses in Heidegger's university politics rest in large part on an important philosophical mistake (the belief in a fundamental ontology) that he later corrected (as a philosophical "lesson learned"). Second, and admittedly more provocatively, because the underlying project that led Heidegger to National Socialism is motivated by a deeply insightful critique of the university he continued to refine after the war, and this prescient critique has only become increasingly relevant ever since (as I argue in Thomson 2001). Certainly Heidegger realized by 1937 that it was too late to redirect the National Socialist movement into the ontological revolution he never stopped pursuing (Rickey 2002), but he did not give up on his long-developed program for radically reforming the university, nor did he abandon the positive project of transforming higher education so that it would serve his life-long philosophical cause (Thomson 2003a, b). It is thus to this critique, and Heidegger's positive vision of the university, that I believe at least some of the discussion concerning Heidegger's politics should be shifted.

Notes

1 We will thus seek to address what Dreyfus rightly calls "the central question," namely "to what extent was Heidegger's support and then rejection of National Socialism a personal mistake compounded of conservative prejudices, personal ambition, and political *naïveté*, and to what extent was his engagement dictated by his philosophy?" (Dreyfus 1992: 19).

2 For Bourdieu, it is Heidegger himself who represses the fact that his "philosophy is political from beginning to end" (Bourdieu 1991: 96). According to Bourdieu's reductive "socio-analysis," Heidegger's repressed "id, his unthought – that of an 'ordinary university professor' – and the entire train of social phantasms [generated by Heidegger's position in the academic field] . . . led around by the nose this small bearer of a cultural capital . . . whose 'fixed assets' were in danger" (in Wolin 1991: 277).

3 Rorty (1998) imagined that Heidegger could have lived a politically blameless life and written essentially the same works. Few Heidegger scholars find this edifying "other possible world" plausible, however, since it denies the existential intertwinement of life and thought Heidegger himself insisted on before 1933.

4 In letters to Jaspers in 1950, moreover, Heidegger mentions his sense of "shame" when thinking of Jaspers's Jewish wife, refers to "the worst evil [that] set in with the vile persecutions," and says that "from year to year, as more viciousness came out, the sense of shame also grew over having here and there, directly and indirectly, contributed to it. . . . Then came the persecution of the Jews, and everything fell into the abyss" (Biemel and Saner

2003: 185, 189). The full context of this politically important correspondence would need to be carefully unpacked. Before 1934 Heidegger and Jaspers were "comrades-in-arms" in the project to revolutionize the university, but they remained permanently estranged afterward owing to Heidegger's unwillingness to apologize to Jaspers for the above-mentioned letter (which also contained a politically threatening allusion to Jaspers's "liberal democratic circle of Heidelberg intellectuals" (ibid.: 209)). Nevertheless, Jaspers would finally conclude in 1966 that Heidegger expressed "the usual clichés about '"the international [Jewish conspiracy],' etc., but without inner-conviction. He was no 'anti-Semite'" (ibid.: 281, note 5).

5   As Dreyfus (2000) shows, *Being and Time* presupposes a neo-Aristotelian understanding of practical wisdom as operating beyond the domain of principles – and so outside the space of possible "derivations" of praxis from theory – without, for that reason, being "decisionistic" in the objectionable sense of *arbitrary*, let alone "blind and uninformed" (Wolin 1990: 52).

6   I make this argument in a longer essay (Thomson 2003a), section 3 of which contains an earlier and abridged version of the following analysis.

7   Heidegger's sole exception to this rule concerns the positive science of theology, in which the guiding ontological posit is accessible only to faith, not to phenomenological analysis. This, ultimately, is what Heidegger means by his oft-repeated, provocative assertion that "philosophical theology" is an oxymoron, "wooden iron."

8   To recognize this further connection, it helps to introduce a terminological distinction. "Historicality," *Geschichtlichkeit*, is often translated as "historicity," but this is misleading when discussing the views of the early Heidegger. The later Heidegger does indeed use *Geschichtlichkeit* to convey his recognition that being has a history (his hard-won recognition of the fact that humanity's most fundamental sense of reality changes with time), and this is precisely what most of us mean by the notoriously slippery term "historicity." Indeed, I take Heidegger's increasingly radical "historicization of ontology" – to which he is driven by his *Destruktion* of metaphysics – to be one of the definitive characteristics of his famous "turn" (or *Kehre*), the philosophical transformation which distinguishes the "early" (pre-1937) from the "later" Heidegger (see Thomson 1999). This means, however, that we cannot read the doctrine of "historicity" back into 1927's *Being and Time*, where Heidegger pursues a "fundamental ontology" ultimately incompatible with a radical historicization of ontology (as I argue below). It should not be surprising, then, that the early Heidegger's use of *Geschichtlichkeit* is quite different. Let us thus disambiguate *Geschichtlichkeit* by introducing a distinction Heidegger's lifelong use of the term tends to elide, using *historicality* to refer to the being of history (the early ontological understanding of what history is), and reserving *historicity* for the history of being (the later *Seinsgeschichte*, with its radical historicization of ontology). This helps to clarify that historicality and historicity are distinct but developmentally related concepts (as Guignon, chapter 24 in this volume, shows). More importantly, for our purposes, distinguishing historicality from historicity helps us to recognize another connection between "authentic historicality" and Heidegger's politics. *Being and Time*'s notion of authentic "historicality" seeks to explain philosophically what it is that makes an entity *historical*, properly speaking. As we have seen, this understanding of the *being* of history is what enables historians to distinguish historical from non-historical entities and events. Through the notion of authentic historicality, then, Heidegger was himself seeking to provide a positive science (namely history, or "historiography") with its guiding ontological posit. (As Guignon explains, Heidegger sought to "derive" an account of authentic "historiography" from his understanding of authentic historicality.) This makes Heidegger's discussion of authentic historicality in *Being and Time* the beginning of an attempt actually to *legislate* philosophically the ontological understanding that should guide

45

the research of another science, although I think it clear that here too the project did not yield the kind of determinate, science-guiding results for which Heidegger hoped. Unfortunately, rather than abandoning that task in 1927, Heidegger simply pushes it back to his even more ambitious quest for a fundamental ontology capable of guiding all the positive sciences.

9 In his Rectoral Address, Heidegger adds "language" (a category meant to map onto his understanding of the pre-Socratic *logos*) to the regional ontologies of nature and history (which he traces back to *phusis* and *alētheia*), suggesting that the university should be reorganized into twelve academic disciplines, which would be unified as four different ways of approaching and elucidating the three regional ontologies (Neske and Kettering 1990: 9).

10 Instead of asking when exactly Heidegger brought his critique of technology to bear on the university, it is better to recognize that this critique of technology *grew out of* his critique of the university. De Beistegui jumps the gun a bit when be writes that the target in "The Self-Assertion of the German University" is already "the university of the *Gestell*," but he is right that "Heidegger's attacks on . . . technology, still somewhat veiled in the Rectoral address, will become most explicit in the *Contributions to Philosophy*" (de Beistegui 1998: 60, 50; see also Thomson 2000c). When one reads the critique of the university Heidegger elaborates in his 1929 Inaugural Address and his 1933 Rectoral Address from the standpoint of his later work, one can indeed see that Heidegger is beginning to develop his critique of "enframing" there. Nevertheless, this critique of our Nietzschean, "technological" understanding of the being of entities remained veiled *even to Heidegger himself* in 1933. After the failure of his Rectorate, Heidegger sought to understand the deeper ontohistorical etiology responsible for the crisis of the university, first fully sketching this underlying understanding of the history of being in his 1936–7 *Contributions to Philosophy* (Thomson 2003b).

References

Agamben, G. (1999) *Remnants of Auschwitz: The Witness and the Archive* (trans. D. Heller-Roazen). New York: Zone Books.

Bambach, C. (2003) *Heidegger's Roots: Nietzsche, National Socialism, and the Greeks*. Ithaca, NY: Cornell University Press.

Biemel, W. and Saner, H. (eds.) (2003) *The Heidegger–Jaspers Correspondence* (trans. G. E. Aylesworth). Amherst, NY: Humanity Books (original work published 1990).

Boden, M. A. (ed.) (1996) *The Philosophy of Artificial Life*. Oxford: Oxford University Press.

Bourdieu, P. (1991) *The Political Ontology of Martin Heidegger* (trans. P. Collier). Stanford, CA: Stanford University Press (original work published 1988).

Crowell, S. (1997) Philosophy as a vocation: Heidegger and university reform in the early interwar years. *History of Philosophy Quarterly*, 14(2), 255–76.

Dallmayr, F. (1993) *The Other Heidegger*. Ithaca, NY: Cornell University Press.

De Beistegui, M. (1998) *Heidegger and the Political: Dystopias*. London: Routledge.

Derrida, J. (1989) *Of Spirit: Heidegger and the Question* (trans. G. Bennington and R. Bowlby). Chicago: University of Chicago Press (original work published 1987).

Dreyfus, H. L. (1992) Mixing interpretation, religion, and politics: Heidegger's high-risk thinking. In C. Ocker (ed.), *Protocol of the Sixty-first Colloquy of the Center for Hermeneutical Studies*. San Anselmo, CA: Center for Hermeneutical Studies.

Dreyfus, H. L. (1993) Heidegger on the connection between nihilism, art, technology, and politics. In C. Guignon (ed.), *The Cambridge Companion to Heidegger*. Cambridge: Cambridge University Press.

Dreyfus, H. L. (2000) Could anything be more intelligible than everyday intelligibility? Reinterpreting division I of *Being and Time* in the light of division II. In J. E. Faulconer and M. Wrathall (eds.), *Appropriating Heidegger*. Cambridge: Cambridge University Press.

Edler, F. (1990) Philosophy, language, politics: Heidegger's attempt to steal the language of revolution in 1933–34. *Social Research*, 57(1), 197–238.

Fritsche, J. (1999) *Historical Destiny and National Socialism in Heidegger's* Being and Time. Berkeley: University of California Press.

Fynsk, C. (1993) *Heidegger: Thought and Historicity*. Ithaca, NY: Cornell University Press.

Gadamer, H.-G. (1989) Back from Syracuse? (trans. J. McCumber). *Critical Inquiry*, 15, 427–30 (original work published 1988).

Guignon, C. B. (1983) *Heidegger and the Problem of Knowledge*. Indianapolis: Hackett.

Harries, K. and Jamme, C. (eds.) (1994) *Martin Heidegger: Politics, Art, and Technology*. New York: Holmes and Meier.

Heidegger, M. (1973) *The End of Philosophy* (trans. J. Stambaugh). New York: Harper & Row (original work published 1954).

Heidegger, M. (1987) *Nietzsche, volume 3: The Will to Power as Knowledge and as Metaphysics* (ed. D. F. Krell; trans. J. Stambaugh, D. F. Krell, and F. Capuzzi). New York: Harper & Row (original work published 1961).

Heidegger, M. (1991) Only a god can save us. In R. Wolin (ed.), *The Heidegger Controversy*. New York: Columbia University Press (original work published 1976).

Husserl, E. (1965) Philosophy as a rigorous science. In *Phenomenology and the Crisis of Philosophy* (trans. Q. Lauer). New York: Harper & Row (original work published 1910).

Löwith, K. (1994) *My Life in Germany Before and After 1933* (trans. E. King). London: Athlone Press (original work published in 1986).

Löwith, K. (1995) *Martin Heidegger and European Nihilism* (ed. R. Wolin; trans. G. Steiner). New York: Columbia University Press (original work published 1983 and 1984).

Lang, B. (1996) *Heidegger's Silence*. Ithaca, NY: Cornell University Press.

Losurdo, D. (2001) *Heidegger and the Ideology of War: Community, Death, and the West* (trans. M. and J. Norris). Amherst, NY: Humanity Books (original work published 1991).

Lyotard, J.-F. (1990) *Heidegger and "the Jews"* (trans. A. Michel and M. Roberts). Minneapolis: University of Minnesota Press (original work published 1988).

Marcuse, H. (1988) The struggle against liberalism in the totalitarian view of the state. In *Negations: Essays in Critical Theory* (trans. J. J. Shapiro). London: Free Association Books (original work published 1934).

Milchman, A. and Rosenberg, A. (1997) Martin Heidegger and the university as a site for the transformation of human existence. *Review of Politics*, 59(1), 75–96.

Neske, G. and Kettering, E. (eds.) (1990) *Martin Heidegger and National Socialism: Questions and Answers*. New York: Paragon House (original work published 1983).

Nietzsche, F. (1909) *On the Future of Our Educational Institutions*. In O. Levy (ed.), *The Complete Works of Friedrich Nietzsche, volume 6* (trans. J. M. Kennedy). Edinburgh: T. N. Foulis.

Olafson, F. A. (2000) Heidegger's thought and Nazism. *Inquiry*, 43(3), 271–88.

Ott, H. (1993) *Martin Heidegger: A Political Life* (trans. A. Blunden). London: Basic Books (original work published 1989).

Rickey, C. (2002) *Revolutionary Saints: Heidegger, National Socialism, and Antinomian Politics*. University Park: Pennsylvania State University Press.

Rorty, R. (1998) A master from Germany. *The New York Times Book Review*, May 3 (http://www.nytimes.com/books/98/05/03/reviews/980503.03rortyt.html).

Rorty, R. (1999) On Heidegger's Nazism. In *Philosophy and Social Hope*. New York: Penguin Books (originally published as "Another possible world," *London Review of Books*, February 8, 1990).

Safranski, R. (1998) *Heidegger: Between Good and Evil* (trans. E. Oslers). Cambridge, MA: Harvard University Press (original work published 1994).

Schürmann, R. (1990) *Heidegger on Being and Acting: From Principles to Anarchy* (trans. C.-M. Gros and R. Schürmann). Bloomington: Indiana University Press (original work published 1982).

Sluga, H. (1993) *Heidegger's Crisis: Philosophy and Politics in Nazi Germany*. Cambridge, MA: Harvard University Press.

Thomson, I. (1999) The end of ontotheology: understanding Heidegger's turn, method, and politics. Philosophy dissertation, University of California at San Diego.

Thomson, I. (2000a) Ontotheology? Understanding Heidegger's *Destruktion* of metaphysics. *International Journal of Philosophical Studies*, 8(3), 297–327.

Thomson, I. (2000b) From the question concerning technology to the quest for a democratic technology: Heidegger, Marcuse, Feenberg. *Inquiry*, 43(2), 203–16.

Thomson, I. (2000c) What's wrong with being a technological essentialist? A response to Feenberg. *Inquiry*, 43(4), 429–44.

Thomson, I. (2001) Heidegger on ontological education, or: How we become what we are. *Inquiry*, 44(3), 243–68.

Thomson, I. (2003a) Heidegger and the politics of the university. *Journal of the History of Philosophy*, 41(4), 515–42.

Thomson, I. (2003b) The philosophical fugue: understanding the structure and goal of Heidegger's *Beiträge*. *Journal of the British Society for Phenomenology*, 34(1), 57–73.

Wolin, R. (1990) *The Politics of Being: The Political Thought of Martin Heidegger*. New York: Columbia University Press.

Wolin, R. (ed.) (1991) *The Heidegger Controversy: A Critical Reader*. New York: Columbia University Press.

Young, J. (1997) *Heidegger, Philosophy, Nazism*. Cambridge: Cambridge University Press.

Zimmerman, M. (1990) *Heidegger's Confrontation with Modernity: Technology, Politics, and Art*. Bloomington: Indiana University Press.

Further reading

Neske and Kettering (1990) and Wolin (1991) collect many of the primary texts at the heart of the controversy surrounding Heidegger's National Socialism. The best succinct introduction to the philosophical issues is Dreyfus (1993). The two most important in-depth treatments remain the critique by Wolin (1990) and defense by Young (1997). Safranski (1998) is less philosophical but provides a balanced narrative. Zimmerman (1990), Sluga (1993), and Losurdo (2001) are invaluable for an understanding of the broader context. On the specific philosophical views responsible for Heidegger's attempt to transform the university, see Crowell (1997), Milchman and Rosenberg (1997), and Thomson (2001, 2003a). On Heidegger and the Shoah, see Agamben (1999).

4

Heidegger and Husserl: The Matter and Method of Philosophy

STEVEN GALT CROWELL

"Phenomenology, that's Heidegger and I – and no one else." According to legend Husserl spoke these words in the early 1920s, when he was at the height of his fame in Freiburg and Heidegger, his young assistant, was grappling with the ideas that would become *Being and Time*. In 1927 Heidegger dedicated that work to Husserl "in respect and friendship," writing in a footnote that "If the following investigation has taken any steps forward in disclosing the 'things themselves,' the author must first of all thank E. Husserl, who, by providing his own incisive personal guidance and by freely turning over his unpublished investigations, familiarized the author with the most diverse areas of phenomenological research during his student years in Freiburg" (SZ: 38, n. 1). But in 1923 he was writing privately to Karl Löwith that "I am now convinced that Husserl was never a philosopher, not even for one second in his life" (Husserl 1997: 17). And while dedicating *Being and Time* to his mentor, Heidegger was writing to Karl Jaspers that "if the treatise has been written 'against' anyone, then it has been written against Husserl" (Husserl 1997: 22). For his part, Husserl struggled to understand how Heidegger's work fit into his own project of transcendental phenomenology and ultimately came to the conclusion that it did not: "my antipodes, Scheler and Heidegger," he wrote to Roman Ingarden in 1931 (Husserl 1968: 67).

As these conflicting statements attest – and they could easily be multiplied – the relation between Heidegger and Husserl, one of the philosophically decisive encounters of the twentieth century, cannot be constructed as a simple *pro* or *contra*. Nor is it – at least on Heidegger's side – a matter of uniform development from initial enthusiasm to ultimate rejection. Rather, there is from the start a dynamic of attraction and repulsion in Heidegger's attitude toward Husserl's work, one that has to do not with this or that aspect of philosophical doctrine, but with the *matter* and *method* of philosophy as such. Attraction and repulsion are evident in the fact that Heidegger defends Husserl's phenomenology against its neo-Kantian and neo-Hegelian detractors, while rejecting the Cartesian language Husserl uses to formulate his views. It is evident in the fact that Heidegger publicly acknowledges Husserl's influence only in very general (if formally generous) ways, while appropriating Husserlian analyses into his own work without comment. And it is evident in the fact that Heidegger saw his lectures of the early 1920s as "wringing the neck" of "the old man" (Husserl 1997: 17), while he managed to take over nearly every significant Husserlian theme: philosophy as science, as transcendental inquiry; the centrality of description, intuition, and *Evidenz*; the critique of naturalism and the reduction to meaning; the rejection of traditional metaphysics; the focus on temporality; the appeal to first-person philosophical self-responsibility; and so on. To be sure, in taking them over Heidegger did not leave these themes unaltered. Still, despite its many other sources (Aristotle, Kant, St Paul, Kierkegaard, Dilthey), it is not too much to say that the shape of Heidegger's early philosophy is essentially Husserlian.

Some may dispute this claim on the ground that the apparent connections between Heidegger's early thought and Husserl's are in fact superficial, to be explained by the circumstances of Heidegger's academic career. Needing support for his promotion to a professorship, it is suggested, Heidegger maintained the fiction of *Symphilosophieren* precisely as long as was necessary to become Husserl's successor in Freiburg. The curious attraction and repulsion may then be understood as a natural outcome of this Oedipal situation – Heidegger aching to "burn and destroy" Husserl's "sham philosophy" (Husserl 1997: 17, 22) while nevertheless having to present himself as part of the latter's phenomenological school. On this view Husserl's influence constitutes a detour in Heidegger's itinerary, an academically motivated distraction from the true wellspring of his thought.

Whatever its merits (and academic politics certainly plays a role in the Husserl/Heidegger relation), this view entails that one dismiss, or at least downplay, the achievement of *Being and Time*, which, all agree, brings with it much Husserlian "baggage." To do so, however, is to go further than Heidegger himself; for though he abandoned the project of *Being and Time*, he would maintain, as late as 1953, that "its path remains nevertheless a necessary one even today, if our Dasein is to be stirred by the question of being" (SZ: vii). If *Being and Time* remains an achievement worthy of philosophical attention, then, a look at the issues involved in Heidegger's relation to Husserl cannot be without profit. Before we turning to some of these issues, it will be useful to sketch how the intellectual relationship unfolded in its academic context.

The Academic Relationship

In 1963 Heidegger recalled that as a young seminarian (1909–10) he was "fascinated" by Husserl's *Logical Investigations*, reading it "again and again . . . without gaining sufficient insight into what fascinated me" (Heidegger 1972: 75). Husserl was then in Göttingen, and Heidegger, having switched in 1911 from theological to philosophical studies, was working to define his own position in the then-current debate between neo-Kantians and neo-Scholastics over the nature of logic. In his earliest scholarly publication, "Neuere Forschungen über Logik" (1912), he comments that logical meaning belongs neither to the domain of empirical science nor to that of metaphysics but to a "realm of validity" that "in the entire course of the history of philosophy has never been given its due in a fully conscious and consequent manner" (GA 1: 24). Husserl's refutation of psychologistic approaches to logic in the *Logical Investigations* provided Heidegger with ammunition for his 1913 dissertation, a criticism of five psychologistic theories of judgment that ends with the question "What is the meaning of meaning?" (GA 1: 171). Two years later, in his Habilitation thesis, Heidegger adopted the language of Husserl's recently published *Ideas for a Pure Phenomenology and Phenomenological Philosophy* to explore the "noetic" and "noematic" foundations of Thomas of Erfurt's theory of categories and pure grammar. Though ostensibly a work in the history of philosophy, the book seeks to make a contribution to "modern logic" and praises scholastic thought for its powerful "moments of phenomenological observation" (GA 1: 202). Heidegger is writing under the nominal direction of the neo-Kantian, Heinrich Rickert, but it is Husserl's theory of "pure consciousness" in *Ideas* that has provided "a decisive overview of the treasures of 'consciousness' and has destroyed" the neo-Kantian thesis of the "emptiness of consciousness in general" (GA 1: 405). Though the neo-Kantian philosopher, Paul Natorp, had dismissed Husserl's exploration of consciousness as a "relapse" into psychologism, Heidegger rejects this accusation. For him, "a purely 'objective' general theory of objects remains incomplete"; the domain of logically valid meaning cannot be clarified without bringing "subjective logic" into focus through phenomenological investigation (GA 1: 404).

A conclusion added to the Habilitation thesis in 1916 points in a different direction: logic and its problems can be properly understood only in a "trans-logical" or "metaphysical" context (GA 1: 405–6). Philosophy of logic must penetrate to the "historical living spirit" and even to what mystics like Eckhart had in view. But though these themes – life, history, spirit – were never abandoned, Heidegger would not develop them under the neo-Scholastic aegis of "metaphysics" but, for the next decade, under the aegis of Husserl's phenomenology. Two things account for this: first, in 1916 the Chair of Catholic Philosophy that Heidegger had hoped to get on the basis of his Habilitation went instead to Joseph Geyser, and, in the same year, Husserl came to Freiburg as Rickert's successor.

During the period between 1919, when Heidegger took up teaching as a lecturer after the war, and 1923, when he gave his last Freiburg course before leaving for Marburg, Heidegger turned repeatedly to the main theme of Husserl's 1911 programmatic essay, "Philosophy as Rigorous Science," namely the peculiar character of philosophical inquiry, which is cognitive (makes truth-claims) but not "theoretical," not an explanatory system of propositions governed by laws. In the *Logical Investigations* Husserl had argued that philosophy is not a theory that explains knowledge causally but a reflection that clarifies knowledge phenomenologically. Heidegger radicalizes this idea, turning it against Husserl himself. In a 1919 lecture course, for example, he argues that even Husserl's insistence that philosophy abjure theoretical constructions and cleave to what is directly given in experience involves a distortion of the phenomena, since "givenness" is itself already a theoretical construct (GA 56/57: 89). The givenness of meaning to consciousness – intentionality as consciousness of objects – conceals its own condition, which Heidegger now begins to call "being." Before being a reflection on intentionality (Husserl's view) phenomenology is to be an "understanding, an *hermeneutic intuition*" (GA 56/57: 117), a self-interpreting process in which "factic life" intuits itself in its practical, pre-theoretical unfolding.

Thus, while Husserl was moving phenomenology toward transcendental idealism, Heidegger was imagining it as a "hermeneutics of facticity." In this notion he linked the Husserlian idea of philosophy as "primal science" with the Aristotelian idea of philosophy as a doctrine of categories, an ontology. As Heidegger tells us, while he "practiced phenomenological seeing, teaching, and learning in Husserl's proximity after 1919,"

51

he was simultaneously exploring "a transformed understanding of Aristotle" (Heidegger 1972: 78). Husserl's theory of categorial intuition had made such a reading possible by "for the first time concretely pav[ing] the way for a genuine form of research capable of demonstrating the categories" (GA 20: 97–8), but Husserl disputed Heidegger's view that research into the categories of factic life was the ultimate task of primal science.

Both the demand for an account of the ultimate conditions of intentionality and the turn toward practical comportment of human beings were also part of Husserl's work during this period, work that Heidegger, as Husserl's assistant, knew well, though it remained unpublished for decades. In lectures and research manuscripts beginning in 1905 and collated by Edith Stein in 1917 (to be published under Heidegger's editorship only in 1928), Husserl located the ultimate conditions of object-consciousness in the pre-intentional absolute flow of inner time-consciousness. The structure of this analysis – though not the details – would reappear in Heidegger's *Being and Time*, where temporality is the "horizon" for the "meaning of being" in general. Heidegger also knew Husserl's work on "nature and spirit" – meant for the second volume of *Ideas* – in which Husserl argues for the primacy of the embodied, practical comportment of the "person" over any form of purely theoretical attitude. Whether Heidegger was influenced by these analyses, or whether, as he says, Husserl took note of "[Heidegger's] objections from my lecture courses in Freiburg" and "[made] allowances for them" (GA 20: 167) is a matter of some dispute. What is clear is that Heidegger was not satisfied that Husserl's concept of the person was a phenomenologically adequate categorial account of the "being who is intentional."

This formulation appears in a lecture course delivered in 1925, shortly after Heidegger had moved from Freiburg to Marburg. In 1917 Paul Natorp had approached Husserl about Heidegger's suitability for a professorship at Marburg, but Husserl (who at that time had had little personal contact with Heidegger) was non-commital. By 1923, however, Husserl had come to see Heidegger as the great hope for carrying on his phenomenology, so that when Natorp again inquired about Heidegger Husserl was enthusiastic. One of Heidegger's first projects upon finding himself in the capital of Marburg neo-Kantianism was to develop a radically anti-Marburg interpretation of Kant. Reading "the *Critique of Pure Reason* anew and . . . as it were against the background of Husserl's phenomenology . . . opened my eyes," he writes in 1927 (GA 25: 431). For instance, Husserl's concept of intuition allowed Heidegger to grasp the significance of Kant's faculty dualism (pointedly rejected by the Marburg School); and Husserl's approach to inner time-consciousness helped Heidegger to recognize, in temporality, the crucial link between the transcendental imagination and the schematism. But at the same time Heidegger was beginning to settle scores with Husserl, in particular with the transcendental idealism of *Ideas*, which he condemned as a foreign, neo-Kantian transplant into phenomenology (GA 20: 145).

As the representative of phenomenology in Marburg, Heidegger begins his 1925 lecture course by defending the genuine sense of Husserl's achievement from then-current misunderstandings. Nevertheless, he argues that Husserl's "breakthrough" to phenomenology in the *Logical Investigations* had been compromised by its subsequent subordination to a "traditional idea of philosophy" (GA 20: 147). Heidegger accuses Husserl of foisting on phenomenology the Cartesian demand for a philosophical science based on absolutely certain foundations, when in fact it should be a radically new approach to ontology. Though Husserl does outline certain ontological determinations of consciousness, Heidegger argues that these are not drawn from the "being who is intentional" but from those aspects of consciousness that make it suitable to become the object of an epistemologically foundational science. That Heidegger's own view of phenomenology as ontology is equally derived from a "traditional idea of philosophy" – one borrowed from Aristotle, rather than Descartes – is obvious, though like Husserl he will claim that it arises solely from the immanent logic of phenomenology itself.

In 1925, again supported by Husserl, Heidegger became a candidate for Nicolai Hartmann's Chair and, in a rush, submitted the unfinished *Being and Time* for publication. On the basis of galley proofs the Minister of Education deemed it "insufficient," but once it had been published in Husserl's *Jahrbuch für Philosophie und phänomenologische Forschung* this judgment was reversed, and in 1927 Heidegger was promoted to full professor. Between 1927 and 1929, when he moved to Freiburg as Husserl's chosen successor, Heidegger continued to develop his reinterpretation of phenomenology. Husserl's marginal remarks in his copy of *Being and Time* show that he was troubled by Heidegger's apparent departures from his own position, but he reports that "Heidegger steadily denied that he would abandon my transcendental phenomenology, and he referred me to his future second volume [of *Being and Time*]" (Husserl 1997: 23).

In order, perhaps, to get to the bottom of their differences, Husserl invited Heidegger to collaborate on an article for the *Encyclopaedia Britannica*. Heidegger's revisions recast Husserl's original so as to highlight the continuity between ontology and transcendental phenomenology, but Husserl saw only the (not inconsiderable) departures from his view and the collaboration collapsed. This was effectively the collapse of the academic and personal relation as well. In 1928 Heidegger did contribute an essay, "On the Essence of Ground," to Husserl's *Festschrift*, but the tenor of the piece – with its long historical analyses of the concept of "world" and its attempt to trace the Husserlian themes of intentionality and reason to the "more primordial" ground of "Dasein's transcendence" – was confrontational. So was Heidegger's inaugural lecture in Freiburg, "What Is Metaphysics?," delivered in 1929. Taking over the Chair of the founder of phenomenology, who had always held philosophy to be rigorous science, Heidegger does not mention phenomenology, sharply distinguishes philosophy from science, and grounds all science in "the Nothing." This lecture begins a chapter in Heidegger's thought where Husserl's influence is mainly absent. The early 1930s were years in which Husserl had little to do with Heidegger, developing his ideas instead in conversation with his former assistant, Eugen Fink, while Heidegger lectured on Nietzsche, Hölderlin, and the pre-Socratics. On Husserl's death in 1938 Heidegger – who in the meantime had become the first National Socialist Rector of the University of Freiburg and, in the wake of controversy, had subsequently retired from public academic politics – did not attend the funeral.

Because both Husserl and Heidegger believed that phenomenology radically transformed philosophical inquiry – standing "opposed to those pseudo-questions which parade themselves as 'problems,' often for generations at a time" (SZ: 28) – it can be difficult to assess each's claim that the other lacked "radicality." Such a claim is possible only if there is common ground; but if, as each held, the matter and the method of philosophy are inseparable, objections to an account of the matter can always be parried by a claim that the method has been misunderstood. This, in fact, was Husserl's general response to Heidegger's criticisms. The present chapter is not the place to adjudicate such disputes; instead, it focuses chiefly on how *Heidegger* constructed the differences with Husserl. Regarding the matter of philosophy, the dispute turns on the question of whether philosophy is essentially an inquiry into "being" or a "science of consciousness"; regarding method, the dispute concerns a nuance in the concept of phenomenological "reduction."

Contested Philosophical Issues, Part I: The Matter of Philosophy

Heidegger holds that philosophy has "forgotten" the "question of being" (What is being? What does "being" [*Sein*] mean?). What for the Greeks had been the source of deepest wonder has become a desiccated branch of logic that concerns itself with laws of the empty "something in general." Husserl, for instance, distinguished between "regional ontologies" (the *a priori* categorial frameworks governing the empirical sciences) and "formal ontology" (the categories governing cognitive "objecthood" as such). Though Heidegger also distinguishes between regional ontologies and ontology proper, he does not construe the latter as a *formal* inquiry; rather, it is the Aristotelian question of the "unity" in the "manifold senses of being," an inquiry into the meaning of being as such. Husserl could make no sense of this question. When, in his 1929 *Kant and the Problem of Metaphysics*, Heidegger writes that "we understand being and yet we lack the concept," Husserl responds in the margin: "We lack it? When would we need it?" (Husserl 1997: 465). Beyond the formal category "something-in-general" there is, for Husserl, nothing to say about being as such, but for Heidegger it is precisely phenomenology's task to overcome such "forgetfulness" and ask about the sense of being presupposed in formal and regional ontologies alike.

By placing phenomenology in the service of the question of being Heidegger had, in Husserl's eyes, failed to grasp its radicality. For Husserl, all objectively oriented science, including ontology, is naive, that is, uncritical with regard to its own possibility. This is not to dismiss such science but to indicate the need for a different sort of inquiry, one that explores the conditions presupposed by objective inquiry. Phenomenology thus takes the form of an investigation into "consciousness" – not consciousness as the object of the science of psychology, but "pure" or "transcendental" consciousness as the *subjective* as such, the site where all objectivity, "whatever has for me sense and validity as 'true' being" (Husserl 1969: 19), is given. Pure consciousness is not an entity in the world, but subject for the world; its philosophically salient characteristic is intentionality: all consciousness is consciousness *of* something *as* something, thanks to which all entities present themselves with a certain "content" or meaning (*Sinn*). Phenomenology is thus to be an analysis of how that content, presupposed in all scientific and pre-scientific dealings with entities, gets constituted through "acts" of consciousness and their "syntheses." Since such acts condition the givenness of any possible beings, all ontological inquiry presupposes the science of transcendental consciousness.

The deepest differences between Husserl and Heidegger concern this idea of an inquiry "prior to" ontology, for in *Being and Time* Heidegger apparently demands something similar. In order to answer the question of the meaning of being one must first clarify the conditions under which it can be raised in a meaningful way – the first of which, Heidegger argues, is that one have something like a pre-ontological "understanding of being" (SZ: 5). Thus ontology proper must be preceded by "fundamental" ontology – a phenomenological explication of how an understanding of being is possible. This entails examination of that being who is possessed of such an understanding – which Heidegger, using the ordinary German expression for "existence," calls *Dasein*. Just as Husserl's transcendental consciousness is not equivalent to psychological (human) consciousness, so Dasein, though precisely the entity that "each of us is himself" (SZ: 7), is not equivalent to the *anthropos*. But – and the source of all friction lies here – it is not equivalent to transcendental *consciousness* either. Heidegger acknowledges that Husserl's "formal phenomenology of consciousness" is possible (SZ: 115), but he argues that such an "analytic description of intentionality in its apriori" (GA 20: 108) cannot fulfill the larger goal of accounting for the *possibility* of intentionality, the origin of that content through which "there is" something. For consciousness itself rests upon an ontological basis that has the character of "being-in-the-world." Heidegger's fundamental ontology proposes to show how the structures of being-in-the-world make consciousness in Husserl's sense – the intentionality of acts of perception, judgment, imagination, etc. – possible.

Husserl understood the problem of intentionality to be the problem of how a "transcendent" (mind-independent) object can be "there" for consciousness. How is it, for instance, that perception gives its object as a real entity in the world, and what sort of modification of perception is involved when the same object is remembered, hallucinated, or merely imagined? Heidegger, in contrast, held that this kind of ontic transcendence – the meaning of entities as correlates of intentional acts – depended upon an ontological transcendence to which Husserl was blind, namely the transcendence of Dasein as being-in-the-world. Consciousness of objects is possible because Dasein transcends beings as a whole toward their *being*: because Dasein "understands something like being," individual beings can show up *as* what they *are*. In contemporary terms, intentional content cannot be understood as a function of consciousness alone but must be seen as deriving from the structure of being-in-the-world as a whole, that which enables our understanding of being.

This point may be brought out by a series of contrasts between what Heidegger took to be Husserl's views and his own account of the structures of being-in-the-world. As previously noted, Heidegger traced Husserl's problems to the latter's adherence to a traditional Cartesian idea of philosophy. Heidegger admits that Husserl makes essential advances beyond Descartes (GA 17: 261–2), yet he argues that Husserl's commitment to a science of consciousness undermines these advances. Heidegger thus formulates his own position as a response to what he sees as Husserl's residual individualism, rationalism (theoretism), and internalism. We may begin with individualism.

For Husserl, the basic structure of intentional experience is the Cartesian *ego-cogito-cogitatum*. Because the "I think" (I judge, I remember, etc.) belongs to every intentional act, the field of meaning is essentially a field of *individual* consciousness. If one asks about the character of the "I" here, Husserl will point out that there are various attitudes in which the question can be answered. In the personalistic attitude, for example, I grasp myself as a social, practical, valuing, being; in the naturalistic attitude, in contrast, I appear as the bearer of "psychic experiences." But considered in its deepest ("transcendental") significance the ego is a unique, "indeclinable" instance, the genuine first-person irreducible to any third-person descriptions, a monadic spontaneity that "constitutes itself for itself in, so to speak, the unity of a 'history'" (Husserl 1969: 75; translation modified). Here Husserl not only faces the problem of solipsism, but embraces it: though he recognizes that any account of intentional content must refer to a community of egos in communicative interaction ("transcendental intersubjectivity"), he nevertheless insists that this intersubjectivity must itself be egologically constituted. Heidegger registers his objection at just this point. Agreeing with Husserl that an account of intentional content must make reference to social norms and hence to a social subjectivity, Heidegger argues that this very fact renders contradictory the idea of a pre-social subject, which would have to constitute sociality from its own individuality. As being-in-the-world I am always being-with-others. For Heidegger, then, the problem is not to explain how the social world can be constituted from my "monad," but to explain how anything like *individuality* is possible. On Heidegger's view I understand myself in terms of the typical roles, inherited customs, and standard ways of doing things prevalent in my time and place. I belong to *das Man* (the They), the anonymous "others" from whom, "for the most part, one does *not* distinguish oneself" (SZ: 118). Because such interchangeability is a condition for intelligibility, Heidegger conceives individuation not as prior to the social but as a modification of it; "authenticity" does not constitute sociality but merely occupies it in a different way.

Being-in-the-world, then, is not equivalent to the traditional idea of subjectivity as individual consciousness. One philosophically significant consequence is that the understanding of being that makes ontological inquiry possible is not first of all a matter of what takes place in an individual mind but is, rather, an intelligibility that resides in the shared social practices prevalent in a particular culture at a particular historical moment. Such an understanding is not, therefore, a function of a hidden reason, supported by an implicit transcendental logic, as Husserl supposed was the case for the domain of intentional consciousness. Instead, it is groundless, resting upon nothing more than the way things are done. For Husserl, this entailed an unacceptable relativism; for Heidegger it is the necessary consequence of the fact that Dasein is "care" (*Sorge*) before it is reason.

What this means emerges from Heidegger's criticism of a certain rationalism or theoretism in Husserl's account of intentionality. According to Heidegger, the intelligibility of things derives from Dasein's practical gearing into the world, its "projects." Self-understanding is not initially a theoretical self-awareness but is embedded in these projects – that is, in practices that involve my abilities and skills. Abilities and skills entail norms of success or failure, and because they do, things can show up in *significant* ways – that is, as hammers that "nicely fulfill" their function, or as bicycles that are "too rickety to ride." On Heidegger's view, the satisfaction conditions inherent in such projects are what make intentionality in the Husserlian sense possible. Thus, to say that Dasein is "care" before it is reason is to say that what things are or mean depends on their involvement in a totality of significance ("world") anchored in my practical concerns – ultimately, in my concern for my own being. Heidegger believes that Husserl, on the contrary, misconstrues the character of such experience thanks to a rationalist presupposition built into his focus on intentional *acts*, one that leads him to propose something like a "theory theory" of intentional content.

Thus, for example, Husserl recognizes that our ordinary experience is one of using hammers, tables, and chairs, but he argues that it is phenomenologically founded in something more basic – namely, the thing as merely perceived, an identity in the manifold of perceptual properties such as color, orientation in space, weight, and so on. Upon this basis the thing comes to exhibit its practical and other "evaluative" properties through a series of further act-syntheses that yield our seamlessly rich experience of it. Using Heidegger's terms, Husserl treats experience as though things were initially given as merely "present at hand" and only subsequently taken up into practical activities. In Husserl's favor, it would appear to be a logical or conceptual requirement that if I use a hammer I also see (or feel) a physical thing-with-properties; indeed, Heidegger himself admits that "only by reason of something present-at-hand, 'is there' anything ready-to-hand" (SZ: 71). But he denies that the ready-to-hand is thereby founded on the present-at-hand in the phenomenological sense. The logical requirement is not a phenomenologically *evident* one; it is only when our smooth dealings with things break down that the kind of intentionality characteristic of simple perception or explicit propositional determination emerges. To read these structures back into pre-theoretical experience is to exhibit a rationalist prejudice. Husserl's account is thus a "theory theory" in the sense that it substitutes analytic desiderata, based on the demands of a cognitively foundationalist theory, for unprejudiced description of how things show up for us.

In arguing that being-in-the-world is essentially social and practical, Heidegger has undercut two core elements of the Cartesian view of intentional content, to which, he believes, Husserl is committed. Together these imply rejection of a third element, "internalism" or representationalism. Husserl staunchly maintained that his theory of intentionality had left all forms of Cartesian subjectivism behind, but for Heidegger any appeal whatsoever to consciousness as the ground of intentionality brings with it a kind of representationalism, since it construes our basic openness to the world (which he calls "disclosedness") as a kind of *forum internum* with its own laws and structures. In Husserl this shows up in his theory of the "noema," the idea that entities are given by way of noemata, or "senses," that are immanent to consciousness. Heidegger's claim that Dasein's understanding of being is equivalent to the disclosedness or revelation of things is meant to undercut this sort of view on ontological grounds.

If internalism is the view that intentional content is sufficiently determined by *mental* content ("what is in the head"), then it is doubtful that Husserl's theory of the noema is truly internalist. He rejects the idea that intentionality can be explained psychologically, in terms of mental representations. To ground object-reference in the individual psyche ("narrow content") is to court skepticism by severing the *way* things are given from the things themselves. Husserl's noema is meant to include both, and it is no more in the head than it is in the world; it belongs to "transcendental" consciousness as such. From this point of view – a full explication of which would require an account of the reductions – the transcendent thing is itself "immanent" to consciousness and can play the role sometimes attributed to "external" factors in accounting for intentional content. To say, for instance, that the intentional content of my state when I refer to water is partly determined by the micro-structure of that substance, whether that structure is known to me or not, is not to say that such content is determined by something external to the *noema*, since the latter includes within itself reference to an open-ended process of determining that thing – whatever it is – to which I stand in relation by means of its being given in a certain way. From the noematic point of view, a causal theory of reference is not a *causal theory* (i.e. an explanation that supervenes on phenomenological factors) but an explication of how the sense of certain noemata (intentional content) is constituted by reference to a particular sedimented causal history. But while this causal history, as an intentional implication of the noema, belongs within the field of consciousness, this does not mean that the causal history *itself* is internal to the mind. Even if Husserl's position is not internalist in the ordinary sense, however, Heidegger finds that Husserl's talk of the "constitution" of the thing by means of a "synthesis" of various intentional acts remains caught in the Cartesian trap. Though he nowhere rejects Husserl's theory of the noema explicitly, Heidegger's argument that intentionality (the "discoveredness" of entities) depends on Dasein's transcendence, that is, on the prior disclosedness of being-in-the-world, involves elements that undermine what Husserl took to be the self-sufficiency of an account of meaning in terms of consciousness. For Heidegger, disclosedness is a matter of three equally necessary aspects of Dasein's being – understanding, disposition, and discourse – none of which is an intentional act in Husserl's sense. We have already mentioned how understanding functions as "project": the meaning that informs practical activity cannot be grasped as the correlate of an act of consciousness, a noema. But a deeper contrast with Husserl's alleged internalism requires a look at the equally decisive role of disposition, since by its means the "factic" character of Dasein's disclosedness comes to light.

Disposition (*Befindlichkeit*) names that dimension of being-in-the-world that structures the affects: moods, feelings, emotions. For Husserl, it is through affect that things have value for us, claim us, and so possess meaning in the sense of weight or bearing. For Heidegger, too, it is through moods that things matter to us, but whereas Husserl saw mood as a distinctive kind of intentional act (with "value" as its distinctive intentional object), Heidegger links affectivity to the pre-intentional disclosure of being-in-the-world as a whole. Less formally, it is through mood that the world as a *whole* – the context of significance co-structured by my projects – is opened up as mattering in a certain way. When I am bored it is the world as a whole that is boring, hence individual things in it can strike me as tedious; when I am joyous I am warmly attuned to things as a whole, hence I can find particular things enchanting. At the same time, moods tell me something about myself. As Heidegger puts it, they reveal my "thrownness" or "facticity" – the "burdensome character of Dasein," that "it is and has to be" (SZ: 135). Moods thus attest that I am not a pure egological spontaneity but am passively *exposed* to the world. Such exposure marks my being as finite, a designation that Heidegger explores in his analyses of anxiety, being-towards-death, and historicality.

To the extent, then, that Husserl can be seen to claim that nothing essential to the constitution of meaning lies outside (transcendental) consciousness, Heidegger's analysis of disposition – of the passivity and finitude of being-in-the-world – would seem to contest such internalism. As the way in which the world as a whole comes to matter at all, disposition yields a condition on all intentional content (exposure to the world, facticity) that cannot itself be conceived as a correlate of consciousness. *Finding* oneself in a world cannot be recovered reflectively as a product of intentional activity; yet it is necessary for there to *be* intentionality.

Does this mean that Heidegger should be counted among the externalists who argue that intentional content is partly determined by what lies outside consciousness? Certainly, if consciousness is understood in Cartesian fashion: Heidegger denies that some complex system of mental representations could be identical to the content of our experience. Yet it is not clear that Heidegger's externalism differs radically from Husserl's internalism. For instance, Heidegger's appeal to the world in which I find myself is not equivalent to the metaphysical naturalism typical of externalist theories, which treat the causal and micro-structure that determines aspects of certain intentional content as something unavailable to phenomenology. As he tells us in *Being and Time*, "the 'nature' by which we are 'surrounded' is, of course, an entity within-the-world" (SZ: 211); that is, it is not the world itself but a kind of intentional content, something that shows up *in* the world. The "nature" of naturalistic accounts is thus immanent to being-in-the-world in much the same way it is immanent to consciousness for Husserl, and precisely this structural similarity allowed Heidegger to dismiss Husserl's charge that *Being and Time* was merely an "anthropologistic" misunderstanding of transcendental phenomenology. Heidegger's emphasis on the factic and worldly character of existence cannot mean that a philosophical account of intentionality is to be supplemented by historical, sociological, anthropological, or biological theories. What then can it mean? With this question, Heidegger's view of the matter of philosophy can no longer be explicated without reference to its *method*.

Contested Philosophical Issues, Part II: The Method of Philosophy

For Heidegger, as for Husserl, philosophical method must be distinct from that of non-philosophical inquiries; it can be neither inductive nor deductive, neither experimental nor dialectical. "Only as phenomenology is ontology possible" (SZ: 35). Husserl characterized phenomenological method as reflective, intuitive, and descriptive, and in some places Heidegger appears to embrace, while in others he appears to contest, each of these. Since an account of Heidegger's phenomenology is reserved for another chapter in this volume, the focus here is on the issue of method most closely bound up with the dispute over the matter of philosophy, namely, the issue of Husserl's *reductions*. By means of eidetic, phenomenological, and transcendental reductions Husserl sought to define the specific character of philosophical knowledge, and while Heidegger appears to dismiss them as useless "technical devices" (SZ: 27) antithetical to the ontological aims of phenomenology, his own position remains within the scope of the reductions save at one crucial point, where an existential moment asserts itself within the framework of what both Heidegger and Husserl call the "*transcendental* knowledge" of philosophy (SZ: 38) .

For Husserl, philosophy is not an empirical but an *a priori* discipline, a science of "essence." Thus phenomenology might begin with an example drawn from experience, but its goal is not an exhaustive description of the example. Rather, it seeks insight into what is essential to things of that kind, gained by varying the example in imagination until the limits of its variability-within-identity become clear. Husserl terms this process the "eidetic reduction." Many objections have been raised against such a procedure, but there can be little doubt that Heidegger agrees with its outcome. For him philosophical knowledge is eidetic. Early in *Being and Time* Heidegger warns that his analysis of "average *everydayness*" will exhibit "not just any accidental structures, but essential ones which, in every kind of being that factical Dasein may possess, persist as determinative for the character of its being" (SZ: 16–17). Heidegger does not describe the process whereby he attained insight into these essential structures, but his conception of philosophical knowledge remains within the *scope* of the eidetic reduction. Thus his 1925 claim that ideation is "the most fundamental of misunderstandings" when applied to Dasein (GA 20: 152) is curious. And the argument that, since Heidegger holds philosophical inquiry to be grounded in factical, historical existence, any claim to essential knowledge is inconsistent with his position, shows at most that Heidegger is inconsistent since he *does* lay claim to such knowledge.

For Husserl, philosophical knowledge is distinct from all other knowledge in that it may not "presuppose the world," and a second, "phenomenological," reduction (or *epoché*) makes this explicit. Often described as a "bracketing of being," the *epoché* would seem to be ruled out by the very nature of Heidegger's enterprise as an inquiry *into* being. Indeed, in 1925 Heidegger specifically rejects the "phenomenological reduction" as a "disregarding" that is "in principle inappropriate for determining the being of consciousness positively" (GA 20: 150). However, as with the eidetic reduction, the positions of Husserl and Heidegger are not as far apart as they initially appear. For by "bracketing" of being Husserl means, first of all, that philosophy cannot take over results from other sciences. It can reflect upon scientific claims as *claims* to truth, but in its effort to clarify the essence and possibility of scientific knowledge philosophy may not presuppose the validity of those claims. Heidegger affirms just this point – so contrary to contemporary naturalism – when he argues that philosophy does not "limp along" behind science, investigating its status "as it chances to find it," but rather "leaps ahead, as it were, into some area of being" and "discloses it for the first time in the constitution of its being" (SZ: 10).

Husserl's reduction of "being" to "phenomenon" might appear to go further, but in fact it merely extends the *epoché* of the positive sciences to the factual claims inherent in everyday experience. For Husserl, to bracket being in order to focus on the phenomenon is to consider the entity precisely as it gives itself without *committing* oneself to the claims that the entity makes for itself. The *epoché* does not "disregard" being but sets a specific sort of epistemic commitment out of play. This pen and paper before me, for instance, certainly present themselves as real; but to investigate how this presentation-as-real, as a kind of intentionality, is constituted I need not *use* my commitment to its reality. In bracketing it I neither deny the reality of pen and paper nor eliminate the possibility of inquiring into what reality means. Because philosophy is not an explanatory factual science, the bracketing of being does not compromise inquiry into its sole concern: the phenomenon as such. In contrast, a science like psychology *must* commit itself to the factual existence of what it studies since it aims at laws that explain matters of fact, thus laws that depend on the real existence of the evidence that lies at their basis. Understood as a bracketing of epistemic commitment, Heidegger too accepts the phenomenological reduction. It merely expresses the anti-naturalism he shares with Husserl.

Having focused philosophical reflection on the phenomenon by means of the *epoché*, Husserl proposes a further, "transcendental," reduction whereby the phenomenon's conditions of possibility are disclosed. For Husserl, these conditions lie in "absolute" consciousness, which is said to "constitute" all being as phenomenon. Heidegger will part company with Husserl on this point, but again not without embracing a good many of the methodological implications of the transcendental reduction.

First, Heidegger informs us of the difference between Husserl's and his own version of this reduction:

> For Husserl, the . . . reduction . . . is the method of leading phenomenological vision from the natural attitude of the human being . . . back to the transcendental life of conscious-ness and its noetic-noematic experiences, in which objects are constituted as correlates of consciousness. *For us*, . . . reduction means leading phenomenological vision back from the apprehension of a being . . . to the understanding of the being of this being (projecting upon the way it is unconcealed). (GA 24: 29)

That this is a form of the transcendental reduction becomes clear if one recalls that to lead phenomenological vision back from the entity to the understanding of its being is, for Heidegger, to thematize the conditions for the disclosure, manifestation, of the entity *in* its being. Nevertheless, because the understanding of being depends on being-in-the-world, Heidegger's reduction would appear to conflict with Husserl's since the latter attains an absolute – that is, "worldless" – transcendental consciousness. In a famous passage Husserl imagines the "annihilation of the world" in order to argue that while all worldly being is relative to consciousness, consciousness is absolute in the sense that it needs no "real" thing in order to be – "*nulla 're' indiget ad existendum*" (Husserl 1982: 110). Heidegger, in contrast, insists that the very *thought* that the world does not exist cannot be entertained. In order to locate the true point at which Heidegger parts company with Husserl it will be instructive to examine this famous dispute a bit more closely.

"The question of whether there is a world at all and whether its being can be proved makes no sense if raised by *Dasein* as being-in-the-world; and who else would raise it?" (SZ: 202). Heidegger here targets Kant and, behind him, Descartes's claim that the world, appearing just as it does in experience, might not exist; that it might be a very coherent dream or the product of an evil demon. Though he never says as much, Heidegger appears to target Husserl here as well. But in contrast to Descartes, Husserl nowhere implies that we have reason to doubt the existence of the world. On the con-trary, he argues that if the "pertinent regularities" of our experience actually persist it is *inconceivable* "that the corresponding transcendent world *does not exist*" (Husserl 1982: 111). The *evidence* for the existence of any worldly thing, and so of the world itself considered as the sum-total of worldly things, is never sufficient to establish that existence apodictically; it is always presumptive; but Husserl does not treat this as a reason for the sort of Cartesian skepticism that Heidegger dismisses. In imagining the world's "annihilation" he refers, instead, to a situation in which the above-mentioned "pertinent regularities" *fail* to obtain. In such a case the "being of consciousness . . . would indeed be modified," but "its own existence would not be touched" (Husserl 1982: 110); that is, even if law-governed identities did not present themselves in the ways they do in fact present themselves – i.e. such that there are physical things for us – there could still be something like psychic functioning. Indeed, certain stages of infantile consciousness must be very much like this.

Such a position does not conflict in any essential way with Heidegger's. First, it does not imply that *Dasein* could be without a world. Being-in-the-world is indeed unthinkable under the conditions of "annihilation" in Husserl's sense, and if Heidegger is right that consciousness depends on Dasein, then consciousness could not be without a world either. Yet, second, one should proceed here with caution: Heidegger's arguments about the dependence of consciousness on Dasein show only that *intentionality* could not be without Dasein, not that "consciousness" in some other sense could not be. And this is consistent with what Husserl says, since for him too "annihilation" of the world eliminates intentionality, though not consciousness. Consideration of infants, animals, and other apparently conscious creatures provides some reason to think that consciousness can in some sense exist without "world"; indeed, Heidegger makes just this point when he denies "worldhood" – though surely not sentience – to animals. This suggests that while Heidegger must reject Husserl's claim that the transcendental reduction establishes "absolute" consciousness as the ground of an account of intentionality, this is not because the move to a transcendental perspective itself somehow conflicts with the "worldly" character of Dasein. Dasein's worldliness is *itself* transcendental. What finally forces the transformation of transcendental into existential phenomenology is to be sought in a different direction altogether.

Husserl developed the method of the reductions in order to do justice to what he took to be the fundamental norm governing philosophy, namely the norm of "ultimate philosophical self-responsibility." Because philosophical inquiry can take nothing for granted – neither from the sciences nor from previous philosophies – it must be radically first-personal. Only what I can validate on the basis of my own evidential insight can stand as actual philosophical knowledge; the assertions of others are initially merely "empty," mere truth-claims that I must demonstrate for myself against the things that "fulfill" them. To take responsibility for evidential fulfillment defines the *practice* of philosophizing. The various reductions, then – including the reduction of one's own being to transcendental consciousness – are meant to stake out the kind of *Evidenz* that measures up to the norm, the first-person experience within which any possible claim to meaning and being must be assessed.

For Heidegger, too, the norm of evidential self-responsibility defines the practice of philosophy. Taking over Husserl's distinction between empty and fulfilled judgments, Heidegger treats philosophical concepts not as material for dialectic – "free-floating constructions" (SZ: 28) – but as empty or "formal" indications that point toward a first-person "evidence situation" (GA 61: 35) in which their claims can be fulfilled or thwarted on the things themselves. Heidegger was more attuned than was Husserl to the way traditional philosophical concepts can distort what the philosopher "sees," so his phenomenology includes a "destruction" (*Destruktion*) – or critical examination – of the tradition that aims at "access to those primordial 'sources' from which the categories and concepts handed down to us have been in part quite genuinely drawn" (SZ: 21). In speaking of access to primordial sources, however, it is clear that destruction is not an alternative to first-person insight but its handmaid, an approach to tradition that aims to free up, here and now, "those primordial experiences" from which our understanding of ourselves has grown (SZ: 22). Further, the demand for evidential self-responsibility is built into the structure of *Being and Time*. An inquiry into Dasein (the being possessed of an understanding of being) as the ground of intentionality is, by the same stroke, an inquiry into its own conditions of possibility as inquiry. And because one of those conditions is that I be able to take *responsibility* for what I see and say, Heidegger must develop the analysis of Dasein beyond the account of its everyday lostness in the anonymity of *das Man* to that point where Dasein can genuinely say "I," that is, recover its "own" self and so *be* responsible to itself. This is the methodological significance of the chapters on death, conscience, and authenticity as resoluteness.

But this has a serious implication for the theory of the transcendental reduction. It is possible for the phenomenologist to bracket her commitment to the existential claim made by any object of consciousness without thereby sacrificing the very possibility of attaining truth, since the phenomenon yields all the basis she needs for the kind of *a priori* and essentialist truth phenomenology seeks – including truth about meaning and being. However, when the inquiry concerns the transcendental *conditions* of such ontological inquiry – as it does when I am inquiring into my own being as a cognitively responsible being – the being of the inquirer cannot be bracketed. For I cannot bracket my commitment to *being* a philosopher (to the practice of philosophy as taking responsibility for the distinction between what is truly seen and what is only emptily asserted) without thereby losing the very topic of inquiry. Commitment to being, in the form of carrying out philosophy as evidential self-responsibility, is at this point – but *only* at this point – irreducible. As Heidegger was the first to see clearly, phenomenology must become existential because it is here, in the being of the philosopher, that the matter and method of philosophy become one.

References and further reading

Bernet, R. (1994) Phenomenological reduction and the double life of the subject. In T. Kisiel and J. van Buren (eds.), *Reading Heidegger from the Start: Essays in his Earliest Thought*. Albany: State University of New York Press.

Bernet, R. (1988) Transcendance et intentionalité: Heidegger et Husserl sur les prolégomènes d'une ontologie phénoménologique [Transendence and intentionality: Heidegger and Husserl on the prolegomena to a phenomenological ontology]. In F. Volpi et al. (eds.), *Heidegger et l'Idée de la phénoménologie* [*Heidegger and the Idea of Phenomenology*]. Dordrecht: Kluwer Academic Publishers.

Carman, T. (2003) *Heidegger's Analytic: Interpretation, Discourse, and Authenticity in* Being and Time. Cambridge: Cambridge University Press.

Crowell, S. G. (2001) *Husserl, Heidegger, and the Space of Meaning: Paths Toward Transcendental Phenomenology*. Evanston, IL: Northwestern University Press.

Crowell, S. G. (2002) Does the Husserl/Heidegger feud rest on a mistake? An essay on psychological and transcendental phenomenology. *Husserl Studies*, 18, 123–40.

Dahlstrom, D. O. (2001) *Heidegger's Concept of Truth*. Cambridge: Cambridge University Press.

Dreyfus, H. and Haugeland, J. (1978) Husserl and Heidegger: philosophy's last stand. In M. Murray (ed.), *Heidegger and Modern Philosophy*. New Haven, CT: Yale University Press.

Heidegger, M. (1962) *Being and Time* (trans. J. Macquarrie and E. Robinson). New York: Harper & Row (original work published 1927).

Heidegger, M. (1972) *On Time and Being* (trans. J. Stambaugh). New York: Harper & Row.

Hopkins, B. (1993) *Intentionality in Husserl and Heidegger: The Problem of the Original Method and Phenomenon of Phenomenology*. Dordrecht: Kluwer Academic Publishers.

Husserl, E. (1968) *Briefe an Roman Ingarden* [*Letters to Roman Ingarden*]. The Hague: Martinus Nijhoff.

Husserl, E. (1969) *Cartesian Meditations: An Introduction to Phenomenology* (trans. D. Cairns). The Hague: Martinus Nijhoff (original work published 1950).

Husserl, E. (1982) *Ideas Pertaining to a Pure Phenomenology and to a Phenomenological Philosophy* (trans. F. Kersten). The Hague: Martinus Nijhoff.

Husserl, E. (1997) *Psychological and Transcendental Phenomenology and the Confrontation with Heidegger (1927–1931)* (ed. and trans. T. Sheehan and R. Palmer). Dordrecht: Kluwer.

Keller, P. (1999) *Husserl and Heidegger on Human Experience*. Cambridge: Cambridge University Press.

Kisiel, T. (1993) *The Genesis of Heidegger's* Being and Time. Berkeley: University of California Press.

Marion, J.-L. (1998) *Reduction and Givenness: Investigations of Husserl, Heidegger, and Phenomenology* (trans. T. A. Carleson). Evanston, IL: Northwestern University Press.

Okrent, M. (1988) *Heidegger's Pragmatism: Understanding, Being, and the Critique of Metaphysics*. Ithaca, NY: Cornell University Press.

Philipse, H. (1998) *Heidegger's Philosophy of Being: A Critical Interpretation*. Princeton, NJ: Princeton University Press.

Stapleton, T. J. (1983) *Husserl and Heidegger: The Question of a Philosophical Beginning*. Albany: State University of New York Press.

Taminiaux, J. (1994) The Husserlian heritage in Heidegger's notion of the self. In T. Kisiel and J. van Buren (eds.), *Reading Heidegger from the Start: Essays in his Earliest Thought*. Albany: State University of New York Press.

Tugendhat, E. (1970) *Der Wahrheitsbegriff bei Husserl und Heidegger* [*The Concept of Truth in Husserl and Heidegger*]. Berlin: Walter de Gruyter.

Von Herrmann, F.-W. (1974) *Subjekt und Dasein: Interpretationen zu "Sein und Zeit"* [*Subject and Dasein: Interpretations of "Being and Time"*]. Frankfurt am Main: Vittorio Klostermann.

5

Heidegger and German Idealism

DANIEL O. DAHLSTROM

Heidegger's early relationship to the German Idealists has its ups and downs. Late in life he recalls how, in the "exciting years" between 1910 and 1914, he had developed a "growing interest in Hegel and Schelling" (GA 1: 56). A decade later he had clearly soured on both thinkers, especially Hegel, whom he accuses of "confusing us with God" (GA 21: 267). At the conclusion of his Habilitation in 1916, after pleading for investigation of "the living, historical spirit" out of which categories emerge, he does call for critical engagement with Hegel's system, "the most powerful in its fullness as in its depth, reach of experience, and conceptual formation" (GA 1: 410ff). However, in his initial lectures after the war, presenting himself as a phenomenologist for whom the future of philosophy consists in a "non-theoretical science" that breaks with traditional ontology, Heidegger finds himself squarely at odds with German Idealism, which he saw as the "acme" of theoretical consciousness. Convinced that "the idea of the *system* . . . was illusory," he speaks of forming a "front against Hegel." He takes Natorp's system and Rickert's philosophy of value to task as descendants, respectively, of Hegel's "absolutizing of the theoretical" and Fichte's doctrine of the primacy of practical reason (Strube 2003: 94ff).

Schelling is not mentioned in this context, probably because Heidegger considered him merely a "literary figure," or at least he did until 1926 when, prodded by Jaspers, he began reading Schelling's writings – especially his *Philosophical Investigations on the Essence of Human Freedom* (hereafter "Freedom Essay") – in earnest. In a letter to Jaspers from this period, Heidegger writes: "Schelling ventures much further philosophically than Hegel, even though he is conceptually less orderly" (Heidegger and Jaspers 1990: 62; Gadamer 1981: 432). Though Heidegger offers an early seminar on Schelling's Freedom Essay in 1927–8, his reading of Schelling does not bear fruit that Heidegger deems worthy of publication for another decade or more.

Toward the end of *Being and Time*, Heidegger does discuss Hegel's attempt to explain how the human spirit and time are related and, thereby, how the history of the human spirit can transpire in time. Yet, while part of Heidegger's motivation is to call attention to Hegel's under-appreciated concept of time, his main aim is to drive home the distinctiveness of his interpretation of human existence in terms of temporality by contrasting it with Hegel's conception of the relation of time and spirit. In this light, he chides Hegel for taking the bearings for his analysis of time from an overly simplified ("vulgar"), albeit traditional, concept of time as an ever-present sequence of nows. In addition, he makes the controversial point that, contrary to Hegel's "construction" of a connection between spirit and time, the existential analysis of Dasein begins in the "concretion" of factically thrown existence "in order to reveal temporality as what originally enables it [existence]" (SZ: 435–6; Sell 1998: 76ff).

This discussion of Hegel's concept of time and its connection with spirit, while highly critical, marks the beginning of a basic change in attitude toward the German Idealists (hereafter simply "Idealists"), as Heidegger's early dismissal of them gives way to ever-mounting respect and critical engagement. From this point on, Heidegger repeatedly challenges conventional wisdom by arguing that the aftermath of German Idealism marks not its collapse, but rather a deterioration of philosophical thinking to a level far below it. The philosophical creativity, radicalness, and raw metaphysical ambition of Schelling, Hegel, and Fichte increasingly become a cause of wonder to him and, more importantly, a challenge he cannot ignore. Taking the time finally to read the Idealists for himself (as he puts it in a letter to Jaspers; Heidegger and Jaspers 1990: 123), Heidegger could not help but recognize a series of similarities with his own ambitions: resisting the untested presuppositions of scientific naturalism, religious dogmatism, a worldless, ahistorical subjectivity and the philosophically ungrounded worldviews engendered by them – and resisting them in favor of a thoroughgoing attempt to think things through completely, radically, and concretely. Not surprisingly, many aspects of their thought can be and, indeed, were read – to Heidegger's dismay, in some cases – as anticipating his thinking in *Being and Time*. Yet whether critics provided the spur to Heidegger's rediscovery of the Idealists or not, this first serious reading of their works also helped him to appreciate not only that the critics had a point but also that the Idealists command an essential place in the history of Western metaphysics and, hence, in his project of deconstructing it (thereby considerably expanding the originally planned second part of *Being and Time*). Moreover, after Heidegger moves away from the transcendental phenomenology and fundamental ontology of *Being and Time*, his thinking incorporates issues and insights introduced in the context of Idealist meta-physics, a fact that, at the very least, raises questions about his allegedly post-metaphysical turn. For all these reasons, Heidegger lectures and writes frequently on works of the Idealists, seizing each interpretation as an opportunity to clarify his own thinking by comparison and contrast.

Following the publication of *Being and Time*, Heidegger's relationship to the Idealists passes through four principal phases (though the third and fourth phases overlap for a time). The first phase, his awakening to the significance of German Idealism, coincides with his initial efforts, in the first few years following the publication of *Being and Time*, to elaborate fundamental ontology as a "metaphysics of Dasein." In this first phase, dominated by lectures on "German Idealism," given in 1929, Fichte figures more prominently than do Schelling or Hegel. In the second phase, the major turn in Heidegger's thinking after 1929 away from fundamental ontology begins to take shape precisely as Heidegger lectures on the "crossroads" of his thinking with Hegel's (Sell 1998: 26ff; GA 32: 113). While this second phase is transitional, the same cannot be said for the last two phases, each dating from the mid-1930s, as Heidegger attempts to prepare for a new, non-metaphysical beginning for philosophy, what he deems "think-ing being historically," i.e. thinking being as an event in which human beings play an essential role (GA 65: 422–3, 431). In the third phase Heidegger lectures twice (1936 and 1941) on Schelling's Freedom Essay as "the pinnacle of the metaphysics of German Idealism," which nonetheless makes some "individual thrusts" in the direction of Heidegger's new beginning, indeed, "driving German Idealism from within beyond its own basic position" (GA 42: 6/Heidegger 1985: 4). In the fourth and final phase of Heidegger's encounter with the Idealists, he clarifies his post-metaphysical turn by distinguishing it from Hegel's metaphysics as the culmination of Western metaphysics (Heidegger 2003: 89ff). In the series of studies from 1936 to 1958 that mark this fourth phase, Heidegger is concerned with establishing Hegel's trenchant elaboration of the modern conception of being, yet as a legacy of Greek thinking. The import of the exercise is to provide an indirect argument for a new beginning, one that takes its bearings not from metaphysics' leading question ("What is?"), but from the basic but forgotten question of being ("What is being?" or, alternatively, "What does it mean to be?").

Earlier I mentioned the overlap between the third and fourth phases, dominated respectively by Schelling and Hegel. Although Heidegger early on found, as noted, a particular resonance with Schelling's thinking, he increasingly takes pains after 1940 to compare and contrast Schelling's and Hegel's thinking, a move which probably facilitated the change in focus from Schelling to Hegel after 1945 (GA 49: 181–5). In any event, after 1930 Heidegger does not lecture again on Fichte nor after 1945 on Schelling; but extended references to Hegel and treatments of his works can be found from 1916 to 1958.

There is much to be said for the charge that Heidegger's readings of the Idealists are in various respects tendentious, a point ably made even by authors highly appreciative of Heidegger's thinking, e.g. Walter Schulz, Hans-Georg Gadamer, Otto Pöggeler, David Kolb, Annette Sell. The following study attempts not to address these various criticisms, but to help to lay the groundwork for assessing them. Its aim is to highlight Heidegger's central contentions in each phase of his engagement with German Idealism and to do so with a view to their significance for his own thinking.

The First Phase: Fichte's "Metaphysics of Dasein" and Its Systemic Betrayal

Heidegger's brief initial engagement with the Idealists demonstrates to him just how much his fundamental ontology, especially in its deliberate appropriations and departures from Kant's transcendental philosophy, coincides with their efforts to develop a post-Kantian metaphysics. In their reconfigurations of Kant's theories of imagination and judgment in particular, Heidegger recognized unmistakable anticipations of his own Kant-interpretation (GA 28: 108–13, 163–71, 260–3). Not surprisingly, the last chapter of Heidegger's *Kant and the Problem of Metaphysics*, published the same year that he delivered the lectures on German Idealism, essentially overlaps with the opening chapter of the published lectures.

In both settings Heidegger presents his project of fundamental ontology as the only legitimate inference to be drawn from the two basic tendencies of contemporary philosophy at the time, namely philosophical anthropology (the search for a unified conception of humanity in the face of a proliferation of approaches and findings) and a new metaphysics (the effort to overturn a one-sidedly epistemological orientation and to renew questions about the totality and ultimacy of things). Heidegger appreciated the inseparability of these two tendencies, but located their unity, not (like Scheler) in philosophical anthropology, but in fundamental ontology. Heidegger's fundamental ontology holds that a human being's most basic determination (prior to its place in the cosmos) is its understanding of being. There is, he accordingly stresses, "an inner connection" between the basic question of metaphysics and the metaphysics of Dasein (GA 28: 18–23, 46). In other words, Heidegger attempts to drive home that inner connection through his readings of the Idealists, just as he had in his interpretation of Kant (as the substitution of essentially the same material in both the lectures and the Kantbook already suggests). Indeed, the issue had become more pressing in the wake of recent critics' anthropological misunderstandings of *Being and Time*, some of which he addresses in these lectures. Thus, he reads Fichte's *Foundation of the Entire Doctrine of Science* as a "metaphysics of Dasein" and "foundation of metaphysics" (GA 28: 103, 132–9, 241).

At one level this reading appears counterintuitive since Fichte is working toward an absolute system. But Heidegger turns to Idealist systems precisely to demonstrate the supposedly ineluctable finitude of human understanding of being and, thus, human existence itself (the "always already" factual, historical contextuality of being-here: *Da-sein*). Accordingly, one of his strategies is to demonstrate how the dialectical method of these systems, first introduced by Fichte, presupposes not only what it sets out to prove, but also what it does not set out to prove yet gives the proof whatever trenchancy it has. In this way Heidegger finds corroboration for his conception – at the time – of the fundamental convergence of the basic question of metaphysics and a hermeneutically circular metaphysics of human existence.

The 1929 lectures on German Idealism have been dubbed "the Fichte lectures," because well over two-thirds of them, following the opening chapter just discussed, are taken up with the three parts of Fichte's "Doctrine of Science" (*Wissenschaftslehre*): (a) its presentation of the basic principles of the entire doctrine, (b) its foundation of theoretical knowing, and (c) its foundation of a science of the practical. In each part Heidegger finds treatments of themes that accord strikingly with his own thinking, though most of his focus is directed at the first part. There Fichte introduces the judgment "I think" as the first principle of the *Doctrine of Science* with the argument that it is the supreme and unconditioned condition of all judging because it expresses an action that consists in nothing other than bringing forth the thought of the ego. This account of the ego amounts, Heidegger remarks, to a "self-positing" that is "the essence of the ego's being" (GA 28: 65). The remark is approving because Heidegger sees affinities here with the discipline and the content of his existential analysis, i.e. a refusal to appeal to something outside human existence itself and a recognition that human existence defines itself in its own projection. Fichte's account of this first principle also reveals in Heidegger's eyes a genuine understanding of the distinctiveness of being a self in contrast to being something merely "on hand" (*vorhanden*) (GA 28: 53, 65, 68). In view of this discovery of Fichtean subjectivity, as Jürgen Stolzenberg notes, Heidegger would have to revise his previous sweeping indictment of the Western tradition for treating human existence as something simply "on hand" (Stolzenberg 2003: 80ff).

Fichte's second principle, not derivable from the first, is the necessary positing of the "not I," i.e. of something opposed to the ego. As Heidegger reads this principle, it does not refer to an entity or collection of entities standing opposite the ego, itself construed as an entity. Instead, that "not I" in Fichte's second principle, posited as it is in and for the ego, is essential to the ego. It is the *horizon* and *elbow room* within which the ego comports itself as ego. Obviating the contradiction that obtains between the first two principles, Fichte's third principle – a "decree of reason" (Fichte 1982: 106) – posits not their mutual exclusion, but their mutual limitation. In this principle, together with the second, Heidegger finds an appreciation for understanding human existence as whole yet as inherently finite, two central themes of his own existential analysis. Invoking a crucial notion of that analysis, Heidegger characterizes this finitude as the contextual "facticity of the I" (GA 28: 77, 79n.8, 90ff).

But this factual finitude and the decree introducing it, Heidegger also urges, are incompatible with the certainty and "absolute ideal of a science" that Fichte otherwise claims for his system and its deductions. In fact, in a patent inversion of Fichte's idealism, Heidegger claims that this finitude drives the entire first part of the *Doctrine of Science*. In other words, on Heidegger's reading, the first and unconditioned principle in Fichte's *presentation*, i.e. the self-positing ego, has its seat in the finitude expressed by the third principle. But Fichte systematically betrays this insight because of the priority that he – following Descartes – attaches to method over content and certainty over truth, "the basic character of metaphysics as science of knowledge" (GA 28: 91). In this same connection, echoing the joint concern of his readings of Kant and the Idealists at this time, Heidegger makes the critical observation:

> In the dominance of the dialectic within German Idealism, the basic conception of the I as absolute subject makes itself known, i.e., this is ultimately grasped *logically* and that means that this metaphysics severs itself from the basic question in which all metaphysics, as far as its possibility is concerned, is grounded: the question of the being of human existence [*Dasein*] from which alone the universal and fundamental question of being can be posited at all. . . . Precisely here in the most resolute endeavor at metaphysics, being is not present at all! (GA 28: 122)

The criticism is vintage Heidegger with its charge that *being is forgotten* – and by no means coincidentally – in the Idealist epitomization of metaphysics, the science supposedly concentrating on being. But the similarities between the Idealists' metaphysical project and his own undoubtedly helped him to appreciate the pitfalls of the metaphysical horizons in which he couches his own project toward the end of the 1920s. Indeed, it is not hard to imagine that this appreciation contributed to his abandonment of the project of a "metaphysics of Dasein" and helped to usher in the next phase in his thinking and ongoing conversation with the Idealists.

The Second Phase: Onto-theo-ego-logy and the Question of Infinity at a "Crossroads" with Hegel

Heidegger's lectures on the opening chapters of Hegel's *Phenomenology of Spirit* in 1930/1 contain his first sustained treatment of the work that he considers the heart and soul of Hegel's philosophy. The lectures are transitional, both for Heidegger's own thinking and for his engagement with the Idealists. Though Heidegger continues explicitly to clarify the project begun in *Being and Time* (this time by way of contrast with Hegel's thinking), these lectures are no longer in the ambit of the metaphysics of Dasein. Thus, after characterizing the science of the phenomenology of spirit as "the fundamental ontology of the absolute ontology and, that means, the onto-logy in general," Heidegger immediately adds that it is at the same time "the endstage of any possible justification of ontology" (GA 32: 204).

The difference that Heidegger's thinking has undergone between the first and second phases is also evident in one of the initial contrasts that he draws between his thinking and Hegel's. In the course of arguing for the fundamental importance of Hegel's system of science in the *Phenomenology of Spirit* (as opposed to Hegel's Frankfurt, Jena, and *Encyclopedia* "systems"), Heidegger contrasts the Greek conception of philosophy as science, "radically completed" by Hegel, with his own claim that philosophy is not a science – a clear departure from his portrayal of philosophy as phenomenology and phenomenology as the science of being, i.e. ontology, just a few years earlier. Hegel manages to consummate the Greek conception of a science of being because the meaning of being is determined from the beginning by an absolute that is already with us. "One must say it to oneself again and again: Hegel already presupposes what he gains at the end" (GA 32: 43). Heidegger interprets the genitive "science of experience" in the original title of the *Phenomenology of Spirit* as an appositive genitive (like "city of Boston"), indicating that the experience in which absolute knowing comes to itself (or, alternatively, in which the spirit appears as a relative phenomenon in the process of coming to itself) is precisely the science (the knowledge of being) in question. Heidegger introduces the term "absolvent" to characterize the way in which the absolute "frees itself" from the limitations of a merely relative knowing (consciousness) by "dissolving" and "replacing" it (GA 32: 71–2). This absolute knowing (subjectivity) that is presupposed at every juncture of the *Phenomenology* is thus infinite, when matched against the finite perspectives of consciousness charted in the work.

This infinity marks one of the ways in which Heidegger finds himself in these lectures at a crossroads with Hegel. The talk of a "crossroads" and "crossing" seems to serve more than one purpose. It indicates, even if only rhetorically, Heidegger's acknowledgment of the intersection of his thinking with Hegel's, particularly in the similar ways that they take up yet distance themselves from Kant's transcendental philosophy (GA 32: 92, 113–14, 151–2). At the same time, to the extent that crossroads call for a decision, the image accords with Heidegger's claim that there is something irreducibly finite about being. Thus, Heidegger's attempt "to fashion *the* kinship, that is necessary in order to understand the spirit of his [Hegel's] philosophy," amounts to an insistence on considering both his concept of finitude and Hegel's concept of infinity in connection with the question of being (GA 32: 55). Though this approach is clearly self-serving, it allows Heidegger to draw some basic distinctions between him and Hegel regarding the problem of being. While Hegel conceives being as infinite, a conception that becomes accessible to absolute knowing only at the cost of time, Heidegger conceives time as "the original essence of being" (GA 32: 17, 210ff). Further evidencing the turn but also the continuity in his thinking, Heidegger distinguishes his time-oriented questioning as "ontochrony" from ontology (GA 32: 144). In this connection

Heidegger also faults Hegel not so much for the claim of the superiority of an infinite, absolute knowing over the finite knowing considered in the *Phenomenology* as for the inadequacy of his inherited (even if dialectical) grasp of the finite (GA 32: 55, 101–14).

One of Heidegger's final encounters with Hegel is his much-touted 1957 essay, "The Onto-theo-logical Constitution of Metaphysics." Yet the concept of onto-theo-logy and, with it, that of onto-theo-ego-logy already figure prominently in the lectures of 1930/1. At times Heidegger employs the term "onto-theo-logy" to designate a traditional way of thinking and knowing (*logos*) beings (*onta*) by inquiring into their ultimate ground, the supreme being (*theos*). This linking of ontology to theology, introduced by Aristotle, is a paradigmatic expression of what Heidegger understands as Western metaphysics' obliviousness to being – paradigmatic because the question of what being is gives way to the question of what beings there are and how they are related to one another (e.g. creating and created). But Heidegger also uses the expression "onto-theo-logy" for how specific conceptions of what is (ontology), what is primarily (theology), and what it is to determine something as something (logic) serve as "mutually determining perspectives of the question of being" (GA 32: 183). Emphasizing this mutual determination is especially relevant in Hegel's case since his science of logic is at once an ontology and a theology as he makes his case that being is, in the final analysis, the absolute spirit, "the absolute self-conception of knowing" (GA 32: 142).

Heidegger's aim in portraying Hegel's (and, later, Schelling's) thinking as onto-theo-logy is to demonstrate how the basic question of philosophy gets sidetracked by the leading question of metaphysics. Onto-theo-logy is thus another way in which Heidegger marks the crossroads at which he stands with Hegel. For Heidegger, the *basic* question is the question of the sense of being and the answer, at least in part, lies in time (later, time-space). Traditional ontology, by contrast, allegedly forgets this basic question in its pursuit of the *leading* question of metaphysics, the question of what is, which it frames not in terms of time, but in terms of a certain kind of talk (*logos*: concepts, statements, inferential grounding, theoretical cognition) about beings. So, too, Hegel is said to pre-empt the question of whether being is essentially finite by reconfiguring all finitude in terms of the infinity of absolute knowing, indeed, to such a degree that philosophy itself becomes equated with this reconfiguring (*Aufheben, Dialektik*). Yet the very distinction between finite and infinite being, Heidegger submits (albeit with far too little argument), is evidence of Hegel's indifference to the basic question of being (GA 32: 106).

If Heidegger exploits the term "onto-theo-logy" to expose the Aristotelian roots of Hegel's thinking, the expanded term "onto-theo-ego-logy" is meant to indicate its distinctively modern character. In Heidegger's commentary on the transition from consciousness to self-consciousness in the *Phenomenology of Spirit*, he applies the expression "ego-logical," borrowed from Husserl, to characterize the justification for the transition, i.e. the claim that consciousness of things and thinghood is only possible as self-consciousness. Hegel himself, it bears recalling, characterizes self-consciousness as "the native realm of truth," adding that in it "the concept of spirit is already at hand for us" (Hegel 1977: 104, 110). In the transition to self-consciousness, Heidegger accordingly submits, lies Hegel's appropriation and revision of the modern grounding of beings in subjectivity, from the Cartesian *cogito* to Kant's apperception and Fichte's absolute ego. The self in self-consciousness is the ego of the "I think" that, by positing itself, enacts the infinite identity of identity and difference, itself as subject and its object. On this account, being (i.e. spirit which first makes its appearance in self-consciousness) is infinite and its infinity is inseparably logical and subjective, inasmuch as the absolute identity of the "I think" coincides with the mode of conceiving it. Reminding his students that the absolute for Hegel is the spirit, Heidegger sums up Hegel's "onto-theo-ego-logical" approach to being with the observation: "The spirit is knowing, *logos*; the spirit is I, ego, the spirit is God, *theos*; and the spirit is actuality, beings purely and simply, *on*" (GA 32: 183). Each of these dimensions of Hegel's absolute conception of being expands beyond any previous philosophical pretensions the scope of what is considered to be (e.g. history, objective spirit, art). Yet Heidegger's critical point is that, precisely in this process of realizing metaphysics' claim to utter universality and explicability, the *basic* question of what is meant by saying that these various entities exist is not posed. Instead, in the last analysis, i.e. in the constant and complete presence of the development of things, an old, refurbished answer is presupposed. But Heidegger also recognizes that he cannot make this same criticism, at least not without much further ado, of the "system" of Hegel's leading contemporary critic and one-time friend: Schelling.

The Third Phase: Schelling on the Basic Distinction, the Primal Being of the Will, and the Existence of Evil

Schelling's "Freedom Essay" is, Heidegger declares, "the pinnacle of the metaphysics of German Idealism" in the sense that Idealist metaphysics can climb no higher yet from its heights the shape and necessity of another beginning, i.e. Heidegger's own project, can be seen. For this reason, with the exception of a brief review of Schelling's early writings in the 1929 lectures, the Freedom Essay is the primary focus of Heidegger's engagement with Schelling. "The genuinely philosophical reason" for working on this essay, Heidegger tells his students, is that "it is at its core a metaphysics of evil and with it a new essential impulse enters into philosophy's basic question of being" (GA 42: 169/Heidegger 1985: 98; see GA 65: 202). In perhaps the strongest statement of the extent of Schelling's capacity to break through the metaphysical tradition that reaches back to the Greeks, Heidegger maintains: "The genuinely metaphysical accomplishment of the Freedom Essay [is] the establishment of an original concept of being," a concept that no longer makes the onhandness or presence of things the measure of being (GA 42: 147/Heidegger 1985: 85; GA 42: 212/Heidegger 1985: 122).

In the essay, Schelling initially frames the question of freedom's fit within a philosophical system, but the systematic fit in question involves not freedom and nature, but freedom and God. The answer to the question of freedom's fit is to be found in a "correctly understood pantheism" in which the ground of the dialectical identity of God and everything else requires freedom. Yet everything turns on the sort of freedom entertained here since the Idealists, including the young Schelling, had already posited a freedom-centered pantheism. For while the Idealists' dynamic concept of being has, in

Schelling's opinion, the better of a "one-sided realism" (Spinoza's fatal assumption of the inertness of things), the formal conception of freedom in Idealist systems ("self-determination") still leaves us "clueless" because it fatally overlooks what is distinctive about human freedom, namely a capacity for evil. Moreover, in the process it renders God irrelevant. In these ways, Heidegger stresses, Schelling identifies the basic limits of idealism (Schelling 1936: 20–5, 61ff; GA 42: 156–72/Heidegger 1985: 90–9).

Schelling's key to reconciling the human capacity for evil with God is a distinction between ground and existence. Though the distinction refers to two inherent aspects of each being, it is not a merely logical or useful distinction but, Schelling submits, "a very real" one that he first uncovered in his philosophy of nature. The distinction is rooted in the observation that all things are in the process of coming to be, eternally in case of God, finitely in the case of created things. Only in and as this becoming are they what they are. Thus, every being, God included, comes to be, i.e. to exist from a ground. Though distinct, ground and existence are inseparable, like darkness and light. The ground is contracting, chaotic, self-centered; existence is expansive, orderly, universal. The ground is the ultimate power for evil and it is *in* God yet distinct from God's existence (Schelling 1936: 33ff, 51). In this way, Schelling sets the metaphysical stage for explaining God's creation of the possibility of evil, i.e. of human nature.

Heidegger regards the introduction of this distinction as the "centerpiece" of the essay. Employing his own terminology, he characterizes the distinction as "the fit of being" (*Seynsgefüge*), adding that, for the conception of being that the distinction entails, "the determination of entities in the sense of the presence of something on hand [*Anwesenheit eines Vorhandenen*] . . . no longer suffices" (GA 42: 191/Heidegger 1985: 109; GA 42: 211/Heidegger 1985: 121; GA 42: 236ff/Heidegger 1985: 136ff). For the ground remains ever "incomprehensible" in every being since being itself is the movement to the "light" and "intelligibility" of existence, a creative event in which "the ground and the existence, the self-concealing and the determining" strive toward one another in their "clearing unity" (GA 49: 84–9). These remarks are telling since they betray no qualms about recasting Schelling's thinking in the very terms that Heidegger is using to pose and address the basic question of being. In any case, if Fichte's conception of the dynamic process of the subject begins to break the ontological mold in Heidegger's eyes, Schelling's distinctive elaboration of this dynamism and extension of it to the entire creation and to the Creator Himself raises this newfound ontological sophistication to new heights.

These new heights can be gathered from the human imagery invoked by Schelling to capture the crucial relation between ground and existence. Thus, in the course of marking the advance of idealistic over Spinozistic systems, Schelling contends: "There is in the last and highest instance, no other being at all than willing. Willing is primal being" (Schelling 1936: 24). He accordingly calls the ground in God the unconscious will and the longing for existence and understanding. Corresponding to the longing, "an inner reflexive representation" is produced in God, by means of which God sees himself in His own image, an image that he also equates with the understanding, "the word of that longing." The "eternal spirit" is said to be the unifying unity of ground and existence, longing and word, a unity that, motivated by love, unifies without collapsing them, in effect "letting the ground ground." More precisely, this spirit is "the

73

breath of love," leading Schelling to posit love as higher than the spirit (Schelling 1936: 35ff, 51ff). But this act of love is also God's self-revelation via creation of His Other (in His image and likeness): humanity. Hence, far from manufacture, creation for Schelling is, Heidegger stresses, a kind of individualization and stratification in which at once the ground is deepened and existence expanded (GA 42: 224–38/Heidegger 1985: 129–37). But in this process of divine self-differentiation motivated by love, humanity's difference from God is precisely its capacity to dissolve the loving unity of ground and existence. Evil is the substitution of one's own will for the universal will, the perversion of the divine harmony of the universal will with the will of the ground. In the loving act of letting the ground ground, God wills not evil but human existence and human existence is a freedom for good *and* evil.

Heidegger's lectures on Schelling coincide with his efforts to think being as the self-concealing yet revealing event between humans and God, in which the contest between a recalcitrant earth and a malleable world is waged. Being, so conceived, is in need of Dasein, the time-space of its "concealing clearing," as much as Dasein is in need of it. As already suggested, Schelling's account of being (creation) in terms of the dynamics of ground and existence and, not least, their groundless unity parallel Heidegger's efforts too closely to be coincidental (GA 42: 230ff/Heidegger 1985: 133ff; Sikka 1994). The parallels, which can only be suggested here, underlie Heidegger's positive statements, cited at the outset of this section, about Schelling's "original concept of being." They also form the backdrop for his defense of Schelling against charges of anthropomorphism, charges advanced, Heidegger points out, from the presumption of an adequate understanding of human existence. Here again, the parallel with Heidegger's own project is patent as he argues that being, grounding and grounded in Dasein, first grounds human being (GA 42: 283ff/Heidegger 1985: 163ff; GA 65: 317–18).

Perhaps because of the parallels mentioned, Heidegger's criticisms of Schelling are less sharply developed than his criticisms of the other Idealists. Still, he faults Schelling for falling prey to the same onto-theo-logical tendencies and subordinating the question of being to a conception of a supreme and all-encompassing being as an absolute subjectivity (GA 28: 90–122). But Heidegger's criticisms are directed at Schelling's thinking even as it departs from Idealism. He addresses, for example, Schelling's observation that, while there is a system in the divine intellect, "God Himself is no system, but a life" (Schelling 1936: 78). Though the observation is probably directed at the Idealistic conception of the absolute as intelligence, it places the ground outside the system, thereby vitiating, Heidegger contends, the universal pretensions of the system itself. So, too, struggling to identify what is determined by the first (albeit eternal) distinction of ground and existence ("what was there before the ground and the existing (as separated) were, but was not yet as love"), Schelling calls it "the primal ground [*Urgrund*] or much more the *nonground* [*Ungrund*]" – a notion that verges on Heidegger's own discussion of the abyss (*Abgrund*) of being (Schelling 1936: 87; GA 65: 379–88). But in this crucial respect, Heidegger claims, Schelling fails to see "the necessity of an essential step," namely the inference from the fact that being cannot be predicated of the absolute to the conclusion that "finitude is the essence of all being" (GA 42: 279ff/Heidegger 1985: 161ff). Thus, in Heidegger's view, Schelling fails to answer the questions that he poses for himself because he is unable to resolve how the difference and the unity of ground and existence relate to the system. But given the "individual thrusts" that Schelling makes at the same time toward a new concept of being, his "failure" is anything but insignificant in Heidegger's eyes.

What makes this failure so meaningful is the fact that Schelling thereby merely brings out difficulties posited already in the beginning of Western philosophy and posited as insurmountable by this beginning, given the direction it takes. For us that means that a second beginning becomes necessary through the first, but one that is possible only in the complete transformation of the first beginning, never through merely letting it stand (GA 42: 279/Heidegger 1985: 161).

The Fourth Phase: Hegel's Completion of Western Philosophy and "Getting over" Metaphysics by Thinking Its Forgotten Ground

Whereas Heidegger initially reads the Idealists in view of the broadly conceived "Kantian" project of fundamental ontology, his later engagements with Hegel and Schelling have a more "Nietzschean" accent, not least because he views all three of them as "finalizers" of Western metaphysics (Heidegger 1985: 184ff; GA 65: 203–4). In the 1930/1 lectures on Hegel, Heidegger had already set for himself the task of elaborating the "inner motivation of the Hegelian position as the completion of Western philosophy" (GA 32: 183). But this theme looms even larger in his final, lengthy encounter with Hegel. In this encounter, ranging over two decades, Heidegger is intent on elaborating the underlying continuity of Hegel's modern version of metaphysics with its Greek beginnings and, in the process, plumbing the forgotten ground of metaphysics. But Heidegger pursues this task with the express aim of demonstrating the need not merely to negate but to "get over" (*verwinden*) metaphysics and make a new, post-metaphysical beginning.

Accordingly, in order to appreciate Heidegger's observation – "The completion of metaphysics begins with Hegel's metaphysics of absolute knowing as the will of the spirit" – we have to look both back to the origins and forward to the completion of metaphysics, as Heidegger views it (Heidegger 2003: 89). By the Greek origins of metaphysical thinking, Heidegger has in mind their propensity to equate an entity's being with its presence, a primarily temporal designation (though not recognized as such) that, because of the inseparability of time and space ("time-space"), is also a spatial and relational term in the sense of the placement of something before someone (itself or another). In short, being is conceived as the present presence of something, a presence that is potentially present to someone. By raising the pervasive look or appearance (*idea*, *eidos*) that something gives of itself, to the status of something constant and common, Plato allegedly crystalizes this conception of being as a standing presence. Heidegger claims that the modern appropriation of this conception (the conversion of Platonism into idealism) occurs when the idea is equated with the perception or representation that includes, along with the perceiving and the perceived, one's certainty, in perceiving, of their connection. Hegel culminates this development with his conception of the idea as "the absolute self-appearing of the absolute," an idea which necessarily includes, as Heidegger puts it, "being-present-with-us, the parusie" (Heidegger 1970: 30, 48ff; GA 65: 202–3, 208–22). Thus, what the Greeks single-mindedly associated with the nature of objects and the moderns (at least Descartes and Kant) just as single-mindedly identified with a subjectivity irreducible to nature, Hegel synthesizes in terms of a historical, yet ever-present, absolute. As a result, the Greek conception of being as presence achieves an unprecedented systematic universality and historical concreteness as Hegel extends it to the objectivity of objects, the subjectivity of subjects, and their developing, self-mediating relation. What it means for an object or a subject or anything else to be is determined by the presence of this absolute subjectivity.

To understand Hegel's place in the history of metaphysics, however, it is necessary, as noted, to look forwards as well as backwards. Given that his metaphysics of absolute knowing first surfaces publicly in the *Phenomenology of Spirit*, to which Schelling's metaphysics of evil is in part a response, Heidegger's comment about Hegel marking the beginning of the finalization of metaphysics by no means excludes Schelling. Indeed, Heidegger emphasizes the convergence of Hegel's thought with Schelling's (and Nietzsche's) by insisting that the dialectical movement of thought is an expression of the "will" of the absolute (Hegel 1977: 47; Heidegger 1970: 34ff, 40). Yet the completion of metaphysics begun by Hegel reaches beyond the work of Schelling and Nietzsche and coincides with the very dispensability of philosophy, i.e. its replacement by sciences ultimately in the service of technology. Thus, while Hegel's notion of absolute subjectivity represents the beginning of the completion of metaphysics and Nietzsche's will to power its penultimate stage, "technology" constitutes its utter completion (Heidegger 2003: 89–96). It is this alleged connection between technology and a metaphysics of absolute subjectivity that, in this fourth and final phase of Heidegger's engagement with the Idealists, explains Hegel's particular importance for him and his argument for a new beginning for thinking.

This connection underlies Heidegger's repeated rejection (mentioned earlier) of the commonplace about the collapse of Hegelian philosophy after Hegel's death. "In the 19th century," he contends, "this philosophy alone determined the reality of things," albeit not in the form of a heeded doctrine, but "as metaphysics" (Heidegger 2003: 89; 1998: 327; GA 65: 213ff). The alleged boundlessness of human thinking and production, the *presentability* and manageability of everything that is, is secured by the self-certainty of an absolute subjectivity for which nothing – or, more precisely, no object, let alone no subject – is alien. Referring to this moment when the technological devastation of the earth is first willed but not known, Heidegger comments: "Hegel grasps this moment of the history of metaphysics in which absolute self-consciousness becomes the principle of thinking" (Heidegger 2003: 110). Heidegger makes a similar point after observing how Hegel identifies "the innermost movement of subjectivity" with the speculative dialectic, referring to the latter as "the method." The method is "the soul of being," the production process through which the web of the absolute's entire realty is fabricated. This talk of method as the "soul of being" might seem like fantasy but, if so, Heidegger remarks, "we are living right in the midst of this supposed fantasy" (GA 9: 432/326). The remark testifies to Heidegger's considerable confidence in metaphysical thinking's ability to elaborate an epoch's basic (albeit unprobed) understanding of being, a feat that he praises even as he sees the need to supersede it with another kind of thinking. Yet, the connection that he is proposing here, however provocative, is forced to a fault. Far more argument than he provides is required to demonstrate the "inner" connection of the method of modern physics ("the being of beings dissolved into the method of total computability") and Cartesian method with Hegel's conception of method in the sense of speculative dialectic as the fundamental trait of all reality (Heidegger GA 9: 431ff/326ff).

This "indictment" of Hegel's philosophy might also seem far-fetched, given the basic roles played by negativity and history in his thinking. These roles suggest a sensitivity to the supposedly forgotten dimensions of being, e.g. the absence, loss, hiddenness, and so on that, no less than an entity's presence, define its being. Heidegger himself recognizes that "genuine negativity" is for Hegel something absolute, "the 'energy' of what is absolutely actual" (GA 68: 22; GA 28: 260). He further observes that we need "to begin a conversation with Hegel" because he thinks "in the context of a conversation with the previous history of philosophy" and is "the first who can and must think in this way" (Heidegger 2002: 43ff). Nevertheless, Hegel's way of relating negativity and history reinforces in Heidegger's mind his contention that Hegel's metaphysics epitomizes Western obliviousness to the basic *question* of what it means to be. (This obliviousness means that Western metaphysics has an understanding of being but does not place it in question.) Hence, with the aim of demonstrating the "incomparability" of metaphysics and his own project of thinking being historically, Heidegger differentiates Hegel's approaches to both the history of philosophy and the concept of negativity from his own. Though "entering into the force of earlier thinking" is, for both thinkers, the criterion for a dialogue with the history of philosophy, Heidegger claims to seek this force not, like Hegel, in what has already been thought, but in what is not thought, "from which what is thought receives its essential space" (Heidegger 2002: 48; GA 68: 4, 34). According to Heidegger, what is unthought by Hegel is the origin of his conception of negativity (not unrelated in Heidegger's eyes to a supposed lack of seriousness in Hegel's treatment of death).

Heidegger specifies that origin in two ways. Metaphysically speaking, it is the ontological difference between being and entities (being is *not* an entity; entities are *not* being) (GA 68: 14ff, 20–5; Heidegger 2002: 47, 70ff). Yet this way of elaborating the negativity not considered by Hegel but underlying his conception of negativity is metaphysical, according to Heidegger, since the distinction posits on the same level what it distinguishes, thereby reducing being to the status of an entity. Hence, his preferred, post-metaphysical expression for it is a clearing or original time-space, an abyss (*Abgrund*) that, far from being any thing or entity, is removed from any ground among entities (GA 68: 43–8; Heidegger 2002: 67, 71ff). This abyss is the difference from – that also allegedly makes all the difference to – Hegel's concept of being as the actuality of an all-embracing, self-referential totality (spirit).

Here the similarities and dissimilarities with Heidegger's Fichte-interpretation are noteworthy. In 1929, as noted above, Heidegger stresses how an unthought finitude (the "facticity of the I") carried Fichte's argument, lending it whatever trenchancy it possesses, yet ultimately undermining its pretensions to "absolute certainty and derivation" (GA 28: 92). So, too, a decade later Heidegger contends that what is decisive but unthought in Hegel's argument is the clearing in which entities come to light, a clearing that is not itself explicable by or grounded in any entity, and, indeed, is not any entity at all. This clearing is "nothing and yet not *nil* [*doch nicht nichtig*] . . . the abyss as ground . . . the event" – all metonyms for what Heidegger understands by "being" (GA 68: 45ff). Instructively, in this same context, he cautions against talk of the finitude of being (the centerpiece of his Fichte-interpretation) for being too easily mis-interpreted and too pejorative. What is meant by it, he advises, is the essential inher-ence of this "nihilating dimension" (*Nichten*) in being (GA 68: 47). Hegel's concept of being, despite its recognition of the "power of the negative," fails in Heidegger's eyes to appreciate this basic opacity of being, the concealment, absence, inaccessibility that are as essential to it as overtness, presence, and accessibility are. "Hegel's negativity is no negative because it never takes 'not' and 'nihilating' seriously – having already can-celled and taken them up in the 'yes'" (GA 68: 47).

Accordingly, while "Hegel thinks the being of beings in a speculative-historical fashion" that gathers up (*legein*) what has been thought into an absolute presence, Heidegger is bent on thinking what it leaves unthought. With a confidence in the power of thinking, unrivaled even by Hegel, Heidegger draws a further contrast that is reminiscent of his earliest misgivings with Hegelian theorizing. Heidegger claims that thinking being historically – in contrast to speculative metaphysical thinking – sets the stage for a decision and transformation of human beings into *being-here* (*Dasein*) as guardians of being (Heidegger 2002: 45, 72ff; GA 9: 428–9/324–5; GA 65: 232ff, 242).

In sum, Heidegger came to appreciate that German Idealism makes a genuine advance in understanding the concrete and historical manifoldness of beings and in conceiving being itself as more than the perceptible onhandness of things or, in Kantian terms, the objectivity of objects. Still, Heidegger contends that being itself, as the eventful interplay of presence and real absence, is not merely "unthought" and obscured, but completely closed off by the ways in which the Idealists, despite their dif-ferences, incorporate the ancient metaphysical identification of being as presence into a modern understanding of the ineradicably subjective dimension of reality (Heidegger 1970: 69ff; GA 9: 441–4/333–5). But therein lies the Idealists' very importance for Heidegger. For while the overlooked sense of being itself is, in his view, the most press-ing matter for thinking, it is so only for a thinking that has struggled with and trans-formed the quintessentially metaphysical, i.e. the Idealist conception of being.

References and further reading

Fichte, J. G. (1982) *The Science of Knowledge*. Cambridge: Cambridge University Press (originally published 1794).

Gadamer, H. G. (1981) Heidegger und die Geschichte der Philosophie. *The Monist*, 64(4), 434–44.

Hegel, G. W. F. (1977) *Phenomenology of Spirit*. Oxford: Oxford University Press (originally pub-lished 1807).

Heidegger, M. (1970) *Hegel's Concept of Experience*. New York: Harper & Row (originally published 1950).

Heidegger, M. (1985) *Schelling's Treatise on the Essence of Human Freedom*. Athens, OH: Ohio University Press (originally published 1971).

Heidegger, M. (2002) *Identity and Difference*. Chicago: University of Chicago Press (originally published 1957).

Heidegger, M. (2003) Overcoming metaphysics. In *The End of Philosophy*. Chicago: University of Chicago Press (originally published 1954).

Heidegger, M. and Jaspers, K. (1990) *Briefwechsel, 1920–1963* (ed. W. Biemel and H. Saner). Frankfurt am Main: Klostermann.

Kolb, D. (1981) Hegel and Heidegger as critics. *The Monist*, 64(4), 481–99.

Pöggeler, O. (1995) Hegel und Heidegger über Negativität. *Hegel-Studien*, 30, 145–66.

Rockmore, T. (ed.) (2000) *Heidegger, German Idealism, and Neo-Kantianism*. New York: Humanity.

Schelling, F. W. J. (1936) *Of Human Freedom*. Chicago: Open Court (originally published 1809).

Schulz, W. (1971) Über den philosophiegeschichtlichen Ort Martin Heideggers. In O. Pöggeler (ed.), *Heidegger*. Cologne and Berlin: Keipenheuer und Witsch.

Sikka, S. (1994) Heidegger's appropriation of Schelling. *Southern Journal of Philosophy*, 32, 421–48.

Sell, A. (1998) *Martin Heideggers Gang durch Hegels "Phänomenologie des Geistes"*. Bonn: Bouvier.

Stolzenberg, J. (2003) Martin Heidegger liest Fichte. In H. Seubert (ed.), *Heideggers Zweigespräch mit dem Deutschen Idealismus*. Cologne: Boehlau Verlag.

Strube, C. (2003) Die ontologische Wiederentdeckung des deutschen Idealismus. In H. Seubert (ed.), *Heideggers Zweigespräch mit dem Deutschen Idealismus*. Cologne: Boehlau Verlag.

6

Early Heidegger's Appropriation of Kant

BÉATRICE HAN-PILE

In *Being and Time*, Heidegger praises Kant as "the first and only person who has gone any stretch of the way towards investigating the dimension of temporality or has even let himself be drawn hither by the coercion of the phenomena themselves" (SZ: 23).[1] Kant was, before Husserl (and perhaps, in Heidegger's mind, more than him), a true phenomenologist in the sense that the need to curtail the pretension of dogmatic metaphysics to overstep the boundaries of sensible experience led him to focus on phenomena and the conditions of their disclosure: thus, the "question of the inner possibility of such knowledge of the super-sensible, however, is presented as thrown back upon the more general question of the *inner possibility of a general making-manifest* [*Offenbarmachen*] *of beings* [*Seiende*] *as such*" (GA 3: 10, emphasis added). So Kant should be read not as an epistemologist (contrary to Descartes, for example), but as an ontologist:[2] "Kant's inquiry is concerned with what determines nature as such – occurrent beings as such – and with how this ontological determinability is possible" (GA 25: 75). Heidegger sees this investigation into the "ontological determinability" of entities as an *a priori* form of inquiry: "what is already opened up and projected in advance i.e. the horizon of ontological determinability . . . is what in a certain sense is 'earlier' than a being and is called *a priori*" (GA 25: 37). This *a priori* character of ontological determinability forms the main link between Kant's critical project and fundamental ontology, itself characterized as a form of transcendental philosophy: "transcendental knowledge is a knowledge which investigates the possibility of an understanding of being, a pre-ontological understanding of being. And such an investigation is the task of ontology. *Transcendental knowledge is ontological knowledge*, i.e. *a priori* knowledge of the ontological constitution of beings" (GA 25: 186). Thus Heidegger presents his own inquiry into the nature of being as a way to address the same issue as Kant: "what is asked about is being – *that which determines entities as entities*, that on the basis of which entities are already understood, however we may discuss them in detail. The being of entities 'is' not itself an entity" (SZ: 6, emphasis added). So Heidegger agrees with Kant on the object of the investigation (the determination of entities), and on the idea that the structure of ontological determination is not itself ontical. What remains unclear, however, is the extent to which Heidegger modifies the Kantian definition of the *a priori*, and, more generally, whether his project of describing the non-ontic structure of our understanding of being is enough to make him a transcendental philosopher – and if so, of which kind.

There are many ways in which this question, central for a chapter concerned with Heidegger's *appropriation* (and not merely interpretation) of Kant, can be spelled out. William Blattner's analysis of the two meanings of the transcendental in Kant is helpful here as a starting point (Blattner 1999: 236). According to him, the idea of a transcendental standpoint can refer to the position (which Blattner calls "epistemological") one occupies when inquiring into the *a priori* conditions for the possibility of knowledge and thus, in the more Heideggerian terms I have used so far, into the non-ontic conditions of ontological determinability. But it can also refer to the standpoint resulting from the bracketing of these conditions, when one inquires about the nature of things regardless of the conditions under which they are disclosed to us (what Blattner calls the properly "transcendental" standpoint). Most commentators, even the ones who, like Hubert Dreyfus, don't see Heidegger as a transcendental philosopher, would probably agree that there is a transcendental element in fundamental ontology in the first of these two senses. Although he insists that Dasein cannot be properly understood in a decontextualized, word-less manner, the way in which Heidegger spells out the structure of the existentials is transcendental in that it requires a shift from the *post hoc* (beings) to the *a priori* (being), and inquires about our understanding of being as a set of non-causal, non-compositional conditions for the determination of entities. (What Taylor Carman, for example, openly refers to as the Allisonian notion of an "epistemic condition" and calls "hermeneutic conditions." Thus Taylor Carman sees these conditions as expanding on Allison's notion of an "epistemic condition." See Allison 1983: 10ff.) However, there is considerable dissent on whether Heidegger can (or should) be understood as a transcendental philosopher in the second of the above mentioned senses: Blattner is (to my knowledge) the only one who holds that the stronger notion of the transcendental standpoint as a bracketing of the epistemological perspective is operative in Heidegger, while others, in particular Dreyfus (1991: 253–65), Taylor Carman (2003: 157–203) and David Cerbone (chapter 15 in this volume) think that the thrust of Heidegger's position lies precisely in refuting the possibility (or at least showing the philosophical futility) of such a standpoint.

Similarly, commentators disagree on the question of whether there is anything like transcendental determination in Heidegger's work. Another useful distinction here can be borrowed from Mark Sacks, who differenciates between what he calls "transcendental constraints" and "transcendental features" (Sacks 2003: 211–18). The first indicates a "dependence of empirical possibilities on a non-empirical structure" (Sacks 2003: 213). It denotes a strong sense of transcendental determination, in which the conditions of such a determination are definable in isolation and in anticipation of what they determine (in the way the transcendental organization of the faculties can be spelled out completely independently of experience in Kant, and in such a way that experience must conform to them). Transcendental features, on the contrary, "indicate the limitations implicitly determined by a range of available practices . . . to which further alternatives cannot be made intelligible to those engaged in them" (ibid.). They refer to a much weaker sense of transcendental determination, (in Heidegger's case) the fact that beings are dependent, to be disclosed, on our having an understanding of being which, while it is not ontic, is nevertheless historically situated and thus dependent on ontic practices. Most people, I think, would agree that our having an understanding of being can be construed as a transcendental feature. However, few would grant that there is anything like a transcendental constraint in Heidegger's work – Blattner being, again, the only one who holds this view (by arguing, first, that ontology does not depend upon, and is not open to refutation and revision by, empirical, scientific inquiry, and, second, that from the fact that there is an *a priori* connection between being and temporality, one can infer that entities must have a temporal structure).

Thus the really problematic question is not whether Heidegger can be construed as a transcendental philosopher in general, but (a) whether anything of substantial importance rides on his being able to endorse the transcendental standpoint in the strong sense, and (b) whether fundamental ontology involves anything like a transcendental constraint. I shall begin with the second point, and focus on the problem of transcendental determination (what Heidegger calls the "ontological determinability," or the "constitution of being" of entities; GA 25: 37). This, in turn, raises a very difficult question: what does Heidegger mean by "entity" (*Seiende*)? He clearly uses the word as a generic term for what there is, without any of the specific connotations linked to the notions of "object" (*Objekt*) (as a mental representation) or "thing" (*Ding*) (as what gathers, in the later work). But how do entities relate to what he calls the "phenomenon" (*Phänomen*)? In which sense can entities be said to be "phenomena" (*phainomena*)? In particular, by "entity," should we understand something as it is in itself, independently of the conditions of its disclosure, and which we could know independently of such conditions? Or does the word "entity" structurally involve a form of ontological determination, in which case it would be impossible to dissociate its what-being (as a disclosed entity) from the "how" of its disclosure (although, as we shall see, it would be wrong to think the former single-handedly determined by the latter, as in subjective idealism)? And if such is the case, how does our knowledge of entities relate to what is?

The problem is that *Being and Time* is very ambiguous on this point, and both sides can find substantiating quotes. Thus, while Blattner focuses on the claim that "being is that which determines entities *as entities*" (SZ: 6, emphasis added), Carman is quick to point out that for Heidegger "entities *are*, quite independently of the experience by which they are disclosed, the acquaintance in which they are discovered, and the grasping in which their nature is ascertained" (SZ: 183). This ambiguity is partially caused by the fact that Heidegger did not devote any section of *Being and Time* specifically to the problem of the nature of entities, a lack probably due to his concern for changing the focus of the tradition and completing metaphysics by shifting from the Aristotelian question *ti to on* to the question of being (see, for example, GA 3: 221). The closest candidate, however, is a notoriously difficult passage, "The Concept of Phenomenon" (SZ: ¶7A), which none of the aforementioned interpreters has examined in its entirety.[3] The beginning of the passage provides an ontic definition of the "phenomenon" (*Phänomen*), as "that which shows itself in itself, the manifest" (SZ: 28). Thus the " 'phenomena' are the totality of what lies in the light of day or can be brought to the light – what the Greeks sometimes identified simply as *ta onta* (entities)" (ibid.). At this stage, it is impossible to draw any conclusion about the nature of entities and their relation to being (the definition just indicates that entities are whatever is in the sense of being presenced). The second meaning of the phenomenon, "semblance" (*Schein*), is also an ontic one: it refers to an entity showing itself "as something which it is not", or "looking like something or other" (ibid.). Heidegger does not give any example, but optical illusions (such as Descartes's seemingly broken stick) seem to be a plausible option (see SZ: 30). Semblance is structurally dependent on the first signification of the phenomenon in the sense that it presupposes the possibility of something being able to show itself in itself in the first place – thus one must be able to see that the stick is not broken (when it is removed from the water) to realize that the perception of it as broken is a case of semblance, and not just the phenomenon of a broken stick showing itself as it is in itself. Thus Heidegger concludes that the term "phenomenon" should be reserved for the "positive and primordial signification of *phainomenon*" (SZ: 29), i.e. entities, while semblance is just a privative modification. Again, this does not help much *per se* to clarify the relation of entities to being, although it has important implications for Heidegger's understanding of truth (in the sense that without this distinction between the two first meanings of the phenomenon, ontic truth as correspondence would not be possible, for we couldn't ascertain whether an entity is disclosed in itself or not).

However, the situation changes with the next two definitions, "appearance" (*Erscheinung*) and in particular "mere appearance" (*blosse Erscheinung*). Unexpectedly, because Heidegger introduces them by saying that both phenomenon and semblance have "proximally nothing at all to do with what is called an appearance, or still less a 'mere appearance'" (SZ: 29). However, as we shall see, the way Heidegger analyses them shows that, in fact, they have a lot to do with each other, and that this exaggerated warning is mostly motivated by his worry that "the bewildering multiplicity of 'phenomena' designated by the words 'phenomenon', 'semblance', 'appearance', 'mere appearance' cannot be disentangled" (SZ: 31) unless they are carefully distinguished. Heidegger's emphasis that all are "founded upon the phenomenon, though in different ways" (SZ: 31), is *per se* indicative that his warning should not be taken literally. By contrast with the first two cases, in which what is shows itself, respectively as what it is (entities as ontic phenomena) or as what it is not (semblance), appearing is a "not showing itself" (SZ: 29), specified as "an announcing itself through something that shows itself" (SZ: 29). Appearing is a way for an entity to indicate its presence, but without revealing itself directly, and therefore through the disclosure of another entity – thus, says Heidegger, measles announces itself through spots. So the spots are, considered in their own right, a phenomenon (they show themselves as what they are); but considered with respect to what is hidden and which they indicate (the disease), they are an appearance. As both what "announces itself" (SZ: 30) (the disease) and what does the announcing (the spots) are entities, this definition of appearance, like that of semblance, is an ontic one: appearance "means a reference-relationship which is *in an entity itself* and which is such that what does the referring . . . can fulfil its possible function only if it shows itself in itself and is thus a 'phenomenon'" (SZ: 31, emphasis added). Consequently (as in the case of semblance), the relation between appearances and phenomena is not symmetrical: the possibility of there being appearances in the first place rests on the ontic definition of the phenomenon as that which shows itself in itself (without which the spots couldn't be disclosed): thus "phenomena are *never* appearances, though on the other hand every appearance is dependent on phenomena" (SZ: 30; strictly speaking, Heidegger should say that *considered in themselves* phenomena are never appearances).

So what is can show itself as what it is (as an entity, a phenomenon in the ontic sense) or as what it is not (semblance), or not show itself at all and appear through some other entity that indicates it. However, there is an even more complex mode of disclosure for entities, introduced as a complication of the referring structure of appearance. In the case of "mere appearances," "that which does the announcing and is brought forth does, of course, show itself, and in such a way that, as an emanation of what it announces, it keeps this very thing constantly veiled in itself. On the other hand, this not showing which veils is not a semblance" (SZ: 30). According to what we have just seen, appearances and mere appearances are both phenomena in the ontic sense (they "show themselves"); but whereas appearances indicate what announces itself in such a way that its presence can be made indirectly manifest (through the reference structure), the indication performed by mere appearances is such that what announces itself must structurally remain hidden. Both appearances and mere appearances are referred by Heidegger to Kant in the following way: "according to him, appearances are, in the first place, the 'objects of empirical intuition.' . . . But what thus shows itself (the 'phenomenon' in the genuine primordial sense) is at the same time an appearance as an emanation of something which *hides* itself in that appearance" (SZ: 30). It is difficult to interpret this passage simply from the perspective of *Being and Time*, which remains fairly allusive. In particular, the temptation is great to read it, as Blattner does, in the light of Kant's remarks on noumenal causation, and to identify the "something which hides itself" to a thing-in-itself, and "mere appearances" to its manifestation (its "emanation" (*Ausstrahltung*) in the empirical realm). This, in turn, would suggest that Heidegger holds the so-called "two-world" view, according to which things-in-themselves, as super-sensible beings, are substantially different from phenomena (in the Kantian sense) themselves considered as mental representations which can only obscure the true nature of the in-itself. If such was the case, then the mode of disclosure intrinsic to mere appearances would be hopelessly metaphysical (and without any relevance whatsoever to Heidegger's own position regarding entities) for three reasons: (a) mere appearances (and appearances) would not be entities, but subjective representations; (b) mere appearances would not refer to entities anymore (contrary to appearances in the Heideggerian sense), but to things-in-themselves; and (c) the objects of the reference structure (i.e. the things-in-themselves) would be forever beyond our reach.

However, both the *Phenomenological Interpretation of Kant* and *Kant and the Problem of Metaphysics* are helpful in correcting this view. Heidegger returns twice to the notion of "mere appearances" (which indirectly underlines its importance), and makes it clear that both appearances and mere appearances are entities, not mental representations: "the general discussion of the thing-in-itself and appearance should make clear that appearances mean objects or things themselves. The term *mere* appearance does not refer to mere subjective products to which nothing actual corresponds. Appearance as appearance or object does not need at all still to *correspond* to something actual, because appearance itself *is* the actual" (GA 25: 100). Throughout the two Kant books, Heidegger is very insistent that one should avoid endorsing the two-worlds view of transcendental idealism, which he calls the "grossest misunderstanding": "appearance is also appearance of something – as Kant puts it: the thing itself. However, in order to eliminate right away the grossest misunderstanding, we must say that appearances are not mere illusions, nor are they some kind of free floating emissions from things. Rather appearances are objects themselves, or things."[4] Thus Heidegger's reading of Kant anticipates the so-called "deflationary" or "two-aspects" interpretation of transcendental idealism put forward by Bird and Allison.[5] In doing so, Heidegger opposes stronger interpretations of transcendental idealism,[6] which commit Kant to a substantial definition of the thing-in-itself as an intelligible entity, with specific properties which we can think (but not know) – for example, immortality for the soul, or free noumenal agency.[7] This clarifies two points in *Being and Time*. First, it explains why the "not showing which veils" of mere appearances is not a semblance. Semblance refers to an entity showing itself for what it is not (a "mere illusion"); mere appearances are entities which show themselves for what they are, but which, in doing so, also indicate something else. Second, it suggests that the indication performed is very unlikely to refer to noumenal causality (Heidegger says that is not a "free-floating emission," a theme that takes up that of "emanation" in *Being and Time*), in particular because of Heidegger's emphasis on the *identity* between the things-in-themselves and appearances: "appearances are also not other things next to or prior to the things themselves. Rather appearances are just those things themselves, which we encounter and discover as occurrent within the world" (GA 25: 98; see also GA 3: 32). In fact, Heidegger endorses the two-aspect view to such an extent that his commentary on the *First Critique* leaves entirely out the notion of noumenal causality.

So both appearances and mere appearances are entities; however, the nature of what is indicated by the latter still remains obscure. From Heidegger's strong rejection of the two-world view, we can infer that it is not the thing-in-itself as an intelligible entity. We also know that the indication is not arbitrary (not "free-floating"), and that what is indicated must, at least prima facie, remain hidden by the showing itself of the entity. Again, *Kant and the Problem of Metaphysics* provides an important clue: "the 'mere' in the phrase 'mere appearance' is not a restricting and diminishing of the actuality of the thing, but is rather only the negation of the assumption that the entity can be infinitely known in human knowledge" (GA 3: 34). The "mere" is thus an indication of human finitude, by opposition to the infinite knowledge of an *intuitus originarius*, which would not need external input and could produce the thing it knows in the purely intuitive act of knowing it. But what makes us finite, for Heidegger, is the need for sensory data and for the synthetizing activity of thought, which, in turn, both involve *a priori* conditions (in Kant, time and space as the *a priori* forms of sensibility and the pure concepts of the understanding). Consequently, it makes sense to think that "mere appearances" refer not to another entity, nor to a thing-in-itself, but to the transcendental framework that all entities, as spatio-temporal (or temporal only), must conform to if they are to count for us as entities. Very importantly, this is an *ontological* form of indication: entities, as mere appearances, *structurally* refer to the transcendental conditions of their disclosure. Conversely, these are built into them in such a way that to be an entity in the sense of a mere appearance is tantamount to being a (spatio)-temporal object: since both the *a priori* forms of sensibility (time and space) and the categories (such as causality) are transcendentally involved in the determination of entities, it belongs to the very nature of these entities to be spatio-temporal, and to interact causally. Thus, "appearances as appearances, as beings so encountered, are themselves spatial and intra-temporal. *Spatial and temporal determinations belong to that which the encountered being is*" (GA 25: 156, emphasis added). *Kant and the Problem of Metaphysics* extends this point to the pure concepts of the understanding: these "by means of the pure power of imagination, refer essentially to time. . . . For this reason they are, in advance, *determinations of the objects, i.e. of the entity insofar as it is encountered by a finite creature*" (GA 3: 86, emphasis added). Very importantly, another passage generalizes this inbuilt reference of entities to their transcendental conditions to *all* appearances: "the expression 'mere appearances' indicates the beings which are accessible to a finite being. *This is the primary meaning of the Kantian concept of appearance*" (GA 25: 100–1, emphasis added; the following page indicates that such appearances are "things encountered in daily life", in "prescientific experiential knowledge"). So for Kant, all appearances (i.e. all entities) are mere appearances in that they both obey and indicate the transcendental conditions under which they must be disclosed.

This, in turn, allows Heidegger to uncover in Kant's work a second, ontological meaning for the notion of "phenomenon", distinct from the first ontic sense examined above (that which shows itself in itself, i.e. entities). He begins by pointing out that there are two ways of thinking of the phenomenon, both derived from its original definition as "that which shows itself": the first one is the "formal" or "ordinary" conception, which we arrive at if "by 'that which shows itself' we understand those entities which are accessible through 'empirical intuition' in . . . Kant's sense" (SZ: 31). This definition refers to mere appearances, and more generally to appearances in the Kantian (but not Heideggerian) sense. However, with the right method of investigation a second meaning for the phenomenon can emerge from the first: "we may then say that that which already shows itself in the appearance as prior to the 'phenomenon' as ordinarily understood and *as accompanying it in every case*, can, even though it thus shows itself unthematically, be brought thematically to show itself; and what thus shows itself in itself (the 'forms of the intuition') will be the 'phenomena' of phenomenology" (SZ: 31, emphasis added). As we have seen, all appearances structurally involve ("in every case") a reference to the spatio-temporal framework which is built into them as the entities we can have access to. This framework (the "forms of intuition") is "prior" to phenomena in the ontic sense because it is presupposed by them as a condition of possibility for their disclosure: it is thus an ontological kind of phenomenon. But contrary to these entities, it does not show itself directly (which is the reason why Heidegger said earlier of mere appearances that what they indicate "*hides* itself in that appearance"), and it is not itself an entity. However, it is not irretrievable: "manifestly space and time must be able to show themselves in this way as the phenomena of phenomenology – they must be able to become phenomena – if Kant is claiming to make a transcendental assertion grounded in the facts when he says that space is the *a priori* 'inside-which' of an ordering" (SZ: 31). So while phenomena of the first order (entities) are directly accessible to us, and do not require any elaboration to be understood, the phenomena of phenomenology, i.e. the transcendental conditions of the disclosure of entities, can only *become* a phenomenon in the first sense (i.e. show themselves as they are) if uncovered by a specific method, phenomenology. Correlatively, the latter must, because of the nature of its object, be defined as a *transcendental* form of inquiry which traces entities to their ontological conditions of possibility: in doing so, phenomenology discloses the way(s) in which ontic phenomena are constituted. It is very important, however, to understand such a constitution as transcendental and to distinguish it carefully from any causal process: both Heidegger and Kant are very clear that we do not create the entities which we access (this would only be the case if we were infinite beings); nor are the properties disclosed arbitrarily attributed to them. In fact, neither the mode of disclosure nor the properties are up to us, since we do not choose our framework, and we do not decide whether what is can or cannot be determined by it, a point to which I return in conclusion.

A careful reading of ¶7 of *Being and Time* thus uncovers two meanings, both for appearances and for the phenomenon. At the ontic level, phenomena are entities, and appearances are entities that refer to other entities, which appear through them (like measles does through spots). At the ontological level, all appearances should be seen as "mere appearances" in that they refer to the transcendental conditions that a finite entity like Dasein needs to be able to access anything. Correlatively, the phenomenon in the ontological sense is identified with these conditions, which are hidden by the entities themselves and can only become accessible to the phenomenologist. This means that while all entities are phenomena (in the first sense) and structurally involve the phenomenon (in the ontological sense), not all phenomena are entities (since the transcendental framework is not ontic). Phenomenality is a condition of possibility for entityhood, but not the reverse, which is the reason why (as Blattner insists) phenomenology is not primarily a theory of perception. However, so far the ontological meaning of appearances and phenomenon has been established only within the context of Kant's work. What I want to suggest now is that while appearances in the Heideggerian sense are a very limited case of ontic reference (partially taken up in the later analysis of the kind of indication performed by signs and symbols, SZ: 77–83), mere appearances analogically provide us with a way to understand how *Heidegger*, and not only Kant, thinks of entities as structurally involving a reference to being as both their condition of intelligibility and thus of existence *as entities*. I will try to establish this point before outlining the limits of the analogy and its consequences on the debate about realism.

In my view, the key to the analogy is given by the final section of ¶7, i.e. "The Preliminary Conception of Phenomenology," where Heidegger expresses his own views about the nature of phenomena and entities. Just as in his analysis of Kant, he starts with the ontic meaning of the phenomenon: "the expression 'phenomenology' may be formulated in Greek as *legein ta phainomena*, where *legein* means *apophainesthai*. Thus 'phenomenology' means *apophainesthai ta phainomena*" (SZ: 34). Because it deals with phenomena in the formal sense (i.e. as entities; see above), Heidegger calls this the "formal" meaning of phenomenology, which he sees encapsulated in the Husserlian formula "back to the things themselves!" (i.e. back to entities, as opposed to things-in-themselves). Thus, "the signification of 'phenomenon', as conceived both formally and in the ordinary manner, is such that any exhibiting of an entity as it shows itself in itself, may be called 'phenomenology' with formal justification" (SZ: 35). However, such a conception, both of phenomenology and of the phenomenon, must be "deformalized"; hence the question: "What is it that must be called a 'phenomenon' in a distinctive sense?" (SZ: 35). Heidegger's answer is that "that which remains *hidden* in an egregious sense . . . is not just this entity or that, but rather the *being* of entities" (SZ: 35). Thus "in the phenomenological [i.e. ontological] conception of the 'phenomenon' what one has in mind as that which shows itself is the Being of entities, its meaning, its modifications and derivatives" (SZ: 35). However, the crucial point here is that this definition of the phenomenological understanding of the phenomenon is, structurally at least, strikingly identical to the ontological definition of the phenomenon in Heidegger's reading of Kant. Indeed, Heidegger indicates that "manifestly, being is something that proximally and for the most part does not show itself at all: it is something that lies *hidden*, in contrast to that which proximally and for the most part does show itself; but at the same time it is something that *belongs to what thus shows itself*, and it belongs to it so essentially as to constitute its meaning and its ground" (SZ: 35, emphasis added). Just as time and space, the transcendental forms of intuition, "hide" in Kantian appearances, being, the phenomenon of phenomenology, "lies hidden" within entities (i.e. "that which shows itself," the ontic definition of the phenomenon). At this point, Heidegger even mentions explicitly (and rejects) *vis-à-vis* being the possibility which he previously refuted in the case of mere appearances, i.e. the idea that "the being of entities could ever be anything such that 'behind it' stands something else 'which does not appear'" (SZ: 36), i.e. a thing-in-itself. On the contrary, both the Kantian forms of intuition and being "belong to what thus shows itself," not as a property, but as what "constitutes its meaning and its ground," i.e. as what allows what is to be determined as intelligible (for Heidegger) or cognizable (for Kant), and therefore as an entity (or as a phenomenon in the Kantian sense). In both cases, such a transcendental form of constitution is seen as necessary: thus the phenomenon of phenomenology is something which "by its very essence is *necessarily* the theme whenever we exhibit something *explicitly*, i.e. when we shift from the ordinary mode of disclosure to the phenomenological one" (SZ: 35).

The correlate of this is that the conditions of transcendental determination must be reflected, in a way that can be transcendentally clarified, by the ontological structure of entities: as we have seen, according to Kant one can analytically infer from the fact that time and space are *a priori* forms of sensibility that phenomena are spatio-temporal. In ¶7, the fact that being is bound up with the structure of entities as ontic phenomena (it "lies hidden" within them) is suggested by the claim that it is necessary to start from the entities themselves in order to exhibit the phenomenon in the ontological sense as what is, in each case, *their* being: "because phenomena in the ontological sense, as understood phenomenologically, are never anything but what goes to make up being, *while being is in every case the being of some entity*, we must first bring forward the entities themselves if it is our aim that being should be laid bare" (SZ: 37, emphasis added). Later in the text, Heidegger makes a similar point about the relation of world (understood ontologically) to entities: "what can be meant by describing the 'world' as a phenomenon? It means to let us see what shows itself *in 'entities'* within the world" (SZ: 63; note Heidegger's use of scare quotes). Conversely, "entities must likewise show themselves with the kind of access which *genuinely belongs to them*" (SZ: 37, emphasis added). For such a "belonging" to be "genuine," or for the being of each entity to be "its" being, access must be impossible to dissociate from the very concept of the entity considered. In turn, this suggests that there is an *internal* relationship between entities and being, which makes it impossible to separate their what-being *as entities* from the how of their disclosure. This relationship is the transcendental determination performed by Dasein. In the final part of *Kant and the Problem of Metaphysics*, where he defines his enterprise as a "retrieval" (GA 3: 208) of the Kantian project, Heidegger strongly reasserts that ontological determination must be understood in its intrinsic connection with the nature of entities as entities, and gives some indications as to its nature:

> in the question as to what the entity as such might be, we have asked *what generally determines the entity as an entity*. We call it the being of the entity. . . . This determining should be known in the How of its determining. . . . In order to be able to grasp the *essential determinacy of the entity through being*, however, the determining itself must be sufficiently comprehensible. (GA 3: 222–3, emphasis added; see also GA 3: 283, where Heidegger speaks of the "transcendence of man" as a "*formative* comporting towards entities," emphasis added)

A few pages later, Heidegger specifies how this "determining" should be seen by stating that

> the existential analytic of everydayness . . . should show that and how all association with entities, *even where it appears as if there were just entities*, i.e. even where entities seem to be independent from our "association" with (or, in terms used so far, access to) them, already presupposes the transcendence of Dasein – namely, being-in-the-world. With it, the *projection* of the being of the entity, although concealed and for the most part indeterminate, takes place. (GA 3: 235, some emphasis added)

This allows us to understand better the kind of transcendental determination that is specific both to Dasein and to entities. Indeed, for Heidegger, the idea of a "projection" of being as the horizon of ontological determination is an analogical transposition of the opening of the pure horizon of temporality by the schematizing activity of transcendental imagination in Kant's work. In the same way, temporality is understood by Heidegger himself as the "*transcendental primal structure*" that underlies both care and being-in-the-world (GA 3: 242; Blattner has shown that this is already the case in *Being and Time*). As we shall see below, this means that, as suggested by Blattner, all entities are *a priori* determined as temporal.

There are, of course, limits to the analogy between Kant and Heidegger, most of which were identified by Heidegger himself. First, in focusing the search for the conditions of ontological determinability on the transcendental subject as a detached, disembodied ego, Kant chose the wrong starting point. He remained trapped within the Cartesian understanding of the subject as a thinking substance, which led him to think of Dasein as a worldless entity, an occurrent compound of body and soul (GA 25: 160–1). This is why Kant was able to provide, at best, a regional ontology of the occurrent (because he failed to replace theoretical cognition within the wider context of understanding as grounded in our everyday practices) (see, for example, GA 25: 199). Thus,

> the fundamental and crucial deficiency in Kant's posing of the problem of the categories in general lies in misconstruing the problem of transcendence – or better said, in failing to see transcendence as an original and essential determination of the ontological constitution of Dasein. Insofar as it factually exists, Dasein is precisely *not* an isolated subject, but a being which is fundamentally outside of itself. (GA 25: 315)

This failure to understand the ecstatic nature of Dasein as being-in-the-world explains Kant's second shortcoming, i.e. his shrinking back from his own insight into the temporally projective nature of transcendental imagination as the "common root" between the pure forms of sensibility (time and space) and the pure concepts of the understanding (the categories). According to Heidegger, in the A edition of the *Critique of Pure Reason*, Kant did recognize the synthetic role played by transcendental imagination, and established that both the *a priori* forms of sensibility and the "I think" of transcendental apperception are dependent on its syntheses: thus, "the origin of pure intuition and pure thinking as transcendental faculties is shown to be based on the transcendental power of imagination" (GA 3: 138). Consequently, Kant defined time as pure self-affection, and spelled out the connection between the three imaginative syntheses (apprehension, reproduction and recognition) and the three dimensions of temporality (respectively, present, past and future) (see GA 25: sections 20–24; on time as self-affection, see GA 25: 386–99; on the three syntheses, 403–24). But although he glimpsed the horizontal nature of temporality and thus came close to uncovering the constitutive link between time and being, Kant "shrank back" from his own intuition, and demoted imagination to being a purely empirical faculty in the B edition.[8] Thus he looked on imagination as "the dimension of human Dasein . . . only to be scared away from it" (GA 25: 279). However, it is crucial to note that these limitations do not affect the reading of Heidegger that I have suggested. Heidegger does not criticize Kant for claiming that entities are transcendentally determined (as spatio-temporal): on the contrary, *he blames him for not developing the idea of transcendental determination far enough*, and in particular for not having seen (or rather having "shrunk back" from the idea) that temporality is not only an *a priori* form of sensibility, but also underlies the "I think" of transcendental apperception and the syntheses of transcendental imagination. Heidegger does not question the claim that entities get their "essential determinacy" through being, and thus that they must not be dissociated from the transcendental framework that determines them. On the contrary, he establishes that temporality underlies that framework *at all levels*, not only as far as occurrentness is concerned. The consequence of this is that although no empirical property can be ascribed in advance to entities, all entities are *a priori* determined by Dasein as temporal. Just as, on Heidegger's dual-aspect reading of Kant, we can analytically infer, from the fact that time and space are *a priori* forms of sensibility, that phenomena are spatio-temporal, in the same way we can infer from the fact that temporality underlies the structure of being-in-the-world and of care that entities are temporal (although one cannot infer any such thing about what is independently of the conditions of transcendental determination).

This has important consequences, however, on the existing debate about Heidegger's realism. On the one hand, some commentators, like Dreyfus, hold that "Heidegger never concluded from the fact that our practices are necessary for *access* to theoretical entities that these entities must be *defined in terms of* our access practices" (Dreyfus 1991: 253). This position was recently radicalized by Carman, who reads Heidegger as an "ontic realist," ontic realism being "the claim that occurrent entities exist and have a determinate spatio-temporal structure independently of us and our understanding of them" (Carman 2003: 157). Both these options associate two positions: ontological realism (there is a way entities are in themselves) and epistemological realism (we can know them as they are in themselves). On the other hand others, like Blattner, who think that Heidegger is a transcendental (or temporal) idealist, do so on the opposite assumption that entities (like phenomena for Kant) cannot be defined as such independently of the conditions of their disclosure: thus, "being determines entities by making up the criterial standards to which entities (or aspects of what is) must conform in order to be entities at all. *Being is a framework of items without which entities would not be entities*" (Blattner 1999: 5, emphasis added). On the strength of this strong definition of transcendental determination, Blattner attributes to Heidegger a position broadly similar to Kant's,[9] namely a combination of transcendental idealism and ontic realism, where ontic realism has a very different meaning from the one suggested by Carman as it combines a limited form of epistemological realism (we can know phenomena/entities as they are at the empirical level/from Dasein's perspective) with the idealist epistemic claim that we cannot know things as they are in themselves, i.e. from the transcendental (in the strong sense) standpoint.[10]

Both the Kant books and *Being and Time* ¶7 suggest that Blattner is right; in particular, in the idea that entities get their "essential determinacy" through being, and this, *a priori*, tends to invalidate the claim, put forward by Carman, that "although Heidegger maintains that cognition is founded on being-in, and that occurrent reality is interpretable for us only against the horizon of our own worldliness . . . , occurrent entities themselves nevertheless do not depend on Dasein's being-in-the-world" (Carman 2003: 134). The main argument offered is that if such was not the case, then Dasein's naive realism would be unjustified.[11] But as we have seen, entities depend on being-in-the-world, not in the sense that they are created by Dasein, or that Dasein attributes to them arbitrary properties, but because they are *a priori* determined as temporal entities. This does not mean that what is *as such* depends on being-in-the-world (otherwise Heidegger would be committed to a form of subjective idealism), but that as long as it is determined by our framework of intelligibility and is disclosed as entities, the nature of these entities *is* bound-up with their mode of disclosure. Therefore the claim that "Heidegger takes occurrent entities to exist and have a determinate causal structure independently of the conditions of our interpreting or making sense of them" (Carman 2003: 159) is inconsistent: occurrent entities can only be occurrent if they are ontologically determined as entities by Dasein. Similarly, their having a causal structure is due to the fact that causality is, as Carman puts it himself (in rather Kantian terms), an "ontological category," an "*a priori* category of the understanding, the content of which is precisely the content of Dasein's naive realism about objects as existing independently of us and our understanding" (Carman 2003: 136). In his (legitimate) concern to avoid subjective idealism, Carman commits Heidegger to a form of pre-critical realism (equally suggested by his claim that "contrary to Kant's prohibition . . . there is no good reason to deny that we can and do have knowledge of things as they are in themselves"; Carman 2003: 159). This is not to say that Heidegger is not a realist – he is, but not of the kind suggested by Carman. He is an ontic realist in the *critical*, Kantian sense suggested (but not fully developed) by Blattner: he does think that we can know entities as they are, but not independently of their mode of access. Whether it is possible for us to know more than this is the question that I now turn to.

To answer it, we need to ascertain the extent to which Heidegger is committed to the theoretical correlate of transcendental determination, i.e. the Kantian idea that one must distinguish between phenomena and things-in-themselves, and that the latter are unknowable. This, in turn, involves finding out exactly how much of transcendental idealism Heidegger endorses and, in particular, whether and how the idea of a transcendental standpoint makes sense in the context of his work. In answer to this question, I shall try to establish two sets of claims. First, *per se*, Heidegger's commitment to the notion of transcendental determination does entail two theses that are central to the deflationary interpretation of transcendental idealism outlined above: (a) that there must also be a way in which things are in themselves, independently of us and of the kind of determination we perform, and thus that it makes sense to speak of the transcendental standpoint in the strong sense; and (b) that such things are not substantially different from the entities which are accessible to us, but are the same things, considered under different aspects. I will suggest that Heidegger's name for things considered in this way is the "Real" (*das Reale*). Second, this position commits Heidegger neither to the notion of a thing-in-itself in the strong sense (which he explicitly rejects; see GA 25: 98–9), nor, more polemically, to the idea that we cannot know what is (although we cannot know it as it is, i.e. from a God's eye perspective). While the first is consistent with the deflationary reading of transcendental idealism, the second is not, as Allison, following Kant, insists on the non-spatiality and non-temporality of things-in-themselves, a point I discuss below with reference to Heidegger.

The first two theses have already been touched upon in the course of this chapter. They are explicitly stated by Heidegger with reference to Kant, as both the Kant books aim at establishing that the difference between an appearance and a thing-in-itself, although real, is not a difference in kind, but one of perspective. Thus, "the entity 'in the appearance' is the same entity as the entity in itself, and this alone" (GA 3: 31). But while all appearances are by definition cognizable by us,

> what remains closed off to us is the thing itself insofar as it is thought as object of an absolute knowledge, i.e. as object of an intuition which does not first need the interaction with the thing and does not first let the thing be encountered, but rather lets the thing first of all become what the thing is through this intuition. (GA 25: 98)

To understand the difference between phenomena and things-in-themselves, then, one must differenciate between two modes of cognition, not two sorts of entities: on the one hand, "divine knowing" as a "representing which, in intuiting, first creates the intuitable being as such," and therefore does not bear "the mark of finitude" (GA 3: 24) as it is bounded neither by a pre-existing thing nor by the need to access it through sensibility and thought; on the other hand, "finite knowledge," which perforce must "let the thing be encountered," i.e. received through the *a priori* forms of sensibility and synthesized through the activity of imagination and judgment. Thus, the thrust of Heidegger's argument about Kant is that "a discussion of the difference between finite and infinite knowledge with a view to the difference in character between what is known in each respectively now points out that these concepts of appearance and thing-in-itself, which are fundamental for the *Critique*, can only be made understandable and part of the wider problem by *basing them more explicitly on the problematic of the finitude of the human creature*" (GA 3: 35, emphasis added).

This, however, has a crucially important consequence. Although Heidegger and Kant do not understand finitude in the same way (for the reasons mentioned above), they both agree on the idea that the *defining* feature of Dasein (or human beings, for Kant) is their finitude. The main difference is that whereas for Kant the hallmark of finitude is the need for the conjoined operations of sensibility and thought, for Heidegger it is Dasein's "transcendental neediness" for an understanding of being (GA 3: 236), and the fact that this understanding is constitutively covered up in forgetfulness (GA 3: 233, see also 234). It follows that Heidegger's very grounding of the distinction between things as they are and things as they are disclosed to us in the notion of finitude requires him, *analytically*, to extend the distinction to his *own* position: "in truth, however, the essence of finitude inevitably forces us to the question concerning the conditions of the possibility of a preliminary being-oriented toward the Object, i.e. concerning the essence of the necessary ontological turning-toward the object in general" (GA 3: 73), i.e. in Heidegger's thought, to a consideration of temporality as underlying care as the "transcendental unity of finitude" (GA 3: 237). As finite beings, we cannot be in the world unless we transcendentally determine entities as temporal. However, there is no reason to think that such a determination is the only possible one, nor that it would apply to what is if our transcendental conditions were bracketed. Correlatively, we are required to accept that transcendental determination is also dependent on external conditions: "we can say negatively: finite knowledge is noncreative intuition. What has to be presented immediately in its particularity must already have been 'at hand' in advance. Finite intuition sees that it is dependent on the intuitable as a being which exists in its own right" (GA 3: 25). Another passage states that finite knowledge is "confronted" with and is a "conforming" (GA 3: 31) to what is already there. The notion of "conformity" is a very important one as it prevents Heidegger's position from turning into subjective idealism. What is must conform to the conditions of transcendental determination to be disclosed as entities; but conversely, such conformity is not something that can be determined *solely* by these conditions. It is very important to note, however, that this does not mean that transcendental determination works (either in Kant or in Heidegger), by imposing form on some pre-existing matter. Because we are thrown, entities are always *already* determined by us, there is no pure matter to which we could first relate and then shape (this is the background of Kant's rejection of atomism, and of Heidegger's refutation of skepticism about the existence of the external world).

However, there is an important difference between Heidegger and Kant here: although both are committed by their insistence on the finitude of Dasein to the distinction between the two standpoints, empirical and transcendental, it does not follow that they must have the same understanding of the transcendental standpoint (and consequently, of the nature of things considered in themselves). The reason why they differ is that contrary to Kant, Heidegger does not believe in the existence of God or, consequently, in the possibility of infinite knowledge. Thus,

> along with the assumption of an absolute intuition, which first produces things, . . . the concept of a thing-in-itself also dies away. . . . One denies the philosophical legitimacy and usefulness of such an assumption, which not only does not contribute to our enlightenment but also confuses us, as it becomes clear in Kant. (GA 25: 99–100)

93

This means that the transcendental standpoint cannot be identified anymore with the perspective of a "representing God" (GA 25: 99), for whom the cognition and the creation of things would be one and a single operation. However, what it does *not* mean is that one should drop the notion of a transcendental standpoint altogether. For one thing, we have seen that Heidegger's analysis of finitude suggests that it is analytically entailed by the notion of ontological determination. Moreover, the relevance of the transcendental standpoint to Heidegger's own thought has been established by Blattner's analysis of *Being and Time* (SZ: 211–12; see Blattner 1999: 240–51), which shows that it should not be seen as the perspective of a "*deus faber*" (GA 25: 99), but as the *bracketing of the conditions under which transcendental determination operate* (namely Dasein's projective understanding of time). In response to Cerbone's objection, this bracketing does not need to be thought of as an existential possibility for Dasein: this would be tantamount to requiring that Dasein should be able to *occupy* the transcendental standpoint, which is excluded by definition (since that standpoint only obtains when Dasein's perspective does not apply) (see Cerbone, chapter 15 in this volume). The bracketing of transcendental conditions can only be a *logical* possibility, analytically entailed by the notion of transcendental determination itself.[12] However, even as such, it is not without any value (in answer to Carman's comment that Heidegger would be "pointing out the vacuity and futility of all efforts to stake out a distinct transcendental standpoint"; see Carman 2003: 171). Although it cannot fulfill any positive epistemological function (as it prevents by definition the formation of any synthetic knowledge), such a bracketing has an important *ethical* role to play: it can counterbalance what Heidegger calls our tendency to be "constantly under the domination of an absolutisation of our finitude" (GA 25: 159), i.e. to fall into the trap of metaphysical realism and to believe that our knowledge is not only of entities, but also of things considered in themselves – this has important consequences, to which I return in conclusion.

The claim that the transcendental standpoint should be defined not as that of a divine intellect but as a bracketing of transcendental (in the weak sense) conditions is precisely the position defended by Henry Allison. Thus, "the task of a transcendental justification of the concept of the thing-in-itself . . . is to explain the possibility and significance of considering 'as they are in themselves' the same objects which can know only as they appear; it is not, at is frequently assumed, to license appeal to a set of unknown entities distinct from appearances" (Allison 1983: 239). According to him, this entails the important consequence that things-in-themselves should be thought of not substantively, as intelligible entities, but problematically, as the logical "correlates of a non sensible manner of cognition" (Allison 1983: 242). Thus Allison argues for the identification of the thing-in-itself with the transcendental object (suggested by Kant himself in A366), as the "correlate of the unity of apperception" (A250), or "something in general = X" (A346/B449), i.e. an object considered apart from the sensible conditions under which things can be intuited by the human mind. Another passage from Kant explains why the notion is important, and further identifies the transcendental object with the noumenon understood in its negative sense:

> in the process of warning sensibility that it must not presume to claim applicability to thing-in-itself but only to appearances, the understanding does indeed think for itself an

object in itself, but only as a transcendental object, . . . which can be thought neither as quantity nor as reality nor a substance, etc. . . . If we are pleased to name this object "noumenon" for the reason that its representation is not sensible, we are free to do so. (A288–9/B344–5)

Very interestingly, Heidegger too refers to the transcendental object in the *Metaphysical Foundations of Logic*, in order to distinguish it from the substantive concept of the thing-in-itself. He returns to the question of the usefulness of the concept of a thing-in-itself and indicates that it "cannot be set aside by solving it epistemologically, but that this concept . . . can only be removed if one can show that the presupposition of an absolute understanding is not philosophically necessary" (GA 26: 164). The reason why such a removal cannot be "epistemologically" justified is that there is no contradiction in thinking of what is either as determined by transcendental conditions or independently of such conditions. As we have seen, the denial of the thing-in-itself as the correlate of divine cognition is tied to Heidegger's rejection of Kant's implicit theology. However, he also points out that such a rejection does not have any consequence on the possibility of thinking what is from the transcendental standpoint (as a bracketing of epistemic conditions): "proceeding from appearance, one can show the 'X' immanent in it *qua* thing-in-itself, which is not, however, the 'thing-in-itself' in the strict sense, i.e. as the correlate of divine understanding" (GA 26: 164). Thus although the positive concept of a thing-in-itself requires additional theological assumptions, that of the transcendental object does not: it is analytically entailed by the notion of appearance as the object of finite cognition.

Allison's interpretation has come under much criticism, in particular from K. Ameriks[13] and R. Pippin (see Pippin 1982: 200ff), who attacked it on the grounds that it dilutes the meaning of transcendental idealism to such an extent that the concept would apply to any alternative to transcendental realism which endorses an equivalent to transcendental determination (in particular, constructivist views of language). However, although this is a worry for an interpretation of *Kant*, it is not so for the kind of reading of Heidegger I suggest, since I never claimed that Heidegger endorses Kantian transcendental idealism *as such*, only that his position is most of the time (but not always) analogous to it. Indeed, I now turn to my second hypothesis, namely the idea that *Being and Time* involves an analogon of the noumenon as a negative concept, although there is nothing in it that could be read as a thing-in-itself in the strong sense. Heidegger introduces the "Real" by contrasting it with "reality" (*Realität*). He indicates that "the term 'Reality' is meant to stand for the being of entities present-at-hand within-the-world (*res*)" (SZ: 209; see also SZ: 183): reality is thus the mode of being of occurrent entities. However, Heidegger adds that "entities *within-the-world* are ontologically conceivable only if the phenomenon of within-the-world-ness has been clarified" (SZ: 209). This, in turn, requires an analysis of being-in-the-world and ultimately of care as the "structural totality of Dasein's being" (SZ: 209) – another passage indicates that "in the order of the ways in which things are connected in their ontological foundations . . . *Reality is referred back to the phenomenon of care*" (SZ: 211). As we have seen, this means that all entities are transcendentally determined as temporal. Heidegger thus concludes that he has "marked out the foundations and the horizons which must be clarified if an analysis of Reality is to be possible" and, importantly, that "only in this connection, moreover, does the character of *the 'in-itself' become ontologically intelligible*" (SZ: 209, emphasis added). This idea is clarified three pages later by the following claim: "but the fact that reality is ontologically grounded in the being of Dasein, does not signify that only when Dasein exists and as long as Dasein exists, can the Real be as that which in itself is" (SZ: 212). This suggests that while reality, as a mode of being, is dependent on care and thus on transcendental determination, the Real refers to what is "in-itself," i.e. independently of care, which confers on it a position analogical to that of the noumenon, as "a thing insofar as it is not an object of our sensible intuition" (B307). Following on the analogy with the two aspects view examined so far, one would expect Heidegger to say that the real is not substantially different from entities, but that it is determined *as* entities by Dasein. As it happens, this is exactly what Heidegger says: "*the Real is essentially accessible only as entities within-the-world*, which does suggest that the Real, considered in itself, i.e. independently of transcendental conditions, is not entities. All access to such entities is founded ontologically upon the basic state of Dasein, Being-in-the-world; and this in turn has care as its even more primordial state of Being" (SZ: 202, emphasis added).

Heidegger differs from Kant in that he distinguishes several ways in which the Real can be accessed, and thus asks a question which Kant himself could not have asked: "and finally we must make sure what kind of primary access we have to the Real, by deciding the question of whether knowing can take over this function at all as opposed to more primordial non-theoretical, practically engaged forms of understanding" (SZ: 202). But just like Kant, Heidegger rejects the claim that the Real could be known it itself, independently of its ontological determination into entities. This is made clear by his refutation of Dilthey's position, which follows his analysis of reality: "to be sure, the Reality of the Real can be characterised phenomenologically within certain limits without any explicit existential-ontological basis. This is what Dilthey attempted in the article mentioned above. He holds that the Real gets experienced in impulse and will, and that Reality is *resistance*, or, more exactly, the character of resisting. He then works out the phenomenon of resistance analytically" (SZ: 209). The example of resistance is interesting because it was already used by Schopenhauer with the same aim in mind, namely to try to identify positively the thing-in-itself as will (an identification that both Kant and Heidegger reject). Against this possibility, Heidegger argues that it is impossible to attribute the property of resisting to the Real as such, since resistance can only be experienced on the background of the disclosure of the world, which by definition precludes it from applying to the Real. Thus "the experiencing of resistance . . . is possible ontologically only by reason of the disclosedness of the world. *The character of resisting is one that belongs to entities within-the-world*" (SZ: 210, emphasis added). Therefore the Real cannot be defined as what resists but only negatively, as the correlate of the transcendental standpoint in the strong sense (i.e. the bracketing of our understanding of being).

I hope that I have now clarified the extent to which early Heidegger appropriates Kant's thought in both the Kant books and in *Being and Time*, ¶7. The analysis of the ontological reference structurally performed by "mere appearances," and of the way in which Heidegger extends it to his own thought, show that any pre-critical form of epistemological realism (i.e. things could be known as they are independently of our mode of access to them) must be rejected, although a *critical* form of realism (we can know all entities as they are, but what they are as entities cannot be dissociated from the transcendental perspective that is the only one possible for us) is perfectly acceptable.[14] Heidegger "retrieves" Kant's project by showing that entities are ontologically determined as temporal by Dasein, and therefore cannot be considered as such independently from it. As we have seen, it does not follow from this that Heidegger is a subjective idealist (and neither is Kant). Moreover, the dual claims that the need for ontological determination is definitive of Dasein's finitude, and that the latter is inescapable, entail that although *for us* there is nothing but entities, we are not entitled to universalize the kind of transcendental determination we perform and think that it is the only possible one. Therefore, the possibility of bracketing our transcendental conditions and of referring to what is in itself (the Real) must be allowed, although such a reference must remain purely negative, and such a bracketing cannot by definition be performed by Dasein itself. Yet its logical possibility is essential to prevent the "absolutization" of our finitude. For Kant, such an absolutization is due to reason's forgetfulness of its limitations (the need for sensory input) and thus to its driving "desire" (A796/B824) to overstep the boundaries of experience (which generates the illusions analysed in the "Transcendental Dialectics"). In my view, there is an analogical element in Heidegger's thought, which is falling (*Verfallen*): as a "primal metaphysical factum in Dasein" (GA 3: 233), falling is a structural feature of Dasein, and cannot be avoided. *Kant and the Problem of Metaphysics* defines it as our inescapable tendency to forget that we need (and have) an understanding of being, a forgetfulness which is "nothing accidental or temporary, but on the contrary is necessarily and constantly formed."[15] Such a forgetfulness is tantamount to forgetting the existence of ontological determination, which in turn can lead to pre-critical realism: entities are seen as what is in itself. Conversely, the task of fundamental ontology is to "wrest the forgetfulness away from what is apprehended in the projection of our understanding of being" (GA 3: 233). In this context, to insist on the independence and unknowability of the Real *as such* is essential to prevent the illusion arising that the way in which Dasein must disclose the Real is the way in which the Real is *per se*, and therefore the anthropocentric claim that Dasein's perspective on what is should be the only one.[16]

However, it does not follow from this that the Real cannot be known at all. As far as Kant's position is concerned, Allison contends that our impossibility to know things-in-themselves can be analytically deduced from the fact that transcendental conditions are determinative of representations. Thus, the "forms of sensibility or, more properly, the content of such forms, must be assigned solely to the cognitive apparatus of the human mind and, therefore, cannot . . . also be attributed to things considered as they are in themselves" (Allison 1996: 9). This, in turn, is the ground for the famous claim that things-in-themselves can be neither in space nor in time.[17] According to Allison, the two claims (the impossibility of knowing things-in-themselves and the idea that they are neither in time nor in space) do not conflict because while the first refutes the possibility of forming a *synthetic* knowledge of things-in-themselves, the second rests on an *analytic* inference from the nature of transcendental determination. Thus, the claim that things-in-themselves are neither in space nor in time "does not involve any synthetic a priori judgments about how things *really are* in contrast to how they merely *seem* to us. On the contrary, they involve merely analytic judgments or, perhaps more accurately, methodological directives, which specify how we must conceive of things

97

when we consider them in abstraction from the relation to human sensibility and its *a priori* forms" (Allison 1983: 241). Heidegger agrees that while entities are fully knowable, the Real cannot be known *as it is*, independently of Dasein's mode of access to it. However, the two-aspect view, if taken seriously, entails that phenomena must not be seen as radically distinct from noumena: they are the *same* things, considered either within a transcendental framework or without. This, in turn, has an important consequence for Heidegger: since entities are not substantially different from the Real, the ontic knowledge we can acquire of entities must somehow *pertain* to the Real. We cannot say *how* the properties of entities pertain to the Real, as this would require us to occupy *de facto* the transcendental standpoint and to form synthetic judgment about the nature of the Real. But although we can never be sure of the ways in which our knowledge applies to the Real, it would nevertheless be wrong to think that our framework does not capture at least some of its properties – on the contrary, this is *analytically* entailed by the two aspects view of transcendental idealism. What makes this debatable within the context of Kant's doctrine is that there are other elements in his thought (in particular in the Transcendental Dialectics and in the *Second Critique*) which incline toward a two-world view. However, Heidegger differs from Kant in that he unequivocally supports the two aspect view. Therefore, although metaphysical realism is not a legitimate position for him, the idea that the Real would be by definition completely closed off from us is not acceptable either.

Notes

1 Heidegger's main writings on Kant are *Being and Time*, Heidegger's 1927 course (*A Phenomenological Interpretation of Kant's* Critique of Pure Reason, GA 25), *Kant and the Problem of Metaphysics* (1929, GA 3), and the section of the *Basic Problems of Phenomenology* (GA 24) devoted to "Kant's thesis about Being." Among the later texts, *What Is a Thing?* (GA 41) is the most relevant, and recontextualizes Heidegger's reading of Kant within the history of being.

2 This is also the reason why Heidegger was so opposed to the interpretation of the *First Critique* put forward in his own time by N. Hartmann. This is made particularly clear by GA 25: 75–6, where Heidegger criticizes the three successive "mistakes" (metaphysical, epistemological, psychological) made in interpreting Kant.

3 Blattner comes the closest, but his exegesis stops before the crucially important notion of "mere appearances" is introduced. The reason for this omission is indirectly given in a footnote (Blattner 1999: 11), which dismisses "mere appearances" as "the somehow products of entities in the world." Blattner sees this as Heidegger's misreading of "Kant's few remarks about noumenal causation of appearances"; as will become apparent, Heidegger's reading of Kant is correct, it is Blattner's (quite understandable) assumption that the passage is referring to noumenal causation that is mistaken.

4 GA 25: 98. See also GA 25: 55: "when Kant brings about the Copernican revolution in philosophy – when he has the objects hinging on knowledge rather than knowledge hinging on objects – this does not mean that real beings are turned upside down in interpretation and get resolved into mere subjective representations." Guyer's (1987) attacks on Allison's position are a good representative of the kind of mistake that Heidegger has in mind here. Guyer grounds his criticism of the two-aspect view on the Kantian statement that epistemic

conditions, particularly space and time, are "merely subjective," in which case they would be imposed on entities (hence the charge of "impositionalism") and all we would know would be our own mental representations of things. However, while the claim that space and time are "merely subjective" denies them *transcendental* applications, it does not mean that they do not have *empirical* validity, quite the contrary. This is the reason why Kant can describe himself as a transcendental idealist and an empirical realist. Another similar criticism is provided by Langton (2001). Like Guyer, she assumes that when Kant speaks of space as "ideal," "subjective," or a "mere representation," he is expressing a kind of phenomenalism (or empirical idealism) about space. But Kant insists on the "objective validity" and "empirical reality" of space (A35–6).

5   Such a position can be broadly characterized by the two following sets of claims: (a) transcendental conditions exist, can be analysed *a priori*, and form the framework necessary for things to be constituted as phenomena; (b) it makes sense, however, to bracket these transcendental conditions and to refer to the *same* things thus considered in themselves, as endowed with independent properties which we cannot know, although we are driven by the very nature of human reason to think about them.

6   Heidegger's interpretation of the *Critique of Pure Reason*, perhaps because it leaves the Transcendental Dialectics aside completely, is mostly concerned with Kant's account of the conditions of the constitution of phenomena, and very little with the latter's positive suggestions about the nature of things-in-themselves. Thus Heidegger anticipates more contemporary readings, in particular Graham Bird's and Henry Allison's, in trying to establish the meaning of transcendental idealism exclusively from the *First Critique*. There are some differences between Heidegger's and Allison's interpretations of Kant, in particular on the question of the nature of self-affection and the status of the "I think" of transcendental apperception; but as none of them are relevant to the question of Heidegger's *appropriation* of Kant, I won't develop them here.

7   Such interpretations, such as Karl Ameriks's, argue that it is not desirable to read the *Critique of Pure Reason* in isolation from other works, in particular the *Second Critique* and the *Groundwork*. However, this is precisely what Heidegger does, with just a fleeting reference to the notion of respect in the *Critique of Practical Reason* (as also dependent on the activity of transcendental imagination). Cf. GA 3: section 30, "Transcendental Imagination and Practical Reason."

8   Heidegger thinks that part of the reason for this lies in Kant's remaining influenced by the scholastic division of the faculties, and the need to reinforce the traditional prevalence of the understanding over both sensibility and imagination.

9   Similar but not identical, because Blattner thinks that Kant is an ontic idealist (Blattner 1999: 245, fn25). Much as I sympathize with Blattner's views in general, I disagree on this particular point, which is also strongly denied by Heidegger's own reading of Kant.

10   Hence Blattner's analysis of SZ: 212, and his rejection of what he calls the "weak" interpretation of the passage, according to which the contrast between "now" and "then" should be seen as merely ontic, opposing two empirical possibilities (Dasein's existence versus a time when there would have been no Dasein).

11   It should become clear in the course of this chapter that the version of realism I suggest also supports Dasein's "naive realism." It is also perhaps worth noting that one of the reasons for Carman's rejection of the strong notion of transcendental determination, which results in his endorsement of a pre-critical notion of realism, is that his reading of Kant inclines toward the two-world view that Heidegger himself rejected. Thus, "Kant often sounds like a realist in another sense, of course, inasmuch as he seems to regard things in themselves as constituents of a kind of ultimate reality that exists independently of human

cognition, notwithstanding the fact that 'reality' and 'existence' are themselves mere categories of the understanding which is tantamount to accusing Kant of being a metaphysical realist" (Carman 2003: 156).

12 This is the basis of Allison's "semantic reading" of Kant, which argues that there is a logical implication between the consideration of something as an appearance and the possibility of considering the same thing in itself.

13 Ameriks points out the "substantive character of things-in-themselves with non spatio-temporal characteristics." Allison's (1996: 20) response to him is that the intelligible objects referred to by Kant are the *ideas* of pure reason, not things-in-themselves. While the notion is central to the "Transcendental Dialectics," this metaphysical account should not be used within the context of the "Analytic of Principles."

14 There are some passages, in particular in the *Metaphysical Foundations of Logic*, which resist this interpretation and tend to support a more naive view of realism by suggesting that entities are what they are independently of whether we access them or not. See, for example, GA 26: 194–5, where Heidegger asserts that "beings are in themselves the kinds of beings they are, and in the way they are, even if, for example, Dasein does not exist." However, Heidegger continues in the following way: "only insofar as existing Dasein gives itself anything like being can beings emerge in their in-themselves, i.e. can the first claim likewise be understood at all and be taken into account." This suggests to me that the first claim ("beings are in themselves the kinds of beings they are") is implicitly made from the *empirical* standpoint, from which indeed what neither beings' existence nor what they are is dependent on Dasein. However, the seemingly naive realism of this claim is qualified by Heidegger's second sentence ("only insofar as Dasein gives itself anything like being can . . . the first claim likewise be understood at all"), which reasserts the dependence of the empirical standpoint on its transcendental counterpart: from the transcendental standpoint, beings can only be "in their in-themselves" if we have an understanding of being, i.e. if they are ontologically determined as beings.

15 GA 3: 233. In *Being and Time*, falling refers to the movement by which Dasein seeks to hide from its ontological lack of essence by covering it up with ontical identities and roles. However, the two definitions are not inconsistent. Dasein can only identify fully with a role provided by the "One" if it remains unaware of the fact that such a role is merely an existential possibility among others. This entails a misconception of itself as a being endowed with a nature (understood as a fixed set of essential properties), which, in turn, is only possible if Dasein forgets that its real essence lies in the lack of such a nature, and thus in its having a projective understanding of being.

16 I do not have enough space to develop this second point further, but it is particularly important in the light of the development of Heidegger's thought after *Being and Time*, which is more and more concerned with the danger of anthropocentrism. Thus, Heidegger's well known reversal, in the *Letter on Humanism*, of the relation between Dasein and being (Dasein is characterized as the "shepherd" of being instead of being the entity on whom being depends for its projection, and thus the starting point for fundamental ontology) is another strategy meant to counter the risk of an absolutization of our finitude. Similarly, I have suggested that the introduction of "earth" in the *Origin of the Artwork* could be seen as a reworking of the notion of the Real in *Being and Time* (see Han-Pile 2003: 120–45).

17 This claim has been criticized by many commentators, in particular Strawson (1989: 60 and the appendix to the book) and Guyer (1987: chapter 16), mainly on the grounds that (a) it is not supported by the Transcendental Aesthetic and (b) it clashes with the idea that we cannot know things-in-themselves. See, for example, Kemp-Smith (2003: 113–14). Similar objections were raised in Kant's time, in particular by Mendelssohn (see Allison's discussion in "The non spatiality of things-in-themselves for Kant"). I also found a very

useful overview of these arguments in the yet unpublished manuscript of Sally Sheldon's very interesting PhD thesis, "The problematic meaning of transcendental idealism" (University of Essex 2001). Allison's reply to the first line of criticism is that it is possible to find such evidence in the Transcendental Aesthetic (see Allison 1983: chapter 5). For his reply to the second, see the main text of this chapter.

References and further readings

Allison, H. E. (1983) *Kant's Transcendental Idealism.* New Haven, CT: Yale University Press.

Allison, H. E. (1996) *Idealism and Freedom: Essays on Kant's Theoretical and Practical Philosophy.* Cambridge: Cambridge University Press.

Blattner, W. D. (1999) *Heidegger's Temporal Idealism.* Cambridge: Cambridge University Press.

Carman, T. (2000) Must we be inauthentic? In M. Wrathall and J. Malpas (eds), *Heidegger, Authenticity, and Modernity.* Cambridge: Cambridge University Press.

Carman, T. (2003) *Heidegger's Analytic: Interpretation, Discourse, and Authenticity in* Being and Time. Cambridge: Cambridge University Press.

Dreyfus, H. (1991) *Being-in-the-World: A Commentary on Heidegger's* Being and Time, *Division I.* Cambridge, MA: MIT Press.

Guyer, P. (1987) *Kant and the Claims of Knowledge.* Cambridge: Cambridge University Press.

Han, B. (2002) *Foucault's Critical Project* (trans. E. Pile). Stanford, CA: Stanford University Press.

Han-Pile, B. (2003) Transcendence and the hermeneutic circle: some thoughts on Heidegger and Marion. In J. Faulconer (ed.), *Transcendence in Philosophy and Religion.* Indianapolis: Indiana University Press.

Kemp-Smith, N. (2003) *A Commentary to Kant's Critique of Pure Reason.* London: Macmillan.

Langton, S. (2001) *Kantian Humility: Our Ignorance of Things-in-themselves.* Oxford: Oxford University Press.

Pippin, R. (1982) *Kant's Theory of Form.* New Haven, CT: Yale University Press.

Sacks, M. (2003) *Objectivity and Insight.* Oxford: Oxford University Press.

Strawson, P. (1989) *The Bounds of Sense.* London: Routledge.

7

Heidegger's Nietzsche

HANS SLUGA

A productive thinker devoting himself in detail and over some time to the work of another such thinker – that surely demands attention. Something is likely to be learned about one or the other of the two as well as about the issues and conditions that brought them together.

One must remind oneself of this when considering Heidegger's prolonged engagement with Nietzsche's thought. For the outcome of this engagement is by no means easy to fathom. Those sympathetic to Nietzsche have often found reasons to complain that Heidegger has failed their philosopher. They object that he considers only selective elements of Nietzsche's philosophy and often interprets them against their author's stated intention. Heidegger's sympathizers, on the other hand, are apt to quote his comment: "Nietzsche has destroyed me" ("*Nietzsche hat mich kaputt gemacht*"; Müller-Lauter 2000: 17). He meant by this, perhaps, only that his "confrontation with Nietzsche," as he called it, had demanded an overwhelming effort. But two factors must be considered to fully explain this remark. The first is that Heidegger approached Nietzsche from within his own philosophical problematic and not from a neutral, scholarly position. The second is that he turned to Nietzsche only *after* he had abandoned the assumptions and doctrines of *Being and Time* and *after* 1929 when he had embarked on new lines of thought. Nietzsche accompanied him only in the later phases of this process from about 1933 onwards. Still, it is plausible to assume that the engagement with him both accelerated and influenced the course of his thinking.

Heidegger had read *The Will to Power* "in the exciting years between 1910 and 1914" (GA 1: 56; note also the passing reference to Nietzsche in Heidegger's 1916 *Habilitationsschrift* on Duns Scotus, GA 1: 196), but the work was to become important to him only some twenty years later. In *Being and Time* he gives Nietzsche, in any case, remarkably short shrift. Nietzsche makes, indeed, only three appearances in that work – and marginal ones at that. In the first, Heidegger simply borrows the Nietzschean phrase "becoming too old for one's victories" without any indication of its original context (SZ: 264). Next, he mentions Nietzsche casually in a footnote on the interpretation of conscience together with Kant, Hegel, Schopenhauer, and several others (SZ: 272). Nietzsche's third appearance is admittedly more interesting, though it, too, does not take us far. Heidegger draws our attention to the essay on "The Use and Abuse of

History" – a text which he was to examine at length in 1938 but which serves him here only as a foil for his own philosophical concerns. He calls Nietzsche's observation that history can be either used "for one's life" or abused "unequivocal and penetrating" but immediately goes on to chide him for failing to say that this is because "one's life is historical in the roots of its being, and that therefore, as factically existing, one has in each case made one's decision for authentic or inauthentic historicality." He also praises Nietzsche's distinction between monumental, antiquarian, and critical history, but once again complains that he does not explicate "the necessity of this triad or the ground of its unity." One must suppose, Heidegger adds, "that he understood more than he has made known to us" (SZ: 396). *Being and Time* points us in this way to Nietzsche's *Untimely Meditations* and to his *Genealogy of Morals* but to no other writings and specifically not to *The Will to Power*. The Heidegger of *Being and Time* reveals, in fact, no interest in Nietzsche's thoughts on art, in his metaphysics, his doctrine of the will to power and of the eternal recurrence of the same, no interest in his theory of knowledge, his critique of nihilism, or his concept of the overman – all themes that will come to matter to him later on. Nietzsche appears in *Being and Time* simply as a moral psychologist and philosopher of history.

Heidegger's intensive engagement in Nietzschean thought belongs to the decade of the mid-1930s to mid-1940s. His Rectoral Address of 1933 gives us the first hint of a new assessment of Nietzsche (Heidegger 1990a). On that public and official occasion Heidegger calls for a political renewal of Germany through a renewal of the German university. What is needed, above all, he argues, is reflection on the nature of science (*Wissenschaft*) itself and in this there are two historical moments to consider. The first is Greek philosophy, which "thought science not merely a means of bringing the unconscious to consciousness, but the power that hones and encompasses all existence" (Heidegger 1990a: 7). The second moment is due to Nietzsche, "that passionate seeker of God and last German philosopher" who said that God is dead. "If we must be serious about this forsakenness of modern human beings in the midst of what is, then what is the situation of science? . . . Questioning is then no longer merely a preliminary step that is surmounted on the way to the answer and thus to knowing; rather, questioning itself becomes the highest form of knowing" (Heidegger 1990a: 8). This as yet only rhetorical appeal might be dismissed as Heidegger's bow to the man who has just been declared the philosopher of the National Socialist revolution. But the external factors detract in no way from the seriousness with which Heidegger is now beginning to look at Nietzsche's thought. Still, his understanding of Nietzsche is as yet only sketchy. Somewhat rashly, he identifies Nietzsche with a view that he himself is moving to – the idea that philosophical thought must resist answers and learn to see questioning as "the highest form of knowing." That this is inadequate as an interpretation of Nietzsche will, however, begin to dawn on him soon after. By 1935 he will have reached a more nuanced and at the same time more critical view of what Nietzsche stands for and it is at this point, finally, that his intensive engagement with Nietzsche's thought begins.

This engagement elicits three sets of questions. (a) *Why* did Heidegger begin to read Nietzsche so intensively in the 1930s? What relation did he see at the time between Nietzsche and his own thought? (b) *How* did he read Nietzsche? What paths did he follow in trying to unravel Nietzschean thought? How did he mean to distinguish his reading from alternatives offered at the same time by Alfred Baeumler and Karl Jaspers? (c) *What* was for him the outcome of this engagement? How did it bear on his critical rethinking of metaphysics? What political lessons did he draw from his reading? What role did Nietzsche play in his critical reassessment of the modern age and its characteristic mode of technological thinking?

Why Heidegger Reads Nietzsche

One thing is certain. The man who devotes himself so intensively to Nietzsche is no longer the Heidegger of *Being and Time*. That Heidegger had sought to elicit an ontology of being from a hermeneutics of Dasein. But the project had collapsed under Heidegger's inability to complete the argument of *Being and Time*. Three sketchy observations will have to suffice in indicating the new course he was taking. (a) In his inaugural address at Freiburg in 1929 Heidegger said that metaphysics had to concern itself with the question of nothingness but that no scientific metaphysics or ontology of the kind envisaged in *Being and Time* could do so. (b) In the essay on "Plato's Doctrine of Truth" from the same period he, furthermore, dismissed the classical concept of truth as correspondence and proposed instead its characterization as unhiddenness. The Platonic conception of truth, he argued further, had also been the source of a mistaken humanism and subjectivism. (c) Also in 1929 Heidegger was criticized by his friend Oskar Becker for omitting any discussion of art and for being, in effect, unable to accommodate a philosophy of art in *Being and Time*. Becker objected that the book saw everything from the perspective of Dasein, whereas art could not be accounted for in that manner.

Heidegger sought to respond to these challenges from 1929 onwards but the issues did not reach a critical point until he delivered his lecture course *Introduction to Metaphysics* (EM) of 1935 and wrote his essay "On the Origin of the Work of Art" (GA 5). These texts define, in fact, the setting of his new concern with Nietzsche. The lecture course is more of an introduction to what is problematic in metaphysics than an introduction to metaphysics itself. Metaphysics, so Heidegger argues, has always concerned itself with the nature of beings. This has been its leading question. It has ignored, on the other hand, the fundamental question of the nature of being itself. The metaphysical mode of thought was due to Plato and Aristotle, with whom therefore the decline of philosophy had begun. Heidegger concludes that we must reverse this decline. *Introduction to Metaphysics* ends, therefore, with a number of programmatic conclusions. The first is that "seen metaphysically, we are staggering" (EM: 155). Metaphysics, in other words, can no longer give us a hold. Second, "being must therefore be experienced anew, from the bottom up and in the full breadth of its possible essence" (EM: 155). But, third, "the question of being is intimately linked to the question of who the human being is" (EM: 156). The crucial question is, finally, how the distinction between beings and being is to happen. "Where can philosophy start to think it?" (EM: 156). *Introduction*, thus, ends with questions and the issue at hand for Heidegger must be where to turn next. His essay on art from the same year sought equally to turn the tables on *Being and Time*. Heidegger agreed now with Becker that art could not be understood from the perspective of human Dasein. He was certain, in any case, that "modern subjectivism" could not account for art since it "misinterprets creation, taking it as the self-sovereign subject's performance of genius" (GA 5: 64/Heidegger 1971: 76). But even his own analysis of Dasein in *Being and Time* could not explain why precisely in great art "the artist remains inconsequential as compared with the work, almost like a passageway that destroys itself in the creative process for the work to emerge" (GA 5: 26/Heidegger 1971: 40). One had to see that in the work of art a world opens itself up. In it "truth is thrown toward the coming preservers" (GA 5: 63/Heidegger 1971: 75). And with this concept Heidegger has, in effect, left the conceptual framework of *Being and Time* behind. That work had recognized the thrownness of Dasein and had spoken of Dasein being thrown toward death and toward history, but there had been no reverse throw in which truth is thrown toward (*zugeworfen*) human Dasein. Genuine poetic projection is now characterized as the opening up of the earth, which is the "self-closing ground" on which a historical people "rests." With this Heidegger has adopted Becker's "para-existential" conception of art according to which the specific condition of artistic existence is its being borne (*Getragenheit*; see Becker 1963: 34). Like *Introduction to Metaphysics* the essay ends with questions. We are left asking after the nature of art. We are left asking "whether art is or is not an origin in our historical existence." We are left asking whether our existence is "historically at the origin" and whether we know the nature of the origin (GA 5: 66/Heidegger 1971: 78).

The questions, thus generated, by *Introduction to Metaphysics* and "The Origin of the Work of Art" took Heidegger directly back to Nietzsche. Had Nietzsche not presented himself as a radical critic of metaphysics and of the whole metaphysical tradition since Plato? And had Nietzsche not developed such a critique in the name of art? Heidegger's two new preoccupations – the critique of metaphysics and the philosophy of art – seemed, thus, to have been anticipated by Nietzsche. But at the same time, it was becoming quickly evident to him that his own way of addressing these two concerns might conflict with Nietzsche's. He makes this explicit in the *Introduction to Metaphysics* and the same critical attitude is built into "The Origin of the Work of Art" – that is, even before he begins his long engagement with Nietzsche. In the *Introduction to Metaphysics* Nietzsche is, in fact, a pervasive presence, both named and unnamed. But Heidegger's remarks about him are surprisingly critical. He deplores, first of all, Nietzsche's dismissal of the concept of being as a mere vapor and an error. Because of this view, he thinks, Nietzsche remains confined to the metaphysical question of the nature of beings. "Merely to chase after beings in the midst of the oblivion of being – that is nihilism. Nihilism thus understood is the *ground* for the nihilism that Nietzsche exposed in the first book of the Will to Power" (EM: 217). Nietzsche is, in other words, a victim of the very nihilism he diagnoses. Second, because of his failure to deal adequately with the question of being, Nietzsche holds on to an absolute opposition between being and becoming and hence, in Greek philosophy, an absolute opposition between Parmenides and Heraclitus. "To be sure, Nietzsche fell prey to the commonplace and untrue opposition of Parmenides and Heraclitus. This is one of the essential reasons why his metaphysics never found its way to the decisive question" (EM: 133). To this Heidegger adds significantly, though, that "Nietzsche did reconceive the great age of the inception of Greek Dasein in its entirety in a way that is surpassed only by Hölderlin" (EM: 133). The remark is worth noting because of Heidegger's positive assessment of Nietzsche's rethinking of Greek philosophy and also for its comparison of Nietzsche with Hölderlin – a comparison which will gain increasing significance for Heidegger in the following years and which already at this point reveals his ultimately placing of the poet above the thinker. A third critical remark on Nietzsche occurs at the end of *Introduction to Metaphysics* in the course of an attack on the neo-Kantian theory of value as yet another piece of ungrounded metaphysics. He turns his critical gaze in this context also on the Nietzschean conception of created values and writes: "Because Nietzsche was entangled in the confusion of the representation of values, because he did not understand its questionable provenance, he never reached the genuine center of philosophy" (EM: 213–14). Against Nietzsche, Heidegger argues that we cannot make intrinsically valueless things valuable by an act of human willing. That assumption is steeped in the subjectivist tradition, which Heidegger has come to reject. This critical observation has far-reaching consequences. In dismissing Nietzsche's view of man as the originator of values, Heidegger is, in effect, questioning not only Nietzsche's conception of art, but also, as it will turn out, his doctrine that the world is to be conceived as will to power.

Such critical comments raise the question why Heidegger should have embarked a year later on his prolonged study of Nietzsche's work. The answer must be that despite his criticisms he believed Nietzsche to have something important to offer. That this is so becomes evident from his words at the start of his first lecture course on Nietzsche in 1936. Heidegger says on that occasion: "The task of our lecture course is to elucidate the fundamental position within which Nietzsche unfolds the guiding question of Western thought and responds to it. Such elucidation is needed in order to prepare a confrontation with Nietzsche. If in Nietzsche's thinking the prior tradition of Western thought is gathered and completed in a decisive respect, then the confrontation with Nietzsche becomes one with all Western thought hitherto" (GA 6.1: 3/Heidegger 1979: 4). Heidegger was never to reverse his judgment on the limitations of Nietzsche's philosophizing. We can see that most clearly from the essay "Nietzsche's Word: 'God is dead'" which Heidegger first delivered in 1943 but which was meant to be "based upon the Nietzsche lectures that were given between 1936 and 1940."[1] But when we look carefully at his lectures in the 1930s and 1940s we see that he became increasingly more convinced of the crucial importance of Nietzsche for understanding the modern world. The paradoxical fact is then that Heidegger's assessment of Nietzsche became increasingly more positive as he was moving beyond him.

How Heidegger Reads Nietzsche

Heidegger was convinced that Nietzsche's thought is not as readily accessible as the tone of his writings suggests. In 1936 he says that Nietzsche's "words and sentences provoke, penetrate, and stimulate. One thinks that if only one pursues one's impressions one has understood Nietzsche." But, we must "unlearn this abuse" and first of all "learn to 'read'" Nietzsche's writings (GA 6.1: 474/Heidegger 1982: 47). In 1944 he declares "the appearance of being easy and easy-going" the real difficulty in Nietzsche's philosophy, since it "seduces us into forgetting the thought over the impressiveness and magic of its language" (GA 50: 106). Finally, in 1951 he warns most emphatically that Nietzsche cannot be read in a haphazard way and that his work makes "demands to which we are not equal." In fact, he advises his audience to "postpone reading Nietzsche for the time being, and first study Aristotle for ten or fifteen years" (GA 8: 78/73).

One kind of difficulty Heidegger perceives in Nietzsche's writings is that they are full of "incoherencies, contradictions, oversights" and that his expositions are "overhasty and often superficial and arbitrary" (GA 6.1: 63/Heidegger 1979: 66; translation modified). We must therefore, first, strip away what is flawed to get at the philosophical essence of Nietzsche's thinking. In saying in 1936 that we must first learn to read Nietzsche, he warns us that this demands a stripping away, in particular, of Nietzsche's biologism – that is, of his preoccupation with life, blood, the metabolism, digestion. (There cannot be any doubt that Heidegger's remarks are meant here to critique National Socialist readings of Nietzsche as a biological racist.) Just as important for Heidegger is to set aside Nietzsche's borrowings from physiology and psychology, his various attempts to ground philosophical doctrines in physics, his pervasive reliance on the natural sciences and more generally his attraction to positivism. It is indisputable that "Nietzsche went through a period of extreme positivism. . . . Such positivism, though of course transformed, became a part of his later fundamental position also. But what matters is precisely the transformation"(GA 6.1: 156–7/Heidegger 1979: 154). The important point to remember here is that "no result of science can ever be applied *immediately* to philosophy" (GA 6.1: 42/Heidegger 1979: 45). For this reason we must separate Nietzsche's thought from these detrimental borrowings. We will see then that what Nietzsche deals with "is not a matter for psychology, nor even for a psychology undergirded by physiology and biology. It is a matter of the basic modes that constitute Dasein, a matter of the ways man confronts the Da, the openness and concealment of beings, in which he stands" (GA 6.1: 41/Heidegger 1979: 45).

Heidegger means, in fact, to separate Nietzsche from everything characteristic of the nineteenth century. "In order to draw near to the essential will of Nietzsche's thinking, and remain close to it," he declares emphatically, "our thinking must acquire . . . the ability to see beyond everything that is fatally contemporary in Nietzsche" (GA 6.1: 128/Heidegger 1979: 127). For Heidegger, Nietzsche's own time is a "complicated and confused historical and intellectual milieu." Two great streams mingle in it: "the genuine and well-preserved tradition of the great age of the German movement, and the slowly expanding wasteland, the uprooting of human existence" (GA 6.1: 84/Heidegger 1979: 85) The fame of Schopenhauer and Wagner is for Heidegger a product of this dubious milieu. Their influence on Nietzsche is therefore also best ignored. We must, furthermore, set aside Nietzsche's curious obsession with music and his entire aestheticism – both products of nineteenth-century culture. Instead, we must connect him with Kant, Schelling, and Hegel and the great movement of German Idealism. His doctrine of the will to power must, for that reason, be traced back not to Schopenhauer (as seems most plausible) but to Schelling and Hegel.

For Heidegger, Nietzsche belongs to the "essential thinkers" who as "exceptional human beings . . . are destined to think one single thought, a thought that is always 'about' *beings as a whole*. Each thinker thinks only one *single* thought" (GA 6.1: 427/Heidegger 1982: 4). With this characterization Heidegger is adopting a decidedly advanced view of the philosopher. From his death in 1900 to the 1930s, Nietzsche had

107

mostly been treated as a literary figure and cultural critic. Philosophical amateurs like Thomas Mann or the members of Stefan George's circle might identify with him, but to the neo-Kantians who still dominated the philosophical scene in Germany Nietzsche was of small interest. All this was changing by the time Heidegger turned to Nietzsche. In 1931, Alfred Baeumler, known until then for his work on Kant's aesthetics, had published a provocative book titled *Nietzsche as Thinker and Politician* that proposed to treat Nietzsche seriously as a metaphysician whose doctrines had at the same time strongly intended political implications. Shortly before Heidegger embarked on his lectures, Karl Jaspers had, in turn, published his comprehensive study *Nietzsche: An Introduction to the Understanding of His Philosophizing*, likewise emphasizing the metaphysics of the will to power and taking note also of Nietzsche's commitment to a great politics. There is no doubt that Heidegger's own concern with Nietzsche was, at least initially, influenced by these two interpreters and must be understood in relation and in contrast to them.

Just like these two others, Heidegger was determined to read Nietzsche as first and foremost a metaphysician. He agreed, moreover, with Baeumler initially that Nietzsche's metaphysics was fully expressed in the posthumously constructed *Will to Power*. From this work and this work alone, both men assumed, a coherent philosophy could be derived. Jaspers, on the other hand, had argued that all of Nietzsche's writings, both published and unpublished, had to be used in the interpretation of his philosophy. Given the variability of Nietzsche's thoughts, that meant, however, that no philosophical system could be extracted from this material. Heidegger was in these respects closer to Baeumler, but he disagreed, from the start, with both men over the exact content of Nietzsche's metaphysics. Baeumler saw it contained in the concept of the will to power and was inclined to dismiss Nietzsche's doctrine of the eternal recurrence of the same as a mystical and poetic intrusion into the philosophical system. For Jaspers, both the will to power and the eternal recurrence were genuine elements of Nietzsche's philosophizing, but he, too, thought that the two doctrines could not be fully reconciled. Nietzsche's thought could therefore not be appropriated as a systematic and theoretical unity but only existentially as the expression of a personal and radical search for limit experiences. In contrast to both, Heidegger insists throughout the course of his engagement with Nietzsche that the will to power and the eternal recurrence of the same are components of a single and coherent metaphysical conception. In fact, he never waivers from the line he lays down in the first of his Nietzsche lectures, where he declares: "Baeumler's reflections on the relationship between the two doctrines do not press in any way toward the realm of actual inquiry. . . . For Baeumler the doctrine of eternal recurrence cannot be united with the political interpretation of Nietzsche; for Jaspers it is not possible to take it as a question of great import, because, according to Jaspers, there is no conceptual truth or conceptual knowledge in philosophy" (GA 6.1: 20/Heidegger 1979: 22–3).

Despite such criticisms, Heidegger's reading remains indebted to Baeumler. He agrees with him, in particular, that the genuinely philosophical Nietzsche reveals himself not in the published writings but in the unpublished aphorisms of the late 1880s. In his 1936 lecture course he follows Baeumler also in thinking that *The Will to Power*, with its selections from the late aphorisms, gives us the outline of Nietzsche's intended main work. This book must then be for Heidegger the center of his interpretation of Nietzsche. But his reading of that work is highly selective. He completely ignores book 2 with its critique of religion, Christianity, morality, and philosophy. In book 3 he passes over Nietzsche's discussion of "the will to power in nature" (section 2) and of "the will to power as society and individual" (section 3), disregarding thus the naturalistic and the political elements of Nietzsche's philosophy. He skips likewise over the first section of book 4 ("Order and Rank"), with its discussion of politics, the masters of the earth, and the great human being. All in all, he ignores about 310 of the 550 pages of the book.

Heidegger's focus on Nietzsche's work was eventually to broaden. In the summer of 1937 he shows an increasing concern with the unpublished aphorisms as a whole. He now declares that "only an investigation of the notes in Nietzsche's own hand provides a clearer picture" of the doctrine of the eternal recurrence of the same.[2] This leads him to be increasingly critical of the compilation of texts in *The Will to Power*. By 1944 he will speak of the "arbitrary and thoughtless" manner in which Elisabeth Förster-Nietzsche and Peter Gast have "grabbed pieces together" in the production of "this disastrous book" (*dieses verhängnisvollen Buches*) (GA 50: 109). With his increasing interest in the doctrine of the eternal recurrence and its development, Heidegger also begins to pay attention in 1937 to *The Gay Science* and to *Thus Spoke Zarathustra* and, particularly, the latter will come to have increasing importance to him over time. Yet, throughout this course of development, Heidegger remains convinced that every great thinker entertains a single thought, which is metaphysical in character and concerns beings as a whole. For that reason he will continue to think that the late aphorisms, with their focus on the doctrines of the will to power and the eternal recurrence of the same, express most clearly the central aspects of Nietzsche's thought. But he also increasingly sees that thought as having different facets. Thus, by 1941/2 he can speak of Nietzsche's metaphysics as built around five essential concepts: the will to power, nihilism, the eternal recurrence, the overman, and justice (GA 50: 6). But even then he maintains that every term "names at the same time what the others say. The naming of each basic word is exhausted only when one also thinks with it what the others say" (ibid.).

In later stages, it is Nietzsche's idea of the overman that attracts Heidegger's greatest attention and for that reason *Thus Spoke Zarathustra* becomes a decisive text for him. In his first postwar lecture course at Freiburg he characterizes Nietzsche as predominantly concerned with the question of what it means to be human. The overman, we are also told, "is the man who first leads the essential nature of existing man over into its truth, and so assumes that truth" (GA 8: 62–3/59). But this does not mean that Heidegger has abandoned his old preoccupation with Nietzsche's metaphysics. For "man himself is the metaphysical" (GA 8: 62/58), and "Zarathustra teaches the doctrine of the overman because he is the teacher of the eternal recurrence of the same" (GA 8: 109/106). For Heidegger, the overman thus merely casts Nietzsche's metaphysics in a new light. Once again, he declares that every thinker thinks only a single thought which for Nietzsche is now said to be unquestioningly the idea of the eternal recurrence of the same. *Thus Spoke Zarathustra* "thinks this thinker's one and only thought: the thought of the eternal recurrence of the same" (GA 8: 53/50), and "the eternal recurrence of the same is the supreme triumph of the metaphysics of the will that eternally wills its own willing," i.e. the will to power (GA 8: 108/104).

Despite his shifting focus, Heidegger's concern with Nietzsche remains thus remarkably the same. That means, specifically, that he continues to see Nietzsche throughout as a metaphysical thinker and largely ignores Nietzsche as critic of nineteenth-century culture, as psychologist, genealogist, and political thinker. He therefore also largely passes over such works as Nietzsche's *Birth of Tragedy, Human, all too Human, The Genealogy of Morals*, and *Beyond Good and Evil*. Even *Zarathustra* is for him only a prologue to the late aphorisms and, thus, an entry point into Nietzsche's metaphysical concern with beings as a whole.

What Heidegger Learns

Heidegger, we may say, learned three different lessons from his engagement with Nietzsche. The first concerns metaphysics, the second politics, and the third the world historical situation.

Nietzsche and the end of metaphysics

Heidegger approaches Nietzsche's metaphysics through his philosophy of art. That undertaking convinces him quickly within the course of a semester that he cannot find common ground with Nietzsche's conception of art. But the examination has not been useless for that matter because, so Heidegger concludes, it has given him a deeper access to Nietzsche's metaphysical doctrines and these are not only central to Nietzsche's own thought but can help to illuminate the precarious nature of all metaphysical thinking. Heidegger summarizes Nietzsche's conception of art in five statements – each of which gives rise to critical objections. Art must, according to Nietzsche, "be grasped in terms of the artist" and his work constitutes "the distinctive countermovement to nihilism." Art is, in fact, worth more than "truth." Understood in this fashion, it must be seen as "the most perspicuous and familiar configuration of the will to power," and all beings must be conceived in these terms as "self-creating" and "created" (GA 6.1: 68–73/Heidegger 1979: 71–5). Heidegger is quick to point out that this conception of art constitutes nothing but an inverted Platonism from which Nietzsche could never twist himself free.[3] In the footsteps of Plato, he treated art as mere semblance and as something standing in opposition to truth. To understand art in Nietzsche's way means to see it "under the optics of the artist," to estimate it and everything else "according to its creative force" (GA 6.1: 223–4/Heidegger 1979: 219–20). This means also to understand art as "the supreme configuration of the will to power" (GA 6.1: 221/Heidegger 1979: 218). But, Heidegger argues, this metaphysical conception of art must ultimately fail "because creation itself is to be estimated according to the originality with which it penetrates to being" (GA 6.1: 224/Heidegger 1979: 220). And with this conclusion, Heidegger has twisted himself free from Nietzsche's philosophy of art. Though it was the failure of the philosophy of *Being and Time*, its inability to deliver a philosophy of art, the criticisms of his friend Becker, and his own efforts to devise a philosophically satisfactory account of art that had initially attracted him to Nietzsche, he would not find it necessary after his 1936 lectures to return to Nietzsche's reflections on art; instead, he would now devote himself directly to Nietzsche's metaphysics.

The critique of metaphysics that Heidegger had inaugurated in his inaugural lecture at Freiburg in 1929 and, thus, well before his engagement with Nietzsche was to be sharpened through this encounter with Nietzsche's thought. Through Nietzsche, Heidegger would come to appreciate the difficulty involved in the project of overcoming metaphysics. He learned, in particular, that the desire to escape from metaphysics does not guarantee its success. Nietzsche may have been convinced of "the senselessness of metaphysics" (see Nietzsche 1967: section 574), but his concepts of the will to power and of the eternal recurrence of the same are nevertheless, on Heidegger's view, themselves metaphysical in character. This is, indeed, a dilemma which readers of Nietzsche have to face and which has called forth a number of interpretative strategies. Thus, some have argued that seemingly metaphysical assertions are not genuinely so since for Nietzsche all truth is perspectival and an interpretation. Others have dismissed Nietzsche's apparently metaphysical claims as passing remarks to be found mainly in his unpublished notebooks. Heidegger is justifiably wary of such defensive maneuvers. He understands that a perspectival interpretation of the world may still turn out to be a piece of metaphysics and he is also rightly convinced that someone who thinks and writes like Nietzsche and under Nietzsche's condition, someone who wants to hide from common men, who wants to wear a mask and keep his own truths to himself, may well not have entrusted his deepest and most important thoughts to print.

Like all metaphysicians, Nietzsche fails, as Heidegger sees it, to escape from the metaphysical preoccupation with the nature of beings as a whole. He seeks to characterize the nature of beings as a whole with his concepts of the will to power and the eternal recurrence of the same. But in the pursuit of the leading question of all metaphysical thinking, Nietzsche fails to confront the grounding question of metaphysics. Like all metaphysical thinkers he is thus caught in a forgetfulness of being. He dismisses the concept of being as "gaseous" and an "error," and fails to confront the question of being itself. Such a critique depends, of course, on Heidegger's distinction between beings and being, between beings as a whole and being itself, which, despite his persistent attempts at justification and clarification, has continued to be thought of as problematic and by some readers even as metaphysical in character. If the latter is true, then Heidegger's attack on Nietzsche is conducted in terms of yet another metaphysics; his belief that Nietzsche's is the last form of metaphysics in the West is mistaken and Heidegger just like Nietzsche has failed to escape metaphysical thinking. This is how it has seemed to Jacques Derrida but this is also how it must appear to any determined positivist. Heidegger's critique of Nietzsche will, in any case, be compelling only to those who can grant him his own fundamental philosophical assumptions.

But given the conflict between Nietzsche's programmatic critique of metaphysics and his apparent advocacy of a particular metaphysics, one may justifiably ask why we should not dismiss the latter and concentrate, instead, on the former. Heidegger resists such a "positivistic" reading of Nietzsche because he considers metaphysics to be decisive for the history of the West and possibly crucial to any kind of human thought. Nietzsche serves him, in fact, as evidence that metaphysics is not easily escaped from even when we are trying to do so. And the reason for that is, in Heidegger's eyes, that behind the errors of metaphysics lies a valid concern with something that is never explicitly manifested. Metaphysics always asks for the nature of beings as a whole, but behind this kind of inquiry lies the question of being itself. On Heidegger's view metaphysics is, thus, not only forgetful of being but also, at the same time, haunted by the question of being. This is particularly evident for him in Nietzsche, who therefore has a specific importance to him as a witness to the hidden underpinnings of all metaphysical thinking. That is the reason why Nietzsche's doctrine of the eternal recurrence is so important. That doctrine is genuinely metaphysical in character but it gestures at the same time beyond itself to the question of being. In the ten years of his intense engagement with Nietzsche, Heidegger therefore insists again and again – in contrast to other readers and, in particular, in contrast to Baeumler and Jaspers – that the will to power and the eternal recurrence of the same are correlated notions, that they form the woof and the warp of Nietzsche's metaphysics. Over the years, he draws repeatedly on section 617 in *The Will to Power* to support this claim. Nietzsche writes there: "To impose upon becoming the character of being – that is the supreme will to power. . . . That everything recurs is the closest approximation of a world of becoming to a world of being: high point of the meditation" (Nietzsche 1967: 330). On Heidegger's picture, then, Nietzsche's metaphysics is a metaphysics of becoming which approximates being through the concept of the eternal recurrence. One might take Nietzsche to have meant here simply that the idea of a constantly changing but constantly recycling universe introduces an appearance of stability into the picture of continuous becoming. But Heidegger prefers to read Nietzsche's remark in the light of his own understanding of the concept of being and takes the doctrine of the eternal recurrence of the same to be a part of Nietzsche's metaphysics that points beyond metaphysics to the question of being itself. In his 1951 lectures *What Is Called Thinking* he speaks finally of the idea of the eternal recurrence as a component of Nietzsche metaphysics that is at the same time "wrapped in thick clouds – not just for us, but for Nietzsche's own thinking" (GA 8: 111/108). He chides Nietzsche, in this context, for having been led "curiously astray" in his attempts to demonstrate this doctrine and goes on to say: "The thought of the eternal recurrence of the same remains veiled – and not just by a curtain" (GA 8: 112/109). For that thought constitutes – and here comes the decisive conclusion – "Nietzsche's attempt to think the being of beings" and if the doctrine of the eternal recurrence is difficult for both Nietzsche and us this makes clear that "all thinking, that is, relatedness to being, is still difficult" (GA 8: 112/110). Heidegger concludes his lectures in the summer of 1951 with the declaration: "The being of beings is the most apparent; and yet, we normally do not see it – and if we do, only with difficulty" (GA 8: 113/110). It is evidently the merit of Nietzsche that in thinking the eternal recurrence of the same he has not shied away from that difficulty even though he has failed to identify its true source.

Nietzsche and "the essence of being German"

When Heidegger embarked on his first lecture course on Nietzsche in 1936, he had seen himself as resolutely opposed to Baeumler's "political" reading. He might have aimed a similar criticism against Jaspers at the time, since he, too, had been looking at Nietzsche politically. The two had done so, however, in very different and, indeed, opposed ways. Baeumler had sought to picture Nietzsche as the natural forerunner of

Hitler and his National Socialism (Sluga 1993: 129–31). Jaspers, on the other hand, had attempted to show that Nietzsche stood "in opposition to the National Socialists" even though they had made him their philosopher (Jaspers 1981: preface to the second and third editions, no page number). Heidegger contrasted himself to both Baeumler and Jaspers by avoiding any direct discussion of Nietzsche's political thought. Even so, he meant to use Nietzsche for political purposes but in a different direction from those adopted by his two competitors. His Nietzsche was to be an "anti-political" politician and the political lessons to be derived from him were to be in turn anti-political in character. Where Baeumler and Jaspers had used Nietzsche to speak either for or against National Socialism, Heidegger sought to separate actually existing National Socialism from a new and idealized alternative. Through the examination of Nietzsche he sought to attack the existing system as committed to an empty will to will and to a consequent rush into technological machinations. But with Nietzsche's help he sought at the same time to spell out a purer national and social German identity.

Nietzsche, or, rather, Nietzsche in conjunction with Hölderlin, was for the Heidegger of the mid-1930s and 1940s the guide to a deeper conception of what it means to be German. That question had been his concern since his Rectoral Address and still more outspokenly so since his *Introduction to Metaphysics*. In the latter work he had argued that the dilemma of modern and Western existence manifested itself most severely in Germany, "the land of the middle." He had declared dramatically that the German people "lie in the pincers. Our people, as standing in the center, suffers the most intense pressure – our people, the people richest in neighbors and hence the most endangered people, and for all that, the most metaphysical people. . . . Precisely if the great decision regarding Europe is not to go down the path of annihilation – precisely then can this decision come about only through the development of new, *spiritual* forces from the center" (EM: 41; on Heidegger's politics in *Introduction to Metaphysics* see Sluga 2001b). Such a development, he had continued, required the recognition that Nietzsche had correctly diagnosed the question of being as a mere vapor and error for modern man. "Nietzsche's judgment, of course, is meant in a purely dismissive sense," Heidegger had commented (EM: 42). We, on the other hand, must recover that question against the whole metaphysical tradition. Only in this way, Heidegger was convinced, could the middle be saved and the dilemma of modern man be resolved. The question of being and the question of the German identity thus belonged in a mysterious way together.

Heidegger seeks to clarify this astounding claim in the decade from 1935 to 1945 by confronting Nietzsche again and again with Hölderlin. For the poet is, according to Heidegger, the only one who can resolve the dilemma which Nietzsche has diagnosed. He is the one who can open for us once again the question of being and he is also the one who can point the way to a new and deeper way of being German. It is for this reason that Heidegger's discussion of Nietzsche in the decade between 1935 and 1945 is interwoven with an examination of Hölderlin's hymns. We can clearly recognize this intercalation when we look at the courses Heidegger gave on Nietzsche and Hölderlin in this period:

WS 1934/5	Hölderlin's Hymns "Germania" and "The Rhine"
WS 1936/7	Nietzsche: The Will to Power as Art

SS 1937	Nietzsche's Basic Metaphysical Position in Occidental Thought: The Eternal Recurrence of the Same
WS 1938/9	On the Interpretation of Nietzsche II: Untimely Meditations: One, The Use and Abuse of History
SS 1939	Nietzsche's Doctrine of the Will to Power as Knowledge
Second Trimester 1940	Nietzsche: European Nihilism
WS 1941/2	Announced but not given: Nietzsche's Metaphysics. Instead: Hölderlin's Hymn "Remembrance"
SS 1942	Hölderlin's Hymn "The Ister"
WS 1944/5	Announced but cancelled: Introduction to Philosophy: Thought and Poetry

Some comments are needed to fully bring out how the two sets of courses are interwoven. In the first of the Hölderlin lectures Heidegger had initially proposed a whole series of lectures on Hölderlin's hymns. Instead, he proceeds from 1936 onwards to a sequence of courses on Nietzsche. For the winter of 1941 Heidegger announced yet one more course in that series but substituted for it at the last moment the course on Hölderlin's "Remembrance." This he followed up with another course on the poet in the summer of 1942. Finally, in the winter of 1944–5 Heidegger had planned to lecture on Hölderlin and Nietzsche together but the war intervened and the lectures were never given. From his notes for the course we learn that he had intended to speak about the interdependence of thought and poetry in German culture, exemplified "in Nietzsche, who as a thinker is a poet, and in Hölderlin, who as a poet is a thinker" (GA 50: 95–6). As such, the two were strictly distinct but nevertheless belonged together. Heidegger had said as much previously in his interpretation of Hölderlin's hymn "Remembrance" when he declared: "The recent fashion which puts Hölderlin and Nietzsche side by side is completely misleading. . . . Abysmally different, the two together, nevertheless, determine the nearest and the furthest future of Germany and the West" (GA 52: 78).

The philosopher and the poet belonged together because Nietzsche was the thinker of the godlessness and worldlessness of modern man, Heidegger wrote in his undelivered notes in the Winter of 1944. Nietzsche had considered the gods and all things to be "products" of creative man and in this he had given voice to the destiny of Western man. "In the absence of the gods and in the decay of the world homelessness is specifically assigned to modern, historical man" (GA 50: 116). Nietzsche had, in this way, correctly diagnosed the modern condition. Hölderlin, by contrast, was the poet of homecoming. His deepest insight was to have seen that historical man is not initially familiar with his home at "the beginning of his history, that he must first become not at home, in order to learn from the other, by departing to it, the appropriation of his own, and that he can come to be at home only in the return from this other" (GA 53: 23). We, too, as Germans and moderns, so Heidegger had argued, are called to share in the poet's concern. And if we do, "then there is kinship with the poet. Then there is homecoming. And this homecoming is the future of the historical essence of the German" (GA 4: 30). But the home of which the poet had spoken was not to be conceived as geographical place in which the Germans live. Home was rather the hearth and the hearth was being itself. To come home means then to come home to the question of being and to face that question as a question. Nietzsche had been right when he had characterized science as the capacity to live in the face of the question and without answer, but in characterizing the world metaphysically he had fallen back into attempting an answer. He had lost sight of the question of being which the poet had faced more squarely and poetry could, in this way, claim pre-eminence over philosophical thought.

How the poet might help us in defining "the essence of being German" had been Heidegger's concern from the moment he began to engage himself seriously with Nietzsche's philosophy. This becomes apparent in the first of the Nietzsche lectures from 1936. Even at that early moment in his confrontation with Nietzsche Heidegger was comparing and contrasting the poet and the philosopher and the way they might assist us in revealing the essence of being German and even then he was sure that the poet ultimately excelled over the thinker. The issue at stake is for Heidegger in 1936 the distinction between the Apollinian and the Dionysian. Heidegger says in his lectures that Nietzsche may lay claim to its "first public presentation." But he insists that Jacob Burckhardt may well have drawn it already in lectures Nietzsche attended at Basel. What is more, Heidegger continues: "Of course, what Nietzsche could not have realized, even though since his youth he knew more clearly than his contemporaries, who Hölderlin was, was the fact that Hölderlin had seen and conceived of the opposition in an even more profound and lofty manner" (GA 6.1: 104/Heidegger 1979: 103) On Heidegger's interpretation, "Hölderlin's tremendous insight" is contained in a letter to his friend Böhlendorf from December 4, 1801. It is a letter Heidegger will quote repeatedly in subsequent lectures and it plays a decisive role in his overall reading of Hölderlin's hymns. In the letter in question Hölderlin had written to his friend: "As I see it, clarity of presentation is original to us and just as natural as the fire from the sky is to the Greeks." Heidegger took this to mean in 1936 that the poet was contrasting "the holy pathos" of Greek culture with the "Occidental Junonian sobriety of representational skill" of the Germans and this contrast he took to correspond, in turn, to Nietzsche's distinction between the Dionysian and the Apollinian (GA 6.1: 104–5/ Heidegger 1979: 103–4). Not only that, but the poet had expressed this distinction even more deeply than the philosopher. This is, of course, a daring and questionable interpretation since for Nietzsche Greek culture was itself defined by a balance between the Apollinian and the Dionysian and the distinction was not meant to characterize different national identities. But for Heidegger it was clear that "by recognizing this antagonism Hölderlin and Nietzsche early on placed a question mark after the task of the German people to find their essence historically." And to this he added somberly: "Will we understand their cipher? One thing is certain: history will wreak vengeance on us if we do not" (GA 6.1: 105/Heidegger 1979: 104).

In the contest that Heidegger staged in this manner between Nietzsche and Hölderlin there is more at stake than the question of who had priority in drawing the distinction of the Apollinian and the Dionysian. At stake was, for him, at the same time, the entire relation of philosophy and poetry and thus the question of the status of the whole philosophical enterprise – a matter that had exercised him ever since the recognized failure of *Being and Time*. If philosophy could not be a science, as he had once envisaged, then what was it to be? Was truth perhaps, revealed more deeply and more directly in poetical than in scientific, metaphysical, or even philosophical language? Heidegger's peculiarly ambiguous relationship to Nietzsche must be seen in the light of his subsequent faith in the power of poetry and his abandonment of philosophy in the name of thinking. By 1944 it was Nietzsche, the poet among the philosophers, who mattered most to him. Heidegger's undelivered lectures from the winter of 1944 reveal no longer any interest in Nietzsche's philosophy of art. That part of Nietzsche had been dismissed, easily enough, as a consequence of his doctrine of the creation of values which, in turn, had its origin in Nietzsche's metaphysics of the will to power. What mattered to him, instead, was Nietzsche's actual poetry. His best diagnosis of modern homelessness was to be found not in his philosophical writings but in the poem "Without Home" (GA 50: 116ff). No wonder then that Heidegger's postwar interest in Nietzsche was focused so sharply on the philosophical poem *Thus Spoke Zarathustra*.

Nietzsche and the world-historical situation

Heidegger's concern with "the essence of being German" appears now as dated and as, at best, of local interest. Heidegger himself abandoned it with the end of the war and the collapse of Hitler's regime. After this he strove to restate his thought "without referring to nationalism" since "society has taken the place of the nation (*Volk*)" (Heidegger 1990b: 46).

Nietzsche became for him the thinker who thinks what is now and thus the diagnostician of the modern age. "Nietzsche is that thinker who thinks what is now," he had written in the winter of 1944/5 (GA 50: 103). He is "the last thinker of the modern age," who thinks "the modern essence of the West as being at the same time the historical essence of the modern world history of the globe" (GA 50: 97). Nietzsche's thought is "authentic European-planetary thinking" (ibid.). The "innermost fate of the history of the West" finds expression in Nietzsche's thought (GA 50: 106). In 1951 Heidegger added: "In a decade when the world at large still knew nothing of world wars, when faith in 'progress' was virtually *the* religion of the civilized peoples and nations, Nietzsche screamed out into the world: 'The wasteland grows . . .'" (GA 8: 52/49). Nietzsche had seen that "the devastation is growing wider. Devastation is more uncanny (*unheimlich*) than destruction . . . devastation blocks all future growth and prevents all building. . . . Mere destruction sweeps aside all things including even nothingness, while devastation on the contrary establishes and spreads everything that obstructs. . . . Devastation is the high-velocity expulsion of Mnemosyne" (GA 8: 31/29–30). The character of this age was, in fact, correctly analyzed in Nietzsche's metaphysics of the will to power and the eternal recurrence of the same. It was characterized by its subjectivist, value-creating, technological, and ultimately nihilistic mode of thinking. Nietzsche had thought what is now and now was "the moment when man is about to assume dominion of the earth as a whole" (GA 8: 61/57). His thinking reveals "the essence of modern technology" in the "the steadily rotating recurrence of the same" (GA 8: 112/109). Heidegger had been concerned with the "hopeless frenzy of unchained technology" since at least 1935 (EM: 40). This frenzy, he had said then, had its consequence in a "measureless on-and-on of what is always the same and indifferent" (EM: 48; translation modified). Being had thus become "set into calculation" and beings had been turned into something "that can be ruled in modern, mathematically structured technology" (EM: 207). But it was to take him until the 1940s to connect this technological frenzy of the "always the same" and its mathematical structures with Nietzsche's metaphysics. He then turned Nietzsche into the philosopher of "the struggle for the unlimited exploitation of the earth as the sphere of raw materials and for the realistic utilization of the 'human material,' in the service of the unconditional empowering of the will to power" (GA 5: 257/Heidegger 1997: 101). That interpretation appears to overlook the cosmogonic and vitalist meaning of the Nietzschean concept of the will to power as well as the tragic vision embodied in it – a vision in which the world appears as

> a monster of energy, without beginning, without end . . . a sea of forces flowing and rushing together . . . out of the stillest, most rigid, coldest forms toward the hottest, most turbulent, most contradictory, and then again returning to the simple out of this abundance, out of the play of contradictions back to the joy of concord, still affirming itself in this uniformity of its courses and its years, blessing itself as that which must return eternally . . . my *Dionysian* world of the eternally self-creating, the eternally self-destroying. (Nietzsche 1967: section 1067)

There is, however, no doubt of the profound seriousness with which Heidegger reads Nietzsche as the philosopher of modern technology. As such, Nietzsche is for him the first to raise the question: "Is man as he has been and still is, prepared to assume that dominion? If not, then what must happen to man as he is, so that he can make the earth 'subject' to himself" (GA 8: 61/57). Heidegger's critical reflection on Nietzsche's "technological" philosophy turns, thus, into a critique of the whole modern and Western mode of thinking. Insofar as actually existing National Socialism (together with other current political and cultural conceptions) was a product of this form of thinking, the critique of Nietzsche could thereby serve him at the same time as an implicit critique of this whole modern syndrome of ideas. As a genuine and original thinker, Nietzsche gives for Heidegger expression to the way being manifests itself in the modern age. Nietzsche is for him, in fact, both a diagnostic and a symptomatic thinker. He reveals the nihilistic condition of modern, technological man and shows how the history of metaphysics from Plato onwards leads inevitably to a now imminent *denouement*. At the same time, however, he also exemplifies what he analyzes. Heidegger concludes his examination of Nietzsche in 1951 appropriately enough with a quotation from Aristotle: "Just as it is with bats' eyes in respect of daylight, so it is with our mental vision in respect of those things which are by nature most apparent." What is in this way most apparent, Heidegger adds, is "the presence of all that is present" (GA 8: 113/110). Nietzsche was a thinker who saw more clearly than most of us "all that is present," for he thought what is now. But his eyes still did not penetrate far enough, glimpsing, perhaps, only occasionally and with difficulty what is there to be seen.

Conclusion

Heidegger's encounter with Nietzsche was profoundly personal in nature and motivated, on the one hand, by the internal dynamics of his thought and, on the other, by the needs of the historical moment. But precisely because it is all those things, we cannot simply take over his reading of Nietzsche. Neither Nietzsche nor Heidegger is, in fact, committed to the idea that there can be only one correct reading of a text, of a thinker, or an epoch. Every interpretation, as Heidegger reminds us, is a translation and thus a transition from our own initial place to another one and from there back again to our own. How we read, interpret, and translate something will therefore always depend on who we ourselves are and what shore we stand on or whether we have any shore to stand on (see Sluga 1997).

Heidegger's pointed reading of Nietzsche can in this way highlight other possibilities of doing so. Heidegger, we have seen, read Nietzsche in the direction of his own thought and that means in the face of the question of being. That question has been forgotten in our tradition. Metaphysical thought in the form that Nietzsche has given it can serve as the most eloquent witness of this forgetfulness. But the forgetfulness of being is, on Heidegger's view, not due to willful human choice; it is not the result of modern man's or Nietzsche's autonomous action. It is instead, as Heidegger sees it, that being itself has withdrawn from us. Heidegger's reading thus intends to make manifest the withdrawal of being in Nietzsche's thought and also how metaphysics in obscuring the question of being is at the same time forced to gesture toward it. In Nietzsche's doctrine of the eternal recurrence of the same the question manifests itself despite Nietzsche's contrary intentions. But if being has now withdrawn why should we not let being be being and turn our back on the question of being itself? Why can we not, in contrast to Heidegger, accept the fate of being and then read Nietzsche as facing away from the question of being? That would mean, first of all, to read him from the perspective of a "happy positivism" that Foucault has claimed for himself. Nietzsche would from this perspective still appear as the thinker who thinks what is now but we would see him facing the question what it means to be human directly and without the intent to reach out to the question of being. We would see his attempt to think what is now not as metaphysically but as genealogically motivated. In contrast to Heidegger, we would look at Nietzsche not as the last metaphysician but as the first genealogist. Such a reading would force us, moreover, to interpret the concept of the will to power in the opposite direction from the one that Heidegger followed. Heidegger explicated this formula in the direction of its first term; he understood will to power as will to will. This will to will expressed itself for him inevitably in the technological imperative of an endless will to more. Heidegger's critique of Nietzsche's doctrine of the will to power turns for this reason on a critique of the will on which he had been embarked since *Being and Time*. If we read Nietzsche's formula, however, in the opposite direction, we will seek to explain the will to power, instead, in the direction of power. Will to power will then come to mean to us as much as the power to power, that is, the power to have, manipulate, and, multiply power. Such a power, when considered genealogically, will prove not one thing but many. We will have to conclude that there is, strictly speaking, no such thing as power but only power relations. These will have different configurations and may manifest themselves in our time in the sturdy, non-metaphysical phenomena of biopower. In short, when we read Nietzsche in the direction away from Heidegger, we will encounter Foucault's reading of him. Heidegger's singular confrontation with Nietzsche may, thus, reveal as its sharpest alternative the use that Foucault has made of Nietzsche's thought.

To highlight this contrast is not, of course, to say that we have to choose between these two opposing appropriations. It means, rather, that we may have to pursue our own understanding of Nietzsche by working first through Heidegger's and then through Foucault's reading. In this undertaking we will have to note that Heidegger subjects Nietzsche to a more sustained critical examination than Foucault. Reading Nietzsche in Foucault's direction still leaves us, therefore, with the task of determining whether we can indeed construct a full genealogy of what is now in terms of the notion of power. That question will take us not only beyond Heidegger but also beyond Foucault. But in this undertaking we can certainly still learn from Heidegger. For he has shown us how deeply one must engage oneself, if one is to appropriate the thought of a productive thinker. Heidegger's sustained effort in exploring Nietzsche's work sets, in other words, a decisive standard for our own undertaking.[4]

Notes

1 Heidegger's characterization is taken from William Lovitt's "Introduction" to Heidegger (1977). For a discussion of "The Question Concerning Technology," see Sluga (2001a).
2 GA 6.1: 12–13. "*Erst der Einblick in den handschriftlichen Nachlaß gibt ein deutlicheres Bild.*" Krell's translation makes this misleadingly "an investigation of the posthumously published notes" as if Heidegger was still referring here to *The Will to Power* (Heidegger 1984: 15).
3 Krell's translation speaks misleadingly of an "overturning of Platonism" where Heidegger refers to an *Umdrehung des Platonismus* (Heidegger 1979: 200).
4 I am grateful to my colleague Hubert Dreyfus above all others for helping me to improve this chapter with his trenchant questions.

References and further reading

Becker, O. (1963) *Dasein und Dawesen*. Pfullingen: Neske.
Heidegger, M. (1971) *Poetry, Language, Thought* (trans. A. Hofstadter). New York: Harper & Row.
Heidegger, M. (1977) *The Question Concerning Technology and Other Essays* (trans. W. Lovitt). New York: Harper & Row.
Heidegger, M. (1979) *Nietzsche*, volume 1 (trans. D. F. Krell). San Francisco: Harper & Row.
Heidegger, M. (1982) *Nietzsche*, volume 3 (trans. D. F. Krell). San Francisco: Harper & Row.
Heidegger, M. (1984) *Nietzsche*, volume 2 (trans. D. F. Krell). San Francisco: Harper & Row.
Heidegger, M. (1990a) The self-assertion of the German university. In G. Neske and E. Kettering (eds.), *Martin Heidegger and Nation Socialism*. New York: Paragon House.
Heidegger, M. (1990b) The Spiegel interview. In G. Neske and E. Kettering (Eds.), *Martin Heidegger and National Socialism*. New York: Paragon House.
Jaspers, K. (1981) *Nietzsche. Einführung in das Verständnis seines Philosophierens*, 4th edn. Berlin: Walter de Gruyter.
Müller-Lauter, W. (2000) *Heidegger and Nietzsche. Nietzsche-Interpretationen III*. Berlin: Walter de Gruyter.
Nietzsche, F. (1967) *The Will to Power* (trans. W. Kaufmann). New York: Vintage.
Sluga, H. (1993) *Heidegger's Crisis. Philosophy and Politics in Nazi Germany*. Cambridge, MA: Harvard University Press.

119

Sluga, H. (1997) Homelessness and homecoming. Nietzsche, Heidegger, Hölderlin. In D. v. d. Meij (ed.), *India and Beyond. Essays in Honor of Frits Staal.* London: Kegan Paul International.

Sluga, H. (2001a) Heidegger and the critique of reason. In K. M. Baker and P. H. Reill (eds.), *What's Left of Enlightenment?* Stanford, CA: Stanford University Press.

Sluga, H. (2001b) "Conflict is the father of all things": Heidegger's polemical conception of politics. In R. Polt and G. Fried (eds.), *A Companion to Heidegger's Introduction to Metaphysics.* New Haven, CT: Yale University Press.

8

Heidegger and the Greeks

CAROL J. WHITE

Heidegger claims that, though the pre-Socratics originally glimpsed the role of being as the cultural ordering of what-is, this insight, and hence being itself, has sunk further and further into "oblivion" as the history of metaphysics has unfolded. The pre-Socratics grasped the relationship between the cultural practices and how things show themselves as well as the role of Time in the presencing of the being of what-is, but Heidegger's contribution to the history of being is the explicit recognition of what they only tacitly recognized (see Okrent, chapter 29, and Guignon, chapter 24, in this volume).

The reader should be forewarned that Heidegger's reflections assimilate a philosopher's thinking into his own view of the history of metaphysics. He does not attempt to give what we might regard as a "historically objective" analysis of their views. But, then, Heidegger's work brings into question the meaning of historical objectivity. Here I only try to trace his own vision, not argue with him about what a philosopher really meant.

The chapter starts with a discussion of the beginning of Dasein's history in ancient Greece, and then we examine Heidegger's account of the rise of metaphysical thinking with Anaximander. The third and fourth sections examine the contribution of Heraclitus and Parmenides to the discovery of the being of what-is. The last two sections of the chapter explore the new and fateful direction that metaphysical thought takes with the work of Plato and Aristotle.

The Primordial Beginning

In Heidegger's view, what made the Greeks special was that they themselves recognized the distinctive estrangement that sets humankind apart from all other beings. Sophocles in "Antigone" says that, of all the strange things in the world, nothing surpasses man in strangeness (EM 112/146; parallel citations to EM refer to Heidegger 1959). As he who "breaks out and breaks up," man breaks into an environment in which birds and fish, bull and stallion, earth and sea live in their own rhythm and precinct. However, "into this life . . . man casts his snares and nets; he snatches the living creatures out of their order, shuts them up in his pens and enclosures, and forces them under his yokes" (EM 118/154). This breaking-up opens what-is as sea, as earth, as animal, and, more generally, as the being of what-is. Sophocles also noted, Heidegger claims, that the "sweep of time" both lets what-is emerge into the open and conceals what once appeared (GA 54: 209).

The Greeks were not the first people to domesticate animals or plant crops, of course, but Heidegger's account suggests that they may have been the first to tell themselves that the way they did this made them distinct from other creatures.[1] And, more importantly, to tell themselves what things must be that they could use them so. Heidegger does not think that the questioning of being only begins with those thinkers whom we regard as the first philosophers. His credit to Sophocles shows that. For him, thinking about what-is does not even have to be expressed in propositions or formed into an explicit system (GA 9: 241/185). An answer to the question of "what it is to be" can be posed, for example, in art without expression in propositions or in poetry without articulation in an explicit system. Indeed, besides artists, poets, and thinkers, Heidegger also mentions statesmen as among those who pose an answer to the question of being (EM 47/62), perhaps thinking of Solon and Lycurgus or even Hitler.

In fact, Heidegger thinks of artwork in terms of letting the being of what-is appear, or, as Heidegger would say, unconceal itself. The Greek tragedies both articulate and critically alter the dying Homeric world and usher in a new order. The light cast by the creator's insight lets The "gods and the state, the temple and the tragedy, the games and philosophy," the works which were wrought to tell the Greeks who they were, bring things into focus (EM 80/105ff; see Dreyfus, chapter 25 in this volume).

What prepares the ground for Dasein's fateful insight, what sets up the world in which Dasein finds itself, is being. For Heidegger, the world-building accomplished in a work of art such as the temple is not the invention of human beings but of being revealing itself in human activity and through the insight of authentic Dasein (see GA 5: 28ff/Heidegger 1971: 42ff). Human beings gain their outlook on themselves and what-is in general when being is revealed in a new way through the temple. However, the builders of the temple were responding to the culture's practices: its traditional stories of the gods, its understanding of how to approach them, its dealings with animals and plants dear to the gods, and so forth. Human beings only come to understand their outlook on themselves when it becomes articulated by and focused in a work like the temple.

Perhaps the first written question and answer to being occurs in the poetry attributed to Homer, though not in so many words and certainly not in propositions. Heidegger invokes a passage from Homer to show that this poet reflected on "*ta onta*," or what-is (*to on*) regarded as a plurality of different things. Homer mentions the ability of the seer Kalchas to see all that is, will be, or once was. Homer used the term "*ta eonta*" (the extra "e" is archaic) not just for things of nature but also "the Achaeans' encampment before Troy, the god's wrath, the plague's fury, funeral pyres, the perplexity of the leaders, and so on" (GA 5: 350/Heidegger 1975: 38). Perhaps such poetry inspired the philosophers to think explicitly about the being of what-is.

Anaximander and the Beginning of Metaphysics

Metaphysics is "the kind of thinking which thinks what-is as a whole in regard to being" (GA 15: 125/Heidegger 1993: 75). Unlike the insight manifest in a work of art such as the temple, metaphysical thinking articulates the order of what-is in words. Heidegger believes that the ancient Greeks were inspired to think about what-is as a whole which manifests a certain being not just by their language's copula verb but by the ambiguity of a single verbal term: the Greek word "*on*." As both participle and noun, this word "says 'being' in the sense of *to be* something-which-is; at the same time it names *something-which-is*. In the duality of the participial significance of *on* the distinction between 'to be' and 'what-is' lies concealed." Heidegger adds that what seems like grammatical hair-splitting is "the riddle of being" (GA 5: 344/Heidegger 1975: 32–3).

If metaphysics has its beginning in the emergence of the duality of being and what-is from "the self concealing ambiguity" of the term "*on*," then, Heidegger argues, metaphysics begins with the pre-Socratic thinkers (GA 5: 176/Heidegger 1970: 107). They were the first to think explicitly about the nature of everything with which they dealt. The emergence of the duality is the emergence of the "ontological difference" between being and what-is. However, the emergence of the difference between what-is and being does not guarantee that they emerge explicitly recognized as distinct. In fact, Heidegger says that at no time – presumably until he came along – has the distinction between what-is and being been designated as such. He argues that, from the beginning of thought about what-is, being has been forgotten and "the oblivion of being is the oblivion of the distinction between being and what-is." But, then, in what sense does such a distinction emerge with the pre-Socratic thinkers? Heidegger suggests that the two things distinguished, being and what-is, unconceal themselves but they do not do so as explicitly distinguished (GA 5: 364/Heidegger 1975: 50).

Thus, the original oblivion of the distinction between being and what-is is not the complete oblivion of being and what-is as such but the oblivion of the distinction between them. The early Greek thinkers thought about being insofar as they thought about the being of what-is which "unconcealed" itself to them. But they did not think explicitly about being itself or its relation to the things which show themselves as being in a certain way. Hence, they did not think explicitly about the distinction between being and what-is. For Heidegger, until the distinction between being and what-is is comprehended we have really understood neither being nor what-is, since they only appear "in virtue of the difference" (Heidegger 2002: 64, 131).

But, if the ontological difference was never explicitly recognized until Heidegger came along, if previous thinkers had never seen the connection between how things show themselves in the background practices and what we think about them, then what is the point in saying that this distinction has been "forgotten"? Heidegger thinks that the distinction, though not explicitly recognized as such, can "invade our experience . . . only if it has left a trace which remains preserved in the language to which being comes" (GA 5: 365/Heidegger 1975: 51). Heidegger funds this "trace" of the nature of the distinction in the language and thought of Anaximander, Heraclitus, and Parmenides. Though they did not realize the full nature of the difference, they did glimpse the dependence of what-is on the understanding of being that is embedded in the cultural practices. Heidegger thinks that they tried to articulate this relationship with their notions of *chreon*, *logos*, and *moira*.

For Heidegger the early Greek philosophers divide into three distinct groups: Thales, Anaximenes, et al.; Anaximander, Heraclitus, and Parmenides; and Plato and those

123

after him. Since Heidegger's views on other philosophers are frequently regarded as idiosyncratically bizarre, I will call upon a scholar of Greek philosophy to help to make one of Heidegger's basic points about these thinkers. Preparing for his discussion of Parmenides, Alexander Mourelatos remarks:

> At the dawn of philosophic speculation some bold spirits startled their contemporaries with direct pronouncements such as "It's all water" or "It's the opposites at war." It was an advance in self-conscious thinking when these sages were able to refer to what appears on the right-hand side of these intriguing identity statements as *phusis* or *aletheia*, or *to eon*. Both the practice of employing a concept, and the words referring to this employment, had come to be developed. The radical shift comes with Parmenides. (Mourelatos 1970: 216)

In a thinker such as Thales we can see someone grappling with the nature of what-is, yet he has not really distinguished the "it" from the water of which he says it is made. We take a step closer to metaphysical thinking with Anaximander, who asserts that what-is is ordered by necessity; but the more significant advance comes when Heraclitus and Parmenides identify what-is as some sort of whole, as *phusis* or *aletheia* or *to on*, which reveals itself as having some particular being. This, Heidegger thinks, is quite different from seeing things as made of the same "stuff."

Heidegger dismisses Thales and Anaximenes from the usual list of the first thinkers without much comment. Heidegger does suggest that Thales is the first thinker to answer the question of being by reference to a being (GA 24: 453). He says that "to be" is to be water. One might argue that claims such as "it's all water" or "it's all air" seem to assert something about material composition, and the "it" here is understood as a "totality" in the same way that water is conceived as a totality made up of all particular configurations of water from drops and puddles to lakes and oceans. The predicate then names the "stuff' thus totalized. But the metaphysical notion of "what-is as a whole" is not that of a cumulative mass, and its "being" is not its material composition. We might say that Heidegger regards Thales as offering, so to speak, an ontic theory of the nature of what-is, with Anaximander providing the first authentically ontological inquiry.

As the first ontological thinker, Anaximander points the way for the others to follow. Heidegger agrees with Mourelatos that a "radical shift" in Greek thinking occurs with Parmenides, but, for Heidegger, Parmenides is the second pivotal thinker after whom philosophy begins to move away from the original Greek insight into being and toward traditional metaphysics and the fateful model of knowledge. Anaximander gets metaphysics off the ground, but the thinkers after Parmenides give this grounding a different character.

Heidegger focuses on Anaximander's idea of *"to chreon"* or "necessity" as it is expressed in the one fragment of quotation which has come down to us from him. Things come into and pass out of existence "according to necessity," says Anaximander, "for they pay one another recompense and penalty for their injustice." The "they" which compensate one another according to necessity are, Heidegger tentatively suggests, *"ta onta"* or the multiplicity of what-is.[2] Anaximander's term *"to chreon"* is,

Heidegger argues, "the oldest name in which thinking brings the being of what-is to language" (GA 5: 363/Heidegger 1975: 49).

Homer may have thought about *ta onta*, but Anaximander is the first to name the being of what-is which *ta onta* have and to glimpse the context in which they have their place. "Necessity" is the name for that which unifies or makes a whole of everything that is, even though *ta onta* are still a multiplicity. Heidegger understands Anaximander's notion of *chreon* as, to use his terminology, a "gathering" which both "lights" and "shelters" what-is (GA 5: 369/Heidegger 1975: 55), making it what it is. Heidegger takes the notion to be expressing the original glimpse of being that is developed more explicitly in both Heraclitus and Parmenides. "Gathering" is the activity of the cultural background practices which let things show up in various ways in one unified clearing.

Heidegger insists that we must try to understand the significance of the Greek word for "necessity" in its historical, etymological context, In a rather dubious etymology, he suggests that the term *"chreon"* is connected with *"he cheir,"* which refers to the hand, and *"chrao,"* which means to "get involved with something" or "reach one's hand to something," as well as to "place in someone's hands" or "let something belong to someone." Hence, Heidegger proposes to translate *"to chreon"* into German as *"der Brauch,"* which means "usage" or "custom," relating the term to the verb *"brauchen,"* which means "to need," "to employ," "to engage." In his translation Heidegger is trying to capture the notion of a necessity that arises out of practical involvement and the demands of everyday activity (GA 5: 366/Heidegger 1975: 51–2), but also suggests that things solicit us, engage us, in this involvement. The "world" of *Being and Time* is the context of involvement which "necessarily" must be in order for things to "be," the world that Dasein does not create but enters in its engagement with the being of things.

We should not take this sense of "usage" as being purely pragmatic or implying that the order of things is dependent solely on what human beings want to do with them. Heidegger takes the word *"brauchen"* back to what he regards as its root-meaning: to enjoy, to be pleased with something and have it in use. To "use" is supposed to suggest letting something be involved in one's being-at-home in the world (GA 5: 357/Heidegger 1975: 53). Thus, the trees that surround one's house or the river that flows through the park are as much "useful" as one's shoes or hammer. Tying in Parmenides with Anaximander's *chreon*, Heidegger suggests that the root-meaning of Parmenides' *"chre"* indicates turning something to use by handling it but that this has always meant "a turning to the thing in hand according to its way of being, thus letting that way of being become manifest by the handling" (GA 8: 198). Tending grapes or grain, using leather for shoes or bronze for shields, involves letting these things be what they are. This is not simply a matter of our purposes, though in its modern evolution Dasein is tempted to think so.

To amplify his notion of usage Heidegger quotes some lines from Hölderlin's "The Ister River":

It is useful for the rocks to have shafts,
And for the earth, furrows.
It would be without welcome, without stay [*ohne Weile*].

Heidegger adds that without food or drink, without the crops sprouting from the furrows or the well-water bubbling from the shafts, there is no welcome for us, no "stay" or "lingering" in "the sense of dwelling at home [*Wohnens*]." He explains:

> "It is useful" says here: there is a way of being together of rock and shaft, of furrow and earth, within that realm of being which opens up when the earth becomes a habitation. The home and dwelling of mortals has its own site. But its situation is not determined first by the pathless places on earth. It is marked out and opened up by something of another order. From there, the dwelling of mortals receives its measure. (GA 8: 194)

We, as Dasein, have an understanding of this being which is manifested most primordially in our everyday dealings with things such as, in this period, finding wells and plowing the land. But we do not create being. It reveals itself to us through what-is. That a piece of land is fertile or water potable is a matter of their being, not just ours, although they show up as such only in a context of concern.

In his discussion of Homer and Anaximander, both of whom he considers to be articulating the distinctively Greek understanding of being, Heidegger extracts their understanding of what-is. He says that the Greeks equate what-is with (a) what we are "at home with" in our everyday dealings, and (b) what-is-present (*das Anwesende*). These senses are mingled in the term that Heidegger considers to be the Greeks' most precise name for what-is: "*ta pareonta*." He suggests that the prefix "*par*" shares a meaning with the German preposition "*bei*," indicating "at" or "near" as well as "during" or "while." "*Bei*" also means "at the home of," similar to the French "*chez*." This supposed connotation is especially appropriate since the *pareonta* are, Heidegger says, the things which we come across in the "neighborhood" of unconcealment, that is, our familiar territory (*Gegend*) (GA 5: 346/Heidegger 1975: 34). Thus, Heidegger believes that the Greeks originally thought about the being of what-is primarily with regard to the objects of their everyday concerns such as tools, crops, furnishings, the earth, and the sky. This orientation toward the ready-to-hand is supposed to mark a clear break with myth and magic.

At least from the time of Homer and renewed contact with Eastern cultures, the Greeks did have a sense of the distinctiveness of Greek life and the unique social and political order that made their world a whole. Heidegger claims that the early Greek thinkers understood the importance of this cultural ordering as the condition for things to come forth and show themselves as what they are. In this realm Anaximander's *ta onta* make their presence known: "Anaximander's *chreon*, as the being of what-is, is not a 'something' which stands 'behind' or within separate objects but rather is that which 'gathers' things into a neighborhood." Heidegger also finds in the early Greek thinkers traces of the Temporal significance of presence, the second point above. He comments: "The Greeks experience what-is as what-is-present, whether at the present time or not, presenting in unconcealment" (GA 5: 349/Heidegger 1975: 36–7). For Homer and Anaximander, *ta onta* referred to what is past and what is to come, as well as what is present at some here and now. "Both are ways of presencing, that is, the presenting of what is not presently present" (GA 5: 346/Heidegger 1975: 34). The seer Kalchas, understanding the being of what-is, comprehends what was, is, and will be. Anaximander, according to the traditional version of his fragment, thinks that things come to be and pass away "according to necessity." *Ta onta* pay each other compensation for "injustice" according to the "dominion of time" (GA 5: 341/Heidegger 1975: 29–30).

Thus, Heidegger argues that the locus of reality for the early Greek metaphysical thinkers was their here and now. What is past was present once; what will be becomes present later. They shift from a mythological orientation in which the "really real" existed at some indeterminate "once upon a time" and "once at a place" to an understanding of being according to which even the gods manifest themselves at some here and now, as on the battlefield at Troy.

Heidegger also takes the early Greeks as having at least a glimpse of the way that the understanding of being is dependent upon the quite different sort of time in which we are "in time with" the temporality of being. His analysis of Anaximander's notion of *ta onta* "compensating" each other for their "disorder" according to the "dominion of time" draws on this idea (GA 5: 353–64/Heidegger 1975: 40–50). We will see the nature of this dominion more clearly once we have examined Heidegger's version of the thought of Heraclitus and Parmenides.

Heraclitus

According to Heidegger, Heraclitus' notion of *logos* involves a similar force of necessity which maintains the order of what-is. Heidegger himself takes this *logos* to be the *legein* which "lays out" the world as the context of significance in which things are dealt with in various ways. *Logos* should be understood as not language or reason but rather as the ordering of what-is by cultural practices. Indeed, Heidegger suggests that, if Heraclitus had explicitly recognized the relationship between language and the *logos*, the history of being would have gotten off to a very different start (GA 7: 220/Heidegger 1975: 77), perhaps one not so ignorant of its indebtedness. *Logos* lets what-is manifest itself as what it is, as, for rxample, chiseling let the stone show itself as a column or wine-making let the grapes show themselves as fermented juice.

Heraclitus says that the *logos* reveals that "all is one," that is, *"hen panta."* Making the next move in the history of being, Heraclitus does not just see *ta onta*, the multiplicity of what-is, but rather thinks there is a unity and oneness to what-is. He discovers *to on*, what-is as a totality. In spite of all the apparent diversity of things, there is a sameness to the multiplicity which makes them into a "one." But, Heidegger questions, what does the statement that everything is one mean? He warns us not to jump quickly to the conclusion that Heraclitus is offering "a formula that is in some way correct everywhere for all times" (GA 7: 211/Heidegger 1975: 69). That is, Heraclitus is not making, with universal and eternal intent, a particular metaphysical claim about what-is. He is not proposing the first traditional metaphysics comparable to the Platonic "being is *idea*" or the Aristotelian "being is *ousia*." Rather we could say that Heraclitus is making the first claim about the relationship between being and what-is. He is saying that, thanks to *logos*, what-is is revealed as having some common bond. He does not, however, specify "what" this common bond is, as if it were a common property. In the language of *Being and Time*, Heraclitus offers a glimpse of an existential analysis, not some one existentiell understanding of being.

127

Thus, Heraclitus' dictum only suggests that traditional metaphysics is possible. He is not making any specific claim about the character of the one – about the being of what-is – which is all things. He only describes what it accomplishes. As Heidegger puts the point: "The *hen panta* lets lie together before us in one presence, things which are usually separated from and opposed to one another, such as day and night, winter and summer, peace and war, waking and sleeping, Dionysos and Hades" (GA 7: 213/Heidegger 1975: 71). If everything is one, then even opposites are placed together in such a way that we can find some common bond gathering them.

Instead of trying to make Heraclitus' dictum into a formula of traditional meta-physics, Heidegger suggests that we should think of "*logos* as *legein* prior to all profound metaphysical interpretations, thereby thinking to establish seriously that *legein*, as the gathering letting-lie-before, can be nothing other than the essence of unification which assembles everything in the totality of simple presenting" (GA 7: 220/Heidegger 1975: 70). The things so assembled may exhibit a different unity at different times, and there-fore no "formula" describing their unity as a common property (as "*idea*" or "created by God" or "stuff to be dominated") will remain adequate at all places and times. Heidegger suggests that *legein*, in its letting-lie-together-before, means that "whatever lies before us involves us and therefore concerns us" (GA 7: 203/Heidegger 1975: 62). We are involved with and concerned about things in different ways in different periods of our history, and this difference lies behind the history of traditional metaphysics, that is, the history of the revelations of being.

Heidegger takes note of Heraclitus's use of the image of lightning to describe the context created by the way being unifies what-is: Heraclitus says both that *logos* steers all things through all things and that the thunderbolt steers all things. Heidegger's own notion of this cultural context as a "lightening" or "clearing" in which things show themselves plays on this same imagery. The *logos* lets everything be gath-ered into a unified totality, but our understanding of the character of this totality can be changed in a flash – a lightning flash of insight which casts new illumination on our world.

Heidegger thinks that Heraclitus indicates that he recognizes the ambiguous rela-tionship between being and what-is when he remarks that the one does not want and yet does want to be called Zeus. In order to make Heidegger's point clearer, we can compare the phrase "*hen panta*" ("all is one") to Heidegger's phrase "the being of what-is," which itself refers to the unity of all that is. If we understand "all is one" with the emphasis on the "one" as in the *being* of what-is, then we see the one as a manifesta-tion of *logos* and hence as "what lets what-is-present come to presencing." But then, Heidegger points out, "the *hen* is not itself something present among others" (GA 7: 215–16/Heidegger 1975: 73). All is one emphasizes the being of what-is, that is, it is the *logos* or cultural practices which gather things into what they are. And then the one is not willing to be called Zeus because it is not a thing at all but rather that which lets everything, including things like gods, be present in the clearing and show them-selves as what they are.

On the other hand, Heidegger continues, "if the *hen* is not apprehended from itself as the *logos*, it appears rather as *panta*; then and only then does the totality of what is present show itself under the direction of the highest present thing, as one whole under this one" (GA 7: 216/Heidegger 1975: 74). Then, Heidegger says, this one, now under-stood as the highest one of *all*, and similarly as the highest being of *what-is*, is willing to be called "Zeus." Under this aspect, Zeus becomes one among the all or something-which-is, and he executes the one's "dispensation of destiny" (GA 7: 216/Heidegger 1975: 73). Zeus is regarded as a particular something-which-is and the moving force of the history of being.

Heidegger thinks that the same sort of fruitful ambiguity between being and what-is, the ambiguity of *on* and of the one as Zeus, arises in Heraclitus' comment that "*phusis* loves to hide." Heraclitus evidently conceives of *phusis* both as a characteriza-tion of the *logos* and as what-is. Thus *phusis* is both the activity which lets what-is man-ifest itself and that which is manifest. As the activity of manifesting, it itself does not show itself, and thus it hides; but this activity reveals *phusis* as "nature," as the being of what-is. This way of being, however, is hidden from those who, unlike Heraclitus, do not understand that everything is one, and so only see a scattering of things with each one different from the others. It is hidden from those who live in the Anyone but not from those who are authentically Dasein and can see things through the eyes of Heraclitus.

Heidegger provides his own definition of *phusis*, which becomes one of his favorite terms to capture his notion of being. He says of *phusis*: "It denotes self-blossoming emer-gence (*das von sich Aufgehende*) (e.g., the blossoming of a rose), opening-up, unfolding, that which manifests itself in such unfolding and preserves and endures in it; in short the realm of things that emerge and linger on" (EM 11/14). Notice that this realm includes two distinct aspects: the self-blossoming emergence (being) and that which manifests itself in such unfolding (what-is). In Heraclitus the relationship between these two aspects has not been forgotten. Hence, in his use of the term, "*phusis*" indi-cates the same sort of ambiguity as the two-faceted "*on*."

Parmenides

Parmenides takes the next step in the history of being. Connecting him with the first thinker to name the being of what-is, Heidegger claims that the essence of Parmenides' notion of "*moira*" or "fate" is intimated in Anaximander's conception of *chreon*. Chreon is "the first and most thoughtful interpretation of what the Greeks experienced in the name *moira* as the dispensing of portions" (GA 5: 369/Heidegger 1975: 55). We can support Heidegger's point about the development of metaphysics by noting the connection between "*chreon*" and the necessity referred to in Parmenides' famous dictum. Parmenides used a form of the same word, "*chre*," in saying, as the sentence is usually translated, "It is necessary to say and think what is." George Redard has explored the meaning of Parmenides' phase and shown that the core meaning of "*chre*" is that of adaptation or accommodation to the requirements of a given context.[3] Adding to this idea, Heidegger claims that the context is created by practical activities.

Heidegger also argues that Parmenides' notion of *moira* is similar to Heraclitus' notion of *logos* as a "letting-lie-before which gathers." Connecting Heraclitus and

Parmenides, Heidegger comments that "in the beginning of its history being opens itself out as emerging (*phusis*) and unconcealment (*aletheia*)." (EP 4/403). While translated as "truth," another one of Heidegger's favorite terms to describe the activity of being, "*aletheia*" or "unconcealedness" etymologically indicates the opposite of oblivion. To Heidegger it suggests the same sort of revealing, of un-concealing, as *phusis*. Just as Heraclitus called what-is "*phusis*," Parmenides equates what-is with *aletheia*. But, unlike his predecessors, Parmenides speaks not of *ta onta* or *hen panta* but of *to on*. The many have become one. And an important new factor also enters in: a special sort of apprehension or *noein* is recognized as the distinctive way of grasping this oneness as the being of what-is.

Referring to one of Parmenides' key themes, Heidegger indicates that he takes Parmenides' notion of *to on* as remaining within the fruitful ambiguity of the *on*. He says:

> In its ambiguity, *on* designates both what is present and the presencing. It designates both at once and neither as such. In keeping with this essential ambiguity of *on*, the *doxa* of *eonta*, that is, of *eonta*, belongs together with the *noein* of the *einai* that is, the *eon*. What *noein* perceives is not truly what-is as against mere semblance. Rather *doxa* perceives directly what-is-present but does not perceive its presencing. This presencing is perceived by *noein*. (GA 5: 176/Heidegger 1970: 107)

Parmenides distinguishes two paths to the understanding of what-is: the way of *doxa* or opinion and the way of *noein* or apprehension. A third path cannot be traversed by mortals (see GA 8: 179/175; EM: 84–7/110–14). Viewing the distinction from his own perspective, Heidegger suggests in the above quote that *doxa* perceives what-is-present in its multiplicity, that is, *doxa* perceives *ta onta*. In contrast, *noein* perceives the "to be" (*einai*) of what-is (*on*). Thus *noein* perceives the presencing or being of what-is as a totality, *noein* is the Parmenidean equivalent of *Being and Time*'s moment of insight or, more exactly, of our special capacity as Dasein which enables us to have this insight.

Heidegger thinks that Parmenides, unlike his successor Plato, does not separate the appearance of the multiplicity of *ta onta* from its being as if separating the illusory – the mere semblance or appearance from what truly is – the *on* as unified. Rather, as Heidegger says in the quotation above, Parmenides thinks that *noein* perceives the "to be" *in* what-is-present. We are supposed to group Parmenides with the thinkers of the first beginning of metaphysics who adhered to the ambiguity of *on*. He belongs with them rather than with the thinkers in the history of traditional metaphysics who, like Plato, divided what-is into two distinct realms, one the realm of the illusory and the other the realm of what truly is, with the latter as the locus for whatever being the former was able to manifest even through its illusory appearances (GA 5: 176/Heidegger 1970: 107). Of course, the illusory realm for Plato turns out to be the world of our everyday life.

But, then, precisely what is the distinction which Heidegger thinks Parmenides is making between *doxa* and *noein*? By the time of Plato, *doxa* has become "mere opinion," suggesting a belief which is imagined or supposed but perhaps wrongly so. It is the epistemological relationship that one has to the illusory, sensible world when one mistakenly attributes to it a reality it does not possess. However, Homer and Pindar both use the word to mean simply expectation, opinion, or judgment without any negative impli-cation as to its truth or reliability. Heidegger's above quoted comments about *doxa* strongly tempt one to relate his notion of Parmenides' *doxa* to his own notion of the Anyone, although, as far as I know, Heidegger never explicitly makes such a connec-tion. In his essay on Parmenides, he does say: "Mortals accept (*dechesthai, doxa*) what-ever is immediately, abruptly, and first of all offered to them. They never concern themselves about preparing a path of thought. They never expressly hear the call of the disclosure of the duality" (GA 7: 245–6/Heidegger 1975: 99). *Doxa* simply accepts the things that present themselves, without further thought as to their being, as does the person who lives comfortably in the Anyone.

Mortals, as Heidegger here calls those who are inauthentically Dasein, are absorbed in dealing with the things that show themselves, and, failing to "run before" their death, they never become a forerunner of a new revelation of being. Although the point may seem far-fetched, perhaps it is no coincidence that one descriptive term Heidegger uses in *Being and Time* for the authentic future ecstasis of timeliness is etymologically similar to Parmenides' term when he says that no mortal will be able to "outstrip" ("*par-elassei*," meaning "to drive by" or "to overtake") he who grasps the path to well rounded *aletheia*. The "outermost" or "most extreme" possibility that Dasein "foreruns" in authentically being toward death cannot be outstripped.

Correlatively, *noein*, like being authentically Dasein, involves a "choice" of being. As Heidegger says, "apprehension is no mere process but rather a decision" (EM: 128/167). As we saw in the discussion of resoluteness such a decision is not a matter of a particular person's judgment or choice within the realm of the Anyone, but rather is the decision made from Dasein's ownmost self which brings about a "separation" in "being, unconcealment, appearance, and non-being" (EM: 84/110). In other words, as we saw in the ird section of this chapter, the decision involves taking a stance toward the question of what it is to be. Interestingly enough, Mourelatos suggests that "Parmenides emphasizes that what-is has been gathered apart as a result of a *krisis*, a 'decision' or 'separation.'" Significantly for Heidegger's case, he adds that Parmenides also thinks that what-is "abides *kath' auto*, 'by itself'" (Mourelatos 1970: 135).

At least Parmenides, unlike Plato, recognizes that a "decision" founds the under-standing of being. He thinks that an insight into the being of what-is must be achieved. But this decision is not *ad hoc* or arbitrary or even a matter of "free will." It is an insight into the way being reveals itself and thus into the way what-is abides "by itself." However, the cultural practices revealing being are not independent of the sort of "deci-sion" of which Heidegger speaks. The being of what-is can be both a matter of decision and abide by itself because of the curious, ambiguous relation between being and Dasein, the "there" in which being is revealed.

In discussing Parmenides, Heidegger analyzes this curious relationship as that between *legein* and *noein*. Heidegger describes "*noein*" as a "taking-to-heart" or "taking-heed" of what shows itself in *legein*, the "letting-lie-before-us." He comments: "*noein* whose belonging together with *eon* we should like to contemplate, is grounded in and comes to be from *legein*. In *legein* the letting-lie-before of what-is-present in its pres-encing happens. Only as thus laying-before can what-is-present as such admit the *noein*, the taking-heed-of" (GA 7: 235/Heidegger 1975: 89). The "laying-before" of the cul-tural practices grants the insight into being, and therefore the insight is not arbitrary.

131

To use again a much later example, Descartes and Galileo did not just dream up the idea that everything is capable of mathematical treatment; they were responding to the way things were beginning to reveal themselves in the culture. In apprehension "we gather and focus ourselves on what lies before us" (GA 8: 212/209).

Conversely, apprehension also has an effect on the cultural practices. In *What Is Called Thinking?* Heidegger addresses the intertwined nature of the relationship:

> *Legein* is prior to *noein* and not only because it has to be accomplished first in order that *noein* may find something it can take to heart. Rather *legein* also surpasses *noein* in that it once again gathers, and keeps and safeguards in the gathering, that of which *noein* takes heed; for *legein*, being a laying, is also *legere*, that is, reading. . . . Thus *legein* and *noein* are coordinated not only in series, first *legein* and then *noein*, but each enters into the other. (GA 8: 211–12/208)

Noein's insight into what-is gives cultural practices sense and order, like arranging letters to make words, but Heidegger also is saying that in turn *legein* reads *noein*.

In the rest of the passage above Heidegger suggests that reading involves a gathering or gleaning of the sense that the letters of words give to us. *Legein* responds to the sense-giving activity of apprehension by "reading" the letters that *noein* arranges. Cultural practices respond to the focused articulation that occurs when Dasein apprehends the being of what-is, and, indeed, this is the crucial impetus for the history of being. Thus, *legein* and *noein* "enter into each other" because they engage in a mutually effective dialogue, *legein* abides "by itself' and makes the apprehension of the being of what-is possible, but it also responds to the choice of a possible way to be involved in the insight into being. Consequently, the insight into being found in great philosophers, artists, poets, and statesmen leads to cultural changes which in turn lead to new insights.

This dialogue can be seen from the very beginning of thought about what-is: drawing on comments by Herodotus, Gregory Nagy points out that "the Greeks owed the systemization of their gods – we may say, of their universe – to two poets, Homer and Hesiod." The poets had to try to respond to and unify diverse city rituals in which a god with the same name may appear to have radically different characteristics. Their poetry brought about a similar pan-Hellenic pantheon and encoded "a value system common to all Greeks" (Nagy 1982: 43, see also 46–9).[4] The articulation brought the values into focus in a way that not only united the Greek culture but opened these values up to later questioning by the tragedians and philosophers and hence led to new insights.

The process of focusing and adapting, of reading and responding, indicates the Temporal character of being. In the language of Anaximander's insight, what-is pays "compensation" for its "injustice" according to the "dominion of time." Focusing on one manifestation of the being of what-is to the neglect of others makes them assert themselves to receive their "due." Plato's *idea* left out the concrete reality of things, which subsequently demanded attention from Aristotle. To illustrate this idea we might also think of the way that the technological understanding of what-is as mere stuff to be dominated and manipulated for our purposes has provoked the "ecological" backlash, both in the realm of theory and in the reality of pollution.

Heidegger claims that one of Parmenides' famous maxims captures for the first time the essence of being human (EM: 126/165–6). As Heidegger translates the dictum, Parmenides says that "needful is the gathering setting-forth as well as the apprehension: what-is in its being" (EM: 85/111). The human essence understood as a demand to gather and to apprehend what-is in its being is, in fact, the human essence understood as Dasein. This human essence, Heidegger says, is the relation which first reveals being to people (EM: 130/170). Thus Parmenides is pictured as the thinker who first makes explicit both the role of Dasein as the site in which being reveals itself by gathering what-is and the task of humans as those who apprehend the being of what-is.

Heidegger invokes Parmenides' remark about the "untrembling heart of unconcealment" and suggests that this is "the place of stillness which gathers in itself what grants unconcealment to begin with. That is the opening of the open." He adds:

> We must think *aletheia*, unconcealment, as the opening which first grants being and thinking their presencing to and for each other. The quiet heart of the opening is the place of stillness from which alone the possibility of the belonging together of being and thinking, of presence and apprehending, can arise at all. (Heidegger 1969: 75/Heidegger 1972: 68)

That Parmenides should think about the being of what-is at all is then the "wonder of wonders" that launched the history of philosophy (GA 9: 307/234). Parmenides is not only the thinker who brings to fulfillment the first, essential beginning of metaphysics. He also positioned philosophy for an easy, downhill slide into the start of traditional metaphysics with Plato and Aristotle. Certainly this seems true given that tradition's own reading of Parmenides. Though Heidegger is trying to keep him grouped with his predecessors, his successors have given Parmenides' notion of the being which underlies the many the sort of interpretation that already places him on the downhill side of the slide, which Heidegger describes in the following passage:

> Since the gathering that reigns within being unites everything which is, an inevitable and continually more stubborn semblance arises from the contemplation of this gathering, namely the illusion that being (of what-is) is not only identical with the totality of what-is, but that, as identical, it is at the same time that which unifies and even is the highest-which-is. *For representational thinking everything becomes something-which-is.* (GA 7: 232/Heidegger 1975: 87)

The background context of being recedes into oblivion as the things looming large in the foreground blot it out. Parmenides' being was pictured as some sort of super-substance, the sum total of what-is, which does not change. In this view the changing things around us become illusory.

Heidegger maintains instead that, as with Heraclitus's one, Parmenides' being is the assembled "totality of simple presenting" which arises out of the unification of *legein*. However, thanks to this totalizing activity, Parmenides' being can also be regarded, as was Heraclitus' one, as the totality of what-is or some highest thing rather than the unity manifest by the activity of *legein*. Perhaps Parmenides himself invited this reading by emphasizing one term of the ontological ambiguity, focusing on *aletheia* as what-is rather than as being. Furthermore, *aletheia* is considered with regard to how *noein* grasps it, thus giving the disclosure of truth an orientation toward knowledge (GA 6.2: 202–3/Heidegger 1982: 170) rather than unconcealing.

Plato

While metaphysical thinking in general may begin with the emergence of the duality of what-is-present and its presencing in the pre-Socratic thinkers, Heidegger suggests that, if we think of metaphysics as making a division between a suprasensible and a sensible world with the former as what truly is and the latter as appearance, then metaphysics begins with Socrates and Plato.[5] However, he thinks that this "second start" of metaphysics is only a specifically oriented interpretation of the initial duality of the *on* (GA 8: 44/107), though it is one which endures, in one form or another, through Nietzsche. The slide into traditional metaphysics starts when the ambiguity of *on*, traced out by Anaximander, Heraclitus, and Parmenides, is "forgotten" by Plato. Then the ontological difference is "forgotten" as the difference between how we understand ourselves in being ourselves or understand a hammer when we are hammering and how we understand things reflectively as something-which-is.

The slide into traditional metaphysics begins because of the very nature of thinking. Heidegger argues that the Platonic emphasis on theory involves a "constructive violation of the facts" which rips the thing out of its context of significance and hence forgets being. When Heidegger emphatically asserts that "for representational thought everything becomes something which is," he is not simplistically arguing that thinking reifies everything, turning what is not an object into one. The phrase "something-which-is" refers to universals as well as individuals, to properties, essences, processes, etc., as well as "things." All of these are "things" in the broadest sense of the word or something about which we say "is." Heidegger is arguing that metaphysical thinking by its nature tends to ignore the context of practical significance in which things have their being and to focus instead on the characteristics of that which shows itself in this context.

Plato's thinking is not yet representational thinking, which starts with Descartes, but it prepares the way to such thinking. For Heidegger representational thinking involves a split between subject and object. Plato conceives of what-is as something constant and permanent, thus placing it beyond the influence of human decision and activity, but he does not conceive of it as "object," that is, something set over against the human subject. Heidegger argues that both Plato and Aristotle think of what-is as "the constant" or that which stands on its own and endures. However, he adds that "we would certainly not be thinking like the Greeks if we were to conceive of the constant as that which 'stands *over against*' in the sense of the objective" (GA 9: 246/188).[6] In objectification we understand our relationship to what-is as mastery or dominion, but the Greeks, including Plato and Aristotle, remain in touch with the idea that it is *phusis* which has dominion over what-is, not human beings.

Heidegger examines Plato's allegory of the cave looking for the "unspoken event" "whereby *idea* gains dominance over *aletheia*" (GA 9: 230/176). In his essay "Plato's Doctrine of Truth," Heidegger originally argued that Plato identifies unhiddenness with the self manifestation of the *idea*, and, in doing so, introduces a new concept of the nature of *aletheia* as truth. The "unhiddenness" of earlier thinkers changes to correspondence or correctness. In later remarks Heidegger will not specifically blame Plato for this move, but he still thinks that the distinction between the two ways of viewing truth is fundamental. He acknowledges that no dramatic change takes place in the concept of truth or the notion of *aletheia* and that even from the time of Homer truth was regarded as a matter of correctness, that is, *orthotes*, rather than unhiddenness. However, as he did in *Being and Time*, Heidegger still argues that unhiddenness is the primordial phenomenon (Heidegger 1969: 77ff/Heidegger 1972: 70ff). Truth appears as correctness because we take what-is as what-is present-at-hand, disengaging ourselves from active involvement with it and contemplating its nature.[7]

Plato thinks of the being of what-is as *idea*; what is really real about something is the essence that it imperfectly manifests as an item of the sensible world. Indeed, the *idea* is truly what-is, and the items of the world are a cross between what-is and *me on* or non-being. Heidegger argues that for Plato the being of a thing is not just its outward appearance or *eidos* since it itself is not ultimately real. Istead it is the *idea* that shows itself, however imperfectly, through this appearance.[8] The *idea* is also what lets many things manifest the same outward appearance, thus grouping them into natural kinds. The *idea* lets things be present as what they always are, e.g. dog, cat, table, chair, and therefore Heidegger says that Plato identifies the presenting of being with the "what-being" ("*Was-sein*") of what-is (GA 9: 225/173).

The allegory of the cave represents the ideas by the things which are manifest in the daylight outside the cave, and the sun itself is taken to be the symbol of that which makes all ideas manifest, the "idea of the Good." Heidegger describes the sun as "the 'image' for the Idea of all ideas" (GA 9: 215/165), He seems to identify the Good with the possibility of essence, not in some abstract sense of possibility but as what gives reality its organization into essences (see GA 9: 230/176–7). And once again he tries to connect a thinker's notion of the necessary organization of reality with the notion of use. Heidegger comments: "in Greek thought *to agathon* [the good] means that which is of use to something and which makes something useful" (GA 9: 227/174). Hence, the idea of the Good lets the ideas be useful.

Although Heidegger himself does not pursue the question of the nature of this usefulness in his essay on Plato, we might consider whether it is similar to Anaximander's *to chreon*. It seems that for Plato the ideas are useful for knowing the world, for having correct understanding of what things are, rather than for handling them or putting them to practical use. This would confirm the claim that truth as correspondence or correctness of apprehension and declaration (GA 9: 231/177) is more fundamental than truth as the unhiddenness which lets us be at home with things in everyday life. Heidegger comments that the idea of the Good makes knowing, the knower, knowledge, and what-is as what-is possible; and the term that he uses suggests the knowing of "knowing that" rather than "knowing how" (*Erkennen*) (GA 6.2: 200/Heidegger 1982: 168). We know that the thing is a hammer rather than knowing how to hammer.

True, Plato's notion of the correct knowledge of what things are may appeal to their use or function, but this is not the same as understanding how to use them. He does seem to take the human skill of *techne* as his model for the creation of the universe, but he pays attention to the craftsman's possession of an image of what he wants to create and not the practical skill involved in the actual creation. Things are created according to *ideas*, not "know how." The focus on function is especially inadequate when it comes to the question of what it is to be human, Parmenides' glimpse of the "essence" of human beings is lost when Plato compares the "function" of our soul to the function of eyes and pruning knives. Here we apparently have the first example of what Heidegger regards as our inevitable tendency to understand ourselves in terms of the objects we use.

To Heidegger Plato denigrates the everyday world in favor of the suprasensible realm of ideas; According to Plato, the ordinary man in the cave, which the vast majority of us are, does not realize that "what they take for the real might have the consistency of mere shadows" (GA 9: 215/165). Heidegger thinks, however, that the problem with Plato's thinking is not just that the being of what-is is characterized as *idea* and transferred to some realm beyond the everyday. As he puts it, "the crux of the matter is not that *phusis* should have become characterized as *idea* but that the *idea* should have become the sole and decisive interpretation of being" (EM: 139/182). Plato, unlike Parmenides, seems unaware that his interpretation is founded on a *krisis* or decision about being. Plato thinks that the structure of the reality which he apprehends is eternal, unchanging; and entirely independent of the activities of human beings. However, the metaphysics that begins with Socrates and Plato is not some final solution to the question of being but, Heidegger suggests, "merely a specifically oriented interpretation of that initial duality within the *on*" (GA 5: 177/Heidegger 1970: 107). This orientation is toward conceptual knowledge, toward knowing that things manifest certain essences, and not toward knowing how to deal with them. The former sort of knowledge can be acquired from a philosopher, the latter from a farmer, a cook, etc.

A second problem is reflected in the first: Plato identifies being with the being of what-is and understands this as a special sort of thing which is, the *idea*. He neglects to think of the ambiguity of the *on* which Heraclitus and Parmenides heeded, the unthought difference between understanding being and this way of understanding the being of what-is, between the revelation of being in the cultural practices and the conception of the nature of what-is which it makes possible, spurs on the traditional metaphysics which Plato inspires. Heidegger even comments that "this thoughtlessness can then constitute the essence of metaphysics." He adds: "As it remains unthought, so does the *logos* of the *on* remain without foundation. But this groundlessness is what gives ontology the power which is its essence" (GA 5: 177/Heidegger 1970: 108).

The *logos* has its "foundation" in cultural activities. However, if Plato's thinking grows out of the "oblivion" or "forgottenness" of being, this is not because of some simple "forgetfulness" or absent-mindedness on his part. Rather "the oblivion of being belongs to the self-concealing essence of being" (GA 5: 364/Heidegger 1975: 50). The background practices do not yield themselves up to explicit thought, or, if they do so, it is with difficulty and only against the background of other practices. At least Anaximander, Heraclitus, and Parmenides recognized the necessity of the practical articulation of reality. Plato neglects the background in his attempt to make explicit some unchanging, permanent structure of the foreground, that is, to make explicit the *idea* as the being of what-is.

But, then, in what way does being, as the *logos* which gathers and reveals, evoke the Platonic interpretation of what-is? We must remember that for Heidegger this view of reality was no arbitrary invention on Plato's part, no more than the discovery of mathematical conception of reality hundreds of years later by Descartes and Galileo. Being revealed itself in what-is as *idea*, and Plato apprehended this. Heidegger says that we must bear in mind that, "because being is in the beginning *phusis*, the emerging and disclosing power, it discloses itself as *eidos* and *idea*" (EM: 150/197). Plato did not arrive at his conclusion through some abstract philosophical exegesis; rather it is an insight into being resting on a decision. Arguments come later.

Insight into being involves a leap of thought that is not determined beforehand. The "essence of things" which, Heidegger says, first became a matter of thought with Plato (GA 7: 262/Heidegger 1975: 113), has remained a matter for thought in traditional metaphysics down to the time of Nietzsche. The nature of the essence changes from epoch to epoch and thinker to thinker. In the history of metaphysics being has revealed itself as the being of what-is in various ways: as, for example, *idea*, *ousia*, *actualitas*, *perceptio*, the transcendental making possible the objectivity of objects, the dialectical mediation of Absolute Spirit, the historical process of production, and the will to power, positing values. However, thanks to Plato, the quest of metaphysics remains the same. The effort of thought is devoted to discovering immutable structures in what-is. *Logos* is transformed into reason as the impression of those structures or speech as the expression of words; and *noein*, now contrasted with *doxa* as mere opinion, ceases to involve a leap of insight and becomes instead the source of propositional knowledge, that is, justified true belief.

Aristotle

Heidegger sees Aristotle's thinking as standing in an ambivalent relationship to that of his predecessors. Like Plato, Aristotle regards the "beingness" of what-is as something permanent and eternal. He said in Book VII of the *Metaphysics* that the question of the being of what-is is a question about the essence of a thing, and he predicted that it would always remain so. Yet, according to Heidegger, Aristotle thinks that the question of just what this "beingness" is remains everlasting, as Heidegger himself did (GA 8: 215/212). Heidegger thinks that Aristotle is "more Greek" than Plato because his thinking is closer to that of the pre-Socratics than is Plato's.

Heidegger suggests that "beingness" ("*Seiendheit*") is the only adequate translation of Aristotle's term "*ousia*," rather than "essence" or "substance." The latter terms suggest interpretations of *ousia* which are too much under the sway of Platonic or later Roman thought (GA 9: 259–60/199). Heidegger distinguishes two important elements in Aristotle's notion of *ousia*; an idea of constancy and, more important for the primordially Greek conception of being, an idea of becoming-present "in the sense of coming forth into the unhidden, placing itself into the open" (GA 9: 272/208). For Aristotle, Heidegger argues, the term "*phusis*" has the same two-faceted meaning as "*ousia*." It indicates both a coming-to-be into unhiddenness and the state of nature achieved in this process, thus corresponding to *ousia* in its aspects of both becoming-present and constancy. Furthermore, Aristotle seems to recognize a relationship

137

between these two sorts of *phusis* similar to that posed by the earlier Greeks. He claims that *phusis* in the sense of coming-to-be is the path to *phusis* in the sense of the nature reached (*Physics* 193 b 12). That which lets things show themselves as what they are lets them endure *as* what they are.

Unlike Plato, Aristotle regards the everyday things around us as having being-ness. He does not dismiss what we encounter in our daily lives as not fully real or real only in a shadowy sense. Heidegger suggests that Aristotle's term "*ousia*" still draws on its original, ordinary meaning of "house" and "home," "possessions" and "present holdings" (GA 9: 260/199). His notion of "presence" is supposed to capture the same meaning of familiar territory.[9] Things other than those from *phusis* also have their being on the basis of familiarity. Aristotle's thought at least hints that the *techne* which the craftsman follows in his production of objects is not some abstract knowledge of essences but a know-how and skill at dealing with everyday objects (GA 9: 251/192).

Werner Marx comments that "one of the great intellectual accomplishments in the history of philosophy is that Aristotle, unlike Plato, did not define moveable, transient being, *on gignomenon*, as non-being, as *me on*; rather he saw something intransient 'in' it, and thus 'saved' or 'delivered' the transient individual into the eternal actuality of being of a nonetheless moveable order" (Marx 1977: 29). Heidegger even finds a passage in Aristotle which allows him to connect this idea of the "moveable order" with his account of the early Greek notion of "*logos*," thus denying its "eternal actuality." Aristotle considers *morphe* or form to be the crucial element which gives "order" to *ousia*; it is contrasted with *hule* as the "order-able." He comments that *morphe* means "*to eidos* which is in accordance with *logos*" (GA 9: 275/210).

Heidegger's own interpretation of this sentence lets him suggest that for Aristotle, unlike Plato, the *eidos* is a manifestation not of some immutable order independent of human activity but rather of an order articulated by *legein*. Juxtaposing Aristotle's view with Plato's notion that the *eidos* was idea, Heidegger remarks: "But Plato, over-whelmed as it were by the essence of *eidos*, understood it in turn as something inde-pendently present and therefore as something common (*koinon*) to the individual 'what-is' that 'stands in such an appearance'" (GA 9: 275/210). Aristotle, in Heidegger's interpretation, does not think that the *eidos* stands on its own; it has its grounding in the *logos*.

Aristotle also speaks of the being of what-is as "*energeia*." This being is evidently found both in things which have their "origin and ordering" from *phusis* and in those which have this from *techne*. Both something brought into unhiddenness by its own self production and something unhidden through human production are "*ergon*" or "work." The character of the presence of a work is, Heidegger says, that which occurs in "production" in a distinctively Greek sense. This sense is supposed to be captured by Aristotle's notion of *energeia* in that it suggests an activity or "energy" apparent in being "at work" or involved (see GA 5: 370/Heidegger 1975: 56).

The epoch of Greek thought comes to an end with the translation of Greek notions into Latin terminology and into the Roman understanding of being. Then a different sense of production begins to reign, one which suggests that the human task is to dom-inate and control what-is. The fateful translation of terms indicated a change in the understanding of being. The active, involved *energeia* becomes "*actualitas*," just brute factuality, and the understanding of the being of what-is as actuality will in turn become the notion that reality is "objectivity" (GA 5: 317/Heidegger 1975: 56). The understanding of the being of what-is is set on a path where thinking will find itself "set off against being in such a way the being is placed before it and consequently stands opposed to it as object" (EM: 89/116).

Notes

1 For example, in "Antigone" Sophocles cites the accomplishments of humankind. We plow the earth, snare light-gliding birds, hunt the beasts of the wilderness and the native creatures of the sea. We yoke "the hirsute neck of the stallion and the undaunted bull." We have the courage to rule over cities, and we build shelter to "flee from exposure to the arrows of unpropitious weather and frost." Heidegger quotes the relevant lines in EM (112–13/147).

2 Heidegger admits that the term "*ta onta*" may not be Anaximander's own word, but he seems to end up saying it ought to have been (see GA 5: 340–2, 353/Heidegger 1975: 28–31, 40). Most scholars take this term to be referring back to "the opposites," but, as mentioned in note 1, Heidegger seems to ignore this aspect of Anaximander's view. Eric Havelock indirectly casts doubt on Heidegger's prescription (see Robb 1983: 63).

3 See Mourelatos (1970: 277). This confirmation of Heidegger's interpretation is especially interesting since Heidegger's etymological support for his claims is also frequently regarded as idiosyncratically bizarre.

4 I am indebted to John Hamilton, SJ, for this reference.

5 In such comments Heidegger seems to regard "Socrates and Plato" as one thinker, and the emphasis is on Plato's contribution. However, in *What Is Called Thinking*, Heidegger suggests that Socrates is a thinker after his own heart: Socrates does not give an answer to the question of being or propose any metaphysics but insists on the questionableness of being (GA 8: 20/17).

6 Heidegger's word play between "*das Ständige*" ("the constant") and "*Gegen-ständige*" ("the objective") is lost in English. "*Gegen-ständige*" suggests a "standing over against," which is the meaning at stake here.

7 For criticism of Heidegger's original analysis of Plato's notion of *aletheia*, see Friedländer (1964: 221–9) and the reply in Nwodo (1979). See also Kahn (2003: 363–6).

8 Unlike Plato, Heidegger makes a distinction between *eidos* and *idea*, perhaps emphasizing the slide from the ordinary use of the former to the technical use of the latter.

9 In ordinary language Heidegger's term *Anwesen* means "real estate" or "premises."

References and further reading

Friedländer, P. (1964) *Plato: An Introduction* (trans. H. Meyerhoff). New York: Harper & Row.

Heidegger, M. (1959) *Introduction to Metaphysics* (trans. R. Manheim). New Haven, CT: Yale University Press.

Heidegger (1969) *Zur Sache des Denkens*. Tübingen: Niemeyer.

Heidegger, M. (1970) *Hegel's Concept of Experience* (trans. K. R. Dove). New York: Harper & Row.

Heidegger, M. (1971) *Poetry, Language, Thought* (trans. A. Hofstadter) New York: Harper & Row.

Heidegger, M. (1972) *On Time and Being* (trans. J. Stambaugh). New York: Harper & Row.

Heidegger, M. (1975) *Early Greek Thinking* (trans. D. F. Krell and F. A. Capuzzi). San Francisco: Harper & Row.

Heidegger, M. (1982) *Nietzsche*, Volume 4 (ed. D. F. Krell). San Francisco: Harper & Row.

Heidegger, M. (1993) *Heraclitus Seminar* (trans. C. H. Seibert). Evanston, IL: Northwestern University Press.

Heidegger, M. (2002) *Identity and Difference* (trans. J. Stambaugh). Chicago: University of Chicago Press.

Kahn, C. (2003) *The Verb Be in Ancient Greek*. New York: Hackett.

Marx, W. (1977) *Introduction to Aristotle's Theory of Being as Being* (trans. R. Schine). The Hague: Martinus Nijhoff.

Mourelatos, A. P. D. (1970) *The Route of Parmenides*. New Haven, CT: Yale University Press.

Nagy, G. (1982) Hesiod. In T. J. Luce (ed.), *Ancient Writers*. New York: Scribner.

Nwodo, C. S. (1979) Friedlaender versus Heidegger: aletheia controversy. *Journal of the British Society for Phenomenology*, 10, 84–93.

Robb, K. (1983) *Language and Thought in Early Greek Philosophy*. La Salle, IL: Hegeler Institute.

9

Logic

STEPHAN KÄUFER

Introduction

As part of his phenomenology of human existence, Heidegger develops an interesting and substantial philosophy of logic. His basic thesis is: "Logic grounds in metaphysics and is itself nothing other than the metaphysics of truth" (GA 26: 132). However, it is hard to discern the details of this positive view behind his flashier and more infamous criticisms of logic. In his "What is Metaphysics?" lecture Heidegger says that "the idea of logic itself dissolves in a vortex of more originary questioning" (GA 9: 117). Mild interpreters reduce such polemics to the innocuous claim that he did not find studying logic useful as a preparation for philosophy. Harsher critics pin on him the claim that philosophical thought eschews the rules of logic, such as the law of non-contradiction. This harsh view is tantamount to rejecting Heidegger wholesale as a philosopher, and in fact Carnap, the first and most influential critic of Heidegger's anti-logical stance, recommends precisely this. Carnap compares Heidegger's metaphysics to lyrical and expressive uses of language; he says that Heidegger only turns to words because he lacks Beethoven's talent for music (Carnap 1959a: 78ff). This image of Heidegger as an a-logical, mystical wordsmith is inaccurate, though it appears to fit some of his flashier statements. So before I present Heidegger's positive philosophy of logic, I will first explain what he rails against when he seems to reject logic.

Logic in the Nineteenth Century

It is important to recall that logic changed substantially during the nineteenth century and the first few decades of the twentieth century. Today philosophers may argue technical points – for instance, whether identity or basic rules of arithmetic are part of logic – but by and large we all agree that logic is a family of formal languages that model argument and thought. We also mostly agree on the role logic plays in philosophy. It is a central discipline that establishes important results about the limits and possibilities of systems of inference. It is an important tool for other philosophical disciplines, such as metaphysics or epistemology, but by itself logic does not produce substantial claims about the nature of reality or the structure of knowledge. This current conception of logic is relatively recent. Mathematicians like Boole and Schröder developed parts of the formalism in the 1850s and Frege invented its current form in 1879. Peano and Russell introduced the most commonly used notation in the first decade of the twentieth century. Their invention did not become widely accepted by philosophers as *the* logic until the 1930s. In 1930 Carnap still had reason to complain that "the majority of philosophers have even now taken little cognizance of the new logic" (Carnap 1959b: 134) and he is right to point out that philosophers on the continent were slower to adopt it than their British colleagues.

After Kant, German philosophy of logic was gripped by a debate that made advances in formal logic seem all but irrelevant. Simplifying a bit we can say that philosophers debated the *nature* of logic, while they took much of the *content* of logic as having been established once and for all by Aristotle. They hardly tinkered with the ancient list of syllogistic forms and blithely ignored Frege's revolutionary new way of modeling inferences. Instead they fervently debated whether logical principles are metaphysical, epistemological, or psychological. These questions arose because Kant had invented transcendental logic, a system of *a priori* principles that govern the appearance of things that humans can encounter in experience. Kant himself took pains to distinguish his transcendental logic from "general logic," by which he means Aristotle's syllogistic. But some of Kant's followers thought that this distinction made no sense. Hegel, for one, maintained that transcendental logic, fully understood, shows that the basic rules of logic are also the basic laws of reality and that logic therefore was metaphysics. Neo-Kantians of various stripes – including Friedrich Lange, Hermann Cohen, Wilhelm Windelband, and Heinrich Rickert – interpreted Kant's critical philosophy as the foundation of scientific epistemology. They argue that Kant's transcendental logic constitutes the necessary basis of scientific cognition, and neo-Kantian logic flowers into a *Wissenschaftslehre*, a theory of science that explains the basic concepts and principles of scientific knowledge. Logic, for them, is nothing other than the study of the most general relations that obtain among the most basic concepts of science. Pioneers of empirical psychology, led by Wilhelm Wundt, claimed that Kant had grounded the rules of logic in the psychological makeup of the subject, and that in doing so he had pointed the way to a scientific study of the subject that could express and demonstrate these rules. Wundt wrote a *Logik* that helped lay the foundation of a widespread psychologism that Frege, and later Husserl, took pains to refute.

Paradoxically, this busy re-examination of the nature of logic caused philosophers to overlook the technical advances of symbolic logic. Many thought that such technical progress was laudable, but not properly philosophical. Insofar as they knew of Frege's work at all, the neo-Kantian philosophers I mentioned above consider him a "mere" mathematician and distinguish his "logistics" from real, philosophical logic. Every standard logic book from Leibniz up to the 1930s, including Kant's logic lectures and the transcendental analytic of his *Critique of Pure Reason*, is divided into three parts: the doctrines of concepts, judgments, and inferences. Only the doctrine of inferences, which covers the syllogistic forms, resembles logic as we now know it. It is a symbolic, general survey of forms of reasoning and concluding. But the vast majority of philosophers of logic of the nineteenth century were far more interested in the former two parts of logic. In the doctrine of concepts philosophers tried to work out the interrelations among concepts that are so general that without them thought would be impossible: quantity, number, time, place, quality, subsumption, and so forth. Some even thought they could work out a complete and systematic hierarchy of such basic concepts that would succeed where Kant's table of categories failed. In the doctrine of judgments philosophers investigated various meanings of the copula "is," or the relation of grammatical and logical forms of sentences. They thought these questions were central to an analysis of truth, since sentences are the bearers of truth and falsity.

It is pretty clear, then, that the bulk of "logic" done in philosophy departments in Germany throughout the nineteenth century was concerned with topics that we today consider to be outside of logic, and that we perhaps think logic cannot possibly have anything to say about. What is the origin of thought? What is the relation between numbers and time? It seems equally clear that much of the nineteenth-century discussion of philosophical logic steers clear of the basic topics of contemporary logic, either because they are taken for granted or because they seem irrelevant to the exciting developments in post-Kantian transcendental philosophy. Indeed, "logic" in the field of nineteenth-century continental philosophy takes on a range of meanings from "metaphysics" to "theory of science," from "critical epistemology" to "first philosophy." And debates about the nature of logic were intertwined with competition to inherit the mantle of Kant and with it the future direction of German philosophy. Each new logic book staked a new claim in a century-long expansionist turf war among philosophical trends.

Consider the logical idealism of the Marburg school. In German philosophy, Hegel and his followers dominated the beginning third of the nineteenth century. The middle third saw a bevy of reactions to Hegel, mixed with rising naturalism and a revival of classical scholarship. The final third belonged to the neo-Kantians, a loose community of leading philosophers united by the aim to settle fundamental philosophical upheaval and bring systematic inquiry back to the field. "Back to Kant," they proclaimed. The Marburg school was one of the two major schools of this movement. They grouped around Hermann Cohen's brilliant 1871 book *Kant's Theorie der Erfahrung*, one of the few comprehensive interpretations of Kant's critical project. Cohen argues that the most important type of experience that critical philosophy analyzes is natural-scientific cognition. Transcendental philosophy, therefore, provides the epistemological basis for natural science. Cohen, followed by his younger colleague Paul Natorp and by his doctoral student Ernst Cassirer, developed this interpretation of Kant into a systematic epistemological project that aims to show how the objectivity of possible cognition is grounded in an *a priori* hierarchy of conceptual functions. Besides their epistemological interpretation of Kant and their orientation toward mathematical natural science, these authors are united in rejecting Kant's basic distinction between the two stems of cognition. The forms of sensibility, they argue, are grounded in acts of the understanding. Hence there is no need for a transcendental aesthetic, or a schematization of categories, only for a thorough analytic of concepts. Transcendental idealism turns into straightforward *logical* idealism, and Cohen can call his founding work of this systematic conception the *Logic of Pure Cognition*. Here the various strains that frame the debate about logic are clearly visible: an interpretation of Kant, a penchant for epistemology and natural science, and a systematic conception of philosophy come together as a "logic." Only, it is not so obvious what Cohen's logic book has in common with the subject as we understand it today.

Hermeneutic Phenomenology and the Critique of Logic

Carnap argues that Heidegger attacks the law on non-contradiction. We gain a better perspective on Heidegger's critique of logic once we see how deeply he is entrenched in these nineteenth-century debates about logic. He first studied philosophy under Heinrich Rickert, the most prominent neo-Kantian of the Southwest school. Heidegger's doctoral dissertation was a critical review of a number of psychologistic approaches to logic, and in 1912 he wrote a survey of contemporary works and problems in the philosophy of logic. He even tries his hand at solving some thorny dilemmas pertaining to the logical form of sentences such as "it rains" (GA 1: 186). At this point he professes that as a philosopher he is above all interested in logic. Heidegger did not simply change his mind between these youthful works and his mature philosophy of the *Being and Time* period. Rather, he realized that particular logical problems inevitably point back to a wider philosophical context and that one cannot be a logician without a commitment to a basic explanation of the structure of experience as a whole. *Pace* Carnap, with his critique of logic Heidegger is not rejecting ancient rules of inference and thought, but carving out a position in the massive tangle of views that tie into the central questions of philosophical logic.

The position Heidegger carves out is the hermeneutic phenomenology of everyday existence that he presents in *Being and Time*. Of course this important book contains much more than another philosophy of logic in the nineteenth-century style. But the key to understanding Heidegger's thought on logic is to see that the analysis of Dasein is *also* a philosophy of logic; it provides answers to all the questions the neo-Kantians debated fervently. The best way to see this, I think, is to take note of two very important moments in Heidegger's development of his *Being and Time* view in which he explicitly confronts the logical idealism of the Marburg school. They show that his analysis of Dasein and his criticisms of logic are two sides of the same coin.

The first of these moments comes in 1919, when the young *Privatdozent* Heidegger begins to lecture in philosophy. He had eagerly studied Husserl and found that phenomenological descriptions of experience were a promising starting point for philosophical analysis. In his *Logical Investigations*, Husserl analyzes many central concepts of philosophical logic – such as truth, judgment, content, representation, etc. – by showing that they are grounded in constitutive elements of ordinary experience. These analyses differ markedly from the traditional approach that focuses on pure conceptual derivations of basic concepts. Husserl's approach aims to make the full content of ordinary experience philosophically relevant. In his very first lecture course, Heidegger argues that for these reasons phenomenology is a more suitable analysis of human experience than the epistemological logic of the Marburg school. Phenomenology can account for the structure of *Erlebnis*, of "lived experience." By contrast, Cohen and Natorp thought philosophy should focus on analyzing scientific cognition; they abstract from ordinary experience in order to find a more pure expression of the content of their transcendental logic. As Heidegger notes about Natorp, his "systematic, panlogistic

144

basic orientation prevents him from any free access to the sphere of lived experience, to consciousness. . . . [He] has not exhausted all the possibilities and with his purely theoretical disposition, i.e. the absolutization of logic, cannot exhaust them" (GA 56/57: 108–9). This argument has far-reaching consequences for the debate about the nature of logic. In this early lecture course, Heidegger already suggests that the categories, which the Marburgers hold to be products of the spontaneity of the understanding, may be grounded in the pre-logical significance of ordinary experience. If so, logical idealism is false, and the epistemological approach to transcendental logic is at best derivative. It presumes an analysis of quotidian significance. The logical analysis of categories of thought must be grounded in the phenomenological analysis of Dasein.

The second moment of confrontation with the Marburg school comes around the time Heidegger writes *Being and Time*. Along with that book, Heidegger presents his own comprehensive interpretation of Kant's *Critique*. I have argued that Heidegger carves out a position in the ongoing debate surrounding philosophical logic and that this debate centered on readings of Kant. In order to position his view in the philosophical field, Heidegger needs to explain how his new existential phenomenology can handle the questions that a century of philosophy had raised about Kant's notion of transcendental logic. In several lecture courses and in his 1929 book *Kant and the Problem of Metaphysics*, Heidegger argues that *Being and Time* is not only compatible with Kant's transcendental idealism, but actually prefigured by it. In particular, Heidegger takes care to point out that Kant's analysis of the categories in the transcendental analytic shows them to be grounded in a pre-logical comportment toward the whole of entities. According to Heidegger, Kant points towards this proto-phenomenological view in the schematism chapter of the *Critique* and in his suggestion that the understanding is grounded in the transcendental imagination. However, unlike Heidegger, Kant was not able to make this point clearly or consistently, because he adhered to the strictures imposed by a traditional predilection for logic in metaphysics. Kant often goes back to affirming the priority of the understanding, against his own better insights. This unquestioned adherence to the primacy of the logical in constituting experience is already a fault in Kant, and it is only compounded by the Marburg school's logical idealism. Nevertheless Heidegger concludes that the *Critique* "shakes up the dominion of reason and the understanding. 'Logic' is deprived of its long evolved pre-eminence in metaphysics. Its idea becomes questionable" (GA 3: 243). Heidegger thinks that through the fog of a traditional, logic-dominated framework Kant has already shown that logic grounds in phenomenology.

Heidegger is not interested in motivating a mystical language that eschews basic commitments to consistency and conceptual rigor. With his critique of logic he partakes in the post-Kantian debate that seeks to place logic in the context of metaphysics, epistemology, and psychology. Heidegger's proposal is to ground logic in the phenomenological analysis of everyday existence and his criticisms of logic go hand in hand with his development of hermeneutic phenomenology. He thinks this approach has distinct advantages over logic-dominated metaphysics, such as the logical idealism of the Marburg school. In a 1934 lecture, Heidegger claims that for ten years the primary aim of his philosophy has been precisely "to shake logic from the ground up" (GA 38: 11).

145

It is interesting, but marginal, to note a rebellious rhetorical note in Heidegger's commentary on traditional logic. His criticisms of traditional logic are based on philosophical argument; but they mix with a fervor to develop a new kind of philosophy and leave behind old approaches and systems. In letters to his friend Jaspers, Heidegger sounds a pugnacious note about his battle against entrenched professors. He calls himself and Jaspers a "community of fighters" and hopes to "give life to philosophy again" (Heidegger 1992: 15, 29). He also avers that he gains little from conversation with his senior colleagues and that he prefers to reform philosophy through teaching the young. Many of his students attest to Heidegger's fascinating seminars in which he taught them to engage with the issues directly. In contrast to the habits of many older philosophers, who used the same textbook to lecture year in and year out, Heidegger's classes indeed seemed a revival of philosophy. Heidegger's lectures and writings are affected by his disdain for established views, and his language sometimes is derisive, and sometimes vehement. For example, in an early lecture he complains about the Marburg school's approach: "The system brings about that the dead is made alive, not for the living, but for the dead who have ventured the suicide of existence in order to gain for it the life of thinking" (GA 59: 193). Buoyed by his appointment to Husserl's chair in Freiburg, Heidegger makes even more colorful claims in his inaugural *What Is Metaphysics?* lecture.

How to Read *What Is Metaphysics?*

What Is Metaphysics? has been at the center of misunderstandings of Heidegger's view on logic since he gave the lecture in 1929. Commentators from Carnap onwards take it as obvious that Heidegger here proclaims that philosophical language use is not bound by the rules of logic (Carnap 1959a; Fay 1977: 115; Philipse 1998: 15; Witherspoon 2002). But Heidegger says no such thing. The lecture is much less concerned with logic than these commentators presume, and insofar as it touches upon the issue it states his basic view, that logic grounds in the phenomenological analysis of everyday human existence.

The lecture is about metaphysics, or, as Heidegger defines it, the analysis of entities *as* entities, i.e. the analysis of what it means for something to be. It argues that philosophy cannot make headway in metaphysics unless it differentiates between entities and the being of entities. Heidegger calls this difference the "ontological difference" and it is the most basic distinction of his philosophy. The being of entities, Heidegger says, is not itself an entity. In *What Is Metaphysics?* Heidegger tries to make this point by calling being "the nothing." This odd approach is justified, in a sense; for according to Heidegger's thesis, from the point of view of ontic inquiry, i.e. inquiry that is concerned exclusively with entities, the being of entities appears as nothing at all. Commentators react to two distinct elements in the lecture. First, they find that Heidegger deliberately and disastrously violates the rules of logical syntax by using "the nothing" as if this refers to a thing, rather than quantify over a domain. This issue is best addressed by a careful interpretation of Heidegger's analysis of the nothing. Here I will only point out that such an interpretation does not centrally involve questions about logic; and that Heidegger's argument remains substantially the same if we replace occurrences of "the nothing" with "being" or with "world" in the sense that Heidegger gives those terms in *Being and Time*. Second, commentators worry about three passages in which Heidegger himself addresses the apparent conflict between his approach to metaphysics and the common rules of logic. After defining metaphysics and stating the question concerning the nothing, Heidegger indicates a conflict between metaphysics (talk about the nothing) and logic in a passage I call the "absurdity passage" (GA 9: 107). He immediately challenges the basis of the absurdity argument in the "negation passage" (GA 9: 107ff). Next he analyzes anxiety and the nothing (GA 9: 108–16); this analysis makes up the core of the lecture and argues that philosophy must make the ontological difference. At the end of the analysis, Heidegger reprises the negation passage (GA 9: 116ff) and concludes, in the infamous "dominion passage," that the conflict between logic and metaphysics dissolves (GA 9: 117).

Let us begin with the absurdity passage:

> Accordingly every answer to this question ["what is the nothing?"] is impossible from the start. For it necessarily assumes the form: the nothing "is" such and such. With regard to the nothing, question and answer are equally absurd. . . . The commonly cited ground rule of thinking as such, the principle of non-contradiction, general "logic," defeats this question. For thinking, which is always essentially thinking something, would, as thinking the nothing, have to act contrary to its own essence. (GA 9: 107)

Some commentators think that Heidegger here outright admits that he wants to circumvent the basic rules of logic. But Heidegger does not endorse the argument he puts forth in this passage. He mentions it only to reject it immediately and turn to a more adequate analysis of the phenomena. In fact Heidegger places a condition on the absurdity passage and hints that "the seeming absurdity of question and answer regarding the nothing rests solely in the blind conceit of a roaming intellect" (GA 9: 108). He uses the same stratagem in the early lectures when he argues against Natorp (GA 59: 144), and he leaves no doubt about the status of the argument when he repeats it almost word for word a few years later in his Nietzsche lectures. Here he says about the absurdity argument that "no-one will want to deny that such 'reflections' convince easily and are 'compelling' – that is, as long as one moves in the realm of the easily understood and merely manipulates words and lets oneself be beaten about the head with thoughtlessness" (GA 6.2: 42).

Heidegger is not serious in the absurdity passage because it rests on a presumption, which Heidegger states and rejects in the "negation passage":

> Because we cannot at all turn the nothing into an object, our question about the nothing is already at an end – under the presumption that "logic" is the final arbiter in this question, that the understanding is the means and thinking the way to get an originary grip on the nothing and to decide about the possibility of its unveiling. . . . But is this presumption so certain? Does the not, negatedness and hence negation represent the higher determination under which the nothing falls as a specific kind of the negated? . . . We assert: The nothing is more originary than the not and negation. (GA 9: 107–8)

In the logical order of a hierarchy of definitions, a concept A is more originary than another concept B if B is defined in terms of A. This, for instance, is how Cohen uses the origin-metaphor in his *Logik der Reinen Erkenntnis*. The absurdity argument defines the nothing as a species of negation. As Heidegger well knows, indicating genus (negation) and species (nothing) is a traditional way of defining: "*definitio fit per genus proximum et differentiam specificam*" (SZ: 4). However, he points out that such a definition can be given only for entities, not for being (SZ: 4). In the first statement of the absurdity argument Heidegger only says that the nothing "is precisely *different* from entities" (GA 9: 107, emphasis added), not that it is the negation of entities. The key to unraveling his dialectic is to understand this difference as the ontological difference. "Being is not an entity" states the ontological difference, while "an entity is not an entity" states a contradiction.

Heidegger rejects the absurdity argument because philosophical logic is incapable of getting an *originary* grip on the nothing. It is not a basic concept in a hierarchy of categories. How else can we understand "originary"? In Heidegger's vernacular a phenomenon A is "more originary" than another B if A explains what B is, i.e. if A makes sense of the possibility of B. An example of an originary encounter is using equipment appropriately: "The less we just stare at the hammer-thing and the more we seize hold of it and use it, the more originary our relationship to it becomes, and the more unveiledly it is encountered as what it is – as equipment" (SZ: 69). The basic thesis of Heidegger's phenomenology of everydayness is that through know-how and skills we disclose a familiar world within which things make sense. Specific entity-directed comportments, including negation, presume prior disclosure of the world. As Heidegger puts it, "negation can only negate if something negatable has been pregiven" (GA 9: 116). "Pre-given" means that the being of entities is disclosed, that Dasein already understands them *as* entities. Disclosure is more originary than subsequent comportments; it makes such comportments possible.

Heidegger makes a threefold distinction between predicative ontic, pre-predicative ontic, and ontological levels of encountering being. On the predicative level we make assertions about entities, including negative existential assertions. Predication is rooted in a pre-predicative manifestness of entities (GA 9: 130). In *Being and Time* Heidegger argues that explicit assertions derive from articulated encounters of available equipment (SZ: 157ff). Before laying out entities in explicit assertions, we must discover entities as such by finding ourselves amidst them and dealing with them in articulated, purposive practices. Heidegger calls such pre-predicative discovering "ontic truth" (GA 9: 130) or "pre-logical manifestness" (GA 29/30: 494). Pre-logical manifestness, in turn, is guided by Dasein's understanding of being, which reveals the being of entities. Practical comportment grounds in Dasein's understanding of the being of equipment, i.e. in Dasein's familiarity with the possibilities that make up the world. The nothing makes understanding of being possible and hence belongs to the revealedness of being, which Heidegger calls "ontological truth" (GA 9: 131).

Metaphysics analyzes pre-predicative conditions of encountering entities, while logic articulates the structure of predicative encountering. The dominion passage – perhaps the most infamous and widely misunderstood passage in Heidegger's works – concludes that logic presumes a distinct layer of more originary, metaphysical analysis: "The nothing is the origin of negation, not the other way around. If the power of the understanding in the field of questions concerning the nothing and being is thus broken, then with this the fate of the dominion of 'logic' within philosophy is also decided. The idea of 'logic' itself dissolves in a whirl of more originary questioning" (GA 9: 117). Breaking the dominion of logic does not mean taking refuge in illogical sentences; it means penetrating into the conditions that make logical articulation of encountering of entities possible. "Pre-logical" does not and *cannot* mean "illogical." "We understand pre-logical here in a very specific sense as that which makes the *logos* as such possible in all its dimensions and possibilities" (GA 29/30: 510ff). Further, "we must see that understanding of being lies before all logical asserting and determining and makes possible even this" (GA 27: 320). Attunements, skills, and know-how constitute understanding of being. These ways of making entities manifest are neither logical nor illogical, because originary disclosure is not predicative. They constitute the possibility of logical articulation and prior to such articulation there can be neither consistency nor contradiction. In his book on Kant Heidegger says that originary disclosure (in this case he discusses the transcendental imagination) "is the foundation of both the possibility and the impossibility of contradiction" (GA 3: 195).

The Metaphysics of Truth 1: Assertion and Its Background

Let us turn to Heidegger's positive philosophy of logic, expressed in his thesis that logic is the metaphysics of truth. As we should expect from our brief survey of nineteenth-century philosophy of logic, Heidegger – for all his fervor to rework logic from the ground up – is rather conservative about the content of logic texts. In his lectures on logic he refers his students to the common, outdated logic textbooks of Mill, Sigwart, and Lotze. "Shaking the foundations" of logic is not about replacing the traditional principles of logic with others, or about developing new rules of inference. Heidegger makes concrete criticisms of the going theories of judgment; but he accepts basic logical principles and remains unmoved by detailed issues within logic. He finds textbook logic correct, but aims to make the subject less superficial by arguing that the structure and possible truth or falsity of judgments can only be explained by reference to Dasein's unveiling of being. He also argues that the traditional principles of logic – non-contradiction, identity, excluded middle, and sufficient reason – are not logical but transcendental in his sense of the word, i.e. these principles express structures that belong to Dasein's being-in-the-world.

Heidegger finds available logics superficial for three interrelated reasons. First, logic, as he finds it, takes many terms as basic and undefinable. In some cases this is explicit. Since Lotze, for instance, "*Geltung*" (validity) names the way of being of the logical and is taken to be a basic category that cannot be explained further. "Truth" is often taken to be defined (in terms of validity, in fact); however, such definitions explain what it means for propositions to be true without explaining what truth itself is (GA 21: 74). An explanation of truth itself, for Heidegger, analyzes the conditions that make ontic truth possible. These conditions, he argues, lie in Dasein's understanding of being, or, as Heidegger also calls it, Dasein's "transcendence"; hence understanding of being is "metaphysically originary being-true" and Heidegger concludes: "Truth lies in the essence of transcendence, it is originarily transcendental truth. But if the basic topic of logic is truth, then logic itself is metaphysics, since the problem of transcendence . . . is the fundamental theme of metaphysics" (GA 26: 281). The basic terms of logic are explained in terms of transcendental preconditions, and logic, properly understood, is metaphysical.

Second, the basic terms of received logic are ambiguous. Heidegger points out that "validity" commingles at least three notions: truth of propositions, the relation of propositions to their intended entities, and the normative bindingness of true propositions on the subject (GA 21: 81). Something similar holds for the copula "is." Here traditional logic has produced at least six distinct meanings, which Heidegger reduces to three: what-being (essence), that-being (existence), and being-true (GA 24: 290ff). For Heidegger this means that the tradition has not posed the question radically enough, "for an ambiguity in the meaning of one and the same word is never arbitrary" (GA 24: 276). Analyzing the transcendental preconditions of ontic phenomena shows why a word has various meanings and how they are connected in a unified ground.

A third argument leads to metaphysics via the historical origin of logic in Aristotle. "Logic is the discipline of philosophy that has suffered the most from an ossification and detachment from the central problems of philosophy" (GA 24: 252). Logic was born as a twin to an investigation into the meaning of being. But through subsequent interpreters it took on a hollow life of its own. (Only Kant and Hegel, says Heidegger, have taken steps to once again understand logic as philosophy, i.e. to understand that the problem of logic is the problem of being.) Specifically, logic is concerned with the explanation of truth and most logic texts focus on judgment, or assertion, because assertion is the "bearer of truth." Assertions are true or false and nothing else is. Heidegger grants that the possible truth or falsity of assertion is the central phenomenon of the *logos* and therefore the topic of logic; however, traditional efforts fall short in their understanding of assertion. Heidegger goes back to Aristotle, the last philosopher to analyze assertions without being influenced by mistaken preconceptions.

Heidegger analyzes Aristotle's *logos apophantikos*, the speaking that determines and points out, in almost every lecture course from 1924 to 1930 and he develops his own view of assertion in these analyses. Assertions point out a determination of entities. Heidegger argues that they can only do so on the basis of a prior inexplicit understanding of the entity. "Entities must already be unveiled, so that an assertion about them is possible" (GA 24: 299). We have such prior understanding due to our constitutive familiarity with the world. So, we encounter particular entities in the world by comporting ourselves toward them on the basis of our "fore-having," a way of appropriating the overall significance of the world in terms of purposive projects. To experience an entity as meaningful in a determinate way is to see it as playing a role in a structured activity. Dasein must always "come back" from the fore-having to entities. In Heidegger's analysis purposive chunks of the world play the role that concepts play in traditional (and contemporary) *Urteilslehre*; we experience a particular entity by "subsuming" it under a general type. But Heidegger argues that making sense of an entity does not presume cognizing it through a concept; such cognition is a derivative mode of the more fundamental possibility of encountering entities through inexplicit, practical mastery of their background.

Traditional logic mistakes the structure of assertion because it does not recognize that background involvement is an *essential* part of assertions. Logicians tend to conceive assertions as isolated subjects being determined by isolated predicates, "formally and indirectly from their external structure" (GA 21: 151n). This approach ignores the context of competent comportment within which an assertion can have sense in the first place. "We need to keep our eyes on this in order to see what nonsense is current in traditional logic, when it takes as its standing example of determining . . . 'the rose-things have the property or state of blossoming'" (GA 21: 157–8). Logic analyzes assertions in order to explain truth. Mistaking its formal structures as the essential feature of assertions, though, traditional logic cuts itself off from the possibility of a complete analysis of truth. Accordingly, Heidegger's philosophical logic begins with the argument that assertions only make sense against a background of inexplicit familiarity with entities as a whole. Heidegger's analysis of assertions shows that if we leave out the inexplicit background of familiarity, we cannot explain the important features that assertions wear on their sleeves: the fact that they are about entities; the fact that they are internally unified; and the fact that they can be true or false. Truth and other fundamental concepts of logic are grounded in the structure of this familiarity.

The Metaphysics of Truth 2: Norms, Ground, and Inferences

Heidegger's analysis of assertion does not suffocate the details of logic under a blob of "holism." The background of assertions has a structure and the basic concepts and principles of logic have their origin here. They are structural moments of the world that enable and govern general features of assertoric truth and falsity. Heidegger analyzes this logical ur-structure from three overlapping angles. First, the background is articulated by the "as"-structure. This is the structure of understanding, both in its inexplicit form when we deal competently with our surroundings and in its explicitly articulated form when we deliberately pick out a feature or function of an entity. To make sense of an entity means to encounter it *as* something, as useful, as obstructive, as irrelevant, etc. Nothing shows up unless it shows up with some determinacy. Heidegger explains the universality of the "as"-structure in experience from the temporal constitution of existence, which is the most fundamental analysis of the conditions of experience that he ever gives. Dasein projects ahead and comes back to what is present on the basis of what already is. It is part of the essential nature of temporal beings that they experience presence in terms of "something as something," and this "as"-structure provides the ground for logic as a science of the structure of experience.

Heidegger's holism follows from the second, more specific structure of the background. He bases his analysis on practical comportment, and here the structure of the background shows up as serviceability (*Dienlichkeit*). Frameworks have the character of projects and are articulated into chunks of possibilities that relate to each other through with-which, towards-which, and for-the-sake-of-which relations. These relations of serviceability together with the "as"-structure constitute *networks* of meaningful entities and possibilities. If we experience entities as meaningful within a project, then we can also experience other entities towards which, or with which these first entities make sense. Heidegger focuses his analysis on tools, and these seem to be only one kind of entity that we encounter and can say things about. But, Heidegger claims, "this constraint is not a constraint at all" (GA 38: 143). The reason for this is that Dasein essentially has the structure of living for-the-sake-of itself. Though we are not constantly busy building bookshelves, we do constantly live for the sake of some self-understanding. This is enough to introduce serviceability-structures into even the remotest, least tool-like corner of the world. They structure significance in general.

The "as"-structure explains how we understand entities against a background; the serviceability-structures give details about how this background, the world, is organized and what we can understand entities as and hence what determinations of entities we can articulate. "Every *logos* can only point out, i.e. lay apart, what is already prelogically manifest" (GA 29/30: 502). Yet the world "overshoots" entities (*übertreffen, überschwingen*, GA 26: 278; GA 9: 167ff). Possibilities always exceed the actual. So, to use Heidegger's example, while it is logically impossible to encounter the third root of 69 in a German forest at night, and factically impossible to meet the Persian shah there, it is nevertheless possible to encounter any of several kinds of entities: a bush, a deer, etc. There is a halo of possibility around everything actual, and only for this reason can understanding, and derivatively assertions, be true or false. If entities could only be determined in one way, then there could be no question of making true or false statements, nor of saying anything specific at all. "In order to have the basic function of pointing out, the *logos* must have the possibility of being adequate to that which it points out, or of missing it. . . . The *logos* requires in and for itself a space of adequacy and inadequacy" (GA 29/30: 502). So the paradigmatically *logical* feature of assertions – the possibility of truth and falsity and the normative role of entities towards our experience of them – derive from the relation between actuality and its background of possibility.

The halo of possibility is a "space of adequacy and inadequacy" because entities are normative for assertions about them. Heidegger studies this normativity, which he sometimes calls "bindingness" (*Verbindlichkeit*, GA 29/30: 496ff) and sometimes "powerlessness" (*Ohnmacht*, GA 26: 279) in his analysis of world-forming (*Weltbilden*) and his related analysis of the origin of the principle of ground (or principle of reason, *Satz vom Grunde*). This analysis goes to the heart of Heidegger's conception of logic, for "the principle of ground is not [merely] a rule and norm of assertions, but rather the first principle of logic as metaphysics" (GA 26: 282).

Normativity inheres in the social practices in which Dasein participates. To participate in a practice is to understand a situation and know how to deal with entities within that practice. On the one hand such participation makes manifest the whole of entities and possibilities that constitute the practice; on the other hand it binds Dasein to these entities as they are made manifest in this projection. "[Dasein's] being open for . . . is by its nature a free holding-over against itself and letting itself be bound to that which is given as entities" (GA 29/30: 496). Heidegger gives the example of classroom practices. If we participate in classroom practices, as teachers, students, or more marginally, entities within the classroom show up as having significance. We understand chalk, blackboards, and so on. At the same time we are bound by these entities. The blackboard itself is the standard for what it means for a blackboard to be inconveniently located, say. Whether our comportments toward (including our assertions about) black-boards are adequate or not depends on what the blackboard *is*. And what the black-board is becomes manifest in our understanding of classrooms. Our understanding the being of entities makes those entities themselves the norms for what we say about them and what we do with them. Note that the entities do not produce the norms. Dasein's understanding of being produces norms in such a way that the entities govern the ade-quacy of Dasein's comportments. We could never explain this normative structure by starting from the idea of already manifest entities. "We cannot explain bindingness from object-hood, but the other way around" (GA 29/30: 525).

Heidegger says that the origin of bindingness is freedom (GA 29/30: 496ff). Dasein is constitutively free insofar as it encounters entities by understanding possibilities. "To be free is to understand oneself out of possibilities" (GA 26: 278), so Dasein's freedom makes up the excess of possibilities within which Heidegger defines logical adequacy and inadequacy. Now, Heidegger further says that insofar as freedom is the origin of bindingness, it is also the origin of ground, or of reasons. "The originary phenomenon of ground is the for-the-sake-of that belongs to transcendence. Freedom, holding the for-the-sake-of out in front of it and binding itself to it, is freedom for the ground" (GA 26: 278). This means that Dasein, being bound by entities that it understands out of possibilities, encounters these entities in terms of ground-relations (whatever those relations may be; Heidegger explains several modes in which entities can metaphysi-cally ground or be grounded). Heidegger thus posits a metaphysical version of the prin-ciple of ground: "the ground-character of ground in general belongs to the essence of being in general" (GA 26: 283).

Heidegger's metaphysical version of the principle of ground implies an ontic one: "Because science is ontic (is about entities) it must give reasons" (GA 26: 283). This is Heidegger's statement of the principle of reason of traditional logic, and also of the basic presumption of contemporary logic. Assertions that discover entities stand in inferential relations to other assertions. Heidegger does not systematically explore the inferential relations themselves. Like his predecessors he takes it for granted that they have been codified in a syllogistic theory of inference. He merely says that the logical principles that govern inferences – the laws of non-contradiction and of identity – derive from the principle of ground and are themselves transcendental in character (GA 26: 283; GA 9: 173).

But Heidegger explains why assertions about entities necessarily come in inferential groupings. It is because they are about *entities*. Recall that entities are articulated as entities in a social practice. Dasein is socialized into such practices and understands the being of entities. Now, the manifestness of entities has two basic features. First, it is holistic: entities are manifest in structured networks. Second, entities are normative for assertions about them: they provide standards of adequacy against which assertions can be true or false. The holism means that if we can understand a given entity as such-and-such, then we can also understand other entities in other articulated ways. Now in each case our articulated understanding of an entity can give rise to explicit pred-icative assertions about the entity, so from the holism of entities follows a holism of pos-sible assertions. Heidegger's explanation of normativity implies that the truth or falsity of these possible assertions is governed by the holistic network of the entities them-selves. So the truth of one assertion is holistically connected to the truth of others, and that is just to say that these assertions are inferentially linked. This is what Heidegger means by saying that the ontic principle of reason derives from a metaphysical one. Assertions imply one another not because of features internal to their structure, but because of the structure of Dasein's understanding of being.

Heidegger thus develops an essential connection between the holism of entities, the normativity that entities exercise on assertions, and the inferential interrelations of assertions. In Heidegger's philosophy of logic, this inferential holism is more fundamental still than the fact that assertions can be true or false. "Man is primarily not a no-sayer, nor is he a yes-sayer; he is a why-asker. And only because that is what he is, he can and must say yes and no, not occasionally but essentially" (GA 26: 280).

Conclusion

With his metaphysics of truth Heidegger aims to explain, not merely state, the basic features and principles of logic, and to show how they derive from a single origin. The origin, he argues, is Dasein's constitutive understanding of being. Heidegger derives the structure of assertions, assertoric truth, and the inferential structure from this origin, and he indicates derivations of the basic laws of logic. Some aspects of Heidegger's derivations may seem foreign to our conception of logic. However, we must recall that his approach is motivated by the challenge to explain the basic principles of logic in their unity, i.e. to show what makes a set of basic definitions coherent.

While Heidegger's metaphysics might seem strange to some, we should be rather familiar with the picture of predicative logic that Heidegger derives. He holds that logic is necessary for Dasein. It comes with the temporal constitution of existing beings that experience has logical structure. The limits of logic are not to be found within our experience; only at the total breakdown of death do the ground structures of logic lose their grip. Heidegger also claims that logic is *a priori*, in the best sense that he can give to that phrase. This is part of the import of his claim that the principles of logic are transcendental. We do not come to know the rules of logic in the same way in which we can come to know about entities in the world; we always already know them.

References and further reading

Carnap, R. (1959a) The elimination of metaphysics through logical analysis of language (trans. A. Pap). In A. Ayer (ed.), *Logical Positivism*. New York: The Free Press (original work published 1932).

Carnap, R. (1959b) The old and the new logic (trans. I. Levi). In A. Ayer (ed.), *Logical Positivism*. New York: The Free Press (original work published 1930).

Cohen, H. (1914) *Logik der Reinen Erkenntnis* [*Logic of Pure Cognition*]. Berlin: Bruno Cassirer.

Fay, T. (1977) *Heidegger: The Critique of Logic*. The Hague: Martinus Nijhoff.

Friedman, M. (2000) *A Parting of the Ways*. Chicago: Open Court.

Heidegger, M. (1992) *Martin Heidegger/Karl Jaspers Briefwechsel 1920–1963* [*Heidegger/Jaspers Correspondence 1920–1963*] (ed. W. Biemel and H. Saner). Munich: Piper.

Husserl, E. (1992) *Logische Untersuchungen* [*Logical Investigations*] (ed. E. Ströker). Hamburg: Meiner.

Käufer, S. (2001) On Heidegger on logic. *Continental Philosophy Review*, 34, 455–76.

Philipse, H. (1998) *Heidegger's Philosophy of Being*. Princeton, NJ: Princeton University Press.

Witherspoon, E. (2002) Logic and the inexpressible in Frege and Heidegger. *Journal of the History of Philosophy*, 40(1), 89–113.

10

Phenomenology

EDGAR C. BOEDEKER JR

The period from 1919 through 1929 has appropriately been called Heidegger's "phenomenological decade" (Kisiel 1993: 59). Here Heidegger maintains that "Phenomenology is . . . the method of ontology" (GA 24: 27; cf. SZ: 27) and thus that "*Ontology is possible only as phenomenology*" (SZ: 35). Nominally, the same goes for Husserl's transcendental phenomenology, out of which Heidegger's own thought emerged. It will therefore prove instructive to begin this discussion of Heidegger's phenomenological method for conducting ontology with Husserl's.

Husserl's Phenomenological Ontology

Ontology, the study of the being of entities, is for Husserl either *formal* or *regional*. *Formal* ontology is the study of "formal categories," i.e. structures of possible entities, by means of the structures of the judgments we make about them. ("Judgment" must here be taken in a broad sense to include such "pre-predicative" phenomena as the simple perception of an object.) Its method is *formalization*, a kind of abstraction that begins with (the expression of) a concrete judgment, and turns a constant into a variable, thus resulting in a (relatively) formal structure. Repeated operations of formalization give rise to a hierarchy of ever-more-abstract formal structures. *Regional* ontology is the study of *domains* of possible objects. Its method is *generalization*, which begins with a particular predicate and constructs a hierarchy of ever-more-abstract species and genera under which it falls. Such predicates are *material categories*, each of which corresponds to a *region* of possible objects. Because Husserl rejects the view that existence is a predicate (GA 20: 78), each material category must have *some* content. For Husserl, the highest, most abstract division among such categories is that between *mental* and *physical*; these predicates thus mark out the most basic distinction among regions of possible entities.

Husserl's phenomenology appears tailor-made for this twofold ontological project. On Heidegger's sympathetic gloss, Husserl's phenomenology differs from the natural sciences in being the "analytic description of intentionality in its *a priori*" (GA 20: 108). Each of the four key concepts in this slogan can be "unpacked" as follows.

Intentionality is that feature of consciousness that it is *about*, or *directed toward* some object, whether or not it really exists. A natural-scientific approach to intentionality postulates various psycho-physical relations between the mind and the objects toward which it is directed. A phenomenological approach, however, examines just the descriptive, or semantic, content of our intentional acts – *what* we think, as opposed to what we think *about* – that Husserl calls the "intended-as-such," "sense," or "noema" of a mental act. In the everyday, or "natural," attitude, we constantly make use of these semantic contents. For our minds are always directed toward everyday intentional objects as described by some intended-as-such. Nevertheless, in the natural attitude our minds are not directed explicitly toward the intended-as-such. The first step in Husserl's phenomenological method must therefore be the "transcendental reduction," in which we direct our consciousness away from everyday intentional objects and toward their intendeds-as-such.

Whereas empirical science explains phenomena using theoretical models, phenomenology aims to be an entirely descriptive enterprise. In keeping with Husserl's call to arms – "To the matters themselves!" – phenomenology seeks only to *clarify* intendeds-as-such, just as they are given to consciousness. For Husserl, this implies that phenomenology must allow no epistemic "gap" between the intended-as-such and the assertions it makes about it. Husserl thus intends for phenomenology to be a science utterly without presuppositions, including those about the nature or existence of the intentional objects of the natural attitude. Phenomenological assertions must be guaranteed absolute rational certainty, and for Husserl this can occur only if their objects, intendeds-as-such, are absolutely given to the mind. Accordingly, Husserl insists that the transcendental reduction be accomplished by the *epoché*, in which we "withhold," or "bracket" our judging that the intended-as-such is correct – that it in fact corresponds to the world – thus leaving only its unasserted semantic content. The *epoché* therefore guarantees that phenomenological descriptions are free from the numerous unjustified presuppositions that plague the natural attitude. Furthermore, phenomenology restricts itself only to making judgments about what is adequately given to the mind. Indeed, Husserl employs the concept of adequate givennness to define *phenomenon*. A phenomenon in a broad, formal sense is any (intentional) object. A phenomenon in the strict, phenomenological sense is just one that can be absolutely given to the mind (Husserl 1950: 14, 9ff). And for Husserl, these phenomenological phenomena include (aspects of) intendeds-as-such.

Whereas natural-scientific analysis aims to dissect objects into their constituent parts, *phenomenological analysis* (GA 21: 198; Heidegger 1987: 150) aims to demonstrate the transcendental conditions of possibility of intendeds-as-such. Husserl holds that these transcendental conditions include the logical form of judgments, and, crucially, our understanding of time. Our consciousness of internal time consists in the complex of "protending" anticipated future sense-data, "retaining" past ones, and "attending to" those presently given. In perceiving a physical object, we not only receive present sensations, but also experience these sensations as *of* that object as seen from a particular perspective. And this is possible only because the intended-as-such includes the complex set of "adumbrations" of the intentional object, i.e. "views" of it as it would be seen from every possible perspective. The intended-as-such of a perception of a physical thing *is* just such a temporally ordered set of such adumbrations, and thus a set of verification-conditions. In Husserl's terms, the intended-as-such *constitutes* the intentional object as we intend it.

Unlike empirical natural science, Husserl's phenomenology is *a priori*, or "pure." That is, its object-domain includes neither individuals nor particular properties or relations holding among them, but rather only formal or material categories. We arrive at these categories in the second step of Husserl's method, the "eidetic reduction." Here, we begin with a particular intended-as-such, and then explicitly focus on, or emphasize, the formal and material categories instantiated in it. The eidetic reduction thus includes both formalization and generalization, and results in a relatively abstract intended-as-such, which Husserl calls the (intentional) object of a "categorial intuition." Husserl's analysis of time-consciousness plays a crucial role in intuiting material categories. For they are intuited by abstracting away the features peculiar to a particular intended-as-such (e.g. which particular colors or shapes are involved in its verification-conditions) and leaving only the essential temporal structures common to a class of them. Although these temporal structures are found only in the intended-as-such, and not the intentional object, they can nevertheless be employed in regional ontology. Husserl accomplishes this by defining a region of entities as the set of entities that could be given to consciousness in a particular temporal manner. The region of the *mental*, e.g. sensations, is the class of objects capable of being absolutely given to consciousness at *just one* point in time. The region of the *physical* is the class of objects that, since they are intended as enduring through time in three dimensions, can *never* be absolutely given to consciousness (for protention and retention are essential features of our intentions of physical objects, but are incapable of absolutely giving their objects). And the region of the *universal* can be defined as the class of objects that can be absolutely given *at will* and at *any* point in time. Universals are thus "constantly present," or, more accurately, constantly present*able*. Now Husserl maintains that formal and material categories can be intuited at will and at any time. Since they comprise the domain of the *a priori*, everything *a priori* is universal.

Heideggerian Ontology

Heidegger maintains that ontology properly studies what it is for an entity to be *as such*. Now since Husserlian regional ontology only classifies entities by their (temporally constituted) predicates, it can at best say what it is to be mental, physical, or universal. But it cannot say what it is to *be* as such. Husserl's "regional ontology" thus cannot be genuine ontology. And his "formal ontology" is no better off. For it can at best categorize possible intentional objects as individuals, predicative states of affairs, relational states of affairs, etc. (correlative to the various structures of judgments). And the highest, most abstract formal category, *possible object* (correlative to *possible semantic content of a judgment*), is completely empty. Formal ontology must thus remain silent on what it is for an object to *be* in such a way that would make the corresponding judgment correct. The *being* of entities that Heidegger, following Husserl, calls "presence-to-hand" (*Vorhandenheit*) must thus lie outside the scope of formal ontology. Indeed, since Husserl's *epoché* involves "bracketing" judgment, placing it at the beginning of all phenomenological investigations systematically prevents his phenomenology from investigating the nature of both judgment as such and, correlatively, the presence-to-hand that it posits (cf. GA 20: 150ff). Thus all of Husserl's *a priori* categories fall on the ontic side of the "ontological difference" (GA 24: 22) between entities and their being.

Presence-to-hand is neither a super-property nor a formal structure common to everything existent. Instead, it is one of several ways in which we can *encounter* entities. It is to be contrasted, for example, with "readiness-at-hand" (*Zuhandenheit*), in which we encounter entities in terms of their usefulness (or uselessness) to our practical projects. Crucially, because presence-to-hand and readiness-at-hand are just different *ways of encountering* what Heidegger calls "intraworldly entities" – a term coextensive with "physical objects" – they are *not* different kinds of *entities*. For the same entity – a hammer, for example – could in principle be encountered in different ways of being: once as a present-to-hand object weighing two kilograms, and another time as a ready-at-hand item of equipment useful for hammering. These are thus two modes of the *how-being* of intraworldly entities. *How* we encounter an entity is distinct from *what* we encounter it as – i.e. predicative what-being, or *essentia*, the material categories of which form the basis of Husserl's regional ontology – or the fact *that* it exists – i.e. that-being, or *existentia*, which, along with identity, predication, and modal concepts, forms the basis of formal ontology.

As Heidegger uses the terms, someone can encounter entities in a particular way of how-being (or "being" for short) just in case she *understands* that way of being. Understanding a way of being is not a matter of knowing *that* something is the case; rather, it is a capacity, or ability – a knowing *how* to do something. Since there can be no capacities unless there are havers of such capacities, "only as long as Dasein, i.e. the ontic possibility of understanding being, *is* 'is there' being" (SZ: 212). Now all encounters of entities are interpretive; that is, they have the structure of taking the entity *as* something, one of the family of phenomena that Heidegger calls *discourse* (*Rede*; SZ: 161ff). An entity's *meaning* (*Bedeutung*; SZ: 87) is what we encounter it *as*. Whereas an encountered entity is generally actual, meanings are possibilities – namely, possible ways of encountering that entity, whether correctly or falsely (in the case of the present-to-hand) or appropriately or inappropriately (in the case of the ready-at-hand; cf. SZ: 83). In an encounter of a present-to-hand entity, the entity's *meaning* consists of the properties that we interpret it as having, or the relations to other present-to-hand entities in which we interpret as standing.

Apophantic Interpretation

In encountering an entity, then, we allow it to show itself, show up, or be seen (in a broad sense, not restricted to vision), as something. In Heidegger's broad, or "formal," sense, an entity is a *phenomenon* for someone just as long and insofar as it shows itself to her as something. Heidegger calls encounters of present-to-hand entities *apophantic interpretations* (SZ: 158). Their unique goal is *apo-phansis*, allowing entities to show themselves from themselves just as they are in themselves (SZ: 154; cf. 32, 34; GA 29/30: 462–4). The caveat "just as they are in themselves" means that one goal of *apophansis* is to make *correct* interpretations of the entities in question. The "from

159

themselves" ("*apo*") implies that *apophansis* has the further goal of employing concepts in these interpretations that are *appropriate* to the entities in question, i.e. which illuminate them not just one-sidedly, but fully (whatever this may ultimately mean). Heidegger describes the "commitment" (GA 25: 26; GA 29/30: 496) involved in the perception of a present-to-hand thing as a new determination of the being of the entity, in which we focus on the entity *itself*, as opposed to its usefulness in our projects (cf. SZ: 69ff). Such a commitment is demonstrated in one's readiness to modify, in the light of further experience with the entity, both what one interprets it as, and the concepts one employs in such interpretations.

It is not the case, however, that apophantic interpretations always make good on their implicit commitment to allow what they are about to show itself from itself just as it is in itself. Indeed, there is surely a continuum between complete readiness to modify one's interpretations and concepts, and complete unreadiness or unwillingness to do so. Heidegger calls the latter "con-course" (*Gerede*). Con-course is dis-course (SZ: 155) characterized by an implicit uncritical acceptance of "what one treats as valid and what one does not" (SZ: 127), i.e. of common beliefs, concepts, and ways of looking at things – in large part as these are conveyed by language. Thus Heidegger writes that in con-course, "what is pointed out . . . get[s] covered up as it is passed on" (SZ: 155; cf. 224). Indeed, for Heidegger, con-course is the "default" position of the interpretation of entities (cf. GA 20: 75; SZ: 169).

Heidegger distinguishes correctness (i.e. the ordinary concept of truth) from "un-concealment" (*a-letheia*), which he misleading calls "truth" (SZ: 219; cf. Heidegger 1969: 77; GA 15: 297). All ways of encountering entities involve unconcealment. In the case of apophantic interpretations of the present-to-hand, "un-concealment" has a fourfold sense. First, it is the mere intention of an object (as something); in this sense, an object is brought out of concealment as we become conscious of it. Second, un-concealment is the confirmation, or "fulfillment," of our intention of the object. This occurs in an "intuition," in which we experience that the intended-as-such is identical to the intentional object (SZ: 218; GA 20: 66ff), thereby removing the "concealment" of the correctness of the intended-as-such. Third, un-concealment involves gaining the right sort of "access" to the entity, without which we cannot properly interpret it. In the case of ordinary perception, such access is secured by moving our body into the optimal position(s) for viewing the object. In science, it requires employing the proper methods of investigation. Fourth, un-concealment is the process of "wresting" the entity away from being distorted by the use of inappropriate concepts (SZ: 222; cf. 36).

The task of the largely unpublished treatise entitled "Being and Time" (SZ: 39) is to pose and, insofar as this is possible, answer the question of being: "What is being as such?" (SZ: 6). Being as such is the articulated unity (GA 24: 24; cf. SZ: 3, 196) of ways of how-being. (Unless otherwise noted, we will follow Heidegger in referring to being as such, or being *per se* [*überhaupt*], simply as "being.") The task of ontology is to be "the science of being" (GA 24: 17). Since for Heidegger science "objectifies" (SZ: 363) its objects, ontology must be an "objectification of being" (GA 24: 456–9). In other words, ontology consists of apophantic interpretations of being. In what follows we will examine Heidegger's phenomenological method in terms of the fourfold sense of the un-concealment involved in apophantic interpretations as applied to being.

160

Phenomenological Reduction and Formal Indication

As apophantic interpretations, one thing that ontological assertions must do is to bring being out of concealment by turning it into a phenomenon. By and large, however, Dasein is not explicitly concerned with being, but rather with entities – whether itself, others, or intraworldly entities. Although Dasein does, in virtue of its ability to encounter entities in various ways, have an implicit, or "preontological" (SZ: 12), understanding of being, this is not by and large thematic. The first step in conducting ontology is therefore to make entities' how-being – the "phenomenality" of phenomena – into a phenomenon, i.e. to get it to show itself to us (cf. SZ: 31). Heidegger calls this "leading the phenomenological gaze [away] from grasping the entity . . . toward the understanding of this entity's being" the *phenomenological reduction*, emphasizing that this is quite different from what Husserl means by the term (GA 24: 29).

Note from the passage quoted in the previous paragraph that what gets thematized in the phenomenological reduction is not being itself, but rather Dasein's *understanding* of being. Heidegger devotes Division I of *Being and Time* to explicating Dasein's being – i.e. to fundamental ontology, or the existential analytic of Dasein – only because Dasein is the entity to whose being belongs an *understanding* of being as such (SZ: 13). This means that Dasein is essentially capable of encountering not just itself, but also intraworldly entities and co-Dasein (i.e. fellow Daseins as such). Heidegger proposes to explicate being on the basis of a "preparatory" (SZ: 39) analysis of Dasein's being because an explication of Dasein's being must thus include an explication of its understanding of being as such. Dasein is thus the entity *of which* we ask the question of being (SZ: 13).

Since Dasein's understanding of being is by and large implicit, Heideggerian ontology does not consist of *arguments* in the traditional sense of drawing conclusions from explicit premises accepted as true. Rather, it consists in the "circular" process of using concrete examples of Dasein's encounters of entities as the basis for explicit interpretations of its understanding of being, and then confirming or revising these ontological interpretations in the light of further concrete cases. This process has been called the *hermeneutic circle* (cf. SZ: 7, 153, 315), in the first of four senses we will examine.

From at least 1920/1 through *Being and Time*, Heidegger employs the term "formal indication" to characterize the preliminary assertions, found toward the beginning of an ontological investigation, that are intended to get us to perform the phenomenological reduction. "Formal indication" has a dual sense. First, it means something much like Husserl's "empty intention," as contrasted with *intuitive confirmation*. That is, the assertions made at the beginning of an ontological investigation (e.g. SZ: 12, 33, 38) at first appear "dogmatic" (cf., respectively, SZ: 147, 220, 436). Throughout the course of the investigation, however, their correctness – or, as the case may be, incorrectness – gets "demonstrated" in phenomenological observation of concrete cases of the ontological phenomena in question. Second, "formal indication" is to be contrasted with *differentiated description*. Much like a signpost pointing toward a town, as opposed to a detailed description of it in a tourist guidebook, the descriptive content of a formal indication is relatively impoverished. Heidegger's introductory formulations of ontological phenomena get further articulated in the detailed analyses that make up the bulk of *Being and Time*.

Formal indications in both senses play the *positive* role of pointing *toward* the phenomena in question, thus facilitating subsequent confirmation and differentiation. But they also serve the *negative*, or "defensive," function of warnings or "cautionary measures," by pointing *away* from phenomena that might easily be confused with the ones in question (GA 60: 63; SZ: 41). Most importantly, formal indications are intended to get the reader to understand that the ontological structures in question are *not* those of present-to-hand entities. For this reason, Heidegger explicitly contrasts his formal indications with both Husserl's *generalization*, which operates on present-to-hand predicates, and Husserl's *formalization*, which isolates the logical structures of possible present-to-hand entities (GA 60: 64).

Phenomenological Construction as Ontological Interpretation

The second step in Heidegger's phenomenological ontology consists in making and confirming assertions about being, thus removing the prior "concealment" of their correctness. Heidegger calls this "positive bringing oneself toward being itself . . . and its structures" *phenomenological construction* (GA 24: 29). This brings us naturally to the topic of the nature of Heidegger's phenomenology as *descriptive*, and thus interpretive.

In Being and Time ¶7A, Heidegger explicates his concept of *phenomenon*. Although he does not explicitly mention Husserl here, it is clear that he intends for this to be a devastating critique of Husserl's phenomenology. And the notes that an outraged Husserl wrote in his copy of SZ indicate that this was not lost on him (Breeur 1994: 16). Heidegger begins with a discussion of what he calls the "formal" concept of *phenomenon*, which is the genus neutral with respect to what he calls its "ordinary" and "phenomenological" species. Phenomenological phenomena ("pp's" in what follows) are the proper "objects," "content," or "matter" of phenomenology.

Beginning with his formal definition of "phenomenon" as what shows itself, Heidegger then makes a twofold distinction among kinds of phenomena in this sense. First, a phenomenon can show itself either as it is (in itself) or as it is not, i.e. falsely. Heidegger employs the term "semblance" for the latter, "privative modification of phenomenon" (SZ: 29). Examples of semblances include optical illusions, perceptual errors, etc. Second, some phenomena are *appearances*, examples of which include "indications, presentations, symptoms, and symbols" (SZ: 29). *Appearance* is a three-place relation that holds (at a given time) between a Dasein D and two entities x and y, in which y is a phenomenon that is an appearance to D of x. This is equivalent to saying that y is a phenomenon that indicates x to D; i.e. that x is indicated to D in, by, or through the phenomenon y. Although the appearance y is a phenomenon, *what* appears, x, is not. We can thus see that all semblances and appearances are phenomena, but not all phenomena are either semblances or appearances. Furthermore, the concepts of *semblance* and *appearance* can be defined only by using the concept of *phenomenon*, whereas the converse is not the case. The concepts of *semblance* and *appearance* thus "presuppose," and are thus "in different ways founded in," the "originary" concept of *phenomenon* (SZ: 29–31).

162

Since Husserl holds that something is a phenomenon in the broad, formal sense just in case it is an intentional object of someone's consciousness, we can easily imagine him agreeing with Heidegger's description of the formal concept of phenomenon. And both thinkers distinguish their conception of *phenomenological* phenomenon from what Heidegger calls the "ordinary," i.e. Kantian, conception of phenomena as sensible spatio-temporal objects. Finally, both agree that pp's are the ordinarily implicit, or "*concealed*" (SZ: 35), transcendental conditions of possibility of such ordinary phenomena – analogous to Kant's forms of intuition (SZ: 31). At this point, however, the similarities end. Now it is clear that all Husserlian pp's turn out to be a particular kind of appearance – a *mere* appearance. The concept of a mere appearance has its origin in circumspect locutions of the form: "*y* appears (or 'seems') to indicate *x*," e.g. "The color of *S*'s cheeks *appears to* indicate to *D* that *S* has a fever." Unlike such expressions of the form "*y* indicates *x*" – e.g. "The color of *S*'s cheeks *indicates* to *D* that *S* has a fever" – such expressions do not claim that *y* *is* an appearance of *x*, but *only* that *y* *seems to be* an appearance of *x*. *Y* is not claimed to be a *real* appearance of a *really* existing *x*, but only a *mere* appearance of a *possibly* existing *x*. Since such expressions do not claim that *y* does indicate *x*, they do not commit the speaker to the existence of *x*. As Wilfred Sellars (1956/1997) would point out 29 years later, one feature of such expressions is their incorrigibility – at least with respect to the existence of *x*.

From the use of such harmless words as "appears," "seems," or "looks," however, it is easy to construct a Cartesian monstrosity. All that is necessary is to reify the distinction between (mere) appearances and what appears in them. For Heidegger, this distinction is a *relative* distinction among ways in which things *show up* to us in a *particular* encounter of an entity. The fever that *appears* in someone's cheeks in a non-clinical setting might, upon analyzing the results of various diagnostic tests, be itself an *appearance* of a viral infection. The Cartesian, however, takes the distinction to be one among different kinds of *things* – *defined* in terms of how they can show up to us in *any* encounter of entities. *Mere appearances* are defined as those objects that are immune to the possibility of semblance, whereas *what appears* is defined as what is necessarily always beyond the reach of our experience. That is, a phenomenon *y* is a mere appearance (of *x*) if and only if *y* is an appearance of *x* and *x* can "*never*" show itself, i.e. must "constantly" be "concealed" (SZ: 30). And this is indeed just Husserl's way of distinguishing pp's from ordinary phenomena. Pp's are mere appearances, free of the possibility of semblance. They include sensations and the universals (i.e. predicates and logical forms) employed to organize sensations into intentions of ordinary phenomena. Ordinary phenomena are those physical objects and other minds that can *never* (directly) show themselves – but can only be (indirectly) indicated through pp's.

Heidegger's subterranean criticism of Husserl's conception of pp's is that it suffers from "confusion" (SZ: 30). Besides the reification of the distinction between mere appearances and what appears, Husserl's concept of pp's also makes a conceptual error. For Husserl, the concept *mere appearance*, and the coextensive concept *freedom from the possibility of semblance*, can be understood independently of the formal concept of *phenomenon* as what shows itself, and that thus includes the possibility of semblance. This is because Husserl requires that all phenomenological assertions be based *just* on pp's, without assuming anything, whether factual or conceptual, about the ordinary phenomena that are the intentional objects of the natural attitude. Heidegger, again anticipating Sellars, argues that this is impossible – even for the universals that Sellars does not discuss in his critique of the Cartesian legacy in Empiricism. For the concept of *mere appearance* includes the concept of *appearance*, and thus, as we saw above, that of *phenomenon* in the formal sense. And the same goes for something free from the possibility of semblance. Thus neither concept can be defined or understood independently of the formal concept of *phenomenon*. Now for Heidegger, the history of ontology is replete with evidence that the pp *par excellence*, i.e. "the *being* of entities" (SZ: 35), can indeed be a "semblance," i.e. a "'distortion'" (SZ: 36) of how it is in itself. Thus Heideggerian pp's are not mere appearances. Nor are they *ever* appearances *of* something else (SZ: 36; cf. 151, 325). To conclude: Husserlian pp's necessarily stand *between* us and the ever-unreachable ordinary phenomena. Heideggerian pp's, on the other hand, are what we always already, although ordinarily implicitly, understand *behind* ordinary phenomena – what we "project" them upon in encountering them.

Heidegger does not regard the impossibility of guaranteeing the absolute givenness of pp's to diminish ontology's status as a science. For he rejects Husserl's view that rational certainty and complete freedom from presuppositions are desirable or even possible goals of science in general, and *a forteriori* of phenomenological ontology. During his student years and early teaching career Heidegger experienced first hand the major foundational crises and revolutions in mathematics, physics, biology, history, and theology (SZ: 9f; cf. GA 20: 4–6) that shook the German intellectual world. For Heidegger, appeals to presuppositionless "self-evidence" and the like proved to be entirely useless in such debates about basic concepts and methods. Since Heidegger during this period regarded ontology as a science, the same must apply to it. Thus he writes, with Husserl obviously in mind:

> There is no pure phenomenology . . . according to its essence, it is laden with presuppositions, as is all human activity. And the task of philosophy is not something like doing away with presuppositions at any cost, but rather admitting them and gearing the investigation to them positively and in a manner based in its matters. (GA 21: 279; cf. GA 24: 31)

Consequently, Heidegger frequently and colorfully criticizes Husserl's obsession with the rational certainty of phenomenological assertions as "fantastic" (GA 17: 43), "dogmatic" (GA 17: 303), and "to a certain extent intelligence gone crazy" (GA 17: 43).

Heideggerian ontology must give up on not only the ideal of certainty, but also that of immediate intelligibility. This can be seen in the way in which Heidegger came to modify his concept of *formal indication* in 1929/30, and as foreshadowed already in early 1926 (GA 21: 410). As we have seen, ontology is about the ways in which the individual *herself* encounters entities. It thus differs from natural science in that it literally takes one (Dasein encountering entities in a given ontological structure) to know one (ontological structure). In other words, ontology "is ultimately . . . *ontically* grounded" in the individual's own grasp of each ontological phenomenon in question "as a possibility of being of the respectively existing Dasein" (SZ: 13; cf. GA 29/30: 429). An ontological assertion "in each case points into a concretion of the individual Dasein in the human being," which, in turn, "is always . . . *mine*" (GA 29/30: 429). (Note that this is not a "private object," such as a sensation, but rather the way in which

I encounter *public* entities.) Thus unless I enact the relevant ontological phenomenon in my own case, I will be unable not just to *confirm* ontological assertions about it, but even to *understand* the assertion at all – for I will lack acquaintance with what the terms mean (GA 29/30: 430).

One implication of this ontic basis of ontology is that what would appear to be ontological *assertions* are also really *imperatives*. They "demand" (GA 29/30: 430) that I perform the "task" (GA 29/30: 425) of encountering entities in the manner specified, i.e. "that [my] understanding must first . . . expressly transform itself into the Da-sein in [me]" (GA 29/30: 428). What Heidegger comes to mean by "indication" is just this imperative nature of ontological assertions (GA 29/30: 428). A specifically *formal* indication is one that, like ordinary imperatives, cannot compel, or "cause" (GA 29/30: 429), a reader to enact the structures indicated. And this naturally applies to phenomenological "assertions" found in the later, descriptively articulated stages of an ontological investigation just as much it does to preliminary ones. Thus *all* phenomenological assertions and concepts are formal indications in this later sense (GA 29/30: 435).

Heidegger's 1929/30 view of formal indications brings to light a difficulty peculiar to phenomenological language. Because *ordinary* imperatives are involved in essentially public speech-acts, I can learn the meaning of ordinary imperative words by observing the utterances of *others*, together with the linguistic and non-linguistic consequences of such utterances on them. This appears not to be the case with ontological formal indications. For I cannot learn the meaning of an ontological formal indication until I *myself* have already done what it demands. Until I have done so, there *is* no instance of its being carried out for me to observe, and from which I can learn what it demands. On the other hand, I cannot knowingly carry out what a formal indication demands unless I understand *what* it demands! The comprehension of ontological assertions thus involves a second kind of "hermeneutic circle," not between Dasein's implicit understanding of being and explicit ontological interpretations of it, but between the meanings of ontological terms and the phenomena they indicate. Clearly, this circle is especially difficult "to leap into" (SZ: 315), since until we have done so "in the right way" (SZ: 153), we can't understand the meanings of the terms used. Heidegger thus concedes: "When philosophizing is spoken out then it is given over to . . . that essential *misinterpretation based on its content*" (GA 29/30: 422), which "insinuates itself again and again with infallible certainty" (GA 29/30: 426). The possibility of misunderstanding or incomprehension is endemic to all phenomenological assertions.

Phenomenological Construction as Temporal Analysis

In a manner analogous to Husserl's regional ontology, Heidegger's ontology proceeds by analyzing the temporal constitution of encountered entities. In this respect, however, his analyses differ from Husserl's in two ways. First, whereas regional ontology merely categorizes ways in which entities can be encountered in a single kind of time, Heidegger's make use of two different kinds of time. Second, whereas Husserl's regional ontology deals only with possible present-to-hand entities, Heidegger's "phenomenological chronology" (GA 21: 199–207) differentiates among different ways of *how-being*.

All of Husserl's investigations of time employ what Heidegger calls the "ordinary" concept of time, according to which time is the never-ceasing flow from the protended future that is not yet now, into a punctual present that we can attend to now, and into an ever-receding past that can be retained but is no longer now. Since each point of time can be defined in terms of its relation to the present "now," Heidegger calls the *linear* time of the ordinary conception "now-time," or "world-time," or "intratimeliness" (*Innerzeitigkeit*, parallel to the *intraworldly* entities encountered within it; SZ: 419–22). Because Heidegger rejects Husserl's conception of pp's as mere appearances, he also rejects Husserl's view that "knowing a mere sense-datum" is the proper starting-point of a phenomenology of "the primary and originary consciousness of time," in such a way that "the whole investigation then operates thoroughly around the phenomenon of the temporal passing-away of a tone" (GA 26: 284). Nevertheless, he agrees with Husserl that now-time and the structure of protention, retention, and attention suffice for an understanding of how it is possible to encounter intraworldly entities *as such*. What Heidegger rejects is Husserl's characterization of the temporality of *consciousness*. For Husserl, consciousness is infinitely extended in time, and thus in principle able to survive the annihilation of the physical world, including its body (Husserl 1922: 91–3). Although the *contents* of Husserlian consciousness are constantly in flux, consciousness *itself* is constantly presentable (through the *epoché* and transcendental reduction), and thus a universal (cf. GA 20: 151). For Heidegger, however, Husserl's doctrine of the eternal (non-)temporality of consciousness leaves it entirely incomprehensible why consciousness would ever "bother" with those intraworldly entities that can never be adequately given. What "interest" could it possibly have in going "behind" the absolutely given mere appearances to the necessarily concealed transcendent entities they indicate?

For Heidegger, the key to overcoming Husserl's version of the Cartesian predicament is to explicate Dasein's being. The key here lies in the *existential finitude* and the *circular temporal directional sense* ("TDS" hereafter; cf. Boedeker 2002: 340) of Dasein's being, both of which have a twofold sense (indicated in what follows by superscripts). Dasein's being is finite[1] because it *is* only insofar as it goes about everyday possibilities of itself, such as pursuing a career or being a friend or a family-member, that cannot be pursued without interacting with others, using ready-at-hand tools, and perceiving the present-to-hand. As finite[1], Dasein's own being thus includes the understanding of being as such. Furthermore, the TDS of Dasein's being in the mode of everydayness, or unownedness (*Uneigentlichkeit*), *appears* to be circular[1] (SZ: 153). For it is impossible to specify conditions under which the everyday possibilities of itself, unlike the practical possibilities involved in instrumental dealings with ready-at-hand equipment, could ever be fully *completed*. Being a friend, a family member, etc. does not lead to some goal that, if achieved, would mark the completion, and thus the cessation, of the pursuit of such possibilities (Blattner 1999: 82–6). Indeed, unowned Dasein lives its life in "extensive busy-ness" (SZ: 195), as if its pursuit of these possibilities would never end. The TDS of Dasein's unowned being thus appears to be much like that of the eternal circular[1] motion of Aristotle's heavenly spheres (cf. SZ: 432n1), constantly going about pursuing possibilities that, by their very nature, could never be completed.

The preparatory fundamental ontology of Dasein, undertaken in Division I of *Being and Time*, shows *that* Dasein is finite[1] and apparently circular[1]. What remains unclear from Division I, however, is *why* this must be the case. Demonstrating the latter is one of the main tasks of Division II. There we learn that the apparently infinite TDS of Dasein's unowned being is really just a *semblance*. After all, Dasein will certainly die. It will thus in fact go about the everyday possibilities of itself only a finite number of times. This finitude[2] can be grasped only in the mode of self-ownership (*Eigentlichkeit*). Self-owning Dasein transparently "owns up" to its twofold existential finitude[2] – *both* to the fact that it can *be* only by carrying out everyday possibilities of itself that bring it into contact with others and the intraworldly, *and* to the fact that its mortality implies that it can go about pursuing only a *finite* number of mutually exclusive possibilities of itself (SZ: 285; Boedeker 2001). As revealed by Dasein's finitude[2], Dasein's unowned being *seems* circular[1] only because it flees, or covers over, the certainty of its death.

Self-ownership reveals that the TDS of Dasein's *originary* – i.e. real, as opposed to apparent – being is circular[2] (SZ: 315), something quite different from the apparently eternal circularity[1] of unowned Dasein. One thing that Dasein can glimpse in self-ownership is that in living its life it is constantly and necessarily projecting itself upon possibilities of itself by striving to realize them. Heidegger terms the TDS of projection Dasein's "coming toward [a possibility of] itself." Furthermore, in self-ownership Dasein also glimpses that *every* possibility of itself upon which it projects itself was always already, but usually implicitly, "disclosed" to it as something that it *could* become. This is Dasein's "thrownness," or "facticity," the TDS of which is Dasein's "coming back to [of possibilities of] itself" (SZ: 325). Dasein's originary TDS is circular[2] because each possibility of itself toward which Dasein comes, in striving to actualize it, *is* always an already-disclosed possibility of itself to which it finds itself thrown back. Heidegger characterizes this TDS of Dasein's being as "ec-static," in the sense that Dasein is not a self-contained *substance*, but always "outside itself" (SZ: 329) as it comes toward and back to its own possibilities.

After analyzing Dasein's self-ownership and the originary TDS of its being, Division II concludes by analyzing now-time, the time within which Dasein encounters intraworldly entities. This analysis reveals how very different linear now-time is from Dasein's circular ecstatic temporality. For whereas the essence of circular[2] time lies in the fact that each projected possibility is simultaneously one to which Dasein comes back, the essence of linear time lies in the fact that no point in time can be simultaneously protended and retained. Division II thus leaves thus us with a difficulty. Not only have we not yet seen *why* Dasein's being is finite in the first sense, i.e. why Dasein's being must include the understanding of being as such, but it has become even more unclear *how* this could be the case. For if the now-time within which we encounter intraworldly entities is so different from Dasein's ecstatic temporality, then how is it possible for the two to be related? Hasn't Heidegger put himself in an existentialist version of the mind/body problem?

This problem was to have been dealt with in the never-published Division III of *Being and Time*. Heidegger appears to have had something like the following in mind. In receiving the answer to any question, the questioner *gathers* something that is not identical to the answer. What is thus gathered from answering the question – i.e. the question's *Erfragtes* – is "what is really intended" in the question, i.e. "that by which the questioning reaches its goal" (SZ: 5). For example, if I ask someone how to get to a certain destination, the answer to my question consists in the directions she gives me. What I gather from her answer, however, is the relevant familiarity with the area – in particular, the ability to get to my destination. This familiarity and ability is what makes it possible for her to answer my question, and, once I come to share it with her, for me to understand the answer. Analogously, the *Erfragtes* of the question of *Dasein*'s being is the TDS of its being – ecstatic temporality – since this is what makes it possible for Dasein to understand its own being, i.e. to be able to encounter *itself*. And the *Erfragtes* of the question of being *as such* would be whatever makes it possible for Dasein (as both questioner and questioned) to understand (at first implicitly, and then explicitly) being *as such*. Now, for Heidegger, Dasein's ability to encounter entities in *each* way of being – and thus its understanding of being – involves its being able to project that entity upon a possibility *toward* which Dasein comes by striving to actualize it. And each such projected possibility is always one into whose prior disclosure Dasein finds itself already thrown, and thus toward which Dasein comes *back*. This circular[2] TDS of being as such is thus *identical* to the circular[2] TDS of Dasein's being. Heidegger calls the *Erfragtes* of the question of being as such – what makes it possible for Dasein to understand being – *Temporalität* (SZ: 19; GA 24: 324). Since this is identical to the TDS of Dasein's being, *Temporalität* is Dasein's ecstatic "temporality [*Zeitlichkeit*] insofar as it functions as a condition of possibility of the preontological as well as the ontological understanding of being [as such]" (GA 24: 388; cf. 324, 436). There is no gap between Dasein's understanding of its own being and that of intraworldly entities, for their TDS's are one and the same.

Phenomenological Obstruction as Access to the "*a Priori* Perfect"

Like Husserl, Heidegger frequently characterizes pp's as *a priori* (e.g. GA 20: 100; GA 24: 461). Heidegger, however, claims that his conception of the *a priori* differs from all previous ones (cf. GA 20: 99; GA 24: 27), thus including Husserl's. Recall that the Husserlian *a priori*, encompassing all formal and material categories, is comprised exclusively of universals. And universals are defined phenomenologically as objects that can be given (a) absolutely, i.e. as "mere appearances," exempt from the possibility of semblance, and (b) at any time and at will. We have already examined Heidegger's rejection of Husserl's conception that pp's must be (a). We can now see that for Heidegger they are never (b). And this brings us to the third aspect of ontology as apophantic interpretation: how it properly gains "access" to its phenomena.

We can illustrate this point using three examples, starting with the attempt to turn a semblance into an ontological phenomenon, i.e. to encounter it *as* a semblance. Note that this cannot occur as long as one is being "taken in" by the semblance, but rather only *after* one has come to believe that a phenomenon had been a semblance, and thus after the phenomenon has ceased to be a semblance. One interprets a phenomenon as a semblance only by remembering what the phenomenon used to show itself as while it was a semblance, and comparing this to how one *now* regards the phenomenon. Thus the ontological phenomenon of semblance cannot be extracted from an ordinary phenomenon as long as the latter is actually a semblance. *Semblance* is thus not a universal. Second, insofar as one is actually employing ready-at-hand equipment in the course of a practical project, the ontological phenomenon of readiness-at-hand with its characteristic structure of practical "references" cannot be explicitly or thematically given (SZ: 69). Indeed, Heidegger calls "the *not-announcing-itself*" of these practical references "the condition of the possibility" of employing the ready-at-hand (SZ: 75). For Heidegger, one can explicitly grasp these practical references, and thus the being of readiness-at-hand, "in a *disturbance of reference*" (SZ: 74), or a "break of the referential contexts" (SZ: 75), i.e. when the required tool is either unusable or missing, or when something "obstinate" prevents the practical task from being completed (SZ: 73–5). Thus the ontological phenomenon of readiness-at-hand cannot be extracted from encounters of intraworldly entities as long as the latter are actually ready at hand. *Readiness-at-hand* is thus not a universal. Finally, we have seen that Dasein's originary being is characterized by its projecting entities upon possibilities into which it finds itself thrown. In the mode of unownedness, however, Dasein does not experience all of its possibilities *as* (mere) possibilities, i.e. as something that it *could*, but need not, become. Even in cases of indecision about which of several possibilities to actualize, Dasein projects these possibilities upon some further possibility that it takes as fixed, as *to-be*-actualized, and thus not as a mere possibility. Dasein's possibilities are explicitly disclosed to it *as mere possibilities* (SZ: 187) only in the "extraordinary" mood of anxiety. Anxiety serves "a *fundamental* methodic function for the existential analytic" (SZ: 190) because Dasein's originary being cannot be made into an ontological phenomenon unless Dasein is either in anxiety or remembers having been in anxiety – and remembers it without brushing it off by saying "it was really nothing" (SZ: 187). Thus the ontological phenomenon of Dasein's originary being cannot be extracted from its unowned, anxiety-free being, but only from the extremely rare (SZ: 190) bouts of anxiety. This implies that Dasein's originary being is not a universal.

Ontological phenomena, then, are structures in one's own particular encounters of entities that can be glimpsed only when something out of the ordinary occurs that disrupts the smooth flow of apophantic interpretations, instrumental activity, or living one's life. Only when such disturbances of the ordinary occur does it first become possible to see what had really always been going on already, only unnoticed, or "unthematized." Let us call an ontologically illuminating breakdown a *phenomenological obstruction*. These obstructions are what allow us to gain the right sort of *access* to ontological phenomena – thereby allowing for phenomenological reduction and construction to occur. But since we cannot simply "will" such obstructions into existence at any time, Heidegger's *a priori* is not the traditional eternal, timeless, or universal *a priori* of what is constantly presentable (GA 24: 462). Nevertheless, Heidegger's characterization of the *a priori* retains the traditional aspect of what is "already" understood, "prior to," or "earlier than," particular encounters of entities (GA 20: 99; GA 24: 461). Heidegger's *a priori* is what he calls the "*a priori* perfect" (SZ: 85), i.e. what *always already* structures and makes possible our encounters of entities, but need not be able to be given at any time. Something belongs *a priori* to Dasein's being if and only if Dasein is always already (cf. SZ: 200) thrown into it, and thus something to which Dasein always already comes back. For this reason, Heidegger's *a priori* is a phenomenon belonging not to now-time, but to Dasein's circular temporality.

169

Phenomenological Deconstruction

The fourth and final function of phenomenological apophantic interpretations is to un-conceal being by removing the distortions of it that arise from the use of concepts inap-propriate to it. Heidegger calls this aspect of his method *phenomenological deconstruction* of the history of ontology. He defines this as "a critical dismantling of the traditional concepts that we must at first necessarily employ down to the sources out of which they are drawn" (GA 24: 31; cf. SZ: 21). Rather than being a disparaging criticism of the history of philosophy, deconstruction is really a "positive" (SZ: 21) or "productive appropriation" (GA 24: 31) of the past for the purposes of "today" (SZ: 22). Heidegger's rationale is that contemporary philosophical concepts are in large part our inheritance from the history of philosophy. In many cases, these concepts were coined in the analy-sis of quite particular phenomena, and are entirely appropriate to them. (The concepts of *being* (GA 24: 140–58) and *time* (SZ: 420–7; GA 24: 363–9) are some notable exam-ples.) Subsequently, however, these concepts were applied to phenomena to which they are not appropriate. Going back to the analyses in which these concepts have their origin can thus aid in avoiding such overgeneralizations in one's current investigations. Generally, then, the result of a phenomenological deconstruction is to demonstrate the proper *boundaries* (SZ: 22) of traditional concepts, so that they do not end up distorting the ontological phenomena that we are now interpreting.

Heidegger's insistence on the importance of deconstruction is closely connected with his view of ontology as a science. All sciences necessarily employ concepts in their apo-phantic interpretations. With recent scientific revolutions in mind, Heidegger writes that "The level of a science is determined by the degree to which it is *capable* of a crisis of its basic concepts. In such immanent crises of the sciences, the relation of positively investigating questioning to the interrogated matters becomes unstable" (SZ: 9). In a crisis, the practitioners of a science recognize that its basic concepts fail to do justice to the object-domain, and thereby undertake a revolutionary "revision of the basic concepts" (SZ: 9; cf. GA 24: 467). Now since Husserl's attempts at achieving absolute certainty are designed precisely to immunize phenomenological results against the possibility of radical revision, they end up preventing the discipline from making fundamental progress. The purpose of phenomenological deconstruction is to keep ontology open to the possibility of progress through revolution.

We saw one instance of the hermeneutic circle in the explication of Dasein's preon-tological understanding of being, and a second in the comprehension of ontological assertions. A third lies in the interdependence of construction and deconstruction (cf. SZ: 26; GA 24: 31). Presumably one cannot determine whether a given concept exam-ined in deconstruction is or is not appropriate to a given phenomenon before one has already adequately interpreted that phenomenon – and thus with the use of concepts. But how can one guarantee in advance that these latter concepts are appropriate to the phenomenon until one has critically examined them in deconstruction? For "only through deconstruction can ontology be fully phenomenologically ensured of the genuineness [i.e. appropriateness] of its concepts" (GA 24: 31). The picture that emerges is one quite different from Heidegger's original plan for *Being and Time*, accord-ing to which historical deconstruction was to follow the answer the question of being

(SZ: 39). After publishing SZ, however, Heidegger claimed to the contrary that construction and deconstruction are necessary concomitants that should ideally go together, as two sides of the same coin.

Conclusion

Heidegger's phenomenological method is linked with its results in a manner closer than that of almost any other philosopher. As we have seen, his whole articulation of phenomenological method is guided by an account of apophantic interpretation. His view of the hermeneutic circle in ontology is an application of his general view of understanding and articulation. His definition of *phenomenology* employs a description of the concept of *phenomenon* and the derivative modes of *semblance* and *appearance*. And phenomenological deconstruction is an instantiation of the circular TDS of Dasein's originary being, which Heidegger calls its "historicity" (SZ: 386). Heidegger thus writes that explicating the phenomenological method

> would just be a matter of re-traveling the traversed paths, but only now with explicit reflection upon them. . . . There is no "phenomenology," and if there could be one, then it could never become something like a philosophical technique. For the essence of all genuine method as a path toward disclosing objects lies in accommodating oneself to what itself gets disclosed through it. Precisely when a method is genuine, i.e. gains access to the objects, the progress enacted on its basis and the growing originariness of disclosing necessarily renders that method obsolete. (GA 24: 467)

A methodological explication of Heidegger's phenomenology can thus be nothing but a post-hoc "rational reconstruction" of the path (*methodos*) of research already undertaken. This inextricability of method and result constitutes a fourth and final instance of the hermeneutic circle.

Heidegger's picture during his phenemonological decade was that Dasein can answer the question of being because its originary temporality *is* in fact what is gathered from the question of being. And Dasein gains proper access to its originary temporality, and thus to the sense of being, in moments of anxiety and self-ownership. For it is only in such moments that it gets a complete view of the TDS of its own being. The task of ontology is, *on the basis* of such ontic self-encounters (cf. SZ: 235n1, 338n1), to employ appropriate concepts in correct interpretations about what is thus seen in them. Despite all the differences we have seen between Husserl and Heidegger, Heidegger during his phenomenological decade thus retains Husserl's insistence on the dependence of phenomenological description on "final direct givenness" (GA 20: 120), something much like Husserl's adequate "intuition" (cf. SZ: 363n1).

Although Heidegger never says it during this period, since he equates historicity with the TDS of Dasein's originary being (SZ: 386), and the latter with the TDS of being as such, he is committed to the historicity of being as such. One major difference between his thought during his phenomenological decade that which began to crystalize in the mid-1930s is his view of the nature of the historicity of being. Whereas, in *Being and Time*, Heidegger held that being's historicity could be glimpsed once and for all at one time in anxiety and self-ownership, he comes to hold that it shows itself only "epochally," i.e. by necessarily "withholding," or "withdrawing," itself as it "sends itself" (*sich schicht*). Heidegger thus abandons his phenomenological dream of an adequate intuition of being.

References and further reading

Blattner, W. (1999) *Heidegger's Temporal Idealism.* Cambridge: Cambridge University Press.

Boedeker, E. C. (2001) Individual and community in early Heidegger: situating *das Man*, the *Man-self*, and self-ownership in Dasein's ontological structure. *Inquiry*, 44, 63–100.

Boedeker, E. C. (2002) Phenomenological ontology or the explanation of communal norms? A confrontation with William Blattner's *Heidegger's Temporal Idealism. Archiv für Geschichte der Philosophie*, 84, 334–44.

Breeur, R. (1994) Randbemerkungen Husserls zu Heideggers *Sein und Zeit* und *Kant und das Problem der Metaphysik. Husserl Studies*, 11, 3–63.

Crowell, S. G. (2001) *Husserl, Heidegger and the Space of Meaning: Paths toward Transcendental Phenomenology.* Evanston, IL: Northwestern University Press.

Heidegger, M. (1969) *Zur Sache des Denkens.* Tübingen: Niemeyer.

Heidegger, M. (1987) *Zollikoner Seminare, Protokolle-Gespräche-Briefe.* Frankfurt am Main: Vittorio Klostermann.

Hopkins, B. (1993) *Intentionality in Husserl and Heidegger: The Problem of the Original Method and Phenomenon of Phenomenology.* Dordrecht: Kluwer.

Husserl, E. (1922) *Ideen zu einer reinen Phänomenologie und phänomenologischen Philosophie.* Tübingen: Niemeyer.

Husserl, E. (1950) *Die Idee der Phänomenologie.* The Hague: Nijhoff.

Kisiel, T. (1993) *The Genesis of Heidegger's "Being and Time."* Berkeley: University of California Press.

Sellars, W. (1956/1997) *Empiricism and the Philosophy of Mind.* Cambridge: Harvard University Press.

Stapleton, T. (1983) *Husserl and Heidegger: The Question of a Phenomenological Beginning.* Albany: State University of New York Press.

11

Heidegger's Philosophy of Science

JOSEPH ROUSE

Philosophy of science is not usually considered central to Heidegger's work, at least among English-speaking philosophers, nor is he seen as a significant contributor to philosophy of science. This dissociation is evident in recent work: several comprehensive volumes on Heidegger's philosophy (e.g. Dreyfus and Hall 1992; Guignon 1993) include no essays about his philosophy of science, while Heidegger's views are almost never considered by Anglophone philosophers of science. Yet the dismissal of Heidegger's involvement with philosophy of science is mistaken from both directions.

Understanding Heidegger's philosophy of science requires situating his project with respect to the epistemological turn central to neo-Kantianism and Husserlian phenomenology, and still dominant in philosophy. For both the neo-Kantians (including the logical positivists) and Husserl, philosophical reflection on science concerned scientific knowledge. Science aspired to establish objectively valid knowledge, while philosophy sought to clarify the grounds for its validity. Initially, it might seem obvious that observational evidence is the basis for empirical knowledge. Yet it was not so obvious *how* empirical evidence was related to scientific judgments or statements about the world so as to underwrite their objective validity.

The challenge in accounting for scientific validity or objectivity was complex. First, one had to understand how scientific claims were meaningful, that is, how scientific statements or judgments described the world in one way rather than another. Second, one had to understand how empirical evidence could either justify or challenge such representations. Moreover, there were dual barriers to meeting each challenge. It was not sufficient to establish a contingent motivational or causal relation between making a claim and either having an experience or accepting other claims. Valid claims express what any rational knower *ought* to say, on the *basis* of the relationship invoked as grounds. The grounds for the meaning and justification of scientific claims thus must be normative rather than merely empirically contingent, and their grounding must be intersubjective.

Ignoring otherwise important differences, we can recognize two common features in Husserl's and the neo-Kantians' responses to these challenges. First, the grounds provided for the meaning and validity of scientific knowledge were rationally or transcendentally *necessary* structures or relations. Second, the domain of these necessary structures or relations was independent of the contingencies of the world in which we find ourselves. No mere facts about this world determine what we ought to do or think. Hence, in seeking grounds for epistemic norms, these philosophers consigned their reflections to the "extraworldly" realms of pure logic or transcendental consciousness. Logic was not an empirical science of how people actually reason, but a study of formal structures or norms that actual thinking may not satisfy. Husserlian transcendental consciousness was likewise not a contingent psychophysical domain examined empirically, but a realm of pure meanings that become accessible only when concern with worldly existence is temporarily suspended. In each case, the actual claims made in the sciences in response to contingent empirical events were taken to be meaningful and justified because they (imperfectly) instantiated ideal structures of rational or eidetic necessity.

Heidegger fundamentally objected to thus turning away from the concrete, historical world in which human agents are situated. By locating the normativity of human activity and understanding in ideal necessities of pure logic or transcendental consciousness, Husserl and the neo-Kantians disconnected philosophical reflection from our actual worldly situation. Yet could there be a middle ground between appeals to necessary structures, and a *Weltanschauung* philosophy circumscribed by a particular historical and cultural situation so as to give up any aspiration to a wider philosophical understanding? Heidegger's response to this dilemma challenged the most basic assumptions that led the neo-Kantians and Husserl toward an epistemological conception of science.

Epistemologists treat knowledge as a relation among entities: a knower, an object known, and the knower's representation of the known. The task is then to understand how these entities ought to be related to achieve genuine knowledge. Heidegger thought that unexamined, erroneous presuppositions underlay any such conception of knowers as a special kind of entity (a mind, consciousness, language-speaker, or rational agent), and of knowledge as a relation between entities, insisting that "we have no right to resort to dogmatic constructions and to apply just any idea of being and actuality to this entity [that we ourselves are], no matter how 'self-evident' that idea may be" (SZ: 16). In posing the question of being (of what it means to be, or of the intelligibility of entities as entities), Heidegger sought to circumvent unexamined assumptions about knowledge or consciousness, and engage in a more radical philosophical questioning. Drawing upon Greek and medieval philosophy, he spoke of the "being" of an entity as a way of considering its intelligibility as the entity it is. In taking over this term, Heidegger sought to avoid assuming that the intelligibility ("being") of entities is itself an entity (a meaning, an appearance, a concept, or a thought).

Heidegger's attempt to avoid reifying relations between knower and known by avoiding epistemological presuppositions also led him to reconceive human understanding. Most philosophers take mental states or propositional attitudes (perceiving, judging, desiring) as our basic way of relating to and understanding things. Heidegger talked more encompassingly of our various dealings with or comportments toward entities, and challenged the presumption that such comportments always at least implicitly involve mental or linguistic representation (Heidegger referred to "our" comportments as "Dasein's," a term denoting our distinctive way of being). In everyday comportment, we understand the entities we encounter, but Heidegger construed understanding as practical competence rather than cognition or mental representation (SZ: 143). Cognition and knowledge were supposedly derivative from ("founded upon") such everyday practical understanding.

A central claim in *Being and Time* was that any understanding of entities presupposes an understanding of being. This seemingly obscure claim is clarified by Haugeland's (1998) parallel to chess. One cannot encounter a rook without some grasp of the game of chess. In Heidegger's terms, the "discovery" of chess entities (pieces, positions, moves, or situations) presupposes a prior "disclosure" of chess as the context for their making sense. The "being" of rooks or knight forks is their place within the game, conferring their intelligibility as the entities they are. The game itself only makes sense, however, as a possible way for us to comport ourselves. In any comportments toward entities, then, what we most fundamentally understand is the world as a significant configuration of possible ways for Dasein to be, and our own being-toward those possibilities: "What understanding, as an *existentiale* [an essential structure of our way of being], is competent over is not a "what", but being as existing. . . . Dasein is not something occurrent which possesses its competence as an add-on; it is primarily being-possible" (SZ: 143). The difficult point to grasp here is Heidegger's claim that the "world" (the situation or context) whose disclosure enables discovery of entities is not itself an entity or a collection of entities. If we ask *what* there is, there is nothing but the various and sundry entities we can discover. But we can discover them only because we understand being, and thereby belong to a historically specific situation or "world," a meaningful configuration of possible ways for us to be. The words "possible" or "possibility" can be misleading, however. Heidegger did not mean possible actualities (definite objects, properties, and relations that might have obtained, but actually do not), but actual possibilities (an orientation toward definite but not fully determinate ways for us to be). We can comport ourselves toward possibilities without representing them as such, even implicitly.

We can now ask how Heidegger (in *Being and Time*) conceived of science and its relation to philosophy. Heidegger's early philosophy of science had three principal themes: the priority of fundamental ontology to science, the need for an "existential conception of science," and the ontological significance of science as the discovery of the occurrent (*Vorhanden*).

Heidegger's understanding of philosophy as fundamental ontology sharply contrasted to traditional logical and epistemological conceptions of philosophy's contribution to science. The latter, he thought, "lag behind, investigating the standing a science happens to have" so far (SZ: 10). Such approaches belie the futural orientation of scientific research, and thus utterly misunderstand what matters in science. Heidegger thought that "the authentic [*eigentlich*] 'movement' of the sciences takes place in the more or less radical and self-transparent revision of their basic concepts. The level of a science is determined by the extent to which it is *capable* of a crisis in its basic concepts" (SZ: 9). A philosophy of science that defines its normative task by the already accepted orientation of a particular scientific discipline aims to secure what science itself seeks to surpass. Heidegger thought philosophy could instead contribute "a productive logic, in the sense that it leaps ahead, so to speak, into a particular region of being, discloses it for the first time in the constitution of its being, and makes the structures it arrives at available to the positive sciences as guidelines for their inquiry" (SZ: 10). Heidegger

175

thought philosophy could do this because the sciences, like any other human activities, proceed from a prior understanding of the being of the entities they encounter. Such understanding involves a practical grasp (*not* an articulated description) of what entities are involved, how to approach them in revealing ways, and what would amount to success in dealing with them. The discovery and articulation of what there is in a particular scientific domain draws upon and further develops this prior disclosure of their being. Philosophical reflection upon a particular science's understanding of being (its "regional" ontology) considers the *a priori* conditions of the possibility of investigating entities in its domain (SZ: 11), but it would not thereby seek *a priori* knowledge. Heidegger claimed that "the original sense of the *a priori*" had nothing to do with knowledge (GA 20: 34). He instead used the term "*a priori*" to designate what is ontologically prior, the conditions of possibility of entities themselves (as the kind of entities they are) rather than conditions of possibility of our *knowledge* of entities. Heidegger's call for reflection upon the *a priori* conditions of possibility of entities thus directly opposed any armchair philosophy seeking *a priori* knowledge. Heidegger instead noted approvingly that many contemporary scientific disciplines (specifically mathematics, physics, biology, the historical sciences, and theology) were engaged in renewed reflections upon their conceptual foundations, and that such developments were appropriately philosophical turns within those disciplines (SZ: 9–10). Philosophical ontology should be continuous with such scientific developments. His explicit models for philosophical ontology were the contributions of Plato, Aristotle, and Kant. In the latter case, he thought, "the positive outcome of Kant's *Critique of Pure Reason* lies in its contribution to working out what belongs to any nature whatsoever, not in a 'theory' of knowledge" (SZ: 10–11). Kant's work was not "prior" to Newton, but a philosophical (ontological) engagement with Newtonian physics.

Philosophy could distinctively contribute to ontological reflection within any particular science, for two reasons. The most important reason was that the "regional" disclosure of being within any particular scientific domain was supposedly dependent upon an understanding of being in general. Just as understanding rooks requires understanding chess, and chess is understood as a possible mode of Dasein's being-in-the-world, so Heidegger thought that disclosing the being of entities within any scientific domain presupposes an understanding of being in general. Until this understanding of being had been clarified, any regional ontology, "no matter how rich and tightly linked a system of categories it has at its disposal, remains blind and perverted from its ownmost aim" (SZ: 11).

The second reason why early Heidegger saw philosophical reflection as essential for science turned upon his proposed "existential" conception of science. Heidegger thought an "existential" conception of science was needed, because "sciences, as human comportments, have [Dasein's] way of being" (SZ: 11). Dasein's way of being is future-oriented; it "presses forward into [its] possibilities," and does so out of concern for its own being. Dasein's most basic relation to itself is not self-consciousness, but care: Dasein is "the entity whose own being is at issue for it" (SZ: 42), such that everything it does responds to that issue. Note that for Heidegger, terms such as "care," "concern," or "solicitude" refer not to mental states, but to whole ways of comporting oneself. An existential conception of science would not emphasize public behavior over private mental states, however; Heidegger sought to avoid familiar distinctions between

176

"inner" and "outer" or public and private realms. The important contrast was tempo-ral: an existential conception of science emphasized scientific possibilities, in contrast to "the 'logical' conception which understands science with regard to its results and defines it as an 'inferentially interconnected web [*Begründungszusammenhang*] of true, that is, valid propositions'" (SZ: 357). Heidegger thus focused upon science as some-thing people do, rather than scientific knowledge as acquired and assessed retrospec-tively. Understood existentially, science is not the accumulation of established knowledge, but is always directed ahead toward possibilities it cannot yet fully grasp or articulate.

Heidegger gave philosophical priority to his existential-ontological conception of science, but also thought that the greater familiarity of logical and ontical conceptions showed something important about science. Although science always presupposes an understanding of being, the scientific project of discovering what and how entities are within its domain obscures the understanding of being that makes inquiry possible. Its determined focus upon the *entities* it investigates takes for granted the understanding of being that provides its focus. We can now grasp the second reason why Heidegger thought that philosophy was indispensable to science, as a challenge to a "normalizing" tendency inherent in scientific research itself (Haugeland 1998: chapter 13; 2000). Thomas Kuhn's (1970) account of normal science eloquently expresses that tendency in scientific work which Heidegger thought made it inevitably dependent upon philosophical questioning (regardless of whether it is scientists or philosophers who raise such questions). For Kuhn as for Heidegger, "normal" science avoids controversy over fundamentals in order to develop with greater detail and precision its unquestioned conceptual and practical grasp of a domain of entities. Left to their own devices, both thought, the sciences suppress any fundamental questioning of how their domains constitute fields of possible inquiry. When such questioning becomes unavoidable through the breakdown of positive research into a particular domain, scientists do not then undertake ontological inquiry for its own sake, but seek only to reconstitute their ability to attend carefully to entities without having to inquire into their being. Where Kuhn and Heidegger diverged was that Kuhn endorsed this closing off of ontological inquiry, whereas Heidegger did not.

Heidegger saw scientific normalization as an essential ontological dimension of science, rather than a contingent and possibly objectionable psychological tendency or social pressure. Here emerges the final theme in Heidegger's early philosophy of science, the connection between science and "occurrentness" (*Vorhandenheit*) as a mode of being. Although Heidegger insisted even in *Being and Time* that being was not itself an entity, there could still be a science of being (fundamental ontology) because there were articulable distinctions within the understanding of being. These "fundamental" distinctions did not define the regional ontologies demarcating *domains of entities* studied by positive sciences (nature, mathematics, language, history, and the like), but instead marked different *ways of being*, of intelligibility as entities. Most basically, Heidegger distinguished the being of Dasein (being-in-the-world) from "innerworldly" ways of being. He was not always careful to distinguish us, the entities whose way of being is Dasein, from Dasein itself as a mode of intelligibility, but the distinction is crucial. Heidegger sought to understand being, not do empirical anthropology.

Heidegger initially distinguished Dasein's way of being from the "occurrentness" of things (such as a mind, soul, ego, body, or person). He then argued, however, that the entities we deal with in our ordinary everyday lives are not occurrent either. Equipment is not a collection of entities with intrinsic properties. Something can only be a hammer, in his familiar example, in "relation" to nails, boards, carpentry, and ultimately those human activities for which hammering and fastening are integral. These interrelations are more ontologically basic than the relata: "Strictly speaking, there is no such thing as *an* equipment. . . . [Equipmental] 'things' never show themselves initially for themselves, so as to fill out a room as a sum of real things. What we encounter as closest to us, although unthematically, is the room" (SZ: 68). Moreover, equipment works best when we needn't think about it at all, and can focus on the task at hand (what is ahead of us). The being of equipment is not the occurrentness of an entity with properties, but the availability of such normally tacit functionality.

One kind of equipment does call attention to itself, however. Signs only function when we notice them. Signs still have the being of equipment, signifying only within a larger practical context. Assertions, however, are signs that allow things to show up differently. Assertions point out entities and make them communicable. Heidegger thought that assertion is in this respect dependent upon everyday practical involvement. Talk about things as occurrent presupposes a practical understanding of an equipmentally interconnected "world."

The ontological significance of science for early Heidegger was bound up with linguistic assertion as a derivative mode of interpretation. To this extent, Heidegger's early philosophy of science remained quite traditional. Science *describes* entities, and thereby strips them of ordinary human significance. Some assertions do place entities within a local, practical situation. In science, however, we discover entities shorn of their practical involvements, as merely occurrent. We then talk about a hammer not as appropriate and available for a task at hand, but as an object with mass and spatiotemporal location. It thereby acquires a new mode of intelligibility. Its local, contextual involvements are displaced by a theoretical contextualization:

> What is decisive for the development [of mathematical physics] . . . lies in *the mathematical projection of nature itself*. This projection discovers in advance something constantly occurrent (matter), and opens the horizon to look for guidance to its quantitatively determinable constitutive aspects (motion, force, location, and time). (SZ: 362)

In talking about a "mathematical" projection, however, Heidegger was emphasizing science's prior ontological determination of entities, not its partially quantitative character: "*Ta mathēmata* means for the Greeks that which man knows in advance in observing entities and dealing with things: the corporeality of bodies, the vegetable character of plants, the animality of animals, the humanness of man" (GA 5: 78). This ontological understanding of theoretical interpretation served two roles. The disclosure and theoretical articulation of entities as occurrent was a genuine, truthful accomplishment of empirical science. This accomplishment, however, was doubly dependent upon its clarification through philosophical ontology.

In the most obvious dependence, science and cognition more generally are derivative modes of understanding. Assertions about occurrent entities are intelligible only through Dasein's prior immersion in a world. Fundamental ontology then clarifies the relation between assertions in theoretical science and the understanding of being they presuppose, for example, by showing how the theoretical discovery of occurrent entities arose by modifying everyday involvement with available equipment (SZ: ¶69b). But scientific assertion was also supposedly derivative in a more troubling way. Assertions can correctly "point out" entities as occurrent. But assertions also thereby indispensably allow what-is-said (*das Geredete*) to be passed on in "idle talk" (*Gerede*) that obscures understanding. Assertions are "ambiguous" in that they can be uttered with or without understanding and, most important, with or without responsibility to what is being talked about. In making understanding communicable, assertion also makes possible a mere semblance of understanding.

Grasping why Heidegger thought scientific assertions relentlessly turn us away from genuine understanding requires further consideration of Heidegger's treatment of assertion and meaning. Most of his philosophical contemporaries, impressed by the need to understand error and thought about non-existent things, posited meanings as intermediaries between thought and things. We can talk and think about what does not exist, or falsely about what does exist, because our grasp of meanings is more basic than our acquaintance with things. Heidegger rejected such appeals to semantic intermediaries. Assertions "point out" entities themselves, not meanings: "The assertion ['the picture on the wall is hanging crookedly'] . . . in its ownmost meaning is related to the real picture on the wall. What one has in mind is the real picture, and nothing else" (SZ: 217). Like advocates of causal theories of reference nowadays, Heidegger accounted for linguistic articulation by situating talk within a larger pattern of interaction, rather than within a linguistic or theoretical structure. Error is a holistic relation to the entities with which we actually interact discursively, not a direct grasp of meanings that fail to represent anything correctly. Heidegger differed from today's advocates of a causal theory of reference in taking our more basic dealings with our surroundings to be practical-normative rather than causal. They make common cause, however, in construing language as interaction with the world rather than as a formal structure of meanings connected to the world only indirectly.

For Heidegger, however, the claim that assertion is a comportment toward entities gives heightened and ironic significance to the possibility of repeating what is asserted. By making what-is-said communicable, assertions can become distant from the entities they point out and are accountable to. Their proximate grounds then become not the entities themselves, but other assertions. There are two distinct ways in which such "idle talk" substitutes other assertions for the entities talked about as what is primarily understood. Most obviously, assertions can be grounded in testimony: I can make an assertion not from my own understanding of how things stand, but as merely passing on what others say, with the anonymous authority of what "one" says. But assertions can also be grounded inferentially upon other assertions, with their authority mediated by complex networks of other claims. These two forms of interdependence are intertwined, for developing and sustaining complex networks of belief requires sharing and passing on what others say.

179

The indispensability of inferential networks for scientific understanding highlights Heidegger's insistence that his account of idle talk is not altogether disparaging. He did not reject articulated theoretical understanding, but only recognized that in developing more extensively articulated theoretical networks, the sciences risk becoming more invested in their own vocabularies and theories than in the things to be understood. Contrary to the sciences' familiar fallibilist image, Heidegger worried that the development of a science *closes off* the possibility that entities might resist our familiar ways of encountering and talking about them. For Heidegger, science needed philosophy in order to remain "in the truth." The greatest danger in science was not error, which is more readily correctable by further inquiry, but the emptiness of assertions closed off from genuine accountability to entities (in this respect, Heidegger's concern bears surprising affinities to McDowell 1994). Thus, Heidegger insisted that truth as correct assertion was grounded in a more fundamental sense of truth as "unhiddenness": correctness alone would not yield genuine understanding unless the entities themselves were continually wrested away from burial in mere talk. We can then connect Heidegger's account of science as the discovery of entities as occurrent, and his insistence upon the need to ground science in fundamental ontology. In focusing upon the cognitive discovery of the occurrent, science inevitably pulls us away from its own "highest" possibility, a readiness for and openness to crisis in its basic concepts out of fidelity to the entities in question. Only in "philosophically" turning away from involvement with and idle talk about entities, toward the understanding of being within which entities are disclosed, could science remain open to truthful disclosure of things themselves.

The sciences' inherent tendency to obscure the entities they discover behind a veil of idle talk is recapitulated and reinforced by the dominant epistemological conception of philosophical reflection. The sciences, in their very efforts to discover and describe entities, lose sight of the entities themselves through involvement in an inferentially interconnected web of assertions. Epistemologically oriented philosophers make explicit and deliberate this tendency to "fall" away from understanding of entities themselves. Whereas science aims to understand the world, epistemological philosophers take scientific cognition as their own subject matter, at one remove from scientific concern. For Heidegger, by contrast, the most important philosophical task regarding the sciences was to help to renew their truthful openness to "the things themselves." In this respect, Heidegger's questioning of being would be seriously misunderstood were it seen as turning away from science toward something obscure and "metaphysical." In thinking about the being of entities discovered in science, we do not think about something *else*. Being is not itself an entity, but only the disclosure of entities as intelligible. Heidegger's ontological reflection would not turn away from the subject matter of the sciences, but instead aims to return afresh to "the things themselves" in their essential disclosedness. For Heidegger, Aristotle's sustained reflections upon biology or Kant's upon mechanics were not a failure yet to distinguish philosophy clearly from science, but instead recognized philosophy's highest calling. Here as elsewhere, Heidegger's work has important affinities with late twentieth-century philosophical naturalism (Rouse 2002).

There were nevertheless tensions within Heidegger's early philosophy of science, indicating fundamental difficulties within his project as a whole. Fundamental ontology was an ahistorical, transcendental-philosophical inquiry into human existence as essentially historical and worldly. In their turn to formal structures of pure logic or transcendental consciousness, Heidegger thought his philosophical opponents had irrevocably severed their connection to the worldly phenomena they aspired to understand. Heidegger adamantly opposed any comparable formalization of his own ontological categories. The in-order-to-for-the-sake-of relations that articulate the being of what is available (*Zuhanden*) can, he admitted,

> be grasped formally in the sense of a system of relations. But . . . in such formalizations the phenomena get leveled off so much that their real phenomenal content may be lost. . . . The "in-order-to", the "for-the-sake-of", the "with-which" of involvement . . . are instead relationships in which concernful circumspection as such already dwells. (SZ: 88)

It was unclear, however, *why* the essential structures of fundamental ontology did not also evanesce into ahistorical, immaterial formal relations (Brandom this volume, chapter 13 gives a lucid account of what such a formalization of availability would look like). Heidegger aimed to show how these structures were manifest within the concrete comportments of Dasein as being-in-the-world, but at multiple points, questions arise concerning how the ontological structures connect to the concrete comportments and entities. For example, how do scientific-Dasein's concrete everyday practices of scientific theorizing (conceived "existentially") relate to the abstract ontological category of science as the theoretical discovery of the occurrent? More generally, how were the differences among ways of being (Dasein, availability, or occurrentness) relevant to the ontological determination of scientific domains such as nature or history? How and why, for example, should the human sciences' investigations of human beings as entities be determined by an understanding of Dasein as our way of being? Likewise, what is the relation between us as cases of Dasein and us as biological or physical entities? Finally, Heidegger's account of science incorporated an ontologically decisive but concretely elusive "changeover" from "the understanding of being that guides concernful dealings with entities" to "looking at those available entities in a 'new' way as occurrent" (SZ: 361). This changeover involves both a shift from contextual communication (hammers that are "too heavy" or "misplaced") to thematic assertions about mass or location in spacetime as occurrent properties, and from everyday understanding to "the mathematical projection of nature." Yet Heidegger merely asserted such a changeover without adequately describing it. The associated changeover from Dasein's practical familiarity with linguistic signs as "equipment for indicating" to explicit, decontextualized assertion was likewise both central and obscure in Heidegger's early philosophy of language.

Reflection on science was central to Heidegger's reorientation of his philosophical project in the mid-1930s. Notably, Heidegger abandoned fundamental ontology. His attempt to articulate essential differences among ways of being, and thus make ontology a philosophical "science," was supplanted by an historicized understanding of the intelligibility of entities: "metaphysics grounds an age . . . through a specific interpretation of entities and through a specific conception of truth" (GA 5: 75). Not only did Dasein's way of being thereby lose centrality, but occurrentness and availability also ceased to be basic categories. Science could then no longer have the ontological significance of discovering entities as occurrent.

The abandonment of fundamental ontology significantly transformed Heidegger's phenomenology of science, developed most extensively in "Age of the World-Picture" (GA 5). Having lost its fundamental-ontological significance, science was reconceived as an essential phenomenon of modernity. Heidegger's earlier account of science as the discovery of the occurrent now seemed too reminiscent of traditional accounts of science as cognition or justified assertion. To replace this residue of traditional epistemology, Heidegger characterized modern science instead as research. Scientific research encompasses its practitioners "within the essential form of the technologist in the essential sense; only in this way can [they] remain capable of being effective" (GA 5: 85). Modern science thus does not suspend practical concern with entities, but intensifies it.

Heidegger retained *Being and Time*'s claim that the "mathematical projection of nature" was decisive for modern science, but radically shifted his conception of what that projection accomplished. Previously, the "mathematical" character of physics disentangled entities from their practical involvements so as to thematize them as objects. On his revised view, the mathematical projection of physical entities instead intensified and more stringently governed scientists' dealings with them:

> Every forging-ahead (*Vorgehen*) already requires a circumscribed domain in which it moves. And it is precisely the opening up of such a domain that is the fundamental process (*Grundvorgang*) in research. This is accomplished, in so far as within a region of entities, e.g. nature, a determinate configuration of natural processes (*Naturvorgänge*) has been projected. This projection sketches out beforehand the way that a cognizant forging-ahead must bind itself to the domain opened up. This binding commitment is the rigor of research. . . . This projection of nature is secured, in so far as physical research binds itself to it in each step of its questioning. (GA 5: 77, 79)

Heidegger presented such a rigorously self-binding moving ahead within a projected domain of entities as the first essential characteristic of science that has been transformed into research.

A second distinctive feature of research is its guidance by a distinctive way of proceeding. In advancing further into a projected domain, research must be open to variation and novelty among the phenomena discovered, yet must also sustain the generality and objectivity of its overall conception. This dual demand accounts for the centrality of natural laws in modern scientific explanation:

> Only within the purview of the incessant-otherness of change does the rich particularity of facts show itself. But the facts must become objective. The forging-ahead [of science] must therefore represent the changeable in its changing, holding it steady while nevertheless letting motion be a motion. The stasis of facts in their continuing variation is regularity (*Regel*). The constancy of change in the necessity of its course is law. Facts first become clear as the facts they are within the purview of regularity and law. Empirical research into nature is intrinsically the putting forward and confirming of regularities and laws. (GA 5: 80)

This process of unifying manifold phenomena under more general laws simultaneously extends and legitimates the projection of nature governing ongoing research: "Explanation, as a clarification on the basis of what is clear, is always ambiguous. It accounts for an unknown by means of a known, and at the same time confirms that known by means of that unknown" (GA 5: 80). The facts receive their definitive determination through subsumption under law, whose authority is secured by success in accounting for a multitude of facts.

Heidegger presented the turn to experimental science as a consequence of this novel way of proceeding rather than its basis. Only with nature reconceived as the unification of diverse events under law could the creation of new phenomena in the laboratory be thought to yield fundamental insights rather than just a proliferation of curiosities. "Experiment begins with the laying down of a law as its basis. To set up an experiment means to represent a condition under which a definite configuration of motions is trackable in the necessity of its course, i.e. of being controlled in advance by calculation" (GA 5: 81). This shift is a general imperative of research, however, and not merely the projection of nature as a distinctively law-governed domain. For Heidegger, all modern research methods, from experimentation to historical source criticism, depended upon a comparable play between an explanatory scheme and the particular objects or events subsumed within it. Research inevitably forms specialized disciplines, each pursuing its characteristic explanatory scheme as far as possible.

For Heidegger, this relentless extension of its explanatory frameworks was a third fundamental characteristic of modern science, as *enterprise* (*Betrieb*; the standard English translations of "*Betrieb*" as "ongoing activity" or "continuing activity" miss its overtones of business enterprise and factory works). What drives scientific research is not the significance of the results sought, but the need to secure and expand the enterprise of science itself:

> The way of proceeding (*Verfahren*) through which individual object-domains are conquered does not simply amass results. Rather, with the help of its results, it adapts itself for a new forging-ahead. . . . This having to adapt itself to its own results as the ways and means of an onward-marching way of proceeding is the essence of research's character as enterprising. (GA 5: 84)

Earlier, Heidegger worried that interconnected theoretical assertions obscured the sciences' accountability to the entities they thereby discovered. In the "World-Picture" essay, an analogous tendency becomes the defining *modus operandi* of scientific research. Supplying the incessant demands of the research enterprise for new problems to work on, and new material, conceptual, and institutional resources to apply to those problems, takes precedence over the disclosure and discovery of entities: "What is taking place in this extending and consolidating of the institutional character of the sciences? Nothing less than securing the precedence of their way of proceeding (*Verfahren*) over the entities (nature and history) that are being objectified in research at that time" (GA 5: 84). The enterprising character of modern science also transforms its participants. Researchers are not scholars. Their characteristic virtues are not erudition but incisiveness, not reflection but constant activity, not insight but effectiveness in getting the job done.

183

What is the "job" of science, however? In *Being and Time*, science aimed to discover entities as occurrent. Philosophers could then guide scientific interpretations of entities with insights from fundamental ontology. The modern orientation of science as research presented in "Age of the World-Picture" undermines any philosophical governance, however. It seeks to maximize the flexibility of the research enterprise itself, unconstrained by prior accountability to a domain of entities:

> The predilection imposed by the actual system of science is not for a contrived and rigidly interrelated unification of the content of object-domains, but for the greatest possible free but regulated flexibility in initiating and switching the leading task of research at any given time. The more exclusively science isolates itself for the complete conduct (*Betreibung*) and mastery of its work process, and the more unapologetically its enterprises (*Betriebe*) are transferred to research institutes and professional schools, the more irresistably do the sciences consummate their modern essence. (GA 5: 86)

What makes a research task important is not the intrinsic significance of its projected discoveries, but the possibility of opening new vistas for further research. Here Heidegger emphasized a kinship between modern science and technology, not simply because of technological applications of knowledge or scientific uses of technology. Rather, each relentlessly overrides any accountability that might constrain the expansion of its capacities for calculation and control. There is and can be no further "for-the-sake-of-which" for modern scientific research; it orders and calculates so as to expand the domain of research, by making entities more fully and extensively calculable. Heidegger's characterization of the research enterprise is thus reminiscent of Plato's vision of the tyrant's soul, driven by an insatiable aspiration to mastery that cannot acknowledge any inherent limits or goals.

There was an important practical and political dimension to this criticism of modern science. Throughout his career, Heidegger addressed philosophical governance of the sciences (not just the natural sciences, but all academic disciplines) in terms of the need for university reform (Crowell 1997). His account of the sciences as overriding any wider normative accountability in part responded to his own disastrous attempt five years earlier to give philosophical direction to the University of Freiburg as rector under the Nazis. However one assesses the relation between Heidegger's vision and the Nazis' political program, Heidegger quickly found the university utterly recalcitrant to his philosophical aims.

What would Heidegger's revised conception of modern science imply for philosophy of science, however? Despite abandoning fundamental ontology and the ahistorical conception of science as discovering entities as occurrent, Heidegger continued to place science at the center of a large *philosophical* story about truth and being. The convergence of science and technology was conceived as an essential phenomenon of modernity, and thereby as a focus for metaphysical reflection. Technoscience allowed entities to show themselves as calculable and orderable, and thereby revealed the impending loss of any meaningful differences in the modern world. The source of this tendency was not just a sociological drive toward professional autonomy for scientific institutions, however, but a metaphysical transformation of the intelligibility of entities.

This reconception changed the significance of epistemological conceptions of science. No longer merely philosophical errors, they supposedly express the "errancy" of the modern world itself, as the "age of the world-picture": "World-picture, when understood essentially, does not mean a picture of the world but the world conceived as picture. What is in its entirety [entities] is now taken to be first and only insofar as it is set in place by human representation and production" (GA 5: 89). Heidegger was not thereby endorsing an idealist or constructivist thesis about entities. He was instead claiming that the *being* of entities (their intelligibility, the ways in which they can manifest themselves) is now determined by the demands of human thought and action, in ways that also reconceive humans as subjects. The link between these reconceptions is apparent in treatments of accountability to entities as "objectivity," or correct representation. The ideal of objectivity is to allow the object to show itself as it is, unchanged by how we conceive or deal with it. But what is thereby determined is not the object, but our dealings with it. Taking the right stance toward it or employing the right methods is taken as decisive for whether it shows itself rightly. Human representation and praxis thereby seem to arbitrate what is real.

This conception apparently exalts human beings: our norms and goals govern the intelligibility of anything and everything. But Heidegger thought that sense of mastery was illusory. The relentlessly conjoined objectification of entities and subjectification of our accountability to them inevitably transformed that accountability itself into a further object (a "value") for a subject. Values then need clarification and objective assessment in turn, but their objectification as values to be chosen undermines their authority over the choice. "Value appears to express that one is positioned toward it so as to pursue what is most valuable, and yet that very value is the impotent and threadbare disguise of the objectivity of entities having become flat and backgroundless. No one dies for mere values" (GA 5: 102). This loss of accountability beyond ourselves, and hence of the possibility that what we do could make a significant difference, supposedly conjoined science and technology with the subjectivization of art and the holy as "essential phenomena of modernity."

This historicized conception of philosophy as metaphysics retained Heidegger's earlier negative assessment of the sciences' capacity to understand their own significance and normativity. Science as such could not uncover its "essence," the metaphysics of the world as picture which made the transformation of science into a research enterprise seem appropriate and inevitable. Only philosophical reflection could hold open the possibility of an alternative understanding. This claim depended upon a contentious distinction between science and philosophy, however. In lectures contemporaneous with "Age of the World-Picture," Heidegger acknowledged that Galileo and Newton, or Heisenberg and Bohr, were doing philosophy rather than "mere" science.[1] The need for such gerrymandering suggests difficulties with Heidegger's claim that science inevitably closed off a more fundamental ontological understanding: the most important and influential scientific work had to count as philosophy instead, precisely *because* it was unquestionably insightful.

Throughout his career, Heidegger thus characterized science in ways analogous to his early association of science with idle talk. Science "as such" for Heidegger was never the opening of a genuine disclosure of how entities show themselves, but only an unreflective ("thoughtless") effort to secure entities within a prior disclosure taken for granted. This attitude was made possible, however, by a more fundamental mistake. Science as such cannot be essentially "untruthful" in these ways without an essence in the first place, unless there *is* such a thing as "science as such." Heideggerian essences are always ontological. In *Being and Time*, the essence of science was to discover entities as occurrent. Later, he claimed that modern science projected entities as calculable and orderable, in ways that govern any particular scientific conceptualization in advance: "Physics . . . will never be able to renounce this one thing: that nature reports itself in some way or other that is identifiable through calculation and that it remains orderable as a system of information" (GA 7: 23). What is ontologically crucial about this way of revealing, for Heidegger, is its relentless overriding of any issues or stakes to which the demand for calculability could be held accountable. Science's ordering and calculation of entities only expands the domain of research, making entities more fully and extensively calculable, with no further "for-the-sake-of-which."

Heidegger's rendition of the history of modern science as a relentless expansion of calculative control may seem initially plausible in light of the "Second Scientific Revolution." In the eighteenth and nineteenth centuries, the Baconian sciences of chemistry, heat, electricity, magnetism, and later biology and geology were gradually encompassed within mathematized, experimental science. In the twentieth century, its reach has extended to ever smaller, ever larger or more distant, and even complex or chaotic phenomena. The domain of experimental manipulation and theoretical modeling seems to expand without apparent bounds. Yet Heidegger's construal of science's relentless expansion overlooks that only a few phenomena within these domains matter scientifically. Most truths about the natural world are of no scientific significance whatsoever; scientific research instead focuses its attention on specific phenomena, experimental systems, and theoretical concepts and models that seem to advance scientific understanding. And as Heidegger's own views suggest, such understanding is always oriented toward a subsequent advance, not a retrospective accounting of accumulated knowledge.

Moreover, which phenomena are at issue in a given field or research program has frequently shifted over time, with accompanying shifts in what is at stake there. For example, Hans-Jörg Rheinberger (1997) noted multiple consequential occasions when experimental studies of cancer shifted fairly seamlessly into investigations of "normal" cellular processes now manifest in cancer cells. What mattered scientifically was then no longer the difference between normal and abnormal cells, but common characteristics of their structure and function. The 1973 "November Revolution" in physics marked by the discovery of weak neutral currents is another example, with fundamental shifts in which high-energy events were worth studying (from soft hadron scattering to lepton-lepton interactions and hard scattering of hadrons), and toward symmetries and symmetry-breaking as central issues in theoretical modeling (Galison 1987: chapter 4; Pickering 1984). Such cases cannot be appropriately regarded as impositions of a predetermined orientation toward calculative control upon nature as a plastic resource, for what it matters to understand calculatively, and what is at stake in its success, has shifted. Such shifts instead reflect an openness within science to allowing things to show themselves intelligibly in new ways, and to do so by letting "the actual results guide the decision about what to do next" (Rheinberger 1995: 60).

Far from invariably seeking greater mastery, such shifts may *sacrifice* calculative precision and laboratory control to advance different concerns. Dobzhansky's adaptation of *Drosophila* genetics to study genetic variation in natural populations deliberately sacrificed both experimental precision and mathematical tractability of inheritance (Kohler 1994: chapter 8). Similarly, attention to the semiclassical boundary phenomena characteristic of so-called "postmodern quantum mechanics" forsakes mathematical elegance and systematicity in taking advantage of multiple formally inconsistent models simultaneously, to encourage a physics of irreducible complexity (Heller and Tomsovic 1993). Such a physics of complexity seeks a deeper understanding of "chaotic" phenomena, which recognizes limits to their detailed prediction and control.

Often the stakes in such shifts are fundamental to human self-understanding. Dobzhansky's work helped to form the neo-Darwinian synthesis, which not only placed evolution by natural selection at the center of a more unified biology, but also had wider consequences ranging from the biological eclipse of "race" to classifications of intelligence and culture as evolved adaptations. Postmodern quantum mechanics rejects the quasi-theological fundamentalism governing much of recent high-energy physics, abandoning the quest for a unified "Theory of Everything" in favor of more local, situated comprehension. Similarly, the phoenix-like emergence of developmental biology from the ashes of embryology, and the concomitant eclipse of genetics by genomics, challenge the now-familiar conception of genes and DNA as the calculatively controllable "secret of life" and biological surrogate for the soul (Keller 1992; Nelkin and Lindee 1995; Oyama et al. 2001).

We need to understand these far-reaching shifts in scientific significance (where "understanding" is meant not narrowly cognitively, but in Heidegger's sense of ability to respond appropriately to possibilities). But Heidegger's aspiration to a grand, nostalgic philosophical history of being obscures these and other cases in which meaningful differences emerge from scientific efforts to wrest phenomena from hiddenness. The point of thus speaking about science in ways more akin to Heidegger's remarks on art is not to reverse Heidegger's hierarchy and instead proclaim science as a privileged locus for the happening of truth. Rather, I am questioning any sharp or even significant boundaries between science and other meaningful comportments as practices that allow entities to show themselves intelligibly. My examples were chosen because they can be rightly described neither as scientific determinations of how things matter to us, *nor* as sociocultural determinations of scientific significance. Rather, they show how scientific understanding is integral to a larger historical disclosure of possibilities, within which scientific practices acquire and transform their issues and stakes. Heidegger's treatment of the futural orientation of scientific research as more basic than the retrospective assessment of knowledge constructively contributes to understanding this aspect of science. Developing this contribution further, however, requires abandoning Heidegger's residual essentialism about science, and especially his

187

insistence that science can play only a derivative, even counterproductive, role in making intelligible our situation and its stakes.

Notes

Parts of this chapter are adapted from Rouse (2003). An earlier version was presented to the International Society for Phenomenological Studies in 2002. Translations from *Sein und Zeit* and *Holzwege* (GA 5) are modified. Thanks to William Blattner and Taylor Carman for critical review of revised translations, and to the editors for helpful comments on the entire paper.

1 Heidegger (1967, p. 67). In *Being and Time*, Heidegger cited relativity theory as exemplary of an ontological reawakening in physics (SZ: 9–10). The omission of Einstein's name alongside Heisenberg and Bohr ten years later inevitably invites questions about Heidegger's deference to Nazi campaigns against "Jewish physics."

References and further reading

Crowell, S. G. (1997) Philosophy as a vocation: Heidegger and university reform in the early inter-war years. *History of Philosophy Quarterly*, 14, 255–76.

Dreyfus, H. L. and Hall, H. (1992) *Heidegger: A Critical Reader*. Oxford: Blackwell.

Galison, P. L. (1987) *How Experiments End*. Chicago: Chicago University Press.

Guignon, C. B. (1993) *Cambridge Companion to Heidegger*. Cambridge: Cambridge University Press.

Haugeland, J. (1998) *Having Thought: Essays in the Metaphysics of Mind*. Cambridge, MA: Harvard University Press.

Haugeland, J. (2000) Truth and finitude: Heidegger's transcendental existentialism. In M. Wrathall and J. Malpas (eds), *Heidegger, Authenticity and Modernity*. Cambridge, MA: MIT Press.

Heidegger, M. (1967) *What Is a Thing?* (trans. W. Barton and V. Deutsch). Chicago: Regnery (original work published 1962).

Heller, E. and Tomsovic, S. (1993) Postmodern quantum mechanics. *Physics Today*, 46, 38–46.

Keller, E. F. (1992) *Secrets of Life, Secrets of Death: Essays on Language, Gender and Science*. New York: Routledge.

Kohler, R. E. (1994) *Lords of the Fly: Drosophila Genetics and the Experimental Life*. Chicago: Chicago University Press.

Kuhn, T. S. (1970) *The Structure of Scientific Revolutions*. Chicago: Chicago University Press.

McDowell, J. H. (1994) *Mind and World*. Cambridge, MA: Harvard University Press.

Pickering, A. (1984) *Constructing Quarks: A Sociological History of Particle Physics*. Chicago: Chicago University Press.

Nelkin, D. and Lindee, S. (1995) *The DNA Mystique: The Gene as a Cultural Icon*. San Francisco: W. H. Freeman.

Oyama, S., Griffiths, P. E. and Gray, R. D. (2001) *Cycles of Contingency: Developmental Systems and Evolution*. Cambridge, MA: MIT Press.

Rheinberger, H.-J. (1995) From microsome to ribosomes: "strategies" of "representation." *Journal of the History of Biology*, 48, 49–89.

Rheinberger, H.-J. (1997) *Toward a History of Epistemic Things: Synthesizing Proteins in the Test Tube*. Stanford, CA: Stanford University Press.

Rouse, J. T. (2002) *How Scientific Practices Matter: Reclaiming Philosophical Naturalism*. Chicago: Chicago University Press.

Rouse, J. T. (2003) Heidegger on science and naturalism. In G. Gutting (ed.), *Continental Philosophies of Science*. Oxford: Blackwell.

Part II

BEING AND TIME

12

Dasein

THOMAS SHEEHAN

Well into its seventh decade, Heidegger scholarship in America has yet to reach a firm consensus on what Heidegger's main topic was. But we cannot understand Dasein without first getting clear on the central issue of Heidegger's thought – what he called "the thing itself" (*die Sache selbst*). Therefore, this chapter investigates "the thing itself" as a way of coming to understand Dasein. That may seem like a roundabout approach. But no, it is a straight path to our theme – because Dasein *is* the thing itself.[1]

Or is it? Many scholars still insist that the central topic of Heidegger's work was "being" or "being itself" (*das Sein, das Sein selbst*) despite Heidegger's unambiguous assertion that it was not. In 1962 (Wednesday morning, September 12, to be exact) Heidegger declared emphatically that once we get beyond metaphysics' dispensations of being (*Seinsgeschichte*) and begin to think within *Ereignis* – from that moment on, "being [*das Sein*], rooted as it is in those dispensations, is no longer the proper topic of thinking."[2]

Heidegger made the same point seven years later, on September 11, 1969, during an informal seminar at Le Thor, Provence. First he reiterated his threefold distinction between beings (*das Anwesende*), being itself (*das Anwesen*), and that which *gives* being itself (*das Lassen des Anwesens*). Then he declared that at that third level – which is proper area of his own thought – "there is no longer room for even the word 'being'."[3]

If "being" or "being itself" is not Heidegger's central topic, what is? The first page of *Being and Time* makes it clear that Heidegger's basic question was not about being but about the *meaning* of being, *der Sinn von Sein*.[4] The distinction between being and the meaning of being is utterly crucial – much more important, for example, than the onto-logical difference.[5] It is the clue to distinguishing Heidegger's thought from both tradi-tional metaphysics and Husserlian phenomenology. It is key to unlock *die Sache selbst*. Yet it is frequently, and disastrously, overlooked in Heidegger scholarship.

In studying Heidegger, everything depends on the presuppositions one brings to the task. What inform the present essay are the Aristotelian and Husserlian presupposi-tions that Heidegger says he brought to his own work.[6] This chapter begins by locating Heidegger's topic in contrast to Aristotle's metaphysics and Husserl's phenomenology, and then explains the role Dasein plays in that topic. The goal is to show that Dasein is the answer to the question about the meaning of being.

* * *

We begin by distinguishing Heidegger's own work from classical metaphysics in the objectivist form that Husserl called "ousiology" and that Aristotle called "wisdom," "first philosophy," or simply "the science we seek."[7]

Aristotle's Ousiology

Field and focus

For Aristotle, the field or subject-matter of first philosophy is everything real – whatever is not nothing, whatever is in being. Aristotle expressed that as *to on* (whatever-is), which Heidegger translates by the German neologism *das Seiende* ("beings" or "any being"). Moreover, Aristotle's specific focus on that subject matter, the formal aspect under which he studied it, was nothing less than its condition of being real, its *realness*. Aristotle called this realness the *ousia* (is-ness or being) of whatever-is – which Heidegger renders as the *Seiendheit* of *das Seiende*. As an inquiry into *ousia*, Aristotle's metaphysics is an ousiology. It studies the realness of whatever-is-real, the is-ness of whatever-is, the being of whatever-has-being.[8]

Two moments

On the assumption that being/*ousia* is what makes things real, Aristotle's metaphysics asks two questions about such being: What is its nature? and What is its ultimate source? These questions structure the two moments of Aristotle's metaphysics. When it considers the *nature* of being, metaphysics is ontology; and when it studies the *ultimate source* of being, it is theology (natural as contrasted with revealed theology).

Aristotle's metaphysics/ousiology The theory of the *being* of whatever-is-real	
THE FIRST MOMENT: ONTOLOGY	THE SECOND MOMENT: THEOLOGY
The nature of the being of the real is *energeia*.	The ultimate source of the being of the real is perfect *energeia*.

First Moment: Ontology

The nature of the being of things has been understood differently by different philosophers. Plato, for example, considered the nature of *ousia* to be *idea* or *eidos*, Aristotle took it to be *energeia* or *entelecheia*, and Aquinas understood it as *esse*. But the different expressions aside, there is a convergence on the core issue. Plato, Aristotle, and Aquinas agree on calling a thing "real" if it *is* and is *something*, i.e. if it *exists* and has a *form or essence*. To say that anything "has being" means that it "is-in-a-form" or "has-existence-with-essence." For these three philosophers, the question "What makes anything real?" is answered formally by "being" (*ousia*) and materially by *eidos, energeia,* or *esse*.

Granted the general agreement that "being" is what explains the real, why specifically does Aristotle understand "being" as *energeia*? Aristotle considers existing-in-a-form (*ousia*) dynamically and teleologically: a thing's form is its *ideal* way of being, it is what that thing is *supposed* to be. The governing metaphor here is athletic and ascetic. The Greek noun *to athlon* means "the prize to be won in a contest"; and the verb for "to contend for a prize" is *athleo*. But contending for the prize requires that the athlete continuously work out (*askeo*) in order to get in shape. Being an athlete entails being an ascetic, someone who constantly works to get in form and stay in shape.

To apply the metaphor to Aristotle's ousiology: the only thing that is perfectly in shape is the divine, which truly is its ideal form and perfectly is what it is supposed to be. Everything else is still striving for its ideal so that, short of God, to be real does not mean *being* in one's form so much as *becoming* one's form.[9] Human beings, for example, have not yet reached their ideal goal (*telos*) and hence are not yet completely *en-tel-echeia* ("in-one's-*telos*") or perfectly *en-erg-eia* (in one's finished form, like a completed work of art). Human being is not perfect (*teleion*) but imperfect (*a-teles*), still on-the-way-to-the-goal. On this view, therefore, being-real can mean one of two things: either still becoming one's ideal form or already being it; either still moving to perfection (*kinesis*) or already at rest with one's fully achieved self (*stasis*).[10]

Second Moment: Theology

The first moment of Aristotle's metaphysics explains *to on* – and thus is an *onto*-logy – by laying out the teleological structure of the being of whatever-has-being. But his second and ultimate question asks: What is the source of all being? Presumably that source is the divine, insofar as God is the perfect instance of achieved *energeia*. One says "presumably" because Aristotle did not thematically ground his ontology in his theology. Others, however, have done the job for him. Professor Joseph Owens, for example, has reconstructed a plausible grounding of Aristotle's ontology in his theology by focusing on the essence-moment of essence-and-existence, and then locating the highest instance of being-in-a-form in the perfectly self-coincident Aristotelian God, the ground or cause of lower forms of *ousia*.[11] Aquinas, on the other hand, constructed his own onto-theology by focusing on the existence-moment of essence-and-existence. He interpreted worldly existence as a finite instance of the "act of being" (*esse*), and then traced finite *esse* back to an infinite act of *esse* that freely bestows finite *esse* in creation.[12]

For Heidegger, however, all such efforts merely identify (in God) the highest entitative instance of the real, even if the essence of that supreme entity is pure self-subsistent existing (*ipsum esse per se subsistens*). Whether it is based on essence or on existence, metaphysics gives an ontic answer to the question about being: it explains *to on* by *ousia*, but then explains *ousia* by yet another *on*, the highest one. Aquinas, for example, explains any *ens* (i.e. any *habens-esse*) by the *ens supremum* (the *maxime-habens-esse*), without thereby explaining what *esse* is in and of itself.[13]

Heidegger's Phenomenology

Field and focus

The entry-level difference between Heidegger and Aristotle consists in Heidegger's employment of a phenomenological attitude and method in his work. Heidegger's shift from an objectivist to a phenomenological framework entailed a radical change in what he took to be the field and the focus of philosophy. Aristotle's material object was the real (*to on*), and his formal focus was on the realness of the real, *ousia* understood as independent of the human subject. By contrast, Heidegger's material object is the meaningful (*to alethes* or *to par-on*), and his formal focus is on the meaningfulness of the meaningful (the *aletheia* of the *alethes*, the *parousia* of the *par-on*) in correlation with human interests and purposes.[14] That is, Heidegger abandons an object-focused theory of being (ousiology as *Seinslehre*) for a correlation-focused theory of meaning (parousi-ology as *Bedeutungslehre*) – in a word, phenomenology.

Phenomenology as a *Bedeutungslehre* or theory of meaning investigates the correlation between objects and their intentional constitution. Heidegger's mentor here was the early Husserl, whose *Logical Investigations* (1900–1) had argued that the focal topic of philosophy was neither objects allegedly meaningful in themselves (the "independent-of-my-mind-out-there-now-real") nor subjectivity as either the Cartesian ego separated from the world or the psychological ego embedded in nature. Rather, phenomenology focuses on the *a priori* correlation between *things-as-meaningful* and the *constitution of their meaningfulness*, where "constitution" refers to the bestowal of sense upon objects (*Sinngebung*).

The subject matter of phenomenology: the *a priori* correlation between		
THE MEANINGFUL	*and*	ITS CONSTITUTION
what appears in understanding	*and*	what allows it to appear
the meaningful as it shows up	*in*	the understanding of its meaning

What finally separated Heidegger's phenomenology from Husserl's was their disagreement over the constitution of the meaningfulness of the meaningful. After the *Logical Investigations*, Husserl took a neo-Kantian and Cartesian turn and claimed that *transcendental subjectivity*, in intentional correlation with its objects, was the source of all meaning-giving. Heidegger, on the other hand, argued that the *lived context or world* within which things are encountered – the matrix of intelligibility structured by correlative human interests and purposes – was the source of meaning.[15]

One of the challenges in interpreting Heidegger is to remember that when he uses the language of "being," he means "being" as phenomenologically reduced, i.e. as meaningfulness. When he says *das Seiende* he means not just beings (*to on*) but beings as intelligible (*to alethes*), not "what is out there" but what is meaningfully present (*to paron*) within a human context. In his first lecture course after the First World War Heidegger made the point by pressing his students on what it is they first encounter in their lived experience. Is it things? Objects? Values? No, he insisted, it is:

> the meaningful [*das Bedeutsame*] – that's what is primary, that's what is immediately in your face without any detour through a mental grasp of the thing. When you live in the world of first-hand experience, everything comes at you loaded with meaning, all over the place and all the time. Everything is embedded in a meaningful context, and that context *is what gives it meaning.*[16]

Heidegger makes the same point by interpreting *ousia* as *parousia*, and *Sein* as *Anwesen*. Being as presence (*Anwesen*) does not refer to a thing's spatio-temporal presence "out there." *Anwesen* means *meaningful* presence in correlation with the understanding of that meaning. When Heidegger, as he frequently does, interprets *parousia* or *Anwesen* as "nearness," that nearness is not spatial but a metaphor for significance. The "near" or meaningful thing, he says, is present *within our concerns* even though it "can be far away in terms of distance."[17]

In summary: (a) Heidegger's shift away from classical metaphysics consists in his taking a phenomenological turn from the being of whatever-is-in-being to the meaningfulness of whatever-is-meaningful; from the classical *Sein des Seienden* to the phenomenological *Anwesen des Anwesenden*. (b) In turn, Heidegger's shift away from Husserlian phenomenology to his own hermeneutical phenomenology consists in identifying the world as the source of all meaning. *Die Welt weltet*[18] – the function of a world is to enworld things, the essence of a context is to contextualize things, i.e. to constitute the meaning of the things found within it, by providing the medium whereby they make sense.[19]

Two moments

Heidegger's phenomenological theory of being-as-meaning asks two questions about the meaningfulness of the meaningful: What is its nature? And what is its ultimate source? We may call these two questions, respectively, the "lead-in question" and the "fundamental question." They provide the two structural moments of Heidegger's thought from *Sein und Zeit* all the way up to his last essays.

Every theoretical question seeks an answer or explanation which, Heidegger and Aristotle agree, is the *aitia* or *arche* or *logos* of (the cause of, source of, or reason for) whatever is being investigated.[20] What Heidegger investigates is not meaningful *things* but their *meaningfulness* – not classical *Sein* but phenomenological *Anwesen*. The meaningfulness of things is the *Anwesen* of the *Anwesendes*, the *aletheia* of *to alethes* or the

197

parousia of *to paron*. The nature of that meaningfulness is the subject of Heidegger's lead-in question, just as its cause or source is the subject of his fundamental question.[21]

Heidegger's phenomenology
A theory of the *meaningfulness* of whatever is meaningful

THE FIRST MOMENT	THE SECOND MOMENT:
The structure of meaningfulness is *presence* (analysis of world)	The ultimate source of meaningfulness is *pres-absence* (analysis of movement)

Before treating the two moments in detail, we may note in summary-form the structural parallels and material differences between Aristotle's problematic and Heidegger's.

The starting point:

Aristotle: things insofar as they are real, that is, the realness of the real (*to on hei on*, that is, *ousia*).
Heidegger: the meaningful insofar as it is meaningful, i.e. the meaningfulness of the meaningful (*to alethes hei alethes*, that is, *aletheia*; *to paron hei paron*, that is, *parousia*).

The lead-in question:

Aristotle: What is the realness of the real? What is *ousia*? (Answer: *energeia*, as what constitutes reality.)
Heidegger: What is the meaningfulness of the meaningful? What is *parousia* or *aletheia*? (Answer: world, as what constitutes meaning.)

The fundamental question:

Aristotle: What is the ultimate source or *Wesen* of *energeia*? (Answer: absolute *energeia*.)
Heidegger: What is the ultimate source or *Wesen* of any world? (Answer: radical finitude.)

The First Moment: The Structure of Meaningfulness

Heidegger begins with the "wonder of all wonders," the fact that things are full of meaning, indeed that there is meaningfulness at all.[22] On that basis, his first question seeks the cause of and explanation for that meaningfulness. Heidegger's answer is "world," and the process of arriving at that answer is his "world-analysis."[23]

Being and Time begins with the everyday lived experience of using things to carry out tasks, but it quickly shifts from the *things* that are meaningful to *how they get* their meanings. That is, Heidegger prescinds from the things that participate in meaningfulness, and focuses instead on their meaningfulness of and by itself (*aletheia* in itself, *parousia* in itself, *das Sein selbst*). When things are meaningful, where does that meaning come from? What is responsible for it? Heidegger's response: what constitutes the meaning of things is the context of human involvement within which those things are met, the matrix of human purposes ordered to human interests and ultimately to human survival – that is, a world.

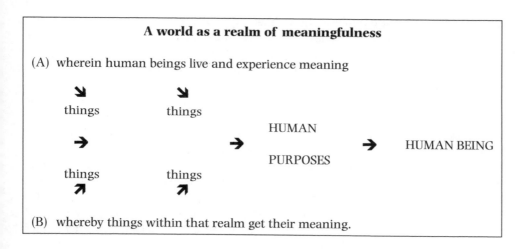

A world as a realm of meaningfulness

(A) wherein human beings live and experience meaning

things   things

               HUMAN

                                        HUMAN BEING

               PURPOSES

things   things

(B) whereby things within that realm get their meaning.

Each human world opens up or un-locks (*a-letheuei*: dis-closes) the meanings that can accrue to the things found within it. It does so by providing, and indeed being, a set of possible relations in terms of which things get their significance. In the context of a downpour, for example, a piece of rough canvas has a different significance than it might in an elegant living room. Of course human beings live in many distinct worlds at the same time. A father, for instance, makes business phone calls from home while rocking his child to sleep. Each of those worlds – his job, his parenting, his need to stay dry in the rain – has the function of providing the range of possible sense-making within its specific region.

In the chapter entitled "The Essential Structure of World," *Being and Time* examines the lived world of practical activity in order to derive the general structure of any world at all. That is, Heidegger's description of particular worlds of praxis (the worlds of the carpenter, the writer, the tailor, and the shoemaker) is only for the purpose of demonstrating the *common structure* of those worlds, the "worldhood" of any world.[24] As Heidegger defines its structure and function, a world is both (a) the "place wherein" human beings live out their interests and purposes, and (b) the "relations whereby" things within that realm get their meaning. A world is the range of human possibilities in terms of which anything within that context can have significance. All such possibilities are ultimately (i.e. teleologically) ordered to human being, by way of fulfilling

199

human purposes. The world, therefore, is what-constitutes-meaning (*to aletheuein*) insofar as it is the relational context, ordered to the final cause of human fulfillment, that lets things make sense.[25]

Heidegger sees a fundamental distinction within meaningfulness, between the meaningful *thing* and its *meaning*, i.e. between any instance and its class, or (in the language of being) between *das Seiende* and its *Seiendheit*.[26] Things do not come with their meanings built in but get *constituted* as meaningful. Discursive meaning occurs only in a synthesis, and synthesis presumes a prior distinction between the elements that will get synthesized into a meaningful whole.[27] Affirming that so-and-so is a philosopher assumes that she does not exhaust the class "philosopher" – she and the class are distinct – even though she can be identified, in a synthesis, as being one member of that class. Heidegger's world-analysis shows how the structure of synthesizing and distinguishing is intrinsic not only to discursive *acts* of making-sense (e.g. the assertion "She is a philosopher") but above all to the *world itself* within which such acts are performed. He argues that the world's very structure as synthesis-and-differentiation is the condition of all discursive sense-making.

"World" is what Heidegger means by "being" (*das Sein*),[28] and he uses many terms and metaphors for this meaning-constituting structure. Each of the terms has both a *static-intransitive* and a *dynamic-transitive* meaning. For example, "world," when viewed statically and intransitively, is the *place* of meaningfulness. But viewed dynamically and transitively, it is the *placing* of things in meaning, the enworldling and contextualizing of them within a set of possibilities that makes things able to be known and used in terms of those very possibilities. Likewise "being," when taken intransitively, indicates "presence," but when taken dynamically and transitively, it names the "presenting" of things, the act of *allowing* them to be meaningfully present."[29] Heidegger's other names for world include the following.

1 *The open that opens things up* (*das Da, das Offene*).[30] Heidegger draws this and cognate terms from Aristotle's description of the human soul as the *topos eidon*, "the place where meaning shows up."[31] The world is the self "writ large" or "opened out," with no "inside" where it might take refuge.[32] Read statically and intransitively, this *Da* or *Offene* is the open field (*die Gegend*) in which all forms of meaningfulness (all instances of "being") occur. Read dynamically and transitively, this open *opens things up* for possible use and appropriation, i.e. makes them accessible and significant to human comportment. (In the language of being, the world lets beings *be*, sc. meaningful.)[33]

In Greek philosophy, which always hovers in the background of Heidegger's work, the condition of being-open indicates imperfection. For Aristotle, closure (self-closure upon oneself, i.e. realization of all one's possibilities) means perfection, completion, accomplishment – the achievement of the *telos* (*en-tel-echeia*). Therefore, by describing the meaning-giving world as "open" rather than "closed," Heidegger is indicating that the game is not over yet – there is still time to play, and room to maneuver (*Zeitraum, Spielraum*). The goal of full intelligibility may be near and even impending, but it never completely arrives. As open, the world – which is human being – is always incomplete and finite. That is why everything it constitutes – every form of meaning or being that appears within it – is also ineluctably finite.

2 *The arena of dif-ference and tension, of in-between-ness and mediation* (*Unter-schied, diaphora; Austrag, polemos; das Zwischen, die Vermittlung, die Mittelbarkeit*).[34] That the

world and the meanings it makes possible are always finite is evidenced by the fact that making-sense always consists in partially synthesizing the never-completely-synthesizable. Difference and distinction always outride efforts at unification (*diairesis* > *synthesis*, *diaphora* > *henotes*), and the structure of world is responsible for that fact. Meaningfulness requires mediation, relations that connect, for example, these tools to that task. But the prerequisite for mediation is a *medium*, a field of possible relations within which the connections can be made. Read statically and intransitively, the world is the medium (the *id quo*) of intelligibility. Read dynamically and transitively, the world as medium *mediates* tools and tasks (as well as subjects and predicates) *to each other*, with the result that sense occurs.

Meaningfulness for human beings is not, and can never be, gathered into perfect unity with itself, as always already is the case with Aristotle's self-coincident God, the thinking that immediately thinks of nothing but itself as thinking.[35] Thus the "open" as what makes meaning possible is never a self-coincident unity but is always "drawn out" (cf. *Austrag*), always a tension (*polemos*) between togetherness and apartness, unity and separation, synthesis and difference. The world is a "setting apart" (*Aus-einander-setzung, Gegen-setzung*) that also holds the separated elements into a tentative unity of sense.[36] That is why our acts of sense-making approach unity but never achieve it. The assertion "Socrates is an Athenian" (i.e. *one* Athenian) indicates that he does not exhaust the category. The same for tools and tasks – they never perfectly coincide. This hammer can do the nailing, but if all else fails, I might use this rock for the job.

3 *The "free" that frees things; the power that empowers them* (*das Freie, das Machtende, das Tauglichmachende*).[37] Read intransitively, the "free" is an open and empty space, and "power" is a reserve of untapped energy. But read transitively, the free *frees* things within the world, and power *empowers* their significance. Insofar as the world is the realm of relations between, for example, tools and their possible utility, it *liberates* those tools from their "just-there-ness" by revealing their aptitude (*Bewandtnis*) for ful-filling this or that purpose.[38] As a dynamic matrix of relations that orients things to human purposes, the world enables things to be significant. In that regard Heidegger compares "world" to what Plato's *Republic* calls "the good." Heidegger translates *to agathon* as *das Tauglichmachende*, the "empowering," insofar as, for Plato, it makes intel-ligibility possible, both the person's ability to understand and a form's ability to be understood. So too the world as the constituting source of intelligibility *empowers* the things within that world to be understood, and *enables* human beings to understand them.[39]

4 *The opening that clarifies things; the unfolding that lets them appear; the birthing that brings them forth* (*die Lichtung*; *aletheia*; *physis*).[40] The original meaning of *Lichtung* is any static opening (e.g. a window) that lets in the light.[41] But read actively and transitively, that opening *brings clarity* to things in the room by letting light shine on them and show them as this or that. In another image, the world is *aletheia* – intransitively, the self-unfolding of world itself; and transitively, the unfolding of things (*to aletheuein*) by bringing them into meaning. In yet another image, the world is *to phyein* or *physis*: intransitively, the world's "arising" or self-emergence; transitively, the birthing that brings things forth into the open, where they can appear as this or that.[42]

These last two terms for world have a specifically kinetic sense, and Heidegger claims that Parmenides and Heraclitus, by naming "being itself" with such terms as *aletheia* and *physis*, revealed their implicit understanding of this movement-character of world. The word *aletheia* indicates "emergence from hiddenness," and the verb *aletheuo* means "to bring from hiddenness."[43] The verb *phyo*, which underlies *physis*, means "to arise" (middle voice) and "to give birth to" (active voice). These terms, Heidegger argues, show that Heraclitus and Parmenides understood that every sense-constituting world is somehow an emergent movement (intransitive moment) that in turn moves things into meaning (transitive moment). Thus Heidegger paraphrases *physis* as the "movement of appearance" (*die Bewegung des Erscheinens*), where the *des* indicates a double genitive: (a) the world's own movement into presence and appearance (intransitive moment) and (b) the world as *moving things* into their present appearance (transitive moment).[44]

But what *is* this movement, and what *causes* it? Parmenides and Heraclitus got no further than the intimation that world is kinetic. They did not take the next step and ask what Heidegger calls the "fundamental question" (*die Grundfrage*). If the world is somehow "moved into position," what is the source of that movement? What causes the emergence of any meaning-giving context?

The Second Moment: The Source of Meaningfulness

The first moment of Heidegger's work examines the world as *Lichtung* – the open that opens things up, the clearing that clarifies them, the ever-present presence that allows things their current meaning.[45] But his final aim is to move beyond the nature and function of world so as to discover the ultimate source of world: the *arche* of all forms of *aletheia*, the *aitia* of any mode of *parousia*, the *Wesen* of *das Sein selbst*. We noted above that "world" is what Heidegger means by "being" (*das Sein*).[46] But his final goal is not being or world but the *meaning* of being, the *source* of world.[47] Hence his fundamental and final question is: "*Woher und wie gibt es die Lichtung?*"[48] Where does world come from? What causes or "gives" any world as a meaning-constituting context? In the language of being: what is the *Wesen* of *Sein*?

Whatever answers to that question will be the thing itself. And Heidegger's response is clear: the ultimate source of world is *the ontological movement of human being that opens the clearing*. The answer, in short, is Dasein, and Heidegger's process of arriving at that answer is his Dasein-analysis.

Dasein's world-opening movement is what Heidegger calls *Ereignis*, a term that covers the three moments of a unified process: Dasein's ontological condition of (a) *being-opened-up* so as to (b) *come-into-its-own* and thus (c) *finitely appearing* – emergence, fulfillment, appearance.[49] The key to understanding *Ereignis* – and therefore *die Sache selbst* – is Heidegger's notion of movement, which he retrieved from Aristotle's analysis of *kinesis*.[50] But Heidegger calls *kinesis* "the most difficult thing Western philosophy has had to ponder in the course of its history."[51] Given the difficulty, our discussion will have to take several steps through Aristotle's thought. Perhaps nowhere else is Heidegger's admonition more relevant: "You would be advised to postpone reading Heidegger for the time being and first study Aristotle for ten or fifteen years."[52]

The following discussion of movement is focused not on just any entity but on the exemplar entity, Dasein. As Heidegger puts it in the opening words of *Being and Time*, "we ourselves (which always means 'I') are the entity to be analyzed."[53] The point of what follows is not to reduce Heidegger to Aristotle or to confuse *Ereignis* with Aristotelian *kinesis*. Heidegger always takes distance from Aristotle's thought to the degree it is metaphysical. However, he also adapts Aristotle's proto-phenomenological insights to his own ends, and frequently uses Aristotelian terms as "limit-ideas," background against which he formulates his own thinking. The point, then, is to find out where Heidegger's thought came from and how he retrieved *Ereignis* from *kinesis*.

Movement as Being-opened-up and Coming-into-one's-own

Perfection

Heidegger's understanding of movement is informed by Aristotle's teleological view of *kinesis*, which in turn flows from Greek philosophy's "top-down" understanding of being. Aristotle shares the classical Greek conviction of the normativeness of the ideal, the perfect, and the whole. In this view, philosophy reads reality "backwards," as it were, from the *de jure* perfect to the *de facto* imperfect, from the *a priori* to the *a posteriori* – rather than "forwards" from the imperfect to the perfection it strives for. Philosophy begins with a sense of the ultimate and perfect (how else would it know anything as imperfect?) and then works down from the ideal to the real, from the fully achieved to what is still on-the-way, from the whole to what participates in it.[54]

By perfection (*to teleion*) Aristotle means self-possession. A thing is perfect and complete when "it possesses its *telos*," i.e. "when not the least part of the thing can be found outside of it."[55] Such perfect self-possession is also called "wholeness" or "ownness" (*to holon*). Something is whole and its own, Aristotle says, when "it lacks no part of what belongs to it by its essence."[56] These ideas converge in Aristotle's key terms: *en-tel-echeia*, "being-wholly-fulfilled," and *en-erg-eia*, "being a finished work." To be perfect means to have arrived at one's essence, to have come into one's own. And since, for Aristotle, "perfection," "wholeness," and "ownness" are not univocal but analogous terms, we must say that every entity *is* perfect *to the degree* that it has come into its own.

Movement is measured by perfection

Such normative perfection gives Aristotle the high ground from which he works down to a definition of imperfection and movement. If the perfect is a finished work already at rest in itself, the imperfect is what is still striving to fulfill its essence. But what is still on the way to its goal is bivalent. On the one hand, it *participates* in the goal without entirely possessing it. (You speak *some* Italian even if not *perfect* Italian.) On the other hand, participation without full possession is inherently deficient or *a-teles*, still coming into its own.

Aristotle combines these two moments into his notion of "participation-as-deficient-perfection." That, in fact, is what he means by movement: *energeia ateles*, the perfecting of the imperfect, or partial perfection striving for complete perfection, or participation on the way to plenitude.[57] Movement, in short, is the state of becoming, and in Aristotle's words, "becoming is the transition to being," indeed, "becoming is *for the sake of* being."[58]

Telos *as mover and as the "giver-of-presence"*

In this dynamic vision of reality, the *telos* of a thing *actively moves* the thing by drawing it towards its own fulfillment. The *telos* is not up ahead somewhere, but always *within* the thing. In Aristotle's view, every being wants itself, wants to become and finally be its own. Thus everything in Aristotle's universe is either telic or erotic, either already itself or desiring to be itself. In the former case, the *telos* is wholly present, informing and fulfilling the entity. In the latter case, the *telos* is still drawing the entity, from within, not to anything outside of itself but to its own self-fulfillment.[59] Self-fulfillment is what Aristotle means by "the good." It is the ultimate reason why anything is at all (*to hautou heneka*), and it is what everything desires. *Kinei hos eromenon* – the *telos* moves us by being desired. Our very being, insofar as it is imperfect, draws us on to ourselves, because self-fulfillment is what we long for.[60]

What then is a moving entity? And what is Dasein as a "self-moving" entity? Answer: a moving entity is actually a "moved" entity (drawn on by its *telos*), and Dasein is "self-moved" insofar as it is drawn on by its own desired fulfillment.[61] Any moved entity – and especially Dasein as self-moved – is defined by its relative *absence-from-perfection*, which is equally its erotic *presence-to-perfection*. In shorthand: ABSENCE (relative rather than absolute absence, since the unfulfilled but desired *telos* draws us to ourselves) GIVES (i.e. lets be, allows for, is the source of) PRESENCE. Dasein's movement is pres-abs-ence; our imperfect presence is the gift of our presence-bestowing absence.

This ontological condition of Dasein is evidenced in its ontic comportment.[62] Alison, for example, is studying for the doctorate: that is her *raison d'être* at the moment. The doctorate is relatively absent yet, as desired, gives Alison her presence, the world of meaning in which she currently lives, that of "being-a-graduate-student." The relatively absent desideratum – still unattained but proleptically present in the desire for it – bestows presence. It gives world. *Es gibt Sein.*

Movement as Bestowing World

Perfect imperfection

But exactly what kind of presence does Dasein's relative self-absence bestow? We mentioned that Heidegger both takes distance from Aristotle and frequently transforms Aristotle's notions to his own ends. We can see how Heidegger radically differentiates his own idea of Dasein's movement from Aristotle's notion of natural movement by considering three analogous meanings of becoming and perfection.

1   Perfectly perfect. In the case of God, perfection means having already attained perfection and indeed having always been there. The divine has always-already come into its own. There is no becoming in God.[63]
2   Imperfectly perfect. An artifact under construction (e.g. wood being assembled into a table) participates in its future perfection, but possesses it only deficiently. It is still being moved towards its fulfillment, and once it reaches it, the movement of becoming-a-table will stop.

3   Perfectly imperfect. Dasein – the human essence – is whole and complete *in* its
    incompleteness. Its ontological perfection is to be imperfect, with no prospect of
    achieving an ideal perfection in the future. Like God, Dasein has always-already
    come into its own, but its own-ness is its human finitude. Ontologically Dasein is
    "frozen" in its movedness or becoming (even though ontically it is always becom-
    ing this or that).

Let us contrast Dasein with the other two entities mentioned above. (a) Dasein
and the table-under-construction are both instances of becoming (coming-into-
its-own) but with this difference: in the case of the table, the becoming will cease
once the construction reaches its goal, whereas Dasein's becoming is always an end
in itself rather than a step towards a further goal. (b) Dasein and God are both instances
of perfection, but with this difference: whereas the divine is always whole and
perfect in its state of unending rest, Dasein is always whole and perfect in its state of
mortal finitude. Ontologically Dasein is going nowhere – because it always already *is*
where it is supposed to be: in the state of coming-into-its-own. Dasein's unique ontological movement is neither diachronic progression over time (as in change of place,
quality, or quantity) nor ontological transformation into something it essentially was
not before (as in the case of substantial change). Rather, Dasein's perfection is to be
imperfect.[64]

Meaningfulness is measured by perfection

The kind of perfect imperfection that characterizes Dasein tells us what kind of presence Dasein's absence bestows upon it. In the Greek view of being, reality is not only a
matter of perfection (coming-into-one's-own), and but ultimately a matter of "shining
forth" and "appearing" – being present and accessible, i.e. meaningful both to oneself
and to other entities. Being and meaningfulness, or perfection and intelligibility – *einai*
and *aletheia* – are interchangeable.[65] Therefore, the greater an entity's degree of being,
the greater its degree of meaningfulness, in the double sense of intelligence (ability to
know itself and others) and intelligibility (ability to be known by itself and others). But
meaningfulness – like being, perfection, and wholeness – is analogous: it comes in different degrees at different levels of perfection. The most perfect entity is all light and no
darkness – pure knowing and knowability – whereas an imperfect entity is *chiaroscuro*,
only partially knowing and knowable.

For Aristotle, knowing is a matter of *being one* with the known. (God's perfect self-
knowledge is the paradigm.) But since "knowing" is also an analogous term, a knower
is one with the known *to the degree* that the knower is perfect. God, as perfectly self-
coincident, is entirely one with the proper object of its knowledge (namely itself).[66] But
with imperfect beings, it is the degree of their *presence to their relatively absent telos* that
gives them their measure of intelligence and intelligibility. The relatively absent goal, to
the degree that it is proleptically present as desired, gives the moving entity its degree
of ability to make sense of things. Dasein, the perfectly *imperfect* intelligent entity, is
structurally a finite knower – it never has the immediate relation to the known that God
has. Dasein knows mediately, by bonding the knowable to itself via a matrix of mediating relationships. Dasein makes sense of itself and of others only by way of world.[67]

In short: Dasein's *imperfect* being engenders an *im*perfect locus of meaning: the world as the dynamic-transitive realm of mediation. With that, Heidegger has reached his goal. He has grounded the theory of meaning in ungroundable Dasein, the theory of presence in the ontology of absence.[68]

Conclusion: *Ereignis*

Dasein has always already come into its own, and its own is its perfectly imperfect finitude. Human being, therefore, is ontologically bivalent. (a) Insofar as it is *imperfect*, it is a lack; but that lack is also a longing (a desire), and a belonging – even if there is nothing to belong *to*, and no "something else" to long *for*. This means that human being is off-center, eccentric, a protention that is going nowhere – Dasein is essentially self-absent. (b) But insofar as it is *perfect*, Dasein also has presence, although a radically finite presence: not self-coincident but distended; not a unity but parts-outside-of-parts; not a pure mind but a self-concerned body. Yet for all its distension, human being is held together in a tension of difference and synthesis. In fact, it *is* that tension. This self-concerned, self-aware body, this distended tension that ultimately intends itself, is the *world* engendered by human being. In fact it *is* human being itself.

The early Heidegger called this state of affairs "being thrown open" (*Geworfensein*), whereas the later Heidegger called it "being drawn out into its own" (*Ereignetsein*).[69] But whether interpreted as *thrown* into its openness or *pulled* into its openness, it is the same movement of human being. Dasein is (a) opened-up into openness and thereby (b) comes-into-its-own-perfect-imperfection and (c) appears as the self-intending distended tension that it is – world. These three moments constitute *Ereignis*, the unique ontological movement that is Dasein.

1   As drawn out and opened up by its own imperfection, Dasein opens up the mediating realm that frees things from unintelligibility, the clearing that clarifies them, the unifying-of-difference that draws them into tentative aggregates of sense.
2   This draw-out, opened-up, and mediating state of imperfection constitutes Dasein's ownmost perfection, its always-having-come-into-its-own.
3   Having always already come into its perfect imperfection, Dasein appears as what it is: not just the *topos eidon* – the place where meaning appears – but above all the *eidos eidon*,[70] the very appearing *of* appearance, the wellspring of meaning, the *aitia*, *arche*, and *logos* – the cause of, source of, and reason for the wonder of all wonders: that there is appearance at all, meaningfulness at all, "being" at all.

And each of us does this not as a modern subject or metaphysical ground but only in utter poverty and in spite of ourselves. In fact, we cannot properly say "we" do it. Rather, it is "done unto" us: we *are moved* by our perfect imperfection in such a way that world occurs. This happens without us being fully ourselves, and not because we spontaneously "become" ourselves, but rather because we *have* to become ourselves: we are "pulled" by our own self-absence. We are the *opened-up* opening of meaning, the *empowered* empowering of sense. Always approaching but never arriving, we are – as Stephen Daedalus puts it – "almosting it." We are always – in Heraclitus' word *agchibasie* – "getting near without ever arriving."[71] And the outcome is meaningfulness.

Notes

This chapter is dedicated to Professor Richard M. Capobianco of Stonehill College, Massachusetts, whose questions about "being" (summer 2003) woke me up from a long dogmatic slumber.

1 (a) By "Dasein" I mean human being as the *essence* of human beings. (b) In the following notes "GA" abbreviates Martin Heidegger, *Gesamtausgabe* (Frankfurt am Main: Klostermann, 1975ff), and "SD" abbreviates Martin Heidegger, *Zur Sache des Denkens* (Tübingen: Max Niemeyer, 1969). Citations in this chapter usually refer to texts by page and line, separated by a period. (The line-count does not include the "header" at the top of the page or any empty lines on the page, but it does count the lines of section titles.) Thus, for example, "SD 44.4–7" means "*Zur Sache des Denkens*, page 44, lines 4 to 7," and GA 15: 365.17–18 means "*Gesamtausgabe*, volume 15, page 365, lines 17 and 18." Unless otherwise noted, all translations are my own.

2 SD 44.4–7.

3 GA 15: 365.17–18: "Wenn die Betonung lautet: Anwesen *lassen*, ist sogar für den Namen Sein kein Raum mehr." Cf. SD 40.18–31.

4 GA 2: 1.9–10.

5 GA 77: 245.1–3: "Aber anfänglicher denn dies [the difference between Being and beings] ist das *Seyn*, auf das die Unterscheidung von Sein und Seiendem . . . nicht anwendbar ist."

6 Martin Heidegger, "Vorwort" to William J. Richardson, *Heidegger: Through Phenomenology to Thought*, 4th edn (New York: Fordham University Press, 2003; originally The Hague: Nijhoff, 1963), ix.21–xiv.17. Also GA 8: 78.8–9, 99.16–19, and SD 87.11–20.

7 (a) Re Husserl: Edmund Husserl, *Vorlesungen über Ethik und Wertlehre, 1908–1914*, Husserliana XXVIII, ed. Ullrich Melle (Dordrecht: Kluwer, 1988), Beilage XIV, p. 377: "Die reale Ousiologie behandelt die Wesenslehre realer Gegenständlichkeit in allgemeinster Allgemeinheit." (b) Re Aristotle: wisdom, *Metaphysics* I 1, 981b 28–29, I 2, 982a 5–6; first philosophy, VI 1, 1026a 16, 24, 30; XI 4, 1061a 19; the science we seek, I 2, 983a 21; III 1, 995a 24; XI 1, 1059a 35 and 1059b 22. Aristotle refers to "theological" science or philosophy at *Metaphysics* VI 1, 1026a 19 and XI 7, 1064b 3.

8 *Metaphysics* VII 1, 1028b 2–4 taken with IV 1, 1003a 20.

9 Hence Pindar's *genoi' hoios essi* ("Become what you are"). Pythian Odes, II, 72, in *The Works of Pindar*, ed. Lewis Richard Farnell (London: Macmillan, 1932), III, 56. Cf. GA 2: 194.3 ("werde, was du bist") and GA 56/57: 5.34 ("werde wesentlich").

10 *Nicomachean Ethics*, VII 14, 1154 b 27: *energeia kineseos* and *energeia akinesias*. Thomas Aquinas reiterates the point in *Summa Theologiae* I–II, 31, 2, ad 1: actus imperfecti, actus perfecti. Re *telos*: The word indicates consummation (not end or cessation), i.e. entrance into a complete and perfect state. *Telos* retains the sense of a "circling round" (hence "completion"); both *telos* and "circle" are derived from the Indo-European root kwel-, to revolve, to move in a circle, to dwell. Cf. Richard Broxton Onians, *The Origins of European Thought* (Cambridge: Cambridge University Press, 1951, 1988), pp. 442–3. Aquinas reads the *finis* (*telos*) as that on which a thing is dependent *for its whole existence. De Veritate* 21, 1, ad 4 (ad fin.). The Greek word *entelecheia* means "being in or at one's fulfillment" and is paralleled by,

but not etymologically connected to, the Latinate word "accomplish," from *ad + con + plere*: to be at the point of complete fullness. "Perfect" means etymologically "completely or thoroughly done" (*per + factum*).

11 Joseph Owens, *The Doctrine of Being in the Aristotelian "Metaphysics"* (Toronto: Pontifical Institute of Mediaeval Studies, third revised edition, 1978), pp. 455–73. Aristotle specifically did not ground *Metaphysics* VII–IX in *Metaphysics* XII, but there are indications of that possible connection. At *Metaphysics* XI 7, Aristotle declares the object of a unified onto-theology to be *on hei on kai choriston* (1064a 29), thereby intimating that the real in its true realness is separate and immobile being (*choriston, akineton*: a 33–4). "And if there is any such *physis* among beings, it must be there where the divine is, and it must be the first and most noble principle" (1064a 36–1064b 1).

12 Cf. Thomas Aquinas, *In metaphysicam Aristotlelis commentaria*, ed. M.-R. Cathala (Turin: Marietti, 1926), p. 102 (no. 296, re *Metaphysics* II, 1, 993b 29–30): "necesse est ut omnia composita et participantia reducantur in ea, quae sunt per essentiam, sicut in causas." ("All things that are composite and that participate [in being] necessarily have as their [final] causes things that have being by their very essence.") On creation cf. Thomas Aquinas, *De Potentia Dei* (*c.*1259–68), q. 3, a. 3, sed contra, ad fin: "creatio nihil est aliud realiter quam relatio quaedam ad Deum cum novitate essendi." ("Creation is nothing else in reality than a certain relation to God, with newness of being.")

13 Re ipsum esse subsistens: Thomas Aquinas first established this characterization of the divine, c.1252, in his commentary on the *Sententiarum libri quatuor* of Peter Lombard: *Scriptum in IV Libros Sententiarum: In I Librum Sententiarum* (distinctio. 8, quaestio 1: "divina essentia per hoc quod exercitae actualitati ipsius esse identificatur, seu per hoc quod est ipsum esse subsistens . . ."). He reiterates it in his *Summa Theologicae* (1265ff), I, 4, 2, c: "Deus est ipsum esse per se subsistens," and I, 13, 11, c: "cum esse Dei sit ipsa eius essentia . . ."

14 Just as *on* is the neuter singular present participle of the very *eimi, einai*, so too *paron* (*para + on*) is the same participial form of the verb *par-eimi, par-einai*, "to be present." Hence *to paron* means "the present" in the sense of "something-that-is-present." See below for Heidegger's understanding of "the present" as "the meaningful," and "presence" as "meaningfulness."

15 In the first edition of *Logical Investigations* Husserl declared he was unable to find a pure ego behind intentional experiences, but in the second edition (1913) he reversed himself and declared he had found it. See Edmund Husserl, *Logical Investigations*, trans. J. N. Findlay (London: Routledge and Kegan Paul, 1970), pp. 43, 549 note ("I have since managed to find it . . ."), and 551. I am indebted to Professor Robert Sokolowski of Catholic University of America for this information on *Logical Investigations*. On the disagreement of Husserl and Heidegger see Edmund Husserl, *Phenomenological and Transcendental Phenomenology and the Confrontation with Heidegger (1927–1931)*, ed. Thomas Sheehan and Richard Palmer (Dordrecht: Kluwer Academic, 1997).

16 A free but faithful translation of GA 56/57: 73.1–5. Heidegger repeats the negative point (not things, not values) at GA 2: 91.33–92.2.

17 GA 8, 241.14–18. The idea of "meaningful" as "near" goes back at least to *Sein und Zeit*: GA 2: 137.3–7, etc.

18 On "Die Welt weltet" see GA 5: 30.30–1. Also GA: 9, 219.31–2 ("welten" as expressing the "Wie des Seins") and 164.10; GA 7: 181.15; 183.27. In each case, "welten" refers both to the *intransitive* "coming-to-be" of world and to the *transitive* activity of the world as constituting the significance of things (GA 7: 181.14–15: "Welt west, indem sie weltet"; cf. also GA 52: 64.25).

19 GA 9, 157.1–3: "Welt . . . 'ist' . . . das, aus dem her das Dasein *sich zu bedeuten gibt*, zu welchem Seienden und wie es [Dasein] sich dazu verhalten *kann*." That is: world or lived

context is that whereby or that in terms of which (*id quo*) Dasein is able to make sense of what is encountered.

20 In spelling out the structure and function of theoretical questioning, Heidegger takes a very traditional Aristotelian approach (GA 2: 7.3–20). For Aristotle, knowing something means grasping the constitutive proximate causes that explain it (*Posterior Analytics* I 2, 71b 9–12; *Metaphysics* I 3 983a 24–6) – where "cause" (*aitia* or *aition, to dia ti* [*Physics*, II 3, 194b 19] or *to dioti* [*Metaphysics* I 1, 981a 28]) does *not* have the sense of one thing exerting a quasi-mechanical effect on another (GA 9: 245.31–2). Aristotle understands the cause to be the "source" of the thing in question (*Metaphysics*, V 1, 1013a17), and Heidegger calls such a source the "*Wesen*" of the thing – not "essence" in the traditional sense but rather "the empowering source," that which makes possible, lets be, constitutes, enables, allows for, is responsible for, and explains something (see SD 40.21, 30; GA 4: 53.11; GA 9: 114.26–7 and 228.8, 24; GA 24: 405.13; GA 68: 51.5). On *logos* as *arche* see Aristotle, *Metaphysics* IV 6, 1011a 9 and 1011a 12. The cause or empowering source of a thing, insofar as it can be understood and articulated by human beings, is called the *logos* (Latin, *ratio*, English *reason*) of and for the thing. In Greek a *logos tinos* is the *explanans*, the explanation or account of something, and giving such an account is called *logon didonai tinos*: Plato, *Sophist* 230a 5, *Republic* 344d 4–5, *Protagoras* 336c, *Gorgias* 465a 3–5. When used of the *explanandum*, *logos* refers to the thing's essence, structure, reason, or ground insofar as it can be grasped by human understanding.

21 Heidegger designates the lead-in issue as the "*Anwesen*lassen [des Anwesenden]" (SD 40.5, 8), i.e. "letting-*things-make-sense*" by "placing-them-*into-context*" ("freigeben *ins Offene*," ibid., 40.13; cf. "ins Offene . . . eingelassen," 40.15). He designates the fundamental issue as "Anwesen*lassen*" (SD 40.6, 18–24), "allowing-*the sense-making-world*-to-emerge."

22 GA 52: 64.24–5: "[das Wunder] nämlich, daß überhaupt eine Welt um uns weltet . . . ," i.e. that "a meaning-giving context constitutes the meaning of everything around us." Cf. also GA 9, 307.23–2: "das Wunder aller Wunder: *daß* Seiendes *ist*," i.e. "the fact *that* things *are* meaningful."

23 GA 2: 116.35–117.1: "*die Bedeutsamkeit . . . ist . . . die Struktur der Welt*." 164.35–165.1: "die Bedeutsamkeit, d.h. die Weltlichkeit." Also GA 2: 116.25–6: "Den Bezugscharakter dieser Bezüge des Verweisens fassen wir als *be-deuten*" and William J. Richardson's commentary on these texts is exactly right: "The relational character of the relations within the matrix [context or world] will be said 'to give meaning' (*be-deuten*), namely it is the relations which constitute the purposefulness of the instruments. The entire matrix of these relations will be called 'Meaningfulness' (*Bedeutsamkeit*), and it is this which constitutes the structure of the World." Richardson, *Heidegger*, 57.1–6.

24 GA 2: sections 15–18. The carpenter's world shows up all over GA 2: sections 15–16. The writer's world gets next billing (GA 2: 92.25–7), and the tailor and cobbler receive only a nod or two at, respectively, GA 2: 92.10 (Nähzeug), 94.14 (Schuh, Schuhzeug), and 94.25 and 32 (Leder, Faden, Nägel).

25 More fully, Heidegger defines a world as the togetherness of (a) a "wherein" (*das Worin*) that focuses on human beings and (b) a "whereby" (*das Woraufhin*) that focuses on the things found within a world. (a) The "wherein" designates a world as a place-of-our-concerns wherein we live our lives for the sake of our purposes and ultimately for the sake of the survival of our own being. Thus, human being is the ultimate "goal for the sake of which" we live (the *telos hou heneka*. On life and its happiness as *praxis teleia* – an act that is an end-in-itself – see *Metaphysics* IX 6, 1048b 22–3 and 8, 1050a 36–1050b 2; *Nicomachean Ethics* I 7, 1097b 20–1: *autarkes . . . telos*.) (B) That *telos hou heneka*, in turn, serves as that whereby or in-terms-of-which (*das Woraufhin*) the things we meet within that world get their meaning. In using those things for our purposes, we use them ultimately for the sake of

human being (and its survival), which therefore is *that-in-terms-of-which* they get their significance. Putting the two together: the world as (a) the place wherein we are directed to our final goal is also (b) the set of relations that directs tools to tasks for the sake of that same final goal. Heidegger brings the two together at the culminating sentence of his world-analysis, GA 2: 115.34–116.1: "*Das Worin . . . als Woraufhin . . . ist das Phänomen der Welt.*" This conjunction of the *Worin* and *Woraufhin* is Heidegger's phenomenological reformulation of Aristotle's position on the sameness (cf. *to auto*) of knower and the known in knowing: *De Anima* III 5, 430a 19–20 and 7, 431a 1–2, and *Metaphysics* XII 7, 1072b 18–21.

26 This is the *metaphysical* difference (see GA 77: 244.19–245.3). By contrast, Heidegger designates the difference between "Welt" and "Ding" as the *ontological* difference GA 12: 21.27–22.2.

27 GA 2: 211.14–20; also GA 4: 53.22–4.

28 See Richardson, *Heidegger*, 167, note 15: "World is equivalent to Being . . . the equivalence is genuine. . . . [Eventually] the term 'Being' replaces the term 'World'." Also op. cit., 36, note 21: "the problem of World becomes more and more explicitly the problem of Being." On the equivalence of *Sein, Welt*, and *Geviert* in the essay "Das Ding" (GA 7: 167–87) see Richardson, 571–2, esp. 571.23–5 taken with 572.14–15.

29 GA 15: 363.27–9: "der tiefste Sinn von Sein [ist] das *Lassen*. Das Seiende sein-lassen. Das ist der nicht-kausale Sinn von 'Lassen' in 'Zeit und Sein.'"

30 On "open": Martin Heidegger, *Zollikoner Seminare. Protokolle–Gespräche–Briefe*, ed. Medard Boss (Frankfurt am Main: Vittorio Klostermann, 1987), 9.6–9: 156.35–157.1; 157.30–2; 188.14–15. GA 5: 40.1. GA 9: 184.11, 184.25, 185.29, 187.32, 188.21–2, 201.30–2. GA 49: 56.20, 27–8, 31–2. GA 65: section 205, 328.28; 331.23. Also Heidegger's "Lettre à Monsieur Beaufret (23 novembre 1945)," in Martin Heidegger, *Lettre sur l'humanisme*, ed. Roger Munier, (Paris: Aubier, 1957), 184.3.

31 *De Anima*, III 4, 429 a 27–8. Cf. GA 15: 335.16–18. On *eidos* or *idea* as a name for *ousia*, i.e. the form-*qua*-intelligibility: GA 45: 172.16–17 and GA 9: 301.20–22.

32 In calling the world "the self writ large," I do not intend either (a) the analogical and comparative sense that Plato employs in *Republic* II, 368b 7–369a 3, or (b) the notion that the self has any other possibility than *to be* the world – that is, there is no alternative "inner"self, "writ small," as it were. Rather, being-the-world (*Lichtung-sein*, GA 69, 101.12; a.k.a. *Welt-sein*, a.k.a. *In-der-Welt-sein*) is the ontological-existential status of human being. The self *is* world-as-such.

33 GA 2: 137.32. The noun "Gegend" is related to the preposition "gegen" and indicates the "open *country* that lies *before* one." Cf. Latin *contra*, "over against," and Late Latin *contrata*, "the land opposite." (In the Left Coast's Bay Area that would be "Contra Costa County.") Early on Heidegger called this "das Entgegen," GA 9: 184.8. Later he employs the archaic term "Gegnet," GA 77: 114.12–13.

34 (a) For *diaphora, Unter-schied, Unterscheidung, Zwischen*, and *Austrag*, see GA 12: 22.1–23.11; GA 49: 97.16–20. (b) For *polemos*, GA 40: 66.8, 16, etc. (c) For *Vermittlung* and *Mittelbarkeit*, GA 4: 61.15–23.

35 *Metaphysics*, XII 9, 1074b 34–5; also 1075a 4–5 with the premises laid at XII 7, 1072b 18–21.

36 GA 4: 53.22–4. Cf. GA 15: 289.29–31: "Hierzu erinnert Heidegger daran, daß das Denken von seinen Anfängen an in der Dimension der *Einheit* denkt."

37 (a) *Das Freie*: GA 8: 137.21; GA 77: 114.1; *Zollikoner Seminare*, 9.9; and Martin Heidegger, *Nietzsche* (Pfullingen: Neske, 1961), II, 412.18. (b) *Machtende*: GA 4: 53.11.

38 GA 2: 111.21 (*freigeben*) and 107.13 and 112.12 (*Bewandtnis*). On "*Bewandtnis*" as "aptitude" (*dynamis*) see GA 22, 174.24-30 and 202.13–16.

39 GA 9: 228.10; cf. 227.32–3. For other expressions of the same notion, see SD 40.21, 30; GA 4: 53.11; GA 9: 114.26–7 and 228.8, 24; GA 24: 405.13; GA 68: 51.5.

40 For *aletheia*, GA 9: 201.32, etc. For *physis*, GA 40: 16.23 ff.

41 Jacob Grimm and Wilhelm Grimm, *Deutsches Wörterbuch* (Leipzig: S. Hirzel, 1854–1960), 16 volumes, vol. VI (L, M), 1885: s.v. "Lichtung," p. 893: "Öffnung oder Ausschnitt in einer Thür zum einlassen des Tageslichtes" and p. 877, s.v. "Licht," II, 18-a: "Fenster."

42 In addition to the four sets of terms already discussed, other formulations for "world" include: (a) *logos* (i.e. *synthesis-diaphora*) as the "house" of meaning: GA 9: 313.13–14. (b) "*Entwurfsbereich*," i.e. the region wherein meaning is opened up: GA 9: 201.31. (c) Time ("die Zeit als der Vorname für die Wahrheit des Seins": GA 9, 376.11; and "Zeit als Vorname des Entwurfsbereichs der Wahrheit des Seins. 'Zeit' ist . . . Lichtung des Seins selbst": GA 49: 160.1–4). All of these name what Heidegger calls *das transcendens schlechthin*: GA 2: 51.9.

43 GA 15: 331.5–6.

44 GA 15: 343.24–5: "Bewegung des Erscheinens." Cf. GA 15: 331.7. As regards the phrase "the world's *own* movement into presence," see SD 40.23–4: "in das zugelassen, wohin es gehört."

45 "Current meaning" translates "Anwesenheit." On "all-present" (allgegenwärtig, die Allgegenwart) see GA 4: 52.11, 20, 24; 53.8, 18–19. On *Welt* and *Da* as *Lichtung*: GA 65: section 193, 316.27 and section 204, 327.14–15. GA 9: 325.20–1. See "Lichtung . . . erbringt . . . Anwesen (Sein)": Heidegger, "Vorwort" to Richardson, *Heidegger*, pp. xxi.29–30. Also Heidegger's re-interpretation of the phrase "Zeit und Sein" as "Lichtung und Anwesenheit," SD 80.23–4.

46 See note 28 above.

47 See GA 9: 201.30–3: "Die entscheidende Frage (*Sein und Zeit*, 1927) nach dem *Sinn*, d.h. (*S.u.Z.* S. 151) nach dem *Entwurfbereich*, d.h. nach der *Offenheit*, d.h. nach der *Wahrheit* des Seins, und nur nicht des Seienden" (emphasis added). At GA 2: 201.21–2 (= *S.u.Z.* 151) Heidegger defines "Sinn" as the "id quo" of intelligibility: "das Woraufhin des Entwurfs, aus dem her [= aus dem Woraufhin] etwas als etwas verständlich wird." Meaning is the means whereby, and thus the reason why, things show up and can be related to by human beings. This is a formal definition that can be applied to either *things* or *world*, to either *Seiendes* or *Sein*. In each case the question "why" asks for the "because" (*das Woraufhin*), and the answer supplies the "that-because-of-which." In the first case: Q. Why do things show up as intelligible? A. The meaning-giving region held open by Dasein's aheadness is that because of which (*to hou heneka*, *das Woraufhin*) things are understandable. (2) In the second case: Q. Why do worlds show up as meaningful and meaning-giving? A. Because of Dasein's relative absence (finite being) that issues in relative presence (finite worlds).

48 SD 80.25. Or in another formulation at SD 40.16–17: "von woher und wie es 'das Offene' gibt."

49 In GA 71, *Das Ereignis* (1941–2), which, as of this writing, is still unpublished, Heidegger spells out this meaning of *Ereignis* (ms typed by Fritz Heidegger, page 100) by way of his glosses on the Grimm brothers' etymology of "*Ereignis*" and cognate terms in their *Deutsches Wörterbuch*, III (1862), 699, 784–5. See Thomas Sheehan, "A Paradigm Shift in Heidegger Research," *Continental Philosophy Review*, 34 (2001), 183–202, especially 196–8.

50 On "retrieval" (Wiederholung) see GA 3: 204.3–16.

51 GA 9: 283.25–6.

52 GA 8: 78.7–8. Of course he said "Nietzsche" rather than "Heidegger."

53 GA 2: 56.5–6, with Heidegger's footnote "je 'ich.' "

54 See GA 9: 244.32–5 and more generally 244.12–35 on *epagoge*.

55 Re *teleion* and *holon*: *Metaphysics* V 16, 1021b 12–13, 23–5, and 31–2.

56 *Metaphysics* V 26, 1023b 26–7.

57 *Energeia ateles*: *Physics* III 1, 201a 10–11 and 27–9; 201 b 4–5; III 2, 201 b 31–2. At *De Anima* III 7, 431 a 8 Aristotles calls movement *tou atelous energeia* ("the current perfection of what is on-the-way-to-perfection"). The Latin is "actus imperfecti": Thomas Aquinas, *Summa Theologiae*, I–II, 31, 2, ad 1; *In IV Sententiarum*, 17, 1, 5, solutio 3, ad 1; *De Veritate* 8, 14, ad 12.

58 *De anima*, III 9, 432b 15–16; *Topics* VI 2, 130b 20; *On the Parts of Animals*, I 1, 640a 18–19. I am grateful to Professor Peter Maxwell of Loyola University Chicago for directing me to the first of these three references. Whereas Aristotle understands *genesis* as getting fulfilled in *ousia*, Plato radically contrasts them: *Republic* VII, 525b 5–6.

59 Thomas Aquinas makes this Aristotelian point quite well when he discusses the twofold "moving power" of the *telos*: the *telos* (= *finis vel bonum*) is an active moving power (*virtus motiva*), and there are two ways of understanding it (*alia ratio*). It actively moves an entity (a) when that *telos* is completely present and informing the entity (in which case it makes the entity rest *in* itself); and (b) when that *telos* is still imperfectly achieved and therefore relatively absent (in which case it makes the entity be moved *unto* itself): "Est autem alia ratio virtutis motivae ipsius finis vel boni, secundum quod est realiter praesens, et secundum quod est absens: nam secundum quod est praesens, facit in seipso quiescere; secundum autem quod est absens, facit ad seipsum moveri": *Summa Theologiae* I–II, 30, 2, c.

60 Re *to hautou heneka*: see *Platonis opera*, ed. John Burnet (Oxford: Clarendon, 1907), V, *Horoi*, 413a 3. Re *kinei hos eromenon*: *Metaphysics* XII 7, 1072b 2. Aristotle is referring here specifically to the first mover, but the principle applies analogously to other *tele*.

61 For the soul as self-moving (*psyche to hauto kinoun*) see: *Platonis opera*, V, op. cit., 411c 7. Heidegger generally prefers "moved-ness" or "being-moved" (*Bewegtheit*) rather than "movement" (*Bewegung*): GA 2: 461.16, 495.30–1; GA 9: 283.17ff. He employs that former term to emphasize that the movement is teleological and that its moving source is the *telos hou heneka*.

62 This is in keeping with the overarching methodological principle that governs all of Heidegger's work: *operatio sequitur esse*. He states the principle, for example, at GA 4: 65.27–8: "während es [= ein Jegliches] doch in Wahrheit je nur das leistet, was es ist."

63 But see GA 9: 284.15–21.

64 (a) Re God: *Nicomachean Ethics* VI 3, 1139 b 22–6 on God as maximally necessary, eternal, ungenerated, and incorruptible, as well as VI 14, 1154 b 26–7: *energeia akinesias* v. *energeia kineseos*. (b) Re Dasein: SD 58.26–9: "[Endlichkeit] nicht mehr aus dem Bezug zur Unendlichkeit [Gottes], sondern als Endlichkeit in sich selbst gedacht wird: Endlichkeit, Ende, Grenze, das Eigene – ins Eigene Geborgensein."

65 *Metaphysics* II 1, 993b 30–1.

66 *Metaphysics* XII 9, 1074b 26 1074b 34–5 (divine knowing as immediate self-knowing); and *Metaphysics* I 2, 982b 1–2 (most knowable); cf. *Nicomachean Ethics* VI 3, 1139b 26 (*matheton*).

67 (a) Re Dasein, no immediate relation to the known: see *De anima* III 8, 431b 21 and III 5, 430a 14–15. Also GA 3: 280.30–1. (b) Dasein bonds the knowable to itself via world: GA 2, 201.12–14: "Wenn innerweltliches Seiendes *mit dem Sein des Daseins* entdeckt, das heißt zu Verständnis gekommen ist, sagen wir, es hat *Sinn*" (first italics added). That is, entities have meaning only to the degree they are discovered *along with* – i.e. *within* – the world that is the being of Dasein.

68 (a) Dasein engenders world: GA 2: 483.22–3, 25–7: "Sofern Dasein sich zeitigt, *ist* auch eine Welt. . . . Die Welt . . . zeitigt sich in der Zeitlichkeit." That is, insofar as a human being is becoming itself, a world *is*. Worlds are generated from out of the human being's movement "into the future." (b) Theory of meaning: GA 2: 220.29–30: "Die Bedeutungslehre ist in der Ontologie des Daseins verwurzelt."

212

69   *Geworfensein*: GA 2: 449.30 and 453.20. A comparison of these two texts shows that *Geworfensein* is the same as *Geworfenheit*. The equivalence of *"geworfen"* and *"ereignet"* is clearly indicated at GA 65: s.122, 239.5, s.182, 304.8, and s.134, 252.24.

70   *De anima*, III 7, 432a 2.

71   (a) Re opened-up opening, see GA 27: 135.13: erschließend erschlossenes. (b) Re "almosting it": James Joyce, *Ulysses*, New York: The Modern Library (new edition, corrected and reset), 1961, (Episode 3, "Proteus"), 47.6; cf. "homing" at 51.6 (ad fin.). (c) Re getting near/*agchibasie*: The late tenth-century Greek lexicon *Suda* or *Suidas* (the title is from a Latin loan word for "fortress") is the first to record the term *agchibasie*, cited without context, as a word of Heraclitus: *Suidae Lexicon*, ed. Immanuel Bekker (Berlin: Georg Reimer, 1854, in one volume), p. 20a, s.v. *agchibatein*; also in the series *Lexicographi Graeci*, of which volume one in five parts is *Suidae Lexicon*, ed. Ada Adler (Leipzig: B. G. Teubner, 1928–38; reprinted Stuttgart: Teubner, 1967–71), Pars I (1928), p. 41, number 398. The word is noted in Hermann Diels, *Die Fragmente der Vorsokratiker*, 6th rev. edn, ed. Walther Kranz (Berlin-Grunewald: Weidmann, 1951), 3 volumes, I, 178.6–7, number 122. *Agchibasie* is related to *agchibateo*, "to draw near," from *agchi* (poetic for *eggus*): nigh + *baino*, to move, step, go. The *Suda* claims (a) that *agchibateo* was an Ionic usage for *amphisbateo*, "to go asunder," hence "to disagree," and by implication (b) that *agchibasie* is the Ionic form of *amphisbetesis*, "dispute, argument, stand-off." However, in *Les Présocratiques*, ed. Jean-Paul Dumont, Daniel Delattre, and Jean-Louis Poirier (Paris: Gallimard, 1988), Dumont translates *agchibasie* as "rapprochement" (p. 173) and comments (p. 1242), "Ce mot ne se retrouve pas ailleurs chez Héraclite. S'agirait-il d'un *rapprochement* des contraires? Rien ne l'atteste." Heidegger uses the word as the title of the first fictional dialogue in GA 77 and indicates therein at 152.18ff the meaning we employ above. *In sabbato sancto* 4.10.04.

13

Heidegger's Categories in *Being and Time*

ROBERT BRANDOM

Introduction

In Division I of *Being and Time* Heidegger presents a novel categorization of what there is, and an original account of the project of ontology and consequently of the nature and genesis of those ontological categories. He officially recognizes two categories of Being: *Zuhandensein* (readiness-to-hand) and *Vorhandensein* (presence-at-hand). *Vorhandene* things are roughly the objective, person-independent, causally interacting subjects of natural scientific inquiry. *Zuhandene* things are those that a neo-Kantian would describe as having been imbued with human values and significances. In addition to these categories, there is human being, or Dasein, in whose structure the origins of the two thing-ish categories are to be found. This chapter concerns itself with three of Heidegger's conceptual innovations: his conceiving of ontology in terms of self-adjudicating anthropological categories, as summed up in the slogan "fundamental ontology is the regional ontology of Dasein"; his corresponding anti-traditional assertion of the ontological priority of the domain of the *Zuhandensein* to that of the *Vorhandensein*, which latter is seen as rooted in or precipitated out of that more basic (Heidegger says "primordial") world of human significances; and the non-Cartesian account of awareness and classificatory consciousness as social and practical.

Section I presents an interpretation of Heidegger's notion of fundamental ontology, and its relation to the "vulgar" ontology practiced by previous philosophers. Section II introduces *Zuhandensein* – the world of equipment, each element of which is experienced as having some practically constituted role or significance. Section III offers a reading of *Mitdasein*, the social mode of being, which institutes the world of equipment. Finally, section IV discusses the move from a world of equipment, about which there are no facts over and above how things are *taken* to be by all the bits of Dasein involved, to a realm of things which have properties not exhausted by the possible roles in Dasein's practical dealings.

Brandom, Robert, "Heidegger's Categories in *Being and Time*" from *The Monist* 66, no. 3 (1983): 387–409. © 1983 *The Monist: An International Quarterly Journal of General Philosophical Inquiry*, Peru, Illinois, USA 61354. Reprinted with permission.

I

What is most striking about Heidegger's account of categories is his distinction between "vulgar" ontology and "fundamental" ontology, and the coordinate claim that fundamental ontology is the regional ontology of Dasein (the kind of being we have). Vulgar ontology is the cataloguing of the furniture of the universe. Fundamental ontology is said to be deeper and more difficult than the vulgar variety, requiring the investigation of the significance of ontological categorization. For vulgar ontology in its most careful versions, whether we consider Leibniz, Hegel, Frege, or Quine, a specification of such general kinds takes the form of a specification of *criteria of identity* and *individuation* for entities of those kinds. As an ontologist in this tradition, Descartes inaugurated the modern era with a bold reincarnation of a Platonic idea: things are to be distinguished according to criteria of identity and individuation couched in terms of *epistemic* privilege. In particular, he invented a new kind of thing, according to the scheme: an event or object is *mental* (or subjective) just in case it is whatever it is taken to be by some individual.[1] The rest of the (non-divine) universe he relegated to the physical or objective realm. These were things which are what they are regardless of how any individual takes them to be.[2] The contribution of the nineteenth century to this scheme was Hegel's notion (see section III) of a third category of *social* entities. What is at issue here is the domain of social *appropriateness* in which, as in etiquette, social practice is the highest court of appeal. Thus a group or community can be thought of as having the same sort of criterial dominion or authority over, and hence privileged access to, social things that individuals have over subjective things.

Before describing how Heidegger develops this idea into a detailed model of social practice and significance in *Being and Time*, let us consider some consequences which adding such an ontological category to the Cartesian two-sorted ontology can have. In particular, we can ask the question of fundamental ontology: What is the ontological status of the distinction of entities into three kinds (subjective, social, and objective) based on the source of criterial authority for them? In particular, is the division of things into subjective, social, and objective a subjective distinction (as Berkeley would have it), a social distinction, or an objective one?[3] The conceptual status of such a question is unusual enough to warrant the citation of a few more familiar examples which exhibit the same structure.

First, consider the distinction between differences of *quality* and differences of *quantity*. Is this difference, we may ask, a qualitative or a quantitative one? Engels notoriously takes himself to have transformed the philosophical tradition by suggesting the latter response in place of the former. Whatever merit that suggestion may have, the issue it seeks to respond to seems to be perfectly intelligible.

Another example can be observed in the medieval notions of "*distinctio rationis*" and "*distinctio realis.*" The distinction between form and matter is only a distinction of reason, for we can never have one without the other. Only by, for example, rationally considering the relations a bronze cube stands in to a bronze sphere and a marble cube can we "separate" its being bronze from its being a cube. Between a piece of bronze and a piece of marble, on the other hand, there exists a real distinction, for these can be non-metaphorically separated without reliance on rational abstraction by comparison.

215

But now we must ask, as did the Scholastics, whether the distinction between rational and real distinctions is itself a rational or a real distinction. Although issues of great moment for the debate about the ontological and epistemological status of universals turn on the answer to this question, our concern is with the structure of the question rather than with the plausibility of various answers to it.

A final example should make clear the phenomenon being pointed out. The US constitution gives the three broad branches of the federal government distinct responsibilities and jurisdictions. As part of the relations of authority and responsibility which exist between the branches (the "checks and balances" that regulate their interaction), the judiciary is given the authority and responsibility to interpret the proper region of authority and responsibility of *each* branch, itself included. In matters of constitutional import, we may say, the judiciary is given the authority to draw the boundaries between its own authority and that of the executive and legislative branches.

It is not easy to describe the structure which these examples share. In each case a family of concepts pertaining to identity and individuation is examined, and the root of the identity and individuation of those concepts is found to reside in one of them. (In the last example, instead of a concept with an extension including various things, we have a social institution with a jurisdiction including various things.) In each case the question can be raised whether one of those concepts (institutions) is *self-adjudicating* in the sense that it applies to the sort of identity and individuation which distinguishes it from the other concepts or institutions in that family. To raise this second-order sort of question about a scheme of ontological categories is to engage in fundamental ontology. And Heidegger's claim that fundamental ontology is the regional ontology of Dasein is the claim that Dasein-in-the-world-of-the-ready-to-hand is ontologically self-adjudicating in this sense. Not only is the distinction between the ontological categories of the ready-to-hand and the present-at-hand intelligible only in terms of the sort of being that Dasein has, but the difference between Dasein's sort of being and readiness-to- and presentness-at-hand must itself be understood in terms of Dasein. It is this central feature of his early work which led the later Heidegger to dismiss *Being and Time* as "merely anthropological."

The ontological primacy of the social can be justified by appeal to a more specific thesis: pragmatism concerning *authority*. This is the claim that all matters of authority or privilege, in particular *epistemic* authority, are matters of social practice, and not objective matters of fact.[4] The pragmatist about authority will take the criterial distinctions between ontological categories to be social in nature, for those categories are distinguished precisely by the locus of criterial authority over them. The category of the social must then be seen as self-adjudicating, and hence as ontologically basic, so the broader claim of the ontological priority of social categories follows from the narrower doctrine concerning the social nature of authority. In what follows it will be argued that Heidegger develops precisely this line of thought in Division I of *Being and Time*.

II

According to Heidegger, Dasein finds itself always amidst an already existing world of equipment, consisting of significant things each of which is experienced *as* something.

The readiness-to-hand of a piece of equipment consists in its having a certain significance. This significance in turn consists in its appropriateness for various practical roles and its inappropriateness for others. "But the 'indicating' of the sign and the 'hammering' of the hammer are not properties [*Eigenschaften*] of entities. . . . Anything ready-to-hand is, at worst, appropriate [*Geeignet*] for some purposes and inappropriate for others" (SZ: 114). Properties, by contrast, are what characterize the present-at-hand independently of human practical ends – what would be taken to be true of objects before human beings "attach significances" to them on the neo-Kantian picture Heidegger wishes to invert. Heidegger's problem in the first part of *Being and Time is* to explain how such a category of objective Being could be constructed or abstracted out of the primitive system of appropriatenesses and significances which makes up the world in which we always already find ourselves.

How are we to understand this category of the ready-to-hand? To inhabit a *world* is to *take* each thing in that world *as* something. A piece of equipment is something experienced *as* something. Several points about this "as"-structure must be appreciated in order to understand the ready-to-hand as the kind of being or significance a thing exhibits by being taken as something. First, the something$_1$s which are taken as something$_2$s must be understood as themselves things which are ready-to-hand as ways of taking still other pieces of equipment. "In interpreting we do not, so to speak, throw a 'signification' over some naked thing which is present-at-hand, we do not stick a value on it."[5] The something$_1$s which are given with respect to one set of takings must themselves have been socially constituted. Second, it must be understood how thoroughly non-Cartesian and unsubjective is Heidegger's notion of the classificatory activity in virtue of which things show themselves *as* something$_2$s. The world of the ready-to-hand is what we can be aware of, *as* we are or would be aware of it. For Heidegger, as for others, there is no awareness or experience without classification. But the "awareness" which is the appropriation of some bit of equipment *as* having a certain significance is a public behavioral matter of how the thing is treated or responded to, not a mental act. For Heidegger the confused notion of the subjective arises when the category of the present-at-hand has been achieved, as that coordinate mental realm which must be invoked when one mistakenly takes the present-at-hand as ontologically primary, and looks for something to *add* to it to explain the everyday world of the ready-to-hand. If this antisubjectivism is overlooked, the use of the notion of classification to bridge the gap between Heidegger's "as"-structure and traditional notions of consciousness will be misleading. Finally, it must be noted that modeling understanding on taking-as is a device for interpreting the text, not a rendering of its terminology. Officially, discussions of "as"-structure are restricted to the level of interpretation (which develops out of understanding) where something is noticed *as* a hammer not when it is hammered with (as the model of understanding would have it) but only when it is discarded as inappropriate for, or searched for as required by, some practical project. The broader usage has an exegetical point, however, and the specific differences between understanding and interpretation can be accommodated within it, as we shall see. The positive account of treating or taking *as* has three features. First, takings are public performances which accord with social practices. Second, such performances are individuated as and by *responses*. Third, the responsive dispositions which constitute the social practices are related to one another so as to satisfy a strong systematicity condition. We examine these points below.

Where do the sorts or kinds or characters which are the something$_2$s according to which something$_1$s are classified come from? Any concrete object or event is similar to any other in an infinite number of respects, and dissimilar to it in an infinite number of others. For a respect of similarity is just a shared possible partial description, and these can be gerrymandered as we like. The practical discrimination of objects and performances into those appropriate for or according to some practice and those not is precisely the recognition of *some* of these infinitely numerous abstractly generable respects of similarity as having a special privilege over the rest. Heidegger should be interpreted in accord with the pragmatist thesis about authority, as taking this privilege to consist in its social recognition; that is, as a matter of how some community does or would respond to things. Something$_2$s are response-types, and classifying something$_1$s as a particular something$_2$ is simply responding to it with a performance of that type. Equipment is originally introduced in ¶15 as consisting of *pragmata*, "that which one has to do with in one's concernful dealings." The ready-to-hand is generically characterized by serviceability (*Dienlichkeit*): "Serviceability . . . is not an appropriateness of some entity; it is rather the condition (so far as Being is in question) which makes it possible for the character of such an entity to be defined by its appropriatenesses" (SZ: 115, H: 83). "Serviceability" is thus the potential which objects have to be caught up in the practices which institute specific respects of appropriateness. For something to be so caught up is for it to be *involved*: "The Being of an entity within the world is its involvement [*Bewandtnis*]" (SZ: 116, H: 84). Such involvement in turn comprises a system of references or assignments: "To say that the Being of the ready-to-hand has the structure of reference or assignment [*Verweisung*] means that it has in itself the character of *having been assigned or referred*" (SZ: 115, H: 84). The appropriatenesses which are the significance of a particular entity exist in virtue of such reference or assignment. Referring or assigning is instituting relations among equipment (pen, ink, paper, etc.) and clearly is something that is *done*, though we must not assume for that reason that it is something any one of us can do, or even that it is something the whole community can do (except in a derivative sense), rather than something done by the community's practices as constitutive of those practices."[6] These assignments exist in virtue of the responsive dispositions which are appropriate in a community.

A further doctrine is that "An entity is discovered when it is assigned or referred to something, and referred as that entity which it is" (SZ: 115, H: 84). Discovering an entity is taking it *as* something (the non-Cartesian notion of awareness as behavioral classification). Referring or assigning is to be understood not only as instituting the social appropriatenesses which are the significances of objects and performances, but also as making possible the appropriation of such significances by those who discover objects in terms of them. "Appropriation" [*Zueignung*] is Heidegger's non-subjective epistemic activity. To discover something ready-to-hand, to appropriate it, is to take it as something, to respond to it in a certain way. In one of his rare examples, after telling us that signs can be taken as paradigmatic of equipment in general, Heidegger says that "the kind of behaving (Being) which corresponds to the sign [a turn-signal arrow] is either to give way or stand still with respect to the car with the arrow" (SZ: 110, H: 79).

Here it is precisely how it is appropriate to respond to the turn-signal in a context that makes it the bit of equipment it is. To take it *as* such a signal (discover it as such) is just to respond to it with the appropriate behavior. The systematicity requirement may be put broadly by the claim that "Taken strictly, there 'is' no such thing as *an* equipment. To the Being of any equipment there always belongs a totality of equipment, in which it can be the equipment that it is" (SZ: 97, H: 68). Anything ready-to-hand is so only in virtue of the role it plays in a "referential totality of significance or involvements." "As the Being of something ready-to-hand, an involvement is itself discovered only on the basis of the prior discovery of a totality of involvements" (SZ: 118, H: 85).

In terms of what relations are such roles to be understood, and how must they fit together to form the appropriate kind of totality? Heidegger gives his answer in ¶18, "Involvement and Significance – the Worldhood of the World." Although the account offered there deploys an unfamiliar set of technical terms, its basic characteristics may be straightforwardly set out. The bearers of the social significances making up readiness-to-hand are of two kinds: objects and performances. Objects and performances are what can be constitutively judged to be (in the sense of being responded to as) appropriate or not according to the social practices which are the medium of social significance. Heidegger calls those practices "in-order-to's" (*das Umzu*). Fastening one board to another by driving a nail would be an example. An object can be caught up in such a practice either by being used in the practice or by being produced in that practice. In the former case, Heidegger calls the object (for example, a hammer or a nail, used in the different senses of "employed" and "consumed" respectively) the "with-which" (*das Womit*) of the practice, and in the latter case he calls the object which is produced the "towards-which" (*das Wozu*). The assignments of objects are the relations between them instituted by relations between the practices in which they are involved in these two ways. The role of an object (its involvement) is determined by those practices in which it is appropriately used, and those practices in which it can appropriately be produced.

Particular performances are called "in whiches" (*das Wobei*). A social practice may be thought of as a class of possible performances, that is as a performance *type*. Such an in-order-to consists, namely, of just those performances which are or would be (taken to be) appropriate according to it. For something to be (ready-to-hand as) a hammer is for it to be appropriate to respond to it with a performance of the hammering type, i.e. to hammer with it. It is performances of using and producing objects which make up the social practices in virtue of which those objects acquire their involvements and significances. Social object-types are then instituted by social practice types of the performances in which they are appropriately used or produced. In the world of the ready-to-hand, in which things are whatever they are (or would be) responded to as, then, the individuation of objects (by their roles as with- and towards-whiches) is determined by the individuation of social practices. Object types are instituted by performance types. So where do the appropriateness equivalence classes of performances, which are the social practices, come from?

As with objects, performance tokens exhibit infinite numbers of objective respects of similarity and dissimilarity. The privilege which one type or co-appropriateness class of performances exhibits as a practice can only have its source in its social recognition; that is, in how the type-privileged (co-typical) performance tokens would be treated or

219

taken, or more generally responded to by the community in question. The performances comprised by a social practice are of the same type in that there is some other responsive performance type (something$_2$) such that each of the tokens of the instituted performance type (something$_1$) is, according to the community whose recognitions are constitutive in this domain, appropriately responded to by some performance belonging to the instituting type. A performance is recognized as being of the type by being responded to as such. For instance, what makes a certain class of performances all instances of the type *constructings of tribally appropriate dwelling huts* is that each of those possible performances would be appropriately responded to by a performance of the type *tribe members treating the produced object as a dwelling* – that is, *being prepared to dwell in it under suitable circumstances*. Whenever what is produced by one practice is used by another, the using practice plays the role of responsive recognition performance type (rrpt) with respect to the producing practice. The role of a social performance type in a "totality of involvements" is specified by saying what performance type is its rrpt, and what performance type it is an rrpt for.

The requirement of systematicity or of the autonomy of significance may then be stated in two parts. First, with respect to objects, every object-type appropriately produced by one social practice must be appropriately useable in or by some other practice. The converse need not hold, for Heidegger says several times that *natural* objects are ready-to-hand as objects usable in human practice, but not requiring to be produced by it.[7] Second, with respect to performances, every performance type which is an rrpt for some performance type must have some other performance type as its own rrpt. Again the converse need not hold, since we can respond to natural events. To specify the role of an object in such a system is to specify these practices with respect to which it functions as towards-which, and those with respect to which it functions as a with-which. To specify the role of a performance (in-which) is to specify the practice; that is, the performance type to which it belongs. And to specify such an in-order-to is to specify its rrpt and what it functions as an rrpt of. Doing so determines all of the assignment relations and involvements which hold between socially significant objects as such, as well as the instituting responsive relations defining social performance types. The non-Cartesian epistemic notion of appropriation of significance or discovery of the ready-to-hand is also given a natural social-behavioral reading on this account. For to grasp the involvement of an object is to achieve practical mastery of its various assignments. And such mastery consists simply in being able to act (use, produce, and respond) appropriately according to the practices which institute those involvements. To respond to an object or performance which is appropriate according to a practice *as* appropriate according to that practice – that is, to respond appropriately to it – is to discover it as what it is, as ready-to-hand for what it is ready-to-hand for. Such practical capacities can be described without invoking anything subjective on the part of the practitioners. The inhabitant of a Heideggerian world is aware of it as composed of significant equipment, caught up in various social practices and classified by the involvements those practices institute. But this awareness is practical, social, and behavioral, consisting entirely in the exhibition of differential responsive dispositions according appropriately with those of the community.

The account suggested of the nature of the referential totality of significance within which we encounter the ready-to-hand explains the concept of the worldhood of the

220

world in at least one straightforward sense. For the remarks above can be expressed in a first-order quantificational language. Such a language would need two different sorts of indivdual constants, to stand for object types and performance types, and three different predicates (corresponding to the three sorts of "assignment or reference" distinguished above): U(o, p), interpreted as saying that object o is used in practice p; P(p, o), interpreted as saying that object o is produced by practice p; and R(p, p'), interpreted as saying that p' is the rrpt of p. It is easy to see that the two halves of the systematicity condition can be expressed as quantificational sentences in such a language. It is equally easy to see how the model theory for such a language might go. Theories in the specified language that include the sentences codifying the systematicity conditions would be interpreted by model structures which consisted of domains of object and performance types (represented as sets of tokens) and relations between them of using, producing, and responding. A Heideggerian world is such a structure satisfying in the usual sense a first-order theory of the sort described which contains the systematicity conditions.[8] At the end of ¶18 Heidegger summarizes the structure he discerns:

> The "for-the-sake-of-which" signifies an "in-order-to"; this in turn a "towards-this"; the latter, an "in-which" of letting something be involved; and that in turn the "with-which." These relationships are bound up with one another as a primordial totality; they are what they are *as* signifying. . . . The relational totality of this signifying we call "significance." (SZ: 120, H: 87)

This passage emphasizes the systematic structure of social significance and retraces the relations of use and response described above. It mentions the further technical expression "for-the-sake-of-which" [*das Worumwillen*], which marks the point of contact of the categorial structure with the existential concerns of Division II and so cannot be discussed here. A practical "in-order-to" gives a point to performances of some type by providing a use for the "towards-this" (a particular "towards-which") produced by such performances. Those performances are "in-which"s individuated as types by their overall role or involvement in use of "with-which"s as means or production of "towards-which"s, as those "towards-which"s are individuated not only by their involvement in being produced by performances of a certain kind from raw materials of a certain kind, but also by their involvement in a further practice (an "in-order-to" whose performances are themselves "in-which"s) which makes use of them. The communities whose responsive recognitive practices generate these structures of social significance will be considered next.

III

> We have interpreted worldhood as that referential totality which constitutes significance. In Being-familiar with this significance and previously understanding it, Dasein lets what is ready-to-hand be encountered as discovered in its involvement. In Dasein's Being, the context of references or assignments which significance implies is tied up with Dasein's ownmost Being. (SZ: 160, H: 123)

Nothing like a full account of Dasein's kind of Being can be essayed here; that is the topic of the whole of *Being and Time*. On the other hand, something must be said about the constitution of the community in whose dispositions (for appropriate responsive recognitions or takings) significance originates. Happily the features of Dasein's kind of Being which must be understood if the precipitation of the present-at-hand out of the ready-to-hand is to be intelligible can be explained with the materials already available.

The first point, of course, is that Dasein's Being is *social* in nature: so far as Dasein is at all, it has Being-with-one-another as its kind of Being (SZ: 163, H: 125), Not only is Being-toward-Others an autonomous, irreducible relationship, as Being-with, it is one which, with Dasein's Being, already is (SZ: 162, H: 125). Dasein in itself is essentially Being-with (SZ: 156, H: 120).

Next, Dasein's sociality is essential to the practical activity which constitutes worldly significance: "Dasein-with remains existentially constitutive for Being in-the-world" (SZ: 157, H: 121; compare also SZ: 163, H: 125). Third, it is only in the context of such Dasein-with that individuals can be spoken of: "In Being with and towards Others, there is thus a relationship of Being [*Seinsverhaltnis*] from Dasein to Dasein. But it might be said that this relationship is already constitutive for one's own Dasein" (SZ: 162, H: 124). "In terms of the 'they' [*das Man*] and as the 'they', I am given proximally to myself" (SZ: 167, H: 129).

These doctrines can be understood according to the Hegelian model of the synthesis of social substance by mutual recognition. To belong to a community, according to this model, is to be recognized as so belonging by all those one recognizes as so belonging. Hegel's idea was that community constitutive recognition is transitive *de jure* – that one must recognize those who are recognized by those one recognizes. The reflexive self-recognition that makes one a Hegelian individual will then follow if one can establish *de facto* symmetry; that is, achieve recognition by those one recognizes. To be entitled to recognize or regard oneself as an excellent chess-player one must be entitled to be regarded as such by those one so regards.

Of course, for an account along these lines to be helpful in interpreting Heidegger, recognition must not be taken to be a mental act, but as with awareness and classification must be given a social behavioral reading in terms of communal responsive dispositions. What sort of response (rrpt) is taking or recognizing someone *as* one of us, a member of *our* community? Clues are to be found in two passages: "In that with which we concern ourselves environmentally, the Others are encountered as what they are; they *are* what they do" (SZ: 163, H: 126). What is it that other community members as such do? They take objects and performances as ready-to-hand with respect to various practices by using them and responding to them in various ways. How does such behavior constitute the practioners as other members of one's own community? "By 'Others' we do not mean everyone else but me – those against whom the 'I' stands out. They are rather those from whom for the most part one does not distinguish oneself – those among whom one is too" (SZ: 154, H: 118).

Not everyone is a communal Other, but only those one recognizes or responds to as such. To respond to them as such is not to distinguish them from oneself. But in what regard? The previous passage said that the Others are what they do, so it is their doings which one does not distinguish from one's own. And this is to say that one treats their *responses* and dispositions as one's own. What they take to be appropriate performances and usings and producings of equipment, one also takes as such. To give one's own responses no special status or priority in this way is to treat the kinds they institute as social. It is to take the authority over appropriateness boundaries to reside in the community, which is constituted by that very recognition.[9]

The suggestion is that my recognizing someone as a co-community member is responding to him in a certain way. That way is for me to respond to his responses as having the same authority to institute kinds and appropriateness equivalence classes that my own responses have. In particular, my recognitions of others *and myself* as members of the community have no special authority. My recognitions of myself as community member count only if they are taken to count by those I take to be community members. Their so taking my recognitions is in turn simply a matter of their recognizing me; that is, treating my responses as equally authoritative as theirs in determining appropriatenesses. The community, *Mitdasein*, then differs from the ready-to-hand in that its members are constituted not only by being recognized or responded to in a certain way, but also by their recognizings and responses as recognizers.

Being-together-with in the sense of forming a recognitive community is accordingly the existential basis of the consilience of practice which constitutes the category of the ready-to-hand and hence, as we shall see, the category of the present-at-hand as well. The distinction between the existential and the categorial terminologically marks that between recognizers, and the merely recognizeds which do not have the kind of being of one of us. The practical agreement of recognizing each other's recognizings can be called "communication" "in a sense which is ontologically broad":

> "Communication" in which one makes an assertion – giving information, for instance, is a special case of the communication which is grasped in principle existentially. In this more general kind of communicating the Articulation of Being-with one another understandingly is constituted. Through it a co-state-of-mind [*Mitbefindlichkeit*] gets "shared," and so does the understanding of Being-with. (SZ: 205, H: 162)

In the next section we investigate the genesis of the category of the present-at-hand out of the sort of understanding which consists in shared precognitive pratice permitting communication about a world of equipment each bit of which is whatever it is recognized-by-us as.

IV

The claim to be developed in this section is that the category of the present-at-hand consists of ready-to-hand things which are appropriately responded to by a certain kind of performance, *qua* things that can *only* be appropriately responded to by such a performance. That categorially constitutive kind of responsive recognition performance type is *assertion*. Since Heidegger holds that "assertion is derived from interpretation, and is a special case of it,"[10] the story must begin with the notion of interpretation (*Auslegung*). Interpretation is a coordinate notion to that understanding which consists

223

in the practical mastery of a totality of significations or assignments required if one is to live in a world at all. For "we never perceive equipment that is ready-to-hand without already understanding and interpreting it."[11] Four features of interpretation must be recognized. First, interpreting characterizes practical activity: "Interpretation is carried out primordially not in a theoretical statement but in an action of circumspectful concern . . . [e.g.] laying aside the unsuitable tool" (SZ: 200, H: 157). Second, interpreting involves making something one's own. Interpretation is described as "the working-out and appropriation of an understanding."[12] "In understanding there lurks the possibility of interpretation – that is, of *appropriating* what is understood" (SZ: 203, H: 161; see also SZ: 191, H: 150). Taking something as something was the form of the act of understanding, that discovery of a bit of equipment which also disclosed a totality of equipmental involvements. What is it practically to appropriate such an understanding?

The answer is offered by a pair of passages, worth citing at length, which for the third point introduce the crucial *conditional* structure of interpretation, out of which the possibility of inference and hence assertion develops.

Circumspection operates in the involvement-relationships of the context of equipment which is ready-to-hand. What is essential is that one should have a primary understanding of the totality of involvements. . . . In one's current using and manipulating, the concernful circumspection . . . *brings* the ready-to-hand *closer* to Dasein, and does so by *interpreting* what has been sighted. The specific way of bringing the object of concern closer we call *deliberating* [*Ueberlegung*]. The schema particular to this is the "if . . . then . . ."; if this or that, for instance, is to be produced, put to use, or averted, then some ways, means, circumstances or opportunities will be needed (SZ: 410, H: 359).

Interpretation classifies according to personal ends or projects, and hence appropriates. What new element is indicated by the invocation of the "if . . . then . . ." as what is in this way brought closer to oneself?

> But if deliberation is to be able to operate in the scheme of the "if . . . then . . . ," concern must already have "surveyed" a context of involvements and have an understanding of it. That which is considered with an "if" must already be understood as *something or other*. . . . The schema "something-as-something" has already been sketched out beforehand in the structure of one's pre-predicative understanding. (SZ: 411, H: 359)

Understanding appropriates equipment. It is exercised in taking something as something, e.g. as a hammer. Interpretation at the level of deliberation adds to this use and appropriation of equipment, the use and appropriation of equipmental *understanding* of particular involvements. One can not only take something as a hammer, but take a hammer as one of the tools required for a certain pratical project. What is appropriated is then the conditional serviceabilities of things. One uses and produces conditional understandings of the significance of particular $something_1$s as $something_2$s.

The fourth point is that this non-Cartesian cognitive notion of interpretation as the personal practical appropriation of a conditional appropriateness of equipmental involvement brings us closer to the notion of linguistic assertion. "In the significance itself, with which Dasein is always familiar, there lurks the ontological condition which makes it possible for Dasein, as something which understands and interprets, to disclose such things as 'significations'; upon these, in turn, is founded the Being of words and of language" (SZ: 121, H: 87).

"Significations" are the conditional appropriatenesses into which the totality of significations can be "dissolved or broken up."[13] What makes the transition to language possible is that one can come to respond differentially to (and hence disclose practically) not just things and performances but the signification which are their conditional dependencies. Deliberation develops towards asserting when what is surveyed from the point of view of a practical end is a field of "if . . . then . . ."s, each of which may then itself be used or laid aside, just as with first-order equipment. Deliberation accomplishes a special kind of abstraction, requiring responsive recognition of the serviceabilities of equipment, rather than merely of the equipment itself.

The key to the precipitation of the present-at-hand out of the ready-to-hand lies in assertion:

> The leveling of the primordial "as" of circumspective interpretation [the "existential-hermeneutical 'as'"] to the "as" with which presence-at-hand is given a definite character [the "apophantical 'as'"] is the specialty of assertion. Only so does it obtain the possibility of exhibiting something in such a way that we just look at it. (SZ: 201, H: 158)

The articulation leading to the discovery of the present-at-hand begins in the "if . . . then . . ." of interpretation of the ready-to-hand. What matters is "what is awaited"[14] in the "then . . ." part. In the basic case of interpreting something merely ready-to-hand, what is "awaited" is the useability or producibility of some actual or envisaged objector performance – that is, the projection of a practical possibility. In presence-at-hand, the primary consequence of an "if (something as something) . . ." is the appropriability of some *claim* or assertion. The difference between responding to something as present-at-hand and as merely ready-to-hand is that things which are present-at-hand are appropriately responded to as such only by producing a particular kind of performance, namely assertions. The "then" is still something ready-to-hand when we thematize (i.e. respond to something as present-at-hand), but it is an assertion, a very special kind of equipment.

The question is then: "By what existential-ontological modification does assertion arise from circumspective interpretation?" (SZ: 200, H: 157). The answer in brief is that assertions are equipment appropriately used for *inference*. Assertion is the topic of ¶33, which offers three "significations" of assertion. The central one of these is that "assertion means communication."

> As something-communicated, that which has been put forward in the assertion is something that Others can "share" with the person making the assertion. . . . That which is put forward in the assertion is something which can be passed along in further retelling. (SZ: 197, H: 155)

> What is expressed becomes, as it were, something ready-to-hand within the-world which can betaken up and spoken again. (SZ: 266, H: 224)

225

Asserting thus has the significance of issuing a reassertion license to other community members. The assertion is produced as something usable by others.

The other two features by which assertion is introduced are "pointing-out" some subject of assertion, and "giving it a definite character" by predicating something of it. What is shared, in other words, is the taking of something as something. Where before taking something as something (pointing it out and characterizing it) was something one could only *do*, now it becomes something one *can say*. What was implicit in performance now becomes an explicitly producible and usable bit of equipment, which one can appropriate and make available for others to appropriate. The pointing-out of a subject is socially transitive across authorized reassertions, and so guarantees communication in the sense of securing a common topic: "Even when Dasein speaks over again what someone else has said, it comes into a Being-towards the very entities which have been discussed" (SZ: 266, H: 224). Such social preservation of a common subject-matter is a necessary condition for the possibility of agreement and disagreement of assertion, as opposed to mere change of topic.

Predication, as explicitly communicable characterization, further extends the authorizing dimension of asserting. For predicates come in inferential families: *if* what is pointed out is appropriately characterizable by one speaker as red, *then* it is appropriately characterizable by another as colored. The practical conditional appropriatenesses of assertion which make up such familes of predicates guarantee that an asserting licenses more than just reassertion, licensing others to draw conclusions beyond what was originally claimed. As members of inferential families, the predicates used to characterize objects in assertions codify the conditional significations responded to as such already in deliberation. It is in virtue of the socially appropriate inferential consequences of an asserting that it conveys information, authorizing a specific set of performances (including other assertions) which would have been inappropriate without such authorization. The taking of something, as something$_2$ of pre-predicative understanding becomes explicitly usable and sharable once linguistic terms are available as equipment for publicly pointing out something$_1$s, and predicates codifying as inferential significances the conditional serviceabilities discerned by deliberative interpretation are available as equipment expressing explicitly the involvements implicit in the something$_2$s things were taken as.

Understanding asserting as authorizing reassertion and inference specifies the *use* to which assertions, as bits of equipment, may appropriately be put. The recognitive responsive performance type of any asserting-type will be the set of assertions which it may appropriately be seen as licensing, namely those which follow from it according to the inferential practices of the community. But this is only half the story. What about the appropriate circumstances of *production* of this new sort of ready-to-hand equipment? Corresponding to the dimension of authority governing the use of assertions as equipment-for-inference is a dimension of responsibility governing their production. For in producing an assertion one does not simply authorize others to use it inferentially, one also undertakes the responsibility to justify one's claim.

> Assertion communicates entities in the "how" of their uncoveredness. . . . If, however, these entities are to be appropriated explicitly with respect to their uncoveredness, this amounts to saying that the assertion is to be *demonstrated* as one that uncovers.

The assertion expressed is something ready-to-hand. (SZ: 266, H224, emphasis added)

As ready-to-hand, assertings are subject to social appropriatenesses of production as well as use. These concern when one is entitled to commit oneself to the claim, or in Heidegger's terminology, "appropriate" it, so that the inference and reassertion license is in force: "It is therefore essential that Dasein should explicitly appropriate what has already been uncovered, defend it against semblance and disguise, and assure itself of its uncoveredness again and again" (SZ: 265, H: 222).

The responsibility to justify or defend one's claims undertaken as a matter of course in their appropriate production is essential to the special sort of communication which emerges with assertion. For even when Dasein speaks over again what someone else has said, though it comes into relation to the things pointed out and uncovered "it has been exempted from having to uncover them again, primordially, and it holds that it has thus been exempted."[15] That is, he who relies on the authority of a previous speaker in reassertion is absolved of the responsibility to justify his claim which he would otherwise have undertaken by his performance of producing that assertion. His reliance upon the authority of the first assertor just is his acquisition of the right to defer justificatory responsibility for his own assertion to the original speaker. The response which socially constitutes taking someone to have appropriately made an assertion (fulfilled or be able to fulfill his justificatory responsibility) is to treat his assertion as genuinely authoritative as licensing others; that is, to recognize as appropriate any deferrals of justificatory responsibility for that claim and its consequences to the original assertor by those relying upon that authority. It is in this way that the dimensions of responsibility and authority, of appropriate production and use, are related so as to constitute assertions as equipment-for-communicating.[16]

This sketch of Heidegger's notion of assertion puts us in a position to understand the category of the present-at-hand. The crucial point to understand here is that the move from equipment ready-to-hand, fraught with socially instituted significances, to objective things present-at-hand, is one not of decontextualization, but of recontextualization. Asserting and the practices of giving and asking for reasons which make it possible are themselves a special sort of practical activity. Responding to something by making an assertion about it is treating it as present-at-hand. Presence-at-hand is constituted by special appropriatenesses of response.

> In characterizing the change-over from manipulating and using and so forth which are circumspective in a "practical" way, to "theoretical" exploration, it would be easy to suggest that merely looking at entities is something which emerges when concern *holds back* from any kind of manipulation. . . . But this is by no means the way in which the "theoretical" attitude of science is reached. On the contrary, the tarrying which is discontinued when one manipulates can take on the character of a more precise kind of circumspection. (SZ: 409, H: 357–8)

Claims, equipment for asserting, represent "more precise" interpretive responses because in them the significations which are merely implicit in ordinary equipment become explicit or "thematized," accessible to claims and inferences and hence to demands for justification. Treating something as present-at-hand is not ignoring its social significance, but attending to a special sort of significance it can have, namely significance for the correctness of assertions about it. Corresponding to a new social mode of response, asserting, there is a new kind of being, presence-at-hand, constitutively uncovered by that response: "Thematizing objectifies. It does not first 'posit' the entities, but frees them so that one can interrogate them and determine their character 'objectively.' Being which objectifies and which is alongside the present-at-hand within-the-world is characterized by *a distinctive kind of making-present*" (SZ: 414, H: 363).

The present-at-hand may thus be defined as what is ready-to-hand as a with-which for the practice of assertion; that is, as what is responded to as such only by making a claim about it. We have seen what kind of performance assertings are. What is the relation between what is responded to as ready-to-hand for assertion and what is pointed out as present-at-hand in the assertion? Heidegger explains this in terms of a transformation:

> The entity which is held in our fore-having – for instance the hammer – is proximally ready-to-hand as equipment. If this entity becomes the "object" of an assertion, then as soon as we begin this assertion, there is already a change-over in the fore-having. Something *ready-to-hand with which* we have to do or perform something turns into something "*about which*" the assertion that points it out is made. Our fore-sight is aimed at something present-at-hand in what is ready-to-hand. . . . Within this discovery of presence-at-hand, which is at the same time a covering-up of readiness-to-hand, something present-at-hand which we encounter is given a definite character in its Being-present-at-hand-in-such-and-such-a-manner. Only now are we given access to *properties* or the like. . . . This levelling of the primordial "as" of circumspective interpretation to the "as" with which presence-at-hand is given a definite character is the specialty of assertion. Only so does it obtain the possibility of exhibiting something in such a way that we just look at it. (SZ: 200, H: 158)

The present-at-hand is first discovered *in* something already ready-to-hand which we are related to by being practically involved with it. It is then possible to adopt a special stance, shifting from the original practical context to that of assertion. The referentiality of the relation to the original piece of equipment is inherited by assertions about the object discovered in it. Dealing with the object in such a context, where practical significance is restricted to significance for inference, is attributing properties to something present-at-hand pointed out in the assertions about it.

One question remains. In what sense does responding to something by making an assertion about it count as treating it as having objective properties? What sort of independence of the social appropriatenesses of use and production constitutive of the ready-to-hand is attributed to the present-at-hand when we understand its defining precognitive responsive performance type to be asserting? Equipment as such is always equipment serviceable for the pursuit of some practical end. Significance flows from the practically orienting projects to the "with-which"s and "towards-which"s whose involvements are their roles in instrumental practices. The objectivity of the present-at-hand consists in the indifference of the appropriatenesses of assertion to the practical ends motivating assertors. Taking something as a hammer is taking it as appropriate for hammering. When the property of heaviness is discerned in the present-at-hand object which was ready-to-hand as a hammer, a claim is made whose appropriateness is not a matter of serviceability for or obstruction of any particular practical ends or projects. The justifiability and hence appropriateness of such a claim is not a matter of answering to some practical need.

The autonomy of justification and inference with respect to the pursuit of practical projects is the source of the autonomy of the properties of the present-at-hand with respect to the appropriatenesses of practice. It is this autonomy that is invoked when it is said that the truth of assertions answers to the things pointed out in assertion. Authority is a social matter, and in the game of asserting and giving and asking for reasons authority over the appropriateness of claims has been socially withdrawn from the sphere of usefulness for practical ends.

The claim that the objectivity of the present-at-hand consists in its insulation by assertion from Dasein's practical activity can be given a strong or a weak reading, and it is important to distinguish these. On the strong reading, the present-at-hand would be entirely irrelevant to practical concerns. On this account, the only appropriate response to something present-at-hand is an assertion, the only use which can be made of assertion is inference, and inference is restricted to *theoretical* inference; that is, inference whose conclusion is another assertion. Assertions are seen as irrelevant to practice, as mere representations of an independent reality indifferent to practical projects. This practical indifference is then inherited by the present-at-hand, since it can only be the subject of such assertions. This idea is present in Heidegger. It is not presence-at-hand, however, but what he calls the doctrine of *pure* presence-at-hand (or, sometimes, "Reality").

> ["Reality"] in its traditional signification stands for Being in the sense of pure presence-at-hand of Things. . . . [But] *all* the modes of Being of entities within-the-world are founded ontologically upon the worldhood of the world and accordingly the phenomenon of Being-in-the-world. From this arises the insight that among the modes of Being of entities within-the-world, Reality has no priority, and that Reality is a kind of Being which cannot even characterize anything like the world or Dasein in a way which is ontologically appropriate. (SZ: 211, H: 254)

Presence-at-hand corresponds to a weaker reading of the insulation assertional practices provide between the objects present-at-hand and practical projects. For although it is correct to see assertions as the only appropriate responses to the present-at-hand as such, and although the only use that can appropriately be made of assertions is inference, it is simply a mistake to think of all inference as theoretical inference. There is also practical inference, whose premises are assertions and whose conclusion is a practical performance which is not an assertion but, in virtue of its genesis as the result of such deliberation, an action. Assertions about the present-at-hand can be practically relevant. We can use information about the merely present-at-hand properties of things, such as the heaviness of the hammer. Without the possibility of language exits through non-assertional performance, theoretical or intralinguistic inference would lose much or all of its point.[17] If it is then incorrect to see the present-at-hand as completely irrelevant to practical pursuits, as in pure presence-at-hand, what is meant by

229

its objectivity? Just this. The *only* way in which the present-at-hand can affect Dasein's projects is by being the subject of an assertion which ultimately plays some role in practical inference. It is not that the present-at-hand is irrelevant to non-assertional practice, it is that its relevance is *indirect*. Assertions are the only interface between the present-at-hand and the rest of our practice. The mistake of the doctrine of pure presence is to see no interface at all.[18] The genuine difference between the present-at-hand (which can be thought of in an extended sense as ready-to-hand for the practices of assertion and inference) and what is ready-to-hand is that one can only make practical use of assertions about the present-at-hand, never of what is present-at-hand itself. Its assertional proxies are serviceable equipment, but the present-at-hand itself is not. Only as represented in assertions can the present-at-hand partake of the equipmental totality of significance which is the world within which Dasein lives and moves and has its being. Discovery of the present-at-hand is an authentic possibility of Dasein's being, instantiated by all human communities ever discovered. Pure presence-at-hand is a philosopher's misunderstanding of the significance of the category of presence-at-hand, and a bad idea.

The categorial nature of the present-at-hand, no less than that of the ready-to-hand (or for that matter the existential nature of Dasein itself as Mitdasein) is constituted by its being appropriately responded to in a certain way, in this case by assertions. In this fact resides Heidegger's ontological pragmatism, and the self-adjudicating nature of Mitdasein-in-the-world. Heidegger sees social behavior as generating both the category of equipment ready-to-hand within a world, and the category of objectively present-at-hand things responded to as independent of the practical concerns of any community. In virtue of the social genesis of criterial authority (the self-adjudication of the social, given pragmatism about authority), fundamental ontology (the study of the origin and nature of the fundamental categories of things) is the study of the nature of social being – social practices and practitioners. Only because Dasein as socially constituted and constituting masters communal practices classifying things according to kind which are whatever they are taken to be "can Dasein also understand and conceptualize such characteristics of Being as independence, the 'in-itself,' and Reality in general. Only because of this are 'independent' entities, as encountered within-the-world, accessible to circumspection" (SZ: 251, H: 207).

We have been concerned with three conceptual innovations presented in *Being and Time*. One of these is Heidegger's hierarchy of non-Cartesian cognitive notions. At its base is understanding – the disclosure of a totality of social significance and the discovery within it of individual pieces of equipment by mastery of communal responsive practices. At the next level is deliberative interpretation by appropriation of the conditional significances implicit in the understanding of the ready-to-hand. Finally there is the discursive appropriation of the present-at-hand through assertion of sentences which in virtue of their social inference potentials explicitly thematize the significations one becomes aware of in interpretation. Second, we have seen how the category of presence-at-hand arises within and yet is distinct from the more fundamental category of readiness-to-hand. Third, in terms of the first two points it is clear that the ready-to-hand is first among equals among the categories because of the self-adjudicating nature of the social (Mitdasein in a world which is a totality of practical significance). Understanding in this way the basic ontological structure of

Heidegger's account in Division I is the necessary preparation for understanding both his account of the individuation of Dasein and the institution of temporality by the personal appropriation of projects in Division II, and his profound reading of that tradition of philosophy which has left us in such a mistaken position that "in general our understanding of Being is such that every entity is understood in the first instance as present-at-hand."[19]

Notes

The general orientation of this chapter owes much to John Haugeland, particularly to his account of transcendental constitution as and by social institution in "Heidegger on being a person," *Noùs*, March 1982, 15–26. I would also like to thank my fellow staff members and the seminar participants at the Council for Philosophic Studies 1980 Summer Institute, "Phenomenology and Existentialism: Continental and Analytic Perspectives on Intentionality," for their responses to an earlier version of the ideas presented here.

1   See Richard Rorty (1970) "Incorrigibility as the mark of the mental." *Journal of Philosophy*, 67(12), 399–424.

2   Of course, Descartes held other views about the substances to which these categories applied as well. He filled in the abstract ontological categorization of epistemic kinds with specifica- tions, e.g. of the objective realm as having its essence exhausted by geometric extension, and of the epistemic subject whose incorrigible "takings" define the mental as itself identi- cal with the sum of mental things it is aware of. The current concern is with the ontologi- cal framework rather than with Descartes's theories about the entities it categorized.

3   In "Freedom and constraint by norms" (*APQ*, April 1977, 187–96) I investigate the sort of norm inherent in the appropriatenesses instituted by social practices. I took it to be signifi- cant that the social–objective distinction can be seen as the origin of the value–fact dis- tinction, and that both naturalists, who want to reduce one category to the other, and non-naturalists, who do not, presumed that it was an *objective* distinction between facts and values which was at issue. I explore the consequences of treating the social–objective, and hence the value–fact, distinction as itself social rather than objective; that is, as a matter of how the community responds to various things, not how they are independently and in themselves.

4   As Rorty has argued (*Philosophy and the Mirror of Nature*, Princeton, NJ: Princeton UniversityPress, 1979), on the plausibility of such a claim rest Sellars's and Quine's twin attacks on the two varieties of unjustified justifiers ("privileged representations") which foundationalists, particularly positivistic ones, had relied on as the foundations of our infer- ential structures. Thus Quine dismantled the picture of *language* as a source of authority immune to social revision ("intrinsic credibility," "self evidence," etc.) for some sentences thought to be true-in-virtue-of-meaning, and Sellars performed the same service for the picture of the mind as a source of supposedly socially impervious privilege for "reports" of thoughts and sensations.

5   SZ: 190, H: 150.

6   Cf. the "sich verweisenden Verstehen" of SZ: 119.

7   See, for example, SZ: 100, H: 70.

8   Such a model must be used with caution, however. Heidegger is concerned that the struc- tures so taken as worlds involve *concrete* relations of use, production, and response, rather than simply structurally analogous relations. He says, "The context of assignments or references, which, as significance, is constitutive for worldhood, can be taken formally

231

in the sense of a system of Relations. But one must note that in such formalizations the phenomena get leveled off so much that their real phenomenal content may be lost . . . the phenomenal content of these "relations" and "relata" – the "in-order-to," the "for-the-sake-of," and the "with-which" of an involvement – is such that they resist any sort of mathematical functionalization" (SZ: 121–2, H: 88).

9   This view represents a normative version of the "conformism" discussed by Haugeland (see introductory note), without what I take to be the ontologically irrelevant account of its ontic genesis that he offers.

10   SZ: 203, H: 160.

11   SZ: 190, H: 150.

12   SZ: 275, H: 231.

13   SZ: 204, H: 161.

14   SZ: 411, H: 360.

15   SZ: 266, H: 224, following the passage on speaking-over quoted above.

16   I have presented the details of an account of asserting along these lines in "Asserting," *Noûs*, 1983, 17, 637–50.

17   Here "theoretical" inference refers to language–language moves, by contrast to "practical" inference involving language-exit moves (in Sellars's sense). In a different sense "theoretical" claims are those which can *only* be arrived at inferentially, and not as non-inferential reports. Discussion of the relevance to the understanding of presence-at-hand of claims which are theoretical in this sense is beyond the scope of this chapter.

18   The semantics of the points of view generated by such "interfaces" – where a set of claims can make a difference to practical deliberations only insofar as it makes a difference to some other set of claims which then affects the deliberations – is discussed in my "Points of view and practical reasoning," *Canadian Journal of Philosophy*, June 1982, 321–33.

19   SZ: 268, H: 225.

14

Early Heidegger on Sociality

THEODORE R. SCHATZKI

Compared to his extensive treatments of other topics such as intentionality, truth, and worldhood, Martin Heidegger wrote relatively little about human sociality in his early works. Yet any number of interpreters credit him with being one of the first contemporary philosophical advocates of the now familiar thesis that human life is essentially social in character, thereby grouping him – and not on the basis of their shared advocacy of just this one thesis – with such contemporaries as John Dewey and Ludwig Wittgenstein. Heidegger's affirmation of this thesis is often portrayed as a piece with his assault on Cartesian accounts of human existence: Dasein, the entity that each of us is, is not a subject that is encapsulated in its own sphere over against the objective world. It is, instead, essentially in-the-world and, as such, inescapably enmeshed with others. I believe that this interpretation is basically correct. Heidegger's scanty remarks on the topic, however, make filling in this outline an interpretive challenge. Continuing interest today in Heidegger's philosophy and in the character of human sociality makes meeting this challenge worthwhile.

Mitsein

The prime object of analysis in *Being and Time*, and in many of the lecture series preceding this book, is the life, or existence, of an individual human being. Correspondingly, the sociality Heidegger examines in these works is the sociality *of* an individual life. More strongly: sociality is treated of *only* as a feature of individual life. As will be discussed, this fact raises questions about the adequacy of his remarks on sociality as an account of sociality.

Division I of *Being and Time* begins by stating that the essence of the entity that each of us is lies in its existence; its ontological characteristics, accordingly, are structures of existence. Heidegger then turns to analyze the fundamental structure of existence: being-in-the-world (*in-der-Welt-sein*). Following extensive treatment of this structure, he announces, in chapter 4 of Division I, that "equiprimordial" with being-in-the-world as a constitutive structure of existence is being-with (*Mitsein*). Human existence is essentially being-in-the-world. It is equally essentially being-with.

I translate *Mitsein* as coexistence. For present purposes, moreover, I treat "coexistence" as equivalent to "sociality." "Sociality" denotes the fact, and character, of the presence, or better bearing, of others (other entities of the sort each of us is) in or on a human life. According to Heidegger, consequently, human existence is essentially social; an essential feature of an individual life is that other lives bear on it. It is worth pointing out that Heidegger does not argue for the essentiality of being-with, nor does he deduce it or infer it from other facts or phenomena. Its essentiality is an experientially informed posit that, like being-in-the-world, proves its cogency on the basis of the perspicuity of interpretive phenomenological analyses carried out on its basis (see Heidegger's (SZ: 314–15) methodological remarks about the idea of existence). As Heidegger states, moreover, coexistence (*Mitsein*) is not the same as interaction, or bodily copresence. Two Daseins can coexist even if they are not interacting or perceptually present to one another. Being alone, for example, far from being an asocial condition, is a way someone who coexists can be, a particular relationship with others. In using a tool, moreover, one coexists with the merchant from whom it was bought, just in opening a gift one coexists with the giver (cf. GA 20: 329). One coexists with all those who bear on one's life.

Heidegger (SZ: 76) characterizes being-in-the-world as "nonthematic circumspective absorption in references or assignments constitutive for the readiness-to-hand of a totality of equipment." Being-in-the-world is, in the first and continuous place, skillfully dealing with tools and other entities on the basis of a familiarity with what can be done with them. Other modes of being-in-the-world include tarrying amid entities and staring at them (as in some "breakdown experiences") and thinking abstractly about entities, the constellations they form, and the principles governing them (as when pursuing theoretical science).

Being-with is not something added to these modes of being-in-the-world. It is not that Dasein is in the world and also coexists. Rather, *in* being in the world Dasein coexists, and *in* coexisting Dasein is in the world. That is to say: Dasein is in the world with others (*mithaften*, SZ: 118), and Dasein coexists in the world. As Heidegger (1992: 7) writes in the 1924 lecture said to be the first run-through of *Being and Time*, "Dasein as this being-in-the-world is at once therewith *being-with-one-another*, being with others." Being-in-the-world and coexistence are coordinate aspects of the single, unified basic structure of Dasein's existence.

There are four basic ways other Daseins bear on a Dasein's existence: (a) one encounters them out of the world; (b) one acts toward them; (c) one shares with them the world in which one lives; and (d) worldhood is largely the same for all involved.

When going about one's business, one encounters not just objects such as tools, machines, and clothes, but other people as well. Objects are encountered as usable objects or as things standing around; thus in their, to use Heidegger's expressions, handiness (*Zuhandenheit*) or occurrentness (*Vorhandenheit*). Other Daseins, by contrast, are encountered as there with (*mit da*) oneself; they are encountered as something of the same sort as is oneself:

> This being of the others, who are co-encountered in environmental things, is not handiness or occurrentness, which pertain to environmental things, but co-Dasein [*Mitdasein*]. This means: the Dasein who is encountered in a worldly encounter is not

a thing, but retains its character as Dasein and yet is encountered out of the world. (GA 20: 330)

Moreover, just as the entities one uses when preceding through one's day are not, for the most part, thematically noticed or attended to when encountered, so, too, does this often hold of encountered others. This unthematicness provides one interpretation of the following passage:

> we must notice in what sense we are talking about "the Others." By "Others" we do not mean everyone else but me – those over against whom the "I" stands out. They are rather those from whom, for the most part, one does *not* distinguish oneself – those among whom one is too. (SZ: 118)

Some encountered others are bodily present in one's perceptual field (*lebhaftig als vorhandene wahrgenommen*; GA 20: 329) Encountering other Daseins, however, does not require meeting with them experientially. Face-to-face interactions are but one type of encounter; non-face-to-face interactions (e.g. using e-mail) are another sort. Other people can also be non-interactionally encountered, for instance, by way of the objects one uses or perceives: when holding a finished good (e.g. a shoe, a tool), for example, those for whom it is intended can be encountered. The owner of a field can be similarly encountered when one walks along its edge (SZ: 117–18). In all cases, moreover, others are encountered "out of the world." In a bodily encounter, for example, the other is encountered as doing such and such with such and such in such and such a setting. In non-interactional encounters, others are likewise encountered as involved with specific entities in the world ("they are encountered . . . in the 'with-which' of their dealings [field, boot] as the one dealing with it"; GA 20: 330): as, for instance, users, owners, occupants of certain jobs and professions; most generally, therefore, as bearers of certain statuses. In most cases, moreover, others, even when they are encountered through entities within the world, show themselves, not as entities within the world, but instead as there (in the world) with the encounterer.

The second way others bear on an individual existence is by being that toward which someone acts. This phenomenon is relatively straightforward and does not require extended exegesis. Heidegger reserves the expression *Fürsorge* (caring-for) for any mode of comportment (*Verhalten*) toward others, from getting out of someone's way on the street and a studied indifference to compatriots, to the "extreme possibilities" of taking over someone else's performance of what they are doing and of awakening someone to the possibility of authentic existence. Although an account of the vicissitudes of caring-for is essential to any full-blooded account of human sociality, it is not crucial for understanding the basic contours of Heidegger's account of coexistence.

The third way others bear on one's existence is that the world in which one exists is the world in which others exist. "In accordance with its way of being *as Dasein*, [the other] itself, in the way of being-in-the-world, is in that world within which it is at the same time encountered" (SZ: 118, italics in original). For the moment, I shall treat this oneness of the world as a matter of different Daseins encountering one and the same entities. When, for instance, farm hands work a field together, the field any one hand works is the one the others do. The world, in short, is given as a common world (GA

20: 339). As something selfsame that different people encounter, the world is a public world:

> Now, insofar as Dasein coexists in being concerned with its world, and as coexisting with others is absorbed in the world, this common world is at the same time the world that each one takes care of as a public environment which one uses, which one takes into consideration, in which one moves in such and such a way. (GA 20: 338)

One might wonder just how inclusive this public world is. Which Daseins, in other words, are the others there with oneself? I address this issue in the next section.

Others bear upon one's existence, finally, in that the worldhood of the world in which oneself and others exist is largely the same in different lives. The worldhood of the world is, formally speaking, that on the basis of which a set of entities forms a world. Fulfilling this function is what Heidegger calls the "referential totality," which is a totality of references (*Verweisungen*) by which entities are entities of specific kinds and others are encountered as, or as doing, such and such. For present purposes, this referential totality can be treated as the ways of being open to encountered entities. Which ways of being are open to encountered entities is tied to the actions it can make sense to someone to perform and the ends, including statuses, for the sake of which it can make sense to perform these actions. As a result, for the worldhood of the world – the ways of being open to encountered entities – to be mostly the same in different lives, is for the range of actions and ends it might make sense to pursue to be the same in these lives. Others thus bear on one's own existence, fourth, in one's being one of them, in one's belonging to them. Full explication of this phenomenon must await the following section.

A number of critics have challenged Heidegger's account of sociality on the grounds that it is monadic. John McGuire and Barbara Tuchanska (2000: 67) write, for instance, that "existentially Dasein is always alone in its monadic . . . being. . . . [A] direct . . . relationship between Dasein and Others . . . is not present in Heidegger's ontology." I began by acknowledging that Heidegger's account is, indeed, monadic – as an account of the sociality of an individual life, it is concerned with sociality only as a feature of individual existence. This focus, as suggested, has implications for the use of Heidegger's account when theorizing human sociality. But being formally monadic does not imply that the account is monadic in other, self-defeating ways. It does not mean, for instance, that Dasein is always "alone" in some sense that undermines its alleged (or at least the spirit of its alleged) sociality, or that Dasein is incapable of maintaining a direct relationship with others. To argue this is to ignore the being of encountered others and what is involved in different Daseins encountering one and the same entities. Other Daseins are *Mitdasein*, coexisting-there: there in the way the encountering Dasein is, involved in the same world out of which they are encountered. "This entity is neither occurrent nor handy, but instead is *as* the freeing Dasein itself – it *is there also and with*" (SZ: 118, italics in original). Dasein, consequently, is hardly alone; the fact that it is a feature of *its* existence that it is essentially there with others does not nullify that others are there with it. When, moreover, others are there with someone in the same setting at work on the same task, those involved are in a "direct and mutual" relationship.

Another version of this monadic worry is Jean-Paul Sartre's (1956) claim that Dasein, according to Heidegger, transcendentally constitutes the Other. This thesis, Sartre holds, nullifies the true otherness of the Other. For an Other, he maintains, can only be encountered. To *constitute* it is to negate its status as Other. In Georg Lukacs's (1966: 139) words, Heidegger advocates the "gnosiological solipsism of subjective idealism." Sartre's claim that Heidegger holds that Dasein transcendentally constitutes the other is correct if this is understood as meaning that it is on the basis of its understanding of type of being X, here Mitdasein, that Dasein is able to encounter a X entity, here another Dasein. But it is important to be clear about the sort of constitution at work. What Dasein is able to encounter on the basis of its understanding of Mitdasein is another Dasein *as Dasein*. What is "constituted" is simply what this other entity is understood to be. This hardly nullifies true otherness. Indeed, it enables a Dasein to be understood precisely as an Other – as another Dasein. Hence, the "constitution" makes an encounter with otherness possible. From Heidegger's perspective, Sartre can only have in mind some radical sort of otherness, which, outside the ken of what Dasein can understand, is in fact unintelligible.

A third version of the charge that Heidegger's account of sociality is debilitatingly monadic is the claim that nothing in it guarantees that one Dasein's world is the same as another's. Heidegger says that Dasein's world is shared with others and that the worldhood of their worlds is largely the same. The worry is that Heidegger says nothing to guarantee that this is the case. As Frederick Olafson (1987: 146) writes,

> Although it is understood that it is an essential feature of *Dasein* that the entities it uncovers are . . . the same entities in the same world that other like entities uncover, and although Heidegger has indicated that the relationships among these uncoverings are not merely additive in character . . . at no point is there any definite indication of why uncovering *must* be joint and convergent.

This criticism is misplaced. Heidegger does not aim to prove that this must be the case; he simply asseverates that it is so, and the course of phenomenological investigation exhibits the cogency of this proposition. I will show below that Heidegger also has the conceptual resources to explain this sameness.

Other commentators have been troubled by the monological character of Heidegger's account of sociality. As opposed, say, to communicative rationality as Jürgen Habermas analyzes it, nothing about existence is intrinsically dialogical (Habermas 1987). The exception is discourse, which is a phenomenon of communication. Thorny problems attending the interpretation of discourse neutralize, however, the significance of this exception. In any event, why is the fact that existence is not dialogical a deficiency? McGuire and Tuchanska (2000: 65, 66) complain that mutuality in relations among Dasein has no ontological status in Heidegger's account of existence. Why, however, should it? Assuming for the sake of argument that by "mutuality in relations" they mean symmetrical dialogue or give-and-take in accommodation, why should such matters be ontological, and not just ontic, features of individual existence: necessary and definitive, as opposed to variable and contingent, such features? Even granting the universality of such relations does not qualify them as ontological.

A sort of reciprocity, furthermore, does reign between any Dasein and others: the world in which others exist, out of which Dasein encounters them, is the same world that Dasein is in, out of which others encounter it. All are and are encountered in the one world. "We all have the same surrounding world [*Umwelt*]; we are in the same space. Space is for us with one another, and we ourselves are there for one another" (Heidegger 2002: 163, translation modified). Reciprocity is an ontological feature of existence.

Admittedly, Heidegger's portrayal of human relations often does downplay ontic mutuality. In *Being and Time*, for example, his illustrative discussion of solicitude (*Fürsorge*) first highlights indifference before addressing the two "extreme" possibilities of leaping in for and leaping ahead of someone, both of which involve individuals insinuating themselves into others' lives (SZ: 121–2). Matters are more complex than they might first seem, however. Heidegger portrays leaping ahead as awakening someone to the possibility of authentic existence (SZ: 298). It is hard to read the following lines as anything but suggesting that some sort of community is possible among authentic individuals: "Oppositely determined is the common taking up of the same matter consequent upon each Dasein seizing itself. This *authentic* togetherness first makes possible the right objectivity that frees the other in his freedom for himself" (SZ: 122). Examining the elements of mutuality and dialogue that might join authentic individuals is beyond the scope of the present chapter.

It might be replied that the phenomenon Heidegger ignores is not mutuality and dialogue, but multiplicity and plurality. This claim is addressed in the following section.

Das Man

The second concept that defines Heidegger's treatment of sociality is *das Man*. (I shall translate this untranslatable German neologism as "the One." This translation reflects the fact that German phrases using "*Man*" or "*man*," for instance, "*Man sagt X*" and "*Er meint, man tut das nicht*," are rendered in English by "One says X" and "He says that one doesn't do that.") Heidegger introduces this topic by way of asking who Dasein is. His discussion reveals that who one can be is twofold: one is either oneself or anyone, either a self authentically or the One self. This distinction has little bearing on Heidegger's analysis of sociality. Because these two ways of being a self mark two ways of living the essential structures of existence, including coexistence, it is the other way around: spelling out the distinction presupposes the analysis.

The One is a particular mode of being of the "there," namely, how the "there" is everyday, i.e. firstly and mostly (*zunächst und zumeist*; cf. SZ: 133). The "there" is the clearing of being within which entities can and do, as Hubert Dreyfus says, show up (as something) for Dasein. The there, more technically expressed, is a space of disclosure. Dasein, Heidegger maintains, is its there. This means that Dasein, more specifically its understanding (or care, or temporality), clears the clearing, opens the space of disclosure. For present purposes, I interpret the there as the space of possible ways entities might show up for Dasein. To say, then, that the One is a mode of being of the there is to say that it is a dispensation of the possible ways things might show up as being.

In the previous section, I construed the worldhood of the world as a space of possibilities. The disclosure contained in world is more or less the disclosure that constitutes the there (cf. SZ: 143). Consequently, because Dasein in being-in-the-world is with others, others are there with Dasein in its being the there. Likewise, Dasein is there with them in their being the there. I take this proposition as implying that, firstly and mostly, there is a single disclosure space, a single there, which Dasein and the others are. Dasein is its there; as coexisting, however, the there that Dasein is is the there of all those with whom it coexists. The neologism, the One, signals that, firstly and mostly, different Daseins are one and the same disclosure space, are in-one-and-the-same-world.

Suggestive evidence for this interpretation lies in Heidegger's use of *Öffentlichkeit* (public or publicness) to characterize the One. "[I]s Dasein as thrown being-in-the-world not exactly, in the first place, thrown into the publicness of the One? And what does this publicness mean but the specific disclosedness of the One?" (SZ: 167). Or again, "[Dasein]'s there is always firstly the co-there with others, i.e. the publicly oriented there, in which . . . every Dasein constantly remains" (GA 20: 350). The One denotes a space of possibilities, into which Dasein is thrown in existing. Indeed, the One is an essential structure of existence because it is something into which Dasein is thrown – inextricably. "To its facticity belongs that Dasein, so long as it is what it is, remains in the throw and is whirled right [*hineingewirbelt*] into the inauthenticity of the One" (SZ: 179).

Heidegger occasionally implies that the One applies to Dasein only insofar as Dasein coexists, e.g. "The One is an undeniable, exhibitable, phenomenon of Dasein itself as coexisting in the world" (GA 20: 341). I think Olafson is wrong to take these occasions as showing that the One is a form of coexistence, more precisely, a deformation of coexistence – Olafson (1994) reads the One as the dimension of anonymity and depersonalization in our relations to others. It is more perspicuous to read the statements involved as claiming that the One is a dimension *of* coexistence (cf. Heidegger's claim that the One is the "*actual how of everydayness, of average, concrete being-with-one-another*"; GA 18: 64). On this interpretation, it is a facet of its coexistence that Dasein is the One space of possibilities. That is to say, Dasein has this space *with* others; it, along with others, is thrown into the same space. "Being with one another in the world, as having it with one another, has a distinctive ontological determination" (Heidegger 1992: 8). In the mode of the One, in other words, entities – the same entities – show up, to different Daseins, with beings of the sorts carried in the One.

This interpretation takes seriously Heidegger's use of *Öffentlichkeit*. The One is a *public space*. The One disclosure space is public in the familiar philosophical sense that anyone who is it has access to the entities that show up within it, including him or herself (cf. the reference to nature, the public world, and accessibility at SZ: 71). This implies that the One is a space within which individuals show up for one another. Thus, it is a public space also in the sense that it is where people encounter one another. "In the foregoing analyses we often used the expressions 'firstly and mostly'. 'Firstly' means the way in which Dasein, in the with one another of the public, is 'the manifest' [*offenbar*], even if 'at bottom' it has existentielly overcome everydayness" (SZ: 370). In being thrown into the One space, moreover, it is indefinite with which others one co-exists; the others are anyone thrown into the public space into which one is thrown: "In this distantiality that belongs to coexistence lies the following: that as everyday coexisting with others Dasein stands in the disposal of the others. . . . These others are not *specific* others. On the contrary, every other can represent them. . . . One oneself belongs to the others and solidifies their power" (SZ: 126).

An important feature of the One is its unity. The One space is one space – which different Daseins, firstly and mostly, are. One piece of evidence for this interpretation is Heidegger's claim that the One has it own ways of being: distantiality, averageness, leveling, and publicness (SZ: 127; GA 20: 338). Another is Heidegger's (SZ: 177) remark that the One is not a general (*Allgemeinen*) that "is 'really' present only in the individual speaking Dasein," which strongly suggests that One space cannot be treated, say, as the presence of the same possible ways of being in each life involved. In claiming that One space is one, I thereby take a stand on a vexed interpretive issue, i.e. the relation between the there and individual existence. On the one hand, Heidegger writes that Dasein is its there, thus seemingly implying that there are as many theres as Daseins. On the other hand, he says several times that the world Dasein is in is shared with others, thus implying that there is one world, one there, despite there being multiple Daseins. Olafson opines that Heidegger never worked his way out of this apparent paradox:

> Whatever the reason, the theory of *Mitsein* is not developed, either in *Being and Time* or later, in a way that contributes to the definition of the relationship in which one *Dasein* stands to another in grounding the *same* world. Because Heidegger fails to given an account of the mediating role of plurality in the relationship between *Dasein* and world. (1987: 72)

Dreyfus (1991: 145), by contrast, believes that the One solves the problem: it is by virtue of being "socialized" into the One that different Daseins, each world-uncovering, uncover the same world – for once socialized they uncover the one world that shows up in the One.

I am basically on Dreyfus's side on this issue. On my reading, the facts that the One is a disclosure space, and that Daseins are thrown into it, entails that they, firstly and mostly, encounter and have to do with entities in the ways maintained in and definitive of that single space. "This common world, which is primarily there, and into which every Dasein who is growing up firstly grows, governs as public all interpretation of world and Dasein" (GA 20: 340; cf. SZ: 127). Indeed, the wording of Olafson's indictment betrays that he underplays the One. There is no question of a "relationship" among Daseins in "grounding the same world." Rather, it is a facet of their inherent coexistence that different Daseins encounter entities as the same and have to do with them in the same ways; that is, it is a facet of the coexistence that is essential to each of them individually that each finds itself in the same there as the others. Daseins do not ground the same world, hence there is no relationship among them in doing so. Daseins perpetuate an already existent clearing, and doing this is intrinsic to their being. Heidegger writes (GA 20: 339):

The One . . . constitutes that, which we in a real sense call *publicness*. Therein lies the idea that the world is always already primarily given as the common world, and it is not the case that on the one side there are firstly separate subjects, thus also firstly separate subjects each with their own world, and that it is a matter of putting together the different individuals' own environments on the basis of some agreement, on this basis working out how one has a common world. This is how philosophers imagine things when they ask about the constitution of the intersubjective world. We say: What is first, what is given, is the common world – the One – that is, the world in which Dasein is absorbed.

Heidegger's wording is redolent of modern social contract theorists, who imagine humans coming together, in some sort of "natural" state, to institute, on the basis of an agreement, either a single government above them or themselves as a single people. This similarity notwithstanding, Heidegger's clear characterization of the position he opposes as an account of the constitution of the intersubjective world implies that the position he defends concerns the metaphysics of the world. And on this issue he clearly maintains that the One is a single world, that Dasein is, in the first place, always bound up with it, and that there is no question of an intersubjective, or even co-, constitution of that single world on the basis of something each individual accomplishes on its own or separately from its being bound up with the world.

There remains the task of reconciling the intuition that there are as many theres as Daseins with the idea of a single One disclosure space. My dissolution of this apparent tension is that different Daseins are thrown into the single publicness of the One and that each projects and presses forward into the possibilities composing this publicness. There is one space but multiple happenings of being thrown into and projecting it; one there, but multiple lives carrying on in its terms. It is for this reason that Heidegger writes (SZ: 384) that the happening of Dasein, its being on the move from its past out of its future, is a co-happening: Daseins are on the move out of their varied futures from the common public world into which they are thrown alike. This solution assimilates Heidegger's early conception of the relationship between humans and the clearing of being to his later conception of this. On the later conception, humans, or rather historical linguistic peoples or groups, "stand into" a clearing that just happens and is distinct from them, even as their language, thinking, and poetry are the place where it happens. Similarly, in the early conception, Dasein is thrown into a clearing that is distinct from its existence, even as it, like other Daseins, projects and lives into it.

An advantage of the foregoing interpretation is that it places Heidegger in a clear lineage between Søren Kierkegaard and Hannah Arendt. Heidegger appropriates the notions of the One and publicness from Kierkegaard. The public, Kierkegaard (1962) writes, in contrast to concrete associations such as groups, is an abstraction created by the press. Consisting, among other things, of public opinion, it is a leveling power that reduces human lives to the same and obliterates the line between public and private. Afoot in salons, newspapers, soirées, and public walkways, the public is a common, social space of doxa and communication that establishes how things are. Heidegger borrows from Kierkegaard the sense of an openness that embraces multiple individuals. Although the One encompasses more than the public, and although Heidegger views the One as an essential feature of human existence, whereas Kierkegaard sees the public as a product of the modern age, the notion of a common space of determinations for individuals remains.

Arendt (1958), meanwhile, construes the public sphere as a space of appearances that opens up among human beings amid a common world. It is a world of visibility in which people appear to one another, their private subjective worlds being but dark reflections of this. Arendt neither confines this space to the modern world nor makes it constitutive of Dasein's being. Unlike the One, furthermore, its existence requires the co-presence of human beings. Arendt also does not presume that the individuals who appear in public space are fundamentally the same, and she further departs from Heidegger in treating people as the sole sort of entity that appears in it. Yet Arendt retains the Kierkegaardian sense of an unavoidable open space, which embraces different individuals who appear in it. As Heidegger writes: "[others] are so encountered co-worldly [*mit-weltlich*] that the others bring the "one oneself" with them. In the co-worldly appearance [*Vorschein*] of those who are encountering, one oneself, along with what one does, "one oneself," his position, reputation, accomplishment, success and failure, is among the others" (GA 63: 99).

Although I have characterized the One as a disclosure space, hence as a space of possible ways to be, I have not more specifically characterized the possibilities that constitute it. Dreyfus, basing himself on Heidegger's claim that the One articulates the referential totality of significance (SZ: 129), holds that the One is the source of all everyday intelligibility (Dreyfus 1991: 161–2). If true, this would mean that the possibilities into which Dasein is thrown are, firstly and mostly, One ones. It is not clear, however, whether this is the case. Heidegger writes, for instance, that

> The understanding self-projection of Dasein is, as factical, in each case already amid a discovered world. From this it takes – and firstly according to the interpretation of the One – its possibilities. This interpretation has already beforehand narrowed the possibilities that can be chosen to the circle of what is known, reachable, endurable, what fits and is appropriate. This leveling of the possibilities of Dasein to what everyday stands proximally at its disposal at the same time effects a dimming of the possible as such. (SZ: 194–5)

Possibilities, accordingly, that are inappropriate, unendurable, not fitting, and not proximal are not One possibilities. But although Dasein surely possesses such, the space of One possibilities might be wider than those embraced by the narrowing interpretations Heidegger describes. Heidegger also occasionally speaks of new or genuine (*echte*) possibilities, interpretations, appropriations, and conceptual articulations (e.g. SZ: 168, 169), in each case claiming that they take off from and arise on the background of the One possibilities. So it is not clear whether the One circumscribes the possibilities through which Dasein firstly and mostly proceeds nor whether the One exhausts its possibilities (for discussion of this issue, see Keller and Weberman 1998: 373–6).

That Dasein's possibilities are wider than those circumscribed in the One emerges clearly in Heidegger's discussions of historicity. In both the so-called "first draft" of *Being and Time* (Heidegger 1992: 19) and the latter itself (SZ: 391–2), Heidegger maintains (a) that the past is repeatable, (b) that when Dasein exists as the One self it is blind to the repeatability and repetition of the past, and (c) that becoming authentically historical involves shedding the presumption that the past has gone by and is present only as material remnants and realizing that the past is possibilities.

The possibilities that constitute the One are norm-governed. I would not go as far as Dreyfus and others do and hold that Heidegger believes that normativity, or the generality and anonymity of One possibilities, are necessary features of human sociality. Perhaps they do enjoy this status. What Heidegger at most claims, however, is simply that any human life is such that the public sphere in which it transpires with other lives is norm-governed. *Vis-à-vis* normativity, moreover, Heidegger's pronouncements can mislead. He writes, for instance, that "We take pleasure and enjoy ourselves as *one* enjoys; we read, see, and judge literature and art as *one* sees and judges; we recoil from the 'great mass' as *one* recoils; we find 'shocking' what *one* finds shocking" (SZ: 126–7). The implication is that, under the social pressure Heidegger calls "distantiality" (*Abständigkeit* – the concern for differences with others), individuals are molded into specific, in effect, prescribed ways of proceeding and thinking. The normativity of the One, however, is, first, acceptability or permissibility, and, only second, shouldness or oughtness. For instance, the One embraces all jobs and roles accepted in society (e.g. GA 20: 336), none of which is prescribed.

As interpreters are wont to point out, moreover, some of Heidegger's characterizations of the One seem peculiarly keyed to early twentieth-century public life in Germany and northern Europe. Occasional lines such as those just quoted that suggest that the One is a matter of conformism and not conformity is one example of this. Others proliferate in his discussion of the everyday being of the there in chapter 5 of Division I in *Being and Time*. For example, his initially non-judgmental discussion of the everyday being of discourse, *Gerede*, which during this initial discussion could be translated as "derivative talk," becomes a thinly veiled denunciation of everyday chatter, thus justifying the translation of *Gerede* as "idle talk." Idle talk is a dubious human universal. Indeed, Joannes Fritsch (1999: 15) opines that the One refers to the destruction of tradition in the big German cities and in the parliament of Weimar. Luckily, not all of Heidegger's formulations reflect the situation of Weimar Germany.

Heidegger is unclear about the source of non-One possibilities. His clearest treatment comes in his discussions of historicity, where, as indicated, the past, for authentic Dasein, is repeatable ways of being. His use of terms such as "heritage" (*Erbe*) suggests that tradition be viewed as the repository of non-One possibilities. On this interpretation, Dasein is thrown into both the One and tradition. At one point, however, Heidegger equates the One with tradition, thus negating tradition as a non-One repository (Heidegger 1992: 9). Talk of tradition also brings with it the notion of a generation: the past, or tradition, into which one is thrown is that of one's generation (SZ: 20). Its generation are those with whom Dasein coexists as part of a tradition. Heidegger, however, says next to nothing about generations and, in general, little on the topic discussed in the present paragraph. The relation between the One and tradition, as a result, is murky. Do traditions, for example, house one or multiple One spaces?

In the previous section, I raised the question of which Daseins are the others *there with* a given Dasein. It has now emerged that there are three analytically distinct, though extensionally overlapping, classes of such others "among whom one is too" (SZ: 118). Those with whom Dasein coexists are (a) those with whom one is active in a particular equipmental context, (b) those from whom one does not differ in carrying on as anyone does (the One), and (c) one's generation.

A number of interpreters have charged Heidegger with eliding the "condition of plurality" that Aristotle and Arendt see as essential to human life. Jacques Taminiaux, for example, avers that Heidegger's appropriation of praxis and phronesis from Aristotle ignores its plural (and political) dimensions (Taminiaux 1991: 129–33). Because Taminiaux is concerned above all with the alleged private and non-relational character of authentic existence, I won't consider its specifics. It is obvious, however, that the One could similarly be accused of "negati[ng] . . . plurality, cancel[ing] . . . the pluralistic sharing of deeds and words, and replac[ing] . . . the pluralistic debate regarding what appears to each and every one" (Taminiaux 1991: 133) with unanimity. As indicated, the One is a figure of unity. A singular space of disclosure into which different individuals are thrown, anyone who unreflectively goes along with its almost all-encompassing ways is the same as anyone else who does so. In just going along, one is not oneself, not a self authentically; one is, instead, anyone, the One self. As various interpreters have stressed, the One, in this regard, is a space of depersonalized possibilities, a space of anonymous ways of being. The only plurality here is the multiplicity of possibilities. Because, however, all there is to Dasein is its ways of being, someone who realizes a given possible way of being is the same as anyone else who does so.

The formal fact that the possibilities involved are no one's in particular, such that Daseins are the same insofar as they realize the same possibilities, does not negate plurality. The One is a space of *acceptable* possibilities. Anyone thrown into it differs from everyone else so thrown by way of realizing a different combination of the acceptable ways of proceeding and thinking. Hence, there is plenty of room for different deeds and words. The existence of a single pool of anonymous possibilities does not negate significant plurality. Given, moreover, that One spaces are parceled out at least one per generation, there exist a plurality of One spaces (in any tradition) and across them.

The analysis of the One does, however, overly unify human life in another way. It is one thing to say that Daseins coexist amid the same entities; it is far stronger to claim that a single space of possibilities governs how entities show up to coexisting Daseins. The singularity of any the One parcels out the possibilities Daseins in general realize into distinct packages and suggests that any given Dasein realizes elements of one package rather than another. This picture, kin to the much-criticized picture of cultures or disciplinary matrices as distinct islands, does not do justice to the facts that not all possibilities are attached to constellations of the breadth of the One and that people live hybrid lives combining possibilities from allegedly different packages. Thus, although the singularity of the One does not deny differences among Daseins, it overly segregates given Daseins into this or that One and denies pluralism and differences of the mongrel sort.

I conclude this section with a brief comment on authenticity, in particular, the relation of authenticity to the One. Heidegger opposes the depersonalized preoccupations of a tranquilized and disburdened inauthentic existence lost in the One with the authentic person's decisive seizure of a possibility of existence out of an awareness of death as its ownmost, non-deligible possibility and an appreciation that all along it has in fact been responsible for how it lives. The difference between inauthentic and authentic existence must be held apart from the One as feature of existence (cf. Keller and

Weberman 1998; Boedeker 2001). Heidegger distinguishes between a structure of and a way of being (SZ: 176). A structure of being is an essential feature of Dasein's existence. An example is the One: *thrown into* the One, no existence can escape it. In this context, by contrast, a way of being is a fundamental way of carrying on a life with such and such essential features. Inauthentic and authentic existence are two examples. Inauthentic existence is a life of carrying out One possibilities while fleeing the truth of existence and the possibility of authenticity. Authentic existence is a decisive seizing of a possibility in an enhanced state of awareness. It never, however, shakes free of the One. "Authenticity is an existentiell modification of the One as essential feature of existence" (SZ: 130). It is, so to speak, a maneuver *vis-à-vis* the One disclosure space, the bulk of the possibilities open to the authentic person remaining those of the One: "Resoluteness . . . discovers what is factically possible, in such a way as to be sure that it takes up what is possible in the way it is possible as one's ownmost being able to be in the One" (SZ: 299). The authentic person, however, also has the past as a fund of repeatable ways of being. Moreover, unlike the inauthentic person, who appreciates "only the '*general lay of things*' and loses himself in the nearest '*opportunities*'," the authentic person recognizes the situation and has thereby moved decisively into action (SZ: 300).

Conclusion: Heidegger and Social Theory

I conclude by considering whether Heidegger's account of coexistence and the One constitutes a satisfactory ontological basis for social theory. Heidegger treats sociality as an essential feature of individual existence: any individual, merely by existing, is enveloped in a tissue of coexistence with others. In existing, moreover, Dasein is thrown into the publicness of the One, where he or she proceeds, thinks, and experiences as others do, and Dasein and the others are mutually accessible. In short, an individual's everyday existence is intertwined with, open to, and directed toward others. Even though Heidegger elaborates these matters only in the depth required for his wider project of fundamental ontology, the thought that his comments might constitute the beginning of a fruitful social ontology is encouraged by Heidegger's own asseveration that "because being-with-one-another is being-with-one-another in a world, being-with-one-another shapes the different possibilities of community as well as society" (GA 20: 333).

Some have challenged this thought on the basis of the monadic and monological character of Heidegger's analysis. I have suggested that its monological character is irrelevant in this context. This is not true, however, of its monadicity. Heidegger, as explained, analyzes not sociality *per se*, but instead the sociality of individual existence. Indeed, his seems to be a largely *cogent* phenomenological analysis of individual sociality. Contrary to some of Heidegger's critics, however, I do not think that this disqualifies his account from contributing elements of an adequate social ontology.

Dasein, Heidegger writes, is there with others; others, meanwhile, are there with it. One might, accordingly, appropriate Heidegger's analyses for an individualist ontology and argue that all social phenomena are grounded in the mutual encountering and understanding of individuals in the publicness of common, normative ways of

245

proceeding, thinking, and experiencing in a common world. It is not true, as McGuire and Tuchanska claim (2000: 70), that Heidegger reduces others, social relations, and communities to structures of an individual Dasein, thus vitiating his claim that Dasein coexists in a common world. One disclosure space, however, is ontologically non-individualist. It is not the case that there are as many One disclosure spaces as there are individuals (thrown into it). What are multiple are the cases of Daseins thrown into and projecting it. Hence, a social ontology that would build upon Heidegger's early phenomenological work would be, ultimately, non-individualist in character.

One limit of Heidegger's account was discussed above. Heidegger seems to believe that in being thrown into the One all of the possibilities through which one firstly and mostly lives are One ones. It is more propitious to think of such spaces as common normative backgrounds against which individual differences develop or are set off. Another limit is that Heidegger's account insufficiently specifies the coexistence that links individuals. As described, coexistence centrally consists in encountering others, even though encountering does not require bodily co-presence. Lives hang together, however, not only via encounters. Causal chains of action, for example, link lives that do not encounter one another. For the purposes of social ontology, Heidegger's account would have to be rounded out by a richer analysis of the modes of coexistence.

Heidegger, furthermore, offers no account of whence the social features of individual existence. From his phenomenological perspective, they are simply given features. Accounting for their source requires transcending Heidegger's monadic phenomenology and theorizing the context within which individual lives proceed. For individual lives come to have the features discussed in the present chapter in part because of the broader context in which they are carried on. Lukacs identifies this context as the material system of society. I would specify it as the nexus of practices. Examining it, however, is the topic for a different essay.

References

Arendt, H. (1958) *The Human Condition*. Chicago: University of Chicago Press.

Boedeker, E. C. Jr (2001) Individual and community in early Heidegger: situating *das Man*, the *Man*-self, and self-ownership in Dasein's ontological structure. *Inquiry*, 44, 63–100.

Dreyfus, H. L. (1991) *Being-in-the-World: A Commentary on Heidegger's Being and Time, Division 1*. Cambridge, MA: MIT Press.

Fritsch, J. (1999) *Historical Destiny and National Socialism in Heidegger's Being and Time*. Berkeley: University of California Press.

Habermas, J. (1987) *The Philosophical Discourse of Modernity* (trans. F. Lawrence). Cambridge, MA: MIT Press.

Heidegger, M. (1992) *The Concept of Time* (trans. W. McNeill). Oxford: Blackwell (original work published 1989).

Heidegger, M. (2002) Wilhelm Dilthey's research and the struggle for a historical worldview. In J. van Buren (ed.), C. Bambach (trans.), *Supplements: From the Earliest Essays to Being and Time and Beyond*. Albany: State University of New York Press (original work published 1992/3).

Keller, P. and Weberman, D. (1998) Heidegger and the source(s) of intelligibility. *Continental Philosophy Review*, 31, 369–86.

Kierkegaard, S. (1962) *The Present Age* (trans. A. Dru). New York: Harper & Row (original work published 1846).

Lukacs, G. (1966) Existentialism or Marxism? In G. Novack (ed.), *Existentialism versus Marxism*. New York: Dell.

McGuire, J. and Tuchanska, B. (2000) *Science Unfettered: A Philosophical Study in Sociohistorical Ontology*. Athens: Ohio University Press.

Olafson, F. A. (1987) *Heidegger and the Philosophy of Mind*. New Haven, CT: Yale University Press.

Olafson, F. A. (1994) Heidegger *à la* Wittgenstein or "coping" with Professor Dreyfus. *Inquiry*, 37, 45–64.

Sartre, J.-P. (1956) *Being and Nothingness* (trans. H. Barnes). New York: Pocket Books (original work published 1943).

Taminiaux, J. (1991) *Heidegger and the Project of Fundamental Ontology* (trans. M. Gendre). Albany: State University of New York Press.

15

Realism and Truth

DAVID R. CERBONE

But why all this creative reconstruction, all this make-believe? ("Epistemology Naturalized," in Quine 1969: 75)

We talk and act. That is already presupposed in everything that I am saying. (Wittgenstein 1983: part VI, section 17)

Overview

My principal aim in this chapter is to consider the question of realism in Heidegger's *Being and Time*. (I also aim to say a few things about his views on truth, though, as we shall see, my remarks on that topic will serve as something of a coda to the discussion of realism.) The issue of whether or not Heidegger is a realist, and likewise whether or not he is an idealist, has been a matter of considerable debate in recent years, with serious interpreters offering a wide array of assessments. Heidegger has been read as committed, variously, to temporal, ontological, and linguistic idealism, as well as ontical, empirical, deflationary, and even multiple hermeneutic realism.[1] In some cases, these labels have been mixed and matched, so that Heidegger comes out as, say, both an empirical realist, and an ontological or temporal idealist. Sorting through the merits and shortcomings of these various readings one by one would be an arduous undertaking which would far exceed the confines of this chapter. Accordingly, though I will at various points engage with a number of the readings already on offer (especially ones depicting Heidegger as ultimately an idealist), I will endeavor to start afresh, with a reading of what I see as Heidegger's stance with respect to the philosophical tradition he wishes to confront and overcome. That confrontation, I will suggest, must be borne in mind when adjudicating such philosophically loaded labels as "realism" and "idealism." Indeed, Heidegger himself does his utmost to skirt such labels, viewing them both as primarily funded by an outlook which puts *epistemology* ahead of *ontology*. By reasserting the primacy of ontology, Heidegger hopes to undermine the whole way of looking at things in philosophy which serves to give epistemology its sense of urgency. As he notes in *The Metaphysical Foundations of Logic*:

> The theory of knowledge . . . has repeatedly made the subject–object relation the basis of its inquiries. But both idealist and realist explanations had to fail because the explicandum was not sufficiently definite. The extent to which the above clarification of the problem determines all efforts to pose the problem is evident in the fact that the consequences of

248

the first refinement of our problem, where it is really carried out and achieved, lead to the disappearance of a possible problem in the sense of the idealist or realistic theories of knowledge. (GA 26: 163–4)

Epistemology and Explanation

Before documenting the "disappearance" of "idealist or realistic theories of knowledge," I first want to say something about how they make their appearance, since how they do so will already begin to reveal what Heidegger finds problematic about both of them. That is, Heidegger's principal aim, as I read him, is to expose and reject the presuppositions common to both realism and idealism. If such presuppositions can indeed be exposed and discarded, then trying to settle the issue of realism versus idealism will no longer appear obligatory.

Notice that in the above passage Heidegger refers to both realism and idealism as *explanations*, and seeing just how they function as explanations will begin to show what is problematic about them. Since Heidegger locates both realism and idealism within epistemology or the theory of knowledge, then what is to be explained is our having knowledge. The central question, framed schematically, is as follows:

1   How is knowledge of X possible?

where X stands for some domain of entities (spatiotemporal objects, other minds, numbers, etc.). For simplicity's sake (and also to focus on the most pertinent case), let us concentrate on the case where X equals spatiotemporal objects. Thus, we have:

2   How is knowledge of spatiotemporal objects possible?

That we have such knowledge seems almost to be beyond question, at least initially. After all, I know what I'm wearing on my feet, I know there are trees outside the room where I'm writing this, I know where my dog is right now, and so on. The answer to the question of what makes it possible for me to have such knowledge is, however, far from obvious, so even if it seems reasonably clear that I do have such knowledge, that only shows that there *is* an answer to (2), not what the answer is.

Consider what one might think is a good beginning at answering (2), what we might think of as, roughly, a *naturalistic* answer (e.g. "Epistemology naturalized" in Quine 1969). A naturalistic answer to (2) is one that strives to provide an explanation for our knowledge of spatiotemporal objects by means of the natural sciences, and as a scientific investigation, it makes "free use" of whatever science has to offer, everything and anything from neurophysiology to quantum theory (the phrase "free use" can be found in Quine 1974: 4; see also Quine 1969, especially 82–3). For example, one of the principal ways that we seem to come to have knowledge of spatiotemporal objects, of both their existence and what they are like, is via perception: by seeing them, hearing them, smelling them, tasting them, and touching them (and even where our experimentation takes us beyond the limits of our perceptual abilities, those abilities nonetheless play an integral role in conducting and analyzing those very experiments). Given this observation, we might imagine an answer to (2) appealing to, among other things, facts about our having variously structured perceptual mechanisms (eyes, ears, noses, etc., along with the underlying "wiring") and our being situated in an environment where light behaves in various ways, sound travels thus and so, and so on. There is certainly nothing trivial about such an explanation, especially as one endeavors to flesh it out beyond the crude sketch I am offering here, and there is certainly something right-headed about what such an explanation offers: staying at the level of the crude sketch, what it says is that without our possessing appropriately structured perceptual systems operating in an appropriately structured environment, we would not have, and would not be able to have, certain kinds of perceptual beliefs and knowledge. So we certainly here seem to be on the right track to providing an answer to (2).

Realism and idealism, I want to claim, make their appearance at precisely this point, since both are expressive of a certain dissatisfaction with the kind of explanation toward which I have just gestured. That is, there might appear to be something *philosophically* unsatisfying about such an explanation, even when spelled out with further scientific details and with greater rigor. There are, for starters, worries concerning whether these explanations are defeasible from the standpoint of what is purely logically or conceptually possible, e.g. might not a "disembodied mind," suitably manipulated by an evil demon, have a variety of perceptual experiences that are, for all the world, qualitatively indistinguishable from ours? And if, the worry continues, another of these conceptual or logical possibilities obtains, then we don't really have *knowledge* of X at all. Of course, if the explanans in my sketch of an explanation above is correct, i.e. we *do* have appropriately structured perceptual systems operating in an appropriately structured environment, then those logical or conceptual possibilities do not obtain. But therein lies the problem, for one cannot simply help oneself to such an explanans, since it appeals to things (perceptual systems, an appropriately structured environment) that fall within the domain, the knowledge of which is to be explained. That is, such an explanation *uses* precisely the kind of knowledge whose possibility is to be explained, and that is no explanation at all. (Hence the now familiar worries as to whether "naturalized epistemology" is epistemology in name only.)[2]

In order, then, to explain in a philosophically satisfying way our knowledge of X, we cannot, on pain of circularity, make use of anything that falls within X. In other words, we must, in accounting for the possibility of our knowledge of X, forswear any appeal to whatever lies within that domain. Otherwise, we will not really understand how such knowledge is possible, and so we will not really have assured ourselves that what we have is indeed knowledge after all. We might call the desired explanation here a *transcendental-epistemological* explanation. The severity of the requirements any such explanation must meet should not be underestimated: to meet its demands, we must deprive ourselves of anything and everything falling within X. When we do so, however, a gap begins to appear between whatever it is we are entitled to use in constructing our answer to questions like (1) and (2) and whatever falls within the particular domain which instantiates X. *Realism*, we might say, unflinchingly acknowledges the possibility of such a gap: for the realist, skepticism is a standing possibility, as it may not be possible to "reach" the domain in question by means of whatever it is we have in our possession when all our claims to X have been suspended. Skepticism and realism are, in other words, two sides of the same coin, since realism concedes, and indeed is predicated on, the legitimacy of skepticism's demands.

There is, however, another response to the threat of a gap, and one that offers more in the way of reassurance than the realist provides. This second response endeavors to show how whatever it is that falls within domain X can somehow be constructed or "constituted" out of whatever it is we seem to be restricted to when we initially "bracket" X.[3] In this way, the "conditions for the possibility" of knowledge of X and the "conditions for the possibility" of anything falling within domain X do not, and indeed cannot, come apart. There is, however, a price for this maneuver, which is that whatever it is that falls within domain X becomes *dependent* upon what we were restricted to in providing our explanation. If X is, for example, the domain of spatiotemporal objects, and what we are restricted to in explaining our knowledge of spatiotemporal objects is our (subjective, immediate) experience, then spatiotemporal objects are, on this response, dependent on experience, and so on the minds whose experiences they are. Hence *idealism*.

Consider, however, a third line of reasoning that might emerge here, again expressive of a kind of dissatisfaction but now directed toward the very demand for the kind of explanation we have lately been considering. Suppose, that is, that there were compelling considerations to the effect that the project of trying to construct transcendental-epistemological explanations is ill-conceived in the sense that the project it envisions is somehow incoherent. It is not so much that what such an investigation proposes cannot in fact be done (that would just be skepticism again, or would at least leave skepticism as a standing worry), but that *what* it proposes to do cannot be intelligibly articulated. Such a third line of reasoning might be considered a transcendental argument against the possibility of a certain kind of transcendental explanation. Quine's naturalism might be seen as one way of mounting such an argument: Quine's rejection of the "museum myth" of meaning and his attending rejection of the analytic–synthetic distinction are meant to preclude in principle the idea of "first philosophy," and so to show that we are always, and must always take ourselves to be, "working from within" our ongoing ordinary and scientific theory of the world. (Quine's animus toward the kind of "rational reconstruction" favored by the logical positivists is a clear instance of the rejection of the kind of transcendental-epistemological investigation I am describing. A rational reconstruction would answer the "How possible?" question by showing how our "access" to whatever it is we seem to have knowledge of can be logically constructed out of elements, our access to which is somehow unproblematic, direct, or immediate.)[4]

Heidegger's critique of traditional philosophy, one of the major themes of Division I of *Being and Time*, might be read, I want to suggest, as likewise mounting such an argument, which aims to unmask as distorted and incoherent a certain set of demands and the kinds of investigation that have been attempted in the service of those demands. All such demands, including a demand for a proof of the existence of the external world, for a refutation of solipsism or a proof of the existence of "other minds," and for an explanation of all phenomena in terms of "material substance," rest, Heidegger argues, on a thoroughly problematic conception of our relation to the world, wherein the "subject" is radically distinct from "objects." If such a conception is indeed

251

incoherent, then the kind of transcendental explanations we have been considering must likewise be lacking in sense: any attempt to explain our "access" to various philosophically significant domains from a standpoint which forswears any appeal to what falls within them is doomed, not because such a task is impossible but because the very terms in which it is couched cannot be made out.

Subject and Object; Dasein and World

Very early on in Division I of *Being and Time* (SZ: ¶13), Heidegger makes explicit his animus toward a certain kind of traditional conception of our relation to the world, a conception which not only privileges *knowledge* as primary but also conceives of knowledge in a way Heidegger finds thoroughly problematic. On such a conception, knowing is conceived of as a possible "relation" between "subjects" and "objects." In saying just this much, Heidegger already complains that the relata in this formula "do not coincide with Dasein and world" (SZ: 60). This complaint is, however, only the beginning, for what Heidegger finds especially problematic is the conception of knowledge itself. On the one hand, "if knowing 'is' at all, it belongs solely to those entities which know," but, on the other, the question of whether or not any such entities know anything at all is not something which can be ascertained in the way, for example, "bodily properties are" (SZ: 60). The knowledge that I "have" whenever I know something "is not some external characteristic," and so, this reasoning goes, "it must be 'inside'" (SZ: 60). It is with this appeal to the notion of an inside that the notion of knowledge begins to appear problematic, if not downright mysterious, since questions of what kind of relation knowledge is and just how it can serve to relate what lies "inside" to what lies "outside" become especially pressing. As Heidegger notes, in a passage whose last sentence quickly recapitulates some of the strands of the discussion of the previous section:

> Now the more unequivocally one maintains that knowing is proximally and really "inside" and indeed has by no means the same kind of being as entities which are both physical and psychical, the less one presupposes when one believes that one is making headway in the question of the essence of knowledge and in the clarification of the relationship between subject and Object. For only then can the problem arise of how this knowing subject comes out of its inner "sphere" into one which is "other and external," of how knowing can have any object at all, and of how one must think of the object itself so that eventually the subject knows it without needing to venture a leap into another sphere. (SZ: 60)

The cluster of problems cited in the second sentence are motivated by the conceit mentioned in the first sentence, namely that "one is making headway in the question of the essence of knowledge" by "presupposing" less and less. That is, such epistemologically oriented questions gain their urgency, indeed their sense, from a demand for a kind of purity, a freedom from any presuppositions which would taint potential answers to "How possible?" questions addressed to knowledge. As Heidegger sees it, however, such a demand is ill-conceived from the start: "With this kind of approach one remains blind to what is already tacitly implied even when one takes the phenomenon of knowing as one's theme in the most provisional manner: namely, that knowing is a mode of being of Dasein as being-in-the-world, and is founded ontically upon this state of being" (SZ: 61).

The idea that knowledge is "founded" on Dasein's being-in-the-world undercuts the primacy of the appeal to the notions of "inner" and "outer" in terms of which the traditional conception of knowledge is framed. The appeal to being-in-the-world effects a reorientation in how one understands both such notions, such that it can be said with equal legitimacy that Dasein is always *both* inside and outside with respect to the world.

> When Dasein directs itself towards something and grasps it, it does not somehow first get out of an inner sphere in which it has been proximally encapsulated, but its primary kind of being is such that it is always "outside" alongside entities which it encounters and which belong to a world already discovered. Nor is any inner sphere abandoned when Dasein dwells alongside the entity to be known, and determines its character; but even in this "being-outside" alongside the object, Dasein is still "inside," if we understand this in the correct sense; that is to say, it is itself "inside" as a being-in-the-world which knows. (SZ: 62)

Undercut as well is thus the kind of explanatory project that is part and parcel of the traditional conception, since any question of how something in a "subject's" "inner sphere" relates to something "outer" requires some antecedent justification for raising the question of knowledge in those terms. Without that justification, just *why* we should take such questions seriously becomes more difficult to make out. Indeed, with the appeal to being-in-the-world as that upon which knowledge is "founded," that kind of explanatory project is, as Heidegger puts it, "nullified." As he notes:

> but if, as we suggest, we thus find phenomenally that *knowing is a kind of being which belongs to being-in-the-world*, one might object that with such an Interpretation of knowing, the problem of knowledge is nullified; for what is left to be asked if one *presupposes* that knowing is already "alongside" its world, when it is not supposed to reach that world except in the transcending of the subject? In this question the constructivist "standpoint," which has not been phenomenally demonstrated, again comes to the fore; but quite apart from this, what higher court is to decide *whether* and *in what sense* there is to be any problem of knowledge other than that of the phenomenon of knowing as such and the kind of being which belongs to the knower? (SZ: 61)

I have framed my discussion of Heidegger and the question of realism versus idealism in terms of Heidegger's rejection of a particular kind of explanatory project where the possession and legitimation of intentional states (beliefs, knowledge, etc.) about worldly entities is at issue. For Heidegger, no such project is necessary because Dasein, as being-in-the-world, is "always already" amidst entities and so an explanation whose explanandum includes an appeal to a "worldless" being is, at best, superfluous, and, at worst, incoherent and delusional ("incoherent" because the very idea of a "subject" which "possesses" states whose putative "success" is at issue already relies upon the phenomenon of being-in-the-world, "delusional" because those who indulge in such "explanations" pretend that such an idea does not). Heidegger's aim throughout Division I of *Being and Time* is to bring the phenomenon of Dasein's being-in-the-world to "an unadulterated givenness,"[5] and one effect of doing so will be to "nullify" the epistemological project of accounting for the possibility of our having "access" to the world and worldly entities. Heidegger argues that any notion of a being who counts as a subject, i.e. of a being who possesses intentionally directed states such as beliefs, is so only by dint of being a being whose way of being is being-in-the-world and the very description of the phenomenon of being-in-the-world already appeals to entities and our being amidst them.

Consider as an example some of Heidegger's preliminary remarks on those entities that play a role in our "concernful dealings," what Heidegger dubs the ready-to-hand or the available. After noting that such entities "become accessible when we put ourselves into the position of concerning ourselves with them," he immediately cautions that this way of putting things is misleading: "Taken strictly, this talk about 'putting ourselves into such a position' is misleading; for the kind of being which belongs to such concernful dealings is not one into which we need to put ourselves first. This is the way in which everyday Dasein always *is*: when I open the door, for instance, I use the latch" (SZ: 67). Thus, there is no room in Heidegger's account for an explanation of how one gets into the position of having concernful dealings with entities from some prior, potentially entity-impoverished condition, and his almost flippant appeal to doors and latches exemplifies his refusal to take seriously, or even fully to understand, the demand that access to such entities be somehow vouchsafed in some more neutral, less entity-laden terms.

Of course, Heidegger *does* provide a kind of answer to questions like (1) and (2) above concerning the possibility of knowledge: in response to the question of how knowledge is possible, his response is that it is possible as a founded mode of being-in-the-world; and there is a long story to tell about how this "founding" works, just as there is a long story for science to tell about how our "perceptual mechanisms" really function. However, from the standpoint from which realism and idealism appear to be viable options, that is no answer at all, no more than Quine's naturalistic answer which makes "free use" of the results of the natural sciences. Heidegger is thus best seen as opting out of epistemology, at least in the traditional sense, and primarily by questioning the legitimacy of the "standpoint" both the realist and the idealist try to occupy: Quine's "first philosopher" incoherently striving for "cosmic exile" (Quine 1960: 275), and Heidegger's realist and idealist are, in this respect, of a piece. Referring specifically to Descartes's *cogito*, but at the same time questioning any philosophical view that incorporates the basic Cartesian view, Heidegger makes clear his rejection of such a starting point for constructing explanations of our relation to the world:

If the "*cogito sum*" is to serve as the point of departure for the existential analytic of Dasein, then it needs to be turned around, and furthermore its content needs new ontologico-phenomenal confirmation. The "*sum*" is then asserted first, and indeed in the sense that "I am in a world." As such an entity, "I am" in the possibility of being towards various ways of comporting myself – namely, *cogitationes* – as ways of being alongside entities within-the-world. Descartes, on the contrary, says that *cogitationes* are present-at-hand, and that in these an *ego* is present-at-hand too as a worldless *res cogitans*. (SZ: 211)

Dasein, Reality, and Explanatory Priority

Realism and idealism are both primarily theses about the possibility of our access to *entities*, and both are intimately connected with the kind of explanatory project Heidegger fulminates against in Division I of *Being and Time*. Again, Heidegger's basic claim is that the very need to assert a philosophical thesis about the "status" of entities, to evaluate the respective merits of apparently competing theses, is predicated on the idea that the status of entities is in some way an *issue*, that our "access" to entities is something which stands in need of explanation (and where the claim to have access stands in need of justification). Both realism and idealism, in their respective depictions of how the actuality of entities either depend or do not depend on the mind or human existence, are responses to an underlying conception of that existence, i.e. of the mind, as fundamentally or essentially *worldless*. The realist demands proof that this is not in fact the case, while the idealist provides reassurance. Either way, worldlessness is a standing possibility: all "attempts such as these which have not mastered their own basis with full transparency, presuppose a subject which is proximally *worldless* or unsure of its world, and which must, at bottom, first assure itself of a world" (SZ: 206).

Heidegger's arguments against the priority of epistemology, of projects whose central concern is the explanation and legitimation of our access to the world and worldly entities, thus serve to undercut the motivations for adjudicating between the competing philosophical theses of realism and idealism. Bringing the phenomenon of being-in-the-world into full view, i.e. properly explicating the way of being of Dasein, renders epistemological questions idle, and so deprives of their imperative any philosophical theses which are primarily responsive to such questions. As he notes in *History of the Concept of Time*:

> When we have seen that the elucidation of the reality of the real is based upon seeing Dasein itself in its basic constitution, then we also have the basic requirement for all attempts to decide between *realism* and *idealism*. In elucidating these positions it is not so much a matter of clearing them up or of finding one or the other to be the solution, but of seeing that both can exist only on the basis of a neglect: they presuppose a concept of "subject" and "object" without clarifying these basic concepts with respect to the basic composition of Dasein itself. (GA 20: 305)

I said before that the idea that knowledge is a founded mode of being-in-the-world precludes the possibility of explaining knowledge from anything other than an entity-laden standpoint. There is, for Heidegger, no standpoint that forswears all commitment to the existence of entities: the very coherence of such a retreat to the "inner sphere" of a "worldless subject" is precisely what Heidegger wants to challenge. Any description of the "basic composition of Dasein" (what both realism and idealism "neglect") always already involves reference to entities other than Dasein. Insofar as Heidegger's position includes taking the assertion of the existence of entities more or less at face value, Heidegger thereby makes a nod toward the realist:

> Along with Dasein as being-in-the-world, entities within-the-world have in each case already been disclosed. This existential-ontological assertion seems to accord with the thesis of *realism* that the external world is Really present-at-hand. In so far as this existential assertion does not deny that entities within-the-world are present-at-hand, it agrees – doxographically, as it were – with the thesis of realism in its results. (SZ: 207)

Heidegger immediately notes, however, that his existential-ontological assertion "differs in principle from every kind of realism; for realism holds that the Reality of the 'world' not only needs to be proved but also is capable of proof" (SZ: 207). The reason for this qualification should by now be reasonably clear: in holding that the "world" (by which Heidegger means the domain of spatiotemporal or present-at-hand entities) stands in need of proof and also can be proved, the realist thereby goes beyond the bare assertion of the existence of such entities to acknowledge the intelligibility of a position where one suspends all commitment to them; only from such a standpoint could such a proof be mounted without threat of circularity. (The failure to convince of Moore's "proof of an external world" illustrates the futility of starting such a proof with the assertion of the existence of mundane entities, Moore's hands in this case; it is not that Heidegger would *deny* those assertions, rather he would reject the use to which those assertions are being put. Of course Moore has hands, but that does not *establish* something that was not already in view from the start.)[6]

Heidegger's nod in the direction of idealism is far more emphatic than in the case of realism. Part of what accounts for his partiality here is what Heidegger sees as an additional commitment on the part of the realist. Immediately after his remark about "neglect" in the *History of the Concept of Time* lectures, Heidegger likewise expresses his notional agreement with realism. He continues by again rebuking the realist, but not because of what he sees as the realist's demand for proof; instead, he complains that realism "falls short in attempting to explain this reality by means of the real itself, in believing that it can clarify reality by means of a causal process" (GA 20: 306). It is far from obvious what the relation is between the demand for proof that Heidegger sees as part and parcel of realism and this predilection for causal explanation. I suggest we understand it this way: one way of trying to express a general epistemological worry is by questioning the causal history of what one has in mind, so to speak, in the form of beliefs and knowledge claims. If the causal history leads back to worldly entities, the putative content of those beliefs and claims, then what one has in mind at least stays in the running as possible knowledge (further worries arise as to how much the one who has such things in mind must also know about those causal relations). If, on the other hand, the causal history were to end with my being asleep in bed or with an evil demon or some other epistemological nightmare, then the credentials of what I claim to know would thereby be destroyed. On this line of reasoning, legitimating our claims to knowledge, justifying our beliefs, takes the form of ascertaining that their causal history is in fact of the right sort. Demonstrating the "reality of the external world" would thus be a matter of proving somehow that the external world is indeed the cause of what I or we believe. This, I take it, is what Heidegger means in talking of the realist's aspiration to "clarify reality by means of a causal process."

If this is correct, then we can see in more detail one dimension of Heidegger's complaint that realism neglects "the basic composition of Dasein." In fixating on the causal history of my or our beliefs, what the realist ignores is the task of accounting for the *fact* of those beliefs: in virtue of what exactly is something one "has in mind" a *belief* at all, and how does a being come to be the possessor of states like beliefs? How, in other words, is intentionality possible? The realist, Heidegger thinks, simply passes those questions by, and were the realist to linger for a while on them, he would thereby lose a grip on the worry that motivates him. As Heidegger puts it in *The Metaphysical Foundations of Logic*, accounting for Dasein's "ontic transcendence" leads back to the "primal transcendence" of being-in-the-world, and this again "always already" involves familiarity with worldly entities:

> The problem of transcendence as such is not at all identical with the problem of intentionality. As ontic transcendence, the latter is itself only possible on the basis of original transcendence, on the basis of *being-in-the-world*. This primal transcendence makes possible every intentional relation to beings. But this relation occurs in such a way that beings are in the "there" of Da-sein in and for Dasein's comportment with beings. The relation is based on a preliminary understanding of the being of beings. (GA 26: 170)

This "preliminary understanding of the being of beings" is what the realist ignores by attending solely to the "causal processes" at work in the formation of beliefs and other intentional states. For this reason, "as compared with realism, *idealism*, no matter how contrary and untenable it may be in its results, has an advantage in principle, provided that it does not misunderstand itself as 'psychological' idealism" (SZ: 207). What Heidegger sees lurking in idealism are at least the glimmerings of the ontological difference, of the distinction between beings and being. The realist's fixation on causes marks either a complete indifference to this distinction or, what is worse, an attempt to explain being in terms of beings, i.e. by accounting for Dasein's understanding of being in terms of the causal impact of what surrounds it. Idealism correctly recognizes that:

> Only because being is "in the consciousness" – that is to say, only because it is understandable in Dasein – can Dasein also understand and conceptualize such characteristics of being as independence, the "in-itself," and Reality in general. Only because of this are "independent" entities, as encountered within-the-world, accessible to circumspection. (SZ: 207–8)

He continues by noting that "if what the term 'idealism' says, amounts to the understanding that being can never be explained by entities but is already that which is 'transcendental' for every entity, then idealism affords the only correct possibility for a philosophical problematic. If so, Aristotle was no less an idealist than Kant" (SZ: 208). By identifying both Aristotle and Kant with the kernel of truth he discerns within idealism, Heidegger thereby signals his own disavowal of the idealist's own position.

Despite what seem to be disavowals, readers of Heidegger have often seen him as ultimately committed to idealism. Perhaps this is because, as noted above, Heidegger's
favorable nod in the direction of idealism is considerably more emphatic than is the case
for realism: idealism's inchoate acknowledgment of the ontological difference, i.e. the
difference between being and beings, gives it "an advantage in principle" over realism.
Idealism, by concentrating on the contours of subjectivity, underscores the importance
of there being an understanding of being "in the consciousness." Furthermore, idealism has the added virtue of not trying to explain those contours of subjectivity in terms
of entities, a sin realism, with its penchant for causes and causal explanation, all too
frequently commits. Where idealism goes wrong is in making subjectivity overly subjective precisely by locating it within an "inner sphere," and by casting the shadow of
subjectivity over entities themselves, pulling them one and all into that very sphere.

Heidegger, for his part, emphasizes the need to separate carefully the various possible dependence claims one might enter here, as can be seen when he writes that
"being (not entities) is dependent upon the understanding of being; that is to say,
Reality (not the Real) is dependent upon care" (SZ: 212). In the following passage,
Heidegger spells out at greater length what he sees as the consequences of the idea that
"being depends on Dasein." Heidegger writes:

> Of course only as long as Dasein *is* (that is, only as long as an understanding of being is
> ontically possible), "is there" being. When Dasein does not exist, "independence" "is" not
> either, nor "is" the "in-itself." In such a case this sort of thing can be neither understood
> nor not understood. In such a case even entities within-the-world can neither be discov-
> ered nor lie hidden. *In such a case* it cannot be said that entities are, nor can it be said that
> they are not. But *now*, as long as there is an understanding of being and therefore an
> understanding of presence-at-hand, it can indeed be said that *in this case* entities will still
> continue to be. (SZ: 212)

Readers of Heidegger have pointed to the contrasts in play in this passage as evidence
of Heidegger's commitment to some kind of idealism (William Blattner's interpretation
of Heidegger as an "ontological idealist" is perhaps the best worked out version).[7] By
tying being to the existence of Dasein, to the being who has an understanding to being,
Heidegger thereby appears to be qualifying considerably his own prior "doxographic"
agreement with the realist: if the being of entities depends on Dasein, how can entities
be without Dasein?[8] This last question appears to make entities in some way dependent
on Dasein after all, and so Heidegger has not so much broken free of the realism–
idealism dichotomy as sided with one of the two available positions.

Careful attention to this passage, however, suggests that Heidegger is here only
drawing out further the consequences of the kind of view he has been advocating
throughout Division I of *Being and Time*. Notice that in the final contrast in the passage,
between "now" and "in such a case," Heidegger is remarking upon what can and
cannot be *said*. In the case where there is no Dasein, "it cannot be said that entities are."
On first blush, this claim may seem trivial, and in some sense it is: since Dasein is the
being who says things such as "Entities are," then of course "in such a case" such a
thing cannot be said (nor can anything else, for that matter). Despite the initial impression of triviality in Heidegger's claims, I think that there is a more substantial point

lurking just beneath the surface. In the final sentence, Heidegger explicates "now" as involving an ordered sequence of possibilities, beginning with an understanding of being, moving to ("and *therefore*") an understanding of presence-at-hand, and ending with "it can indeed be said." Heidegger is here emphasizing the dependence of what can be said about entities (as opposed to the entities themselves) on the understanding of being. If one imagines a case where that understanding of being is absent, then one has thereby imagined a case where the very possibility of saying anything about entities has been removed as well.

Though this last formulation may still appear to be overly trivial, one has to bear in mind how much Heidegger has said by this point in *Being and Time* about the understanding of being. In particular, he has explicated this notion as Dasein's *being-in-the-world*, and what this suggests here is that being able to say (or think) anything about entities cannot be understood in isolation, apart from Dasein's engaged activities in and with the world. In Chapter 5 of Division I of *Being and Time*, where Heidegger discusses at length the notion of assertion, he warns against treating propositions, or the category of the propositional, as self-supporting and self-contained, or what he calls "free-floating" (*freischwebendes*) (SZ: 156). In the passage that contrasts "now" and "in such a case," Heidegger is repeating his earlier warning; he is, in other words, reiterating his prior point that "assertion cannot disown its ontological origin from an interpretation which understands" (SZ: 158). In doing so, he is once again marking his opposition to the idea of a worldless subject, i.e. of a being with the capacity to think, and perhaps say things (to itself, if nothing else), about entities, even in the absence of any dealings with the world and so of any dealings with entities. If one comes to this passage with a commitment to such an idea, as someone who aspires to transcendental-epistemological explanations does, then Heidegger's contrasts are far from trivial. Indeed, they threaten to bankrupt those very aspirations.

Truth and Being True

I said at the outset that I would address the issue of *truth* in *Being and Time*, but that my discussion would serve as something of a coda to what has preceded it. Accordingly, my primary aim in laying out some aspects of Heidegger's views on truth will be to show how those views are consonant with, and indeed reinforce, his principal motivation for rejecting both realism and idealism, namely the rejection of what I have called the transcendental-epistemological project. To put the matter in terms which are foreign to Heidegger, I would suggest that his discussion of truth recapitulates in the formal mode his discussion in the material mode of the founded character of our possession of intentional states like beliefs on our "always already" being amidst worldly entities, on that embodied, engaged way of being which manifests what Heidegger calls "being-in-the-world." That this is so should not be surprising, as one would expect an account of truth to follow closely one's account of belief and knowledge, since the very idea of the latter already involves the notion of truth.

As we saw earlier, Heidegger's discussion of knowledge as a founded mode of being-in-the-world begins with a complaint about how knowledge has traditionally been conceived, i.e. as something residing "inside" the subject who knows. How one continues from this point in spelling out the both the character of this "inner sphere" and that which resides there is a rather delicate matter, as there is a danger of identifying the bit of knowledge the subject has with some real psychological state, some "concrete" state of mind. The danger here is one of psychologism, which threatens to rob the idea of knowledge of precisely the objectivity for which it is standardly esteemed. That is, if one identifies the knowledge I have as a specific state of *my* mind, then it becomes difficult to make out exactly how you and I can both be said to know the same thing. But knowledge would seem to be precisely something that can be shared, held in common, and imparted from one knower to another. To avoid this danger, a separation must be effected between the real psychological state and the *ideal content* that this state somehow instantiates. This would appear to solve the problem of commonality, since you and I can know the same thing insofar as our real psychological states both instantiate the same ideal content.

The solution of one problem, however, brings new ones in its wake. Heidegger's discussion of truth early on addresses this notion of the ideality of the content of judgment, and the general thrust of that discussion is that the unanswered questions this notion raises are sufficient to rethink the idea of truth from the ground up. In particular, Heidegger finds the same sorts of mysteries lurking in the idea of ideal content as he found in the traditional conception of knowledge as a feature of a subject's inner sphere: the postulation of ideal content requires the further postulation of a number of relations, between the knower and the content, on the one hand, and between the content and the thing or state of affairs known. Given the radical differences in the nature of the three relata, it becomes mysterious, to say the least, to ascertain just what kind of relations would do the trick. For this reason, Heidegger suggests we scrap the idea of inquiring into the nature of truth using the notion of ideal content as our guide. Instead, he suggests we look to something more overt and concrete: the assertion. The virtues are obvious, since the assertion is something that is out there, open to view, and easily shared among two or more interlocutors. Indeed, the aim of making an assertion is typically to point out something to someone else. Finally, beginning with the notion of assertion would appear to avoid the dangers of psychologism noted above, as it usually seems quite easy to determine in practice whether you and I have made the same assertion or not.

On Heidegger's view, assertions primarily have the function of pointing something out. When I make an assertion, I am in effect calling attention to something, and I am usually doing so for what I take to be the benefit of the one(s) to whom I am speaking. Heidegger's example involves someone's saying to another "The picture on the wall is askew," while both of the conversants have their backs turned to the wall. *Verifying* the assertion involves nothing more extraordinary here than turning around and seeing how things are with the picture on the wall: if the picture is indeed askew, then a correct assertion has been uttered, otherwise not. As Heidegger sees it, this account of assertion as pointing something out as being thus and so has the virtue of avoiding all the mystery of the ideal content model. Everything, we might say, is open to view: there are the participants in the conversation, the overt assertion, and that to which the assertion calls our attention. There is no need to postulate any additional items or features, in particular nothing mysteriously subjective, mental, or abstract such as representations or ideal content.

This does not mean, however, that Heidegger's account ends with his depiction of how assertions function to point out how things are. On the contrary, his account of assertion marks only the beginning: just as knowledge is a founded mode of being-in-the-world, so too is assertion and likewise assertoric truth. Recall that the founded character of assertion was alluded to above as a clue to what Heidegger is up to in the puzzling passage that contrasts "now" and "in such a case." What Heidegger says when discussing assertions in the context of an inquiry into the nature of truth can be seen to echo those earlier remarks: "Assertion and its structure . . . are founded upon interpretation and its structure . . . and also upon understanding – upon Dasein's disclosedness. Truth, however, is regarded as a distinctive character of assertion as so derived. Thus the roots of the truth of assertion reach back to the disclosedness of the understanding" (SZ: 223). That "the roots of the truth of assertion reach back to the disclosedness of the understanding" shows the truth of assertion to be founded on disclosedness, just as knowledge is founded on being-in-the-world.

Let us go back to our opening questions concerning the possibility of knowledge, in particular:

1   How is knowledge of X possible?

Heidegger provides an answer to such a question (again, as a founded mode of being-in-the-world), while at the same time rejecting the demand for an answer which forswears all commitment to whatever lies in domain X: this maneuver on Heidegger's part exemplifies his rejection of traditional epistemology, of the project of accounting for the possibility of knowledge from a standpoint somehow independent of the domains which are the putative objects of our knowledge. With respect to accounting for the possibility of truthful assertions, Heidegger likewise claims the dependence of that possibility on our already being amidst the entities those assertions concern. As he puts it in *The Metaphysical Foundations of Logic*:

> We are rather always already comporting ourselves towards the beings around us. Statements do not first bring about this relation, but rather the converse is true. Statements are first possible on the basis of an always latent comportment to beings. Dasein, the "I" which makes statements, is already "among" beings about which it makes statements. A first consequence is that making statements, as a stating about something, is not at all a primordial relation to beings but is itself only possible on the basis of our already-being-among-beings, be this a perceptual or some kind of practical comportment. We can say that making statements about X is only possible on the basis of *having to do with X*. (GA 26: 158)

That X appears in both the explanans and the explanandum signals Heidegger's refusal to engage the questions of traditional epistemology, and so his refusal to take seriously the demand to answer such questions from a "presuppositionless" standpoint. Heidegger's impatience with such demands is especially evident in the following passage, which follows closely the one just cited: "Propositional truth is more primordially rooted, rooted in already-being-by-things. The latter occurs "already," before making statements – since when? Always already! Always, that is, insofar as and as

261

long as Dasein exists. Already being with things belongs to the *existence* of Dasein, to its kind and mode of being" (GA 26: 158–9). I argued above that the founded character of assertion was the underlying point of the passages where Heidegger discusses the distinction between beings and entities and further distinguishes between "now" and "in such a case" where Dasein is present in the former and absent in the latter. In the section on truth (¶44), which immediately follows his discussions of reality, realism, and idealism, there are passages that parallel those of ¶43, distinguishing this time between the dependence of truth on Dasein and the independence of what those truths reveal about the world:

> *"There is" truth only in so far as Dasein is and so long as Dasein is.* Entities are uncovered only *when* Dasein *is*; and only as long as Dasein *is*, are they disclosed. Newton's laws, the principle of contradiction, any truth whatever – these are true only as long as Dasein *is*. Before there was any Dasein, there was no truth; nor will there be any after Dasein is no more. For in such a case truth as disclosedness, uncovering, and uncoveredness, *cannot* be. (SZ: 226)

While the truths that we might come to create through the making of assertions depend upon Dasein, the *entities* revealed by means of them do not. Using the example of Newton's laws, Heidegger writes:

> To say that before Newton his laws were neither true nor false, cannot signify that before him there were no such entities as have been uncovered and pointed out by those laws. Through Newton the laws became true; and with them, entities became accessible in themselves to Dasein. Once entities have been uncovered, they show themselves precisely as entities which beforehand already were. Such uncovering is the kind of being which belongs to "truth." (SZ: 227)

With these passages, we can again see Heidegger's nods in the direction of both realism and idealism: realism because of the independence of the entities uncovered by our true assertions, and idealism because Dasein's understanding of being cannot itself be explained in terms of the entities so uncovered.

I have tried to emphasize throughout how Heidegger repeatedly turns the question of realism versus idealism, questions of the "status" of worldly entities, back onto the question of Dasein's understanding of being. In doing so, he takes great pains to avoid traditional distinctions between subject and object, mind and world, internal and external. At the bottom of all such distinctions, and so at the bottom of the very distinction between idealism and realism, lurks a conception of the human subject as detached from its world, cut off and confined to an inner sphere. I want to conclude with the following passage from near the very end of chapter 6 of Division I of *Being and Time*, where Heidegger again returns to the question of the subject and again laments the tendency in philosophy toward its "idealization":

> Thus with the question of the being of truth . . . just as with the question of the essence of knowledge, an "ideal subject" has generally been posited. The motive for this, whether explicit or tacit, lies in the requirement that philosophy should have the "*a priori*" as its theme, rather than "empirical facts" as such. There is some justification for this require-

ment, though it still needs to be grounded ontologically. Yet is this requirement satisfied by positing an "ideal subject"? Is not such a subject *a fanciful idealization*? With such a conception have we not missed precisely the *a priori* character of that merely "factical" subject, Dasein? (SZ: 229)

The debate between realism and idealism is but one example of such a tendency, and so one example of the tendency in philosophy to overlook Dasein in its facticity.[9]

Notes

1 An interpretation of Heidegger as a temporal and ontological idealist, as well as an empirical realist, can be found in Blattner (1999). For an interpretation of Heidegger as a linguistic idealist, see Lafont (2000); for ontical realism, see Carman (2003); for multiple hermeneutic realism, see Dreyfus (1991). My own earlier attempt to interpret Heidegger on these matters been has labeled "deflationary realism" by some: see Cerbone (1995).

2 In tracing out these dissatisfactions and demands, I am very much indebted to the writings of Barry Stroud. See the papers collected in Stroud (2002), especially "Understanding Human Knowledge in General."

3 I have chosen "bracket" deliberately to allude to the phenomenology of Edmund Husserl. One motivation of Husserl's famous phenomenological reduction is to provide an explanation of how cognition of objects in general is possible. Husserl's own conception of such an explanation is predicated on the kind of dissatisfaction with the kind of naturalistic explanation sketched out above. See, for example, Husserl (1970, especially 13–21) and "Philosophy as rigorous science" in Husserl (1965).

4 Again, see "Epistemology naturalized" in Quine (1969) and also Quine (1960), especially chapters I and II, as well as "Posits and reality" in Quine (1976).

5 This phrase appears in GA 20: 332. Though the phrase appears in the context of Heidegger's discussion of the (alleged) problem of other minds, it is, I believe, applicable to epistemological questions more generally.

6 See "Proof of an external world" in Moore (1959). For some discussion of Heidegger and Moore on the question of a proof of the external world, see Cerbone (2000); see also Minar (2001).

7 See Blattner (1994, 1999). For Blattner, ontological and temporal idealism are two distinct theses, where the latter provides an argument for the former. For criticisms of Blattner's views, at least as formulated in his initial interpretation, see Cerbone (1995). What I say below about the relation between this passage and the derivative character of assertion, as well as the implications of this relation for the issue of realism versus idealism, is consonant with my remarks in that paper. For other readings that see idealist implications in this passage, see Schatzki (1992) and Frede (1986).

8 This significance of this question has received opposing interpretations in the work of Frederick Olafson and Taylor Carman. See Olafson (1987, especially 135–41) and Carman (2003, especially 99–203).

9 A version of this chapter was presented at the annual meeting of the International Society for Phenomenological Studies, Asilomar, California, July, 2003. I am grateful to the participants for their comments and suggestions, especially to William Blattner, Hubert Dreyfus, John Haugeland, Jeff Malpas, Wayne Martin, and Joseph Rouse. I would also like to thank Edward Minar for extensive discussion of an earlier draft of this chapter.

References and further reading

Blattner, W. D. (1994) Is Heidegger a Kantian idealist? *Inquiry*, 37, 185–201.

Blattner, W. D. (1999) *Heidegger's Temporal Idealism*. Cambridge: Cambridge University Press.

Carman, T. (2003) Heidegger's Analytic: Interpretation, Discourse, and Authenticity in Being and Time. Cambridge: Cambridge University Press.

Cerbone, D. (1995) World, world-entry, and realism in early Heidegger. *Inquiry*, 38, 401–21.

Cerbone, D. (2000) Proofs and presuppositions: Heidegger, Searle, and the "reality" of the "external" world. In M. Wrathall and J. Malpas (eds.), *Heidegger, Authenticity, and Modernity: Essays in Honor of Hubert L. Dreyfus, Volume 1*. Cambridge, MA: MIT Press.

Dreyfus, H. (1991) Being-in-the-World: A Commentary on Heidegger's Being and Time, Division I. Cambridge, MA: MIT Press.

Frede, D. (1986) Heidegger and the scandal of philosophy. In A. Donagan, A. N. Perovich and M. V. Wedin (eds.), *Human Nature and Natural Knowledge*. Boston: D. Reidel.

Husserl, E. (1970) *The Idea of Phenomenology* (trans. W. P. Alston and G. Nakhnikian). The Hague: Martinus Nijhoff

Husserl, E. (1965) *Phenomenology and the Crisis of Philosophy* (trans. Q. Lauer). New York: Harper & Row.

Lafont, C. (2000) *Heidegger, Language, and World-Disclosure* (trans. G. Harman). Cambridge: Cambridge University Press.

Minar, E. H. (2001) Heidegger's response to skepticism in *Being and Time*. In J. Floyd and S. Shieh (eds.), *Future Pasts: The Analytic Tradition in Twentieth-Century Philosophy*. Oxford: Oxford University Press.

Moore, G. E. (1959) *Philosophical Papers*. London: George Allen and Unwin.

Olafson, F. (1987) *Heidegger and the Philosophy of Mind*. New Haven, CT: Yale University Press.

Quine, W. v. O. (1960) *Word and Object*. Cambridge, MA: MIT Press.

Quine, W. v. O. (1969) *Ontological Relativity and Other Essays*. New York: Columbia University Press.

Quine, W. v. O. (1974) *The Roots of Reference*. La Salle, IL: Open Court.

Quine, W. v. O. (1976) *The Ways of Paradox and Other Essays*, rev. and enlarged edn. Cambridge, MA: Harvard University Press.

Schatzki, T. R. (1992) Early Heidegger on being, the clearing, and realism. In H. Dreyfus and H. Hall (eds.), *Heidegger: A Critical Reader*. Oxford: Blackwell.

Stroud, B. (2002) *Understanding Human Knowledge: Philosophical Essays*. Oxford: Oxford University Press.

Wittgenstein, L. (1983) *Remarks on the Foundations of Mathematics*, rev. edn (trans. G. E. M. Anscombe). Cambridge, MA: MIT Press.

16

Hermeneutics

CRISTINA LAFONT

Among the many philosophical innovations that Heidegger introduces in Being and Time, one of the most significant and rich in consequences is his claim that philosophy is hermeneutics. This claim does not refer merely to the kind of topics with which philosophy should be concerned (interpretation, the methodology of the human sciences, etc.) but aims at a radical paradigm shift within philosophy itself. Indeed, one of the main achievements of *Being and Time* is its articulation of the basic features of the philosophical paradigm of hermeneutics, which had a decisive influence on twentieth-century Continental philosophy (H.-G. Gadamer, K.-O. Apel, J. Habermas, P. Ricoeur, etc.).

To bring about this paradigm shift, Heidegger generalizes hermeneutics from a traditional method for interpreting authoritative texts (mainly sacred or legal texts) to a way of understanding human beings themselves. As a consequence, the hermeneutic paradigm offers a radically new understanding of what is distinctive about human beings: to be human is not primarily to be a rational animal, but first and foremost to be a self-interpreting animal. It is precisely because human beings are nothing but interpretation all the way down that the activity of *interpreting a meaningful text* offers the most appropriate model for understanding any human experience whatsoever. This change of perspective amounts to a major break with traditional philosophy. For the latter has been mainly guided by a diametrically opposed attempt, namely to model all human experience on the basis of our *perception of physical objects*. It is for this reason that in *Being and Time* Heidegger articulates the new hermeneutic account of human experience through a detailed criticism of the traditional philosophical model, the subject–object model.

Although the shortcomings that Heidegger finds in the latter model are virtually innumerable, all of his criticisms are part of a single strategy, namely to show the overall superiority of the hermeneutic paradigm (and thus the need for a "destruction" and new appropriation of the history of philosophy). In order to succeed with this ambitious goal he has to prove that the hermeneutic paradigm can give an appropriate account of all human experience, including the experience that underlies the subject–object model (namely perception and empirical knowledge of objects), whereas the reverse is not the case.[1]

The argumentative strategy that Heidegger develops in *Being and Time* in order to achieve this goal is based on two central objections to the subject–object model. First of all, Heidegger argues that by trying to model human experience on the basis of categories taken from a domain of objects radically different from human beings (i.e. physical objects), traditional philosophy provides an entirely distorted account of human identity. To show this, Heidegger articulates an alternative, hermeneutic model that makes it possible to understand human beings as essentially self-interpreting creatures. Once we understand that human beings are self-interpreting and thus self-misinterpreting beings, Heidegger's ambitious goal can be achieved. For he can then show both why philosophy can only be hermeneutics and how the errors of traditional philosophy are a direct consequence of the kind of beings that humans are. Second, Heidegger argues that by focusing on perception as the private experience of an isolated subject, the subject–object model incorporates a methodological individualism (even solipsism) that entirely distorts human experience with the world (giving rise to nothing but philosophical pseudo-problems such as the need to prove the existence of the external world). To defend this claim, Heidegger offers an alternative, hermeneutic account of our experience that makes it possible to understand human beings as inhabiting a symbolically structured world, in which everything they encounter is already understood as something or other. Once we understand the world in which human beings live as a holistically structured web of significance, Heidegger's overall goal can be achieved in this context as well. For he can show both that the model of understanding a meaningful text is indeed more appropriate for understanding our human experience in the world than the subject–object model, and that the account of perception, knowledge, truth, etc. that the hermeneutic model provides is superior to the traditional one.

In what follows, I will analyze the hermeneutic core of *Being and Time* in order to spell out the main features of this new philosophical paradigm. But before I do so, I will first situate the project of *Being and Time* in the philosophical context from which it emerged and which makes the sense and scope of Heidegger's hermeneutic transformation of philosophy understandable.

Historical Background: Philosophical Continuities and Discontinuities Behind the Project of *Being and Time*

From the point of view of the historical background out of which *Being and Time* grew, the most significant event was the development of the human sciences during the nineteenth century and the difficulties that this development brought to light. The question of how to obtain scientific knowledge of human realities such as history, culture, and religion prompted philosophers of all kinds of persuasions to try to provide a philosophical foundation not only for the conditions of possibility of *explaining natural* processes, but also for the conditions of possibility of *understanding cultural* ones. Taking Kant's critique of pure reason as a paradigmatic example of the first task, neo-Kantians of the Southwest School such as Windelband and Rickert (who was Heidegger's teacher) were trying to extend transcendental philosophy in the direction of a *philosophy of value* that would be able to fulfill the second task. Within the Marburg School of neo-Kantianism, Cassirer's project of articulating a *critique of culture* was similarly motivated. Equally so, Husserl's project of developing a transcendental phenomenology that would provide a foundation for all regional ontologies, not just those that underlie the natural sciences, was an attempt to fulfill the same task. Within the tradition of the historical school, Dilthey's project of complementing Kant's work with a *critique of historical reason* had a similar inspiration.

However, all these attempts to complement Kant's work were confronted with an unprecedented difficulty, namely the need to reconcile the transcendental and the historical without sacrificing one to the other. From this point of view, as the young Heidegger argues, the main difficulty confronting the human sciences is not so much that they lack a scientific foundation, but rather that precisely in trying to apply scientific methodology they lose the possibility of accessing the very reality they aim to understand. Grasping the meaningfulness of human life's experience in its concrete facticity requires a way to gain access to that reality as it is given to us prior to any scientific objectivation. Consequently, the problem of reconciling the transcendental and the historical can only be solved by breaking with the "primacy of the theoretical" and thus with the key methodological assumption built on the basis of this priority, the subject–object model.

Keeping this background of philosophical issues in mind, we can now turn to the very dense Introduction of *Being and Time*. There, Heidegger accomplishes two important tasks. On the one hand, he makes explicit some of the methodological assumptions of his overall project and defends their plausibility by situating *Being and Time* in the context of other transcendental projects (the main references here are to Kant and Husserl). On the other hand, he also introduces the new conceptual framework that will make a hermeneutic transformation of transcendental philosophy possible.

Heidegger's way of situating his own philosophical project in the Introduction to *Being and Time* makes very clear that he shares the conception of philosophy common to the different versions of transcendental philosophy available at the time (phenomenology, neo-Kantianism, etc.) Philosophy is supposed to provide the foundation for the empirical sciences through an *a priori* investigation of their basic concepts, which makes accessible to the sciences their own objects of study in their essential constitution. Heidegger also agrees with his contemporaries on the need for extending Kant's transcendental project to provide a genealogy of the different possible ways of being (beyond the one of "Nature"), but he thinks that this task cannot be properly accomplished without a prior clarification of the meaning of being in general. To the extent that this clarification would provide the *a priori* conditions not only for the possibility of the sciences but also for the possibility of the ontologies themselves, which are prior to them and provide their foundations, it constitutes philosophy's central task: articulating a *fundamental ontology*. Heidegger's short exposition of his specific project for accomplishing this task reveals a further commonality with transcendental philosophy. Heidegger accepts the key methodological assumption necessary for a transcendental strategy, namely the "priority of Dasein over all other entities" (SZ: 13).

As he argues, given that philosophy's central task is a clarification of the meaning of being and that Dasein is the only entity that has an understanding of being, Dasein provides "the ontico-ontological condition for the possibility of any ontologies" (SZ: 13). Thus fundamental ontology must take the form of an existential analytic of Dasein.

But just at this point the commonalities between Heidegger's project and those of traditional transcendental philosophy rapidly come to an end. For, as Heidegger explains in the following section of the *Introduction*, the existential analytic of Dasein focuses on the hermeneutics of a factical Dasein in its average everydayness. Thus, the project of providing a fundamental ontology through an existential analytic of Dasein is the attempt to follow a transcendental strategy without a transcendental subject. To be plausible at all, Heidegger's hermeneutic transformation of philosophy requires cashing out the empirical/transcendental distinction in different terms. This explains the second task that is accomplished in the Introduction, namely to set in motion a new framework of concepts that will make such transformation possible.

The New Conceptual Framework: The *Ontological Difference*

Although the term "ontological difference" is not coined in *Being and Time*, the distinction between "being" and "entities" is introduced at the very beginning of the book. In ¶2 "being" is defined as "that which determines entities as entities, that on the basis of which entities are already understood" (SZ: 6) and "entities" are defined as "everything we talk about, everything we have in view, everything towards which we comport ourselves in any way", including "what we are" and "how we are" (SZ: 6–7).

Taking the ontological difference as the key methodological distinction, Heidegger interprets what is distinctive about human beings (i.e. the priority of Dasein over all other entities) in an essentially different way than does traditional philosophy. In contradistinction to Kant, Heidegger's analysis rests not on *the fact of reason* but on a different fact, namely *the fact that human beings have a "vague average understanding of being"* (SZ: 5). This understanding is what allows Dasein to grasp the distinction between being and beings and thus to have an understanding of itself, the world, and everything that can show up within the world. Here, however, it is important to notice that Heidegger's full interpretation of the ontological difference involves much more than just ascribing to Dasein the intuitive capacity for distinguishing between being and beings. It entails at least the following features:

1   Having an *implicit grasp* of the distinction between entities and their being, that is, between entities and how they are understood (SZ: 6–7).
2   Understanding both as *irreducibly* distinct: "the being of entities 'is' not itself an entity" (SZ: 6).
3   Understanding the *transcendental priority* of being over any entity: "being can never be explained by entities but is already that which is 'transcendental' for every entity" (SZ: 208). Thus "entities are in no way accessible without a prior understanding of their being" (GA 25: 38).

4   Understanding the transcendental priority in *hermeneutic* terms: "there is be-
    ing only in an understanding of being" (SZ: 212). Therefore, "what determines
    entities as entities" is "that on the basis of which entities are . . . understood" (SZ:
    6).
5   To recognize the *detranscendentalized* status of the understanding of being (as con-
    tingent, historically variable, plural, etc.): "what determines entities as entities" is
    merely "that on the basis of which entities are *always already* understood" (SZ: 6,
    emphasis added). This follows from the fact that "the meaning of being can never
    be contrasted with entities" (SZ: 152).

The first feature of Heidegger's interpretation of the ontological difference seems clearly
uncontroversial. At least in its most deflationary interpretation, it seems plausible
to claim that we can intuitively distinguish between the entities we talk about and
the way we understand them. However, the other features are hardly as uncontroversial. This becomes clear if we take into account the philosophical theses that lie behind
each of them and, especially, the philosophical positions that they are meant to
rule out. Acceptance of the ontological difference entails, according to Heidegger, a
strong anti-reductionist commitment: the meaningful and the factual are mutually
irreducible. In virtue of this dualism, hermeneutic philosophy shares with transcendental philosophy its *anti-naturalism*. It also entails a decidedly anti-empiricist commitment: hermeneutic philosophy shares with transcendental philosophy its *opposition to
any kind of metaphysical realism*. However, this opposition is based not on a transcendental but on a *hermeneutic idealism*, that is, on an idealism justified exclusively by
hermeneutic reasons. Here lies Heidegger's hermeneutic transformation of transcendental philosophy.[2] In a nutshell, its main features can be explained as follows. On the
basis of the ontological difference, the transcendental priority of being over entities is
traced back to Dasein's fore-structure of understanding. As a consequence, Dasein's
projections of the being of entities inherit the transcendental status that traditional
philosophy ascribed to synthetic *a priori* knowledge: they are prior to all experience
with entities (1), but determine all experience with those entities (2). However, the
ascription of this status is not due to the alleged universal validity of such knowledge, but it is justified on merely hermeneutic grounds. As we shall see, Heidegger
defends assumption (1) on the basis of a hermeneutic constraint on communication,
namely the assumption that *meaning determines reference*, and assumption (2) on the
basis of a hermeneutic fact about interpretation, namely the *holistic* structure of understanding. As a result of this transformation, the opposition to metaphysical realism
characteristic of hermeneutics involves, in contradistinction to traditional transcendental philosophy, a commitment to *conceptual pluralism* and a strong *incommensurability* thesis.

    An important question in evaluating the strength and plausibility of the paradigm
of philosophical hermeneutics inaugurated by Heidegger is certainly whether and to
what extent Heidegger's interpretation of the ontological difference is a necessary
element of hermeneutics or just a remnant of the transcendental paradigm that
hermeneutic philosophy was meant to overcome. But before we focus on this problem,
we need to analyze first the central steps of Heidegger's development of the paradigm
of hermeneutics in *Being and Time*.

The Hermeneutic Notion of World

As already mentioned, the central feature of Heidegger's hermeneutic turn lies in his replacement of the subject–object model, that is, the model of an *observing* subject posed over against the world as the totality of entities, by the hermeneutic model of an *understanding* Dasein which finds itself always already *in* a symbolically structured *world*. The key for this transformation lies in the introduction of a new notion of world. After the hermeneutic turn, the world is no longer the totality of entities, but a totality of significance, a web of meanings that structures Dasein's understanding of itself and of everything that can show up within the world: "the world itself is not an entity within-the-world; and yet it is so determinative for such entities that only in so far as 'there is' a world can they be encountered and show themselves in their being as entities which have been discovered" (SZ: 72).

The importance of the new notion of world for understanding the paradigm shift from traditional to hermeneutic philosophy cannot be overestimated. For, as we will see, it is on its basis that the hermeneutic model that replaces the traditional subject–object model is built. But although Heidegger is very careful in his introduction of the new notion of world, many commentators of *Being and Time* seem to miss the crucial difference between the traditional and the hermeneutic notions. A common mistake that can be found in many commentaries is the interpretation of Heidegger's notion of world as referring to the totality of equipment with which Dasein is involved in its everyday dealings (i.e. what Heidegger calls "the environment"). Under this interpretation, the difference between Heidegger's notion of world and the traditional one would be that whereas the latter is supposed to be the totality of ocurrent entities as objectified by an observing subject, the former is the totality of available entities which are put to use by an acting Dasein. Thus, the new notion of world would serve the Heideggerian purpose of reversing the ontological priority traditionally ascribed to the ocurrent *vis-à-vis* the available. However, this interpretation is untenable from an exegetical point of view, not just in view of Heidegger's extremely careful definition of his notion of world in ¶14, but at a much more crucial level, namely in view of the ontological difference. As Heidegger made clear in the quote mentioned before, "the world is not itself an entity within-the-world." Consequently, "if we join [such entities] together, we still do not get anything like the 'world' as their sum" (SZ: 72). The world is a "referential context of significance" (*Verweisungszusammenhang der Bedeutsamkeit*, SZ: 123), a system of meaningful relations toward which Dasein comports itself *understandingly* (SZ: 86) and not a totality of entities of any kind, be it ocurrent or available ones.

But, of course, exegetical considerations do not settle the crucial issue here, namely whether Heidegger's use of the term "world" to refer to a totality of meaningful relations is plausible at all. At least, from the point of view of traditional philosophy, it is clearly unprecedented. Traditionally, the notion of world had been understood mainly in one of two ways: either as the totality of entities to which human beings also belong (empiricism) or as the totality of entities constituted by a transcendental, extraworldly subject (transcendental philosophy). However, as we pointed out at the beginning, with the development of the human sciences philosophy saw itself confronted with objects of study such as history, culture, and religion that did not fit well in that mold. Keeping this historical development in mind is very helpful for understanding the need for as well as the plausibility of Heidegger's notion of world. If one is not concerned with natural entities and our activities of coping with them, but with meaningful entities and our activities of making sense of them, it does seem plausible to think of entities such as cultures as totalities of significance (which enable human beings to understand themselves and everything around them as something or other). And it is in virtue of this quasi-transcendental function that in ordinary language we can refer to cultures as "worlds" in expressions such as "the world of the Renaissance man" or "the medieval world." Moreover, in light of this use of the term, the features that Heidegger ascribes to his notion of world seem plausible: cultures are the kind of things that humans can be said to be "in" (or grow up "into") in a non-spatial sense of the term, they are also the kind of things that can be understood or interpreted rather than perceived or manipulated, etc.

Assuming that Heidegger's notion of world is prima facie plausible, we now need to analyze the main features of the philosophical model that this notion makes possible to articulate and which should replace the subject–object model, namely Dasein's fundamental structure of *being-in-the-world*.

In ¶14, Heidegger distinguishes four possible senses of the term "world": (a) "World" in an ontical (extensional) sense means the totality of all ocurrent entities, i.e. the objective world; (b) "world" in an ontological (intensional) sense means the being of a particular realm of entities, that is, the kind of being that all these entities have in common; Heidegger's examples are expressions such as "the world of the mathematician"; (c) "world" in an ontical but existentiell sense means specific social or cultural worlds, wherein a factical Dasein as such can be said to live, for example, "the public world" or "the world of the Renaissance man"; and (d) "world" in the ontologico-existential technical sense means the *a priori* character of wordliness in general.

Heidegger indicates that in *Being and Time* he uses the term "world" in the third signification. In order to show the specific features of his own concept of world, he contrasts it with the traditional notion of world as the totality of ocurrent entities. First of all, he makes clear that, whereas the sense of being "in" the world that corresponds to the traditional notion is the sense of *physical inclusion*, being "in" a cultural world has instead the sense of *involvement*. *Being-in* is not a physical property but rather an *existentiale* of Dasein: it is the ability to understand and be involved with everything that shows up within the world, and thus to have a symbolic and not merely a causal relationship to it. Thus, in virtue of "being-in-the-world" Dasein has the ability to take the internal perspective of a participant in a culture rather than the external perspective of an observer of the physical world. In fact, as mentioned before, one of the crucial aims of Heidegger's analysis of the structure of *Being-in-the-world* is precisely to show that the latter perspective, the subject–object model, is founded in the former.

But there is another aspect of Heidegger's concept of world that entails a deeper break with the traditional paradigm of mentalism. As Heidegger makes clear in the following chapter, the totality of significations that make up the world in which a factical Dasein grows up into is essentially *intersubjectively shared*: "the world is always the one that I share with Others. The world of Dasein is a *with-world*" (SZ: 118). This is a phenomenological fact, however, that can hardly be accounted for within the constraints of the methodological individualism characteristic of the subject–object model. For the public world can be identified neither with the totality of objects nor with the private sphere of the mental acts of an isolated subject.[3] The specific relationship that Dasein has with others in virtue of sharing a public world cannot be modeled on the relationship of a subject either to itself or to objects different from itself. With the introduction of the hermeneutic concept of world, the resulting model reverses the order of explanation characteristic of the subject–object model. It is only to the extent that Dasein first learns to adopt the intersubjective perspective of a participant in its cultural world that it may later learn to adopt the subjective perspective of an (authentic) individual self. Heidegger explains: "By 'Others' we do not mean everyone else but me – those over against whom the 'I' stands out. They are rather those from whom, for the most part, one does not distinguish oneself – those among whom one is too" (SZ: 118). Consequently, "the self of everyday Dasein is the one-self, which we distinguish from the *authentic self*. . . . As one-self, the particular Dasein has been dispersed into the 'one,' and *must first find itself*" (SZ: 129, emphasis added).

Obviously, part of what it takes to grow up into a culture, that is, to become familiar with the whole of significations available within it, is first of all to learn the normative patterns of interpretation and conduct that such a culture prescribes. As Heidegger explains: "We take pleasure and enjoy ourselves as one takes pleasure; we read, see, and judge about literature and art as one sees and judges; likewise we shrink back from the 'great mass' as one shrinks back. . . . The one, which is nothing definite, and which all are, though not as the sum, prescribes the kind of being of everydayness." (SZ: 126–7). If cultural traditions thus *precede* individual subjects, who grow up into them, Heidegger seems right in rejecting the strategy of trying to explain the cultural world as a product of an (individual) subject, even a "transcendental" one. Within the hermeneutic model, the world is not constituted by the subject, but by "the one." Heidegger explains: "If Dasein is familiar with itself as the one-self, this means at the same time that the 'one' itself prescribes that way of interpreting the world and being-in-the-world which lies closest. Dasein is for the sake of the 'one' in an everyday manner and *the 'one' itself articulates the referential context of significance*" (SZ: 129, emphasis added).

However, at this point an important question arises. For in the light of Heidegger's interpretation of the ontological difference, the world is a phenomenon that is hard to situate, given the rigid dichotomy established for methodological reasons between Dasein and all other entities. On the one hand, *Being-in-the-world* is a fundamental structure of Dasein, so "the one" as an element of this structure is an *existentiale*, an ability of Dasein (the ability to take the community's perspective of the "generalized other," in G. H. Mead's terms). But, on the other hand, the articulation of the world precedes each and every individual Dasein (SZ: 364). If it did not, if it were just the product of the meaning-conferring acts of an individual subject, the subject–object model would be re-established. But if "the one" is prior to any individual Dasein and, obviously, is neither an ocurrent entity nor a "transcendental subject" (see SZ: 128–9), how is it constituted? Where is it situated? In his lectures of the summer semester of 1924, Heidegger gives a direct answer to this question:

The *one* is the *genuine how of everydayness, of the average, concrete being-with-one-another*. Out of this "one" grows the way in which man sees the world primarily and usually, how the world matters to man, how he addresses the world. The "one" is the original how of the being of humans in everydayness and *the primordial bearer of the one is language*. The "one" sustains itself, has its primordial dominance in language. (GA 18: 64)

Along the same lines, Heidegger remarks in *Being and Time* that "the 'one' is constituted by the way things have been publicly interpreted, which expresses itself in idle talk" (SZ: 252).

This is another central feature of the hermeneutic notion of world: the world is always intersubjectively shared because it is *linguistically articulated*. It is by virtue of sharing a natural language that Dasein can share the *same* world with others. In this context, it is important to keep in mind one of the crucial differences between the traditional and the hermeneutic notions of world. Whereas the former is supposed to refer to a *single* objective world (to the extent that everything is supposed to be under the same causal laws), the latter admits of a plurality of worlds. Cultural worlds as totalities of significance are *plural*. This is why on the basis of this sense of the term Heidegger can plausibly refer to a factical Dasein *"in seiner jeweiligen Welt,"* in its current world (SZ: 145). This intrinsic plurality of worlds opens up an issue that had no equivalent in the framework of the traditional notion of world. In order to use the hermeneutic notion of world in a plausible way, one must first explain in virtue of what a particular Dasein can be said to share the *same* world with others. Heidegger addresses this issue explicitly in "The Concept of Time" (1924):

> As this being-in-the-world, Dasein is, together with this, *being-with-one-another*, being with Others: having *the same world* there with Others. . . . Being with one another in the world . . . has a distinctive ontological determination. The fundamental way of the existence of world, namely, having world there with one another, is *speaking*. Fully considered, speaking is: oneself speaking *out* in speaking *with* another *about* something. . . . In speaking with one another . . . there lies the specific self-interpretation of the present, which maintains itself in this dialogue. (Heidegger 1995: 12–13; see also SZ: 167–8)

It is the phenomenon of a linguistically articulated world that definitively breaks with the functionality of the subject–object model. For it shows why the attempt to model the common perspective of subjects who share a public world on the isolated perspective of a subject perceiving a physical object must fail: from the private perceptions of isolated subjects there is no way to explain how these subjects could achieve a shared perspective *about the same objects*. The order of explanation is actually the reverse: the subject–object perspective is only possible as a result of success in achieving a shared subject–subject perspective.

As Heidegger explains in *Being and Time*, it is in virtue of sharing a language that speakers and hearers can talk about the same things even if those things are not accessible to all of them to the same extent, either because not all of them are in a position to simultaneously perceive them or because not all of them have the same level of understanding or expertise about those things:

> In the language which is spoken when one expresses oneself, there lies an average intelligibility; and in accordance with this intelligibility the discourse which is communicated

can be understood to a considerable extent, even if the hearer does not bring himself into such a kind of being towards what the discourse is about as to have a primordial understanding of it. . . . We have *the same thing* in view, because it is in the *same* averageness that we have a common understanding of what is said. (SZ: 168)[4]

Now, if this claim is right, if subjects come to share a common world of objects only to the extent that they previously share a common understanding of those objects, the explanatory priority of perception that underlies the subject–object model can be shown to be just wrong. Heidegger explains:

This way in which things have been interpreted in idle talk has already established itself in Dasein. . . . This everyday way in which things have been interpreted is one into which Dasein has grown in the first instance, with never a possibility of extrication. In it, from out of it, and against it, all genuine understanding, interpreting and communicating, all re-discovering and appropriating anew, are performed. *In no case is a Dasein, untouched and unseduced by this way in which things have been interpreted, set before the open country of a "world-in-itself" so that it just beholds what it encounters.* The dominance of the public way in which things have been interpreted has already been decisive even for the possibilities of having a mood. . . . The "one" prescribes one's affectivity, and determines what and how one "sees." (SZ: 169–70, emphasis added)

The Priority of Understanding over Perception

It is in view of the linguistically articulated intelligibility that Dasein shares with others by sharing a natural language that Heidegger can justify the crucial hermeneutic claim of *Being and Time,* namely the *priority of understanding over perception.* As he expresses it, "any mere prepredicative seeing . . . is, in itself, something which already understands and interprets" (SZ: 149). If this claim is right, if every seeing something is already a seeing-as, the possibility of a neutral perception of merely occurrent objects that the subject–object model assumes can be unmasked as just a myth – the Myth of the Given, in Sellars's words. The goal of Heidegger's criticism of traditional philosophy is achieved: the mentalist paradigm collapses. Heidegger explains: "By showing how all sight is grounded primarily in understanding . . . we have deprived pure intuition of its priority, which corresponds noetically to the priority of the ocurrent in traditional ontology. 'Intuition' and 'thinking' are both derivatives of understanding, and already rather remote ones" (SZ: 147).

Heidegger does seem right in claiming that establishing the priority of understanding over perception is all that is needed to motivate the radical shift from the traditional paradigm of mentalism to the hermeneutic paradigm. However, this cannot be achieved merely by pointing to the fact that subjects have a language at their disposal. This would not be news for traditional philosophy. As long as language is understood in the traditional sense, namely as a tool for expressing prelinguistic thoughts about objects that exist independently of language, it is not at all clear why it would be wrong to assume that subjects are set before the open country of a "world-in-itself" so that they just behold what they encounter. Under the traditional conception of language as a bunch of names used to designate objects existing independently of language, subjects were supposed to do precisely that: to merely behold objects in themselves and use an arbitrary sign to name them. To be successful with his overall strategy, Heidegger first has to break with the traditional conception of language as a tool.

The way in which Heidegger tries to do that in his explicit discussion of language in ¶¶33 to 35 can already be hinted at in the context of his crucial argument against the explanatory priority of perception, which takes place in ¶32. There, Heidegger questions the possibility of a neutral perception of "objects in themselves" precisely by questioning the possibility of a neutral designation of such objects. His argument runs as follows:

> the circumspective question as to what this particular available thing may be, receives the circumspectively interpretative answer that it is for such and such a purpose. If we tell what it is for, we are not simply designating something; but that which is designated is understood *as* that *as* which we are to take the thing in question. . . . The "as" makes up the structure of the explicitness of something that is understood. It constitutes the interpretation. In dealing with what is environmentally available by interpreting it circumspectively, we "see" it as a table, a door, a carriage or a bridge. . . . Any mere pre-predicative seeing of the available is, in itself, something which already understands and interprets. (SZ: 149)

Here Heidegger questions the traditional view of designation as a neutral pointing at an object, but he does not offer a specific argument to support his own view of designation. There is, however, an argument to which Heidegger alludes repeatedly, although he never discusses it in detail (for a clear example of this line of argument, see GA 34: 1–3). Perhaps the best way to express it would be with the help of Quine's maxim "no entity without identity." The idea behind it could be made explicit in the following way: communication requires speakers to identify which entities they want to talk about so that they can be distinguished from others. And this cannot be done unless the terms used to designate those entities provide an understanding of what distinguishes them from others, that is, unless they provide the resources to identify entities as *what* they are, that is, in their *being*. To the extent that it is meaningless to purport to refer to entities whose conditions of identity one cannot possibly indicate, our understanding of the being of entities must determine in advance which entities we are referring to, that is, *meaning must determine reference*. This constraint on communication explains why with the terms we use to designate entities "we are not simply designating something; but that which is designated is understood *as* that *as* which we are to take the thing in question" (SZ: 149). And to the extent that the meaning of a designative term provides an understanding of the being of the entities it refers to, it determines at the same time *as what* these entities are accessible to us, it determines our experience with those entities. By designating entities as tables, doors, carriages, or bridges we are at the same time answering the ontological question of what can be in our world (namely tables, doors, carriages, and bridges). As Heidegger explains in his *History of the Concept of Time*: "It is not so much that we see the objects and things but rather that we first talk about them. To put it more precisely: we do not say what we see, but rather the reverse, we see what *one says* about things" (GA 20: 75). Thus Heidegger's claim that there can be no access to entities without a prior understanding of their being is justified by a hermeneutic constraint on intersubjective communication.

If this view is right, linguistic designation does involve much more than the use of a purely arbitrary sign to designate an object as the traditional conception of language assumes. If linguistic signs such as general names provide the individuating criteria of identity for the objects they refer to, without which we could not *identify* objects as something or other in the first place, then language can no longer be seen as merely a system of arbitrary signs. Its essential contribution lies in its *world-disclosing* function (Heidegger develops the view of language as world-disclosing in greater detail after the *Kehre*; see GA 4: 33–48 and GA 12). Language makes it possible for Dasein to share the *same* world with others by articulating a common understanding of the being of entities that can show up in their world. Of course, this contribution is a function not of the arbitrariness of the signs that make up a specific empirical language and distinguish it from others (say English versus German or Swahili), but of the articulation of intelligibility that such a system of signs provides. In order to mark this distinction in *Being and Time*, Heidegger uses the term "language" in an ontical (extensional) sense to refer to the different empirical languages that are the object of study in linguistics, and uses the term "discourse" as an ontological term to refer to the "articulation of intelligibility" that any language provides.[5]

The Fore-structure of Understanding

So far, we have focused on the central feature of Heidegger's hermeneutic model, namely the view of human beings as inhabiting a linguistically articulated world in which everything that might show up within the world is already understood as something or other. As already mentioned, this change of perspective makes it possible to claim that the hermeneutic model of understanding a meaningful text is the most appropriate one for giving an account of any human experience whatsoever. Now we need to know what the implications and consequences of adopting that model are.

If Heidegger is right and human experience does not arise primarily through perception (of entities) and its conditions, but through a prior understanding (of the being of entities) and their conditions, the existential analytic of Dasein must provide an analysis of the conditions of possibility of understanding. This is what Heidegger calls the fore-structure of understanding. Here again a crucial goal of the analysis is critical. For nothing would be achieved by arguing that understanding has explanatory priority over perception if understanding could in turn be explained on the basis of the model of a neutral perception, as traditional philosophy has always done. Thus, in the same way that Heidegger had first to show that there can be no neutral perception of something like a "world-in-itself," he now has to show that there can be no neutral understanding of something like a "literal meaning," no "presuppositionless apprehending of something merely presented to us" (SZ: 150). It has to be shown that understanding is *always* interpretation or, as Heidegger puts it, that "in interpretation, under-standing does not become something different. It becomes itself" (SZ: 148).

At this point in the argument Heidegger takes recourse to the hermeneutic model of textual interpretation in order to show that understanding is necessarily both projective and presuppositional. He does so by appealing to a well known feature of the holistic activity of textual interpretation: the *circle of understanding*. In order to understand the meaning of a text we need to understand the meaning of its parts. But we can only understand its parts by anticipating the meaning of the text as a whole. Thus, as Heidegger puts it, "any interpretation which is to contribute understanding, must *already* have understood what is to be interpreted" (SZ: 152). Without a *projection* of meaning no activity of interpretation can get off the ground. But for this very same reason understanding is always *presuppositional*. There is no such thing as a presuppositionless grasping of a literal meaning (SZ: 152). Consequently, an analysis of the conditions of possibility of understanding must provide an answer to the question of where our anticipations or projections of meaning come from.

To answer this question Heidegger distinguishes three elements of the fore-structure of understanding: *fore-having, fore-sight, and fore-conception*. These are technical terms that Heidegger had introduced and defined in his lectures of summer semester of 1924 (see GA 18: 274–7), and which he describes only very briefly in *Being and Time*. Taking both texts together, the sense of these terms can be explained briefly as follows. "Fore-having" (*Vorhabe*) refers to the prior intelligibility with which we have understood in advance what we want to interpret, the particular way it is presented to us prior to our explicit interpretation. Heidegger's example in *Being and Time* is the way available enti-ties are understood in terms of a totality of involvements prior to any activity of the-matic interpretation. "Fore-sight" (*Vorsicht*) refers to the specific perspective or point of view that guides the interpretation. Heidegger's examples in the lectures mentioned before are the specific understandings of being (ocurrentness, availableness, etc.) that can guide a thematic interpretation. A clear example in *Being and Time* is Heidegger's analysis of three different perspectives from which it is possible to interpret human exis-tence: in the everydayness, Dasein is understood from the perspective of the *available*, in the philosophical tradition Dasein is understood from the perspective of the *ocurrent*, whereas in *Being and Time* Dasein is understood from the perspective of *existence* or care. Finally, "fore-conception" (*Vorgriff*) refers to the specific conceptuality, the particular vocabulary that is at the disposal of the interpretation. Here again the best examples in *Being and Time* are Heidegger's analyses of the matrix of concepts that articulate each specific understanding of being (e.g. his analysis of ocurrentness as articulated through concepts such as substance, location, time, etc.)

According to this view, interpretation is always relative to a particular context, per-spective, and vocabulary (fore-having, fore-sight, fore-conception) that together con-stitute what Heidegger calls the "hermeneutic situation" out of which interpretation evolves and which we cannot transcend at will. This projective view of interpretation presents a clear challenge to the traditional aspirations of absolute objectivity even within the narrow circle of the activity of interpreting a meaningful text. If interpre-tation is essentially contextual and perspectival the hermeneutic ideal of getting the single right interpretation of what a text says, its "literal meaning," makes no sense whatsoever. However, as decades of philosophical hermeneutics have made abundantly clear, recognizing that we are always interpreting out of a contingent, historical, hermeneutic situation may have constructive consequences in addition to the destructive ones. For it makes it possible for us to discover a different hermeneutic ideal that on reflection may be seen as *superior* to the traditional ideal. Precisely by discovering that interpretation entails a moment of application to our own hermeneutic situation, we finally realize what we wanted to know all along: the point of interpreting a text is to find out not so much what its author *literally said* at the time, but first and foremost what he may have to *say to us* now, that is, in our current situation. From this perspective, Heidegger's projective (and thus applicative) view of interpretation offers the basis for a positive contribution to the intricate issues that surround the activity of textual interpretation, as H.-G. Gadamer has convincingly shown in *Truth and Method*.

However, these issues are by no means the target of Heidegger's analysis in *Being and Time*. As already mentioned, Heidegger's underlying strategy is to generalize the model of textual interpretation in order to provide a new account of human identity in terms of "thrown projection," one that should be able to undermine the entirely distorted account of the self that results from the subject–object model. Following this strategy, Heidegger claims that the hermeneutic circle characteristic of the activity of textual interpretation is just a special case of what is in fact a much broader phenomenon, namely the necessarily circular structure of all human understanding: the "circle of understanding . . . is the expression of the existential *fore-structure* of Dasein itself" (SZ: 153). It is Dasein itself who "has, ontologically, a circular structure" (ibid.). These claims point to the task that will be accomplished in Division Two of *Being and Time*, namely to show that the circular structure of understanding derives from the temporality of Dasein.

I cannot discuss here all aspects of the genuinely fascinating account of human identity as "thrown projection" that Heidegger develops on the basis of his projective view of interpretation throughout Division Two of *Being and Time*. Instead, I will focus only on the consequences of his view of interpretation for a specific element of his account of human experience, namely our knowledge of the empirical world. This issue is not only interesting in its own right, but it is crucial to evaluate the strength of the hermeneutic paradigm. For, as already mentioned, Heidegger's success in motivating the shift from traditional to hermeneutic philosophy depends on showing that the hermeneutic model can give a better account of the experience that underlies the subject–object model (namely perception and empirical knowledge of entities).

So far, it already seems clear that Heidegger's projective view of interpretation presents a direct challenge to any aspirations of absolute objectivity. If all human understanding is essentially contextual and perspectival, the ideal of an absolute objective truth is illusory not only with regard to textual interpretation but equally so with regard to our scientific understanding of the empirical world. However, this still leaves a further question open. Similar to what we saw with regard to textual interpretation, it remains to be seen whether by discovering the projective element of all understanding we can still make sense of our scientific activity without appealing to the traditional ideal of absolute objectivity.

Cognition as a Mode of Interpretation

The most challenging feature of Heidegger's application of his projective view of inter-pretation to cognition is the transformation of the traditional conception of *a priori* knowledge that follows from it. This transformation lies behind Heidegger's choice of the term "*fore-structure* of understanding" to explicitly mark the *presuppositional* char-acter of all interpretation. As Heidegger announces in ¶32, the traditional conception of this phenomenon in terms of "*a priori* knowledge" is entirely unsatisfactory, for it does not recognize its internal connection with the phenomenon of *projection*. However, he cannot offer his alternative explanation right away, for this requires first developing his general conception of Dasein in terms of "thrown projection." Thus his explana-tion must wait until ¶69 of Division Two.

In this section, Heidegger shows how his projective conception of interpretation applies to the specific case of cognition by analyzing the historical transformation of science from the ancient conception of nature into modern natural science. In his opinion, the key to this transformation lies precisely in a change of "projection" or, as it is called these days, in a paradigm shift. In an astonishing anticipation of Thomas Kuhn's conception of scientific revolutions, Heidegger explains that this shift does not consist merely in the increasing emphasis on observation or experimen-tation, but in the projection of an entirely different understanding of the being of entities, a new world-disclosure brought about through the establishment and defini-tion of new basic concepts by modern scientists such as Galileo and Newton. To the extent that these new concepts organize all possible experience in advance, the ground-ing postulates or axioms of these modern theories through which these concepts are defined are at the same time responsible for the constitution of objects. To this extent, they have the status of synthetic *a priori* knowledge in the traditional sense. However, and here lies the challenge to the traditional conception, this is a feature of any pro-jection whatsoever. For it is just a consequence of a general constraint on meaningful concept use, namely that meaning must determine reference. As we already saw, in order to use concepts meaningfully, the realm of objects to which these concepts apply must be determined in advance. And this determination requires establishing the cri-teria of identity of those objects *in advance* or, as Heidegger puts it, requires a prior pro-jection of their being. Therefore, this is something that any projection of the being of entities does.

This hermeneutic discovery has very challenging consequences for the traditional conception of *a priori* knowledge. Whereas for Kant the special status of *a priori* knowl-edge was due to the (alleged) fact that no human experience would be possible without said knowledge, according to Heidegger the fact that scientific knowledge is based on an understanding of being as ocurrentness (and its corresponding concepts such as motion, force, space, and time), far from guaranteeing its absolute validity, as Kant thought, merely shows the particular fore-sight and fore-conception on which such knowledge is based. The historical and contingent nature of the prior projection that guides any understanding motivates Heidegger's transformation of the traditional into the hermeneutic conception of apriority or, as he calls it, the *perfect tense a priori* (i.e. the "always already") that is anchored in the circle of understanding.

However, the insight into the contextual and relative character of all projections does not lead Heidegger to question their *absolute authority*, as would be expected. To the contrary, in light of his interpretation of the ontological difference, Heidegger accepts Kant's conception of the synthetic *a priori*, but generalizes it to cover any possible factual projection of the being of entities. As a consequence, such projections still have the normative status of synthetic *a priori* knowledge: they are prior to all experience with entities, and cannot be revised on the basis of the experience with those entities. However, this is the case only for those who happen to share such a historically contingent projection. Only the assumption of uniqueness implicit in the traditional ascription of universal validity to *a priori* knowledge is questioned in Heidegger's conception. This leads Heidegger to draw a very different consequence from Kant's transcendental idealism, namely *conceptual pluralism*.

As mentioned at the beginning, Heidegger's hermeneutic philosophy shares with transcendental philosophy its opposition to any kind of metaphysical realism. Throughout *Being and Time* Heidegger argues that it does not make sense to ask how and what entities are in themselves without a prior determination of which specific meaning of "being in itself," that is, what understanding of being, we have in mind. "Real" or "in itself" are specification-dependent terms. One example of this argument in *Being and Time* is Heidegger's claim that a prior understanding of being as availableness provides the basis on which available entities like equipment "can for the first time be discovered as they are 'substantially' 'in themselves'" (SZ: 88; for a more detailed explanation see GA 24: 292–3).

In this context it is important to refer briefly to a possible misunderstanding of Heidegger's claim. Some commentators interpret it as part of an argument claiming to establish an absolute priority of the available over the ocurrent. According to this interpretation, Heidegger's claim that "available" is the way entities such as equipment are "in themselves" would make him a metaphysical realist about the available, so to speak. In light of the ontological difference, though, it seems clear that Heidegger cannot possibly claim to have discovered the way things are "in themselves" *independently of any prior understanding of being*. On the contrary, as the argumentative context makes clear, the sense of his claim is precisely to show that on the basis of our understanding of being as availableness we are perfectly able to discover available things as they are "in themselves." We can distinguish whether a piece of equipment, say a hammer, is a real hammer or not, whether it is a hammer "in itself" or just a fake hammer, precisely because (and to the extent that) we understand in advance the criteria of appropriateness for that kind of available entity. Given that a hammer is for hammering, a hammer made out of dough, say, is not a "real" hammer. Thus the point of his claim is to question the meaningfulness of the attempt to use terms such as "real" or "in itself" in an absolute sense, that is, independently of establishing in advance a criteria of identity or appropriateness that provides a determinate sense to them. For this very reason, Heidegger's claim that "available" is the way of being of equipment in itself does not mean to exclude that these entities are also "ocurrent" (or as he puts it, that we can discover "something ocurrent in what is available"; SZ: 158). Equally so, he never denies that human beings are also "ocurrent" entities. What he does mean to exclude is the *reductionist* view that would claim that such entities are "really" ocurrent entities, physical objects "in themselves," and only available (or existent) in a "subjective" sense. The scientific understanding of being (as ocurrentness) is as contextual and per-spectival as any understanding always is. Within the parameters of its own fore-having, fore-sight and fore-conception it is a perfectly acceptable kind of interpretation. What is unacceptable is its invasive attempt to monopolize the right to define reality in general and human reality in particular. It is in this sense that the projective view of interpre-tation leads to conceptual pluralism, that is, to the claim that there are many equally acceptable interpretations of reality.

From this perspective, Heidegger's projective view of interpretation definitively chal-lenges one element of the traditional ideal of objecitivity, namely the assumption that there is only one true description of the way the world is. However, the anti-reductionism entailed by this claim is not the only challenging consequence of Heidegger's approach. There is another consequence of the projective view of inter-pretation that challenges the ideal of objectivity even within the limits of the scientific knowledge of the empirical world, however narrowly conceived. It is the strong *incom-mensurability thesis* that Heidegger's conception of interpretation contains. This thesis challenges the most basic element of the ideal of scientific objectivity, namely the assumption that it is possible to compare and evaluate different scientific theories with regard to a single standard of objective truth.

Heidegger illustrates the impossibility of a comparison among different scientific projections by appealing to the holistic structure of understanding. Drawing on what these days is called confirmation holism (i.e. the underdetermination of theory choice by evidence) in *What Is a Thing?* he tries to make plausible the immunity from revision based on experience that he ascribes to the basic principles and axioms of scientific the-ories. Heidegger appeals to the example of different explanations for "one and the same fact" within both the Aristotelian and Galilean paradigms, namely the fact that under normal conditions in the earth's field of gravitation, heavy bodies pass through a determinate distance faster than lighter bodies do. He comments: "Both Galileo and his opponents saw the same 'fact.' But they made the same fact or the same happening visible to themselves in different ways, interpreted it in different ways. Indeed, what appeared to them in each case as the authentic *fact and truth* was something *different*" (GA 41: 90). From this incommensurability among different projections Heidegger infers the impossibility of interpreting their historical change as a process of rational revision based on experience. As Heidegger claims in *Basic Questions of Philosophy*: "it is simply pointless to *measure* the Aristotelian doctrine of motion against that of *Galileo* with respect to results, *judging* the former as backward and the latter as advanced. For *in each case, nature means something completely different*" (GA 45: 52–3; emphasis added).

Here Heidegger offers only the outline of an argument. A *factual* difference in meaning becomes a *normative* argument against the legitimacy of the comparison only under the assumption that meaning determines reference (and thus that a difference in meaning implies *ipso facto* a difference in reference). Given the assumption that what "nature" in each case means determines that to which the respective theories refer, it follows that theories with entirely different conceptions of natural entities cannot be about the same entities. But only if they were would it make sense to think of one as a correction of the other. Consequently, a scientific projection cannot be disproved by a different one; at most, it can be put "out of force" by a different stipulation of what and how things are. And conversely, from the point of view of an old projection, the new one cannot be seen as better or worst but simply as meaningless. In *What Is a Thing?* Heidegger explains this claim with the following remark: "[Newton's First Law of Motion] was up until the 17th century not at all self-evident. During the preceding fifteen hundred years it was not only unknown; rather, nature and *entities in general* were *experienced* in a way with respect to which this law *would have been meaningless*" (GA 41: 78–9; emphasis added). For this reason Heidegger claims in *Being and Time* that "before Newton his laws were neither true nor false" (SZ: 227). From this view it follows that there is no absolute truth across incommensurable understandings of being (see Lafont 2000). They are unrevisable from within and inaccessible (meaningless) from without.

In view of these relativist consequences it seems doubtful that Heidegger's conception of interpretation can make sense of our scientific activity as giving us anything like *objective* knowledge of the empirical world. But precisely these consequences open up a further question, namely whether the assumption that meaning determines reference is the trivial constraint on concept use that Heidegger assumes it is. As we already saw, the hermeneutic idealism entailed by the ontological difference is supposed to follow from a seemingly trivial hermeneutic fact, namely that our understanding of what entities are determines what these entities are for us. However, this claim is not as trivial as it seems. For an essential component of our understanding of what entities are is precisely that they may be different from what and how we understand them as being. This fallibilist insight can be anchored in our practices of concept use without denying the interpretative dimension of these practices if it is possible to use designating expressions in a directly referential way, that is, if, contrary to Heidegger's assumption, the meaning of these expressions does not determine their reference.[6] This issue has been the focus of many contemporary debates in the philosophy of language that I cannot discuss here. But whatever the outcome of this debate may be, at the very least it should be clear that Heidegger's claim is far from being trivially correct. This opens up an important question for those interested in hermeneutics, namely to what extent the insights of Heidegger's hermeneutic turn can be defended without commitment to the hermeneutic idealism entailed by his peculiar interpretation of the ontological difference.

Notes

1   Contrary to what is often claimed, in *Being and Time* Heidegger does provide criteria to judge the validity of an interpretation. From the very beginning of the book, Heidegger uses the term "primordial" (*ursprünglich*) to distinguish valid from invalid interpretations, but he only discusses the issue explicitly toward the end of Division Two. There he provides two further terms as *explanans* of the term "primordial", namely "authentically and wholly" (*eigentlich und ganz*) (SZ: 306). In the context of referring to the quality of specific interpretations, Heidegger disqualifies interpretations as "inauthentic" (*uneigentlich*) by using terms such as "unspecific," "undifferentiated," or "narrow." Accordingly, an interpretation of some subject matter is valid if it can account for what is specific about its subject matter and can do so "wholly," that is, without leaving out any important, specific features of that subject matter. These two formal features, *completeness* and *specificity*, are the basis of Heidegger's claim of

superiority for his own interpretation, the existential analytic of Dasein, *vis-à-vis* the tradi-tional interpretation of human identity. I outline his argumentative strategy along these lines in what follows.

2   According to Heidegger, his claim that "entities are in no way accessible without a prior understanding of their being" (GA 25: 38) is the appropriate way of expressing Kant's tran-scendental idealism in terms of the ontological difference. Paraphrasing Kant's highest prin-ciple of synthetic judgments, Heidegger's hermeneutic idealism could be expressed as follows: the conditions of possibility of understanding the being of entities are at the same time the conditions of possibility of the being of those entities.

3   As Heidegger argues, there is no route from the subjective meaning-conferring acts of an iso-lated subject to the constitution of a genuinely intersubjective, public world. See also GA 20: 339.

4   The possibility of understanding everything in advance of having direct experience of it, which is intrinsic to linguistic communication, generates a kind of communication that Heidegger designates with the negative term *Gerede*, idle talk. However, he also insists that the term should not be interpreted in a disparaging sense, for it points to a genuine phe-nomenon. Here the difficulty lies in the fact that Heidegger is using a single term to refer to both phenomena. On the one hand, as he defines the term, "idle talk is the possibility of understanding everything without previously making the thing one's own" (SZ: 169). Here the term refers to a positive phenomenon, namely the fact that linguistic communication is possible despite the differences in experience and expertise among speakers (the division of linguistic labor, in Putnam's words). On the other hand, he uses the term also to refer to a specific kind of communication that this fact makes possible, namely talking about things one does not really know, which is obviously a negative feature of communication that explains Heidegger's need to use a term with negative connotations.

5   There are further and more important methodological reasons for Heidegger's distinction between "language" and "discourse" in *Being and Time* that I cannot get into here. For a detailed account of the difficulties related to Heidegger's account of the distinction in *Being and Time* see Lafont (2000).

6   For a more detailed analysis see Lafont (2000).

References and further reading

Apel, K.-O. (1980) *Towards a Transformation of Philosophy*. London: Routledge & Kegan Paul.

Dreyfus, H. (1980) Holism and hermeneutics. *Review of Metaphysics*, 34, 3–23.

Gadamer, H.-G. (1994) *Truth and Method*. New York: Continuum.

Gadamer, H.-G. (1976) *Philosophical Hermeneutics*. Berkeley: University of California Press.

Gadamer, H.-G. (1994) *Heidegger's Ways*. Albany: State University of New York Press.

Habermas, J. (2003) Hermeneutic and analytic philosophy: two complementary versions of the linguistic turn. In *Truth and Justification*. Cambridge, MA: MIT Press.

Heidegger, M. (1927) Brief an Husserl. *Husserliana*, 9, 600–2.

Heidegger, M. (1988) *Ontologie (Hermeneutik der Faktizität)*. Frankfurt: Klostermann.

Heidegger, M. (1991) *Kant und das Problem der Metaphysik*. Frankfurt: Klostermann.

Heidegger, M. (1995) *Der Begriff der Zeit*. Tübingen: Max Niemeyer.

Hiley, D., Bohman, J. and Shusterman, R. (eds) (1991) *The Interpretive Turn*. Ithaca, NY: Cornell University Press.

Hoy, D. (1993) Heidegger and the hermeneutic turn. In C. Guignon (ed.), *The Cambridge Companion to Heidegger*. Cambridge: Cambridge University Press.

Lafont, C. (1999) *The Linguistic Turn in Hermeneutic Philosophy*. Cambridge, MA: MIT Press.

Lafont, C. (2000) *Heidegger, Language, and World-Disclosure*. Cambridge: Cambridge University Press.

Philipse, H. (1998) *Heidegger's Philosophy of Being*. Princeton, NJ: Princeton University Press.

Ricoeur, P. (1974) *The Conflict of Interpretations: Essays in Hermeneutics*. Evanston, IL: Northwestern University Press.

Taylor, C. (1985a) Self-interpreting animals. In *Human Agency and Language. Philosophical Papers, vol. 1*. Cambridge: Cambridge University Press.

Taylor, C. (1985b) Theories of meaning. In *Human Agency and Language. Philosophical Papers, vol. 1*. Cambridge: Cambridge University Press.

17

Authenticity

TAYLOR CARMAN

"Authentic" (*eigentlich*) is one of Heidegger's favorite words, and it occurs throughout *Being and Time* in both technical and non-technical senses. Informally, and in ordinary speech, the word is emphatic and simply means *really* or *actually*. Thus Heidegger says early on that that which is to be ascertained (*das Erfragte*) in asking the question of being – namely, the *meaning* of being – is "what is really intended" (*das eigentlich Intendierte*) by the question (SZ: 5).

When it functions as a technical term, by contrast, the word plays two very different roles in *Being and Time*, one evaluative and the other not, though regrettably Heidegger conflates the two throughout. On the one hand, the word *eigentlich* is cognate with *eigen*, which means *own, proper, peculiar*. What is *eigentlich*, then, is what is most Dasein's own, what is most proper or peculiar to it. Indeed, one of the archaic senses of the English word "authentic," according to the *Oxford English Dictionary*, is precisely "belonging to himself, own, proper." Thus Chapman's *Iliad* and Milton's *Eikonoklastes* have Nestor and Justice wielding and putting their "authentic" – that is, *their own* – swords here and there, to various purposes. The point was not that the swords were not forgeries, or unreal, but that they were not someone else's. Words like "proper" and "peculiar" similarly refer to what is authentic to something, what is its own, yet carry unmistakable evaluative content, just as "strange" can mean either *other* or *wrong*. One could accordingly translate *Eigentlichkeit* as "ownedness."

Authentic modes of existence, in this strictly formal sense, are those in which Dasein stands in a directly first-person relation to itself, in contrast to the second- and third-person relations in which it stands to others, and which it can adopt with respect to itself, at least up to a point. This sense of authenticity says nothing about what is better or worse for Dasein, but merely marks a distinction between one's immediate relation to oneself and one's mediate relations to others, or to oneself as another. Authenticity consists in our understanding of the ontological structure of the first person, or what Heidegger elsewhere calls Dasein's "mineness" (*Jemeinigkeit*). The distinction between authenticity and inauthenticity, then, has no evaluative content as long as it simply points up the formal distinction between Dasein's ontologically unique relation to itself in contrast to its relations to others, or to itself viewed from an alienated, second- or third-person point of view. So, for example, Heidegger writes:

> We understand ourselves daily, as we can formulate it terminologically, *not authentically* in the strict sense, not constantly in terms of the ownmost and most extreme possibilities of our own existence, but *inauthentically*, our selves indeed, but as we are *not our own*, rather as we have lost ourselves in the everydayness of existing among things and people. "Not authentically" means: not as we *can* at bottom be our own to ourselves. Being lost, however, has no negative, derogatory significance, but means something positive, something belonging to Dasein itself. (GA 24: 228)

In this non-evaluative, merely perspectival or person-relative sense, then, there can only be a twofold distinction: a comportment or understanding is authentic just in case it relates directly to the person whose comportment or understanding it is; it is inauthentic if it relates to another, or to oneself *qua* other. There is no middle alternative.

On the other hand, and notwithstanding Heidegger's frequent protestations to the contrary (SZ: 167, 175–6, 179; GA 20: 378; GA 24: 228), "authenticity" also obviously functions as an evaluative term describing a desirable or choice-worthy mode of existence; it is something *good*. Under this normative aspect, Heidegger distinguishes not two but three possibilities: Dasein's being, he says, is subject to "authenticity or inauthenticity or the modal undifferentiatedness [*Indifferenz*] of the two" (SZ: 232). Modal undifferentiatedness, or indifference, between authenticity and inauthenticity is what Heidegger calls Dasein's "average everydayness," which is again neither good nor bad, but neutral, and which he insists must be the thematic starting point of a hermeneutic phenomenology, or "analytic," of human existence:

> Dasein must not be interpreted at the outset of the analysis in the differentiatedness [*Differenz*] of a particular way of existing, but rather uncovered in the undifferentiated character it has first and for the most part. This undifferentiatedness of Dasein's everydayness is *not nothing*, but rather a positive phenomenal character of this entity. All existing, such as it is, flows from this mode of being, and back into it. We call this everyday undifferentiatedness of Dasein, *averageness*. (SZ: 43)

Average everydayness is the benign daily background out of which Dasein must emerge as intelligible to itself at all, in any particular way. But the value-neutrality of average everydayness is not the same as that of the distinction between authenticity and inauthenticity understood as the difference between my first-person relation to myself and my second- and third-person relations to others, or to myself as another. Everydayness is an indifferent or neutral form of existence not because authenticity and inauthenticity are themselves non-evaluative notions in this context, but simply because in its average everyday mode Dasein is neither especially authentic nor inauthentic, neither "owning up" and gaining a proper sense of itself nor "disowning" itself and losing its proper self-understanding.

Identifying the two ontologically distinct ways in which Dasein can stand in relation to Dasein, to itself and to others, was, I believe, Heidegger's primary purpose in drawing the distinction between authenticity and inauthenticity in *Being and Time*. Yet the evaluative contrast between better and worse ways of existing clearly surfaces in the analysis and pulls it in another direction. This is because conflating the two distinctions, as

Heidegger does, seems to imply that there is something *wrong* with understanding oneself through, by means of, in relation to, in terms of, or *as* another. But this is a bizarre result, for surely being able to regard ourselves from another's point of view, and generally being attuned to how we appear in the eyes of others, is not just a regrettable lapse or loss of proper perspective on ourselves, but is on the contrary an essential aspect of social existence, a fundamental dimension of Dasein's "being-with" (*Mitsein*). It is bizarre to suggest, as *Being and Time* sometimes does, that all intersecting, overlapping, and intermingling of first- and third-person perspectives on ourselves amounts to a "loss of self" (*Selbstverlorenheit*), a kind of "alienation" (*Entfremdung*) (SZ: 116, 178). If we are to make sense of Heidegger's normative account of inauthenticity as a kind of existential disorientation and estrangement, then, we will have to interpret it as something more than the banal fact that Dasein has at its disposal, in addition to its own first-person attunement to and understanding of itself, second- and third-person social perspectives as well.

What, then, is authenticity, normatively construed? The first association to dispel is the apparent affinity between Heidegger's concept and the Romantic discourse of expressive self-realization that goes back to Rousseau, Herder, and Goethe and includes such nineteenth-century figures as Hegel, Marx, and Dilthey. These "expressivist" thinkers, as Isaiah Berlin and Charles Taylor have called them, understand selfhood as an accomplishment standing in contrast to various deficient conditions, such as alienation, isolation, fragmentation, and incoherence. True selfhood, for them, is the achievement of a kind of wholeness or integrity. In this spirit Charles Guignon has argued that, according to Heidegger, "an authentic life is lived as a unified flow characterized by cumulativeness and direction" (Guignon 1993: 229). Indeed, he says, "such a life is lived as a coherent story" (Guignon 1993: 230). And "like a well-crafted story, there is a beginning, a development, and an ending that gives the whole its *point*" (Guignon 2000: 85).

But this gloss misrepresents what Heidegger actually says. Any such ideal of self-realization, self-actualization, or completion must be impossible in principle for an entity like Dasein, whose being Heidegger describes as a continual "thrown projection" (*geworfener Entwurf*), nothing at all like a finished, completed, or even in principle completable thing. This is no minor quibble, or fastidiousness over metaphors, for to reject the ideal posited by the expressivist paradigm as unintelligible, as unrealizable not just as a matter of social or psychological fact but essentially, as Heidegger does, is to abandon the paradigm altogether.

Heidegger's break from the Romantic tradition is admittedly difficult to see, since so much of his own language remains indebted to the expressivist idiom. One might suppose, for example, that the very distinction between authenticity and inauthenticity makes sense only with reference to a normative ideal of integrated selfhood, of integrity understood as *being oneself*, or *being true to oneself*. And, at first glance anyway, Heidegger's account seems to bear this out. In everyday life, he says, "first and for the most part Dasein *is not itself*," and this is possible only because there is "a determinate mode of being of the 'I' itself" that consists precisely in "a loss of self [*Selbstverlorenheit*]" (SZ: 116). Indeed, one of the modes of falling (*Verfallen*) and inauthenticity is precisely "alienation" (*Entfremdung*) (SZ: 178), a word that captures the normative spirit of expressivism perhaps better than any other.

But while Heidegger's negative characterizations of inauthenticity often remain attuned to the Romantic discourse of self-estrangement and subjective disintegration, I think it is easier to see that his positive account of authenticity as "forerunning resoluteness" (*vorlaufende Entschlossenheit*) has little in common with the corresponding ideal of wholeness, completion, or unified subjecthood taken for granted by the expressivist model. On the contrary, according to Heidegger, Dasein cannot coherently aspire to any kind of complete or total understanding of itself in its being. As early as 1920 in his "Comments on Karl Jaspers's *Psychology of Worldviews*," he explicitly denies that human existence can be intelligible to itself as anything like a whole entity, complete and unified. In his account of what he calls "limit situations" (*Grenzsituationen*) – for example, struggle, death, contingency, guilt – Jaspers makes repeated reference to unity, totality, and infinity in his positive characterization of life, which is thus in principle vulnerable to division, opposition, and destruction. Having cited a number of such passages, Heidegger remarks:

> it should be clear enough by now that it is from this "whole" ("unity," "totality"), taken up as a prior conception [*Vorgriff*], that the talk of "destruction," "division," "opposition" derives its meaning. Man stands within antinomies insofar as he sees himself as a "whole," and so has *this* aspect of life in his prior conception, sees himself as essentially fitted into this whole as something final, experiences his *Dasein* as "bounded" by this unbroken "medium." (GA 9: 12)

But this notion of understanding human life "as a whole" is obscure: "What this 'seeing as a whole' and experiencing the antinomies in infinite reflection is supposed to mean, nothing definite about this is worked out" (GA 9: 13). For Jaspers,

> life "is there" as something that is to be had by looking at it, and which, in this mode of having, is attained as the encompassing whole. . . . The whole of life, life *itself*, is something about which we can say nothing directly. Yet it must be intended somehow, since consciousness of existence arises precisely from looking *at it*. (GA 9: 24)

Indeed, even if we had some coherent notion of speculative self-contemplation, there would still be no reason to suppose that "the meaning of the being of what is observed as such must be primarily accessible in observation" (GA 9: 24). Indeed, as Heidegger argues in *Being and Time*, Dasein's understanding of itself differs profoundly from observational attitudes such as perception or intuition. All notions of a purely observational or contemplative access to the ontological structures of human existence must give way to a phenomenology of engaged practical concern:

> the sense of existence is acquired . . . from the basic experience of a *concerned* [*bekümmert*] relation to itself, which is enacted *prior to* any possible . . . objectifying cognition. To the extent that I seek such knowledge, the observational attitude will become decisive, and all my explications will have an objectifying character, but will repel existence and any genuine relation to it (concern). (GA 9: 30)

Not until Division II of *Being and Time* would Heidegger spell out the positive account of authentic selfhood with which he intended to supplant the method and the metaphysics still evidently informing Jaspers's philosophical anthropology. Although *Being and Time* begins with an interpretation of average everydayness, the ultimate aim of the book, even in Division I, was always "to acquire a phenomenal basis for answering the guiding question concerning the being of the totality of the structural whole of Dasein," and moreover "to grasp the totality of the structural whole ontologically" (SZ: 191).

Division II begins, however, with an admission that the hermeneutic of everydayness, precisely because of its phenomenological immersion in the mundane world of quotidian concern, was incapable of providing an account of Dasein's being *as a whole*. This is because Dasein's own everyday understanding of itself always tends toward averageness, superficiality, and obscurity. Any naively credulous phenomenology of mundane existence is thus in imminent danger of inheriting that same partiality and inadequacy from the phenomenal Dasein it interrogates. Heidegger concludes: "*the foregoing existential analysis of Dasein cannot sustain the claim to primordiality*. Present in its fore-having was always only the *inauthentic* being of Dasein, and this as a *nonwhole*" (SZ: 233).

But if, for human beings, there can in principle be no such thing as a synoptic, speculative grasp of existence, how are we to grasp the being of Dasein "as a whole"? Can we even coherently conceive of such a philosophical effort once we have rejected the methodological and metaphysical preconceptions that led Jaspers astray? Heidegger's response to this dilemma is in effect to change the subject in a subtle but profound way by replacing the very idea of human existence understood *as a unified whole* with a concrete phenomenological account of Dasein *owning up wholly –* that is, *wholeheartedly –* to itself in its existence. To own up to oneself in one's existence is to exist authentically. It is Dasein in its differentiated authentic mode, then, that promises to reveal the deep structure of human existence as falling thrown projection.

When Heidegger talks about authentic selfhood, then, he has in mind something radically different from the kind of subjective integrity envisioned by philosophers like Rousseau, Hegel, and Dilthey. Another way of putting this is to say that, for Heidegger, Dasein cannot be understood at all in terms of the ontological category of subjectivity: "subject and object do not coincide with Dasein and the world" (SZ: 60). This, he says, is because

> the ontological concept of the subject characterizes . . . *the selfsameness and constancy of something always already occurrent.* To define the I ontologically as *subject* means treating it as something always already occurrent. The being of the I is understood as the reality of the *res cogitans.* (SZ: 320)

It might seem uncharitable of Heidegger to dismiss the concept of subjectivity as nothing more than a crude reification of human beings as substances. It seems especially unfair to say, as Heidegger does, that despite his critique of Descartes's substantialism, Kant too ultimately "slips back into *the same* inappropriate ontology of the substantial" (SZ: 318–19). What Heidegger has in mind, however, is a narrower and more refined concept of subjectivity, which can plausibly be ascribed not just to Descartes, but to Kant, Fichte, Hegel, perhaps even Nietzsche.

To understand human beings as subjects in this more technical sense is not simply to construe selves as things, but to assimilate the reflexive structure of our self-understanding to the kind of presence a thing has when we encounter it in an attitude of observation. Our relation to ourselves, according to the subjectivist picture, is one of abiding self-presence. I know myself, or more precisely my own mind, by standing in a privileged observational relation to it. Whether or not they posit a substantial self, that is, subjectivists tend to assimilate or collapse my reflexive or first-person relation to myself to the kind of observational or third-person relation in which I stand to others. As it happens, of course, I stand in much closer epistemic proximity to myself, or my own mind, than I do to others, so I know my thoughts better than I know theirs. Still, the only thing unique or special about the first person is precisely the epistemic privilege that comes along with that peculiar contiguity I enjoy in relation to myself. In this way, subjectivity is in effect a kind of superimposition of the reflexive first-person standpoint and the observational third-person standpoint, an arguably incoherent hybrid.

Heidegger's hostility to the concept of subjectivity in *Being and Time*, then, is not any kind of prejudice directed against phenomena falling outside the orbit of objectivity, but rather a critique of all theoretical attempts to level the structural differences between our first-person understanding of ourselves, which is to say our *own* self-understanding, and the third-person understanding we have of others. Heidegger's concept of authenticity, or "ownedness," is above all a conception of the first-person perspective I have on myself and its irreducibility to any third-person point of view, no matter how descriptively thorough or accurate it may be.

One crucial way in which that structural difference manifests itself is in our understanding of death. The kind of narrative completion that Guignon describes, in which "there is a beginning, a development, and an ending that gives the whole its *point*," is manifestly *not* the sort of completion I am ever in a position to apprehend in my own life, precisely because my own death is the death I don't live to appreciate as the conclusion or *dénouement* of my life. Death understood from that third-person point of view, the death of another, is what Heidegger calls "demise" (*Ableben*), or what one might call death in the *biographical* sense. My own death, death understood from the point of view of the person whose death it is, is "dying" (*Sterben*) proper, or death in the *existential* sense.

But dying in this existential sense turns out not to be the process immediately preceding my demise as a person, but rather "the *mode of being* in which Dasein *is toward* its death" (SZ: 247). And that mode of being turns out to be the mode of being I *always* have *qua* Dasein, that is, as constant thrown projection into my future possibilities. It is true that I die, just like everyone else. There is nothing special about my case, viewed indifferently alongside others, from a third-person point of view. Yet my death, like my body, remains fundamentally different for me precisely by standing in this unique relation to me, its owner. What I understand when I understand my own death under this aspect, as when I understand my own body by *having* it, is what that third-person perspective will never reveal in any objective description of me, no matter how correct and complete.

What Heidegger's existential phenomenology of death discloses, then, is the first-person dimension of death insofar as the death is my own, the death into which I constantly project myself, without ever being able to step out of it, live through it, and stand over against it as I do the deaths of others. "In dying," Heidegger says, "what is revealed is that death is ontologically constituted by mineness" (SZ: 240). Moreover, he adds, echoing Saint Augustine, death in this sense, this death which is essentially mine, is a death I am constantly dying just in virtue of existing finitely, that is, by projecting inevitably into the inherent fragility and vulnerability of my world and my identity, by embracing, either willingly or unwillingly, their subtle but essential tendency to drift, decay, and eventually collapse under their own weight. For Heidegger, "Dasein is facti-cally dying as long as it exists" (SZ: 251).

What then is authenticity? Heidegger's account comprises two seemingly distinct elements. The first is what he calls "resoluteness" (*Entschlossenheit*), a notion inspired by but not identical with Aristotle's account of *phronêsis* in Book VI of the *Nicomachean Ethics* (see GA 19: 48–57). The word *Entschlossenheit* means decisiveness or resolve, but it also literally means unclosing, or disclosing, which is to say remaining open. For Heidegger, that is, resoluteness means openly facing up to the unique concrete "situa-tion" (*Situation*) in which one finds oneself, in contrast to assimilating it to some pre-conceived "general state of affairs" (*allgemeine Lage*) (SZ: 300). Like the *phronimos* who can simply *see* the right ethical moves to make, without subsuming them under general rules, resolute Dasein has a subtle feel for the particular demands of the situation and how to deal with them with intelligence and finesse. Resoluteness thus consists in a kind of focused engagement with things, and with others.

Admittedly, Heidegger's description of resoluteness does not always sound particu-larly Aristotelian, since he ties it to his own somewhat idiosyncratic notion of "guilt" (*Schuld*). "Resoluteness means letting oneself be called forth to one's ownmost (*eigen-ste*) *being*-guilty" (SZ: 305). What is existential guilt? Heidegger's definition might seem hopelessly abstract. Guilt, he says, is "being-the-ground of a [mode of] being defined by a not – that is, *being-the-ground of a nullity*" (SZ: 283). What is it to be the "ground" (*Grund*) of a *not*, or "nullity"? *Grund* here is probably better translated "reason": to be the ground of a nullity is to be the *reason* I am not what I am not. This is not to say that I am to *blame*, but simply that it is *because of me*. Owning up to my guilt is therefore something like recognizing myself as a locus of accountability, which serves as a kind of transcendental condition for regarding myself as literally indebted or solvent, guilty or innocent. I am able to understand myself as guilty or indebted in the ordinary sense of those words only because I understand myself as guilty in the existential or tran-scendental sense.

The second component of authenticity is what Heidegger calls "forerunning" (*Vorlaufen*). Whereas resoluteness carries echoes of Aristotle, forerunning is reminis-cent of Kierkegaard. It is roughly, but only roughly, akin to the famous leap of faith wherein I take up my personal commitments as irreducibly my own, even though they may be irreconcilable or incommensurable with ethical norms applying to everyone, including me. More specifically, for Heidegger, forerunning means "forerunning into death" (SZ: 263), "death" in the existential sense, which is to say the inherent insta-bility of my world and my identity. Forerunning into death, then, means being ready, willing, and able to embrace a particular and essentially fragile set of possibilities, even as they tend to dissolve by their own inertia.

Heidegger's full concept of authenticity as "forerunning resoluteness" (*vorlaufende Entschlossenheit*) (SZ: 302), then, is a kind of hybrid of Aristotelian *phronêsis* and

291

Kierkegaardian faith. Indeed, in the third chapter of Division II of *Being and Time* Heidegger pauses to wonder whether forerunning and resoluteness really have anything to do with each other: "How are these two phenomena to be brought together?" he asks. "What can death and the 'concrete situation' of action have in common?" Perhaps "forcing together resoluteness and forerunning" has yielded an altogether "unphenomenological construction" (SZ: 302). What the two notions have in common, though, is precisely their emphasis on finitude and particularity. Attending to the fine-grained details of the concrete situation and wholeheartedly embracing the inherent inertia and dissolution of possibilities both require that I hold fast to my first-person self-understanding and resist letting it be assimilated into any generic or impersonal conception of people like me in situations like this.

It may appear, then, that although Heidegger has helped to free us from an incoherent concept of subjectivity, much as Wittgenstein did, though by very different means, he nevertheless leaves us without a coherent account of persons. Both Wittgenstein and Heidegger expose traditional accounts of subjectivity as bogus conflations of the first- and third-person points of view, based on the conceit that what I know about myself I know by having a privileged observational relation to the contents of my own mind. The concept of subjectivity, that is, seemed to promise a perfectly harmonized unity of perspectives, so that we could in principle move smoothly and transparently from the one to the other: what I am in a unique position to know of myself I can assert as a fact about my inner experience. But that supposedly seamless unity turns out to be fraught with anomalies, not just epistemically, but especially, as Richard Moran has recently argued, in practical and moral-psychological contexts. It is an epistemological conundrum how or whether I can be said to *know that I am in pain*, or why I cannot say I *falsely believe that p*. It is arguably a more pressing and mundane problem whether I can accept or assert third-person descriptions of myself without in effect relinquishing the commitments that made those descriptions true in the first place. If I act shamefully, and then feel ashamed, I cannot then – as another can – admire my own moral sensitivity, since doing so taints the original feeling of shame and robs it of whatever sincerity might have made it worthy of admiration in the first place.

The problem with slipping into an estranged, third-person, merely observational attitude about oneself, then, is that doing so often involves a slackening of the commitments constitutive of the first-person position one is attempting to observe. This is roughly what Heidegger finds so insidious in the peculiarly alienated standpoint of what he calls "*the one*" (*das Man*), by which he means our ordinary generic conception of ourselves and others as normal or typical agents: one does this, one does that, and you and I do this and that because, well, that is what one does. It is also what Sartre thinks is incoherent in the café waiter's attitude in the famous example in *Being and Nothingness*. The waiter wants to fit into his professional role with no remainder, like a hand in a glove. But doing so means alienating himself from, even disavowing, the first-person commitments that have made it the case that he is a waiter in the first place. Sartre's other example of the woman letting herself be seduced, but pretending that all her options remain indefinitely open, has no close analogue in Heidegger's account, except insofar as the woman is refusing to embrace her own existential death by making a hard choice, one way or the other, and living with it. There is a difference between their accounts because Sartre emphasizes, as Heidegger does not, that I am all the while identical with the third-person aspect or "profile" of myself that is available to others, but only imperfectly, if at all, to myself.

A common, but I think erroneous, reading of *Being and Time* supposes that understanding ourselves in terms of *the one* is nothing more than a deplorable error, craven conformism, a mere distortion of social life. Admittedly, Heidegger often draws a crude distinction between the dominion of *the one* and authentic selfhood: "the self of everyday Dasein is the *one-self*, which we distinguish from the *authentic self*, that is, the self grasped as its own (*eigens ergriffen*). As the one-self, the particular Dasein is *dispersed* into the one and must first find itself" (SZ: 129). Being "lost" in *the one* and not being able to find oneself and grasp one's self as one's own sounds like inauthenticity, and indeed it sounds like something bad. But in fact, as we have seen, in normative contexts Heidegger draws not a twofold but a threefold distinction between authenticity, inauthenticity, and an "undifferentiated" average everydayness. Moreover, average norms of intelligibility constitute the very *being* of entities in our everyday world: "the one-self, for the sake of which Dasein is from day to day, articulates [*artikuliert*] the referential context of significance" (SZ: 129). So too, the fact that "I am 'given' to my 'self' in the first instance in terms of, and as, the one" (SZ: 129), as Heidegger says, does not mean that I am generally corrupt and pathetic in my conformity to the arbitrary demands of custom, but that my sense of self is positively governed by norms defining what makes sense in the particular social world I inhabit. Nor does authenticity consist in simply casting off the shackles of convention altogether, but in taking up a new and different relation to *the one*, which continues to define what will count as normal, proper, and intelligible in this milieu: "*Authentic being-oneself* does not rest on some exceptional condition of the subject, detached from *the one*, rather *it is an existentiel modification of the one as an essential existential*" (SZ: 130).

But alas, even having identified the modally indifferent background of everydayness as something distinct from both authenticity and inauthenticity, Heidegger himself goes on to blur the distinction between indifference and inauthenticity by seeming to dismiss the analysis in the first half of *Being and Time* as not entirely invalidated, but compromised at the outset by its attention to a merely inauthentic mode of existence: "One thing has become unmistakable," he writes at the beginning of Division II, "*the preceding existential analysis of Dasein cannot lay claim to primordiality*." For what it had in view was "only ever the *inauthentic* being of Dasein" (SZ: 233).

It may seem, then, that Heidegger has left us with a rather Manichaean dichotomy between authenticity as forerunning resoluteness in the face of one's finitude and the pervasive banality, anonymity, and inauthenticity of ordinary social life, which is marked by an immersion and dispersal in *the one* and a loss of self. It looks, that is, as if the authentic first-person point of view stands in dramatic contrast to a washed-out impersonal generic self-conception that recognizes no distinction between myself and others, but instead regards me as merely one more among them. Heidegger can paint this strangely impoverished picture of social life only because he has rejected the concept of subjectivity, which, as we have seen, makes false promises concerning the unity and harmony of the first- and third-person points of view. Once we rid ourselves of that illegitimate hybrid, we seem to be left with an account of two incommensurable standpoints, and now the problem lies in seeing how they can be meaningfully interconnected in such a way as to constitute our ordinary concept of a person, which must somehow underwrite and make sense of the very idea of different standpoints converging on one and the same thing, namely *me*. Does Heidegger shed any light on how our ordinary concept of persons ever manages to be intelligible to us in the first place? Or does he in effect propose that we dispense with any such generic notion in favor of a purely first-person point of view, perhaps in tragic conflict with its depraved counterpart, namely myself in the mode of *the one*?

A similar *aporia* emerges in both Wittgenstein and Sartre. Wittgenstein had deep insight into the asymmetry between first- and third-person discourse, so profound in fact that he arguably found himself unable to offer any plausible account of how our concept of the self hangs together as a single concept at all, instead of simply falling apart into avowals or expressive utterances on the one hand, and psychological descriptions of experiences on the other. Wittgenstein occasionally acknowledges the essential interconnectedness of subjective and objective uses of the first person pronoun, but he never develops it into a robust conception of the self. He writes, for example, "The word 'I' does not mean the same as 'L.W.' even if I am L.W. . . . But that doesn't mean: that 'L.W.' and 'I' mean different things" (Wittgenstein 1958: 67). Similarly, he says, characteristically interrupting his own line of thought, "But it is still false to say . . . I is a different person from L.W." (Wittgenstein 1992: 88).

Sartre insists on a comparable asymmetry in his distinction between the self as "transcendence" and the self as "facticity," that is, as freely and consciously directed *toward* the world and as an object *in* the world. Our dual status as both subjects and objects leads Sartre to notorious, disconcertingly paradoxical formulations such as "the being of the *for-itself* [consciousness] is defined . . . as being what it is not and not being what it is," and "We must construe human reality as a being that is what it is not and is not what it is" (Sartre 1943/2003: 32/21, 94/81). Somewhat more plausibly, he points out the essential elusiveness of the phenomenon of *character* from the first-person point of view: "character has distinct existence only in the capacity of an object of knowledge for others. Consciousness does not know its own character – unless in determining itself reflectively from the standpoint of another's point of view" (Sartre 1943/2003: 398/372). My own character remains hidden from me when my consciousness is, as it must be, directed toward the world. And even when I try to turn around and, as it were, see my own profile, it necessarily escapes my gaze. My self, mediated by the consciousness of others, Sartre says, "is like a shadow projected on a moving and unpredictable material" (Sartre 1943/2003: 308/285–6). If this is right, then the only kind of knowledge I can have of my own character must be an estranged knowledge, a knowledge I necessarily borrow from an alien standpoint that I can never fully inhabit.

Does Heidegger leave us with the same sort of bifurcated conception of the self in *Being and Time*? Having dispensed with the concept of subjectivity, Heidegger seems to have made no real progress toward a coherent account of the self. Yet he had at his disposal a richer notion of average everyday self-understanding than the bifurcated conception suggests. This is because his concept of *the one* is not the concept of a wholly alienated view of oneself as another, or as just anybody. It cannot be that notion, for it is absurd to suppose that we go about our daily business with that extreme degree of self-estrangement. I do not ordinarily have anything like an observer's point of view on myself, nor do I typically *predict* what I will do from a third-person standpoint, as opposed to *undertaking* to do it in the first person. Only in highly artificial or even patho-logical contexts am I so alienated from my own behavior that it strikes me as merely numerically distinct from the behavior of another person.

What Heidegger says is that my ordinary self-conception is "modally undiffer-entiated," or indifferent, with respect to authenticity and inauthenticity. It is temp-ting, and Heidegger himself may well have been tempted, to conflate this with the idea that my ordinary self-conception is undifferentiated in the sense that it makes no distinction between myself and others, but paints us all indifferently as "one," or "anyone." This is at least consistent with the way in which, in the mode of *the one*, I unthinkingly conform by aligning my behavior with the behavior of others. But alignment and conformity are not the same as alienation. Ordinary understanding, even in its most egregiously conformist guise, involves subtle and sophisticated forms of competence in steering between first- and third-person points of view on our-selves, in shifting back and forth and substituting one perspective for the other. It cannot be Heidegger's claim that in daily life we routinely lose all sense of our own agency and regard ourselves as if from behind a glass partition, mere spectators of our own actions.

The modal indifference of *the one* must instead be understood as an undifferentiated conglomeration of first-, second-, and third-person points of view, which are in fact dis-tinct, but which are ordinarily fused together in an unprincipled and even partly inco-herent way *as if* constituting a single unified concept of the self. The perspectival complexity of our self-understanding, replete with all the asymmetries, liabilities, and instabilities that Sartre and Moran describe so vividly, is an irreducible fact of ordinary social life. We routinely gloss over those discontinuities as if they were unreal, just as we look past the blind spots in our visual fields and shift our weight from one foot to another, scarcely or not at all noticing the irregularities we are constantly coping with. Thus we learn not to voice every childish thought or feeling that occurs to us because we know how such talk looks and sounds from another's point of view. Dealing with other people is not contingently but essentially difficult business, fraught with conflict and uncertainty, precisely because it demands constant negotiation and compromise among perspectives that fail to fit together seamlessly, but are instead defined by incom-mensurability and asymmetry. Here too, we might say, civilization is founded on an act of violence – in this case the mundane violence involved in fitting my own self-understanding into the, as it were, "one-size-fits-all" concept of personhood.

It would be a mistake, however, to conclude that everyday common sense is just crudely inadequate in its failure to discern the essential structural instability that results from the fissures running between our first- and third-person perspectives on ourselves. Common sense is crude, but its crudeness is also a positive blessing since it facilitates the primitive understanding of personhood that underwrites our grasp of those perspectives as perspectives on one and the same thing, namely ourselves. Our average everyday interpretation of persons in the mode of *the one*, which comprises and indeed blurs together our understanding of the first and third persons, is not just a crass confusion, but the positive condition of the skill with which we subsequently negotiate social life, whether authentically or inauthentically. Being as underarticulated and con-ceptually out of focus as it is, our mundane understanding of ourselves as *the one* may amount to a confusion, but if so, it is the kind of confusion to which we owe whatever self-understanding we can have, just as the crudeness and impoverishment of our peripheral vision allows us to look straight ahead and see what we are looking at as clearly as we do.

References and further reading

Berlin, I. (1998) *The Proper Study of Mankind: An Anthology of Essays* (ed. H. Hardy and R. Hausheer). New York: Farrar, Straus & Giroux.

Dreyfus, H. L. (1991) *Being-in-the-World: A Commentary on Heidegger's "Being and Time," Division I.* Cambridge, MA: MIT Press.

Guignon, C. (1993) Authenticity, moral values, and psychotherapy. In C. Guignon (ed.), *The Cambridge Companion to Heidegger.* Cambridge: Cambridge University Press.

Guignon, C. (2000) Philosophy and authenticity: Heidegger's search for a ground for philosophizing. In M. Wrathall and J. Malpas (eds.), *Heidegger, Authenticity, and Modernity: Essays in Honor of Hubert L. Dreyfus, Volume 1.* Cambridge, MA: MIT Press.

Moran, R. (2001) *Authority and Estrangement: An Essay on Self-Knowledge.* Princeton, NJ: Princeton University Press.

Sartre, J.-P. (1943/2003) *L'Être et le néant: Essai d'ontologie phénoménologique.* Paris: Gallimard. (*Being and Nothingness: A Essay on Phenomenological Ontology* (trans. H. E. Barnes), rev. edn. London and New York: Routledge.)

Sluga H. (1996) "Whose house is that?" Wittgenstein on the self. In H. Sluga and D. G. Stern (eds.), *The Cambridge Companion to Wittgenstein.* Cambridge: Cambridge University Press.

Taylor, C. (1989) *Sources of the Self: The Making of the Modern Identity.* Cambridge, MA: Harvard University Press.

Wittgenstein, L. (1958) *The Blue and Brown Books.* New York: Harper & Row.

Wittgenstein, L. (1992) *Last Writings on the Philosophy of Psychology, volume II* (ed. G. H. von Wright and H. Nyman). Oxford: Blackwell.

18

Human Mortality: Heidegger on How to Portray the Impossible Possibility of Dasein

STEPHEN MULHALL

The Existential Analytic: Terminable or Interminable?

Any reader of *Being and Time* might be forgiven for thinking that Heidegger's existential analytic of Dasein had reached a satisfying conclusion by the end of Division I. His initial introduction of "Dasein" as the being who questions, and hence as the being for whom being is an issue, quickly leads to the claim that Dasein's being is being-in-the-world. To be sure, the subsequent analysis of being-in-the-world in Division I proceeds by isolating and clarifying specific elements of Dasein's worldly mode of being one after the other (first the world, then being-with and being-one's-self, then being-in), and hence can easily give the impression of merely accumulating local insights into Dasein's being without ever bringing or holding them together, so that we might perspicuously survey the whole they constitute. But chapter 6 is explicitly presented as designed to overcome that lack of a unifying perspective. For there Heidegger tells us that there is a specific state-of-mind through which Dasein discloses itself to itself in a simplified way; and its very simplicity is what allows it to give Dasein access to itself as a structural totality. This is the phenomenon of anxiety (angst, dread), a distinctively objectless state-of-mind; and what it reveals is that the being of Dasein means being-ahead-of-itself in being-already-in-(the-world) as being-alongside (entities encountered within-the-world). In short, it tells us that the being of Dasein is care.

It quickly becomes plain, however, that Heidegger is not at all satisfied with this supposedly unifying conclusion; on the contrary, he finds that the perspective it delivers contains the seeds of its own supersession. One might say that, once introduced into his analysis, the concept of angst can no more be anchored to its specific initial role than its existential counterpart can be anchored to its apparent object of concern. In effect, Heidegger finds himself thrown into a state of anxiety about the whole of his analysis in Division I.

To begin with, what anxiety reveals about us is not just our elemental unity, but also the fact that proximally and for the most part we live out our lives in inauthentic ways; we relate to ourselves and Others as "das man," caught up and dispersed or dissociated from ourselves in the realm of idle talk, curiosity, and ambiguity. And this should remind us of Heidegger's warning at the outset of Division I that his phenomenological focus throughout that stretch of the book would be *average* everydayness – that mode of Dasein's existence in which it loses itself, and from which authentic everydayness must be achieved. But how can an analysis which has hitherto focused exclusively on Dasein in its inauthentic modes of being lay claim to having provided a complete or total portrait of that being for whom authentic existence is also a possibility?

Furthermore, one aspect of the structural totality of care itself all but declares that any analysis of Dasein that terminates at this point is not only averting its eyes from its own incompleteness, but also passing over an aspect of Dasein's being that seems to resist the very idea of completeness. For when Heidegger tells us that the care-structure includes Dasein's being-ahead-of-itself, he alludes to what he elsewhere calls Dasein's existentiality – the fact that it projects itself upon existential possibilities, that its existence is a matter of its being endlessly delivered over to the task of actualizing some particular possibility-of-its-being. But this means that, for as long as Dasein exists, it can never achieve wholeness; it will always be ahead of itself, essentially related to a possibility, to something that it is not yet. As Heidegger puts it, Dasein's mode of being is such that something is always left outstanding, or say incomplete; but if Dasein cannot bring its own existence into view as a whole, then how could it produce an existential analytic of its own kind of being that might bring it into view as a whole?

Yet it is plain that Dasein does have an end, and hence is brought to a certain kind of completion or totality – and one that ultimately cannot be separated from the very feature of its being that appears to threaten its possible completeness. More specifically, in being-ahead-of-itself, Dasein does not simply or solely relate to itself as standing out into the future, and hence as incapable of or beyond completion; it also understands itself as relating to – as standing out toward – its own future completion, toward a point at which there will be nothing of itself outstanding. But this endpoint, the point at which Dasein's span of existence completes itself, is also the point of its own non-existence, its "no-longer-being-there" – its death. In other words, human beings relate to themselves as subject to death; it constitutes an ineliminable aspect of their self-understanding, and hence of their understanding of themselves as being ahead-of-themselves. This means that a certain conception of wholeness or completion is inextricably involved in Dasein's conception of its existence as ahead-of-itself.

This is why Heidegger continues to talk of the projective aspect of Dasein's being as indicating its lack of wholeness or essential incompleteness, rather than the distinctive kind of wholeness or completeness that its nature allows. To avoid any apparently paradoxical entanglement of the notion of having-an-end with that of lacking-an-end in his existential analytic of Dasein would be to falsify an inherently paradoxical aspect of Dasein's relationship to its own existence; and since he has already argued that Dasein's relationship to its own being is constitutive of that being, it would also amount to falsifying an inherently paradoxical aspect of that existence itself. His task is rather to achieve a authentically ontological (or rather, existential) understanding of this structural paradox.

This brings us to the second sense in which Heidegger confronts a structural difficulty here. For his existential analytic of Dasein is supposed to result from an application of the phenomenological method in philosophy, which means that it is meant to achieve results by allowing the phenomena to disclose themselves to us as they are in themselves, and in the manner that befits their nature. In other words, his account of

Dasein's being exemplifies the fundamental capacity that his account attributes to Dasein – the capacity to encounter phenomena comprehendingly. But if a complete account of Dasein's being must include an account of its end, and its relation to that end, then this aspect of Dasein's mode of existence at least appears to present a constitutive resistance to Heidegger's philosophical method. For when Dasein reaches its end, when it is no longer essentially related to what is not yet, and hence no longer essentially incomplete, it is also no longer there. Death is not something that any Dasein has or could directly experience; it is not an event in any Dasein's life, not even the last such event. But how then can there be any phenomenological understanding of death? How can a philosophical method which draws exclusively upon Dasein's capacity to allow any and every phenomenon to appear to it as it really is provide any mode of access to a phenomenon that is essentially incapable of appearing to, of being experienced or grasped comprehendingly by, any Dasein?

It is worth noting that the two kinds of difficulty that death poses for Heidegger are in fact best viewed as two internally related difficulties, or perhaps as two aspects of the same difficulty. For in his introduction to *Being and Time*, Heidegger declares that "the roots of the existential analytic . . . are ultimately *existentiell*, that is, *ontical*. Only if the inquiry of philosophical research is itself seized upon in an existentiell manner as a possibility of the being of each existing Dasein, does it become at all possible to disclose the existentiality of existence and to undertake an adequately founded ontological problematic" (SZ 13–14). Philosophical inquiry is one possible mode of being of the being who questions; and that being is one for whom its sense of itself as at once lacking and having an end, an end that is always already yet to come and always already settled, is both constitutive and apparently resistant to understanding. Hence a philosophical inquiry into death could hardly be expected to transcend this constitutive resistance; on the contrary, it is rather more likely that it will be forced to confront in its own terms the very same internal tensions and constitutive difficulties with respect to Dasein's end that characterize any existentiell mode of any Dasein's being. And just as death therefore presents any Dasein with a particularly stark intellectual and existential challenge – that of making sense of itself as a being who must choose whether and if so how to live out its projective existence in the face of its unavoidable death – so it challenges the philosopher in general, and Heidegger in particular, to make his phenomenological encounter with death philosophically fruitful without fleeing from or otherwise falsifying its object. In both cases, or from both perspectives, the achievement of a certain kind of authenticity, and hence the risk of its loss, are at stake.

Death's Representatives: Some Dead Ends

I propose to orient my reading of Heidegger's way of taking up this twofold challenge by relating it to a passage from J. M. Coetzee's recent Tanner Lectures, *The Lives of Animals* (1999). In those lectures, Coetzee tells of a lecture given by a novelist and animal rights activist named Elizabeth Costello, who offers the following remarks as part of her response to some of the things said by philosophers about the relation between human and non-human animals:

> For instants at a time . . . I know what it is like to be a corpse. The knowledge repels me. It fills me with terror; I shy away from it, refuse to entertain it.
>
> All of us have such moments, particularly as we grow older. The knowledge we have is not abstract – "All human beings are mortal, I am a human being, therefore I am mortal" – but embodied. For a moment we *are* that knowledge. We live the impossible: we live beyond our death, look back on it, yet look back as only a dead self can.
>
> When I know, with this knowledge, that I am going to die, what is it . . . that I know? Do I know what it is like for me to be a corpse or do I know what it is like for a corpse to be a corpse? The distinction seems to me trivial. What I know is what a corpse cannot know: that it is extinct, that it knows nothing and will never know anything anymore. For an instant, before the whole structure of knowledge collapses in panic, I am alive inside that contradiction, dead and alive at the same time. (Coetzee 1999: 32)

Without elaborating upon the full complex field of interaction between Coetzee's and Heidegger's thought here, I want at least to note Elizabeth Costello's conception of death as not so much beyond our comprehension because contradictory, but rather comprehensible only as a contradiction or an impossibility. For her, death is a phenomenon that reveals itself to us not insofar as we overcome its capacity to repel us, but only through our capacity to acknowledge it as repellent, as pushing us away – to regard its repulsiveness as our mode of access to it. We can begin to appreciate how this presentation of death might provide a mode of access to Heidegger's struggle with it if I point out that the first half of the first chapter of Division II might fruitfully be read as a philosophical enactment of the way in which death at once invites and resists Dasein's comprehending grasp – or more precisely, invites us precisely through the distinctive ways it resists us. For there, Heidegger tries out a variety of ways in which one might imagine that phenomenological access to Dasein's end, and hence Dasein's wholeness, might be achieved, only to find that they turn out to be dead ends; but it is only his encounter with those dead ends that gives him the clues he needs to reorient his analysis more fruitfully.

The most obvious strategy for gaining access to death that Heidegger contemplates is to make use of the already-established fact that Dasein's being is being-with-Others; for if we cannot directly grasp our own death, can we not experience as intimately and directly as possible the dying and death of other Dasein? Heidegger admits that when we encounter a corpse, we do not encounter a present-at-hand corporeal Thing; we encounter something unalive, something that has lost its life, a being who is no-longer-in-the-world (and who hence manifests a mode of being that is possible only for a being whose being is being-in-the-world). He further acknowledges that deceased people can be an object of respectful solicitude to those who remain, through funeral rites, interment and the cult of graves. In the terms available to those left behind, we can say that the dead person is still with them, with them as someone lost to them; but the loss suffered by those who remain gives us no mode of access to the loss (the loss-of-being as such) suffered by the dying or dead person. Her death, understood as a possibility-of-being that belongs to her own being – death as the end of her life – remains opaque to us.

Heidegger in fact thinks that our tendency to think that being-with-Others in their dying and death might allow death to be phenomenologically representable is an expression of a more pervasive tendency on our part to think that one Dasein might represent (go proxy for, substitute or otherwise stand in for) another. To be sure, one Dasein can vote for another Dasein, or take her place with respect to some specific task or object of concern, or even die in another's place (say by placing oneself in the way of harm that would otherwise be inflicted on another); but no one can take another's dying away from her. Death is not, is never, *the* end; it is my end or yours, or hers. Death, in other words, is in every case "mine," the death of some particular Dasein, the being to whom mineness belongs. Hence, if dying is constitutive of Dasein's totality or wholeness, it must be conceived as an existential phenomenon of a Dasein which is in each case one's own. In other words, the kind of wholeness that Dasein can manifest (or fail to) in its relation to its end is the wholeness of the kind of being to whom mineness belongs; it is not an essentially impersonal or abstract phenomenon, and any attempt to represent it must acknowledge this unrepresentability.

So Heidegger tries again to find a viable mode of access to death, by asking how the notions of "end" and "totality" might be best understood in the specific case of beings with the being of Dasein. He canvasses a number of different inflections of these notions, by asking whether Dasein's relation to its end might be figuratively represented by the rather more clearly understood relationship of other entities to their end – in effect, by asking whether a sum of money, a moon, a piece of fruit, a rainshower, a road, a loaf of bread, or even a portrait might portray or otherwise go proxy for Dasein in this respect. Of course, some proxies look like better candidates than others. A piece of unripe fruit certainly stands in a certain kind of not-yet relation to its ripened state; but then that ripened state constitutes its fulfillment, whereas Dasein's end is not only not intrinsically its fulfillment but may also constitute its lack of fulfillment, even its utter degradation. A newly built road can be unfinished, but then the kind of way in which it breaks off is not that exhibited by a Dasein whose existence breaks off while still 'under construction'; but then, neither does a Dasein whose existence ends in fulfillment (say, with goals achieved, with a "happy" death) exhibit "finishedness" in the way that a portrait may be finished by the last stroke of the painter's brush (or indeed, by the application of varnish). But these specific obstacles to representing death figuratively or by analogy indicate a more fundamental obstacle. No present-at-hand or ready-to-hand object's particular relationship to its end can stand in for Dasein's particular relationship to its end because none manifests the kind of being as such that belongs to Dasein.

The moral is clear: if we are to find a way through this impasse, we must begin from our best available understanding of Dasein's distinctive kind of being as such, or in general. And this implies a further constraint on the resources available to us: we can no more help ourselves to the deliverances of ontic sciences at this point in our ontological inquiries than we can at any point. Heidegger argued extensively in the opening chapter of Division I that fundamental ontology in general, and the existential analytic of Dasein in particular, must be sharply distinguished from the businesses of anthropology, psychology, biology, and theology, and he reiterates his objections in the opening chapter of Division II. To begin with, the results of any ontic science will presuppose a regional ontology that it is necessarily incapable of validating, but which no fundamental ontology can take for granted. But more importantly, the prevailing division of cultural labor between psychology, biology, and anthropology also presupposes a particular conception of the human being that is their common preoccupation; it assumes that the human mind, body, and spirit can be studied in isolation from each other, and hence that the human being is a composite construction from these isolatable elements.

Theology plays a double role in this cultural economy for Heidegger. On the one hand, it can be seen as another ontic science, having to do with the human soul understood in relation to the divine; on the other hand, it also functions as the ontotheological horizon within which this compositional picture of the human being emerged, and through which human conceptions of ourselves as transcendent and comprehending are inflected by their rootedness in a conception of ourselves as made in God's image. Heidegger's aim is to put these horizons of our traditional self-understanding in question, without presuming to think that ontological inquiry can second-guess, displace, or otherwise go proxy for ontic investigations within their legitimate domains.[1]

In this specific context, Heidegger's concerns about biology, or the domain of the life sciences more broadly understood, are particularly sharp; after all, he reminds us, death is a phenomenon of life, and hence it might be thought particularly hard to justify avoiding any reference to the deliverances of scientific studies of animal and plant life in his attempts to understand Dasein's relation to its death. Heidegger responds by introducing a tripartite terminological distinction that has attracted rather more criticism than it has succeeded in averting. He tells us that, while we can refer to the end of anything living as its perishing, and although Dasein "has" its death, of the kind appropriate to anything that lives, it cannot be said, *qua* Dasein, to perish. Rather, it either dies authentically, or it suffers "demise" (which occurs when Dasein ends "without authentically dying" (SZ: 291) – without, that is, realizing that way of being in which it "is" toward its death, of which more later).

It is undeniable that there is a certain instability in Heidegger's talk of "demise," and hence also in his talk of "dying," "perishing," and "life." For example, if demise is the inauthentic mode of dying – if as Heidegger himself puts it, "Dasein can demise only so long as it is dying" (SZ: 247) – why then go on to call it an "intermediate phenomenon" (intermediate between dying authentically and perishing)? And even if Dasein can be understood purely as life (although it is presumably not then being thematized *qua* Dasein), why must that mode of understanding involve what Heidegger calls a "privative" relation to Dasein – which implies that "life" is best understood as the being of Dasein minus something, and hence that the being of Dasein is best understood as life plus something, thereby appearing to reintroduce exactly the compositional account of human being against which Heidegger is supposed to be setting his face? Much of the difficulty here concerns Heidegger's conception of human embodiment, and hence the human relation to animality (another point of intimacy with the Coetzee text with which I began this account); and this can only be systematically explored with reference to texts subsequent to *Being and Time* (pre-eminent among them the 1929–30 lectures series, GA 29/30. I have discussed this text in some detail in the conclusion of Mulhall 2001). Nevertheless, the central negative points Heidegger wishes to make here seem coherent enough, turning as they do upon his unwavering employment of the term "Dasein" as an ontological or existential category, and hence as essentially not synonymous with any biological or zoological category. If "Dasein" is not a synonym for "*Homo sapiens*," any more than it is for "soul" or "self-consciousness" or "human being," then any analysis of Dasein's relation to its end cannot be fruitfully furthered by taking for granted the ontological presuppositions of the results of the ontic life sciences.

The Existential Approach: Death in/from/as Life

How, then, are we to achieve a proper orientation to our topic? In general terms, we need to adopt an existential viewpoint upon it, which means regarding death as one possibility of Dasein's being. Since no Dasein can directly apprehend or encounter its own death, we must shift our analytical focus from death understood as an actuality to death understood as a possibility; only then can we intelligibly talk of death as something toward which any existing Dasein can stand in any kind of substantial, comprehending relationship. In other words, we must reconceive our relation to our death not as something that is realized when we die, but rather as something that we realize (or fail to) in our life.

What, then, is the distinctive character of this possibility of our being, as opposed to any other (such as eating a meal, or playing a game of football, or reading a philosophy book)? Heidegger gives us the following succinct summary: "Death is the possibility of the absolute impossibility of Dasein. Thus death reveals itself as that *possibility which is one's ownmost, which is non-relational, and which is not to be outstripped*. As such, death is something *distinctively* impending" (SZ: 250–1). Death impends, it stands before us as something that is not yet; but unlike any other possibility of Dasein's being, it can only stand before us. A storm or a friend's arrival can impend; but they can also arrive, be made actual. By contrast we cannot relate to our death as anything other than an impending possibility – for when that possibility of our being is actualized, we are necessarily no-longer-Dasein; death makes any Dasein's existence absolutely impossible. Hence, we can comport ourselves toward death only as a possibility; and further, it stands before us as a possibility throughout our existence. A storm or a friend's arrival does not impend at every moment of our existence; but there is no moment at which our death is not possible – no moment of our existence which might not be our last. Hence, death – unlike any other possibility of our being – is always and only a possibility; our fatedness to this purely impending threat makes concrete the articulated unity of our existence as thrown projection, our being always already delivered over to being ahead of ourselves.

Since what impends when death impends is Dasein's utter non-existence, and since Dasein must take over that possibility in every moment of its existence, Heidegger claims that, in relation to death, Dasein stands before its ownmost potentiality-for-being – that possibility in which what is at issue is nothing less than Dasein's being-in-the-world. Since Dasein is certain to die at some point, he further claims that death is a possibility that is not to be outstripped. And to complete his characterization, Heidegger (recalling his earlier claim that no one can take another's death away from her) also claims that, in Dasein's comportment toward its death, "all its relations to any other Dasein have been undone" (SZ: 250) – in other words, that death is a non-relational possibility.

It has been pointed out that the non-relationality of death is hardly unique to it among the vast range of our existential possibilities; if no one else can die my death for

303

me, it is also true that no one else can sneeze my sneezes. It might therefore be worth pointing out in response that sneezing fails to match up to the other two elements in Heidegger's tripartite existential characterization of death (our very existence as being-in-the-world is not at issue when we catch a cold, and at the very least it makes sense to imagine a human being who never sneezed). Furthermore, it is no part of Heidegger's concern to argue that Dasein's relation to its death utterly subverts or suspends its being-with; he has earlier acknowledged a variety of ways in which Others can be with Dasein in its dying and death, and he has also pointed out that ethnological and anthropological studies can reveal the sheer variety of ways in which Dasein interprets and makes sense of its subjection to death, by drawing on differing collective culturally specific understandings of mortality (SZ: 248). If anything, what he is more concerned to stress is that the non-relational nature of death highlights an aspect of Dasein's comportment to any and all of its existential possibilities; for in making concrete Dasein's being-ahead-of-itself, the fact that no one can die our death for us merely recalls us to the fact that our life is ours alone to live.

But before we look more closely at this implication of Heidegger's analysis, we need to take note of the fact that we have so far rather passed over a complication in Heidegger's methodological approach to death. By treating death from an existential point of view, hence as a possibility of Dasein's being, and as one to which it must relate, if it is to relate to it at all, from within its existence, it might seem that Heidegger has overcome death's apparently obdurate resistance to any phenomenological approach. But to draw that conclusion would be to overlook one further remarkable but undeniable feature of death understood as an existential possibility – the fact that it is not really an existential possibility at all. Any authentic existential possibility is one that might be made actual by the Dasein whose possibility it is; we might actually eat the meal we are cooking, or play the game for which we are training. But our own death cannot be realized in our existence; if our death becomes actual, we are no longer there to experience it. In other words, death is not just the possibility of our own non-existence, of our own absolute impossibility; it is an impossible possibility – or more frankly, an existential impossibility. But if it amounts to a contradiction in terms to think of death as an existential possibility, of however distinctive or even unique a kind, then it would seem that Heidegger must be wrong to think that he can achieve phenomenological access to death by analysing it in existential terms.

This is where the real elegance of Heidegger's strategy for overcoming death's resistance to human understanding becomes clear. For if death cannot coherently be regarded as even a very unusual kind of existential possibility (after all, an impossibility is not one genus of the species "possibility," any more than nonsense is a kind of sense), then we cannot understand our relation to our own end on the model of our relation to any authentic possibility of our being – as if our death stood on the same level (the ontic or existentiell level) as any other possibility upon which we might project ourselves. Heidegger's point in calling our relation to our own end our "being-toward-death" is to present it as an ontological (that is, existential) structure, rather than as one existentiell state (even a pervasive or common one) of the kind that that structure makes possible. In short, we cannot grasp Heidegger's account of death except against the horizon of his account of the ontological difference – the division between ontic and ontological matters.

If, however, no authentic (i.e. existentiell) possibility could be omnipresent, ineluctable and owned or individual in the way that death is, why call it an existential possibility at all? Doesn't this choice of terminology actually encourage forms of misunderstanding that Heidegger must then attempt to avert – by, for example, emphasizing that an appropriate relation to one's death is not a matter of actualizing that possibility (say, by suicide), or of expecting it to be actualized at every next moment, or of meditating upon it in those terms? There is, however, a compensating and fundamental advantage, in Heidegger's view. For his terminology underlines his key insight – namely that, although we can't coherently regard death as an existentiell possibility, neither can we understand our relation to our own end apart from our relation to our existentiell possibilities, and thereby to our being-ahead-of ourselves. More specifically, Heidegger's suggestion is that we should think of our relation to death as manifest in the relation we establish and maintain (or fail to maintain) to any and every authentic possibility of our being, and hence to our being as such.

Precisely because death can be characterized as Dasein's ownmost, non-relational and not-to-be outstripped possibility, and hence as an omnipresent, ineluctable, but non-actualizable possibility of its being, which means that it is an ungraspable but undeniable aspect of every moment of its existence, it follows that Dasein can only relate to it in and through our relation to what *is* graspable in our existence – namely the authentic existentiell possibilities that constitute it from moment to moment. Death thus remains beyond any direct existential (and hence phenomenological) grasp; but it is shown to be graspable essentially indirectly, as an omnipresent condition of every moment of Dasein's directly graspable existence. It is not a specific feature of the existential terrain, but rather a light or shadow emanating evenly and implacably from every such feature; it is the ground against which those features configure themselves, a self-concealing condition for Dasein's capacity to disclose its own existence to itself as it really is.

In other words, just as Heidegger earlier reminded us that death is a phenomenon of life, so he now tells us that death shows up only in and through life, in and through that which it threatens to render impossible – as the possible impossibility of that life. Phenomenologically speaking, then, life is death's representative, the proxy through which death's resistance to Dasein's grasp is at once acknowledged and overcome, or rather overcome in and through its acknowledgment. Death can be made manifest in our existential analytic only through a thorough recounting of that analysis in the light of the possible impossibility of that which it analyses. Or, to put matters the other way around: being-toward-death is essentially a matter of being-toward-life; it is a matter of relating (or failing to relate) to one's life as utterly, primordially mortal.

The Modalities of Mortal Existence

What might this amount to? Systematically transposing Heidegger's distinguishing predicates for death onto life, we might say the following. For Dasein to confront life as its ownmost possibility is for it to acknowledge that there is no moment of its existence in which its being as such is not at issue. This discloses that Dasein's existence matters to it, and that what matters about it is not just the specific moments that make it up, but the totality of those moments – its life as a whole. Dasein thereby comes to see that its life is something for which it is responsible, that it is its own to live (or to disown) – that its existence makes a claim on it that is essentially non-relational, not something to be sloughed off onto Others. And to think of one's life as fated to be stripped out, rendered hollow or void, by death is to acknowledge the utter non-necessity of its continuation, and hence its sheer, thoroughgoing contingency at every moment. Simone Weil tells a story about Talleyrand: when he passed a beggar without giving alms, the beggar remonstrated with him, saying "Sir! I must live!" Talleyrand replied "I do not see the necessity." Weil's point is that the hardest lesson of our mortality is its demand that we recognize the complete superfluity of our existence. Our birth was not necessary; the course of our life could have been otherwise; its continuation from moment to moment is no more than a fact; and it will come to an end at some point. To acknowledge this about our lives is simply to acknowledge our finitude – the fact that our existence has conditions or limits, that it is neither self-originating nor self-grounding nor self-sufficient, that it is contingent from top to bottom. But no representation of ourselves is harder to achieve or enact than this one; nothing is more challenging than to live in such a way that one does not treat what is in reality merely possible or actual or conditionally necessary as if it were absolutely necessary – a matter of fate or destiny beyond any question or alteration. Being-toward death is thus a matter of stripping out false necessities, of becoming properly attuned to the real modalities of human existence.

This last perception is what most clearly connects Heidegger's project of representing Dasein to itself as a whole, and his desire to include the possibility of Dasein's authenticity in his general portrait of human everydayness. For an authentic grasp of Dasein's existence as mortal will inflect its attitude to the choices it must make (to its being-ahead-of-itself) in four interrelated ways. A mortal being is one whose existence is contingent (it might not have existed at all, and its present modes of life are no more than the result of past choices), whose non-existence is an omnipresent possibility (so that each of its choices might be its last), a being with a life to lead (its individual choices contributing to, and so contextualized by, the life of which they are a part), and one whose life is its own to lead (so that its choices should be its own rather than those of determinate or indeterminate Others). In short, an authentic confrontation with death reveals Dasein as related to its own being in such a way as to hold open the possibility, and impose the responsibility, of living a life that is authentically individual and authentically whole – a life of integrity, an authentic life.

But, of course, Heidegger does not think that Dasein typically does relate authentically to its own end, and hence to its own life. On the contrary: we typically flee in the face of death. We regard death as something that happens primarily to others, whom we think of as simply more cases or instances of death, as if they were mere tokens of an essentially impersonal type. We encourage the dying by asserting that it will never happen; and on those occasions when it does we often enough see it as a social inconvenience or shocking lack of tact on the deceased person's part – a threat to our tranquilized avoidance of the truth. Although we never exactly deny that it will happen to us, we are happy to contemplate courses of action that might promise to hold it off (whether temporarily, as with fitness schemes, or indefinitely, as with cryogenics); and we tend to regard it as a distant eventuality, as something that will happen, but not yet, and hence as an impending event rather than as the omnipresent possibility of our own non-existence, that impossible but ineluctable possibility without which our existence would lack its distinctively finite significance.

This kind of tranquilizing alienation bears the characteristic marks of Dasein's average everyday existence in "*das man*"; and it suggests that lostness in *das man* is best understood as entanglement in a misplaced sense of the necessities of finite life. For it is part of this everyday mode of Dasein's being that we regard the array of existential possibilities presently open to us, and the specific choices we make between them, as wholly fixed by forces greater than or external to ourselves. We do what we do because that is what one does, what is done, what *das man* does; we displace our freedom outside ourselves, existing in self-imposed servitude to *das man*, unwilling not only to alter that fact but to acknowledge that it is a fact (but no more than that, an actuality and not a necessity). The reality is that we alone are responsible for allowing ourselves to be lost in the range of possibilities that our circumstances have thrust upon us, and we alone are capable of, and responsible for, altering that state of affairs.

Getting Ahead of Ourselves: Heidegger's Analysis between Angst and Conscience

How, then, on Heidegger's account might we regain access to this reality, to the true modalities of our existence as finite beings? Seeing the first part of his answer depends upon recalling what motivated him to reinitiate his existential analytic of Dasein despite its apparently satisfying terminus at the end of Division I in his specification of Dasein's being as care – a certain anxious dissatisfaction with the role he had assigned in that context to the concept of anxiety. For that state-of-mind is, on Heidegger's account, essentially objectless; in contrast to such apparently similar states-of-mind as fear, although anxiety might be triggered by a specific entity or task or possibility, it is not internally or intentionally directed upon one. Fear is always fear of something particular – a dog, a gun, a humiliating public performance – and hence invites us to respond to what we fear in specific ways; but the anxious person is not anxious about anything in particular, and so her state-of-mind cannot find expression or alleviation in the implementation of a particular course of action.

And, of course, it is the objectlessness of anxiety that allows Heidegger to claim that its peculiar oppressiveness is generated not by any specific totality of ready-to-hand objects but rather by the possibility of such totalities: we are oppressed by the world as such – or more precisely, by being-in-the-world. Anxiety gives Dasein access to the knowledge that it is thrown into the world – always already delivered over to being ahead of itself, to situations of choice and action which matter to it but which it did not itself fully choose or determine. In other words, anxiety confronts Dasein with the determining yet sheerly contingent fact of its own worldly existence.

It is no surprise that these formulations from Division I so closely echo Heidegger's present characterizations of what is disclosed in any authentic mode of being-toward-death. For, like any mode of Dasein's being, this mode of projecting one's existence necessarily suffers or undergoes a corresponding state-of-mind; and Heidegger's view is that any properly authentic anticipation of one's mortality will be anxious. The reason for this conjunction of mood and projection is not far to seek; for death's resistance to being understood as just one more existentiell possibility, its essential unrealizability, is the perfect match for the essential objectlessness of anxiety. No object-directed state-of-mind could correspond to an existential phenomenon that utterly repels any objective actualization within Dasein's worldly existence; only a state-of-mind that discloses the sheer worldliness of Dasein's being, beyond any specific world in which it finds itself, could also disclose the sheer mortality of that being, its inherent non-necessity beyond any specific array of contingent circumstances and possibilities it finds itself confronting.

Indeed, since talk of Dasein's worldliness and its contingency might best be thought of as two different ways of alluding to the same thing – to its inherent projectiveness or being-ahead-of-itself – it would be more accurate to say that anxiety is always, fundamentally, keyed to one or another aspect of Dasein's mortality. Only an existentially unspecifiable "object" could conceivably suit this inherently objectless state; no particular, graspable worldly phenomenon could measure up to its lack of specificity. And this in turn suggests that it is as misleading to call anxiety a state-of-mind as it is to call death an existential possibility. Angst is no more a specific mode of Dasein's thrownness than death is a specific possibility of its projectiveness. It is rather an ineluctable aspect of its thrownness, the omnipresent ground and condition of Dasein's specific states-of-mind. One might say: whatever Dasein's particular state-of-mind and project, it is always already anxiously relating to its mortality, whether in resolute anticipation of it or in irresolute, self-alienating flight from it.[2]

But this simply returns us to the question with which we began this discussion of anxiety: if existential angst might take authentic or inauthentic forms – if even the *das man* attitude toward our mortality is an expression of angst – what might permit or invite it to modulate from its inauthentic to its authentic form? This is the question with which Heidegger confronts himself at the very end of his chapter on death and mortality:

> this existentially "possible" being-towards-death remains, from the existentiell point of view, a fantastical exaction. The fact that an authentic potentiality for being-a-whole is ontologically possible for Dasein, signifies nothing, so long as a corresponding ontical potentiality-for-being has not been demonstrated in Dasein itself? . . . [W]e must investigate whether to *any* extent and in any way Dasein *gives testimony*, from its ownmost potentiality-for-being, as to a possible *authenticity* of its existence, so that it not only makes known that in an existentiell manner such authenticity is possible, but *demands* this of itself. (SZ: 265–6)

I lack the space to deal properly with the analysis that aims to meet this demand in the succeeding chapters of *Being and Time*;[3] so I must conclude with some unsystematic, ground-clearing remarks. First, given the key role played thus far by death's resistance to being represented as an existential possibility and by anxiety's objectlessness, it should not be surprising to find that Heidegger will characterize the voice in which Dasein demands authenticity of itself – the voice of conscience – as saying nothing: "conscience discourses solely and constantly in the mode of keeping silent" (SZ: 273).

A demand that activates objectless angst concerning an existential impossibility cannot specify any particular thrown projection as capable of satisfying it; it demands simply that Dasein regard its existence as making demands on it at any and every moment, as being inherently demanding beyond the satisfaction of any specific demands we choose to address in and through that existence.

Once again, the idea is not that the voice of conscience speaks silently at certain specifiable moments; it is rather that any specific existentiell demands we interpret it as making on us always also make the further demand that we regard our subjection to demand as such as unredeemable through the satisfaction of those specific demands. If Dasein's being is inherently being-ahead-of-itself, no meeting of any particular demand in action can eliminate or silence the need to re-encounter that demand (or to choose not to do so) in the next moment of our existence. If we are in this sense essentially incomplete or lacking (Heidegger goes on to call this our being-guilty), then we are also essentially irreducible to what we have hitherto and presently achieved or attained. We are, in other words, inherently self-transcending or transitional, always capable of becoming more or other than we presently are.

This implies that authenticity is a matter not of achieving some particular state, but of acknowledging that no particular achieved state is final or exhaustive of our individuality. Inauthenticity would then be the willingness to believe, and to live as if one believed, that one is identical with one's present state – that the human self is essentially self-identical, capable of coinciding with itself and fulfilling its nature when it does so. For Heidegger, authenticity involves the acceptance and living out of a conception of oneself as intrinsically non-self-identical – Dasein's acknowledging the uncanny non-coincidence of what it is and what it might be. Human mortality and finitude is accepted only insofar as one avoids conflating one's existential potential and one's existentiell actuality, and instead accepts one's inevitable failure to coincide with oneself.

This is the unrepresentable nullity of Dasein's being – its essential relation to what it is not – that being-toward-death aims to grasp, to which angst responds and about which the silent voice of conscience constantly discourses. This endless circling around Dasein's internal relation to negation is how Division II of *Being and Time* attempts to unsettle the insufficiently anxious, excessively complacent air of completeness emanating from the existential analytic of Division I. From the perspective of Division II, the very neatness and self-sufficiency of Division I's culminating summary of Dasein's care-structure, its essential coincidence with itself, attests to its ultimate failure to avoid a philosophical inflection of the very inauthenticity it analyzes. Only by attempting to represent death despite its obdurate resistance to representation, only by representing it as obdurately resistant to representation, and accepting the consequences of so doing (accepting the various ways in which nullity, negation, and nothingness unsettle the architectonic of the text, opening it to forces and vistas that ultimately exceed its grasp), does Division II testify to the ability of the phenomenological approach to meet the demand imposed upon it of grasping the essential uncanniness of Dasein's being.

Notes

1 Although it seems hardly likely that Christian theologians will regard Heidegger's unqualified denial that anyone can take another's dying away from him as really neutral with respect to the doctrine of the Atonement.

2 This is perhaps the most obvious point in my account at which Heidegger's debt to Kierkegaard is made evident, and revealed to be rather more fundamental than Heidegger's ambiguous acknowledgment of it might suggest. But it is not just Kierkegaard's stress on the ubiquity of such phenomena as angst and despair in human existence that has its echo in Heidegger; there is also his emphasis upon the human need to make sense of its existence as a whole, and his assignment of a role to our God-relation that is precisely analogous to the one we have seen Heidegger assign to our relation to death. This makes Heidegger's rather elaborately casual repression of the Christian doctrine of the Atonement a further dimension of significance. For more on this Kierkegaardian inheritance, see Mulhall (1996: chapter 5).

3 Although I have examined the issues in more detail elsewhere: see Mulhall (2001: part II, ss. 38–42).

References and further reading

Coetzee, J. M. (1999) *The Lives of Animals*. Princeton, NJ: Princeton University Press.

Mulhall, S. (1996) *Heidegger and* Being and Time. London: Routledge.

Mulhall, S. (2001) *Inheritance and Originality*. Oxford: Oxford University Press.

19

Temporality

WILLIAM BLATTNER

Why Being *and Time?*

By keeping an eye on this connection [between Dasein and temporality] it should be shown that *time* is that on the basis of which Dasein understands and interprets something like being. Time must be brought to light and genuinely conceived as the horizon of all understanding of being and every interpretation of being. In order to make this transparent [*einsichtig*], we require an *originary explication of time as the horizon of the understanding of being in terms of temporality as the being of Dasein who understands being.* (SZ: 17)

Being and Time sets out to "pose anew *the question concerning the sense of being*" (SZ: 1). To answer this question, to say something about what being means, requires us to acknowledge the role of time: time is the "horizon of all understanding of being," i.e. being makes sense in terms of time. To say this, however, is only to probe so deep, for like many other ordinary words in *Being and Time* (e.g. "death," "guilt," "conscience," "sight"), for Heidegger "time" refers ultimately to something more fundamental than time as ordinarily conceived. It refers to *originary temporality*. Time is not the abstract "container" that we imagine "clock-time" to be, but a basic structure of Dasein's being.

Through his analysis of time as originary temporality Heidegger aims to accomplish several things at once: to offer a new interpretation of the basic contours of human existence; to gain leverage on the development of an ontology; and to lay the groundwork for ontological idealism (the thesis that being depends upon the understanding of being). In this chapter I will explore each of these themes as they emerge chiefly in *Being and Time*. I will rely on other early period texts from Heidegger's corpus, but mostly only to support the analysis of *Being and Time*.

The Temporality of Human Existence

In *Being and Time*, Heidegger not only declares the intimate connection between time and being, but also that between time and Dasein: "*Temporality* will be shown to be the sense of the being of that very entity whom we call Dasein. This account must prove

311

itself in recapitulating the structures of Dasein that were presented preliminarily and interpreting them as modes of temporality" (SZ: 17). In other words, in the final quarter of *Being and Time*, Heidegger wants to return to the fundamental structures of Dasein's being, which were articulated and described in the first 64 sections of *Being and Time*, and redescribe them in terms of their temporal structure. In doing this, he does not think that he is just dropping another layer of jargon over the structure of human existence. Rather, he believes that he is deepening his analysis by revealing the distinctive *unity* of human existence: "*The originary unity of the structure of care lies in temporality*" (SZ: 327; "care" is Heidegger's name for the being of Dasein).

In Division I of *Being and Time*, Heidegger had analyzed the structure of Dasein's being as consisting of three elements: existence, facticity, and falling. These three together make up the "care-structure." Moreover, Heidegger characterizes existence, facticity, and falling in I.6 thus: "The formal existential totality of the ontological structural whole of Dasein must therefore be grasped in the following structure: the being of Dasein means: being-ahead-of-itself-being-already-in-(the-world-) as being-amidst (intraworldly encountering entities). This being fulfills the meaning of the title *care*, which is used purely existential-ontologically" (SZ: 192). Each of these three elements of the "ontological structural whole," moreover, is spelled out in terms of an aspect of temporality: "The ahead-of-itself is grounded in the future. Already-being-in . . . announces in itself beenness [*Gewesenheit*]. Being-amidst . . . is made possible in enpresenting" (SZ: 327). The upshot of all this is that each of the three fundamental elements of Dasein's being (existence, facticity, and falling) is grounded in an aspect of time (past, present, future), and this is meant to shed light on the intrinsic *unity* of care.

In ¶68 of *Being and Time* Heidegger begins to dive into details. "The temporal Interpretation of everyday Dasein should begin with the structures in which disclosedness is constituted. These are: understanding, affectivity [*Befindlichkeit*], falling and discourse. The modes of temporalization that are to be laid bare in light of these phenomena provide the ground for determining the temporality of being-in-the-world" (SZ: 334–5). To cut through a thicket of issues here, suffice it to say that disclosedness is the manner in which Dasein is open to the world. In the passage above, Heidegger identifies four constituent elements of the structure of disclosedness: understanding (or projection), affectivity (or attunement, mood), falling, and discourse. Each of the first three elements discloses one specific moment of the care-structure: understanding discloses existence; affectivity discloses facticity; falling discloses, well, falling. Discourse is the odd man out, in a way, and in ¶68d Heidegger says that discourse is not associated with any one aspect of time (SZ: 349). In short, for our purposes here, we may treat existence and understanding as interchangeable, facticity and affectivity, falling and, well, falling.

Existence is that aspect of Dasein's being that it always is what it understands itself to be. Dasein understands itself by projecting itself forward into some way of life, or as Heidegger puts it, possibility of being. For example, I may understand myself as a musician by projecting myself forward into a musician's way of life. Such projection, moreover, is not a cognitive or intellectual achievement, nor even an imaginative one, but rather a concrete form of conduct. Heidegger characterizes it as "pressing ahead" into the activity of being what one understands oneself to be. So, to project myself forward into a musician's way of life is not to fantasize about being one, nor even to plan being one, no matter how concretely, but rather actually to set about doing what musicians do.

Facticity is that aspect of Dasein's being that it is concrete or determinate. Facticity is Dasein's distinctive form of factuality. This determinateness discloses itself to Dasein through affectivity, which is the way things matter to Dasein. Everything Dasein encounters, from the most significant and oppressive events of one's life, to the most trivial and irrelevant, matter to it. The piano or clarinet I play are alluring and empowering, thus being worthy of ginger care. More importantly, Dasein's own possibilities matter to it. Being a teacher is rewarding and challenging; being a father is fulfilling and animating (and challenging too!). That I am someone determinate or concrete, that I am situated in an ongoing life, in a time and place, rather than just being an abstraction, manifests itself to me in the way in which things matter to me.

Existence and facticity do not just both happen to characterize Dasein's being. Rather, they are equally important ("equiprimordial") and interwoven. In II.2 of *Being and Time* Heidegger describes facticity as the ground or basis (*Grund*) of existence. That is, we project forth into the possibilities we pursue *because* they matter to us as they do. I press ahead into being a father *because* it is fulfilling, into being a teacher *because* it is rewarding. If those possibilities did not matter to me as they do, I wouldn't pursue them.

Finally, the third element of Dasein's being (of the "care structure") and of disclosedness is falling. Before diving into a description of falling, however, we must cut through a significant terminological ambiguity in *Being and Time*. On the one hand, *falling* refers to Dasein's tendency to *fall away from* authenticity and *onto* the world of its mundane concerns in fleeing from the anxiety of a confrontation with death. On the other hand, it names Dasein's essential *encounter with* and *absorption in* non-human things in the course of pursuing its possibilities. Equipment, paraphernalia, gear (*das Zeug*) are available (*zuhanden*) to Dasein as it goes about its daily business. In being a father, I have to do with baseball gloves and bats, with homework assignments and pencils, skillets and eggs, and so on. Primarily and usually (*zunächst und zumeist*) I confront these things; I am not primarily focused on being a father as such. I am busied with the paraphernalia, tasks, and events that are involved in my projects and possibilities. The latter define the former by giving them their place in a cultural matrix of human concerns, projects, possibilities, places, and times. What is more, the paraphernalia always show up in terms of my facticity or affectivity, the way things matter to me.

In what way are these three elements of the care-structure specifically temporal? Let us begin with existence and understanding. Heidegger tells us that Dasein's existence is its being-ahead-of-itself. This "ahead" certainly *suggests* futurity. We cannot, however, take this suggestion in its most obvious terms, for Heidegger admonishes us: "The 'ahead' ['*Vor*'] does not mean the 'in advance' ['*Vorher*'] in the sense of the 'Not-yet-now – but later' ['*Noch-nicht-jetzt – aber später*'] . . ." (SZ: 327). Projection is a matter of pressing *ahead* into some way to be Dasein, but this way to be Dasein is not displaced off into the future; it is not later to come. Consider an event that is later to come, say, tomorrow evening's Silver Spring–Takoma Thunderbolts game. This event is (right now) off in the future. Tomorrow at 7 p.m., it will be in the present, and by about 9:30 p.m., it will belong to the past. It is an event that, as it were, slides through the temporal continuum. (This is true, whether one conceives time as an "A-series"

313

or a "B-series," *à la* McTaggart, be it noted.) It is distinctive (though obviously not fully general), moreover, of such temporal events that while they remain off in the future, they are merely possible: the Thunderbolts game may be rained out, after all. This is to say that the game is possible in the sense that it may become actual. Heidegger denies that this holds for Dasein's possibilities, however. "Possibility, which Dasein in each case is existentially, is distinguished just as much from empty, logical possibility as from the contingency of something occurrent [*vorhanden*], in so far as with the latter this and that can 'happen' ['*passieren*']" (SZ: 143). In other words, the possibility of being a musician is futural, not because it is merely possible, rather than actual. Instead, it is a possibility that can never be actual, a future that can never be present.

> "Future" does not here mean a Now, which *not yet* having become "actual," sometime *will be*, but rather the coming in which Dasein comes toward itself in its ownmost ability-to-be. (SZ: 325)

> Temporalizing does not mean a "succession" ["*Nacheinander*"] of the ecstases. The future is *not later* than beenness, and this is *not earlier* than the present [*Gegenwart*]. (SZ: 350)

In other words, Dasein's possibilities are not the sorts of items that can be actualized in the present. I never can have become a musician, even though I am now pressing ahead into being one. I call this claim *the Unattainability Thesis* (Blattner 1999).

What does it mean to say that I cannot have become a musician? The point is not that there are conditions on being a musician that I cannot satisfy (say, I have no rhythm). The point is rather that understanding myself as a musician is not attempting to bring about some possible, future state of myself. The possibility of being a musician is not an end-state at which I aim; it is not something that I "sometime *will be*" (SZ: 325). Being a musician is always futural with respect to what I am doing now. Of course, one can have attained the social status of being a musician: the prerogatives, obligations, and expectations that devolve upon a person in virtue of occupying a certain station, role, career, or occupation in life. A social status, however, is not the same as an existential possibility, what Heidegger calls an *ability-to-be* (*Seinkönnen*). An existential possibility is a manner of self-understanding with which one is identified in virtue of pressing ahead into it. Social statuses and existential possibilities come clearly apart in the case of the *poseur*. Think of Frank Abignale Jr in *Catch Me if You Can*. He occupies a series of social statuses as which he does not understand himself. He is faking it, yet he is accorded the social statuses *seriatim* of teacher, airline pilot, etc. (even if illegally, in a certain sense), and he is capable of living up to the expectations of these statuses. Social status and existential possibility also come apart in one who has resigned her existential projection, even though she still occupies the social status. If I have resigned or taken back my self-understanding, say, as a father, then I no longer identify with it and no longer press ahead into it, even if my fellows, and the law too, will hold me accountable to the obligations of fatherhood.

The prospect of resigning one's self-understanding points toward an ominous threat that Heidegger believes looms constantly before Dasein, what he *calls* "death,"

314

but which is not exactly what we normally call "death." In II.1 Heidegger defines death as the "possibility of the impossibility of existence" and characterizes it as a "way to be Dasein." Heideggerian death is a way to be Dasein and, therefore, not non-existence *per se*. The latter, the end or ending of a human life, Heidegger calls "demise" (*Ableben*), in contrast with death (*Tod*). For clarity's sake, I will call Heideggerian death "existential death." Existential death is the condition in which Dasein is not able to be or exist, in the sense that it cannot understand itself, press ahead into any possibilities of being. Existential death is a peculiar sort of living nullity, death in the midst of life, nothingness. What would it be like to suffer existential death? To be unable to understand oneself is not for one's life to cease to matter altogether. As Heidegger says early on in *Being and Time*, Dasein's being is necessarily at issue for it. The issue – Who am I? How shall I lead my life? – matters to me, but when existentially dead no possible *answer* matters. All answers to these questions are equally uninteresting. This is what Heidegger calls *anxiety*, although on its face it sounds more like what we today call depression: the total insignificance of the world, including the entire matrix of possible answers to the question: Who am I? Anxiety and existential death are two sides of the same coin: global indifference that undercuts any impetus to lead one sort of life or another (see Blattner 1994a for more detail).

To tie all this together, Heidegger accords the phenomenon of existential death ontological importance, because it signals something about the very nature of human possibilities. If existential death looms constantly as a threat to who I am, then who I am, my possibilities, can never characterize me in any settled way. If they did, then I could never find myself un*able* to be them. Hence, my originary future is not the sort of thing that can *be* present, not a property that can positively characterize me in the way in which a determinate height or hair color, or even a determinate social status, can characterize me. It is a future that is not later than, that does not *succeed*, the present.

Just as the "ahead" in "being-ahead-of-itself" describes a future that can never come to be present, so Heidegger argues that the "already" in "being-already in a world" picks out a past that never was present. Dasein's originary past is, recall, its attunements, the way things already matter to it. I am always already "thrown" into the world and into my life, because I am always attuned to the way it matters to me. These attunements are the "drag" that situates and concretizes the "thrust" of my projection. These attunements, however, are not past events. They do not belong to the sequential past, as the various episodes of my life-history do. In Heidegger's language, they are not "bygone" (*vergangen*). They belong, rather, to the existential or originary past, to my "beenness" (*Gewesenheit*). My attunements were not at one time present, after which they slipped into the past. Rather, at every moment that an attunement characterizes me, even at its first moment, I am already thrown into it; it is already past.

So, it becomes clear that the sense in which care is temporal is exotic, to say the least. Existence or projection is not futural by aiming itself at a possible future state of the self, and facticity or attunement is not past by revealing historical episodes or states. They are futural and past, rather, in a non-successive sense. They make sense in terms of a future that never will come to be present and a past that never was present.

But Why Call It "Time?"

At this point one might certainly suspect that something has gone wrong. One might argue that if Dasein's possibilities are the sorts of things that cannot come to be present, then they are not futural either, and if not futural, then not distinctively temporal. In other words, one might urge that if the argument above holds, the sense of "ahead" in "being-ahead-of-itself" is only metaphorically temporal. Heidegger acknowledges the force of this consideration, when he concedes that his interpretation of Dasein "does violence" to the everyday understanding of human existence (SZ: 311). Still, he believes that his interpretation is required by the phenomena.

Heidegger answers that originary temporality *explains* time, and for that reason it deserves the title originary time.

> So, when we have shown that the "time" that is accessible to Dasein's intelligibility is *not* originary and, what is more, that it arises out of authentic temporality, then we are justi-fied, in accordance with the proposition, *a potiori fit denominatio*, in labeling *temporality*, which has just been exhibited, *originary time*. (SZ: 329)

Time as we encounter it in our everyday experience is not originary. How do we encounter time in our everyday experience? Heidegger distinguishes, in fact, two sorts of everyday time, *world-time* and *time as ordinarily conceived*. Time as we ordinarily *con-ceive* it (*der vulgäre Zeitbegriff*) is time as the pure container of events. Heidegger may well build the term "conceive" into its name, because he wants to emphasize that when we disengage from our ordinary experience and talk about and contemplate time as such, we typically interpret time as such a pure container, as the continuous medium of natural change. When we are pre-theoretically engaged with time, however, we experience it as *world-time*. World-time is the sequence of meaningfully articulated, everyday times: dinner time, bed time, rush hour, the Great Depression, the Cold War Era, the 1960s, and the like.

World-time differs from ordinary time in that the times of world-time are overtly defined in terms of their relation to human interests, whereas ordinary times are con-ceptualized as independent of human interests. Thus, the distinction between world-time and ordinary time shares some of the contours of the distinction between the available and the occurrent. The available (*das Zuhandene*, the ready-to-hand) is the paraphernalia of human life, all of the things that are what they are in virtue of the way they are involved in human practices. A football is a football in virtue of the role it plays in the game of football. Likewise for knives, computers, cornfields, etc. The occurrent (*das Vorhandene*, the present-at-hand), however, is what it is independently of human practices. Electrons and galaxies, and maybe numbers too, would be and be what they are, whether or not humans had ever discovered them and developed theories about them. This parallel is no mere coincidence.

World-time is the temporal medium in which worldly events take place, in which the available is caught up in human activities and in which human affairs run their course. Hammers are actually taken up and put to use in construction in world-time, and the World Series, presidential elections, and birthday parties all take place in world-time.

World-time is *world*-time, both because it is the time in which worldly events are measured and ordered, and because it belongs to the very structure of the world. The world, in Heidegger's technical sense, is the concrete social milieu in which the available has its place and in terms of which human beings understand themselves, hence in which human beings lead their lives. (This is the world in the ontic-existentiell sense, sense 3, defined on SZ: 65, as elaborated in ¶18.) As Heidegger writes, the world is "that '*in which*' a factical Dasein 'lives'" (SZ: 65). This world is articulated temporally: things happen in the world, and they can be measured in part by *when* and *for how long* they happen. The *when* and *for how long* of world-time, however, are not understood in terms of the pure clock-time of nature. To answer *when vis-à-vis* world-time is not to ask for a cosmological or natural specification of time, but rather to ask how an event is situated with respect to dinner time or the American Civil War. These are the contentful, meaningful times in terms of which we lead our lives: they make up world-time.

Ordinary time, however, is the pure flow of clock-time, meaningless, empty, and potentially precise. It is, as Heidegger says, a "pure succession" (SZ: 422). The characteristic "datability" and "significance" of world-time are missing. World-time is datable in that the nows of world-time are essentially characterized in terms of their content: dinner time is dinner time in virtue of its relation to dinner, for example. What is more, because dinner time is defined in terms of dinner, it can be an appropriate or inappropriate time to do something: an inappropriate time to call a friend, an appropriate time to tell your parents why you got detention at school. Ordinary time lacks this datability and significance. It is pure and apparently disconnected from human concerns.

One might infer from all this that ordinary time is somehow "more real" than world-time, because more independent. Whereas world-time depends crucially on human practices in order to be what it is, ordinary time does not seem to do so. To make the point more striking, we may think of ordinary time as natural time – "nature-time" as Heidegger sometimes calls it – the time in which natural events take place. A natural event, such as an earthquake or supernova, is independent of human beings and their practices. They are, and would be what they are, whether or not humans existed. We are thus inclined to infer that the time in which they take place must likewise be independent of us, hence more real than world-time. As natural as these last inferences seem, they are not right, according to Heidegger. Natural time is not so radically independent of human life, nor is it "more real" than world-time. To see why, however, we must explore the contours of Heidegger's temporal idealism, his idealism about time. In the process we will also find the answer to the question of why originary temporality is a form of time after all.

By *temporal idealism* I mean the thesis that time depends on Dasein. As Heidegger puts it in *Being and Time*: "So, when we have shown that the 'time' that is accessible to Dasein's intelligibility is *not* originary and, what is more, that it arises out of authentic temporality" (SZ: 329). In *The Basic Problems* he writes: "There is no nature-time, inasmuch as all time belongs essentially to Dasein" (GA 24: 370). In the most striking statement of the doctrine, he writes, in *Introduction to Metaphysics*:

> There is, in itself, the possibility that humans not be at all. There indeed was a time when humans were not. But strictly speaking, we cannot say: there was a time when humans

317

> *were* not. In every *time*, humans were and are and will be, because time only temporalizes itself in so far as humans are. There is no time in which humans were not, not because humans are from eternity and to eternity, but rather because time is not eternity, and time only temporalizes itself in each case in every time as human-historical. (EM: 64)

No Dasein, no time. (This doctrine is close enough to classical idealist doctrines that it makes sense to call it a form of idealism, even though Dasein is not a subject, and time does not depend on *ideas*.)

More specifically, time depends on Dasein, insofar as it depends on Dasein's originary temporality. Originary temporality is a formal structure of Dasein's being, and so, in this sense, world-time and natural time depend on the being of Dasein. The precise formulation here is crucial: time belongs to Dasein's being. Time is not an entity, but rather an ontological structure. For this reason Heidegger rarely says of time that it "is," except when he is articulating a common or even philosophical misconception. Rather, he uses the verb *sich zeitigen*, which in ordinary German means "to ripen" or "come to fruition." One might try to leverage the term into an interpretation of originary temporality as a form of self-fulfillment, especially if one connects it with the prevalent verb *sich vollziehen* (to perform or fulfill) in *Being and Time*. I believe this would be a mistake, however. In ¶48 Heidegger rejects the applicability of the metaphors of ripening and maturation to Dasein's fundamental structure (which is, obviously, not to say that individuals do not mature). Instead, Heidegger appropriates the verb *sich zeitigen* in order to construct a way of saying "time is" without saying "time *is*." Time *is* not, because time is no entity. As he writes in *Logic: The Question Concerning Truth*: "Time cannot at all be occurrent; it does not have any sort of being – rather, it is the condition of the possibility that it gives [*es gibt*] such a thing as being (not entities). Time does not have the sort of being of some other thing, but rather, it *temporalizes*" (GA 21: 410). Just as Heidegger writes "it gives being" (*es gibt Sein*) – or later, "being obtains" (*das Sein ereignet sich*) – rather than "being is," so he writes "time temporalizes itself" (*die Zeit zeitigt sich*), rather than "time is."

So, to say that time depends on originary temporality is not to say that time would not *be*, if originary temporality were not. Rather, it is to say that if originary temporality did not obtain, world-time and natural time would not obtain either. We are not talking about an existential dependence here, in the logician's sense of "existential," but about something else. But what? As we saw above (SZ: 329), Heidegger writes that time "arises out of" (*entspringt aus*) originary temporality. Recall as well that in the very same passage he pointed to this relation of arising out of to clarify in what sense originary temporality is time. Hence, by understanding what Heidegger means in writing that time arises out of originary temporality, we can see both what he has in mind by way of time's dependence on originary temporality and why he thinks that originary temporality is a sort of time.

By "arise out of," Heidegger refers to a sort of conceptual or phenomenological degeneration. In a well known passage, he writes, "The ontological origin of the being of Dasein is not 'humbler' than what arises out of it; rather, it towers above the latter in power, and all 'arising out of' in the ontological field is degeneration" (SZ: 334). By "degeneration," Heidegger seems to have in mind leveling off, as when he describes ordinary time as leveled off world-time. World-time is leveled off into ordinary time, in that the datability and significance of world-time are "covered up," so that time seems merely to be a "pure succession of nows" (SZ: 422). The full bloom of world-time, as a sequence of datable, significant, spanned, and public nows, is reduced to the narrower disk of a sequence of spanned and public nows. The world-time now is not only significant and datable, as discussed above, but also spanned and public. Nows are spanned, insofar as they stretch from a before to an after, from a no-longer-now to a not-yet-now. Nows are public in that they are not the private possession or horizon of an individual or group, but rather accessible to all as a horizon for measuring events. Ordinary nows are spanned and public, but not datable and significant. Thus, in degeneration the complexity of a phenomenon is covered up, so that some of its crucial features are obscured, and this in turn makes the phenomenon appear to be something different.

Just as ordinary time is a leveled off version of world-time, so world-time is a leveled off form of originary temporality. Just as immediately above, we have a reduction in complexity or features, a narrowing down of understanding from a full-blooded phenomenon to one that is thinner. In this case, however, the thinning out is not the thinning of a *now*. Originary temporality, after all, does not consist of nows. Rather, we have a disconnection of the now from the ontological horizon in terms of which it makes sense. To spell this out, we must return to originary temporality and look into the one dimension of originary temporality that we neglected above: the present.

We saw above that originary temporality consists of an originary future, Dasein's being-ahead-of-itself insofar as it exists or understands itself in terms of some possible way to be Dasein. Originary temporality also involves an originary past, Dasein's being-already-in-a-world, insofar as it is one to whom things already matter in determinate ways. But what of the originary present? In Heidegger's technical language, the originary future and past consist of ecstases and horizons that are coordinated with one another. The ecstasis of the originary future is Dasein's pressing ahead, and the horizon is that into which Dasein presses ahead, namely, its possibilities. The ecstasis of the originary past is Dasein's being already, and its horizon is the way things matter to Dasein. We must now ask ourselves, what are the ecstasis and horizon of the originary present?

Heidegger calls the ecstasis of the originary present *enpresenting* (*Gegenwärtigen*, making-present). The horizon of enpresenting is, Heidegger says, the in-order-to (SZ: 365). The *in-order-to* is Heidegger's general term for the involvement relation that binds the available to the human practices in terms of which they make sense and are defined. Contact cement is involved in home repair, because it is in order to bind objects together. The in-order-to constitutes the significance of the available. Various uses of equipment are appropriate or inappropriate only in virtue of the equipment's defining in-order-to relation. It is, furthermore, only in terms of the web of in-order-to relations that nows themselves can be significant. Significance, the worldliness of the world (*die Weltlichkeit der Welt*), is constituted by the in-order-to. This in-order-to is made accessible to Dasein in enpresenting.

This is all to say that enpresenting or the constitution of worldly significance is one of the three ecstases of originary temporality, and enpresenting's horizon, the in-order-to, is one of the three horizons of originary temporality.

> The schema in which Dasein comes toward itself *futurally*, whether authentically or inauthentically, is the *for-the-sake-of-itself*. We fix the schema in which Dasein is disclosed to itself in affectivity [*Befindlichkeit*] as thrown, as the *in-the-face-of-which* of thrownness, or better the to-which of abandonment. It indicates the horizonal structure of *beenness*. Existing for the sake of itself in abandonment to itself as thrown, Dasein is as being-amidst ... also enpresenting. The horizonal schema of the *present* is determined through the *in-order-to*. (SZ: 365)

Dasein's being-amidst (*Sein-bei*) intraworldly entities belongs to the structure of care, and its temporal meaning is enpresenting. Translated out of the jargon of *Being and Time*, this means that Dasein's relation to the worldly entities and events that surround it, and thus to the meaningful time in which the events and entities take place and find their location, is but one element of the structure of originary temporality. The degeneration of originary temporality into world-time is a reduction in the sense of a disconnection, an abstraction, of the world-time now from its home in originary temporality.

This abstraction of the now, however, should not be thought of on the model of the medieval conception of the standing now (*nunc stans*). The world-time now is not disconnected from its own past and future, i.e. from other world-time nows. The standing now was conceived as a now, a moment of time, with no past and no future, a singular, isolated moment of time. The world-time now, as Heidegger conceives it, is isolated from the *originary* past and future, but not from the world-time past and future. The world-time now is one now in a sequence of nows; world-time is a succession of nows. The world-time now is intrinsically spanned from a world-time past (no-longer-now) to a world-time future (not-yet-now). It is thus spanned, Heidegger argues, because it is a significant now, a now defined by the relations implied in the in-order-to.

The in-order-to binds the available to its function and to its co-equipment. This coffee mug is in order to drink coffee. To be in order to drink coffee, however, the mug must be situated in an equipmental context. As Heidegger famously writes, "Strictly speaking, there never is *a* piece of equipment. To the being of equipment there belongs always an equipmental totality, in which this piece of equipment can be what it is" (SZ: 68). Thus, the in-order-to binds the available to a task or function and from out of an equipmental context. The understanding of these several relations is, moreover, captured in the ecstatic structure of our understanding of the world-time now. As Heidegger writes, "The *expecting* of the in-which in unity with the *retaining* of the with-which of involvement makes possible in its ecstatic unity the specifically manipulative enpresenting of the piece of equipment" (SZ: 353). That is, simply insofar as we enpresent the world-time now, we also expect a world-time future, in which the task in which the equipment is involved will be completed, and we retain the world-time past in which the equipment's co-equipment (the *with-which* (*das Womit*) of involvement) was available for use along with the equipment we are currently wielding. This ecstatic structure Heidegger calls *the temporality of circumspective concern*. Put in comparatively jargon-free terms, Heidegger's point is that insofar as we are immersed in a now in which we deal with the paraphernalia of our world, we are aimed ahead into the completion of our tasks and rely upon the wherewithal of our environment. The world-time now is inherently spanned or stretched from a before to an after. It is significant, datable, spanned, public, and sequential or successive.

This world-time now-structure is, however, embedded in originary temporality as merely one of the latter's ecstases. We wield equipment in order to tackle tasks only because we understand ourselves the way we do: I apply contact cement to my disintegrating formica countertop, because I understand myself as a homeowner. In Heidegger-speak, the in-which of involvement "goes back to" (*zurückgehen*) the for-the-sake-of-which of self-understanding (SZ: 84). Further, I rely on the co-availability of a vise clamp, as I apply the contact cement, only because it makes a difference to me whether my house is falling apart. Again, in Heidegger-speak, we rely on the where-withal or co-equipment of a piece of equipment only because we are capable of relying on anything at all, only because our tasks already matter to us. The structural unity of the ecstases of the temporality of circumspective concern is parasitic upon the unity of originary temporality. The world-time now necessarily spans from the before to the after, because it is embedded in the structure of originary temporality.

Here we arrive at Heidegger's comprehensive explanatory strategy. We can recognize phenomenologically that the now experienced in engaged everyday practice is part of a larger whole, the whole that is the care-structure of Dasein. Heidegger calls the structural unity of care *originary temporality*. When we considered this above, however, we quickly arrived at the question of why originary temporality should be thought of as a sort of *time* at all. Heidegger answers by showing how if we do classify originary temporality as a form of time, we are able to explain aspects of ordinary time that otherwise remain mysterious, such as its continuity. The continuity of natural time is the way in which natural times stretch back to their immediate predecessors and forward to their immediate successors. This continuity or unbrokenness of natural time remains a brute fact about time, unless we can explain it metaphysically. For this reason, metaphysicians have long sought to do so, but always failed. Heidegger's suggestion is, then, to explain the continuity of natural time as a reduced or leveled off form of the span of world-time. The spannedness of world-time, what is more, is merely a leveled off form of the inherent unity of originary temporality, the way in which the originary future and originary past are intrinsically bound up with one another and with the originary present, which opens up the now for us. In short, originary temporality should be called a form of time, because it is explanatorily fruitful to do so. "*A potiori fit denominatio*": the name derives from the more powerful (SZ: 329). (Heidegger believes, moreover, that he can offer explanations of the irreversibility and infinitude of time as well.)

Therefore, Heidegger aims in one stroke to answer two central questions: why call originary temporality "time," and why hold that time is dependent upon originary temporality? In both cases, the answer is that the three varieties of time (originary temporality, world-time, ordinary time) form a degenerating series. If we view ordinary time as a thinned out version of world-time, and if we regard world-time as a disconnected abstraction from originary temporality, we gain explanatory leverage on time. We can now see why ordinary time is continuous, infinite, and irreversible, where beforehand these were bald mysteries. Moreover, if we accept this account in terms of degeneration, we have an excellent reason to regard originary temporality as a form of time: it is a fuller and explanatorily more fundamental form of time.

Residual Issues: Authenticity and Historicality

I have assumed, without arguing explicitly, that originary temporality is "modally indifferent" with respect to authenticity and inauthenticity. This will surprise many readers, for ¶65 of *Being and Time*, which first introduces originary temporality, focuses on *authentic* temporality and follows upon two and one-half chapters devoted to death, guilt, conscience, resoluteness, and authenticity. I contend, however, that Heidegger's initial focus on authentic temporality is merely strategic. Heidegger is concerned with death and anxiety for two reasons. First, the distinction between an existentially authentic or owned life and an inauthentic or unowned life is located in one's response to death and anxiety. Second, death and anxiety reveal important structures of Dasein's being. That Dasein can find itself unable to understand itself and project forth into a way of life, that it can find itself equally indifferent to all human possibilities, shows that it is capable of living as nothing, as a question without even a provisional answer. This, in turn, forces us to recognize that the possible ways to be Dasein are not possible as potentially actualizable, that Dasein presses ahead into a future that never can become present. The latter implies, finally, that originary temporality is not successive. (The preceding is a synopsis of the argument above.)

Thus, Heidegger focuses first on authentic temporality, because the analysis of authenticity makes up the context in which he has nudged us toward seeing just how exotic our mode of being really is. He makes clear along the way, however, that originary temporality as such is modally indifferent. Two passages may serve as representative: "Running ahead [*Das Vorlaufen*, anticipation, the *authentic* version of the future] makes Dasein *authentically* futural, and indeed in such a way that running ahead itself is only possible in so far as Dasein, *as an entity*, always already comes toward itself at all [*überhaupt*], that is, in so far as it is futural in its being at all" (SZ: 325, see also 327). In other words, the authentic future is but one mode of something more fundamental, namely, the originary future. "The schema in which Dasein comes toward itself futurally, *whether authentically or inauthentically*, is the for-the-sake-of-itself" (SZ: 365, emphasis altered). That is, the originary future is specifically neither authentic nor inauthentic. Despite appearances to the contrary, originary temporality is modally indifferent. For this reason, exploring authentic temporality, although it would be relevant here, is not necessary. So, space limitations encourage me to leave the topic to another occasion.

The same space limitations also force me to leave the theme of historicality to another context. Historicality is obviously closely bound up with temporality. I do not believe, however, that originary temporality *just is* historicality (as is at least suggested by Gadamer 1975; Guignon 1983; Pöggeler 1987), nor that the chapter on historicality in *Being and Time* sheds much light on temporality *per se*. As Heidegger says, "the analysis of the historicality of Dasein aims to show that this entity is not 'temporal' because it 'stands in history,' but rather the opposite, that it does and can exist historically only because it is temporal in the ground of its being" (SZ: 376).

The concept of historicality aims to capture the distinctive way in which Dasein stands in time, distinctive in virtue of its originary temporality. In a nutshell, Dasein is historical, in that it inherits its possibilities from its forebears and inherits them as already mattering. Dasein's possibilities are handed down to it by way of tradition. Heidegger's discussion of historicality may be illuminating for its own sake, but it does not spell out originary temporality itself.

One theme we cannot leave to the side, however, is the official and ultimate reason why Heidegger is interested in temporality in the first place: its role in ontology.

Temporality and Ontology

In the course of exploring the relationship between originary temporality, world-time, and ordinary time we have seen the close relationship between world-time and the available, and between ordinary time and the occurrent. Indeed, world-time constitutes the temporal structure of the being of equipment, just as ordinary time is the temporal structure of the being of the occurrent. All this gives us leverage on Heidegger's claim that "*time* is that on the basis of which Dasein understands and interprets something like being" (SZ: 17). The three basic sorts of being (*Seinsarten*) discussed in *Being and Time* are existence (the being of Dasein), being-available (the being of equipment), and being-occurrent (the being of independent objects). For each of these three sorts of being, moreover, there is a corresponding mode of time: originary temporality, world-time, and ordinary time. Whenever we understand something as an entity, that is, in terms of its being, we do so on the horizon of time. We understand being, entities *qua* entities, in terms of time. This is what Heidegger calls the Temporality of being (*die Temporalität des Seins*): "The fundamental ontological task of the interpretation of being as such, therefore, includes working out the *Temporality of being*. The concrete answer to the question of the sense of being is given for the first time in the exposition of the problematic of Temporality" (SZ: 19). Heidegger never completes this task, alas. It would have been center stage in Division Three of *Being and Time*, which he abandoned. Without diving too much into speculation, we can reconstruct some of the basic outlines of his vision, however. Part of Heidegger's goal was to explain the fundamental unity of being in general. What binds Dasein's existence, the availability of equipment, and the occurrence of things together, so that they all count as modes of *being*? We may divide this question in two: what binds the three modes together, and in virtue of what does the whole complex count as being?

As we saw in the preceding section, the three modes of being are all fundamentally structured by modes of time and temporality. These varieties of time are bound together by the complex relations of degeneration and dependence we have explored. Ordinary time is a degenerate form of world-time, and world-time a degenerate form of originary temporality. In some sense, we are learning to see time as ordinarily conceived as a superficial and degraded version of originary temporality. We are learning to see what time "really is." At its conceptual core – which is not a pared down logical scaffolding, but a fuller whole that makes sense of its degenerate faces – time is originary temporality. Because time is at bottom originary temporality, being is at bottom Dasein's existence. "Of course, only as long as Dasein *is* . . . 'is there' ['*gibt es*'] being" (SZ: 212). This is to say that being at large depends on Dasein. It is not to say, however, that entities depend on Dasein: were all humans to pass from the scene, the stars would not blink out of existence. And yes, before humans evolved, the dinosaurs strode the Earth.

It is only to say that the *being* of these things would not obtain, were there no Dasein (see Blattner 1994b for more detail). This is a complex and dark position, but it is Heidegger's. It fits in well with the interpretation we have developed here, and it clarifies the significance of the Temporality of being.

Finally, the oddest question we have asked: why are existence, availability, and occurrentness modes of *being*? Here we have very little to go on, but perhaps the following may crack the door open just a tad. In *Basic Problems* Heidegger writes, "The sequence, mentioned earlier, of projections so to speak arranged one upon another: understanding of entities, projection upon being, understanding of being, projection upon time, has its end with the horizon of the ecstatical unity of temporality" (GA 24: 437). Temporality, or more properly, *Temporalität*, is the final horizon for the understanding of anything at all. Although the argument here is barely a hint, it at least suggests a thought: what better basis for regarding something as *being* than that it constitutes the final horizon of interpretation and understanding? Time is meant to be that horizon, and in its most fundamental mode, time is originary temporality. To end where we began, "In order to make this transparent, we require an *originary explication of time as the horizon of the understanding of being in terms of temporality as the being of Dasein who understands being*" (SZ: 17).

References and further reading

Blattner, W. (1994a) The concept of death in *Being and Time*. *Man and World*, 27, 49–70.

Blattner, W. (1994b) Is Heidegger a Kantian Idealist? *Inquiry*, 37, 185–201.

Blattner, W. (1999) *Heidegger's Temporal Idealism*. Cambridge: Cambridge University Press.

Gadamer, H.-G. (1975) *Truth and Method* (trans. G. Barden and J. Cumming). New York: Crossroad Publishing.

Guignon, C. B. (1983) *Heidegger and the Problem of Knowledge*. Indianapolis: Hackett.

Pöggeler, O. (1987) *Martin Heidegger's Path of Thinking* (trans. D. Magurshak and S. Barber). Atlantic Highlands, NJ: Humanities Press International.

20

Dasein and "Its" Time

PIOTR HOFFMAN

In ¶65 of *Being and Time*, Heidegger finally fulfills the promise given in the Introduction: he shows how the meaning of the being of Dasein, that is, the meaning of care, is indeed temporality. The paragraph's purpose is indicated by its very title, "Temporality as the Ontological Meaning of Care." The three items in the structure of care are now interpreted in temporal terms and are given a grounding in Dasein's temporality. "The 'ahead-of-itself' is grounded in the future, In the 'being-already-in . . .', the character of 'having been' is made known. 'Being-alongside . . .' becomes possible in *making* present" (SZ: 327). These temporal grounds of existentiality, thrownness, and falling are the "ecstases" of Dasein's temporality, and these ecstases are introduced to us as representing an order of "ahead" and "already," although, Heidegger quickly points out, this is not the sort of temporal order we have in mind when we refer to the future and to the past as to what is "later" and "earlier." Still, with this qualification, or rather an account of it, Heidegger is in a position to say quite a few things about the ecstases in general; and he can then go an to offer, in chapter 4 of Division II, a systematic rein-terpretation of Dasein's everydayness in terms of Dasein's temporality.

And so it may come as *something* of a surprise to us when, at the end of the very same chapter, so rich in detailed analyses, Heidegger speaks of "the inadequacy of our explication of temporality" (SZ: 371). We may ask, why inadequacy? What was, what might have been, so inadequate about an "explication" through which Heidegger fulfilled his initial promise from the Introduction by demonstrating how temporality is indeed the meaning of being of Dasein? And what was so inadequate about his having applied this general view as the guiding light for the immediately following reinterpre-tation of Dasein's everydayness in terms of Dasein's temporality? As Heidegger is now telling us, the shortcomings of his "Interpretation of temporality . . . given thus far" (SZ: 372) create the danger of *immobilizing* Dasein. "Have we not hitherto been con-stantly immobilizing Dasein in certain situations, while we have, 'consistently' with this, been disregarding the fact that in living unto its days Dasein *stretches* itself *along* 'temporally' in the sequence of those days?" (SZ: 372). It is not sufficient, then, to explicate Dasein's temporality as a mere order. It will also be necessary to explicate Dasein's temporal stretchedness for, without it, Dasein will be viewed as immobilized, its ecstatic character notwithstanding. But what, precisely, does Heidegger here have in mind?

If we were dealing with the *ordinary* notion of time, we could easily make sense of this distinction with the aid of McTaggart's classical distinction between A-series and B-series. Take three events E, E', E''. If E is earlier than E' and E' is earlier than E''; if, conversely, E' is later than E and E'' is later than E', then the relations of "later" and "earlier" between these three terms are permanent and can never change. In other words, the order of succession is permanent. This is the purely static B-series, But, as a point of common sense, the notion of time does seem to involve some notion of change. For the very same E', fixed forever as "later" than E and "earlier" than E'', was at some point in time "in the future", it then became "present" and, in the end, it lapsed into the "past." The A-series is the series within which these three changing qualities of futurity, presentness, and pastness can be attributed to an event despite its fixed and unchanging position in the order of time.

But while such treatment may be enough to capture the relevant features (the order and the passage) of time as *ordinarily* understood, it is not Heidegger's strategy to stop at that level. Quite the contrary: the central features of the ordinary conception of time must be shown to be derivable from Dasein's everyday concern with time (with time as "world time," in Heidegger's terminology). And where does the everyday Dasein concern itself with the flow, or the passing, of time?

Heidegger has answered this question already in the same place where he first warned us about the danger of "immobilizing" Dasein by disregarding Dasein's temporal stretchedness. Dasein does stretch itself temporally for it is "a fact of existing Dasein that in spending its time it takes 'time' into its reckoning from day to day" (SZ: 371). Now, Dasein's "reckoning" with time has been mentioned and identified even earlier as part and parcel of Dasein's everyday circumspective concern (SZ: 332–3). We are thus given a list of steps we must take, and of concepts we must clarify, in order to avoid that danger of "immobilizing" Dasein. The key move is to bring out Dasein's stretchedness. To do this, in turn, we must focus upon Dasein's everyday behavior of reckoning with time. What is it, then, about Dasein's structure that makes Dasein reckon with time?

Here is how Heidegger answers this indispensable question: "in utilizing itself for the sake of itself, Dasein 'uses itself up' [*verbraucht sich*]. In using itself up, Dasein *uses itself* – *that is to say, its time*. In using time, Dasein reckons with it" (SZ: 333; emphasis added). Thus, Dasein reckons with the time it uses (as when I say: I don't have the time to get through this traffic jam) because Dasein uses *its own* time. But what is Dasein's time? It is, Heidegger explains, the inherently finite time "allotted [*beschieden* may also be rendered as 'apportioned'] to Dasein" (SZ: 410). To put it plainly, when pursuing its for-the-sake-of-which Dasein finds itself consuming its time – the time of which Dasein has only so much to consume. Heidegger's works from the period of *Being and Time* supply numerous clarifications of this limited time that Dasein finds "allotted" to itself (indeed that Dasein "is") and of this time's crucial role in determining the structure of Dasein. Dasein itself can be described as "temporally particular" (GA 20: 205–6, 320–1, 331–3), since its particularity cannot be understood otherwise than as Dasein's being "at its time." "This 'in each particular instance' [*je*], 'at the (its) time' [*jeweilig*], or the structure of the 'particular while' [*Jeweiligkeit*] is constitutive for every character of being of this entity. That is, there is simply no Dasein which would be as Dasein that would not in its very sense be '*at its time*,' temporally particular [*jeweiliges*]" (GA 20:

206). But this "in each instance mine" here mentioned is nothing other than Dasein's "mineness" (*Jemeinigkeit*) we are familiar with from *Being and Time* (SZ: 42–3).[1] And so it makes no sense to speak of Dasein's mineness without viewing Dasein as using up its own time, that is, the finite time alloted to it.

But this is quite enough to understand why Dasein's temporality includes not only the order of ecstases, but also the required dynamical component of the flow or passage of time. Dasein's time is itself passing, for Dasein is always consuming its time. Heidegger himself indicates the relevant conceptual connections which allow him to remove the already signaled danger of "immobilizing" Dasein in the purely static order of ecstases. As he warns us of this danger, and attempts to meet it, he calls upon the phenomenon of Dasein's stretchedness in reckoning with time. We now know that Dasein is temporally stretched and reckons with time insofar as Dasein uses up *its own* finite time – the time that makes Dasein temporally particular, *jeweiliges*. In terms of stretchedness as so understood Heidegger clarifies the dynamical aspect of Dasein's temporality, the aspect he calls "agitation" or "movement." "The movement [*Bewegtheit*] of existence is not the motion [*Bewegung*] of something present-at-hand. It is *definable* in terms of the way Dasein stretches along" (SZ: 374–5, emphasis added).

Furthermore, Dasein's stretching along is, in the last analysis, "the way in which Dasein *stretches along between* birth and death" (SZ: 373). To a Dasein viewed as a temporal particular, i.e. as being only "at its time," the beginning is just as necessary as the end. Indeed, Dasein may be viewed as "being-toward-the-end" where death is only one of the ends of Dasein (ibid.). For without being bounded by its beginning as well, Dasein would not be a "closed round" whole (ibid.). And so both Dasein's beginning and Dasein's "being-towards-the-beginning" (ibid.) are constitutive of Dasein. This is why the two ends of Dasein belong to, and are only possible in terms of, Dasein's structure as care (ibid.). But the structure of care, as well as care's temporal meaning, have already been brought out. Accordingly, just as being-toward-death discloses Dasein's possibility and futurity, so too Dasein's being-toward-the-beginning discloses Dasein's thrownnness and pastness (ibid.). Dasein can thus be described as "the 'between' which relates birth and death" (SZ: 374), and relates them through its own stretchedness as a "movement" of existence.

To some degree, at least, this dynamical aspect of Dasein's temporality did break through the layer of Heidegger's earlier interpretation of the ecstases as an order of "ahead" and "already." In fact, in the passage first introducing the very concept of ecstases, Heidegger has already stressed that temporality's "essence is a *process* of temporalizing in the unity of ecstases" (SZ: 329, emphasis added). But he himself soon came to recognize that it was impossible to do justice to this dynamical aspect of temporality without bringing out Dasein's "movement" as Dasein stretches itself between birth and death. Was it too much to say, as Heidegger did, that this dynamical, processlike quality of temporality is its "essence"? Perhaps it was, since the order of ecstases is just as "essential" to temporality as its passage. But then again: there would *be* no finite temporality with its ecstases if Dasein were not stretched (and hence moving) between its two ends of birth and death.

Couldn't we account for Dasein's "movement" of existence *without* appealing to Dasein's using up the time it finds "allotted" to itself? After all, Dasein is an entity the being of which is an "issue" for it – that is, as an ongoing activity of self-interpretation

327

Dasein is fundamentally *unsettled*. And what else do we need to account for its ever-incomplete and ever-moving temporality? To present temporality as a fixed order of ecstases would be to overlook Heidegger's *dictum*: "temporality 'is' not an *entity* at all. It is not, but it *temporalizes* itself" (SZ: 328). And so, it seems, the very circumstance that Dasein is unsettled would be sufficient to account for the dynamical quality of its temporality.

But I think any such suggestion would be off target as far as Heidegger's view is concerned. It is true, of course, that Dasein's temporality is unsettled; and it is also true that within the ordinary view of the passage of time this element of unsettledness of the temporal flow is glossed over. But if Dasein's temporal passing is unsettled, the unsettledness does not account for the passing. Insofar as Dasein is *using up* its time (and thus taking a stand on it one way or another), Dasein makes its time unsettled; but in order to use its *time*, Dasein must find it *allotted* to itself, and must find it allotted as finite, that is, as bound to be extinguished. At some point Heidegger puts it quite plainly: "because the temporality of that Dasein which must take its time is finite, its days are already numbered" (SZ: 413). That is, while using its time (and thus making it unsettled), Dasein finds its time as *running* out; and this running out of Dasein's time is nothing other than the passing of Dasein's "own" time.

To see why the self's unsettledness *alone* will not be sufficient to account for temporality, let us briefly consider Sartre's account. Quite like Heidegger – indeed, following in Heidegger's footsteps – Sartre views the activity of the self as essentially unsettled. Like Heidegger, too, and in even stronger terms, Sartre stresses the priority of the dynamic over the static aspect of temporality: "the dynamic temporal [is] the secret of the static constitution of time" (Sartre 1956: 130); that is, without the element of temporal flow, the self's ecstases would be fixed and immobilized, and this means that they would cease to be temporal (McTaggart makes the same point about ordinary time: without the A-series, the B-series would lose the element of change and, therefore, would cease to be a temporal series). Unlike Heidegger, though, Sartre thinks that the mere unsettledness of the self – *without* any appeal to the self's "using up" the time allotted or apportioned to it – is quite sufficient to account for the dynamic feature of the self's temporality. This is the issue he takes up in a section titled "The Dynamic of Temporality" (Sartre 1956: 142–9).

As Sartre (1956: 147) himself indicates, his argument here is a straightforward application of his view of consciousness as a being "for itself" lacking any fixed and settled identity and consisting merely in a nihilation of being. Take Sartre's celebrated case of a café waiter. While he unceasingly projects himself toward *being* a waiter (i.e. being a conscious agent with a stable and settled identity, what Sartre calls an "in-itself-for-itself"), he can never actualize such a possibility, for the for-itself can never (fully and stably) *be* anything. As his possibility, the waiter's desired "in-itself-for-itself" is always ahead of him; but as in principle unrealizable this "in-itself-for-itself' is not ahead of him in the sense of something that is not yet actual, but can become so subsequently, later. The Heideggerian lineage of this idea is obvious and Sartre relies upon Heidegger's own concept of "ecstases" to describe this peculiar temporality of the self. Now, in "The Dynamic of Temporality" section Sartre asks us to "imagine" a for-itself endowed with the ecstases void of any element of flow or change internal to them. Such an "ensemble [of ecstases] becomes a *made* totality" (Sartre 1956: 148), an ensemble "which *is*" (ibid.); and this is incompatible with the structure of consciousness as a nihilation of being, since within such an immobilized totality of ecstases nihilation itself would become settled and stable, it would become a mere "*given*" (Sartre 1956: 149). If nihilation is not to be such a mere given (which would establish it as a fully fixed and thing-like being "in-itself"), if it is to be a genuine "spontaneity" (as Sartre explains, he here uses these two terms, nihilation and spontaneity, as equivalent) then it must be seen as an "escape from itself . . . and [an] escape from that very escape" (Sartre 1956: 148). In this consist the "metamorphosis" (Sartre 1956: 144) and the "internal change" (Sartre 1956: 146) of consciousness, that is, the required dynamic element of its temporality.

But why should we view this unceasing spontaneity of consciousness as a *temporal* process? True, when understood in Sartrean terms, that is, as equivalent with nihilation, spontaneity can't be anything other than an unceasing "refusal" of being (Sartre 1956: 148). But this is not *sufficient* to support the claim that such a "spontaneity can't be without temporalizing itself" (Sartre 1956: 148). For the refusal of being (and the refusal of that refusal, etc.) does not, by itself, imply the quality of the specifically *temporal* modification within the self. The noumenal choices whereby the Kantian self modifies and transforms (or freely chooses not to modify and transform) his intelligible character are a glaring example of such a non-temporal spontaneity. In the course of his present argument Sartre briefly considers this Kantian spontaneity and rejects it as amounting to an attribution of an "essence" to the self – Kant's conception is thus deemed incompatible with the self's nihilating structure (Sartre 1956: 149). But even if this criticism is correct, it does not imply that the ongoing unsettledness of the Sartrean nihilating self is *eo ipso* temporal. We cannot attribute temporality to it by situating it within objective time since Sartre, like Heidegger, aims at deriving the objective time from the temporality of the self. But where Heidegger views Dasein's unsettledness as Dasein's activity of using up the finite time "allotted" to it (that is, of using up *its own* time), Sartre has no such or similar concept at his disposal. In fact, since death does not even belong to the ontological structure of the Sartrean "for-itself" (Sartre 1956: 546–7), those much needed Heideggerian concepts could not even be transplanted onto the soil of Sartre's philosophy.

Heidegger relies upon the very same concepts to bring out the structure of Dasein's "historizing." "The specific movement in which Dasein is *stretched along and stretches itself along* we call its 'historizing'" (SZ: 375). To be sure, this definition is still incomplete, for, as historizing, Dasein's movement shows also the "persistence" and the "constancy" of Dasein. Already in Division One of *Being and Time* (¶64) Heidegger has been expounding an a "self-constancy" of Dasein, so different from the purely formal and non-temporal "I" of the Kantian apperception, but still indispensable for securing the unity of Dasein throughout its temporalizing. This is why Heidegger now speaks of "the specific movement *and persistence* which belong to Dasein's historizing" (SZ: 375, emphasis added). And it is only now, he continues, that the problem of self-constancy of the self (imposing as it does, and always did, the requirement of reconciling the self's movement and persistence) can be tackled.

The problem can be tackled because Dasein is "its" time. Dasein's movement and persistence is historizing, *Geschehen*. But *geschehen* means simply "to happen." Now, a happening is certainly something particular: it is always *this* happening and not *that* (or some still other) happening. But it is also temporal: a happening is something that begins and ends. As *Geschehen*, then, Dasein is, once again, *temporally particular* (*jeweiliges*); that is, Dasein's "mineness" must be, once again, understood as Dasein's being at (or simply being) "its" time. Since historizing characterizes a temporally particular Dasein, historizing discloses Dasein's own particular "fate" (*Schicksal*). Dasein historizes itself in many ways. In "primordial historizing" the authentic Dasein takes up its fate "in a possibility which it has inherited and yet it has chosen" (SZ: 384). Dasein can be said to have "inherited" this possibility, for all possibilities of authentic existence come down to Dasein from its heritage (ibid.). Moreover, since Dasein is a communal being, a being-with, "its historizing is a co-historizing and is determinative for it as *destiny* [*Geschick*]" (SZ: 384). In this way Dasein's individual historizing is *eo ipso* historical (*geschichtlich*) in the sense of being a part of the history of a community.

This is not mere historizing any more; it is Dasein's historicality, *Geschichtlikeit*. Still, the latter can be made intelligible only in terms of the former (SZ: 374–5, 382–3). Historizing has already been identified as the "specific movement and persistence" in which Dasein is "its" time. Consequently, if Dasein's historicality is to be made intelligible in terms of Dasein's own historizing, then historicality must "*belong, as an essential constitutive state, to the subjectivity of the 'historical' subject*" (SZ: 382). But how could historicality – i.e. that feature of Dasein whereby Dasein finds itself anchored in a collective, shared history – belong to the "subjectivity" of Dasein's own historizing? There is no mystery here and the link is more solid than the etymological kinship, played upon by Heidegger, between *Geschehen* and *Geschichtlichkeit*. As a temporal particular, Dasein is "its" time. But its time is also the time in which Dasein lives, as when we say of, for example, Stendhal's heroes, that "Fabrizio del Dongo's time was the time of the Napoleonic wars," or that "Julien Sorel's time was the time of the Bourbon restoration." Thus an authentic Dasein can "*take over its own thrownness and be in the moment of vision for 'its time'* " (SZ: 385). Here "for its time" ' (*für "seine Zeit"*) means the time of the historical situation in which Dasein finds itself and in terms of which it must define itself. Dasein is thus historical in the literal sense of the term. But Dasein is historical only because it is "its" time in the still deeper sense of being temporally particular, *jeweiliges*.

To conclude: both Dasein's reckoning with time and Dasein's historicality are grounded in Dasein's using up its own time, the time allotted or apportioned to Dasein. In introducing these concepts, we recall, Heidegger was aiming at accounting for the specifically dynamical aspects of human temporalizing. But this Heideggerian account comes with its own price. In using up its own time Dasein can be said to be consuming it or running out of it; and this indicates the required element of the temporal passage (a *conditio sine qua non* of any time) within Dasein itself. But – and here is the rub – how are we to *conceive* this temporal passage internal to Dasein? Clearly, this cannot be viewed as a case of the flow making up temporal *succession*. To attribute succession to Dasein's temporality would be to violate one of the key tenets of Heidegger's philosophy: "Dasein, in existing, can never establish itself as a fact which is present-at-hand, arising and passing away 'in the course of time,' with a bit of it past already" (SZ: 328). We must, then, ascribe to Dasein some temporal passage which would be very different from succession yet still merit to be called "temporal." In terms of our ordinary, and even circumspective, understanding of time, the concept Heidegger puts forward and employs is thus made up of incompatible components. How could Heidegger justify the use of such a concept and, if he could justify it, why would he persist in speaking here of "time" – as he clearly does when he designates the "primordial temporality" as "primordial time" (SZ: 329)?

To these very pertinent questions Heidegger gives repeatedly the same answer: Dasein's temporality merits being called "time," because time (as understood circumspectively, ordinarily, or even scientifically) can be *derived* from Dasein's temporality (SZ: 329; GA 24: 368–9). As it stands, this answer is not very satisfactory. Take a metaphysician or a theologian who succeeds in "deriving" from God the existence and the essence of the world. This does not yet warrant using the same concepts when speaking of God and of His creation. What is still needed, for that purpose, is the presence of some resemblance, or some common nature, shared by God and the world He has created. By the same standard, in order to show that he can justifiably apply the concept "time" to Dasein's temporality (or that he can even speak of "temporality" – a term which, by itself, indicates some connection, however thin, with time), Heidegger would have to show not only that time is derivable from Dasein's temporality but, in addition, that time and temporality do have some resembling features or some common nature in virtue of which we can indeed speak of "primordial temporality" as "primordial time." To investigate whether or not Heidegger succeeds in carrying out this project would be, of course, a monumental task far beyond the limits of the present chapter.

Happily, though, success or failure of such a derivation (of time from Dasein's temporality) is not the *only* test we can apply to Heidegger's account. For at almost every stage of his analytic Heidegger appeals, and does so as a matter of philosophical principle, to the "attestation" or "testimony" of Dasein itself. For example – but this is a key example indeed – when speaking of Dasein's being-toward-death he states clearly that such a concept would be a "fantastical exaction" if it could not be validated by being "attested" in concrete experiences of Dasein (SZ: 266–7). Dasein's condition as a whole (that is care and its temporal meaning) is attested to in the fundamental moods of *anxiety* and *boredom*. To be sure, there is no analysis of boredom in *Being and Time* itself. But boredom is mentioned in *The Concept of Time* (1924) and in *What Is Metaphysics?* (1929) (See Heidegger 1992: 14E, 16E; GA 9). Above all, *The Fundamental Concepts of Metaphysics* (1929/1930) contains long analyses of boredom and of its pivotal role in disclosing Dasein's temporality (GA 29/30). Now, anxiety and boredom disclose temporality in two different ways. Anxiety discloses temporality as the order of ecstases, while boredom discloses temporality as the passing away of Dasein's time. Needless to say, these different functions of anxiety and boredom can represent only differences in emphasis; for, as we saw earlier, there would be no ecstatic order without Dasein's inherently dynamical stretchedness between birth and death. With this qualification, however, it can be said that anxiety and boredom are indeed focused upon those two different aspects of Dasein's temporality.

Of this function of boredom, the very meaning of *Langeweile* – the German term for boredom – gives us a telling indication. On its deepest and metaphysically most significant level (this is the "profound boredom" Heidegger finds expressed in the phrase "it is boring for one"), boredom operates as the disclosure of the oppressive character of the finite temporality allotted to Dasein. The profound boredom is, in this fundamental respect, quite different from the other two forms of boredom Heidegger also analyzes. In the first form of boredom what is boring is this or that (some particular

331

entity, circumstance, etc.); in its second form, boredom is not focused upon anything determinate (GA 29/30: 172–3). In this second form of boredom, Dasein is bored by time itself, albeit still in a rather superficial way; for in the second form of boredom time is taken merely as an immobilized standing present, cut off from our past and future (GA 29/30: 124–5). Now, in "profound boredom," "time entrances [*bannt*] Dasein, not as the time which has remained standing as distinct from flowing, but rather the *time beyond such flowing and its standing*, the time which in each case *Dasein itself as a whole* is" (GA 29/30: 221). What Heidegger here rules out as entrancing Dasein is the flowing and the standing of time as disclosed in those earlier, more superficial forms of boredom. But, on the other hand, what is this time that Dasein itself "is" (and is "as a whole"), and how can *it* entrance (or "oppress") Dasein in profound boredom? Heidegger answers the question in the following way: "in boredom, *Langeweile*, the *while* [*Weile*] becomes *long* [*lang*]. Which while? Any short while? No, but rather the while whilst Dasein is as such, the while that measures out that tarrying awhile [*Verweilen*] which is allotted to Dasein as such, i.e. the while whilst it is to be" (GA 29/30: 228). Notice what Heidegger explicitly rules out: it is not this or that "short" while that becomes "long" in boredom. Heidegger does not mean a minute as opposed to an hour, an hour as opposed to a day, a day as opposed to a month, a year, a decade and so on. None of the "whiles" which we would ordinarily consider "short" (a minute, perhaps an hour) and none of the "whiles" which we would ordinarily consider "long" (a year, a decade) is what Heidegger here has in mind. The while that becomes "long" in boredom is neither the while of a minute (ordinarily meant as "short") nor the while of a decade (ordinarily meant as "long"). The while that becomes "long" in boredom is neither short nor long in the sense in which these terms are ordinarily understood. Or does Heidegger's "short" while mean circumspective shortness, shortness in terms of the "world-time," as when I say "it will take only a short while to drive from my office to the lake"? No, he does not mean that either, for when he says that in boredom the while becomes long he does not mean what we circumspectively consider a "long" while (as in "it will be a long while before I climb to the top of that mountain"). He can't mean these (circumspectively "long" and "short") whiles for, as he tells us here, the while that becomes long in boredom is "the while whilst Dasein is as such," i.e. the time "allotted" to Dasein. I have already commented upon the conceptual connections here at work. The time allotted to Dasein, indeed the time that Dasein is, is the inherently finite time that Dasein uses up in some way. In thus consuming its own time Dasein is temporally stretched and "moves" between birth and death. What is oppressive in boredom is precisely this sheer dynamical aspect of temporality: the running out of the time allotted to Dasein. But – and this is the key point here – this passing away of Dasein's time is not a succession. For, first, to speak here of succession we would have to say that *this* particular "while" succeeds *that* particular "while," which will in turn be succeeded by *that* (still other) particular "while" and so on. But the while that becomes "long" in this "profound" boredom cannot be this or that particular while (whether "short" or "long" as these terms are ordinarily or circumspectively understood). For this reason, though boredom does disclose the while that Dasein "is" (Dasein's "own time," the time "allotted" to Dasein), it does not disclose it as a succession of whiles. Yet, second, the while that Dasein "is" is finite and, consequently, it must remain "short" in *some* sense of that term. And so it does, as Heidegger here indicates. The while that becomes long in boredom "is this whole while [that Dasein is] – and yet is a short while; and so every Dasein in turn is a short while" (GA 29/30: 228). But if the shortness of Dasein's own while becomes longer in boredom, this does not mean "longer" in the sense of "clock or chronology" (GA 29/30: 229), be that chronology determined circumspectively or within the (ordinary or scientific) pure sequence of "Nows." Profound boredom's lengthening of Dasein's while is only the burden, the "*oppressing*" of Dasein by its own time (GA 29/30: 229); and this oppressing of Dasein by its own time "includes in itself a peculiar indication of its [non-chronological] *shortness*" (GA 29/30: 229), that is, it includes an indication that Dasein's own time is bound to pass away.

Even the way in which Heidegger describes the status of ecstases as they are apprehended in ("profound") boredom conveys that function of boredom. Needless to say, in boredom the ecstases are not obliterated. What oppresses (or "entrances") Dasein in boredom is the temporal horizon of the three ecstases. Heidegger himself says as much (GA 29/30: 217–19, 220–2). But he immediately hastens to explain just *how* the horizon of the three ecstases is oppressive to Dasein in boredom. What is oppressive is "Neither merely the present nor merely the past nor merely the future, nor indeed all these reckoned together – but rather their *unarticulated unity* in the simplicity of this unity of their horizons all at once"(GA 29/30: 222). Let us contrast this with anxiety. Anxiety diseloses the three items of care grounded in the corresponding temporal ecstases and there can be no question of any "unarticulated unity" of these three components as they are brought out in anxiety. Quite the contrary, anxiety is what first discloses in all clarity the relevant different features of Dasein's being-possible ("ahead of itself"), of its being "already" thrown into a world, and of its being "alongside" entities. Even in the temporality of anxiety (SZ: 343–3) – where the focus is not simply on the three components of care, but on their temporal meaning – the three ecstases, albeit apprehended only from within Dasein's past, are still sharply delineated and distinguished from each other. And if, in boredom, the ecstases are brought into their unarticulated unity, it is because boredom discloses the sheer passage of the time allotted to Dasein. The order of ecstases is, in boredom, less important than it is in anxiety, although, to say it again, these two aspects of temporality are both essential to it.

To some degree, at least, this understanding of Dasein's "own" finite time is preserved, however vaguely, in Dasein's everyday moods as well. To be sure, only anxiety and boredom disclose Dasein's finite time without evading it. The everyday moods are evasions from Dasein's thrownness (SZ: 136), where thrownness means always "thrownness into death" (SZ: 308). Dasein's everyday moods are, therefore, ways of evading thrownness into death. But still, in evading this condition of Dasein everyday moods disclose, however dimly, what they evade (SZ: 136). This is why even in the ordinary understanding of time some sense of Dasein's own time as running out on Dasein is still preserved. "Why do we say that time *passes away*, when we do not say with *just as much* emphasis that it arises?" (SZ: 425). Viewing time in a purely detached way, we would find no reason to put more emphasis on passing away rather than on arising. Or is our emphasis due to some arbitrary convention which it would be only up to us to repudiate by beginning to attach more importance to arising? Heidegger thinks not. For "the everyday experience of time *rightly* adheres to" giving "priority to consuming and passing away" (SZ: 431–2; emphasis added). The everyday experience is "right" in this respect, for it expresses Dasein's "fugitive" knowledge of its death, of its "finite futurity" (SZ: 425) – that is, the fugitive knowledge of *its own* time as passing away.[2]

Notes

1   Already in Heidegger's important 1924 Marburg lecture titled The *Concept of Time* (the "original form" of *Being and Time* according to Gadamer) this close link of *Jemeinigkeit* and *Jeweiligkeit* is clearly indicated. See Heidegger (1992: 8E, 10E).

2   Throughout the present chapter I have avoided relying upon *The Concept of Time*, since the work is considered by some (a view I do not share) to have been transcended by *Being and Time*. Be this as it may, the interpretation I have defended in this chapter is greatly strengthened by the material to be found in *The Concept of Time*. Consider the following question Heidegger asks: "What is it *to have one's own death in each case? It is Dasein's running ahead to its past (Vorbei)*" (Heidegger 1992: 12E). But what is this past toward which Dasein is running ahead? Here is Heidegger's answer: "This past, as that to which I run ahead, here makes a discovery in my running ahead to it: it is *my* past. As this past it uncovers my Dasein as suddenly no longer there (*nicht mehr da*); suddenly I am no longer there alongside such and such things, alongside such and such people, alongside these vanities, these tricks, these chatterings" (ibid.). Here Heidegger indicates in unmistakably clear terms that my running ahead to my death as to my past is nothing other than my running ahead toward a point where I myself will be a thing of the past, "no longer there" in the sense of having passed away. I may add that I find it almost inconceivable that the corresponding formula from *Being and Time* (Dasein's "death is the possibility of no-longer-being-able-to-be-there," *Nicht-mehr-dasein-konnens*, SZ: 250) could mean anything different.

References and further reading

Heidegger, M. (1992) *The Concept of Time*. Oxford: Blackwell.
Sartre, J.-P. (1956) *Being and Nothingness*. New York: Philosophical Library.

Part III

HEIDEGGER'S LATER THOUGHT

21

Unconcealment

MARK A. WRATHALL

Truth and Unconcealment

During the two decades between 1925 and 1945, the essence of truth is a pervasive issue in Heidegger's work. He offers several essay courses devoted to the nature of truth, starting in 1925 with *Logik. Die Frage nach der Wahrheit* (GA 21), and continuing with *Vom Wesen der Wahrheit. Zu Platons Höhlengleichnis und Theätet* (Winter Semester 1931/2, GA 34), *Vom Wesen der Wahrheit* (Winter Semester 1933/4, GA 36/37), and *Grundfragen der Philosophie. Ausgewählte "Probleme" der "Logik"* (Winter Semester 1937/8, GA 45). He also includes a significant discussion of the essence of truth in virtually every other lecture course taught during this period. Particularly notable in this regard are the *Parmenides* lecture course of 1942/3 (GA 54), *Einleitung in die Philosophie* (Winter Semester 1928/9, GA27), and *Nietzsches Lehre vom Willen zur Macht als Erkenntnis* (Summer Semester 1939, GA 47).

Heidegger's writings during this period also reflect his preoccupation with truth. In addition to the essay "Vom Wesen der Wahrheit" (GA 9), many of his other works include extended discussions of the essence of truth. These include *Being and Time* (SZ), essays like "Vom Wesen des Grundes" (GA 9), "Der Ursprung des Kunstwerkes" (GA 5), and "Was ist Metaphysik?" (GA 9), and unpublished works like the *Beiträge* (GA 65) and *Besinnung* (GA 66).

Following 1946, there are few extended discussions of "truth" in Heidegger's writings. Indeed, in the last few decades of his work, Heidegger rarely even mentions "the essence of truth" (*das Wesen der Wahrheit*) or the "question of truth" (*die Wahrheitsfrage*) (although other locutions like "the truth of being," *die Wahrheit des Seins*, persist, albeit infrequently, right to the end; see, for example, the 1973 "Seminar in Zähringen," GA 15: 373). But this should be seen as a merely terminological shift. For Heidegger, the essence of truth is always understood in terms of unconcealment, and Heidegger never stops inquiring into unconcealment. Indeed, one is hard pressed to find any work in Heidegger's vast corpus which doesn't have some discussion of unconcealment.

The terminological shift from talk of "truth" to "unconcealment" is a result of his recognition of the misleadingness of using the word "truth" to name unconcealment – a recognition brought about by the gradual realization that the metaphysical tradition's blindness to unconcealment is largely a result of a rather narrow notion of truth. As he explains in 1949:

> In its answers to the question concerning beings as such, metaphysics operates with a prior representation of being necessarily and hence continually. But metaphysics does not induce being itself to speak, for metaphysics does not give thought to being in its truth, nor does it think such truth as unconcealment, nor does it think this unconcealment in its essence. (GA 9: 369/280)

From this point on, Heidegger speaks and writes consistently of the essence of unconcealment rather than the essence of truth. It is also clear that, despite using the word "truth" to name the subject matter of his thought, his primary interest was always unconcealment. As he notes self-reflectively during the "Heraclitus Seminar" (1966–7), "Aletheia as unconcealment occupied me all along, but 'truth' slipped itself in between" (GA 15: 262). But while he is occasionally critical of his own earlier views of the essence of truth (see, for example, GA 65: 351–2), in fundamental outline his view of it remains unchanged.

The fundamental outline, or what I call the "platform," of Heidegger's view of truth forms the basis both for his critique of the metaphysical tradition of philosophy, and for his own constructive account of ontology and the nature of human being. It includes the following planks.

1 Propositional truth (correctness, *Richtigkeit*). An assertion or proposition is true when it corresponds with a state of affairs.

Heidegger understands correspondence (*Übereinstimmung*) as the condition of being succesfully directed toward the world in a propositional attitude:

> What makes every one of these statements into a true one? This: in what it says, it corresponds with the matters and the states of affairs about which it says something. The being true of an assertion thus signifies such corresponding. What therefore is truth? Truth is correspondence. Such correspondence exists because the assertion orients itself [*sich richtet*] according to that about which it speaks. Truth is correctness [*richtigkeit*]. (GA 34: 2)

But this correspondence or agreement, Heidegger argues, cannot be understood on a representational model of language. He argues instead that correspondence exists when our orientation to the world allows what is to show itself in a particular way, and thus it can be understood as a bringing out of concealment.

2 The truth (uncoveredness or discoveredness, *Entdecktheit*) of entities. An entity is "true" when it is uncovered, i.e. made available for comportment.

Propositional truth (1) is grounded in the truth of entities, because a true assertion can only correspond or fail to correspond with the way things are if entities are available as the standard against which the assertion or proposition can be measured. Only because an entity is unconcealed, Heidegger argues, "can we make assertions about it and also check them. . . . Only because the entity itself is true can propositions about the entity be true in a derived sense" (GA 27: 78).

The "truth" – i.e. the uncovering or making manifest – of entities *can* be brought about through an assertion or a theoretical apprehension, but it normally occurs in our practical involvements with things in the world. "Ontic manifesting . . . happens in accordance with an attuned [*stimmungsmäßigen*] and instinctive finding oneself in the midst of entities, and in accordance with the striving and moving comportment to entities that is grounded along with it" (GA 9: 131).

3 The truth of being. There is an unconcealment (*Unverborgenheit*) of being when an understanding of the being or essence of everything that is shapes all the possibilities for comportment in the world.

Ontic truth (2) is grounded in the truth of being, because an entity is made available for comportment on the basis of a prior opening up of the world.

Heidegger's views on the nature of the truth of being undergo considerable change over the course of his career. At various points, he focuses on the following elements of the truth of being.

(A) The disclosure (*Erschlossenheit*) of Dasein and of the world. The idea is that entities can only be available for comportment on the basis of a prior disclosure of the world as the meaningful structure within which entities can show up as what they are. In addition, since entities are uncovered in terms of their availability for comportment, their uncovering requires the prior disclosure of Dasein as an acting and understanding being. In *Being and Time*, Heidegger expressed this idea as follows: "the uncoveredness of entities within-the-world is grounded in the world's disclosedness. But disclosedness is that basic character of Dasein according to which it is its 'there.' Disclosedness is constituted by disposedness (*Befindlichkeit*), understanding, and discourse, and pertains equiprimordially to the world, to being-in, and to the Self" (SZ: 221).

(B) The truth of essence. Entities can be manifest in their truth, that is, as what they really are, only if they are unconcealed in their essence – which means, they (come to) have an essence. Heidegger's catch-phrase for this is: "The essence of truth is the truth of essence" (GA 9: 201; see also GA 45: 95; GA 65: 288; GA 5: 37). This means that the unconcealment of beings requires first an unconcealment of the most fundamental, essential aspect of entities that makes them what they are. This works not by being thought about, but by disposing us to encounter entities in a particular way, as having a particular essence: "the world gives itself an original view (form) that is not explicitly grasped, yet functions precisely as a paradigmatic form for all manifest beings" (GA 9: 158/123).

What both (3A) and (3B) have in common is the insight that entities can only be manifest on the basis of a prelinguistic understanding of and affective disposedness to what makes something the being that it is.

Heidegger eventually comes to believe that the truth of being depends on:

4   Truth as the clearing (*Lichtung*). There is a clearing within which an understanding of being or essence can prevail when incompatible possibilities of being are concealed or held back.

This is the most fundamental form of unconcealment. "Unconcealment," when understood as the clearing, does not name a thing, or a property or characteristic of things,
or a kind of action we perform on things, or even the being of things. It names, instead,
a domain or structure which allows there to be things with properties and characteristics, or modes of being. This is not a spatial domain or physical entity, or any sort of
entity at all. It is something like a space of possibilities.

   (1)–(3) give us possibilities for different kinds of experience of and actions with entities, for different kinds of goals to be pursued, or forms of life to be lived. These possibilities are the possibilities opened up by the understanding of being and essences. But
what is the "space" which allows those possibilities to be actual possibilities – that is,
to be the possibilities that actually shape a given historical existence? This is to ask:
what, given that there has been a progression of different truths of being in history,
allows any particular truth of being to prevail?

   Heidegger's answer is the clearing. The clearing is: that some truth of being prevails
because other truths of being do not.

*   *   *

I call (1)–(4) "planks" in Heidegger's platform for thinking about truth. The platform
describes Heidegger's *considered* view on truth and unconcealment. This is not to say
that he is clear about the relationships between (1), (2), (3), and (4) at every stage of
his career. Indeed, as I discuss in the next section, he is quite critical of his own earlier
works on unconcealment for their failure to recognize (4).

   In what follows, I want to try to explain more clearly what each plank in the platform consists in, and how each plank is grounded in the next one. The first step is to
say something about what holds them together. Heidegger proposes that each plank is
a kind of "truth" only because it involves unconcealment. So, we might ask: what, in
general, is unconcealment? We will then be in a position to explain each plank in more
detail.

Unconcealment in General

The word that is generally translated as "unconcealment" or "unconcealedness" is
Unverborgenheit. This, in turn, is Heidegger's preferred, and rather literal, translation
for the Greek word *alētheia*, itself ordinarily translated "truth." Heidegger uses "truth"
(*Wahrheit*) and "unconcealment" interchangeably for much of his career, well aware
that this practice invites several contrary misunderstandings.

   The first misunderstanding is to think that Heidegger defines propositional truth as
unconcealment; the second is to transfer to the notion of unconcealment features
present in our ordinary understanding of truth. Because the analysis of unconcealment is an analysis of the ground of propositional truth, it should be clear that uncon-

cealment is not to be taken as a (re)definition of propositional truth. Heidegger was emphatic about this both "early" and "late"; compare, for instance, comments from the 1931 lecture course on the essence of truth in GA 34: 11 ("The meaning of the Greek word for truth, unconcealment, above all has absolutely nothing to do with assertion and with the factual context, set out in the customary definition of the essence of truth: with correspondence and correctness"), with the 1964 essay "The End of Philosophy and the Task of Thinking" ("the question concerning *aletheia*, concerning unconcealment as such, is not the question concerning truth" (GA 14: 76); see also the comments in *Being and Time*: "to translate this word [*alētheia*] as 'truth', and, above all, to define this expression conceptually in theoretical ways, is to cover up the meaning of what the Greeks made 'self-evidently' basic for the terminological use of *alētheia* as a pre-philosophical way of understanding it" (SZ: 219); and the 1960 essay "Hegel and the Greeks": "if the essence of truth that straightaway comes to reign as correctness and certainty can subsist only within the realm of unconcealment, then truth indeed has to do with *Alētheia*, but not *Alētheia* with truth" (GA 9: 442/335)). Hence, it is essential to see that the analyses of the unconcealment of beings and the clearing of being are not being offered as definitions of propositional truth. And, just as importantly, propositional truth cannot account for the unconcealment of beings and the clearing of being: "it is never the case that an assertion – be it ever so true – could primarily disconceal an entity as such" (GA 29/30: 493).

In addition, Heidegger's argument for the dependence of propositional truth on the unconcealment of entities, being, and the clearing does not hang in any way on his etymological analysis of *alētheia*. Nevertheless, his argument for the dependence relationship is often confused with his perhaps questionable etymology.

Finally, Heidegger's warnings to the contrary, it is perhaps understandable that readers often confuse unconcealment with what we ordinarily think of as truth. In any event, in response to criticisms from Friedländer about his etymology of *alētheia*, and from Tugendhat regarding the "natural conception of truth," Heidegger eventually disavowed the practice of calling unconcealment "truth" (GA 14: 76). But since Heidegger himself had never confused unconcealment with propositional truth, the disavowal should not be taken to mean that he gave up on the platform or any of the planks of the platform. On the contrary, to the extent that the platform was obscured by the tendency to think of truth only in terms of correspondence, Heidegger hoped to make clearer his commitment to it.

More important than changes in Heidegger's use of the word "truth," but less remarked upon, are changes in his use of the word "unconcealment." Before 1928, Heidegger never spoke of the "unconcealment of *being*" or connected unconcealment with a clearing. In *Being and Time*, for example, the word "unconcealment" only appears in one passage, and it is introduced only to be equated with uncoveredness (*Entdecktheit*) (SZ: 219). It was only starting in the 1928 lecture course *Einleitung in die Philosophie* that Heidegger adopted unconcealment as a term for anything other than the uncovering of entities (see GA 27: 202–3). Between 1928 and 1948, Heidegger wrote of both the "unconcealment of being" and the "unconcealment of entities" – a practice of which his marginal notes were later quite critical (see GA 9: 132–3; also GA 5: 60, 69). This self-criticism is probably a result of the fact that, by 1948, Heidegger came to believe that the metaphysical tradition had only ever thought about the unconcealment of entities, and thus that an important step toward overcoming the metaphysical tradition consists precisely in understanding the unconcealment of being (see, e.g., GA 67: 234). In any event, after about 1948, Heidegger seldom writes of the "unconcealment of *entities*." Instead, from that point on the term "unconcealment" is used almost exclusively with regard to planks (3) and (4) of the platform.

What we want to know, however, is why it is that, at some point, Heidegger speaks of very different kinds of things as contributing to unconcealment or being brought into unconcealment (true assertions, things, human being, understandings of being, and the clearing itself). What makes "unconcealment" and related terms[1] applicable to all these cases is the *privative* nature of the phenomena in question.

Something is "privative" when it can only be understood and specified in relation to what it is not. For example, imperfection can only be understood by reference to perfection – if you don't know what it would be for something to be perfect, then you could not know what is at stake in calling it "imperfect." The *name* for a privative aspect need not itself incorporate a privation marker like "in-" or "un-." To use one of Heidegger's own examples, reticence is a privative aspect in that reticence is not simply *not* making any noise. Something is only reticent insofar as it could speak, but doesn't. So what it is to be reticent is to be understood by way of what the reticent person is *not* doing. Similarly, a stone can be sightless, but it is not blind. To be blind requires that one be in the sight game. Nietzsche's famous account of the good/evil distinction is yet another example. There, "evil" functions as the positive term – the one that is defined first and more clearly. "Good" then gets its meaning as a negation of each of the properties associated with evil (see Nietzsche 1996: I.13).

Thus, given that privative aspects are specifically understood in relation to what they are not, having a privative aspect is different than merely lacking a certain quality. Heidegger's notion of unconcealment applies to things which are privative in just this sense and, he believes, the Greek language's use of a privative word-form to name "truth" shows that the Greeks, too, were aware of the privative nature of material and propositional truth. "The awakening and forming of the word *aletheia*," he writes,"is not a mere accident . . . and not an external matter" (GA 34: 127). Unconcealment is meant to be understood like blindness or reticence. That is, what it is to be unconcealed is determined in relationship to a privative state – here, whatever kind of concealment that does prevail in what is to be unconcealed. With respect to each plank in the platform, then, concealment is the positive term, and needs to be understood before we can get clear about what unconcealment amounts to.

So far, this discussion is very formal. I now try to give it some phenomenological content by looking at each plank in the platform in turn.

The Planks of the Platform

Propositional truth

One typically thinks of truth as a property of things that have as their content a proposition – things like assertions and beliefs. The truth of propositions is, for Heidegger, the right starting point for thinking about unconcealment, because truth or unconcealment (*alētheia*) has often been understood exclusively as a property of propositions, but also because in a phenomenology of propositional truth, we quickly discover that the truth of propositions depends on the uncovering of entities. Thinking about propositional truth thus leads to an inquiry into more fundamental forms of unconcealment.

Heidegger accepts that many propositions are true by corresponding to, or agreeing with, the way things are. But recognizing this fact, for Heidegger, is less an explanation of truth than a basis for further inquiry into its nature.

> The old received definition of truth: *veritas est adaequatio intellectus ad rem, homoiosis,* measuring up, conformity of thinking to the matter about which it thinks – . . . is indeed basically (*im Ansatz*) correct. But it is also *merely* a *starting point* (*Ansatz*) and not at all that which it is commonly taken to be, namely, an essential determination of truth. It is merely the starting point . . . for the question: in what in general is the possibility of measuring up to something grounded? (GA 29/30: 497)

If we admit, in other words, that true assertions agree, measure up to, correspond with, the way things are, still we need to be able to explain what makes such a relationship between an assertion and a proposition possible. By considering this problem, however, Heidegger believes that we are led to a view of truth as uncovering.

The difficulty for the correspondence view is explaining in an illuminating way what a correspondence relationship consists in. There has been a tendency to explain correspondence as a relationship between mental representations and facts or states of affairs in the world. Heidegger, by contrast, argues that truth "has by no means the structure of a correspondence between knowing and the object in the sense of a likening of one entity (the subject) to another (the Object)" (SZ: 218–19). If we are to make sense of the idea of correspondence, he believes, we first need to jettison the idea that it consists in a relationship between a *representation* and things in the world. Instead, Heidegger suggests that correspondence is a characteristic of our orientation to the world – particular, of our "assertative being toward what is asserted" (SZ: 218). Our beliefs and assertions correspond not by representing some state of affairs just as it is, but by giving us an orientation to things that lets the state of affairs appear just as it is (GA 21: 9–10). True beliefs and assertions are true because they make possible a perceiving that "lets what is itself be encountered as it is" (GA 21: 167). A phenomenological description of cases where we confirm the truth of an assertion, Heidegger, believes, shows us that this is in fact how we ordinarily understand the truth of the assertion. "To say that an assertion 'is true'," Heidegger argues, "signifies that it uncovers what is as it is in itself. It asserts, it points out, it 'lets' what is 'be seen' (*apophansis*) in its uncoveredness. The being-true (truth) of the assertion must be understood as being-uncovering" (SZ: 218, translation modified). A true assertion uncovers a state of affairs by elevating it into salience or prominence, thus allowing it to be seen: "the basic achievement of speech," Heidegger argues, "consist[s] in showing or revealing that about which one is speaking, that concerning which there is discussion. In such revealing, the thing that is addressed is made manifest. It becomes perceivable, and, in discussion, the thing perceived gets determined" (GA 21: 6).

343

We are now in a position to see why Heidegger believes that propositional truth is a kind of bringing out of concealment. Concealment reigns in a non-assertoric dealing with the world in the sense that, in such pre-predicative comportments, the world is experienced in a way that lacks determinacy, i.e. propositional articulation. This means that the world is not available for thought, for the discovery of inferential and justificatory relationships between propositional states and worldly states of affairs.

Heidegger believes that, in our everyday dealings with things, we experience the world in precisely such a propositional concealment (see GA 21: 111). In our pre-predicative experience of the world, things are understood as the things they are in terms of our practical modes of coping with them. Such practically constituted things are implicated in a complex variety of involvements with other objects, practices, purposes, and goals, and are understood immediately as reaching out into a variety of involvements. In assertion, by contrast, our experience undergoes an "explicit restriction of our view," and we "dim down" the whole richly articulated situation in front of us to focus on some particular feature of the situation (SZ: 155). The "assertoric determining of a thing," Heidegger suggests, must be understood as a "levelling-off of the primary understanding within [everyday] dealings" (GA 21: 156). He notes that when we make an assertion about what we perceive in our fluid coping with the world, the "assertion makes certain relations stand out from the matter, which is at first apprehended directly and simply in its unarticulated totality" (GA 20: 76–7).

In natural perception, then, we ordinarily perceive a whole context which lacks the logical structure of linguistic categories. When we apprehend things in such a way as to be able to express them in an assertion, however, the act of perception now is brought under the categories of the understanding. The assertion, Heidegger writes, "draws out" or "accentuates" "a state of affairs," thus allowing the entity to "become expressly visible precisely in what it is" (GA 20: 86). In doing this, the assertion "discloses anew" what is present at first in a non-conceptually articulated fashion, so that these things "come to explicit apprehension precisely in what they are" (GA 20: 84). Thus, the assertion manifests things differently than they are given to natural perception. In it, things are defined or determined "as such and so" – as having a particular property or characteristic (see, e.g., GA 21: 66, 133–4). Those properties or characteristics were present in the entity before, but through the assertion they are isolated and cut off from their context, thereby being highlighted or lifted into prominence. This allows us to see an object with a thematic clarity that is not present in our natural perception of it, but we are no longer able to deal with it naturally – for that, we need to see it in its immediacy (GA 21: 144–7).

Thus, the dimming down or leveling off that occurs when we suspend our everyday dealings with things is what first makes it possible to give something a conceptual character by making it possible to uncover the kind of determinate content which allows one to form conceptual connections, draw inferences, and justify one occurrent intentional state on the basis of another. The pre-predicative is a non-conceptual way of comporting ourselves toward the things in the world around us. Rather than a conceptual or a logical articulation, the pre-predicative manifestness of things is articulated along the lines of our practical comportment. In such an articulation, things show up *as* what they are, but in the whole complexity of their involvements.

This makes propositional truth, on Heidegger's view, a privative concept – it is defined relative to the richer, more primordial givenness of the world, which is lost in propositional articulation. Because propositional modes of comportment (believing, asserting, and so on) function by determining and highlighting certain elements of our pre-propositional experience of things, they are a derivative form of comporting ourselves toward things in the world, yet a form of unconcealment all the same.

We will explore the pre-propositional experience of things in more detail in the next section. Before going on, however, we can summarize Heidegger's views in the following way. Our most fundamental forms of comportment are practically rather than conceptually articulated. On the basis of this practical articulation, things show up as making demands on us, and constraining how we can use them. Through language we are able to orient ourselves to objects in a way that is conceptually rather than pragmatically articulated. When our orientation allows us to see a state of affairs just as it is – when it uncovers an object in its condition – we say that it corresponds to the facts or the state of affairs. Thus, we can understand assertions and propositions to be measured in terms of the positive/privative pair "concealing/unconcealing (a fact or state of affairs in the world)." That means that the proper basis for judging the success of a linguistic act is whether it makes manifest a fact toward which we can comport ourselves. The act will fail to the extent that it leaves a state of affairs in concealedness – that is, leaves it unavailable to thought, or leaves thought out of touch with the world. Correspondence, consequently, needs to be rethought in terms of Heidegger's account of how to assess the success or failure of linguistic acts like, for example, assertion. An assertion most genuinely succeeds if it brings a state of affairs into unconcealment for thought (which may well go with a correlative concealing of the practical world). What we now need to understand is the ground of propositional truth – what makes it possible for an assertion to uncover in this way? The answer is a prior uncovering of entities.

The uncoveredness of entities

We have seen that the concealment removed by propositional truth is the unavailability of the world for a certain kind of comportment – namely thought. Propositional truth is, in turn, a specific form of a more general kind of *unconcealment*. In the more general version, what is at issue is the availability of entities for comportment in general. The *uncoveredness* of entities makes entities available for comportment. The concealment which constitutes the privative state of entities consists in their not being available as that toward which or with which we can comport.

Comportment (*Verhalten*) is a very broad term that is meant to include every instance in which we experience something, and everything that we do. Excluded from comportment, then, are physiological or causal events or behaviors. When I grow hair or hiccup, there is no sense in which I am comporting myself. Unlike such causal events or behaviors, comportments have a meaningful structure. But comportment is broader than the class of deliberate actions (although, naturally it includes them), because comportment involves things I do or experience without an occurrent mental state in which I intend to do it or register the experience. Thus, comportment includes automatic actions, for example, which reflect a responsiveness to the meaning of a situation.

Because comportments are tied up with meaningfully structured situation, all comportments involve a relationship to an object of some sort. When I swat at a fly, I am comporting myself toward the fly. When I hear a symphony, I am comporting myself to the symphony (as well as all the instruments, musicians, the conductor, etc.)

An entity is concealed, then, when I can't comport myself toward it – when it is not available as something toward which I can direct myself in a basic intentional comportment. The opposite of uncoveredness, Heidegger says, "is not covering up, but rather lack of access for simple intending" (GA 21: 179). The fly is concealed, for example, when I can't find it to swat at it. The symphony would be concealed if I lacked an understanding of symphonic form (that is, I might be able to hear beautiful music, but I couldn't hear it *as* a symphony). The contrast of comportments with behaviors allows us to see that something can be concealed, even if it is physically operative on me. But because comportment is broader than intentional action, something is not necessarily concealed, even if I have no awareness of it whatsoever – there is a sense in which it is unconcealed as long as it figures meaningfully in my comportment.

The unconcealment of entities, then, will be a privation of the state of affairs in which something is unavailable for comportment. Thus, the unconcealment of entities will consist in all the different ways to make something available for comportment. But the primary mode of comportment to focus on in order to understand uncovering, Heidegger believes, is that in which we have a practical mastery of things. This sort of uncovering, it should be obvious, doesn't require the mediation of language. I can learn to deal with things without any explicit instruction in them, or even any names for them, simply by picking them up and starting to manipulate them, or by being shown how they work. Heidegger writes:

> The predominant comportment through which in general we uncover innerworldly entities is the utilization, the use of commonly-used objects (*Gebrauchsdingen*): dealing with vehicles, sewing kits, writing equipment, work tools in order to . . . , equipment in the widest sense. In dealing with equipment we learn to know this first. It is not that we have beforehand a knowledge of these things in order then to put them to use, but rather the other way around. . . . The everyday dealing with innerworldly entities is the primary mode – and for many often the only mode – of uncovering the world. This dealing with innerworldly entities comports itself – as utilization, use, managing, producing and so forth – toward equipment and the context of equipment . . . we make use of it in a "self-evident manner." (GA 25: 21–2)

Indeed, Heidegger believes it is constitutive of our human mode of being that we always already encounter ourselves in the midst of a world that is uncovered in just such practical terms.

346

But now these claims, phenomenologically grounded, seem to be in tension with the idea that the privative state of being covered up has some kind of priority in understanding our dealings with entities in the world. Nevertheless, Heidegger insists upon this. "When Dasein comes to existence, beings within the range of its existence are already familiar, manifest. With it a certain concealedness has also already occurred with it" (GA 28: 360). Every uncoveredness of the world, in other words, occurs together with a concealing of entities. Moreover, Heidegger insists that the "default" state of entities in the world is being covered over – he even has a slogan for this idea: truth, understood as uncoveredness, is robbery. "The factical uncoveredness of anything is, as it were," Heidegger claims in *Being and Time*, "always a robbery" (SZ: 294). This is not just a passing claim – he repeats it and elaborates on it often: "If this robbery belongs to the concept of truth, then it says that the entity must first of all be wrested from concealedness, or its concealedness must be taken from the entity" (GA 27: 79; see also GA 19: 10–11; GA 28: 359; GA 29/30: 44; GA 34: 10, 126; GA 9: 223). This seems like an odd thing for him to say, however – if entities are always already uncovered, why is our uncovering them a kind of robbery?

The basic reason for this is that entities are independent of us and our wishes, desires, intentions, and purposes for them, as well as our beliefs about them. This fact gives rise to a fundamental concealment in at least two ways. First, it means that uncovering an entity – making it something with which we can comport easily and transparently – demands something of us. It requires us to struggle to foster and develop the right skills, attitudes, and bodily dispositions for dealing with it, that is, those skills that will let it show itself in its own essence. Heidegger illustrates this through the example of walking into a shoemaker's workshop. "Which entities are there and how these entities are available, in line with their inherent character, is unveiled for us only in dealing appropriately with equipment such as tools, leather, and shoes. Only one who understands is able to uncover by himself this environing world of the shoemaker's" (GA 24: 431). This means that, for most of us, the entities in the workshop are not fully uncovered, and could only become uncovered as we acquire a shoemaker's skills. What holds of the shoemaker's shop, of course, holds for the world as a whole:

> it is only in the tiniest spheres of the beings with which we are acquainted that we are so well versed as to have at our command the specific way of dealing with equipment which uncovers this equipment as such. The entire range of intraworldly beings accessible to us at any time is not suitably accessible to us in an equally original way. There are many things we merely know something about but do not know how to manage with them. They confront us as beings, to be sure, but as unfamiliar beings. Many beings, including even those already uncovered, have the character of unfamiliarity. (GA 24: 431–2)

There is a tendency on our part, however, to cover over this unfamiliarity. In point of fact, Heidegger believes that we always inherit an understanding of and disposition for the world that tends to conceal from us the fact that we cannot practically uncover most things. The understanding, dispositions, and skills that Dasein has in the first instant are the banalized understandings, dispositions, and skills of the one (*das Man*; see Schatzki, chapter 14 in this volume). Thus, entities are initially manifest but nevertheless concealed in what they most authentically are. "Because the movements of being which Dasein so to speak makes in the one are a matter of course and are not conscious and intentional, this means simply that the one does not uncover them, since the uncoveredness which the one cultivates is in fact a covering up" (GA 20: 389). Authenticity, by contrast, consists in Dasein learning to "uncover the world in its own way . . . this uncovering of the 'world' [is] . . . always accomplished as a clearing away of concealments and obscurities, as a breaking up of the disguises with which Dasein bars its own way" (SZ: 129; see Carman, chapter 17 in this volume).

A second consequence of the independence of entities from us is that there is always more to entities than we can deal with. No matter how skillful we get in dealing with entities, Heidegger argues, there will always be something about them that we can't focus on or pay attention to: "each being we encounter and which encounters us keeps to this curious opposition of presencing, in which it always holds itself back in a concealment" (GA 5: 40/Heidegger 1993: 178). But this concealment "is not in every case primarily and merely the limit of knowledge," rather, it is precisely what makes it possible for us to deal with the thing in the first place: it is "the beginning of the clearing of what is cleared" (GA 5: 40/Heidegger 1993: 178–9). We get a grip on entities in the world, in other words, by generalizing, by dealing with them as instances of a known type. This leads to the possibility that established ways of dealing with things will make it harder to uncover other possible ways of dealing with them: when "what is familiar becomes known," Heidegger notes, "with that the concealedness of the unfamiliar deepens, and all that is not-known becomes more insistent in its concealment" (GA 28: 361). The way our familiarity depends on getting a certain more or less familiar grasp on things also leads to the possibility that we treat something as an instance of the wrong type – that is, that based on a superficial similarity between one thing and another with which we are familiar, we take something as a thing it is not (or, as Heidegger puts it, "a being appears, but presents itself as other than it is" (GA 5: 40/Heidegger 1993: 179)).

One consequence of Heidegger's account is that something can only be uncovered on the basis of our skillful ability to inhabit a world, because we uncover something only by knowing how it works together with other entities in a context (see SZ, Division I, chapter 3). Thus, the uncoveredness of entities (plank 2) is dependent upon the disclosedness of a world and ways of being within the world (plank 3A). Until it is given at least some minimal foothold in our world by taking a place within a context of involvements, Heidegger argues, the object can at best appear in a privative manner – that is, as something which resists our world. We are now also in a position to see that the uncovering of entities – developing comportments for dealing with them as what they really are – depends on things having modes of being appropriate to them and an essence that is independent of us. Truth as uncoveredness, in other words, depends on truth as the disclosure of being or essence. This leads us to plank (3B).

Unconcealment of the essence (being) of beings

Our ability to practically, reflectively, and linguistically uncover the way things are, we have seen, requires that objects make themselves available to our thought and talk, and that our thought and talk holds itself open to and responsible to the objects in the world around us. The unconcealment of beings is what gives us objects toward which we can be directed, and about which we are responsible for getting it right. Heidegger explains: "if our representations and assertions . . . are supposed to conform to the object, then this being . . . must be accessible in advance in order to present itself as a standard and measure for the conformity with it" (GA 45: 18).

This might seem like a trivial point, but it is only possible for things to manifest themselves in themselves if there is a way that the world really is, and it shows itself to us as it really is. This disclosure of the world – plank (3A) – was the focus of Heidegger's discussion of disclosedness in *Being and Time* (SZ: 221–2). It was also to this that Heidegger refers in passages like the following from the 1928 essay "On the Essence of Truth":

> Human Dasein – a being that finds itself situated *in the midst* of beings, comporting itself *toward* beings – in so doing exists in such a way that beings are always manifest as a whole. Here it is not necessary that this wholeness be expressly conceptualized; its belonging to Dasein can be veiled, the expanse of this whole is changeable. This wholeness is understood without the whole of those beings that are manifest being explicitly grasped or indeed "completely" investigated in their specific connections, domains, and layers. Yet the understanding of this wholeness, an understanding that in each case reaches ahead and embraces it, is a surpassing in the direction of world. . . . World as a wholeness "is" not a being, but that from out of which Dasein *gives itself the signification* of whatever beings it *is able* to comport itself toward in whatever way. (GA 9: 156/121)

What this transitional work added to Heidegger's account in *Being and Time*, however, was the claim that an important contribution of the world to unconcealment consists in the way that "through the world," Dasein "gives itself an original view (form) that is not explicitly grasped, yet functions precisely as a paradigmatic form for all manifest beings" (GA 9: 158/123)

Heidegger subsequently develops this idea in terms of the truth of essence – plank (3B). In the 1929–30 lecture course on *The Fundamental Concepts of Metaphysics*, Heidegger argues that the world should be understood as the prevailing of a "pre-logical manifestness" of beings "as such and as a whole" (GA 29/30: 512–13). But any sufficient inquiry into the origin of the "as" in the "as such" and "as a whole" – i.e. that *as* which entities show up – "must open up for us the whole context in which that, which we intend with 'manifestness of beings' and with the 'as a whole', comes into its essence (*west*)" (GA 29/30: 435–6). This means that, for Heidegger, our actions, thoughts and assertions about things cannot be true (uncover the way things are) unless the things we are thinking and talking about have an essence, a way that they are, i.e. that the objects themselves possess properties in virtue of which they do or do not belong to the extension of the terms of the proposition. Unless there are constraints on what is involved in a thing being some specific sort of thing, our thoughts and assertions about it run the risk of losing touch with anything about which they could be an assertion or a thought. For example, if there are no essential features of a table, then my assertion "there is a table in the room" could be referring to anything, and thus is incapable of being either true or false. So it is a condition of propositional truth that beings come to stand before us as having essential properties.

It must be the case, in addition, that in our comportments, we take the way that things are arrayed and interacting in the world as the measure for the success or failure of our comportment. This point is simply the consequence of the first – namely that what we say is only true or false if something specific in the world satisfies or fails to satisfy the belief or assertion. This means that we must have some grasp of the essence of things; otherwise, there is no sense in which we can take the world as the measure of the success or failure of our propositions. The unconcealment of being thus grounds truth by opening up a world of things with essential properties, a world about which it makes sense to say that we are speaking and thinking either correctly or incorrectly.

The question of the disclosure of being or essences is the question of how there can come to be modes of being or essences which are independent of us in the right sort of way. As it turns out, the answer to this question poses something of a paradox. We can't disclose an essence or mode of being in the way that we would uncover a fact or uncover an entity, because essences and modes of being are neither existing facts nor entities. A comment is in order here on the way that Heidegger thinks of essences.

For some reason, most translators and many commentators are hyper-sensitive about Heidegger's use of *Wesen* ("essence") and related neologisms like *Wesung* ("essencing") and *wesen* with a small "w" – that is, *wesen* as a verb, meaning "to essence" or "to come into its essence." These commentators have *really* taken to heart Heidegger's warning that he does not mean to use *Wesen* in the traditional sense – so much so that they seem to translate the word randomly (as, for example, "perdurance" or "presence" or, my favorite example from the translation of the *Beiträge*, "essential swaying"). All such choices avoid any metaphysical baggage, but at the cost of confusion or incomprehensability. I think it is better to translate "Wesen" in the straightforward way as "essence," but then explain how Heidegger thinks of essences (as hard as that might be).

As I understand it, Heidegger's disagreement with many views of essences are that they define what a thing is in terms of some necessary property that all X things must have, or some universal property that all X things in fact have. In the "Origin of the Work of Art," Heidegger calls this kind of essence the "unimportant/indifferent essence" (*das gleichgültige Wesen*) or the "unessential essence" (*das unwesentliche Wesen*). The traditional way of thinking of an essence, Heidegger notes, thinks of it in terms of the common features in which all things that share an essence agree.

> The essence gives itself in the generic and universal concept, which represents the one feature that holds indifferently for many things. This indifferent essence (essentiality in the sense of *essentia*) is, however, only the unessential essence. What does the essential essence of something consist in? Presumably it lies in what the entity *is* in truth. The true essence of a thing is fixed from out of its true being, from the truth of the given entity. (GA 5: 37/Heidegger 1993: 175–6, translation modified)

The idea is, I believe, relatively straightforward: the essence of a thing is given by that in the light of which it is brought into unconcealment. This way of approaching the issue makes room for something being essentially determined by an aspect or trait that, in fact, it lacks. For example, suppose that the essence of human being is to be rational. If we buy the "unessential essence" view of essences, than puzzles arise whenever we encounter a human-like thing that happens to lack rationality – say a baby or a person in a vegetative state. There might well be a way around such puzzles if the essence of a thing is treated as a property that all X things possess, or a abstract concept which they instantiate; that doesn't matter for present purposes. The point is simply that, in light of such puzzles, it seems a natural thing to say that the essence is fixed not by the property that an entity possesses or an abstract type, but by that in the view of which we take it as that thing it is. So even a person in a vegetative state is a human if she is understood in terms of the essence of being human (in particular, she is understood precisely as failing in some way to measure up to what it is to be human). A person could be a human on this view, even if, in fact, it is factually impossible for her to be rational.

Another example to illustrate how this works for Heidegger is his account of technological entities – the standing reserve. To be a standing reserve, for example, is not a matter of possessing an aspect or trait such as "being always on call." Instead, it is to be experienced in terms of enframing – that is, in terms of the challenging forth that unlocks, exposes, and switches things about ever anew. Because everything is experienced in terms of enframing, particular things are experienced as in a state of privation when they are not always on call as standing reserve. This means that they can have the essence of enframing, even if they are not standing reserve yet. Their essence is determined technologically, because they are seen as being defective when they are not always ordered and on call.

Now, the problem with essences so understood is that they present something of a paradox. Heidegger demonstrates this by comparing these two assertions:

(A)   The lights in this lecture hall are on now
(B)   Truth is the correctness of an assertion

where assertion (B) is intended to specify the essence of truth (GA 45: 77 ff/69 ff). The truth of assertion (A) seems in a straightforward and undeniable fashion to consist in its relating to a particular fact or state of affairs – namely the condition of the lights in the lecture hall right now.

How about the truth of assertion (B)? Heidegger makes two important observations about such assertions. First, while it might well correspond with the facts (the relevant facts would include all particular truths), its correspondence with the facts is not what makes it true. Rather, its being true is what guarantees that it will correspond with the facts. We can see this if we think about what facts we could possibly adduce for (B) to correspond to. If the notion of a fact or a state of affairs is meaningful, it must be some actual (whether past, present, or future) condition of an object or a state of affairs. But essential claims go beyond any claim about past, present, or future conditions to include all possible conditions. This is because the essence of a thing is not picked out by a mere empirical regularity, but must also be maintained in the face of counterfactual situations. If I were to claim that the essence of a table is to be a wooden item of furniture, for instance, it would not establish this claim to merely show that all past, current, and future tables are wooden items of furniture (even if I could, in point of fact, be certain that there is not, never had been, and never would be such a plastic object). It would, in addition, have to be the case that a plastic object with exactly the same shape, resistance, function, etc., would not be a table. This means that for essential definitions, correspondence to the facts is a necessary but not sufficient condition for their being true.

Second, facts come too late for essential definitions, since we need to assume that the definition is true in order definitively to identify the fact or facts to which it corresponds. To get a feel for this, compare two other essential definitions – this time for gold.

(C)   Gold is the noblest of the metals
(D)   Gold is an element with atomic number 79

When it comes to definitively founding simple factual statements like (A), we begin by finding the fact to which it corresponds, and we can do this by first finding the object referred to in the subject phrase – the lights – and then checking their condition. How about (C)? It seems like we would start by locating the object referred to in the subject phrase – gold. In fact, if (C) is an essential definition, the only way we can determine that gold is the noblest of the metals is by first finding some gold, and we do this by looking for instances of the noblest metal. Thus we see that in order to establish the truth of the essential specification, we first have to assume that it is true. And that means that we are never in a position to empirically prove that it is right.

Suppose, for example, we are trying to decide between (C) and (D). The advocates of (C) would round up all the noblest metals to test their definition. The advocates of (D) would round up all the elemental stuff with atomic number 79 to test theirs. Neither camp could ever persuade the other that their essential definition was correct, because, on the basis of their respective definitions, each would reject exactly those particular substances that the other took as decisive evidence in favor of his or her definition. As Heidegger summarizes the situation, "every time we attempt to prove an essential determination through single, or even all, actual and possible facts, there results the remarkable state of affairs that we have already presupposed the legitimacy of the essential determination, indeed must presuppose it, just in order to grasp and produce the facts that are supposed to serve as proof" (GA 45: 79).

It seems that both definitions cannot be right. Even if it so happens that (C) and (D) agree in their extension, we could imagine cases or possible worlds in which the definitions apply to some substance differently. That means that we would have reason to believe that they name, at best, an accidental property of gold.

If the world gives us no basis for deciding which of the competing essential definitions is right, then perhaps we have to conclude that there are no genuine essences in the world. Instead, what we find in the universe is what we (arbitrarily) project into it. And if we conclude that, then we also might be forced to conclude that there is no way that the universe is independently of the way we conceive of it, because it seems that we are free to carve it up in any way that we want. But such anti-essentialist and anti-realist views threaten the possibility of our thoughts and claims being about the world at all, and thus threaten the possibility of their being either true or false.

We can summarize the situation in the following way. It seems that our ability to have truly uncovering comportments and true beliefs and make true assertions about the world depends on things having an essence, and our grasping that essence. This is because we cannot succeed in linguistically referring to things in the world unless they have an essence. However, if an understanding of essences consists in a grasp of a propositional definition, then nothing in the world can make the essential definition true, because nothing in the world could establish one definition as opposed to any other. Thus, it seems to follow, nothing in the world can make our beliefs or assertions true.

Heidegger, in fact, rejects this argument, because he denies that our understanding of essences consists in a grasp of a propositional definition. The "knowledge of essence," he claims, "cannot be communicated in the sense of the passing on of a proposition, whose content is simply grasped without its foundation and its acquisition being accomplished again" (GA 45: 87). This is because the knowledge of essence he is interested in is a way of being attuned to the world; for that, we have to be introduced to the practices that will eventually teach us to have a particular sensibility and readiness for the world. Thus, "the knowledge of the essence must be accomplished anew by each one who is to share it" (GA 45: 87). It is this latter understanding of our knowledge of essences – seeing it as consisting in being attuned by the world to consider certain properties or features of things as definitive – that, Heidegger believes, allows us to see our way clear of anti-essentialism and anti-realism. The unconcealment of being is precisely the way a certain pre-cognitive understanding of essences comes to prevail in an attunement. Through the unconcealment of being, Heidegger says, "human comportment is tuned throughout by the openedness of beings as a whole" (GA 9: 193/147, translation modified).

So, the first thing to say is that our disclosure of essences is not an explicit grasp of what the essence is, nor is it a particular experience or comportment with a particular entity. "Addressing something *as* something," Heidegger notes, "does not yet necessarily entail *comprehending in its essence* whatever is thus addressed. The *understanding* of being (*logos* in a quite broad sense) that guides and illuminates in advance all comportment toward beings is neither a grasping of being as such, nor is it a conceptual comprehending of what is thus grasped" (GA 9: 132/104). Heidegger illustrates this point: "we are acquainted with the 'essence' of the things surrounding us: house, tree, bird, road, vehicle, man, etc., and yet we have no knowledge of the essence. For we immediately land in the uncertain, shifting, controversial, and groundless, when we attempt to determine more closely, and above all try to ground in its determinateness, what is certainly though still indeterminately 'known': namely, house-ness, tree-ness, bird-ness, humanness" (GA 45: 81). As a result, "the essence of things," Heidegger notes, is ordinarily something "which we know and yet do not know" (GA 45: 81). The essence is "not first captured in a 'definition' and made available for knowledge" (here, Heidegger is speaking specifically of the essence of truth; GA 45: 115). This is because, as he explains, the knowledge of essences is originally manifest in the way "that all acting and creating, all thinking and speaking, all founding and proceeding were determined by and thoroughly in accord with the unconcealment of beings as something ungrasped" (GA 45: 115).

We can say, then, that the disclosure of being consists in our being disposed in a particular way for the world. An understanding of being is concealed when it is not operative in our experience of the things in the world. What distinguishes each historical age from another, Heidegger claims, is that each has a different style of "productive seeing," of perceiving things in advance in such a way that they are allowed to stand out as essentially structured (see GA 45, section 24).

We can illustrate this by going back to the gold example above. The fight between medieval and modern conceptions of gold is based ultimately in different ways of picking out salient entities in the world – that is, different ways of responding to some evident property or properties that they possess. One way of being disposed might lead us to find the true being of a thing in the extent to which it approaches God by being like Him. Another way of being disposed might lead us to find the true being of a thing in its ability to be turned into a resource, flexibly and efficiently on call for use. When someone disposed to the world in the first way uncovers a lump of gold, and subsequently defines gold as such and such a *kind* of thing, she will take as essential its nearness to God. When someone disposed to the world in the second way uncovers it, she will take the essential properties to be whatever it is about it that allows us to break it down into a resource, and flexibly switch it around and order it.

In fact, there is, in principle, an indefinite if not infinite number of ways to characterize the properties of any particular thing. A piece of gold, for instance, has a color and a weight and a texture and a shape, but also all sorts of other properties like being good (or bad) for making jewelry, gleaming in a way that seems divine, being directly in front of my favorite chair, and so on. When we decide what kind or type of thing this particular object is, we will do it on the basis of just those particular properties we are responding to, and these properties will be some subset of an indefinite or infinite set of properties we could be responding to.

Given that this is the case, before anything can show up *as* anything, we must have some particular, pre-linguistic disposition or readiness for the world that leads us to see certain features as more important than others. All understandings of what things are thus arise on the basis of a background disposition to the world. We disclose the essences that we do, according to Heidegger, because the way we are moved by or disposed to things allows a particular style of being "to be ascendent" (see GA 45: 129).

As a result, there is no longer any need to see (C) and (D) as incompatible. There might be a culture whose sensibilities for the world lead it to uncover an instance of gold as having just those essential properties specified in (D) – in fact, Heidegger would probably argue, those are just the essential properties we would find in a lump of gold if we were oriented to the world in a technological fashion. We do not need to see (D) as true *a priori*, because whether it is true is up to the world. Instead, we will use our technological disposition to pick out objects as instances of *that kind of resource*; from there it is an empirical matter which features of it make it that kind of a resource. In our age, it seems plausible to say that gold's essential features (in the traditional sense) are found in its atomic structure, because knowledge of the atomic structure gives us the best grasp on how to turn gold into a resource. The possibility of truth is secured because there is a way that the world opens itself up or is unconcealed, a coherent mode of being, and thus the world can serve as a standard for our thoughts and words.

In summary, then, the unconcealment of beings is the "anticipatory gathering" which lays out certain properties and relationships as salient (see GA 45: 121). This means that essences are historical – they show up differently as dispositions for the world change.

The historical nature of essences leads, in turn, to a further question. How is it that changes in historical understandings can arise? Heidegger in reflecting on this question noted:

> entities are reordered, and indeed not merely by an entity that is not accessible to us, and perhaps never will be, but by something concealed which conceals itself precisely when we, holding ourselves in the clearing, are left to the discretion of, or even captivated by, entities. . . . From this we derive an essential insight: the clearing, in which beings are, is not simply bounded and delimited by something hidden but by something self-concealing. (GA 45: 210)

This is a phenomenological observation which Heidegger repeats often in various forms, but without much clarification or argument. The idea seems to be something like the following: the style of being that allows things to show up as having an essence is most invisible when it is most effective. That is, when everything is showing up to us in terms of flexibility and efficiency, for example, we are captivated by things – we are wholly absorbed in our dealings with them. That renders us unable to make ourselves aware of the understanding of being which is shaping our experience of the world. Looked at another way, the ready availability of beings to us depends on our losing sight of the fact that their availability is grounded in a particular understanding of the essence of beings as a whole. Thus, "the concealment of beings as a whole . . . is older than every manifestness of this or that entity" (GA 9: 193–4/148).

So a new understanding of being can establish itself, and a new ordering of beings can become operative, only if there is something like a clearing which conceals any other way of experiencing the world in order to allow this particular way to come to the forefront. The upside to this is it allows us to inhabit a world: the self-concealment of being "leaves historical human beings in the sphere of what is practicable with what they are capable of. Thus left, humanity replenishes its 'world' on the basis of the latest needs and aims, and fills out that world by means of proposing and planning" (GA 9: 195/149). The downside is that, having lost sight of the concealment that makes it all possible, we become convinced of the necessity and unique correctness of our way of inhabiting the world: "human beings go wrong as regards the essential genuineness of their standards" (GA 9: 196/149).

The revealing–concealing of the clearing

This brings us to the last, and most difficult, feature of Heidegger's platform of unconcealment. Because of the historical nature of the disclosure of essences/understandings of being discussed under plank (3), Heidegger was pushed to ask what makes it possible for any one of a plurality of understandings of being or essence to prevail. Part of the answer he arrived at was that there must be a clearing which allows one way of being disposed to the world to come into operation, while withholding other potential ways of being disposed for the world. I conclude with just a few words about the unconcealment of the clearing.

As I have noted already, the clearing should be understood as something like a space of possibilities – it "grants first of all the possibility of the path to presence, and grants the possible presencing of that presence itself" (Heidegger 1993: 445). That is, the clearing makes it possible for a certain understanding of being – a particular mode of presence – to come to prevail among entities. For possibilities to be live possibilities, however, it requires a space from which other incompatible possibilities are excluded. The clearing maintains a world by keeping back (concealing) possibilities that are incompatible with the essence that is currently operative. In order for some possibilities to shape our experience of the world, any other "possibilities" cannot be live possibilities, they can't be possible for us, they must be kept from us.

This might make it sound like the clearing is a gallery of possibilities – that it keeps different determinate ways of being in the world locked in the back room, while exhibiting one at a time. But this would be to think about it incorrectly. The word "clearing" (*Lichtung*) in ordinary language means a glade or clearing in a forest. The forest clearing does not work by keeping some particular trees or shrubs on hand, but out of the way. Rather, the forest clearing is nothing but the condition that there are no trees or shrubs growing.

Similarly, the clearing makes some possibilities possible, not by putting some determinate possibilities in cold storage, but by making it the case that there are no other determinate possibilities available. For the available possibilities to have authority as possibilities, moreover, we cannot be aware that other possibilities are being ruled out or concealed from us. Our experience of the natural world *as* resources, for example, could not authoritatively shape our experience of the world if we were aware that one would be equally justified in experiencing it as God's creation. This means that, paradoxically, the clearing only works as a clearing when it is not uncovered – when it is not something toward which we can comport. Thus, the clearing does not only keep back other possibilities, but it keeps back that it is keeping back other possibilities. The clearing conceals the possibility of other understandings of beings. It is not "the mere clearing of presence, but the clearing of presence concealing itself, the clearing of a self-concealing sheltering" (Heidegger 1993: 448).

Notes

Research for this chapter was funded in part by the David M. Kennedy Center for International and Area Studies.

1   These include discoveredness (*Entdecktheit*) and uncoveredness (*Unverdecktheit*), disclosedness (*Erschlossenheit*), unveiledness (*Enthülltheit*), and disconcealedness (*Entborgenheit*).

References and further reading

Heidegger, M. (1993) *Basic Writings*, rev. and expanded edn (trans. D. F. Krell). San Francisco: HarperCollins.

Nietzsche, F. (1996) *On the Genealogy of Morals* (trans. Douglas Smith). Oxford: Oxford University Press.

22

Contributions to Philosophy

HANS RUIN

When later defending the misguided decision to take on the Rektorat in Freiburg in 1933, as well as his early enthusiastic embrace of National Socialism, Heidegger always insisted that shortly after, he withdrew into a kind of personal philosophical resistance. This self-description was often ridiculed by his critics, taking as evidence his maintenance of a high academic and intellectual profile up the end of the war, including party membership. However, starting in 1989, a series of volumes have been published within the *Gesamtausgabe* that provide a remarkable testimony to what we could now rightly speak of as Heidegger's "secret writings" from the years of dictatorship. The most important, and by far the most discussed, among these works is *Contributions to Philosophy (From Enowning)*, as the title reads of the English translation of *Beiträge zur Philosophie (Vom Ereignis)* (GA 65). But this 500-page volume, composed in the years 1936–8, is only the first of several works from this time, which include also *Besinnung* (GA 66), from 1938/9, *Die Geschichte des Seins* (GA 69), from 1938–40, and the yet to be published *Über den Anfang* (projected as GA 70) and *Das Ereignis* (projected as GA 71).

During this time Heidegger also lectures as intensively as before, mostly on Nietzsche, Hölderlin, and German Idealism, in the 1940s turning more toward the pre-Socratics. Much of this material was also published as lecture courses within the *Gesamtausgabe*, and some of it was edited into books after the war, where the two-volume work on Nietzsche from 1961 stands out as his philosophically most powerful achievement. But aside from this "public" work, we can now begin to see how much of Heidegger's effort during these strange, tumultuous, and for him also very creative years was spent on the writing of texts for no particular purpose, and which he could have cherished no hopes of having published in the then prevalent political and academic situation. This is clearly the case with *Besinnung*, which contains very articulate criticism of contemporary National Socialist ideology and aesthetics, but it is also true of *Contributions*, which takes a clear stand, for example, against the racial and biological conception of history. Yet the main part of the philosophical criticism developed in these writings – which as a whole are essentially *critical* writings, writings from within an acute sense of *crisis*, where the need for *krinein*, for decision and judgment, is more urgent than ever – is not directed explicitly against the immediate present. Instead it is the historical destiny of the Western world as such, interpreted as a mode of thinking and of conceptualizing being, which is at stake. The recurrent reflections on modernity, and the occasional remarks on fascist political ideology, are always incorporated into this larger interpretive scheme.

In these writings Heidegger is on one level speaking to himself in an intensified inner dialogue, as a kind of marginalia to his public historical interpretations, as well as to the present political and intellectual situation. But on another level he is speaking to an unknown future audience. There is a strange form of address – and also a non-address – taking place in these books that differs from the voice in the lectures, which can often be very direct, animated as it is by a pedagogical intention. In these "secret" works, however, Heidegger is speaking of and to the present yet over and beyond it. In one fragment he describes it as a discourse aimed "to the few and the rare" (GA 65: 11). In another introductory note he states that "no one understands what 'I' think here" (GA 65: 8), which a few lines further down is followed up by "and he who will someday grasp it does not need 'my' attempt" (GA 65: 8). The tone will remind some readers of the young Wittgenstein in *Tractatus*, but it also reverberates from a longer tradition of enigmatic self-riddling philosophical discourse that we find already in the Heraclitean fragments.

For Heidegger himself these secret writings, and *Contributions* in particular, were of immense philosophical importance. Here he was free, experimenting with his own thinking and mode of expression, beyond all duties and necessities, in hiding from a degenerating public sphere, anticipating philosophical trajectories which he would continue to pursue during the remaining three decades of philosophical activity. In a letter to Elisabeth Blochmann from December 1935, shortly before he began to work on *Contributions*, he reflects on his recent rereading of *Being and Time*: "I can see now the great impertinence hiding in this book, but perhaps one has to perform such leaps in order to get anywhere at all. The task now is to raise the same question again, but much more original, much more free from everything contemporary, from everything learned and from the learned" (Heidegger and Blochmann 1989: 88). This anticipatory remark can be compared to the famous footnote added to the *Letter on Humanism* when it was published in 1949, where he says that the thoughts presented here, notably what concerns *Ereignis*, the event or enowning, was begun in 1936, i.e. the year when he began writing *Contributions* (GA 9: 313).

When Heidegger started to set up the plans for the *Gesamtausgabe* together with his assistant Friedrich Wilhelm von Herrmann, he was quite aware of the difficulty and inaccessibility of these secret writings. For this reason their publication was projected for a later stage of the whole edition, under the heading "Unpublished dissertations." It was therefore not until fourteen years after the inception of the *Gesamtausgabe* that *Contributions* was released, for the centenary of Heidegger's birth in 1989. During all this time, however, there were people, notably Otto Pöggeler and von Herrmann, who had access to it, and who referred to it in commentaries. Pöggeler's mentioning of it as Heidegger's second major work, after *Being and Time*, had instilled enormous expectations before its publication, expectations that it could not fulfill, and that it – as I think we now can see – was never really meant to fulfill. Von Herrmann still maintains, in his continued and more recent work on *Contributions*, that it should indeed be seen as "the second major treatise" for an inquiry into the grounding question of being (von Herrmann 2001: 109). Nevertheless, the first ten years of reception of *Contributions* were to a large extent focused on coming to terms with the sense of disappointment and frustration that the book provoked among the majority of its readers once it was there, in that open public space, in explicit withdrawal from which it had once been conceived and composed. Daniela Vallega-Neu has summarized well the immediate impression it evokes: "a random collection of repetitive notes, aphorisms, fragments of texts, collections of questions, or list of words and unfinished sentences," before which the reader finds herself "deprived of linking elements providing continuity of thought in a smooth development from one question to the next" (Vallega-Neu 2001: 66).

This impression can partly be explained by the fact that the manuscript was never really finished at the time of its composition. In comparison to the works that have been strictly edited by Heidegger himself, *Contributions* remains a sketch, raw material, "boulders from a quarry, in which primal rock is broken," as he describes it himself in section 257. The confusing impression that it evokes also has to do, however, with the peculiar nature of its theme, and how Heidegger perceived the task of a radical philosophical thinking at the time.

The overall philosophical theme or issue of *Contributions* is the same as in *Being and Time*, namely the question of being which remains the horizon of Heidegger's philosophical pursuits throughout his life. But as *Being and Time* pointed out in its introductory sections, the question of being is the most general and therefore in a sense the most empty of all possible questions. There is a reason why it has been "forgotten" or overlooked, namely that it has appeared throughout history as no question at all. In order to awaken even the relevance of this apparent non-question, its question-worthiness must be called forth. In *Being and Time*, the hermeneutical procedure goes by way of an existential-ontological examination of the questioner himself, i.e. Dasein. The book has a clear and systematic structure, modeled on the great predecessors in the genre, in particular Husserl and Kant. As the book reaches its provisionary end (which was to become its real end, since the promised continuation was never published), it has excavated a series of ontological strata, all related to Dasein's being-in-the-world, culminating in ecstatic temporality, which shines forth as a quasi-transcendental foundation for the meaning of being.

Perhaps the most obvious deviation from the program of *Being and Time* in *Contributions* is precisely the abandonment of the ideal of the *system*. In the very important section 39, where Heidegger comments on the structure and form of the new "inceptual thinking" attempted in *Contributions*, he says that systems belong to the past, that they only have their place in the history of responses to the guiding question of being (GA 65: 81). In the place of the system and of a systematic approach in general he here presents the ideal of "the jointure," *die Fuge*, the fugue. The outline or contribution presented in the book is an attempt to provide a jointure of such an inceptual thinking. Consequently the 281 sections are organized into six parts or chapters, each one of which he speaks of as separate joinings (*Fügungen*) within the overall jointure (*Fuge*). They are called "Echo" (*Der Anklang*), "Playing-forth" (*Das Zuspiel*), "Leaping" (*Der Sprung*), "Grounding" (*Die Gründung*), "Those Who Are to Come" (*Die Zukünftigen*), and "The Last God" (*Die letzte Gott*). These six are followed by a last long section entitled simply "Be-ing" (*Das Seyn*), which was apparently intended for *Contributions*, but its position within the whole was never finally settled by Heidegger himself. There has been a good amount of discussion surrounding the meaning and significance of this metaphorical and enigmatic structure. What is the rationale behind this particular ordering of the material? Is there a progressing or developing argument that motivates it, or is this not rather a random ordering of notes that really does not permit a distinct structure? When discussing the structure himself, Heidegger is evasive, stating that each of the joinings "stand for itself" yet in order to "make the essential onefold more pressing" (GA 65: 82). In another remark he defines the jointure as a possession (*Verfügung*) which complies with the call (*sich den Zuruf fügende*), and thus grounds Dasein (GA 65: 82). The English translation reads "the jointure is the conjoining that enjoins the call and thus grounds Dasein," which is an admirable attempt to preserve the play on *Fuge* but which nevertheless confuses the philosophical sense of the passage. What Heidegger is suggesting is essentially that the structure of the work somehow responds to the matter at stake, which becomes visible, or perhaps audible, for the one who is prepared to listen to its call.

The fugue is also a musical term, which signifies a composition characterized by a recurrent theme which is first presented in an introductory part and which then reappears in several different voices, in an open, partly improvised manner (musically brought to completion by Bach). It is tempting to read *Contribution* as a fugue also in the musical sense, and even to suspect that Heidegger was inspired by this particular form. He himself does not, however, address this connection, so there is not much to build on. The apparent etymological connection is not significant, since the musical term comes from Latin and Italian, recalling an "escaping" (*fugare*) movement of melody, with no connection to the German *Fuge*, in the sense of joint. As another possible inspiration for the specific choice of this term, which does indeed recall musical terminology in a more general sense, one could point to Heraclitus' *harmonia*, from *harmozein*, joining, which Heidegger in his readings, following Diels, translates precisely as *Fügung*. An important fragment in this respect is number B54, which reads: "the hidden attunement is better than the obvious one" (in the translation of Kahn 1979: 65). For Heidegger's interpretation of this sentence and of the other fragments that recall the *harmonia*, understood as *Fügung*, see GA 55: 142ff.

Whatever the exact background of the term may be, it is clear that in organizing his material under these six general joinings, Heidegger at least wanted to suggest a unitary and linear movement of thinking through what first appear more as a random collection of working notes. Consequently some readers have argued forcefully for a systematic reading of this anti-systematic work along these directives, notably its editor von Herrmann. The overall trajectory then begins with recalling, in *Echo*, the loss and forgetfulness of being, which is followed by a stepwise recovery, not so much of the question of being, but of Dasein's own belonging to being, through a *Leap* into original history and truth. As Dasein is led to understand itself not over and against being, but as existing from and through being, thinking takes the form of a second beginning, in relation to classical metaphysics as the first. This is first attempted by the chosen few, poets and thinkers, who thereby anticipate the coming of the last god. Yet, despite the obvious ambition to provide a guidance to such a philosophical path, the general thrust of Heidegger's evasive remarks on the structure and composition of the work, is, I think, that there simply is no privileged systematic composition that can convey and communicate its deepest philosophical motivation. He even admits at one point that the particular path outlined here is the "one way, which an individual can open, foregoing a survey of the possibility of other perhaps more essential ways" (GA 65: 81). Instead of committing oneself to monolinear reading of the text, it is therefore probably wiser to see the movement of *Contributions* as a dispersed yet contained meditation, which, in a pattern reminiscent at times of the musical fugue, seeks to bring its matter to expression in a way that should ideally resonate from the demand of this matter itself. And in this post-systematic ambition to say the absolute, which cannot be expressed in a unitary way, the book is not without its own tradition, a tradition of essentially frag-mented philosophical writing that we find already in Novalis and Schlegel, in Nietzsche of course, but also in such contemporaries as Ernst Jünger, Walter Benjamin, and Theodor Adorno.

The significance of Nietzsche for the style and orientation of *Contributions* is espe-cially important to ponder. Together with Hölderlin, he is the great voice from the past with which Heidegger is seeking to come to terms philosophically during this time. The composition of *Contributions* runs parallel to the initial sequence of lectures on Nietzsche. On a stylistic level we could read *Contributions* as an attempt to work in the spirit of his aphoristic books. Whereas Heidegger pays little attention in his interpretations to the style and format of Nietzsche's thinking, he could nevertheless be seen to respond to it in his own writing. From the viewpoint of this comparison we can also assess the limits and uniqueness of Heidegger's own writing more clearly. The format in which Nietzsche celebrated his greatest triumphs as a writer, the aphorism and the miniature essay, is simply not fit for Heidegger's way of pursuing philosophy. He lacks the wit as well as the capacity for and interest in dialectical twists and turnings of perspective within a contained movement of thought that characterize so much of Nietzsche's best writing. In comparison with Nietzsche, Heidegger shines forth as a somewhat dull and very monotonous writer, with inferior literary skills, an impres-sion that becomes overwhelming if we place *Contributions* alongside, for example, *The Gay Science* or *Beyond Good and Evil*. But it is precisely this monotony, this insistence in pursuing the one question, and taking it to heights or depths where it has not been taken earlier, that constitutes his uniqueness as a thinker and in the end also permits him to accomplish what is arguably the most powerful critical interpretation of Nietzsche.

More important than these stylistic aspects, however, is the presence of Nietzsche in the overall philosophical framework of *Contributions*. This could be described as an attempt to diagnose and come to terms with modernity as a situation of nihilism. For Nietzsche nihilism is a long-term effect of a resentful creation of the ideal as opposed to the real, after which the highest ideals undergo a stepwise abasement to a point where the world itself and life lose their value. In Heidegger's historical conception the guiding question is the fate not of values or ideals, but of being. It is in terms of its understanding and conceptualization of being that the fate of Western humanity (which has also become a global fate) must be grasped. The question of being, and the conceptual responses which it has elicited, constitute a tradition that unites Anaximander and Nietzsche, before and within which we stand. The present crisis is diagnosed in terms of an inability to pose this question in a radical enough manner, and even to experience it as a necessity. Our need, Heidegger often repeats here, is that of a "needlessness." We do not experience our need, and precisely in this it manifests itself. This diagnosis may seem hopelessly aloof, as if the crisis of the West was simply a philosophical conceptual problem concerning ontology. But as in Nietzsche's diagnosis of nihilism, Heidegger traces the reverberations of this for-getfulness of being throughout present day culture, down to its character of "machi-nation" through which it will continue to "pillage and lay waste to the planet" (GA 65: 408–9). How man relates to, understands, and conceptualizes being here becomes the supreme index with the help of which an entire cultural situation and practice is focused.

For Nietzsche, our age is the age of the death of God. Still, it remains unclear whether in Nietzsche's understanding it is also the end of all Gods, especially if we take seriously his reflections on the possible return of a refigured Dionysos as a new tragic divinity. Heidegger is more explicit concerning the "theological" framework of the problem. The modern age is characterized not by the death of God, but by the "flight of the Gods," a formulation he adopts from Hölderlin, who, alongside Nietzsche, is his great interlocu-tor in this matter. The Gods, or more generally the divine and the sacred, are absent, and therefore thinking can also understand itself as a preparation for the return of God, of the "last God," as the final part of *Contributions* is entitled. The philosophical premise for this "theological" discourse is not confessional, and definitely not Christian. The epitaph for this whole part of the book reads "The totally other over against gods who have been, especially over against the Christian God" (GA 65: 403). Heidegger's point is that a presumably "secular" or "atheist" position is itself inevitably situated within Christianity and its metaphysical ontotheology and its nihilistic aftermath. We do not free ourselves from the necessity of thinking the divine, if only in its historical absence, by simply adopting an enlightened atheist viewpoint. Such a position will only reinstate a symptom of modernity itself. God, or the divine, thus appears here as a philosophical category, of equal importance to that of being (which is not to say that being is equated with God). The task of thinking can therefore be defined as a "preparation for the appearing of the last God" (GA 65: 411), but this task is inseparable from the grounding of the truth of being as *Ereignis*, as event or enown-ing of being, as well as the recognition of man's belonging to being. It is a task, and also a decision, but when, if, and by whom it will be taken remains uncertain. Heidegger indicates that this preparation can only be accomplished by rare individuals, who nevertheless prepare the ground for a turning which will ultimately affect the entire planet.

In this overall scheme, oriented by a sense of threat, crisis, decision, and a possible redemption, Heidegger can be said to both affirm and refuse Max Weber's famous analy-sis of modernity as an epoch of "disenchantment." Modernity is indeed here the epoch of the disappearance of the Gods, and more generally of the sacred as such. Yet Heidegger refuses to see this as a definitive historical fate, issuing from the extended application of human rationality. Instead, his whole project in *Contributions* could be described as an attempt to fix historically the character of this modern rationality as a contingent constellation, with its roots in a Greek philosophical metaphysical heritage, and to reflect on it from the point of view of its possible overcoming. And just as the crisis itself is understood in terms of the loss of the sacred, its overcoming must also be grasped in these terms. Still, this could – or rather should ideally – not signify a return to old Gods, cults, and congregations. The appearance of such reactive returns to ancient forms of worship – of which the present world bears even greater testimony than the time of *Contributions* – Heidegger views with the same disdain as would a Weberian critic. The last God, anticipated in the rare attempts to articulate being in a non-metaphysical way, remains a philosopher's God, in the sense that its appearance is only available through a radical philosophical questioning and excavation of the meta-physical heritage. The traditional theological understanding of divinity, on the other hand, belongs to this heritage as just an extension of its paradigm.

Having presented the general theoretical framework of *Contributions*, and discussed some of its formal and stylistic aspects, I now want to move on to a more systematic discussion of its themes, against the background of those of Heidegger's philosophical concerns with which most readers will be more familiar from *Being and Time*. In this way, it is also possible to see in what way *Contributions* constitutes a development and progression along Heidegger's path of thinking.

The task of fundamental ontology is to open again, or perhaps for the first time, an access to the question of the meaning of being. The premise for the argument in *Being and Time* is that this access requires that we critically examine the conditions for the question itself. First of all, we must examine the nature and position of the questioner, which is what leads to the whole existential analytic, culminating in the account of existential temporality as the condition of possibility of meaning as such. We must also develop a critical awareness of the historical nature of the question, how it has been conceived throughout tradition, and in what way we stand in that tradition today. This is the necessity of a destruction of the history of ontology. A consequence of this destruction of ontology is the destruction and critical retrieval of the philosophical con-ceptuality inherited from our tradition. *Being and Time* does not develop a thinking on language like that we find in Heidegger's post-war writings, notably in the collection *On the Way to Language*. Yet the problem of language for philosophy, the problem of finding the appropriate philosophical terminology, which does not simply reproduce the prejudices of tradition, hovers over the whole work and motivates its innovative con-ceptuality. For, as Heidegger writes in an important passage, "in the end it is the task of philosophy to preserve the power of the elementary words, through which Dasein expresses itself from being debased by common sense to incomprehensibility, which in the end gives rise to false problems" (SZ: 220).

In *Being and Time* this "creative" preserving and reactivation of the elementary words is not explicitly connected to the use of poetic language. It is only in the *Origin of the Work of Art*, written in 1934–5, that this thought is developed, and that poetry and poetizing is explored as an event of truth in its own right. Still, in *Being and Time* Heidegger already anticipates what we could speak of as a *crisis* of philosophical lan-guage itself. Whenever the ambition to contemplate and articulate being has resulted in the construction of a metaphysical vocabulary, being has been fixed in the form of a separate mode of being. The inability to preserve and respect the ontological difference between being and beings is intimately connected to the construction of metaphysical language, and to the practice of conceptual thinking as such. The tendency of science and metaphysics to objectify or reify subjectivity has its counterpart in an ever recur-ring reification of being itself. The project of *Being and Time* is to move beyond this delimitation. Through its radical critique of the subject–object distinction and of classical epistemology in general, and its compelling challenge to objectifying categories, it opens a new space for philosophical reflection. Yet it has its internal limits, of which Heidegger himself was very much aware.

The complex philosophical itinerary of *Contributions* must be described in terms of all of these previous concerns. It is an attempt to think being in a non-objectifying way, by moving beyond the subject–object dichotomy and traditional epistemology with its correspondence theory of truth. Decisive in this pursuit is the new understanding of truth as *aletheia*, as the event of disclosure, as *Ereignis* or enowning, as the free and incalculable and abyssal opening in and through which beings obtain their place and significance. But the overall prerequisite is that the thinker is able to reflect on and problematize his or her position with regard to what is to be thought, and the means by which this thinking approaches its theme. As long as the theoretical pursuit itself is, explicitly or implicitly, understood in terms of a thinking subject contemplating an object which it seeks to represent by the use of an appropriate terminology, then it will inevitably reproduce the problems inherent in the metaphysical tradition. For this reason the very relation between the knower and the known must undergo a transformation, a transformation ultimately manifested in the mode of discourse. Thus on the very first page of the book Heidegger states: "it is no longer a case of talking 'about' something and representing something objective, but rather of being owned over into enowning" (GA 65: 3). This is immediately followed by the remark: "this amounts to an essential transformation of the human from 'rational animal' [*animal rationale*] to Dasein." In this elliptic statement the core concern of the work is contained, in a way that I will try to explicate in what follows.

The first part of the statement underscores the point that *Contributions* is a work where the mode of philosophical discourse is a central philosophical theme in itself. How should philosophy speak, how should it articulate its concerns and findings? It should no longer speak *about* something, so as to represent it, because when it speaks in such a way, or rather when it understands its purpose along these lines, then it will only reproduce a representational objectifying discourse in which the forgetfulness of being is enacted yet again. But how should it avoid this trap? Is it not the inevitable fate of language to posit and objectify the entities which it designates? Heidegger's response here evokes the key concept of the whole work, namely *Ereignis*, which in the English translation of *Contributions* has been rendered as *enowning*. The story of its various translations is a theme in its own right. Among the earlier alternatives are "appropriation" as well as "event." "Enowning" is an awkward, but etymologically well founded, possibility, since the German term is composed by the prefix "er" and "eigen," which means "own." Yet the expression "being owned over into enowning" is so strange and unnatural from an English perspective that it risks prohibiting the access to what Heidegger is after from the start. The German expression here is "dem Er-eignis übereignet zu werden" (GA 65: 3). Unlike the English translation, this passage has an immediate and more straightforward meaning in German, where it signifies something like "to abandon oneself to the event." To be sure, *Ereignis* is a concept which in Heidegger's use obtains a depth and philosophical gravity which the undifferentiated notion of "event" can hardly carry. Yet it is a common word in German, which "enowning" in English is not. In forging a philosopheme from out of the neutral term of

Er-eignis Heidegger seeks to reach beyond the subject–object dichotomy, to designate the event of meaning, that which takes place, that which manifests itself and shines forth, as something to which the subject of knowledge also *belongs*. As a descriptive term it therefore short-circuits itself at the root, since the very premise for its use is that it is not an ordinary descriptive term, whereby something is depicted and designated by someone.

From Heidegger's earlier work we are perhaps most familiar with this philosophical aspiration in his discussions and uses of the so called "formal indication," which is first introduced in the lectures from the early 1920s, which is mentioned only in passing in *Being and Time*, but which is again emphasized in the very important lecture course from 1929, *The Basic Concepts of Metaphysics*. The point on which he repeatedly insists is that existential-ontological terminology must be seen not as ordinary objective descriptive categories, but as pointers or precisely "indicators" of a meaning which somehow has to be lived and enacted by Dasein, Because when life is reflecting on itself it is seeking to determine not the meaning of some objective nature, but precisely itself as a source of meaning. In *Contributions* we can see how this self-reflexive nature of the philosophical pursuit is established as its fundamental principle. To contemplate being in a radical enough philosophical manner requires that we recognize from the start that we are not standing over and against a foreign entity, which we can speak "about." Instead it is necessary that we acknowledge the irreducible self-reflexive aspect of this whole endeavor; in other words, that we "abandon" ourselves to that "event" with which we are seeking to come to terms. And to do so means also to understand ourselves from that which we are trying to understand. This is another, and I hope somewhat less opaque way of putting the point of "being owned over into enowning." Yet we should not fool ourselves into thinking that there is some definitive way of translating or clarifying what Heidegger is here saying in a convoluted manner. There is, one could say, a kind of structural opacity built into the very core of the book, which has to do with its philosophical ambition, not simply to report philosophical findings or arguments, but rather to stage a move-ment and an experience of thinking which has to be enacted by everyone in a unique way.

In the particular passage under scrutiny we have seen how the problem of language and mode of description is connected to the overall philosophical orientation of the work, namely to move beyond objectifying thinking. In the second of the two quoted sentences we could also see how Heidegger connects this general remark to the question of man, to an "essential transformation of the human from 'rational animal' [*animal rationale*] to Dasein." For Heidegger, the traditional definition of man as rational animal is tied to an understanding of subjectivity as representation and as foundation. It is what generates an anthropocentric metaphysics which has as its effect an objectifying mode of thought. To fully recognize the epistemic conditions for accessing the question of being it is therefore also necessary to confront the nature of human life. In *Being and Time* the neutral term "Dasein" (with its everyday sense of "existence") was introduced explicitly in order to discharge the prejudices inherent in such terms as man, human being, or subjectivity. As the existential analytic is laid out, this term obtains an ever richer meaning, with a wealth of connections, all gathered in the general definition of "concern," as a condensed expression for "ahead-of-itself-being-already-in-(the-world)" (SZ: 192). Perhaps the most important aspect of this definition is the insistence that Dasein is a being-in-the-world, in other words a being whose essence is relatedness to and interdependency with regard to its environment.

Yet the role and position of Dasein within the context of the phenomenological ontology explored in *Being and Time* remains notoriously unclear. How should it be understood: as a slightly transformed Kantian or Husserlian transcendental subject, the condition of possibility of meaning; or as a being among beings, situated at the clearing of being, exposed to the disclosure of world, in no way its agent, but rather the recipient of its gift? In some of the literature on Heidegger, especially where the role and importance of his "turning," his *Kehre*, is accentuated, one finds the argument that following *Being and Time* he abandons the philosophy of the subject implied in the whole analysis of Dasein and turns instead to a thinking of the history and event of being. Even though there is some truth to this rudimentary scheme, it is invalid if taken to mean that Heidegger somehow abandons the theme of Dasein altogether in favor of a thinking of being as event. The problem of Dasein, the problem of how to philosophically conceptualize the being of man within the horizon of the general question of the meaning of being, remains equally valid in the context of *Contributions*. Indeed, the question of Dasein is, as he says at one point, the very "crisis" between the first and the other beginning (GA 65: 295), and consequently the question of Dasein and the transfigured conception of man implied by this concept reappears throughout the book. Generally, but not always, he writes it here as "Da-sein," in order to emphasize the point that was already articulated in *Being and Time*, namely that Dasein signifies the being of the "there," the *da*, as the openness for beings. In an adjacent entry he declares that in *Being and Time* Dasein was conceived too much under the shadow of "the anthropological and the subjectivistic" (GA 65: 295). Yet, he continues, "the opposite of this is what we have in view." For, as he also writes elsewhere, "Dasein has overcome all subjectivity" (GA 65: 252).

Neither the problem nor the concept of Dasein from earlier has thus been abandoned; instead the reflection on the nature of this openness to and for being is decisive for grasping the whole project of *Contributions*. Now Dasein is the place of the truth of being, which can only be understood from within being itself as *Ereignis*. "The relation of Dasein to being belongs in the essencing [*Wesung*] of being itself," which he also expresses as follows: "being needs Dasein and does not essence [*west*] at all without this enownment [*Ereignung*]" (GA 65: 254, translation modified). Yet Dasein should now be understood not as an epistemic foundation for the meaning of being, but as being's own way of becoming manifest to itself, as its truth. In a seemingly self-contradictory passage he says: "Dasein is the grounding of the truth of being" (GA 65: 170). If Dasein is here understood as a foundation for a structure of true propositions, or as an exemplary mode of being, then the statement seems to deny what he is saying elsewhere. But the point here is that Dasein is a foundation to the extent that it does not focus on itself, but rather to the extent that it abandons itself to being. "The less he insists upon the being which he finds himself to be, so much nearer does he come to being" (GA 65: 170–1). It is in thinking this thought that we have also moved from a conception of man as the rational animal, to man as Dasein, as was said in the passage from which we started out above.

In *Being and Time* temporality is an existential of Dasein, and described as the "meaning" of concern, and thus also as the ultimate projectory domain of the meaning of being. One way to understand the impasse in which the question of being ended up as a result of the previous analysis is that there was no way to get from the temporality of Dasein to the temporality of being itself. In this way the shadow of "subjectivism" mentioned above could also be said to color its account of time. In an important passage in *Contributions* Heidegger comments on the "crisis of the question of being" following *Being and Time*, saying that in order to avoid an objectification of being, it was necessary here to withhold initially the "temporal" exposition of being and to attempt to make the truth of being "visible" independently (GA 65: 451). This remark can be read as one explanation for the surprising lack of any substantial discussion of time and temporality in *Contributions*, where only a handful of sections explicitly deal with this theme. Still, even though the notion of a temporality of Dasein is not part of the vocabulary of *Contributions*, the philosophical problem to which it provided an answer remains. In a section devoted to "Being and Time," both as a theme and as a specific work, Heidegger writes (GA 65: 242): "Time was to become experiencable as the 'ecstatic' free-play [*Spielraum*] of the truth of being." Yet, the ground for the truth of being can no longer be demonstrated, he says, but must be awaited as a "thrust" for which we can prepare historically. Even though the earlier book could not be read as a program for how to achieve this task, it nevertheless still constitutes a valid beginning and a preparation. For, as he writes, the "reaching out into the free-play of time-space [*Zeit-spiel-raum*]" must continue (GA 65: 242). For the important German term *Spielraum*, literally "playspace," there is no good English translation, and "free-play" is a somewhat desperate solution. One way to understand what Heidegger is after with this concept is to see it as an extension of the quasi-transcendental notions of the "there" and the "clearing" in *Being and Time*, as the name for a dynamic space of the emergence of meaning and truth.

Apart from the familiar reservation with regard to the overly systematic aspirations of *Being and Time*, we can note in the quoted passage a significant shift in Heidegger's understanding of time. In the earlier analysis the ontological order of time and space was hierarchical, and it was explicitly stated that spatiality was less fundamental than temporality (cf. section 68, GA 65: 133–4). Throughout *Contributions*, however, he rarely refers to time simpliciter, but more often to "time-space," in other words to an apparently indissociable conjunction of these two parameters. This change confirms a famous remark from a much later phase of his thinking, in the lecture "Time and Being" from 1962 (Heidegger 1968: 24), where he explicitly criticizes his previous attempt to ground spatiality in temporality.

As a parallel term to that of time-space Heidegger occasionally also refers to another significant metaphor, namely that of the *Augenblicksstätte*, translated as "the site for the moment" (GA 65: 375). Just like "time-space," this neologism joins a temporal and a spatial term, moment and site. Sometimes it appears as a refiguration of time-space, but sometimes also as a more fundamental notion, as he speaks of the "unfolding of time-space out of the site for the moment" (GA 65: 375), an origin which is furthermore said to "correspond to the uniqueness of being as enowning." In *Being and Time*, the *Augenblick*, the "moment of vision" (literally "the blink of an eye"), designates the qualified authentic temporality of understanding, and also the authentic repetition of historicity. It is a temporality which cannot be reduced to the now in the traditional sense of the point in time, but it is instead what marks the overcoming of the objectivist "vulgar" conception of time as such. It is the temporality of freedom and of transcendence, and of radical decision. In several ways the *Augenblick* could be described as the conceptual "predecessor" to *Ereignis* in *Contributions*, and as the most important link in the development of Heidegger's thinking on time. In both cases we stand before a term which in itself gathers a criticism of a vulgar concept of time, with a reference to the inescapable temporal and historical situatedness of thinking. For the *Augenblick* is never just a name for a neutral minimal temporal phase, but always connected to a decision, with the need to act, also in thinking. If we follow the longer trajectory of Heidegger's thinking we can see how it emerges from out of his reflections on both the Paulinian and Kierkegaardian sense of *kairos* as a flash of eternity in the finite, but also on Aristotle's reference to *kairos* as the incalculable temporality of *phronesis* or practical wisdom.

The connection between *Ereignis* and *Augenblick* sharpens again the key move repeated throughout *Contributions*, namely that genuine thinking requires that we refuse the temptation of an objectifying gaze, and permit the experience of our belonging to being to permeate our understanding of being. Genuine thinking has no temporal framework; instead it permits time to take shape on the basis of its own decision. It issues from and enacts the *Augenblicksstätte* out of which temporal historical frameworks arise. Only in recognizing our belonging to that which we are trying to grasp can we approach it in a language that must remain a kind of stammering discourse on the verge of syntactical and semantic breakdown.

The reference to the *Augenblick* also permits us to move on to a theme which it recalls, and which unlike that of time receives overwhelming attention in *Contributions*, namely history and historicity. We have already seen how the self-reflexivity of the philosophical task is repeated throughout the book, in relation to subjectivity (Dasein), to language, and to time. But in no context is the situatedness of thinking developed at greater length than in respect to history. One sometimes finds the mistaken view in the literature on Heidegger that following *Being and Time* he abandons the theme of historicity of Dasein and of thinking, in favor of a thinking of the history of being. But the intensified ventures into the history of being attempted in *Contributions* go hand in hand with an even more radical historicization of thinking itself.

Following the passage quoted above, on the "crisis of the question of being," which resulted in the withholding of the "temporal" exposition of being, Heidegger speaks of the necessity of "a more original insertion into history," a process in which thinking will become "evermore historical" (GA 65: 451). These formulations are indications of a basic orientation of the work as a whole, in which questions concerning the historicity of thinking and the relation between philosophy and history are by no means avoided or set aside, but instead emphasized more than ever. It is in relation to history that the new mode of thinking presented in *Contributions* is distinguished. However, "the historical" here primarily defines not the theme, or the method of thinking, but the *mode* in which thinking relates to what is to be thought, to being as well as to truth, its *enactment*. Here the untranslatable distinction in German between what is *historisch* and what is *geschichtlich*, also familiar from *Being and Time*, becomes absolutely crucial. The historical in the sense of *historisch* designates events in chronological time, such as can be the object of historical science. History as *Geschichte*, on the other hand, is the happening and manifestation of being to which we belong. It is not simply the question of a distinction between history as a theoretical enterprise and history as actual historical events. If that was all there was to it, the idea of philosophy becoming more historical, as *geschichtlich*, would have no meaning. The problem with what is *historisch*, and thus also with all kinds of historicisms, is the belief that history, as *Geschichte*, can be grasped and understood as an object of knowledge, of classification and comparison. But history as a science and as a theoretical enterprise is part of the same metaphysical and objectifying configuration that has generated the forgetfulness of the question of being. Philosophy thinks that it becomes more historical by educating itself with the knowledge of past achievements, but in the end it only reaffirms the reign of a subjetivistic paradigm, within which the present sets itself up as the judge of everything past. It is not only unable to think and experience itself from out of history, and thus itself as historical, but it actively prevents this awareness from becoming manifest. Thus he states the apparent paradox: "History [*Geschichte*] emerges only in the immediate skip of what is historical [*das Historische*]" (GA 65: 10). Of course, Heidegger could not be taken to mean simply that we should at one point somehow transcend historical learning and interpretation altogether in an affirmation of blind and future oriented action. Also in his own reconstructions of the history of being, he relies on the meticulous work of generations of philologians. His point is, in the spirit of Nietzsche's "Second Untimely Meditation," that the historical theoretical enterprise can in the end make us blind to the history that we ourselves *are*.

Again, the key word is "belonging," *Zugehörigkeit*. In genuine historical thinking man understands himself as belonging to being in a sense which metaphysical thinking was supposedly unable to see. " 'Historical' here means: belonging to the essential swaying of being itself." (GA 65: 421) The examples of similar formulations could be multiplied. This belonging does not primarily designate a *fact* about the relation between two entities, thinking and being. Instead it marks a recognition of a debt or an exposure, an experienced lack, that constitutes the relation as such. In thinking, man recognizes himself as appropriated by being, but this recognition also implies an active appropriation on the part of thought. This double bind is characteristic of the particular belonging that Heidegger is struggling to convey. There is a constant play between activity and passivity, of being claimed and claiming. In a passage which again mentions the historical nature of thinking, and which also recalls the theme of the joining, the *Fuge*, he writes of the thinking in the other beginning that it is "in a unique way originally historical," in the sense that it is the "submissive possessing of be-ing's essencing," *die sich fügende Verfügung über die Wesung des Seyns* (GA 65: 11, translation modified). From *Being and Time* we are familiar with a similar structure in what it says about the passive–active scheme of thrownness and projection, or in the definition of Dasein's basic comportment as "ahead-of-itself-being-already-in" (SZ: 237).

The qualified historical reflection presented in *Contributions* is enacted as a dialectics of the "first" and the "other" beginning. In the opening paragraph, Heidegger declares that his account will move along a path which is cleared in "passing over to the other beginning" (GA 65: 4), and throughout the book he will repeat this claim. What is the meaning of this eschatological ambition? In *Being and Time*, "repetition" (*Wiederholung*) is the name for the movement that constitutes Dasein's historicity as "destiny," enacted in and through the moment of authentic temporalization. It is an event in which the identity of Dasein is preserved yet transformed, since in this repetition the past possibility of the other is projected as a future for oneself. On a manifest level it is not clear how this connects to the historical scheme in *Contributions*, which makes hardly any thematic use of the term "repetition." Yet the term does appear in one short but very interesting section (section 20, GA 65: 55), entitled "The Beginning and the Beginning Thinking," which is devoted precisely to the dialectic of the first and other beginning. A genuine beginning is here presented as something unsurpassable. It is "self-grounding," "reaching ahead" into a future. To confront such a beginning, within which we always already stand, cannot amount to explaining or deducing it. Our only hope is to encounter it in a "repetition" so as to grasp it in its uniqueness. And "when this encountering is inceptual, then it is originary – but this necessarily as *other* beginning" (GA 65: 55).

In its general structure, this passage does in fact recall the logic of so-called authentic historicity from *Being and Time*, where authenticity or originarity is manifested in the repetition of an origin which the repetition can never fully master, but which it can nevertheless retrieve in anticipation. In *Contributions* the awareness of the first beginning, i.e. the inception of Greek metaphysics, is needed in order to accomplish the other beginning. The opening of thought is possible only under the condition that this first beginning can be articulated, felt, and experienced in its own validity and necessity. Yet the first beginning is never immediately seen or experienced as such. Until it is repeated, it remains concealed under an apparently self-evident practice of "historical" thinking and doing. It is only by being repeated that it become a first beginning, which can enable us to envisage another beginning. "The old, i.e. that which nothing younger can ever surpass in essentiality, manifests itself only to historical encounter and to historically mindful deliberation" (GA 65: 434). Repetition in this sense is obviously not just a matter of retrieving a hidden origin; the agonistic element in this encounter is clearly acknowledged. In a Nietzschean turn of phrase, Heidegger here also speaks of repetition as a challenge that requires strength and courage: "To the genuine passage belongs both the courage for the old and the freedom for the new" (GA 65: 434). What should we expect from this other beginning? *Contributions* remains evasive as to the more concrete effects of this transformation. No specific politics or ethics, no specific institutions, religions, or works are anticipated in the text, yet this new beginning is said to constitute a fundamental shift in man's relation to being. On one level this has to do with the explicitly *preparatory* character of the work. But more importantly it requires us to seek its significance on the level of philosophical thinking as such, precisely as this is enacted in the book. *Contributions* is not a vague blueprint for a new world order, but the self-enacting and exemplary practice of mindful (*besinnende*) philosophical thinking. Its status as another or second beginning rests on the claim that this can only be accomplished through a radical and critical encounter with the original motive and impetus of Western philosophy as a whole.

To step into the play, into the *Spielraum*, of historical happening is also to enter into the play of *truth* as that which comes to pass as an opening or "essencing" of being.

371

The theme of truth, of the essence of truth, as *aletheia*, as openness and clearing, also recalls the problem of the historical as just shown. As long as we think of truth simply as correspondence to how it is, we remain on the superficial level of taxonomies and comparisons characteristic also of historical science. To genuinely confront the phenomenon of truth is to confront the very opening of the space in which a question can be experienced as such. It is the "projection of the very domain of projecting open itself," as Heidegger writes in the introductory entry to the part of the book explicitly devoted to this theme (GA 65: 327). Again we can see both the profound continuity with regard to *Being and Time* and a radicalization of its orientation. If truth as disclosure was previously understood as founded on the disclosure of Dasein, it is now approached as an opening in and of being itself. It is the truth *of* being in the dual sense of the genitive. Still, if this formulation is taken to mean something more "objective" over and against the "subjectivist" conception of the previous analysis the whole point is lost again. Dasein can access this truth of being not by turning away from itself, but rather by turning deeper into itself as a belonging to that which it is trying to grasp.

In order for thought to step into the truth of being, Heidegger writes, "it must at the same time leap into the essencing of truth" (GA 65: 446). Dasein must place itself, or rather permit itself to be placed, in that opening, which it conceptually is trying to grasp. And when it thus permits truth to shine forth in and through itself it can also experience its dual nature. For truth in this sense is never just unconcealment and disclosure, it is likewise and essentially concealment and withdrawal. It is the incalculable play of these two powers. "Both clearing and sheltering-concealing, are not two but rather the essencing of the one, of truth itself" (GA 65: 349, translation modified). In this dionysian experience of a ground that "takes back and towers up" (GA 65: 346), which never consumes itself in full disclosure, but which always returns to itself, we also come across what is perhaps the most profound aspect of *Ereignis*. For this ground, Heidegger writes in the same section, "is *Ereignis* itself as the essencing of being" (GA 65: 346). *Ereignis* is a temporal-historical happening of truth as itself being's way of becoming present. But this repeated gathering of parallel and related, equiprimordial concepts should not be read as another system, but rather as the conceptual debris from the ongoing attempt to keep open the space for this one fundamental experience. It is an attempt to give voice to an experience which has no definitive and appropriate linguistic form, and to give voice to life's belonging to what is, by "turning" toward and thus "attuning" oneself to its demand.

Later, Heidegger will refer to his philosophical development during this period in terms precisely of a "turning," a *Kehre*, a notion which has been the subject of extensive interpretive efforts and some controversy. In *Contributions* this notion does not play a major part. Still, it is here, in the attempt to articulate the experience of *Ereignis* as the abyssal play of truth, accessible only through our own abandonment to its essencing, that the reference to a *Kehre* flashes forth as a philosopheme, in the ultimate section of the book. *Ereignis*, Heidegger says here, "has its innermost occurrence and its widest reach in the turning" (GA 65: 407). What is this turning, he asks. And responds: "Only the onset of being as *Ereignung* of the *Da* leads Dasein to itself and thus to the enactment (sheltering) of the inabiding and grounded truth into the being which finds its site in the lit-up sheltering-concealing of the Da" (GA 65: 407). In other words, the turning is the event of the site of truth whereby Dasein comes to understand itself as the very enactment of this site. We could also add: as belonging to this disclosure which it itself brings about. The turning, the figure of a transformation and transfiguration, has been implicit in most of what has been said so far about the principal issues in *Contributions*. For as a figure of reversal it concentrates the message of the whole book, namely that only when thinking can experience, understand, and articulate the nature of its own dependency upon and belonging to being is a new beginning in philosophical thinking possible.

As the many quotations have amply demonstrated, *Contributions* is an exceptionally difficult and sometimes very awkward text. Its own initially stated ambition, not to describe, explain, or teach, but to constitute that which is to be said as an essencing of being, seems to suggest that here being is simply evoked and presented in complete transparency, as if there was no need of any further explication or commentary. Read in the light of such an ambition the book is a failure. Yet if one is prepared to take the time – and time it requires – then it is possible to begin to discern the key of its melody, and through it the simple and tragic beauty of its message.

Note

The text was written with the support of a research grant from the "Rausing Foundation for Research in the Humanities."

References and further reading

Heidegger, M. (1969) *Zur Sache des Denkens*. Tübingen: Niemeyer.

Heidegger, M. and Blochmann, E. (1989) *Briefwechsel 1918–1969*. Marbach am Neckar: Deutsche Schiller-Gesellschaft.

Herrmann, W. von (1994) *Wege ins Ereignis: Zu Heideggers "Beiträge zur Philosophie."* Frankfurt am Main: Klostermann.

Herrmann, W. von (2001) *Contributions to Philosophy* and enowning-historical thinking. In C. Scott et al. (eds.), *Companion to Heidegger's Contributions to Philosophy*. Bloomington: Indiana University Press.

Kahn, C. (1979) *The Art and Thought of Heraclitus*. Cambridge: Cambridge University Press.

Pöggeler, O. (1987) *Martin Heidegger's Path of Thinking* (trans. D. Magurschak and S. Barber). Atlantic Highlands, NJ: Humanities Press (original work published 1963).

Ruin, H. (1994) *Enigmatic Origins. Tracing the Theme of Historicity through Heidegger's Works*. Stockholm: Almqvist & Wiksell.

Ruin, H. (1999) The moment of truth: Augenblick and Ereignis in Heidegger. *Epoche*, 6, 75–88.

Schurmann, R. (2003) *Broken Hegemonies* (trans. R. Lilly). Bloomington: Indiana University Press (original work published 1996).

Scott, C., Schoenbaum, S., Vallega-Neu, D. and Vallega, A. (eds) (2001) *Companion to Heidegger's Contributions to Philosophy*. Bloomington: Indiana University Press.

Vallega-Neu, D. (2001) Poietic saying. In C. Scott et al. (eds), *Companion to Heidegger's Contributions to Philosophy*. Bloomington: Indiana University Press.

Vallega-Neu, D. (2003) *Heidegger's Contributions to Philosophy: An Introduction*. Bloomington: Indiana University Press.

23

Ereignis

RICHARD POLT

Heidegger's theme is being. No doubt – but the same could be said of Parmenides, Aristotle, or Aquinas. If we want a name for a uniquely Heideggerian theme – his distinctive concern within the generous domain of "being" – we can do no better than the term *Ereignis*. The word plays a central part in his earliest extant lecture course (1919; see GA 56/57). It fades away in *Being and Time*, but makes a triumphant though secret comeback as the "essential" title (GA 65: 3, 80) of the massive and cryptic *Contributions to Philosophy (Of Ereignis)* (written 1936–8, published 1989). *Ereignis* makes cameo appearances in a number of Heidegger's postwar publications and stars in "Time and Being," his last major essay (1962; see Heidegger 1969).

But what does *Ereignis* mean? If it is a name for the ultimate, then it will not do to define it in terms of more proximate, familiar concepts. So we may throw up our hands and simply repeat with Heidegger: *Das Ereignis ereignet*, "Appropriation appropriates" (Heidegger 1969: 24). A more elaborate version of the same gesture might borrow some phrases from the *Contributions to Philosophy*: "Enowning [*Ereignis*] occurs as a turning in-between being's enowning call and Da-sein's enowned belonging" (Vallega-Neu 2001: 72). But if we simply remain within Heideggerian language we are imitating, not interpreting. Alternatively, if we believe Heidegger is trying to say something that we can say better, then *Ereignis* can mean almost anything. If, for instance, we think the analysis of everydayness in Division One of *Being and Time* is what really matters in Heidegger's thought, then *Ereignis* can be what enables us to use things "effectively and familiarly according to recognized norms" (Spinosa 2001: 207) – regardless of the fact that the *Contributions* speak of the "*uniqueness*" and "extreme *strangeness*" of *Ereignis* (GA 65: 252).

The responsible way to gain a sense of *Ereignis* is to combine close reading with independent thought. We must trace the word's roles in crucial texts while keeping in mind its usual meaning, corresponding to the English "event." Furthermore, if Heidegger is right that interpreting is the pursuit of a projected possibility rather than a disengaged staring at the given (SZ: 150), then we have to bring words and concepts of our own to bear on Heidegger's texts – otherwise we are parroting instead of reading. However, these concepts continually have to be tested both against Heidegger's own words and against "the things themselves" (SZ: 153).

Yet our task is still harder, because *Ereignis* seems to have various meanings. As we will see, in 1919 it means, roughly, a kind of experience in which I find myself intimately involved, as opposed to an experience in which I am nothing but an objective viewer. In 1936–8 it means, roughly, the possible happening in which a new dwelling may be founded – a place and age in which a people could cultivate significance. In 1962 it means, roughly, neither an experience nor a happening but an ultimate source that has always already granted us time and being. How are these meanings connected? Is one of them deeper than the others? Or are they all the same in the end?

These problems can hardly be resolved in one essay, but in what follows I try to provide the rudiments of responsible readings of three key texts that employ the word *Ereignis*, as well as reflecting on the promise that these avatars of *Ereignis* hold for our own future thinking.

1919: My Own Event

The "war emergency semester" of January–April 1919 marks Heidegger's emergence as a thinker in his own right (Kisiel 1993: 21–5, 38–59; Kovacs 1994; van Buren 1994: chapters 12, 13). In his lecture course for this term, *The Idea of Philosophy and the Problem of Worldview*, he distances himself from the neo-Kantian value theory of his teacher Heinrich Rickert and aligns himself with the phenomenology of his new mentor and colleague, Edmund Husserl. Heidegger joins Husserl's search for the roots of scientific knowledge in lived experience, and shares Husserl's desire to do justice to what is genuinely shown in our experience instead of imposing a theory upon it. Heidegger's incipient difference from Husserl is that while Husserl holds out hope for a new, more adequate theory of phenomena, Heidegger sees theory itself as the problem. According to Heidegger, the theoretization of life "de-vivifies" it, reducing a situation from an *Ereignis* – an event of one's own – to a *Vorgang*, a "process" that passes before one like a spectacle (GA 56/57: 74–5).

Heidegger attacks the neo-Kantian focus on the norms for theoretical knowledge: "The primacy of the theoretical must be broken, but not in order to proclaim the primacy of the practical . . . but because the theoretical itself and as such refers back to something pre-theoretical" (GA 56/57: 59). What is this pre-theoretical, pre-practical something? How can we encounter and conceive of it?

This problem leads to radical questions. How is anything given to us at all? What is givenness itself? "Is there the 'there is'? . . . Already in the opening of the question 'Is there . . . ?' there is something" (GA 56/57: 62–3). "What does 'there is' mean?" (GA 56/57: 67). Heidegger uses the German idiom *es gibt*, literally "it gives." Even before we specify what is given, the sense of givenness is itself given to us. What is this sense, and how is it given?

At this point, we must "leap into the world as such" (GA 56/57: 63): only if the world is "worlding" can anything in the world be given (GA 56/57: 73). Exploiting our English idiom, we can state the point this way: *there* can be nothing without a *there*. The pre-theoretical "something" is not really any thing (an entity), but the there, the context or world within which entities can present themselves. What are the characteristics of worldhood as such, thereness itself?

Heidegger approaches this question by way of the clichéd but "fitting" word *Erlebnis* (GA 56/57: 66). The word means an experience and is related to *leben*, "to live." It is an experience that one lives through, that forms part of one's life. "Life" here is not the functioning of an organism, but the course of one's fortunes and actions, a course that invites a reckoning of failures and successes. The "life" in *Erlebnis* is *bios* as in "biography," not as in "biology."

Who experiences my lived experience? I do. But this truism may initially seem untrue. In the general question, "Is there something?" no "I" is apparent – at least, no individual "I" (GA 56/57: 66, 68–9, 73). "The 'is there' is a 'there is' for an 'I', and yet it is not I to and for *whom* the question relates" (GA 56/57: 69). However, this abstract, empty "Is there something?" is not part of normal lived experience: "It is the absolutely worldless, world-foreign; it is the sphere which takes one's breath away and where no one can live" (GA 56/57: 112). In normal experience, I inhabit a world of my *own*. "Wherever and whenever 'it worlds' for me, *I* am somehow there" (GA 56/57: 73). This "I" is a concrete, "historical 'I'" (GA 56/57: 74) – an individual with particular capacities and goals, living in a particular cultural context.

The fact that lived experiences are mine does not mean that they happen within my isolated mind, but that they happen within a world, a there, within which I dwell. Heidegger lashes out against the reduction of meaning and truth to subjectivity: "Knowing as a psychic process is in no way explained when I acknowledge it as occurring in a psychic subject" (GA 56/57: 64). Once we think of ourselves as self-contained subjects we will be bedeviled by the insoluble epistemological problems of modern philosophy (GA 56/57: 77–94), problems that are essentially nonsensical because they overlook the phenomenon of the world (GA 56/57: 91–2). By puzzling over the relationship between subject and object – a thinking thing and an extended thing, as Descartes puts it – we lose sight of the non-thing, the world, within which all things are given and in which we are engaged. As in all his subsequent work, Heidegger wants to avoid both subjectivism (the retreat to an "inner" self) and objectivism (the restriction of truth to "external," theoretically established facts).

To use Heidegger's own example: as he enters the classroom, he sees the lectern. It is *his* place, the place where he is to speak. It is a little too high for *his* modest stature. A book lying on it stands in *his* way (GA 56/57: 71). What is given in Heidegger's experience, then, is the lectern as a meaningful thing. It is meaningful thanks to its place in a world, a complex of meaning within which things can belong – or fail to belong. This is Heidegger's *own* world, the context in which he pursues his activities and thoughts. Only by living in such a context can we encounter things at all.

Our encounters, then, are *Ereignisse*, events of appropriation.

> Lived experience does not pass in front of me like a thing, but I appropriate [*er-eigne*] it to myself, and it appropriates itself [*er-eignet sich*] according to its essence. . . . The experiences are events of appropriation in so far as they live out of one's "own-ness" [*aus dem Eigenen*], and life lives only in this way. (With this the event-like essence of appropriation [*Ereignischarakter*] is still not fully determined.) (GA 56/57: 75)

This last remark may be the understatement of Heidegger's career, given that he was to devote hundreds of pages more to the theme. But this climactic passage does give us some crucial insights. The point of the word *Ereignis* is not that I reach out and grab some object, appropriating it "from outside or from anywhere else" (GA 56/57: 75). Instead, I already live within a system of ownness, a network of my own concerns and issues. My concerns are mine not merely because I am currently taking interest in them, but because they define me – the sense of my life. Who Heidegger *is*, for instance, depends on what matters to him, what is meaningful to him: speaking at the lectern, addressing his students, operating as a thinker. All these activities are part of his environing world (*Umwelt*), the environment of an early twentieth-century Freiburg academic.

Heidegger's use of *Ereignis* is a play on words, not linguistic scholarship. *Ereignis* has no etymological connection to *eigen* (own, proper, particular) and its cognates. Instead it is related to *Augen*, "eyes," and originally means something like "coming into view" (Sheehan 2001: 196–8). (Similarly, "transpire" means "come into view" but is used loosely to mean "come to pass" in general.) But because Heidegger focuses on the phonetic similarity between *Ereignis* and *eigen*, the translation "event of appropriation" is apt.

In events of appropriation, the enveloping system of ownness reveals situations and things as appropriate or inappropriate, proper or improper. The book on the lectern is inappropriate: it interferes with Heidegger's immediate goal as a teacher. It would be improper for Heidegger to stand on the lectern and hurl books at his students – not because the lectern is physically unsuited for the action but because his world, which overlaps with the students' worlds, defines this behavior as inapt, as contrary to the meaning of the situation.

Meaningfulness and ownness characterize all worlds. For instance, an African tribesman inhabits a very different world from Heidegger's, so if he were suddenly trans-ported to Freiburg he might take the lectern as a shield or a magical object – or even as "something 'which he does not know what to make of' " (GA 56/57: 72). But this state of being at a loss, encountering something puzzling, is simply a limit case of perceiv-ing something as improper or inappropriate; it is made possible by a world, a context that determines what counts as sensible and senseless.

Heidegger eventually claims that even the general experience that "there is some-thing" can be a genuine *Ereignis* – and even a sign of "the highest potentiality of life" (GA 56/57: 115). It can happen in "gliding from one world of experience to another genuine life-world, or in moments of especially intensive life; not at all or seldom in those types of experience that are firmly anchored in a world *without* reaching, pre-cisely within this world, a much greater life-intensity" (GA 56/57: 115). As a case of "life-intensity" we might think of an artistic breakthrough in which a poet or painter experiences the sheer wonder that there is something instead of nothing. As a case of "gliding" between life-worlds, consider the moment in which one returns from a long trip and settles back into one's house. For an hour or so there is an opportunity to see home with new eyes and to experience oneself neither as traveler nor as resident but as "someone" unsettled, encountering "something" unsettled. Such an experience is still one's *own*, but who one is has temporarily become a problem.

Despite Heidegger's recognition of the importance of everyday familiarity, both here and in later writings he insists that *unfamiliar* moments, such as anxiety or joy, provide the deepest illumination (Fell 1992). Such moments are "pre-worldly" (GA 56/57:

115): they have not yet been articulated into patterns of significations. They tend, however, to push out "'*into* a (particular) world,' and indeed in its undiminished 'vital impetus'" (GA 56/57: 115). This passage suggests that "pre-worldly" moments are founts of meaning, generating systems of sense yet irreducible to these systems (cf. van Buren 1994: 276). These moments experience the given without yet categorizing it as a particular kind of entity within an established life-world. Heidegger does not deny that we all already live in articulated worlds; however, these worlds can be refreshed or transformed by "pre-worldly" encounters with the raw givenness of something as opposed to nothing. The meaning of "there is" is rooted in these basic vital experiences of the "something."

Heidegger states that both the pre-worldly experience of something in general and the worldly experience of things *as* this or that "express the characters of the appropriating event [*Ereignischaraktere*]" (GA 56/57: 117). The workings of *Ereignis*, then, are not limited to events in which we encounter things with a set interpretation; the vague experience of "something" is also an *Ereignis*. Both types of event "live in life itself and [thus] are at once originating and carry their provenance in themselves. They are at once preceptive and retroceptive" (GA 56/57: 117). This passage expresses a nascent concept of temporality, later developed into the insight that we essentially reach out into the future and the past in order to reveal the present (SZ ¶65). We might see this reaching-out as an *Ereignis*: I appropriate my own past for the sake of my own possibilities in order to encounter my own surroundings. Normally this appropriation happens in a "worldly" way, as part of my established way of life; occasionally it happens in a "pre-worldly" way that exceeds the boundaries of any settled world.

In addition to worldly and pre-worldly lived experiences there is the *theoretical* stance, for which "something" in general has no apparent relation to a meaningful life-world, but is a "something of knowability" (GA 56/57: 116) – a mere object to be described in propositions. From this perspective, the lectern is not objectively appropriate or inappropriate, and in fact is not intrinsically a "lectern" at all; it is simply an object that is 1.5 meters tall, weighs 20 kilograms, is composed of pine, and has such and such a geometrical shape. What we do with it and the meanings it may have for us are epiphenomena, "value" judgments that we impose upon the object itself.

This perspective arises from a "de-vivification" (*Ent-leben* or *Entlebnis*) of the primal *Erlebnis* (GA 56/57: 74). The lived experience of a lectern can succumb to a "progressively destructive theoretical infection . . . lectern, box, brown colour, wood, thing" (GA 56/57: 89). Now my encounter with the thing is no longer an *Ereignis* but a *Vorgang*, a process: I watch the thing as if I were surveying a procession that passes in front of me (GA 56/57: 74, 205). Instead of using the lectern, I measure it and make assertions about it. I have gained facts, but lost the connection to vital meaning. Similarly, consider the difference between shouting out to one's teammates in a game (an *Ereignis*) and analyzing a recording of the shout as manipulable and reproducible information (a *Vorgang*).

Without any event of appropriation, the objectified experience would have no sense. The theoretical perspective is a "residue of this event" (GA 56/57: 75, cf. 89). Without the vital experience of the pre-worldly "something," the theoretical "something" as mere object could not arise (GA 56/57: 116); it is, so to speak, post-worldly.

The theoretical perspective also recognizes a difference between lived experience and theoretical truth – but instead of acknowledging its own roots in life, theory tends to explain life theoretically. Theorists might try to account for culture and meaning with theories of evolution, physiology, and psychology. They might claim that the experience of thing-like objects is primary, and meanings and values are accretions: I first receive sense data, then interpret them as a physical object 1.5 meters tall, and then as a lectern. Heidegger counters: "The lectern is given to me immediately in the lived experience of it. I see it as such, I do not see sensations and sense data" (GA 56/57: 85). The meaningful thing and its environment cannot be reconstructed by piling up meaningless data, which are just the result of "dismembering" the original life-world (GA 56/57: 86).

If life cannot be reconstructed by theory, then phenomenology or "primordial science" must be a *non-theoretical* science (GA 56/57: 96). It must not explain lived experience in propositions, but must depend on and evoke lived experience itself; it is not a theory of experience, but an "experience of experience" (GA 56/57: 219). In the concluding hours of his course, Heidegger calls such experience the "back-and-forth formation of the recepts and precepts from which all theoretical objectification . . . falls out" (GA 56/57: 117). Our concepts must both refer back to life and anticipate life, rather than pretending to capture life in a theory.

The point of Heidegger's reflections is not to destroy or disparage theory, but to revitalize it by tying it back to its roots. A genuine theoretical life is an admirable form of existence with its own specific virtue, "veracity" (GA 56/57: 213).

Many of Heidegger's ideas from 1919 are paralleled in *Being and Time*: world and environment as meaningful wholes (SZ ¶¶ 14–24), the problem of the external world as a pseudo-problem (SZ ¶43a), the rooting of theory in pre-theoretical existence (SZ ¶¶ 13, 33, 44b, 69b). The most obvious difference is the use of "being" as the primary name for Heidegger's theme, but the question of being was already present when Heidegger asked in 1919 about the sense of "there is" and the origin of this sense (GA 56/57: 62–3, 67). Now, however, Heidegger frames his entire project as an investigation of what it means to be and how we understand this meaning (SZ: 1).

The term *Ereignis* nearly disappears in *Being and Time*. Heidegger uses it to refer to natural events (SZ: 152), events within the world (SZ: 273), death as a future event (SZ: 250, 253–4, 257), and past events (SZ: 284, 290, 378–9, 382, 389). In almost all these cases, an "event" is something more superficial than the essential temporal constitution of Dasein (i.e. human beings insofar as they understand being). The exceptions may be two passages where Heidegger inquires into the happening (*Geschehen*) of historical "events," and suggests they are not reducible to "processes" in which objects change their location (SZ: 379, 389). These passages introduce "the ontological enigma of the movement of happening in general" (SZ: 389, translation modified).

1936–8: The Happening of Owndom

Does *Being and Time* do justice to the enigma of happening? Not according to the *Contributions to Philosophy*, written a decade later (Vallega-Neu 2003: 7–51). *Being and Time* claimed that Dasein was essentially historical, but "historicity" is treated there as if it were an abstract quality of a timeless human essence. We must explicitly embrace historicity and integrate it into our thought; Dasein itself must be recognized as an historical *possibility* rather than as a given phenomenon (GA 65: 294, 300–1). Instead of conceiving of the meaning of being as circumscribed by the nature of our own understanding, we should recognize that we ourselves have been "thrown" by being (GA 65: 252), which is itself radically historical (GA 65: 32–3). Then we will complete the transition "from the understanding of being to the *happening of being*" (GA 40: 218). As the name for this happening, Heidegger chooses *Ereignis*.

The *Contributions* sketch a transition from the "first inception" of Western thought to the "other inception." In the first inception, the Greeks wondered at beings as such, and asked about their "beingness" – their most general characteristics. "Being" (*Sein*) in this sense is an abstraction from beings (GA 65: 111–12, 183, 293, 425, 458). The guiding question in the first inception is: what are beings as such (GA 65: 75, 179)?

In the other inception, however, we must ask about being in a new sense that Heidegger usually indicates with the obsolete spelling *Seyn* (GA 65: 436), which we can render as "be-ing." Be-ing is not an abstraction from beings: it must be understood "not on the basis of particular beings, but . . . on the basis of its originary essential happening [*Wesung*]" (GA 65: 75). (*Wesung* – a verbal form of *Wesen* or "essence" – suggests a historical, unique truth as opposed to a timeless universal: GA 65: 66, 286–9.) The fundamental question in the other inception is: how does be-ing essentially happen (GA 65: 78)?

But what does it mean to ask about "be-ing" without considering anything that actually *is*? Heidegger's question in 1919 gives us a clue: "Is there the 'there is'?" (GA 56/57: 62); does it give the "it gives"? Yes: the meaning of the givenness of things is itself given to us. But how (cf. Sheehan 2001: 192)? Furthermore, this meaning can come into question; it can become a burning issue, an urgent problem. How? Such questions can never be answered simply by inspecting given beings, because when we encounter them we are already drawing on a meaning of givenness.

"How does be-ing essentially happen?" means, then: how is the meaning of givenness granted to us, and how can it come into question? Heidegger answers: "*Be-ing essentially happens as Ereignis*. That is not a proposition but the nonconceptual, silent telling of the essential happening that opens itself only to the full, historical enactment of inceptive thinking" (GA 65: 260). The meaning of *Ereignis* is not self-evident – in fact, it can never become fully clear. Be-ing "can never be said definitively" (GA 65: 460), so we must cultivate a way of speaking – *Erschweigung* or "telling silence" (GA 65: 78–80) – that never pretends to represent its theme perfectly. As in 1919, Heidegger suggests that only a non-theoretical thinking can do justice to *Ereignis*. Such thinking cannot simply present a disengaged report on *Ereignis*, but must take part in it and flow from it (GA 65: 3, 86, 464), just as "inceptive thinking" (GA 65: sections 20–31) will not merely be *about* the other inception but will participate in its "enactment" (GA 65: 64). The connection between the event of appropriation and our thought of it is supposed to be so intimate that the saying of be-ing "is" be-ing itself (GA 65: 4) (Polt 2001: 31–2). This radicalizes Heidegger's earlier idea that instead of theorizing about experience we can *experience* experience, live through it in a self-interpreting way (GA 56/57: 219).

381

None of the sayings in the *Contributions*, then, is meant as a theoretical proposition (GA 65: 13). But it is still useful to gather some statements that speak of crucial aspects of *Ereignis*.

1   *Grounding the there. Ereignis* is an "abbreviation" for "the *Ereignis of the grounding of the there*" (GA 65: 247). Such a founding is highly exceptional: be-ing "is what is rarest because it is the most unique, and no one appreciates the few moments in which it grounds a site for itself and essentially happens" (GA 65: 255). In these moments, be-ing literally takes place: it appropriates its own domain, inaugurating a place and age in which the givenness of beings can be questioned and cultivated by a people (GA 65: 97). This place and age is *die Augenblicksstätte*, "the site of the moment" or, more loosely, the momentous site (GA 65: 323).

2   *Inception.* "The inception – inceptively conceived – is be-ing itself . . . as *Ereignis*" (GA 65: 58). An inception (*Anfang*), as opposed to the mere starting point of a process (*Beginn*), is an enduring origin that opens up a whole realm of events or meanings (GA 39: 3–4). Only in an inception can the there be grounded, so be-ing happens only as inception. The scheme of the "first inception" and "other inception," then, does not refer to moments in which human beings recognize or fail to recognize an already given state of affairs. To seek the other inception is not merely to hope for a new relation to *Ereignis*, but to prepare for the essential happening of *Ereignis* itself.

3   *Reciprocity.* "Be-ing requires man in order to happen essentially, and man belongs to be-ing. . . . *This counterpoise of requiring and belonging* constitutes be-ing as *Ereignis*" (GA 65: 251). Be-ing *braucht* – both needs and uses – Dasein as its seeker, preserver, and guardian (GA 65: 17, 294). In turn, we cannot enter Dasein (we cannot "be there") unless be-ing takes place. Heidegger calls this reciprocal relation "the turn in *Ereignis*" (GA 65: 407). Due to the turn, the grounding of the there is both the grounding of be-ing and the grounding of Dasein. In less Heideggerian terms: if the givenness of things is to become a living issue for us, then we have to become alive to it – and only then can we reach our highest potential. Some ways of wrestling with the meaning of givenness include art, politics, philosophy, and religion. In a healthy, vigorous "there," people pursue these activities intensely and keep searching for new, deeper forms of them. Givenness then comes to life by coming into question.

4   *Emergency.* "Urgency, which presses round in its essential happening – what if it were the truth of be-ing itself . . . as *Ereignis?*" (GA 65: 46). *Not* (urgency, emergency, pressing need) is a central motif in Heidegger's writings of the 1930s. All necessity (*Notwendigkeit*) is rooted in urgency (GA 65: 45, 97); beings emerge as meaningful only in emergencies, we might say, when what it means for them to be is called into question. The moment of *Ereignis*, should it ever happen, will be a crisis – a moment that demands "decisions," in a sense that involves not only human choice but also the destiny of be-ing (GA 65: 87–91). The emergency in our own age is the lack of emergency (GA 65: 11, 107, 119, 125, 234–7): in a time that is indifferent to crisis, the greatest danger is that be-ing will fail to happen, because we will fail to enter the condition of urgency that *Ereignis* requires.

382

5   *Gods.* "Be-ing essentially happens as *Ereignis*, the momentous site of the decision about the nearness and distance of the final god" (GA 65: 230). A people's relation to the divine is essential to its participation in be-ing (GA 65: 34, 398–9). The "passing of the final god" will be central to the other inception (GA 65: 17, 27, 228, 331, 414). This "passing" is neither a direct revelation nor a disappearance, but a moment in which the problem of god (or gods, GA 65: 437) *matters* to us once again – it becomes an issue calling for decision (GA 65: 405).

6   *History.* "*Be-ing as Er-eignis is history*" (GA 65: 494). Here 'history' does not mean the past or historical information, but the way in which be-ing and Dasein happen. To think in terms of 'the history of be-ing' is not to tell a story about the ways be-ing has been conceived but to grasp how be-ing itself takes place. Be-ing's history must be understood not merely in terms of change (GA 65: 280, 472) but in terms of how we belong (or fail to belong) to a unique dispensation of meaning. The dispensation lays claim to us, and we can succeed or fail in laying claim to it; this dynamic of claiming, or appropriating, is crucial to the happening of be-ing.

7   *Owndom.* "[T]he origin of the self is *own-dom* [*Eigen-tum*]. This word taken here like king-dom. The mastery of propriety or owning [*Eignung*] in *Ereignis*. . . . Insistence in this happening of owndom first makes it possible for man to come to 'himself' historically and be with himself" (GA 65: 320). Only in *Ereignis* can we truly become *our own selves* (GA 65: 311); this does not mean returning to some fixed nature but accepting our role as the beings to whom our own being, and being in general, makes a difference. This can happen only if we enter into "owndom," that is, the there as the realm in which being is an urgent issue for a community (cf. GA 69: 123–6).

To sum up: *Ereignis* is the way in which the givenness of given beings – including ourselves – comes into question for us. This happening is an urgent inception that grounds a site and initiates an age that has its own unique relation to the divine. This event requires Dasein just as much as Dasein requires it.

Heidegger resists taking *Ereignis* as any sort of *a priori* (GA 65: 222–3). In particular, because *Ereignis* is reciprocal, transcendental thinking *à la* Kant becomes impossible: we have already been appropriated, so we as subjects cannot determine the character of appropriation (GA 65: 239, 252–3). For example, "time-space" (GA 65: sections 238–42) is not an *a priori* structure in our sensibility but an aspect of the unique happening of *Ereignis* which can be "empowered" only by a "future grounding of Dasein" (GA 65: 386). The point is not to correct our way of representing time and space, but to "de-range human essence into Da-sein" (GA 65: 372). Time and space will then happen in a new, richer way.

The word *Erlebnis*, which Heidegger adopted with some reluctance in 1919, is used in the *Contributions* only as a term for a superficial form of modern subjectivity. It is a stimulus that keeps us entertained – the sort of "experience" one gets from an amusement park. It goes hand in hand with "machination," the manipulative representation of objects (GA 65: sections 61–9).

This change in usage parallels Heidegger's increasing suspicion of common experience. The *Contributions* are written for a later audience of the "few" and "rare" (GA 65: 11) who will have made their own way to the truth (GA 65: 8) and who are the secret voices of the people's future (GA 65: 319). This elitism is combined with a bleak view of the present age and with apocalypticism, in the double sense of "apocalypse" as revelation and disaster: only in a moment of extreme emergency can be-ing emerge. All this means that it is difficult to find instances of *Ereignis* in our own lives. No longer does an *Ereignis* happen every time I step up to a lectern; it takes place only when a place is established, not in events within an established place.

We cannot simply observe the grounding of the there, since it is not only a rare occurrence but also an event that determines what counts as observation and as the observable. It is still more elusive, then, than the phenomena of lived experience Heidegger addressed in 1919. These phenomena had to be interpreted without theoretical distortion – a difficult trick. But *Ereignis* in 1936–8 can hardly be called a phenomenon at all. Be-ing is intrinsically "self-withdrawing and essentially happens as refusal" (GA 65: 246). We can only hope to respond to this refusal as a special kind of gift (GA 65: 246) and do justice to it with "telling silence." It is no accident that Heidegger no longer describes his project as phenomenology.

Not only is *Ereignis* in the *Contributions* rare and elusive, but it is arguably one, solitary event. Some passages suggest that be-ing can take place many times, but each time in a distinctive way; Heidegger speaks of be-ing's "uniqueness in each case" (GA 65: 460). But at other times, he seeks "what happens one time, this time" (GA 65: 463). *Ereignis*, like *physis* in the first inception, is "unique and singular" (GA 65: 385).

We can go farther: maybe *Ereignis* has never yet happened at all. *Ereignis* is history (GA 65: 494), but "so far, man has never yet *been* historical" (GA 65: 492). Heidegger thus invokes "the future ones" (Part VI), those who can engage with the sweep of the first inception and open the possibility of another unique inception. The *Contributions* are thought in the future tense and subjunctive mood.

If there is any model for the *Contributions'* version of *Ereignis*, it is probably the idealized National Socialism for which Heidegger still held out some hope at this time. (By 1938 or 1939, his manuscripts would be severely criticizing Hitler by name; GA 66: 122–3. The *Contributions* already attack official Nazi ideology – see GA 65: 43, 117, 319, 493 – but cling to the possibility of a revolutionary transformation of the German *Volk*.) Heidegger's political ideal is based not on racism and conquest, but on a Hölderlinian interpretation of Germany's poetic and philosophical mission as creatively inheriting the spirit of Greece. With the right conjunction of thinkers, poets, and statesmen, the German people might experience an *Ereignis*. We can imagine this event as a communal version of the "pre-worldly" experiences of "something" that Heidegger discussed in 1919. A people might be shocked into something analogous to an artistic breakthrough, a fresh way of dwelling amidst things. This shock might be an overt emergency (something like September 11, 2001), but Heidegger would probably expect it to take a subtler form (such as a work of poetry). The effect would be a renewed "there" and a renewed concern with national heritage and destiny.

1962: The Giving of the Own

The further private writings that follow the *Contributions* develop a new mood, turning away from the tense expectation of an apocalypse and toward a patient abiding. Just as the political and military crises surrounding him come to a head, Heidegger retreats from the theme of emergency and abandons the revolutionary tone of his writings of the mid-1930s. For example, whereas the *Contributions* speak of a "will to *Ereignis*" (GA 65: 58) and challenge humanity to "empower be-ing to its essential happening in a unique moment of history" (GA 65: 430), *Besinnung* (1938–9) claims that be-ing lies beyond both power and powerlessness (GA 66: 83, 187–8). *Die Geschichte des Seyns* (1938–40) sets aside the notion of a transition (*Übergang*) to the other inception, which pervades the *Contributions*, in favor of a simple "going" (*Gang*) (GA 69: 45). By the end of the war, Heidegger has embraced "letting-be" (*Gelassenheit*) and "pure waiting" as the only appropriate attitudes (GA 77: 118, 217).

Along with this withdrawal from action and decision comes a dilution of the sense of *Ereignis* as event. In several postwar essays, Heidegger emphatically distinguishes *Ereignis* from an "occurrence" or "happening" (Heidegger 1971: 127; Heidegger 1972: 20; Heidegger 2002: 36). This is a striking departure from the *Contributions*, which freely use locutions such as "the happening of the truth of be-ing" (GA 65: 287) and claim that "only the greatest happening, the innermost *Ereignis*, can still save us" (GA 65: 57). (The *Contributions*' translators attempt to distance *Ereignis* from eventfulness (Heidegger 1999: xx–xxi), but this interpretation forces the *Contributions* into the perspective of the postwar essays.)

These essays culminate in the tightly constructed 1962 lecture "Time and Being," which unites a number of Heidegger's fundamental thoughts in order to introduce *Ereignis*. The lecture's opening steps point out that if being is presence, then being seems to be determined by something temporal: the present. Conversely, time seems to remain constantly, to be present – so it is determined by being. Time and being determine each other (Heidegger 1969: 3/Heidegger 1972: 3). Yet when we look more closely, we are led to a third topic. Neither time nor being is an entity – neither one *is*. We can only say that "it gives" time and being. So what is the "it" that gives them (Heidegger 1969: 5/Heidegger 1972: 5)? What is the origin of both being and time?

This may seem like nothing but a play on words. We cannot simply assume that there is an "it," some object that lies behind being and time and causes them (Heidegger 1969: 17/Heidegger 1972: 16–17). That would confuse the entire issue. What is the issue, then? As in the *Contributions* (GA 65: 75), Heidegger wishes to think of being without basing it on beings (Heidegger 1969: 2/Heidegger 1972: 2). And as in his distant 1919 lectures, his question is how the "it gives" (being as the meaning of the givenness or presence of entities) is itself given (GA 56/57: 62). To resurrect Heidegger's old example: I encounter a lectern. It presents itself to me as something present, it enters my field of concern as well as my field of vision. It *is*, i.e. it is present. Now, how is presence *itself* available to me? How is it possible, in other words, that things make sense to me *as present*? This is no longer a question about a lectern or any other entity, but one about the source of the meaning of entities as such. Heidegger also asks about the source of time, because time and being seem to implicate each other.

Since the "it" that gives being and time is obscure, we can begin by elucidating the giving itself (Heidegger 1969: 5/Heidegger 1972: 5). How is being given? As something "sent" by a hidden source (Heidegger 1969: 8/Heidegger 1972: 8). Being is, as it were, an anonymous donation. The West has always experienced being as "presencing"

(Heidegger 1969: 6–8/Heidegger 1972: 6–8) but has been unable to think of the origin of this gift. For instance, the lectern may be available or unavailable, present or absent; I may speculate philosophically about its way of being present; but the source of presence itself, as the field in which things can become available or unavailable, remains in oblivion.

How is time given? As the "time-space" (Heidegger 1969: 15/Heidegger 1972: 14) or "nearness" (Heidegger 1969: 16/Heidegger 1972: 15) opened up by the extending of future, past, and present. Yet this nearness also involves distancing, since the future and past "presence" in a way that keeps them apart from the present in a narrow sense (Heidegger 1969: 16/Heidegger 1972: 15). When I step up to the lectern, the lecture I am about to give is close to me – it is already prepared and is ready to deliver – so the past and future are there, even though they are not currently actual.

Heidegger finally unveils the word *Ereignis* – which he has carefully anticipated with references to thinking being and time each "into its own element" (*in sein Eigenes*, Heidegger 1969: 5/Heidegger 1972: 5) and discovering what is "peculiar" to them (*das Eigentümliche*, Heidegger 1969: 10/Heidegger 1972: 10). Now he tells us that in the way being and time are given – in the "sending" of being and the "extending" of time – we can discern "a dedication [*Zueignen*], a delivering over [*Übereignen*] into what is their own [*ihr Eigenes*]" (Heidegger 1969: 20/Heidegger 1972: 19). What determines being and time in their mutual belonging, then, is *Ereignis* (Heidegger 1969: 20/Heidegger 1972: 19).

Much of the rest of the lecture is taken up with caveats; Heidegger reveals only two more characteristics of *Ereignis*, both of which discourage us from presuming that we understand it. First, he reveals its non-revelation: *Ereignis* intrinsically withdraws, so that it includes its own "expropriation" (*Enteignis*) (Heidegger 1969: 23/Heidegger 1972: 23). Second, we ourselves are appropriated by *Ereignis*, because it brings "man into his own as the being who perceives being by standing within true [*eigentlichen*] time" (Heidegger 1969: 24/Heidegger 1972: 23). Because *Ereignis* so intimately constitutes us, we cannot objectify it in propositions (Heidegger 1969: 24/Heidegger 1972: 23). Yet (in a move reminiscent of Wittgenstein's *Tractatus*) Heidegger ends his lecture by confessing that he has spoken "merely in propositional statements" (Heidegger 1969: 25/Heidegger 1972: 24). So is the entire lecture a waste of time?

Not really. Heidegger warned us at the start that it is up to *us* to think in terms of more than "a series of propositions" and to "follow the movement of showing" (Heidegger 1969: 2/Heidegger 1972: 2). His lecture brings us to the brink of something that we must ourselves confront (Heidegger 1969: 27–8/Heidegger 1972: 26). How does it indicate this topic?

The main indicator is the word *Ereignis*, which is reserved for the climax of the lecture. This word is not to be taken in its usual sense, as "occurrence and happening," but as "Appropriating [*Eignen*] as the extending and sending which opens and preserves" (Heidegger 1969: 21/Heidegger 1972: 20).

But can extending, sending, opening, and preserving be anything other than *happenings*? Maybe so; maybe the verbs mislead us into picturing "something which is not temporal" as an event that takes place within time (Heidegger 1969: 51/Heidegger 1972: 47). Instead, Heidegger is investigating the workings of time itself – and as he tells us, "time itself is nothing temporal" (Heidegger 1969: 214/Heidegger 1972: 14). Time cannot happen, it would seem.

But then, why take up the word *Ereignis* once again? Is it simply a bad habit? It seems that Heidegger's intention is not to highlight its meaning as "event," but to point us toward *Eignen* – appropriating, owning, belonging. What, then, does "own" mean in "Time and Being"?

When we review Heidegger's uses of *Eignen*, *eigen*, *eigentümlich*, and *eigentlich*, it is hard to distinguish his thoughts from those of a traditional metaphysician, on the hunt for essences. To discover what is *eigentümlich* to time and being, or to bring them into their "own," is apparently to determine their essence. To say that man is "appropriated" by *Ereignis* seems to mean that we cannot properly fulfill our essence unless we stand in an essential connection to being and time – *eigentlich* time (Heidegger 1969: 24/Heidegger 1972: 23), that is, the essence of time. Is there a radical difference between this way of thinking and that of Plato, Aristotle, or Descartes?

Heidegger would deny that his essay is "metaphysics" as he defines the term – a theory of being as the ground of beings (Heidegger 1969: 6, 61–2/Heidegger 1972: 6, 55–6) – but the essay does seem to follow familiar metaphysical patterns of thought. We look for the essence or nature of something distinct from all particular entities (Heidegger 1969: 2/Heidegger 1972: 2), something that must never be confused with a particular (Heidegger 1969: 3–4/Heidegger 1972: 3, 4) – otherwise we are mixing up the "source" and the "river" (Heidegger 1969: 25/Heidegger 1972: 24). This quest can give us a perspective from which to judge particulars (Heidegger 1969: 2/Heidegger 1972: 2) and reveal what makes our experience of these particulars possible; for example, "true time itself . . . is the prespatial region which first gives any possible 'where'" (Heidegger 1969: 16/Heidegger 1972: 16). Heidegger seems to be engaging in transcendental philosophy, in the broad sense of discovering the general conditions of possibility for all particular phenomena.

But it would be hasty to read the late Heidegger as just another metaphysician. At the end of his 1962 seminar on the lecture "Time and Being," he drops another hint about the word *Ereignis* that brings us back to the word "own" in a sense that is strikingly different from the traditional search for essences. "The finitude of Appropriation . . . is no longer thought in terms of the relation to infinity, but rather as finitude in itself: finitude, end, limit, one's own [*das Eigene*] – to be secure in one's own" (Heidegger 1969: 58/Heidegger 1972: 54). The point is not to transcend the particular, then, but to return to it – and not merely as what is not absolute, not infinite, but as the home of a primal rootedness or belonging. This sense recalls Heidegger's early focus on the inhabited, owned world as the pretheoretical source of meaning.

The Promise of *Ereignis*

The next natural question is whether this similarity is only a distant echo or whether it points to a deep consistency in Heidegger's thought. Could it be that in 1919, 1936–8, and 1962 he is saying the same thing? Maybe so. Despite the apparent differences in the three texts, they may all be attempts to respond to the same experience: the same encounter with an enduring theme or "thing" (*Sache*). Some central questions patently endure: how are beings given to us? How is their being given to us? However, showing that Heidegger's *answers* to these questions remain essentially the same would require us to go well beyond the texts, present our own developed account of the "thing" at stake, and argue that Heidegger's various texts are responding to different facets of the same "thing" (cf. Sheehan 2001: 199–200). Here we can only achieve some preliminaries. Staying close to Heidegger's texts themselves, we can, first, sum up the differences that set them apart, at least on the surface. Second, we can begin to look for the most promising way for us to appropriate these texts today.

Textual differences

In everyday German, any change or motion, any happening, can be called an *Ereignis* (although, like our "event," the word can hint at a special and unique quality). Heidegger's usages of *Ereignis* grow increasingly distant from this normal usage.

In 1919, *Ereignis* refers to experiences that belong to my own, meaningful life. Such happenings are the norm, whereas objectified, meaningless processes are products of a theoretical attitude that is neither normal nor philosophically necessary. Even the *Ereignis* of the pre-worldly "something" is an accessible part of human life – "a basic phenomenon that can be experienced in understanding" (GA 56/57: 115). Both everyday, worldly events and extraordinary, pre-worldly events illustrate the workings of appropriation in human existence.

In 1936–8, *Ereignis* has become far more rare, perhaps even becoming a unique future possibility that has never yet taken place. Now it is life as we know it, at least in its everyday modern state, that is drained of meaning and consigned to the "confusion of unbeings" (GA 65: 7). Only through a supreme effort might we begin to take part in the event of appropriation. Only an extreme emergency can illustrate *Ereignis*.

In 1962, *Ereignis* does not seem to be a happening at all. It is a constant aspect of the human condition, even though philosophy up to now has failed to recognize it. *Ereignis* was already "appropriating" in ancient Greece – and indeed, wherever and whenever human beings have existed. Far from being an extraordinary emergency, it seems to be a universal.

It is worth looking closely at the difference between these last two usages, since most interpreters (e.g. Pöggeler 1975) have assumed that the meaning of *Ereignis* is established in the *Contributions* and remains stable thereafter. In this they are following Heidegger himself, who claims in 1962 that the essential structure (*Wesensbau*) of *Ereignis* was "worked out between 1936 and 1938" (Heidegger 1969: 46/Heidegger 1972: 43). However, the evidence indicates important changes after the *Contributions*.

As we saw, the *Contributions* attack the search for the *a priori* (GA 65: 222–3), including all transcendental philosophy (GA 65: 239). They refer to *Ereignis* as a happening (GA 65: 57) and an inception (GA 65: 58) or groundbreaking event. Inceptions are not "supratemporally eternal, but greater than eternity; [they are] *the shocks* of time" (GA 65: 17). Time-space itself seems to *happen* as part of the possible event of appropriation; Heidegger departs from "the usual formal concepts of space and time" (GA 65: 261) to describe a unique eruption of meaning.

The contrast to "Time and Being" is dramatic. In 1936–8, "*be-ing as Er-eignis is history*" (GA 65: 494); in 1962, "what sends as Appropriation [is] unhistorical, or more precisely without destiny" (Heidegger 1969: 44/Heidegger 1972: 41). Since "time itself is nothing temporal" (Heidegger 1969: 14/Heidegger 1972: 14), time-space cannot happen; it is a transcendental in the broad sense, a permanent structure that enables us to encounter anything. As for *Ereignis*, the "it" that gives time and being, it is a still more ultimate condition. Although Heidegger claims *Ereignis* is *a priori* only "From the point of view of metaphysical thinking" (Heidegger 1969: 33/Heidegger 1972: 31), it has now become difficult to find any other perspective. *Ereignis* is now "what has always already happened before we do anything" (Seubold 2003), or "the ineluctable condition of our essence . . . the way we always already are" (Sheehan 2001: 194).

Heidegger's writings seem to swing back and forth between two poles: unique happening and universal structures. The phrase "always already" is ubiquitous in *Being and Time*, where Heidegger uses it to point to inescapable aspects of our condition (SZ: 328). It seems that a certain search for essences and the *a priori* is legitimate according to both *Being and Time* and "Time and Being." But according to the 1919 lectures, any such search needs to be brought back to our unique, concrete, lived experiences; otherwise it runs the risk of abstract objectification. According to the *Contributions*, there is something deeper than lived experience – but it, too, is unique and eventlike rather than *a priori*.

In order to reconcile Heidegger's usages in 1936–8 and 1962, we could discard all the *Contributions*' "apocalyptic language . . . the cosmic drama, the mystical metaphors, the Teutonic bombast" (Sheehan 2001: 201). Before we do so, however, we should meditate on apocalypse: could it be that truth really does take place as a unique moment of crisis?

Alternatively, we could try to find a happening at work beneath the apparent *a priori* structures of the later essays. Heidegger does say that "being takes place [*geschieht*]" (Heidegger 1969: 8/Heidegger 1972: 8). In 1957 he suggests that "a more original [*anfänglicheres*] appropriating" is possible (Heidegger 2002: 37). And as we noted, his 1962 seminar ends by suggesting that appropriation as "one's own" is deeper than any universal structure. *Ereignis* may be more than a formal condition, after all.

Appropriating Ereignis

Whether we reconcile the texts one way or the other, or whether we accept their inconsistency, depends on how we ourselves interpret the matters at stake. It is ultimately a philosophical question, not a textual one. I close with two considerations for our future thought.

First, the texts that adapt themselves to unique happening are more revolutionary than the texts that discover universal structures. According to traditional metaphysics, the unique is ineffable; according to the 1919 lectures and the *Contributions*, all saying springs from the unique, and we might find a unique kind of saying that does justice to this source. This thought is challenging and strange, and for this reason calls for our philosophical attention more than does the quasi-essentialist language of "Time and Being."

Of course, to be revolutionary is not to be right. Maybe the whole project of thinking on the basis of unique happening is incoherent or unworkable. For example, it is difficult at best to think of time-space as a unique happening from which ordinary time and space emerge (cf. GA 65: 372, 386–7). How can anything "happen" except *within* an already given time? To say that time itself takes place seems to be a category mistake. But what is time, then? It seems we have to think of it as an *a priori*, transcendental condition. We are then drawn back into traditional philosophy – unless we somehow manage to think ourselves out of its presuppositions.

Second, if *Ereignis* is either extremely rare (as in 1936–8) or an ultimate that we think without reference to particular beings (as in 1962) then it becomes very difficult to connect it to our own experience. How is appropriation actually manifested in our perceptions, thoughts, and acts? How can we use the concept to help us to understand our own lives?

The late Heidegger might dismiss these questions as philistine; philosophy "is today placed in a position which demands of it reflections that are far removed from any useful, practical wisdom" (Heidegger 1969: 1–2/Heidegger 1972: 1–2). In reply, we might suggest that Heidegger's retreat from ethics (in any normal sense: see GA 9: 356–7/Heidegger 1998: 271) may be more of a personal failing than a philosophical triumph. But even on strictly contemplative grounds, we need to recognize *Ereignis* at work in accessible phenomena. When it becomes a remote future possibility, as in the *Contributions*, it becomes unclear what our basis for speaking of it, much less embracing it, could be (Polt 2003: 193).

It is the 1919 lectures that make the greatest use of *Ereignis* in understanding experience – and maybe it is here, in Heidegger's first great breakthrough, that the greatest potential lies. These lectures, however, are only a beginning; the *Contributions* are the text that goes furthest in thinking through the implications of locating truth in an event of owning. The problem is that this event becomes an epochal grounding with only faint parallels in life as we know it. Could we draw on the *Contributions'* elaboration of the features of *Ereignis* – such as inception, emergency, and owndom – to enrich our explorations of lived experience? We might find, then, that events of appropriation happen countless times in our lives – though not at every time. We might find that every life is touched and sustained by inceptive moments, greater and lesser emergencies in which our own sense of being emerges into its own.

References and further reading

Fell, J. P. (1992) The familiar and the strange: on the limits of praxis in the early Heidegger. In H. Dreyfus and H. Hall (eds.), *Heidegger: A Critical Reader*. Oxford: Blackwell.

Heidegger, M. (1969) *Zur Sache des Denkens*. Tübingen: Niemeyer.

Heidegger, M. (1971) *On the Way to Language* (trans. P. D. Hertz). New York: Harper & Row.

Heidegger, M. (1972) *On Time and Being* (trans. J. Stambaugh). New York: Harper & Row.

Heidegger, M. (1998) *Pathmarks* (ed. W. McNeill). Cambridge: Cambridge University Press.

Heidegger, M. (1999) *Contributions to Philosophy (From Enowning)* (trans. P. Emad and K. Maly). Bloomington: Indiana University Press.

Heidegger, M. (2002) *Identity and Difference* (trans. J. Stambaugh). Chicago: University of Chicago Press.

Kisiel, T. (1993) *The Genesis of Heidegger's Being and Time.* Berkeley: University of California Press.

Kovacs, George (1994). Philosophy as primordial science in Heidegger's courses of 1919. In T. Kisiel and J. van Buren (eds.), *Reading Heidegger From the Start: Essays in his Earliest Thought.* Albany: State University of New York Press.

Pöggeler, O. (1975) Being as appropriation. *Philosophy Today,* 19(2), 152–78 (original work published 1959).

Polt, R. (2001) The event of enthinking the event. In C. Scott et al. (eds.), *Companion to Heidegger's Contributions to Philosophy.* Bloomington: Indiana University Press.

Polt, R. (2003) *Beiträge zur Philosophie (Vom Ereignis):* Ein Sprung in die Wesung des Seyns. In D. Thomä (ed.), *Heidegger-Handbuch: Leben–Werk–Wirkung.* Stuttgart: J. B. Metzler.

Ruin, H. (2002) The moment of truth: *Augenblick* and *Ereignis* in Heidegger. In H. Dreyfus and M. Wrathall (eds.), *Heidegger Reexamined.* London: Routledge.

Seubold, G. (2003) Stichwort: Ereignis: Was immer schon geschehen ist, bevor wir etwas tun. In D. Thomä (ed.), *Heidegger-Handbuch: Leben–Werk–Wirkung.* Stuttgart: J. B. Metzler.

Sheehan, T. (2001) A paradigm shift in Heidegger research. *Continental Philosophy Review,* 34, 183–202.

Spinosa, C. (2001) Derridian dispersion and heideggerian articulation: general tendencies in the practices that govern intelligibility. In T. R. Schatzki et al. (eds.), *The Practice Turn in Contemporary Theory.* London: Routledge.

Vallega-Neu, D. (2001) Poietic saying. In C. Scott et al. (eds.), *Companion to Heidegger's Contributions to Philosophy.* Bloomington: Indiana University Press.

Vallega-Neu, D. (2003) *Heidegger's Contributions to Philosophy: An Introduction.* Bloomington: Indiana University Press.

van Buren, J. (1994) *The Young Heidegger: Rumor of the Hidden King.* Bloomington: Indiana University Press.

24

The History of Being

CHARLES GUIGNON

Heidegger's Use of the Term "History of Being"

The term "history of being" makes its appearance in the *Contributions to Philosophy* (GA 65) and continues to appear in the later writings, including the Nietzsche lectures of 1944–6, the seminar *On Time and Being* of 1962 (Heidegger 1969), and some of the late essays on technology and early Greek thinking. When we come across this term in Heidegger's texts, we might suppose that "the history of being" refers either to the actual history of thought about being that has developed over the course of Western history or to the various epochal understandings of being that have determined the "metaphysics" or "ontotheology" of Western peoples at different times in the course of that history. In so interpreting the term, we would suppose that what is at stake in this notion is the history of the Western world, where this is understood as a set of past occurrences ordered on a time-line and configured into a story by some unifying plot or theme. To do the history of being, then, would be similar to doing the history of philosophy. It would be a matter of correctly (or at least insightfully) capturing the understandings of being that have arisen and had an impact over the course of our history.

There are a number of contexts where Heidegger seems to use the expression "history of being" in just such a sense. In "Nihilism as Determined by the History of Being," an essay written in 1944–6 and published in 1961, he treats the entire history of metaphysics from ancient Greece to Nietzsche as a unified story, and he suggests that this story, the "history of being," just *is* being itself as being (GA 6.2: 327/Heidegger 1982: 221). But in his earlier and more careful writings on the history of being, Heidegger was inclined to reject any notion of history as a story about changing interpretations of being. To think of the history of being in this way, he suggests in the late 1930s, would be to regard history in the traditional way as a set of occurrences in the past which are to be studied by historical science or historiography (*Historie*). For such a traditional conception, "history [*Historie*] means the exploration of the past from the perspective of the present" (GA 45: 34). Such an approach to history may be thought of as a matter of accurately representing the past "as it really was" or as making the past come alive for the purposes of the present. In either case, the subject matter of historiography is regarded as something past.

392

In contrast to such a familiar conception of history, Heidegger proposes an approach he calls "historical reflection," a form of reflection on sense (*Be-sinnung*) aimed at understanding a happening (*Geschehen*) in which we are now immersed and which gets its point from where it is going as a whole. In Heidegger's words, "reflection is looking for the meaning [*Sinn*] of a happening, the meaning of history," where the word "meaning" refers to "the open region of goals, standards, impulses, decisive possibilities and powers" that "belong *essentially* to happening" (GA 45: 35–6). And insofar as the meaning of any happening is determined by what is fulfilled or realized through it, history understood in the Heideggerian sense is not about something that is past. Instead, "the happenings of history are primordially and always the future, that which . . . comes toward us. . . . The future is the beginning of all happening" (GA 45: 36). So "genuine history" is not a sequence of events, but consists of "the goals of creative activity, their rank and their extent," and this forms the subject matter for historical reflection (GA 45: 36).

According to this reflective approach to history, only human beings can "have" a history, for only humans can "*be* historical, i.e., can stand . . . in that open region of goals, standards, drives and powers, by . . . existing in the mode of forming, directing, acting, carrying out, and tolerating" (GA 45: 36). But history in its genuine sense is not primarily a story about the doings and sufferings of human beings. Instead, Heidegger holds that the history of being is a wider happening that catches humans up and carries them along in its unfolding. Creating a conceptual family out of like-sounding words, Heidegger says that the history (*Geschichte*) of being is a happening (*Geschehen*) that constitutes a destiny (*Geschick*). Humans are participants in this "destining" of being but not its sole agents.

It should be evident, then, that the expression "history of being" refers not so much to a series of past events or epochs leading up to today as to an all-encompassing "sending" that is informed by a unifying meaning: the essential unfolding of the event of being (often written with the archaic spelling *Seyn*) as it realizes its mission. Since this peculiar conception of history gains its sense from Heidegger's earlier reflections on the being of history, any attempt to grasp the later conception of the history of being must begin with an account of his early conception of history.

Heidegger's Debt to Dilthey's Vision of History

Though the concept of history played a central role in Heidegger's thought from his earliest lectures and essays until his final writings, his conception of history and its significance changed in important ways. In his early works, by which I mean his earliest lectures up to the publication of *Being and Time*, Heidegger's attempt to characterize history and the "historicity" of human existence was part of his characterization of human existence as having a distinctive temporal structure. A clear and focused sketch of this account is found in "Wilhelm Dilthey's Research and the Struggle for a Historical Worldview" (Heidegger 2002), a series of lectures Heidegger delivered in Kassel in 1925, the year before he wrote *Being and Time*. In these lectures, Heidegger quickly runs through his account of Dilthey's views and then turns to a presentation of his own position. The advantage of starting with these lectures is that they clarify the connection Heidegger makes between temporality and history in *Being and Time*, while also showing the train of thought underlying concepts that are introduced without explanation in the later writings.

The Kassel lectures begin by noting that Dilthey's primary aim throughout his life's work was to pose "the question concerning the meaning of history and of human being" (Heidegger 2002: 154, translation modified). Since "formulat[ing] a question requires that one have a primordial intuition of the object that one is interrogating" (Heidegger 2002: 154), Heidegger says, Dilthey's investigations into the meaning of history must operate with an initial intuition of what is to be found in the question. So Heidegger asks: where does one "find this object 'history,' so that one might read off from it the meaning of its being, i.e., read off its historical being?" Dilthey's answer is that the meaning of the being of history is found in human *life* itself. The being of history is to be discovered by examining human life or, as Heidegger calls it, *Dasein* (Heidegger 2002: 154–5).

Dilthey's way of trying to understand life is through what he calls a "descriptive and articulative [*zergliedende*] psychology," an approach to psychic life that focuses on the interconnected "*whole* of life" as it shows up in pre-reflective experience. The mental context must be understood not causally, but in terms of *motivation*. Psychic life is *purposive*, a "being-in-motion" that cannot be explained in terms of a story about a knowing subject relating to objects in a causal framework. Life is always a "being-with" in the sense of being embedded in a shared context of meaning. It is constantly under way toward reaching a *Gestalt* or defining configuration of meaning. Finally, "the structural context of life is acquired, i.e., it is defined by its history" (Heidegger 2002: 158). As a mode of existence in which humans achieve self-knowledge, life itself is the subject matter of the historical sciences.

Heidegger takes over many of these insights the next year when he writes *Being and Time*. With respect to the actual content of the characterization of life itself, Heidegger agrees with Dilthey in saying that life must be understood as a *whole* and as a *movement*, and he also agrees with Dilthey's view that, because historiography is about life, grasping the subject matter of historiography requires an understanding of the "historicity" of human life. Despite these points of agreement, however, there is one crucial respect in which Heidegger disagrees with his predecessor. Whereas Dilthey portrays life as a stream of life-experiences moving along *in* time, Heidegger claims that Dasein at the deepest level *is* time (see Schatzki 2003). "The *being-there* of Dasein *is* nothing other than *being-time*" (Heidegger 2002: 169). This conception of Dasein as temporality provides the basis for Heidegger's own view of historicity and history.

Heidegger's Early Account of History

After presenting and criticizing Dilthey's views, the Kassel lectures develop Heidegger's own conception of human existence, historicity, and history. Heidegger starts by formulating what he calls a "preliminary determination" of Dasein as being-in-the-world. This preliminary account of average everydayness portrays human existence as engrossed in dealings with an environing world and bound up with others in shared undertakings. In our typical dealings with things, we are scattered into diverse areas of concern, busy with a variety of tasks, doing what *one* does and seeing things as *one* sees them in the public world. As a result, our being in everydayness is characterized by *falling* into publicness in such a way that we are *not* ourselves, but are rather the "one" or "anyone." "The human being," Heidegger says, "is inauthentic in its everyday world" (Heidegger 2002: 164).

The preliminary determination of Dasein as the undifferentiated "anyone" leads Heidegger to ask how, given that for the most part we are *not* ourselves, we are ever going to grasp the being of human existence. The problem with the preliminary characterization of Dasein is that it portrays our lives as dispersed and disjointed, and so as lacking any clearly defined identity. What we need if we are to capture that which is proper to us, then, is a characterization of "human Dasein as a whole, as a unified reality." It might seem that in grasping a life as a whole one can gain access to human existence as a unified totality. But here, Heidegger says, there is an obvious problem. For in the attempt to grasp human reality as a whole, "I can only define human Dasein as a living being that always has before it a not-yet being." In other words, as long as I am alive, there is something outstanding that keeps me from being able to grasp my existence as a whole. So the question becomes all the more pressing: "How can human Dasein be given as a whole?" (Heidegger 2002: 165).

The answer to this question is provided by the concept of death. "A whole requires . . . a sense of being finished," Heidegger says, and Dasein's being is finished at the moment of death. It might seem that this approach leads to another paradox, for "when life comes to be finished in *death*, it is no longer" (Heidegger 2002: 166). But this paradox arises only if we think of life as a *process (Vorgang)*, that is, as a sequentially ordered flow of occurrences through time that terminates in a final state. In order to avoid this way of thinking about life, we need to think of human existence not as a series of occurrences moving toward a finished state, but as a movement or happening shaped by specific structures, with death being one of these structures. Regarded as a structural dimension of life, the concept of death captures the idea of life as a finite, forward-moving, directional project, one that points toward fulfillment even though a final and complete fulfillment is never possible for it as long as it exists. As being-toward-death, human existence is an unfolding movement *toward* the realization of one's identity or being as a person.

To face up to the reality of death is to make a choice about how one will live: it is to be *resolved*. To be resolute is to live in the way that is proper (*eigen*) to one's own structural make-up, and so to be authentic (*eigentlich*) in the sense of being owned-up-to and owned. When one is resolute as being-toward-death, one is able to gain access to a more primordial way of understanding Dasein's being as temporality. As anticipatory "running forward" toward the possibility "which I am not yet, *but will be*," Dasein is *futural* (Heidegger 2002: 169). To say that Dasein is futural is not to say that in addition to living in the present one also exists in the future. In fact, the term "futural" does not refer to a location on a time-line at all. Instead, it refers to a structural component of Dasein's being: its movement toward its self-definition, its "coming toward" itself (*Zukünft*, from *zu* and *kommen*, meaning "coming-toward"). Futurity therefore appears to be identical to what John Richardson calls Dasein's "existential teleology," its being "for-the-sake-of-itself" in all it does.[1] The idea seems to be that our striving to accomplish things in practical affairs is part of our underlying striving to *be* something as humans

– to realize and define our identity (or being) *as* such and such, that is, to make something of ourselves in what we do. Dasein exists as a directional *kinesis heneka tou*, a "being-in-motion for the sake of" that is under way toward the fulfillment of its ability-to-be (*Seinkönnen*).[2]

Properly understood, then, futurity refers not to a position *in* time, but to a *condition for the possibility of there being such a thing as time* as we ordinarily understand it. To say that Dasein is futural is to say that it exists as a *projection* toward its realization. Dasein's futurity in turn brings to life the existential structure of being past, what *Being and Time* calls *beenness* (*Gewesenheit*). When Heidegger says that Dasein's past " 'happens' out of its future" (SZ: 20), he means that the existential teleology definitive of Dasein's being opens up a space of meaning in which what *has been* can come to play a role in relation to Dasein's undertakings. In the words of the Kassel lectures, "in acting in the direction of the future, the past comes alive" (Heidegger 2002: 169). Seen from this standpoint, the existential past is not something that happened at an earlier time and continues to have a residual impact on the present. Instead, it is the structural component of Dasein through which what is opened by Dasein's "thrownness" is taken up and carried forward in undertaking projects for the future.

At the bedrock level of Dasein's authentic existence, then, future and past are "ways of being" or "existential structures" informing all of Dasein's being and making possible time as we commonly think of it. The future does not happen "later than" or "after" the past, and the past does not occur "earlier" than the future. As William Blattner (1999) has shown, primordial time does not have any sequentiality at all. Instead, past, present, and future are structures of Dasein's being that are prior to the time of everyday practical existence. In Heidegger's words, "Time characterizes the wholeness of Dasein. Any instance of Dasein is not only in a moment but rather is itself within the entire span of its possibilities and its past" (Heidegger 2002: 169). Dasein is not *in* time at all; it *is* time. To be human is to be the stretching or stretch that embraces both "coming toward" what one is and carrying forward the possibilities defining one's "beenness." In this picture, Heidegger says, "the present vanishes" (Heidegger 2002: 169). As we shall see, this conception of time underlies Heidegger's thinking about history throughout his life.

Historicity and History in *Being and Time*

The characterization of Dasein's being as embodying a deep underlying temporal structure paves the way to Heidegger's early account of the being of history. According to the Kassel lectures, history (*Geschichte*) "signifies a happening (*Geschehen*) which we ourselves are and in which we are involved" (Heidegger 2002: 173). In historical happening, "the fundamental motion from which history arises" is a "going-forth-in-advance-of-oneself"; it is "through this going-forth that the past is uncovered" (Heidegger 2002: 173). This is the point Heidegger makes in *Being and Time* when he says that the past "is not something which *follows along after* Dasein, but something which already goes ahead of it" (SZ: 20). The past is defined by a specific way of "coming toward" the future.

The Introduction to *Being and Time* offers an initial characterization of Dasein that paves the way to displaying its temporal being. Dasein is the being, Heidegger says, for whom its being is *at issue* or *in question*. That is to say, we are beings for whom our own being, and hence being in general, is something questionable, something *at stake* for us, and so something we *care* about in living out our lives. Because of the questionableness of being, we are constantly in motion, always under way in taking stands that express our attempts to get a grip on what life is all about. This forward-directedness is called *existence*: as Heidegger says, "That being toward which Dasein . . . always does comport itself somehow, we call *existence*" (SZ: 12). As ex-sisting (from *ex-sistere*, standing outside itself) Dasein is always already "out there," engaged in undertakings, directed toward its realization.

Dasein's forward-directedness as "ex-sisting" circles back, appropriates, and carries forward what has been, with the result that Dasein is also structured by *having been* (*Gewesene*). This notion of "beenness" captures the fact that Dasein's being is an undertaking that is always enmeshed in the pre-given context into which it is *thrown*. In confronting its life as an open-ended task to be taken up, Dasein's "essence lies . . . in the fact that in each case it has its being to be, and has it as its own" (SZ: 12). We find ourselves *delivered over* to ourselves, already caught up in a "factical" context of meanings and possibilities that we do not create but must respond to in living out our lives.

Finally, Dasein exists as a *making present* that discursively encounters and deals with (*Ansprechen und Besprechen*) entities in the environing world. As a temporally structured whole, Dasein is the *clearing* in virtue of which entities can show up in various ways. In its full temporal dynamism, Dasein is a "there," a *Da*, where this is understood as a lighting, leeway, or "room for free play" (*Spielraum*) in which things can come into presence *as* counting or mattering in determinate ways.

Toward the end of *Being and Time*, Heidegger turns to an explicit discussion of historicity, history, and historiography. The concept of historicity, he says, is "just a more complete working out of [the idea of] temporality" (SZ: 382). To say that Dasein's being is characterized by historicity is to say that its concrete temporal existence has a cumulativeness and directedness that is always embedded within a specific historical culture. This complicity in and indebtedness to the historical context only becomes fully manifest when Dasein becomes authentic. As authentic, Dasein draws itself back from its dispersal in the "endless multitude of possibilities which offer themselves" in the anyone, and it takes over the defining possibilities of its *heritage* as its own most fundamental commitments (SZ: 383–4). To be authentically historical is to grasp one's own life as bound up with the life of one's "community, of a people [*Volk*]." And it is to see one's own future-directed existence as interwoven into the wider undertaking of the mission or sending of a historical people, what Heidegger calls a *destiny* (*Geschick*) (SZ: 384). Authentic historicity, then, consists in *repeating* or *retrieving* the heritage of possibilities into which one is thrown and taking a resolute stand on what is demanded by one's current situation.

Having discussed *Being and Time*'s account of historicity, we are in a position to examine the conception of authentic historiography in Heidegger's early thought. Heidegger claims that just as the most fundamental structure of Dasein's temporality is futural projection, so historiography must begin with a projection of the possibilities

397

definitive of the "destiny" of the historian's community. Historiography therefore begins with an *anticipation* of where the course of world events is going overall. The reason why the future has priority in this way should become apparent if we consider the nature of historical research. Historiography is feasible as an undertaking only if the historian, in looking at the plethora of what has happened in the past, is able to *select* the events that are to count as historically relevant for a historical account. Such a selection presupposes certain judgments about where history is going and where it ought to be going, and these anticipations concerning the future are essentially *evaluative*: as Heidegger says in his 1915 lecture "The Concept of Time in the Science of History," "the selection of the historical from the fullness of what is given is thus based on a relation to values" (Heidegger 2002: 56).[3]

What is distinctive about authentic historiography is that its appraisal of the destiny guiding events is grounded in a clear-sighted grasp of the most primordial possibilities open to a community, a grasp that results from ongoing "communicating and struggling" aimed at understanding what the current "hermeneutic situation" of the community demands (SZ: 384, 397). Historiography that results from a clear-sighted grasp of the future is *monumental*: it projects an image of what can be achieved through the course of events, and then interprets what has happened in terms of its contribution to realizing or failing to realize that ideal.

In the light of an understanding of the future-directedness of the course of events, the historian engages in a project of *retrieval* or *repetition*: just as Dasein's temporal structure gathers up and carries forward what has been, so the historian carries forward the possibilities into which he or she is thrown. "When the possible is made one's own by retrieval or repetition," Heidegger says, "there is . . . the possibility of reverently preserving the existence that has-been-there" (SZ: 396). In preserving what has come before, historiography is *antiquarian*. As we shall see, this notion of *preservation* becomes central in Heidegger's later writings.

Finally, historiography is *critical* of that which "in the 'today'" is working itself out as the past. In other words, it criticizes commonly accepted interpretations of the historical tradition in order to retrieve and preserve the deepest beginnings and projects that define the heritage. Authentic historiography makes a "reciprocative rejoinder" (SZ: 386) to what current interpretations regard as important for the historian's culture.

It follows from this characterization of historiography that historians can appropriate and own the past in an authentic way only if they cultivate the *hermeneutic situation* in which they find themselves, getting clear about what is demanded by the historical context in which they currently find themselves (SZ: 396–7). This hermeneutic situation in turn provides the resources for making evaluative judgments about what is to come, and so the circle continues in an endless cycle, with no exit to neutral "facts" that could provide a basis for knowledge in the historical sciences.

Being-historical Thinking in the Later Writings

Less than a decade after the publication of *Being and Time*, Heidegger's thought had undergone significant changes. His lectures and writings of the mid and late 1930s formulate carefully thought out responses to some of the perceived shortcomings of *Being and Time*. In response to the charge that *Being and Time* is individualistic in its focus on the existentiell characteristics of the specific (*jeweilige*) Dasein who is philosophizing, Heidegger now generally refers to a historical people (*Volk*) when he speaks about human beings. In reply to the charge that his early thought is voluntaristic and idealistic in the priority it accords to Dasein's *projection* in accounting for the meaning of being, Heidegger puts special emphasis on our *thrownness* into the midst of beings. In the writings of the 1930s, history is no longer a theme tacked on at the end of an account of Dasein. It is instead the central subject matter of the question of being. Heidegger's method explicitly shifts from a transcendental inquiry into the conditions for the possibility of an understanding of being ("fundamental ontology") to a concern with actually enacting a path of thinking that participates in and "corresponds" to the "call" of being. Finally, and most importantly, Heidegger claims that his *real* topic all along has been not "being" – not "beingness" as the traditional metaphysical determination of the "whatness" and "thatness" of beings – but the *truth* of being, where this is understood as the event (*Ereignis*) in which any "constellation of intelligibility" emerges, perseveres, and eventually may be replaced by a new understanding of being.[4]

These new ideas are implicit in the lectures Heidegger delivered in the mid-1930s, but they are even more prominent in the work he was privately composing during that period, the *Contributions to Philosophy: From Enowning*. In this esoteric work, Heidegger tries to accomplish a new form of philosophy, one he calls "be-ing-historical thinking" (*seynsgeschichtliches Denken*). To show that this new thinking goes beyond all traditional metaphysics and transcendental philosophy, Heidegger identifies his subject matter not as *Sein* (being), but as (using an archaic spelling) *Seyn*, a term usually translated with a hyphen as "be-ing." Whereas "being" refers to the type of understanding of beings prevalent during a particular epoch, *be-ing* is thought of as the event of emerging out of concealment that brings about an understanding of being. Any attempt to make sense of the later Heidegger must start out from the conception of be-ing-historical thinking in *Contributions to Philosophy*.

To get a handle on the basic outlook that informs *Contributions to Philosophy*, it might be helpful to look back at Heidegger's discussion of Herder in his lectures of 1919. Herder's "decisive insight" in the development of historical consciousness, according to Heidegger, was to recognize "the autonomous and unique value of each nation and age, each historical manifestation" (GA 56/57: 133). Where Enlightenment rationalism tended to assume that all people are basically the same "under the skin," so to speak, Herder held that each nation has its own center of gravity, its own unique nature, which becomes manifest and is brought to realization only in the course of its development. Seen in this light, the *being* of a people or nation – what they *are* – is something that is defined not by an original seed or germ present at the outset, and not by some essential characteristics constantly present throughout their history. Instead, the being of a people or nation is defined by the actual course of history that unfolds as this community comes to realize a specific form over time.

In Herder's writings, Heidegger says, "the category of 'ownness' [*Eigenheit*] becomes meaningful and is related to all formations of life" (GA 56/57: 134). The concept of ownness provides a basis for thinking of being as an achievement and a happening rather than as a static set of enduring attributes. It lets us think of the being of a people as a matter of "coming into its own," an emergence-into-presence in which *what is its own* comes to definition and form (*Gestalt*). Heidegger observes that Herder's distinctive conception of ownness was taken up by Schlegel, Niebuhr, Savigny, and Schleiermacher as a basis for thinking about literature, law, and religion, and that these developments "decisively influenced Hegel's youthful works on the history of religion, and indirectly also Hegel's specifically philosophical systematic, where the decisive ideas of the German movement reached their apex" (GA 56/57: 134).

Though there is no reason to think that Herder was explicitly in Heidegger's mind when he composed *Contributions to Philosophy*, it is clear that the ideas of this "German movement" underlie the work's thinking about *Ereignis* or "enownment." *Contributions to Philosophy* starts from the intuition that Western history is already under way in its historical unfolding, and that this "happening" of history is to be regarded as an ongoing movement with its own proper (*eigen*) course, an unfolding of events that calls on and appropriates a historical people to an appointed task. In Heidegger's words, "History is the transporting of a people into its appointed task as entry into that people's shared endowment [*Mitgegebenes*]" (GA 5: 65/Heidegger 1971: 77).

The actual thinking that makes up *Contributions to Philosophy* is experienced as a new insertion into the flow of historical unfolding, a thinking that achieves a "crossing from metaphysics to be-ing-historical thinking" (GA 65: 3). This new thinking is called "be-ing-historical" in at least two senses. First, it tries to rethink the history of be-ing in its different epochs from within the movement of the essential unfolding of the *truth* of be-ing, that is, in terms of the interplay of unconcealing and self-sheltering that is characteristic of *truth* in its primal sense. And, second, it no longer treats history as a topic that can be put at arm's length and questioned with regard to its being, but instead understands itself as caught up in and carried along by this happening (Vallega-Neu 2003: 31). Thinking the history of be-ing is therefore not a matter of forming representations about an object set over against that thinking. Instead, such thinking enacts and brings to realization that history: as Heidegger puts it in the 1940s, "Thinking in terms of the history of being lets being arrive in the essential space of man. . . . thinking in terms of the history of being lets being occur essentially as being itself" (GA 6.2: 353/Heidegger 1982: 243).

In the background of *Contributions to Philosophy* is a particular story about the overall course of events in Western history. The story, in crudest outline, seems to go something like this. The starting point for questioning is what *Contributions to Philosophy* calls the experience of "refusal as gifting," the experience of the "openness of the onslaught of the self-concealing" (GA 65: 15). To introduce this idea, Heidegger speaks of the experience that occurs when our easy comportment in the familiar and commonplace gives way and there is the experience of shock or startled dismay (*Erschreckung*) at the onslaught of what is *other* to all familiarity. This "other" is described as that which holds itself in (it "refuses itself") at the same time that it becomes manifest. As that which both comes into the open yet also refuses to be swallowed up in commonplace interpretations (it is "self-concealing"), it manifests the traits of what Heidegger calls the "primal strife" that occurs before the imposition of any human interpretations.

According to the story in *Contributions to Philosophy*, the earliest response to this onslaught occurred in the "first beginning," when ancient Greek thinkers dealt with the onslaught by experiencing the being of beings as *phusis*. The claim is that, in the "first beginning" of the history of being, the givenness of "the gift of the self-refusing" was made accessible in terms of a *there* or *clearing* in the light of which entities show up as emerging-into-presence from out of concealment (the meaning of *phusis*). The interplay of revealing and concealing described here is supposed to capture the earliest Greek experience of truth as *a-lētheia*, literally, un-forgetfulness or un-concealing. To say that beings enter into the "there" in some way or other is to say that truth happens or essentially unfolds (*west*) in a determinate way.

But even though the first beginning brought about an un-concealment of beings, even though it made possible an understanding of the "beingness" of beings, there is something that was overlooked or quickly forgotten in the earliest Greek interpretation of beings. In focusing on the givenness of the given, the first beginning failed to think the *event of giving itself*. As a result, in this initial inception, a particular understanding of being comes to be regarded as "the only game in town" – the way things *are* in an absolute sense – with the result that it then becomes impossible to think either the relation of presencing to absence or the giving of the gift itself.

And because the thinkers of the first beginning were unable to think the giving of the given, they were unable to grasp the role humans have to play in the event of bringing to realization an understanding of being. Human beings, Heidegger says, are pressed into being-there (Dasein) "because the overwhelming as such, in order to appear in its prevailing, *requires* [*braucht*] the site of openness for itself," a site that humans are when they realize their calling as a clearing (EM: 124, translation modified). The point here seems to be that there is an initial onslaught of beings with an initial ordering of some sort, but this ordering only becomes accessible and intelligible when it is appropriated and put in question through human naming, work, the founding of a state, or some other world-defining stance.

What was forgotten in the first understanding of the being of beings is what Heidegger now calls be-ing (*Seyn*). Be-ing is the event of appropriation or "enownment" in which (a) beings are encountered as such and such in a particular understanding of being, and (b) the humans who do the encountering come to be appropriated in such a way that they can play their proper role in the essential unfolding of truth. Through the event of be-ing, beings can show up as counting or mattering in some way or other – they have a determinate being (or beingness) – and humans can come to *be* the site in which beings show up, thereby becoming fully what they are as human beings. Or, to put this differently, in the event of appropriation, humans truly come to *be* the *there* – the concrete form of Da*sein* – that determines that an understanding of being is at issue or in question. Heidegger makes it clear that it is only when the being of beings is made *questionable* in this way that truth can essentially unfold in the fullest sense.

Heidegger's story suggests that the first beginning of Western thought "misfired" or did not come off as it should have if it was to be a full realization of be-ing. There was indeed an understanding of the beingness of beings – a clearing or "ontotheology" – and this has unfolded in various permutations in the ensuing epochs of Western history. According to the epochal account given in Heidegger's writings of the middle period, the understanding of being was first "overpowered" by the idea of *technē* in Plato's conception of being as a plan or *idea* for making something; this in turn was replaced by the idea of being as *ens creatum* in the Middle Ages; and the medieval view eventually gave way to the modern conception of beings as *objects* presented to (and, in Kant, constituted by) subjectivity. The constellations of intelligibility that have unfolded over the course of Western history, according to this story, have all centered on the idea of *making*, and together they constitute what is called the "history of metaphysics."

Throughout the history of metaphysics, there has always been some understanding of being, some "truth," and so there is a sense in which truth has been essentially unfolding (*west*) throughout this history of metaphysics. But in another sense, the history of metaphysics never quite achieved what is necessary for there to be be-ing, enowning or truth in the fullest sense of these words. This is the case because the distinctive event named by these words can be fully realized only if humans, in their thinking and doing, experience their *belongingness* to be-ing and keep the understanding of being in question. Only if there is this sort of *questionability* can there be a genuine site for a clearing (a "there" or *Da*), and only then can there be history in the full sense of this word. For this reason Heidegger says, "Until now man never was historical," though "he 'had' and 'has' a history" (GA 65: 346). Because the giving of the given was never in question, and because such questioning is necessary to history, history in the fullest sense has never yet occurred. And insofar as "be-ing needs man in order to happen" (GA 65: 177), there is a sense in which be-ing has not yet happened (for this point, see Polt 2005).

According to *Contributions to Philosophy*, the permutations unfolding throughout the course of the history of metaphysics have evolved to the point at which the history of being has exhausted all possibilities, so that no new understandings of being are possible. Nietzsche's recognition of the death of God, along with his understanding of being as the Will to Will, have brought about a closure of metaphysics. As a result, we have reached a moment in which the history of the West is up for *decision*: either the future will bring nothing but an endless dark night of minor variations on this "metaphysics to end all metaphysics," as the ever-greater presence of machination and giganticism dominating the world seems to foretell, or it may happen that the "future ones," the ones who might yet respond in the appropriate way to the call of be-ing, will open up a site in which entities can show up in their question-worthiness. If the future ones achieve this sort of site, the history of metaphysics will end and there will be a "totally different domain of history" (GA 65: 161).

It is important to see here that, as in *Being and Time*, the "future" of these future ones is not something that can be plotted on a time-line as occurring at some point "later than" or "after" the present moment. This follows from the fact that, as Heidegger says, history properly understood is not "a sequence in time of events of whatever sort, however important" (GA 5: 65/OWA in Heidegger 1971: 77). As the meaningful happening that first lets events and human beings appear on the scene *as* such and such – that is, as locatable and datable on a time-line – history is not itself a sequence of events. Heidegger points out that at least one "future one" already existed a century ago – the poet Hölderlin – and he implies that his own thinking enacts the opening of a "there" in which questionableness is preserved. The future ones are not so much ones who are to come as they are those who "come toward" the fulfillment and realization of the history of being. They are envisioned as "preservers" and "guardians" who can let

402

themselves be appropriated by the event of *Ereignis* in such a way that they come into their own *as* Dasein.

Retrieving the first beginning and thinking the giving of givenness brings about the "other beginning." The distinctive characteristics of temporality as envisioned in *Being and Time* are still visible in the storyline of the middle period, though they are no longer seen in terms of an individual case of Dasein. What is fundamental to *Contributions to Philosophy* is the *thrownness* of Western humanity into an event that is always already under way, an event in which we can only let ourselves be carried along. This event is one that "throws" to us a task and a calling: it calls on us to think the event of enowning that has been forgotten since the first beginning, to retrieve the first beginning by appropriating what was thought there, to let ourselves be the site or clearing in which beings can show up in their open-ended questionableness, and, in doing so, to *be* what we are meant to be, that is, to come into our own (*eigen*) as Dasein. Only by coming into Dasein, Heidegger says, can humanity become a "Self," where this now refers to a communal understanding marked by a coherent openness that is able to free up entities without imposing static interpretations on them and so to be the "timely space for free play" (*Zeitspielraum*) in which be-ing essentially unfolds.

But even though thrownness is made central to the writings of the middle period, Heidegger continues to give a crucial role to the future in defining the history of be-ing. In *Introduction to Metaphysics*, he defines history as a happening that, "determined from the future, takes over what has been, and acts and endures its way through the present" (EM: 34). As in the Kassel lectures, "the present . . . vanishes in the happening" (ibid.). According to this conception of history, the history of being embodies a *destining* (*Geschick*) that sends it on its way toward its fulfillment and culmination (according to *Contributions to Philosophy*, the other beginning) in such a way that what has come before (the first beginning) is endowed with the meaning and import characteristic of a true beginning (its promise and potential is defined and realized).

We should not be surprised, then, when Heidegger says in a later essay that "being itself is inherently eschatological" (GA 5: 327/Heidegger 1984: 18). The idea that history is future-directed, moving toward a culmination, is rooted in the conception of being he takes up in his retrieval of the thinking of the first beginning. Just as, for the Greeks, the being of any being is defined by the stand it achieves when it runs up against its limit (*peras*) and so comes to have constancy (*Ständigkeit*) and form (*morphē, Gestalt*) (EM: 46), so the being of history is defined in terms of what Heidegger's student Hans-Georg Gadamer calls an "anticipation of completion [*Vollendung*]" (Gadamer 1989: 294?): an anticipation of a possible *telos* or *eschaton* in which the course of events comes to be gathered up into a meaningful, motivated whole.

The History of Being and the Work of Art

Heidegger points out in both *Contributions to Philosophy* and *Introduction to Metaphysics* that the best way to understand the conception of the sort of historically emerging truth he is describing is to examine what happens when a work of art is working. In "The Origin of the Work of Art," he tries to convey a sense of what happens when a monumental work of art comes on the scene in the lives of a historical people. Starting with a description of a Greek temple, Heidegger shows how the temple takes up what is initially inchoate, what lies in the background of a world, and melds it into a world-defining work. According to this description, it is the temple that first lets the valley, the god, and the surrounding environment take on a determinate form so that things come to *count* in specific ways. By holding its ground, Heidegger says, the building makes manifest the violence of the raging storm, and it imparts a distinctive aspect to "tree and grass, eagle and bull, snake and cricket" (GA 5: 28/Heidegger 1971: 42). Most striking in this description, the temple is said to first let human beings emerge into presence *as* the humans they are in this particular world. "It is the temple-work that first fits together and at the same time gathers around itself the unity of those paths and relations in which birth and death, disaster and blessing, victory and disgrace, endurance and decline acquire the shape [*Gestalt*] of destiny [*Geschick*] for human being" (GA 5: 27–8/Heidegger 1971: 42).

The description of the temple shows how a world-defining work of art responds to and takes up a "primal strife" of concealing/unconcealing and defines that strife in a way that keeps it in question in a people's world. One example Heidegger gives, Sophocles' *Antigone*, makes this defining function of the artwork especially clear. In this tragedy, Heidegger says, "nothing is staged or displayed theatrically, but [instead] the battle of the new gods against the old is being fought" (GA 5: 29/Heidegger 1971: 43). The work of art does not *represent* something, such as events in the distant past. Instead, it *presents* those events in such a way that the Greek community now sees what is put in question by those events. The work, "originating in the saying [*Sage*] of a people, . . . transforms the people's saying" so that now what is at issue in their world is vividly brought into focus for them (GA 5: 29/Heidegger 1971: 42). What at first is only tacit and amorphous in a community's background understanding (the shift in Athens from a women's *oikos*-based society to a men's *polis*-based state) is given form and lit up in all its enduring strangeness and question-worthiness. In this way, the work of art enables a people to discover the questionableness of what defines their being as participants in a historical sending, and it thereby discloses the need for decision and measure.

In Heidegger's account of art, it is not the artist who is crucial to the work of art ("the artist remains inconsequential," he says; "it is the work that makes the creators possible"; GA 5: 26/Heidegger 1971: 40). Instead, what determines the being of the work is the "future ones," that is, the coming generations of "preservers" who take up the challenge enshrined by the work and carry it forward in the life of a people. By putting in question everything ordinary and commonplace, a great work of art inaugurates history, where history is understood as a shared project of confronting fundamental questions about how things are to count for a community. Whenever art happens, Heidegger says, "a thrust enters history; history either begins or starts over again" (GA 5: 65/Heidegger 1971: 77).

Seen in this light, the being of a work of art consists in the way it throws an understanding of things toward future preservers. It is a *projection* in which "the concepts of a people's historical essence, i.e., of its belonging to world history, are preformed for that people" (GA 5: 62/Heidegger 1971: 74). But this advance sketch of what it means to be a people of a certain sort is realized and "comes into its own" (it "ownness") only in the specific ways it is taken up and carried forward by preservers. If the preservers do not heed the call, if they let the challenge of the work become stale and calcified, then there is an "abandonment of being," and beings become "unbeings." If, on the other hand, the preservers maintain a dynamic site of questioning, letting both the lighting and self-secluding aspects of things show up, then beings are fully "in being" (*seiend*), and be-ing can come into its own as what it is destined to be. According to this account, then, humans have a crucial role to play in defining and fulfilling the potential of be-ing, and so they are "needed" and "used" by be-ing, and in this sense "belong" to be-ing.

But be-ing itself is much more than what humans do. Be-ing embraces the entire happening of the onslaught of beings, the emergence of a primal strife, the appropriation (*Ereignis*) of humans in the call to prepare a space-time leeway or site (a "*Da*") for being to emerge, and the coming-to-be of a Dasein in which a questioning-understanding of being can be crystallized, defined and carried forward. It is this entire happening that constitutes what Heidegger in his middle period calls the "history of be-ing."

Notes

1   John Richardson, "*Being and Time*'s Teleologies," unpublished manuscript presented at the annual meeting of the International Society for Phenomenological Studes (2001).
2   John van Buren (1994: 331) alludes to the Greek formulation of Heidegger's notion of Dasein's futurity.
3   In a similar vein, Jürgen Habermas argues that the historian must "anticipate end-states from which the multiplicity of events coalesces smoothly into action-guiding stories." This "transcendental condition of possible historical knowledge" is unavoidable, according to Habermas: "Only because we project the provisional end-state of a system out of the horizon of life-practice can the interpretation of events (which can be organized into a story [only] from the point of view of a projected end) as well as the interpretation of parts (which can be described as fragments from the point of view of the anticipated totality) have any information content at all for that life-practice" (Habermas 1977: 350–1).
4   The term "constellation of intelligibility" and much of my account draws on Iain Thomson's (2000) helpful essay.

References and further reading

Blattner, W. (1999) *Heidegger's Temporal Idealism*. Cambridge: Cambridge University Press.
Gadamer, H. G. (1989) *Truth and Method*. New York: Continuum.
Habermas, J. (1977) A review of Gadamer's *Truth and Method*. In F. R. Dallmayr and T. A. McCarthy (eds.), *Understanding and Social Inquiry*. Notre Dame, IL: University of Notre Dame Press.
Heidegger, M. (1969) *Zur Sache des Denkens*. Tübingen: Niemeyer.
Heidegger, M. (1971) *Poetry, Language, Thought* (trans. A. Hofstadter). New York: Harper & Row.
Heidegger, M. (1982) *Nietzsche*, volume 4 (trans. D. F. Krell). San Francisco: Harper & Row.
Heidegger, M. (1984) *Early Greek Thinking* (trans. D. F. Krell and F. A. Capuzzi). San Francisco: Harper & Row.

Heidegger, M. (2002). *Supplements: From the Earliest Essays to* Being and Time *and Beyond* (trans. J. van Buren et al.). Albany: State University of New York Press.

Polt, R. (2005) *The Emergency of Being: On Heidegger's "Contributions to Philosophy."* Ithaca, NY: Cornell University Press.

Schatzki, T. (2003) Living out of the past: Dilthey and Heidegger on life and history. *Inquiry* 46, 301–23.

Thomson, I. (2000) Ontotheology? Understanding Heidegger's *Destruktion* of metaphysics. *International Journal of Philosophical Studies*, 8, 297–327.

Vallega-Neu, D. (2003) *Heidegger's Contributions to Philosophy: An Introduction.* Bloomington: Indiana University Press.

van Buren, J. (1994) *The Young Heidegger: Rumor of the Hidden King.* Bloomington: Indiana University Press.

25

Heidegger's Ontology of Art

HUBERT L. DREYFUS

Introduction: World, Being, and Style

Heidegger is not interested in works of art as expressions of the vision of a creator, nor is he interested in them as the source of aesthetic experiences in a viewer. He holds that "modern subjectivism . . . immediately misinterprets creation, taking it as the self-sovereign subject's performance of genius" (GA 5: 63/Heidegger 1971: 76), and he also insists that aesthetic experience "is the element in which art dies" (GA 5: 66/Heidegger 1971: 79). Instead, for Heidegger, an artwork is a thing that, when it works, performs at least one of three ontological functions. It *manifests*, *articulates*, or *reconfigures* the style of a culture from within the world of that culture. It follows that, for Heidegger, most of what hang in museums, what are admired as great works of architecture, and what are published by poets were never works of art, a few were once artworks but are no longer working, and none is working now. To understand this counter-intuitive account of art, we have to begin by reviewing what Heidegger means by world and being.

World is the whole context of shared equipment, roles, and practices on the basis of which one can encounter entities and other people as intelligible. So, for example, one encounters a hammer as a hammer in the context of other equipment such as nails and wood, and in terms of social roles such as being a carpenter, a handyman, etc., and all such sub-worlds as carpentry, homemaking, etc., each with its appropriate equipment and practices, make sense on the basis of our familiar everyday world. Heidegger calls this background understanding our understanding of being. As he puts it in *Being and Time*, "being is that on the basis of which beings are already understood" (SZ: 7).

When he wrote *Being and Time*, Heidegger thought that he could give an ontological account of the universal structures of Worldhood and thus ground a "science of being." He was, therefore, not interested in what he called ontic accounts of specific sub-worlds and various cultures. It was only in the early 1930s that he realized that, in our Western culture at least, the understanding of being has a history. Then, he saw that the specific way that beings are revealed – what he then calls the truth of being – determines how anything shows up *as* anything and certain actions show us *as worth doing*. For simplicity, we can call the truth of being of a particular culture or a specific epoch in our culture the *style* of that world.

Style is the way the everyday practices are coordinated. It serves as the basis upon which old practices are conserved and new practices are developed. A style opens a disclosive space and does so in a threefold manner: (a) by *coordinating* actions; (b) by determining how things and people *matter*; and (c) by being what is *transferred* from situation to situation. These three functions of style determine the way anything shows up and makes sense for us.

One can best see these three functions of style in another culture. Sociologists point out that mothers in different cultures handle their babies in different ways that inculcate the babies into different styles of coping with themselves, people, and things. For example, American mothers tend to put babies in their cribs on their stomachs, which encourages the babies to move around more effectively. Japanese mothers, contrariwise, put their babies on their backs so they will lie still, lulled by whatever they see. American mothers encourage passionate gesturing and vocalizing, while Japanese mothers are much more soothing and mollifying.

In general American mothers situate the infant's body and respond to the infant's actions in such a way as to promote an active and aggressive style of behavior. Japanese mothers, in contrast, promote a greater passivity and sensitivity to harmony in the actions of their babies. The babies, of course, take up the style of nurturing to which they are exposed. It may at first seem puzzling that the baby successfully picks out precisely the gestures that embody the style of its culture as the ones to imitate, but, of course, such success is inevitable. Since *all* our gestures embody the style of our culture, the baby will pick up that pervasive style no matter what it imitates. Starting with a style, various practices will make sense and become dominant and others will either become subordinate or will be ignored altogether.

The general cultural style determines how the baby encounters himself or herself, other people, and things. So, for example, no bare rattle is ever encountered. For an American baby a rattle-thing is encountered as an object to make lots of expressive noise with and to throw on the floor in a willful way in order to get a parent to pick it up. A Japanese baby may treat a rattle-thing this way more or less by accident, but generally we might suppose a rattle-thing is encountered as serving a soothing, pacifying function. What constitutes the American baby as an *American* baby is its style, and what constitutes the Japanese baby as a *Japanese* baby is its quite different style.

Once we see that a style governs how anything can show up *as* anything, we can see that the style of a culture does not govern only the babies. The adults in each culture are completely shaped by it. It determines what it makes sense to do, and what is worth doing. For example, it should come as no surprise, given the caricature I have just presented of Japanese and American culture, that Japanese adults seek contented, social integration, while American adults are still striving willfully to satisfy their individual desires. Likewise, the style of enterprises and of political organizations in Japan aims at producing and reinforcing cohesion, loyalty, and consensus, while what is admired by Americans in business and politics is the aggressive energy of a *laissez-faire* system in which everyone strives to express his or her own desires, and where the state, business, or other organizations function to maximize the number of desires that can be satisfied without destructive instability.

The case of child rearing helps us to see that our cultural style is in our artifacts and our bodily skills. Since it is not something inner, but a disposition to act in certain ways in certain situations, it is misleading to think of our style as a belief system, scheme, or framework. It is invisible both because it is in our comportment, not in our minds, and because it is manifest in everything we see and do, and so too pervasive to notice. Like the illumination in a room, style normally functions best to let us see things when we don't see *it*. As Heidegger puts it, the mode of revealing has to *withdraw* in order to do its job of revealing things. Since it is invisible and global, our current understanding of being seems to have no contrast class. We can't help reading our own style back into previous epochs, the way the Christians understood the Greeks as pagans in despair, and the Moderns understood the Classical Greeks as already being rational subjects dealing with objects. So how can we ever notice our style or the style of another epoch in our culture?

The Work of Art as *Manifesting* a World

Heidegger answers this question in two stages. First, he shows that art is capable of revealing someone else's world. He shows this by describing a Van Gogh painting of a peasant woman's shoes. (Whether, as art critics debate, the shoes are really a pair of peasant shoes or Van Gogh's own shoes is irrelevant to how the picture works.) Heidegger claims that the shoes are not a symbol; they don't point beyond themselves to something else. Instead, Van Gogh's painting reveals to us the shoes themselves in their truth, which means that the shoes reveal the world of the peasant woman – a world that is so pervasive as to be invisible to the peasant woman herself, who, even when she deals with her shoes, "simply wears them . . . without noticing or reflecting" (GA 5: 23/Heidegger 1971: 34).

The Van Gogh painting, however, manifests the peasant's world to the viewer of the painting. Art, then, can be seen as manifesting a world *to those outside it*. But, of course, a culture's language, its artifacts, and its practices all reflect its style. This leaves open the question: if the style necessarily withdraws, *how can anyone ever come to see the style of his or her own epoch?* To answer this question, we need to look further into Heidegger's account of the special function of art.

The Work of Art as *Articulating* a Culture's Understanding of Being

Heidegger's basic insight is that the work of art not only *manifests* the style of the culture; it *articulates* it. For everyday practices to give us a shared world, and so give meaning to our lives, they must be focused and held up to the practitioners. Works of art, when performing this function, are not merely *representations* of a pre-existing state of affairs, but actually *produce* a shared understanding. Charles Taylor and Clifford Geertz have discussed this important phenomenon.

Taylor makes this point when he distinguishes shared meanings, which he calls *inter-subjective* meanings, from *common* meanings. As he puts it: "Common meanings are the basis of community. Inter-subjective meanings give a people a common language to talk about social reality and a common understanding of certain norms, but only with common meaning does this common reference world contain significant common actions, celebrations, and feelings" (Taylor 1979: 51). Taylor calls the way common meanings work, *articulation*.

A year after Taylor's article, in his famous paper on the cockfight in Bali, Clifford Geertz introduces the notion of style and argues that works of art and rituals produce and preserve a style. "A people's ethos is the tone, character, and quality of their life, its moral and aesthetic *style*. . . . Quartets, still lives, and cockfights are not merely reflections of a pre-existing sensibility analogically represented; they are positive agents in the creation and maintenance of such a sensibility" (Geertz 1973: 451). We might say, then, that art doesn't merely *reflect* the style of a culture; it *glamorizes* it and so enables those in the culture to see it and to understand themselves and their shared world in its light.

To appreciate the way the phenomenon Taylor and Geertz have seen defines art's function, it helps to turn to Thomas Kuhn. In *The Structure of Scientific Revolutions*, Kuhn argues that scientists engaged in what he calls normal science operate in terms of an exemplar or paradigm – an outstanding example of a good piece of work. The paradigm for modern natural scientists was Newton's *Principia*. All agreed that Newton had seen exemplary problems, given exemplary solutions, and produced exemplary justifications for his claims. Thus, for over two centuries scientists knew that, insofar as their work resembled Newton's, they were doing good science.

The Newtonian paradigm was later replaced by the Einsteinian one. Such a paradigm shift constitutes a scientific revolution. After such a revolution, scientists see and do things differently. As Kuhn puts it, they work in a different world. They also believe and value different things, but this is less important. Kuhn is quite clear that it is the paradigm – the exemplar itself – that guides the scientists' practices and that the paradigm cannot be explained in terms of a set of beliefs or values and spelled out using criteria and rules. As Kuhn notes, "paradigms may be prior to, more binding, and more complete than any set of rules for research that could be unequivocally abstracted from them" (Kuhn 1970: 46). Kuhn explicitly describes the work of science as articulating its paradigm: "in a science, . . . like an accepted judicial decision in the common law, [a paradigm] is an object for further articulation and specification under new or more stringent conditions" (Kuhn 1970: 23).

It seems almost inevitable after Kuhn to see whatever articulates a style as a paradigm. And, indeed, Geertz says: "it is [the] bringing of assorted experiences of everyday life to focus that the cockfight . . . accomplishes, and so creates what, better than typical or universal, could be called a paradigmatic human event" (Geertz 1973: 450). To sum up and generalize what Taylor, Geertz, and Kuhn have taught us: a cultural paradigm collects the scattered practices of a group, unifies them into coherent possibilities for action, and holds the resulting style up to the people concerned, who then act and relate to each other in terms of it.

Heidegger was the first to give a satisfactory ontological account of this phenomenon. He takes as his example the Greek temple. To begin with, it is clear that the temple is not a representation of anything; moreover, it is not the work of an individual genius. Nonetheless, the temple opened a world for the Greeks by articulating their style. The Greeks' practices were gathered together and focused by the temple so that they saw

410

nature and themselves in the light of the temple. Everything looked different once the style was articulated. As Heidegger puts it, "tree and grass, eagle and bull, snake and cricket first enter into their distinctive shapes and thus come to appear as what they are" (GA 5: 31/Heidegger 1971: 42).

The temple also held up to the Greeks what was worth doing by manifesting distinctions of worthiness: "it is the temple work that first fits together and at the same time gathers around itself the unity of those paths and relations in which birth and death, disaster and blessing, victory and disgrace, endurance and decline acquire the shape of destiny for human being" (GA 5: 31/Heidegger 1971: 42). The temple thus "gave things their look and men their outlook on themselves" (GA 5: 32/Heidegger 1971: 43). And, like every cultural paradigm, it illuminated *everything*. Thus, as Heidegger says, "the *all-governing* expanse of this open relational context is the *world* of this historical people" (GA 5: 31/Heidegger 1971: 42).

Heidegger is not the first to have seen the role of artistic articulation. Hegel, Nietzsche, and Wagner had already discussed the function of the artwork in giving a people a sense of their identity. But Heidegger is the first to have defined art in terms of its function of articulating the understanding of being in the practices and to have worked out the ontological implications. Thus, Heidegger could argue against Nietzsche and the Romantics that it was the *artwork*, not the experience of the *artist* that had ontological significance. Likewise, he could deny Hegel's claim that philosophy was superior to art, since what art showed symbolically, philosophy could rationalize and so make explicit.

Kuhn saw that the fact that the paradigm cannot be "rationalized" but only imitated is crucial to the paradigm's function. He says: "the concrete scientific achievement, as a locus of professional commitment, [is] prior to the various concepts, laws, theories, and points of view that may be abstracted from it. . . . [It] cannot be fully reduced to logically atomic components that might function in its stead" (Kuhn 1970: 11). The fact that the paradigm cannot be rationalized makes it possible for the scientists to agree without having to spell out their agreement. As Kuhn says, "the practice of normal science depends on the ability, acquired from exemplars, to group objects and situations into similarity sets that are primitive in the sense that the grouping is done without an answer to the question, 'Similar with respect to what?'" (Kuhn 1970: 200). At a time of a scientific revolution, however, Kuhn tells us, the paradigm becomes the focus of conflicting interpretations, each trying to rationalize and justify it.

Similarly, Heidegger holds that a working artwork is so important to a community that the people involved must try to make the work clear and coherent and codify what it stands for. But the artwork, like the scientific paradigm, resists rationalization. Any paradigm could be paraphrased and rationalized only if the concrete thing, which served as an exemplar, symbolized or represented an underlying system of beliefs or values that could be abstracted from the particular exemplar. But the whole point of needing an exemplar is that there is no such system, there are only shared practices. Therefore the style resists rationalization and can only be displayed. Heidegger calls the way the artwork solicits the culture to make the meaning of the artwork explicit, coherent, and all encompassing, the *world* aspect of the work. He calls the way the artwork and its associated practices resist such explication and totalization the *earth* aspect.

411

Heidegger sees that the earth's resistance is not a drawback but has an important positive function.

> To the Open there belong a world and the earth. But the world is not simply the Open that corresponds to clearing, and the earth is not simply the Closed that corresponds to concealment. Rather, the world is the clearing of the paths of the essential guiding directions with which all decision complies. Every decision, however, bases itself on something not mastered, something concealed, confusing; else it would never be a decision. (GA 5: 43–4/Heidegger 1971: 55)

Heidegger understands that if actions were fully lucid, as Sartre would have them be, they would be arbitrary and freely revocable and so not serious.[1] Like disposedness (*Befindlichkeit*) in *Being and Time*, earth supplies mattering and thus grounds the seriousness of decisions.

In "The Origin of the Work of Art," however, earth is understood no longer as an aspect of human being but as a function of the tendency in the cultural practices themselves to open worlds: "The earth cannot dispense with the Open of the world if it itself is to appear as earth in the liberated surge of its self-seclusion. The world, again, cannot soar out of the earth's sight if, as the governing breadth and path of all essential destiny, it is to ground itself on a resolute foundation" (GA 5: 38/Heidegger 1971: 49). Thus, earth is not passive matter, but comes into being precisely as what resists any attempt to abstract and generalize the point of the paradigm.

> The earth appears openly cleared as itself only when it is perceived and preserved as that which is by nature undisclosable, that which shrinks from every disclosure and constantly keeps itself closed up. (GA 5: 36/Heidegger 1971: 47)

> The opposition of world and earth is a strife. But we would surely all too easily falsify its nature if we were to confound strife with discord and destruction. In essential strife, rather, the opponents raise each other into the self-assertion of their natures. (GA 5: 37/Heidegger 1971: 49; translation corrected – *Streit* does not mean striving)

The temple draws the people who act in its light to clarify, unify, and extend the reach of its style, but being a material thing it resists rationalization. And since no interpretation can ever completely capture what the work means, the temple sets up a struggle between earth and world. The result is fruitful in that the conflict of interpretations that ensues generates a culture's history.[2]

Such resistance is manifest in the materiality of the artwork. A Greek tragedy requires the sound of the poetry to create a shared mood for the spectators and thus open up a shared world, so, like all literary works, tragedies resist translation. More generally, Heidegger tells us:

> the temple-work, in setting up a world, does not cause the material to disappear, but rather causes it to come forth for the very first time and to come into the Open of the work's world. The rock comes to bear and rest and so first becomes rock; metals come to glitter and shimmer, colors to glow, tones to sing, the word to speak. All this comes forth as the work

sets itself back into the massiveness and heaviness of stone, into the firmness and pliancy of wood, into the hardness and luster of metal, into the lighting and darkening of color, into the clang of tone, and into the naming power of the word. (GA 5: 35/Heidegger 1971: 46)[3]

What is dark and hidden and what is out in the open differs from culture to culture. How the line between the two is drawn is an aspect of the unique way the style of each particular culture is elaborated.

World demands its decisiveness and its measure and lets beings attain to the Open of their paths. Earth, bearing and jutting, strives to keep itself closed and to entrust everything to its law. The conflict is not a rift (*Riss*), as a mere cleft is ripped open; rather, it is the intimacy with which opponents belong to each other. This rift carries the opponents into the source of their unity by virtue of their common ground. It is a basic design, an outline sketch that draws the basic features of the rise of the lighting of beings. (GA 5: 51–2/Heidegger 1971: 63)

In each epoch, then, the struggle between world and earth and its rift design manifests a different style. The temple requires the stone out of which it is built in order to do its job of setting up the tension between structure and stone; a temple made out of steel would not work. The cathedral, in its different style, uses stone and glass to show the struggle between light and darkness and that light is winning out. We now construct debased works of art like the national highway system, which imposes such an efficient order on nature that earth is no longer able to resist.

The answers to our earlier questions should now be clear: the special function of art is precisely to let each group of historical people see the style of their own culture by showing it in a glamorized exemplar. Moreover, we can now add that such a function is an ontological necessity. As Heidegger puts it, "there must always be some being in [the] open, something that is, in which the openness takes its stand and attains its constancy" (GA 5: 49/Heidegger 1971: 61).

It follows that appreciating artworks when they are working, to talk like Heidegger, is the furthest thing from having private aesthetic experiences (GA 5: 55–6/Heidegger 1971: 68). Yet art is somehow connected with beauty. Heidegger describes art as "the shining of truth" (GA 5: 52/Heidegger 1971: 64), and describes beauty as the way artworks shine: "this shining . . . is the beautiful," he says (GA 5: 44/Heidegger 1971: 56).

But how does the temple shine? It is white, of course, and dazzling in the Greek sun, but what about other artworks such as somber cathedrals or dark tragedies? Do they shine too? Not literally, but remember that thanks to artworks some aspects of things and practices become salient and others marginal and that makes some ways of acting show up as worth doing, and others not show up at all. Thus the Greeks saw life and the cosmos *in the light of* their artworks. This is presumably the metaphorical sort of light Heidegger has in mind.

The way in which art thoroughly spans the being-in-the-world of human beings as historical, the way in which it illuminates the world for them and indeed illuminates human beings themselves, putting in place the way in which art is art – all this receives its law and structural articulation from the manner in which the world as a whole is opened up to human beings in general. (GA 53: 23)

To sum up: the work of art doesn't *reflect* the style of the culture or create it; it *illuminates* it.

Normally the illumination in the room must withdraw to do its work. But sometimes we can see the light bulb and also see everything in its light. In this way the artwork, like the sun in Plato's Allegory of the Cave, makes everything in the world intelligible, yet we can gaze upon it; but with the important difference that Plato thought the ground of the intelligibility of the world had to be outside the world, whereas Heidegger holds that it has to be something within the world. That means that, rather than being eternal like the Good, works of art can cease to work or, as Heidegger puts it, works of art can die.

> The Aegina sculptures in the Munich collection, Sophocles' *Antigone* in the best critical edition, are, as the works they are, torn out of their own native sphere. . . . [E]ven when we make an effort to cancel or avoid such displacement of works – when, for instance, we visit the temple in Paestum at its own site or the Bamberg cathedral on its own square – the world of the work that stands there has perished. (GA 5: 29–30/Heidegger 1971: 40–1)

Another way to express the artwork's fragility is to note that, unlike Plato's idea of The Good, the work of art shows itself to be created. "[A] work is always a work, which means that it is something worked out, brought about, effected. If there is anything that distinguishes the work as work, it is that the work has been created" (GA 5: 45/Heidegger 1971: 56). But this does not mean that Heidegger follows Nietzsche in emphasizing the creator of the work. In fact, Heidegger claims that "art is the origin of the artwork and of the artist" (GA 5: 46/Heidegger 1971: 57). But Heidegger adds that "the impulse toward such a thing as a work lies in the nature of truth" (GA 5: 45/Heidegger 1971: 57; translation modified). Truth for Heidegger means disclosing. So, for Heidegger, opening a world is a way truth sets itself to work. We can now understand this to mean that a culture's practices tend to gather so as to open and illuminate a world, and they use the artwork to do so. Indeed, in his marginal comments to "The Origin of the Work of Art," Heidegger repeatedly notes that what he is referring to here is what he later calls the event of appropriation (*das Ereignis*). That is, what ultimately makes truth and art possible is the way cultural practices tend toward making sense, the way they gather together to bring things out in their ownmost, to let things and people appear in a rich rather than in a banal way.

Thus far Heidegger has pointed out that the function of the artwork (like the accepted scientific paradigm) is to articulate the understanding implicit in the current practices. Paradigms thus reveal the current style to those who share it. But having devoted most of his essay to a description of the temple as the focus of the struggle of earth and world that fixes a culture's style and holds it up to the people, Heidegger has not yet arrived at the origin of the work of art – the way artworks work when they are functioning at their best, nor has he described how the practices come together to create new artworks that disclose new worlds. He turns to these issues at the end of his essay.

Heidegger: Artworks as *Reconfiguring* a Culture's Understanding of Being

Only when he realized that being itself had a history was Heidegger able to describe what he calls the *origin* (*Ur-sprung*) of the work of art. In setting the stage for this further move, he says:

> in the West for the first time in Greece . . . [w]hat was in the future to be called being was set into work, setting the standard. The realm of beings thus opened up was then transformed into a being in the sense of God's creation. This happened in the Middle Ages. This kind of being was again transformed at the beginning and in the course of the modern age. Beings became objects that could be controlled and seen through by calculation. At each time a new and essential world arose. (GA 5: 63–4/Heidegger 1971: 76–7)

Such changes are cultural revolutions and, as in scientific revolutions, they are made possible by the establishment of a new paradigm. As Heidegger says: "at each time the openness of what is had to be established in beings themselves, by the fixing in place of truth in figure" (GA 5: 64/Heidegger 1971: 77). That is, in each such case the being that shines in the clearing not only *configured* the style of the culture; it *reconfigured* it.[4] It follows that each time a culture gets a new artwork, the understanding of being changes and human beings and things show up differently. For the Greeks, what showed up were heroes and slaves; for the Christians, they were saints and sinners. There could not have been saints in ancient Greece; at best there could only have been weak people who let others walk all over them. Likewise, there could not have been Greek-style heroes in the Middle Ages. Such people would have been regarded as prideful sinners who disrupted society by denying their dependence on God and encouraging everyone to depend on them instead.

Once Heidegger describes the function of artworks when they are functioning as *revolutionary paradigms*, he can generalize the notion of a cultural paradigm from a work of art working to anything in the world that not only focuses, or refocuses, the current cultural style, but establishes a new one. Thus, he says:

> one essential way in which truth establishes itself in the beings it has opened up is truth setting itself into work. [The temple as articulating the Greek culture.] Another way in which truth occurs is the act that founds a political state. [Pericles, and, perhaps, Hitler.] Still another way in which truth comes to shine forth is the nearness of that which is not simply a being, but the being that is most of all. [God's Covenant with the Hebrews?] Still another way in which truth grounds itself is the essential sacrifice. [The Crucifixion?] Still another way in which truth becomes is the thinker's questioning, which, as the thinking of being, names being in its question-worthiness. [Philosophers do this by introducing a new vocabulary, like "subject/object," and "autonomy." In this sense, for Heidegger, revolutionary scientists like Galileo and Einstein are thinkers too]. (GA 5: 49/Heidegger 1971: 61–2)[5]

In Heidegger's terms, articulating works of art *establish* a style; now Heidegger tells us, *founding* works reconfigure it. But just how does this founding work? After giving

415

examples of articulators like the Greek temple, the Bamberg Cathedral, and the tragedies of Sophocles, Heidegger suddenly, toward the end of "The Origin of the Work of Art," without examples, offers a few hasty remarks on the function of the artwork he calls founding: "We understanding founding here in a triple sense: founding as bestowing, founding as grounding, and founding as beginning. . . . We can do no more now than to present this structure of the nature of art in a few strokes" (GA 5: 63/ Heidegger 1971: 75). Heidegger's three modes of founding correspond to the past, present, and future. First is *bestowing*, the role of the past. A new understanding of being must be incomprehensible yet somehow intelligible. To account for this possibility, Heidegger returns to an idea already touched on in *Being and Time* (see SZ: ¶74). In a historical change, some practices that were marginal become central, and some central practices become marginal. Reconfiguration is thus not the creation (*schaffen*) of a genius, but the drawing up (*schöpfen*) of the reserve of marginal practices bestowed by the culture as from a well (GA 5: 63/Heidegger 1971: 76). What ultimately bestows the material for the new style is the style of a people's language. Art takes place in a clearing "which has already happened unnoticed in language" (GA 5: 62/Heidegger 1971: 74).

So Heidegger now generalizes language to any form of "poetic projection:" "projective saying . . . brings the unsayable as such into a world" (GA 5: 61–2/Heidegger 1971: 74). "Genuinely poetic projection is the opening up or disclosure of that into which human being as historical is already cast. . . . Founding is an overflow, an endowing, a bestowal" (GA 5: 63/Heidegger 1971: 75–6).

In *grounding*, the present has to take up the marginal practices already in the culture into a new style that makes them central. Given the current understanding, the new style will, of course, seem weird and barely intelligible. "The setting-into-work of truth thrusts up the unfamiliar and extraordinary and at the same time thrusts down the ordinary" (GA 5: 63/Heidegger 1971: 75).

This makes possible a *new beginning* by opening a new future. Of course, a new style does not arise *ex nihilo*. Marginal practices of various sorts are always on the horizon. For example, the printing press and Luther were already moving people toward the individualism and freedom from authority that became central in Descartes's attempt to take over his life and education from the ground up. Thus, when speaking of the new beginning, Heidegger adds that while the new beginning is "a leap," "what is thus cast forth is . . . never an arbitrary demand" (GA 5: 63/Heidegger 1971: 75). He explains: "the peculiarity of a leap out of the unmediable does not exclude but rather includes the fact that the beginning prepares itself the longest time and wholly inconspicuously" (GA 5: 64/Heidegger 1971: 76).

The new beginning sets up a new future, by calling the people in the culture to be preservers.

> Preserving the work does not reduce people to their private experiences, but brings them into affiliation with the truth happening in the work. Thus it grounds being for and with one another as the historical standing-out of human existence in reference to unconcealedness. . . . The proper way to preserve the work is cocreated and prescribed only and exclusively by the work. (GA 5: 55/Heidegger 1971: 68)

416

Heidegger admits he gives no example of reconfiguration. Such examples, Heidegger admits, are only "initial hints" (GA 5: 55/Heidegger 1971: 68). Indeed, the examples he uses are all Greek – the temples, the tragedies, the classical philosophers – and, as such, are powerful articulations of an already existing cultural style. There may well be good reasons for his not being able to find any examples of reconfiguration in Greece. As Kierkegaard remarks in his discussion of the Christian notion of the fullness of time, and Heidegger repeats in his appropriation of Kierkegaard's notion of the *Augenblick*, the experience of radical transformation of self and world is what differentiates the Christian world from Antiquity (SZ: 338, note). After all, the Greeks believed in endless cycles of the same; not in radical creation. The most striking example of such a radical cultural transformation of a new beginning is the transformation of the Hebrew world into the Christian world.

So let us take a simplified account of this transformation as an illustration of the three aspects of founding. We are told that the Jews followed the Law so that one was guilty for one's overt acts, and that Jesus changed all this when, in the Sermon on the Mount, he said that anyone who looks at a woman lustfully has already committed adultery with her in his heart.

Jesus thrusts down or marginalizes the ordinary – the Law and the overt acts it condemns – when he practices healing even on the Sabbath, and he introduces the extraordinary new idea that what really matters is that one is responsible for one's desires. Purity, not rightness of action, is what is essential, and, in that case, one can save oneself not by will power, but only by throwing oneself on the mercy of a Savior and being reborn.

One might reasonably object that this emphasis on desire can't be such a radical change from Judaism after all, since the eighth commandment already enjoins one not to covet anything that is one's neighbor's, and coveting is surely a case of desire, not overt action. But Heidegger would surely be the first to point out that, if Jesus had not had some basis in the previous practices – something bestowed by the past – no one would have had a clue as to what he was talking about, so it was essential that, in his grounding of a new world, he take up and make central a marginal practice already bestowed by the culture. In the unique case of the Ten Commandments, it seems that the amount of marginal practice bestowed by the tradition can be quantified; it is reflected in one out of ten commandments.

But, of course, this is only the beginning. A world transformer such as Jesus can show a new style and so can be followed, as Jesus was followed by his disciples even though they could hardly understand what they were doing. But he will not be fully intelligible to the members of the culture until the preservers become attuned to his extraordinary new way of coordinating the practices – his new beginning – and articulate it in a new language and in new symbols and institutions.

Thus, although Heidegger never says so, it seems there must always be two stages in each cultural revolution: reconfiguration that thrusts down the ordinary and introduces the extraordinary, followed by an articulation that focuses, and stabilizes the new style. Thus Jesus is interpreted in terms of *caritas* by St Paul, Galileo is interpreted in terms of *gravitas* by Newton, and the implications of Descartes's new idea that we are subjects in a world of objects is worked out in terms of *autonomy* by Kant. It is because

417

Kant is merely an articulator that, for Heidegger, Descartes, as a reconfigurer, is a more primordial thinker than Kant.

Conclusion: Can an Artwork Work for Us Now?

Heidegger thinks that our current understanding of being levels all meaningful differences and hides the earth so now there are only negative exemplars of our style – Heidegger takes as an example the power station on the Rhine, and another example might be our walk on the moon. So far the West has not produced any reconfiguring work of art that sets forth the earth and restarts history with a new struggle between earth and world. The question then arises for Heidegger whether our flexible style that turns everything, even ourselves, into resources could ever be reconfigured.

Of course, one cannot legislate a new beginning. But perhaps our marginal practices could gather into a new style, one, for example, in which marginal practices and attunements like awe in the face of nature from our pre-Socratic past would begin to coalesce with the nature worship of the Romantics to affirm what is sometimes referred to as the Gaia Principle, i.e. that nature is god. Perhaps then some new paradigm would make those marginal practices central and marginalize our current practices, which, as Heidegger once put it, "are turning the earth into a gigantic filling station." Preservers might then see nature in the light of the new god, put solar panels on their homes and stop buying SUVs.

It is too early to see how such a work of art manifesting this new understanding of being might begin to work, but a hint of how a different sort of new paradigm almost worked can be found in the music and style of the 1960s. Bob Dylan, the Beatles, and other rock groups became for many the focus of a new understanding of what really mattered. This new style coalesced in the Woodstock music festival of 1969, where people actually lived for a few days in an understanding of being in which mainline contemporary concerns with order, sobriety, willful activity, and flexible, efficient control were made marginal and subservient to pagan practices, such as openness, enjoyment of nature, dancing, and Dionysian ecstasy, along with neglected Christian concerns with peace, tolerance, and non-exclusive love of one's neighbor. Technology was not smashed or denigrated; instead, all the power of electronic communications was put at the service of the music that articulated the above concerns.

If enough people had recognized in Woodstock what they most cared about and recognized that many others shared this recognition, a new style of life might have been focused and stabilized. Of course, in retrospect it seems to us who are still in the grip of the technological understanding of being that the concerns of the Woodstock generation were not organized and encompassing enough to resist being taken over by the very practices it was trying to marginalize. Still we are left with a hint of how a new cultural paradigm might work. This helps us to understand why Heidegger holds that we must foster human receptivity and preserve the endangered species of pre-technological practices that remain in our culture so that one day they may come together in a new work of art, rich enough and resistant enough to reconfigure our world.

Notes

1   This argument is first made by Søren Kierkegaard in his account of the breakdown of the Kantian ethical, and filled in phenomenologically in the freedom chapter in Merleau-Ponty (2002).

2   It is interesting to note that rituals, unlike the temple, do not set up a struggle between earth and world, presumably because they do not try to unify the whole culture. (The Balinese cock-fight Geertz analyses only glamorizes the role of the males.) Cultures that do not have art-works in Heidegger's view do not have a history, since, for him, history means the series of total worlds that result from a stuggle of interpretations as to the meaning of being. But it seem there can be more local works of art. The US Constitution, like a work of art, has nec-essarily become the focus of attempts to make it explicit and consistent, and to make it apply to *all* situations. Such attempts are never fully successful but this is not a drawback. The resulting conflict of interpretations is an important aspect of the history of the republic.

3   The last phrase is a surprise. One would have expected the *sound* of the word as its earthy component. The naming power seems to be what opens a world. This may be simply a mistake on Martin Heidegger's part. But it may not be, since he never corrected it in his marginal notes.

4   Heidegger also says: "whenever art happens – that is, whenever there is a beginning – a thrust enters history, history either begins or starts over again." (GA 5: 64/Heidegger 1971: 77). Heidegger seems to be confused about whether the Greek temple articulated or reconfigured because, in fact, it does neither. As the beginning of the history of being, the Greeks do not yet have a unified understanding of being to renew or to reconfigure. The temple and the Pre-Socratic thinkers had to take the style that was already in the language and, for the first time, focus it and hold it up to the people. According to Heidegger, this is the origin (*Ur-sprung*) of our Western culture.

5   In this connection it is interesting to note that Heidegger, who is infamous for saying that great philosophy can only be done in Greek or German, in GA 54 says that Descartes is a greater thinker than Kant, even though Descartes wrote in Latin and French, and never wrote a word in Greek or German.

References and further reading

Geertz, C. (1973) *The Interpretation of Cultures*. New York: Basic Books.

Heidegger, M. (1971) *Poetry, Language, Thought* (trans. A. Hofstadter). New York: Harper & Row.

Kuhn, T. (1970) *The Structure of Scientific Revolutions*, 2nd edn. Chicago: University of Chicago Press.

Merleau-Ponty, M. (2002) *The Phenomenology of Perception* (trans. C. Smith). New York: Routledge.

Taylor, C. (1979) Interpretation and the sciences of man. In P. Rabinow and W. Smith (eds), *Interpretive Social Science*. Berkeley: University of California Press.

26

Technology

ALBERT BORGMANN

It can be argued that technology is the most important topic of Heidegger's thought. The argument is this. Once he had found his voice as a philosopher, and from then on for the rest of his life, Heidegger tried to understand reality in its deepest and most crucial dimensions, and he did so in three ways: (a) he explored the nature of being; (b) he engaged in a conversation with the great Greek and German thinkers and poets; (c) he analyzed the human condition in the modern era.

These efforts proceeded unevenly and side by side until they converged on Heidegger's understanding of modern technology. Being, Heidegger found, changes through history and from the ground up, and beginning in pre-Socratic Greece, it passed through various epochs to take its present shape as the framework of technology. The great philosophers of the past Heidegger came to see as the framers (along with the artists and politicians) of the kind of reality that finally issued in technology. He saw the great poets, Hölderlin and Trakl in particular, as the witnesses and guardians of a world that was an alternative to technology. The technological culture is for Heidegger the decisive environment of humans in the late modern era, and their most fundamental welfare depends on their ability to pass through technology into another kind of world.

Given the importance of technology, it is perhaps surprising how little Heidegger wrote and lectured about it. It is, however, instructive to read the sequence of Heidegger's works as the gradual emergence of the problem of technology. To be able to do so, we need a preliminary understanding of what is meant by technology in Heidegger's thought.

As soon as technology became an explicit topic of his thought, Heidegger rejected the common notion of technology as an ensemble of artifacts and procedures that for better or worse is subject to human control. Specifically, Heidegger (1) did not think of technology as the use of tools that is as old and universal as the human race; he instead used technology in the sense of *modern* technology. More important still, Heidegger (2) denied that technology is a value-neutral instrument but thought of it as a radically fundamental and comprehensive phenomenon, something like the innermost character of modern culture and reality. Eventually Heidegger came to call the two senses of technology he rejected the anthropological and the instrumental senses. The conception of technology he was intent on illuminating he called the essence of technology.

To get this preliminary notion of Heidegger's concern right, we need to understand that Heidegger's search for the essence of technology is not what these days is called and criticized as essentialism. Critics take exception to essentialism because they think of it as the oppressive imposition of a dominant and timeless mold on what is in fact historically changing and multiple in its appearance. Heidegger obviously does not disagree with the claim that reality changes fundamentally over time. He, along with R. G. Collingwood and Michael Oakeshott, was a pioneer in criticizing the supposed timelessness of philosophical theories. He does, to be sure, oppose the other claim, i.e. that cultural phenomena are too many-sided to exhibit a definite character, and he denies a third claim, often associated with anti-essentialism, to the effect that what discernible shape a cultural phenomenon has is a social construction.

How did the phenomenon of technology become problematic for Heidegger? Martin Heidegger was born in rural and largely pre-technological circumstances. The world of his childhood and youth would have been readily understandable to a medieval peasant or a Roman soldier. It was, moreover, a deeply Catholic and petit bourgeois world. Being Catholic, it was culturally oppressed by the ruling and militant Protestantism of the recently founded German Empire; and even within Catholicism, he belonged to the orthodox party that in his hometown of Messkirch was temporarily overshadowed and repressed by the more affluent and liberal minority that dissented from the dogmas of the recently concluded Vatican Council. Heidegger's father was a sexton and a cooper, and had it not been for the support of the Catholic Church, young Martin would have remained confined to the world of small-town artisans. Thus it is well conceivable that Heidegger early on learned to be skeptical of forces that triumphantly gather power and affluence about themselves. Even so, though the mature Heidegger showed great affection for his native town and country, young Heidegger was chiefly concerned to rise above them. His early work in philosophy was marked by intelligence and ambition; it was also quite academic and conventional.

The philosopher who helped Heidegger to find his voice and vision was Edmund Husserl. His phenomenology promised the best of two worlds: realism and relevance, the turn from abstract and academic subjects "to the things themselves"; and rigor and radicalism, a methodology that would be as compelling and trenchant as that of the sciences. The first of these features taught Heidegger to pay attention to the real world, to analyze it, and to capture its crucial features. Heidegger remained a phenomenologist throughout his life, but it was the initial and fundamental, not to say the lowest, form of Husserlian description and analysis – the direct phenomenology, trained on the character of things – that Heidegger practiced. He refused to follow Husserl's ascent to ever more abstract and complicated modes of inquiry. As for radical rigor, Heidegger never felt the attraction of the mathematical or scientific model. Rigor came to mean depth rather than precision. Thus technology was bound to come into view as a phenomenon both concrete and fundamental.

Being and Time (1927) was the celebrated result though technology so far remained an implicit concern. The notion of being was Heidegger's oriflamme of radicality, and it remained so for the rest of his life. Never defined or rigorously explained, it was Heidegger's spur to reach beyond all prejudices, conventions, and received wisdoms, successfully sometimes, more often not. *Being and Time* failed to grasp technology directly for two reasons. First, it was still committed to the transcendental ambition of uncovering universal conditions of existence. Thus it failed to focus on technology as a modern phenomenon. Second, the finished and published part (two-thirds of the projected work) was preparatory and dealt with human being as the place where being becomes an issue; it did not address being itself. Thus *Being and Time* missed technology as the way being reveals itself in the modern era.

Yet without Heidegger realizing it, *Being and Time* anticipates his philosophy of technology in two ways. First, in discussing the normal and inauthentic condition of human existence – what Heidegger called *the they* (*das Man*) – *Being and Time* reveals less a timeless condition of humans than the debilities of life in the culture of technology (SZ: 114–30). Of the three features that characterize the they, talk (*das Gerede*) is the first. It is a way of knowing and speaking that has lost touch with reality and has become what today we would call public opinion. Heidegger, in less guarded discourse, made the technological framework of such knowledge explicit in his lecture *Fundamental Concepts*, given in the summer semester of 1941:

> That people occasionally "read a book" is a Philistine kind of accounting, quite aside from the fact that we have to ask whether people today who often get their "education" only from lists, magazines, radio reports, and movie theaters, whether such discombobulated, purely American individuals still know and are able to know what it means "to read." (GA 51: 13–14)

Similarly, *curiosity* (*die Neugier*) is, as Heidegger puts it, the kind of "restlessness" and "distraction" that has truly come into its own in the information age. In a pre-modern setting, information is necessarily limited and anchored in the environment. It is only when the modern media push a "tendency toward deracination," as Heidegger has it (SZ: 173), and when they provide a surfeit of information that news no longer engages us and does not have to engage us because as soon as we tire of one news story two others clamor for our attention. Heidegger noticed the resulting curiosity at a time when by contemporary standards the media were few in number and measured in their output.

Ambiguity (*die Zweideutigkeit*), finally, denotes the loss of authority in the way the world is presented to us and the fact that we no longer have to take responsibility for our views insofar as we constitute public opinion (SZ: 170–5). These losses presuppose a mediated world, one that is reported, interpreted, and tendentiously presented rather than one that addresses us in its own right, and they presuppose the anonymity of modern mass society where my vote and my responses to a poll are taken at face value.

The second way in which *Being and Time* implicitly adverts to technology is the discussion of what for Heidegger came to be the positive counterpart to the devastations of technology. It is a world that has depth and coherence and is centered and disclosed in some tangible thing. In *Being and Time* it is the shop whose context of concern and references is gathered in the tool (*das Zeug*) (SZ: 66–88), and it is, more generally, the coherent pre-technological world (SZ: 102–13), as is apparent from one of Heidegger's asides on the fate of familiarity and nearness: "Through radio, for instance, human being brings about a re-moval – yet to be determined in its existential significance – of the world by way of an expansion of the everyday environment" (SZ: 105). As if to bring out the implicit critique of technology, Heidegger amplified this passage in the

1976 edition so that it read: "expansion *and destruction* of the everyday world" (Heidegger 1979: 105, emphasis added).

Being and Time was published in 1927 after a fallow period of eleven years, and it quickly earned Heidegger wide discussion and renown. In 1928, he was appointed to Husserl's position in Freiburg and was able to return to his beloved native region. As we can see, however, from the lectures he gave in the next five years, Heidegger's mood and work were not happy.

Instead of reveling in the pleasures of the academic world that he had conquered and that had rewarded him so well, Heidegger became irritated with and contemptuous of the university and the professoriate. Particularly in philosophy he found the features of the they abundantly in evidence among his colleagues. He found them superficial, smart, smug, and busy. More importantly, Heidegger himself could not find a way of breaking through the conventional wisdom and of passing beyond *Being and Time*. Much of his lecturing was devoted to the analysis of Plato, Aristotle, and the German idealists in an effort to wrest from their writings the clues to productive and illuminating work. There were also efforts to push ahead, in the wake of *Being and Time*, with the exploration of concrete reality.

Heidegger's refusal to rest on his laurels and his tenacity in searching for he-was-not-sure-what were admirable, and his rising dissatisfaction with contemporary culture and his abiding interest in the Greek phenomenon of *techne* pointed forward to his philosophy of technology (GA 33; Feenberg forthcoming). Still, the substantive results as well as the publications of those five years (1928–33) were meager, and it must have been at least in part anger and frustration that made him reach for the rectorship of the University of Freiburg. His goal was, as we now know, to use Nazi power and ideology to promote his thought politically if not philosophically (Ott 1988).

Heidegger's involvement with the Nazi regime was a disaster from every point of view. It was a disaster morally most of all, made worse by the fact that, though it ended within less than a year, Heidegger never came forward with a frank acknowledgment of his implication and responsibility. It was a disaster personally; Heidegger eventually felt rejected and bitter, as he obliquely complained in one of his first lectures after his failed rectorship (GA 39: 136, 208).

Heidegger's alliance with the Nazis was a philosophical disaster because there was little of substance that he was able to propagate from the rector's pulpit. Beyond the deplorable avowals of chauvinism and allegiance to Hitler, all that Heidegger had to offer were the antonyms to the characteristics of the inauthentic they – resolve, dedication, discipline, service (GA 16: 107–17). Later he came to see the totalitarian character of National Socialism as "the encounter of planetary technology and modern humanity" (GA 40: 152) and the holocaust in particular as "the fabrication of corpses in gas chambers and annihilation camps" (GA 79: 27). Technology in Heidegger's sense was surely an ingredient of the holocaust. Its bureaucratic and mechanized features have been widely noted. But to mention Nazism and the holocaust only in connection with technology is to suggest, wrongly, that technology was the nearly sufficient condition of those disasters or to let, reprehensibly, an incidental feature overshadow the moral substance at issue. Heidegger must have sensed that the evil of fascism and racism sprang from depths more profound than those of technology. In one of his Bremen lectures he said: "What is inhuman and yet human is of course more evil and fatal than a human being that would simply be a machine" (GA 79: 37). But he never referred this insight directly to the holocaust.

A new and constructive period in Heidegger's thought began in 1935 when he delivered his lecture on "The Origin of the Work of Art" (GA 5: 1–74). It turns directly to the question of how a world is disclosed in a tangible thing. The tool of *Being and Time* yields to the work of art, to the peasant's shoes in a Van Gogh painting, to the Roman fountain in C. F. Meyer's poem, and to the Greek temple. The essay is sometimes thought to mark "the turn" (*die Kehre*) in Heidegger's thought, the turn of attention from the human condition to the eloquence of reality. What degree of continuity there is in Heidegger's philosophy is a complex question. The 1935 essay, at any rate, resolves the ambiguity in the early Heidegger's writings between transcendental universalism and factual uniqueness and between human decisions and the inescapable givenness of one's situation.

In "The Origin" the unpredictable and fundamental changes of art reflect and, more, occasion like changes in the world entire. The work of art establishes the truth of an epoch, truth not in the formal sense of truth conditions but in the substantive sense of what is eminently and decisively true of a particular time. Epochal truth, moreover, essentially engages the artist and issues from the artist – a relation and notion of freedom that remains problematic in Heidegger's philosophy of technology.

The path that this essay breaks for the philosophy of technology is the possibility of grasping technology too as the truth of a particular epoch, i.e. of our time. More particularly, the truth and the world that the work of art opens up is the precursor of the kind of reality that Heidegger came to see as the salutary alternative to technology. He realized, however, as he indicates in a 1950 postscript, that in the modern era the work of art was no longer the tangible thing that could gather and center a world, far less establish the crucial dimensions of an epoch (GA 5: 67–70).

A year later, in 1936, Heidegger began to write down the investigations and reflections that ever more sharply delineated his philosophy of technology. They were concluded in 1938 and published in 1989 under the title of *Contributions to Philosophy* (*Of the Event*) (GA 65). It is now available in an English translation that can only be called unfortunate (Heidegger 1999). It bristles with neologisms where Heidegger for the most part uses regular German words. Where he does not, the modifications Heidegger makes remain close to common words. The deplorable neologisms needlessly move obstacles into the reader's path, and they expose Heidegger's thought to unwarranted ridicule (Blackburn 2000).

Heidegger was now able to close the gap between his interrogations of the history and philosophy of being and of the great figures of the Western tradition with his investigations of contemporary culture. Technology is seen as the outcome of metaphysics, the concentration on the structure and presentation of objects to the detriment of giving thought to the epochal contexts to which objects owe their fundamental character in the first place.

This sort of obliviousness takes on a characteristic shape in technology. It is the unquestionable conviction that everything there is exists for human *machination*, Heidegger's early term for the essence of technology. It leads to a leveling down of traditions and landmarks and a pervasive regularity that is the more distressing the more it is becoming concealed. But all this springs from the character of the epoch we live in. It is neither a social construction nor the fault of individuals. Alongside the analysis of technology, the eventual counter to the distress of technology emerges as well in the *Contributions*. The work of art is replaced by the simplicity of an inconspicuous thing, the wine jug. The world of earth and sky becomes the fourfold of earth and sky, mortals and divinities.

In addition to providing new insights into technology, *Contribution* also reveals how Heidegger reached them and what experiences he drew on in articulating them. By 1936, Heidegger had broken through the seemingly unyielding walls of the post *Being and Time*, pre-Nazi period. Thoughts, discoveries, and hunches rained down on the page, fixed for the moment, taken up and elaborated in later passages. Heidegger used diagrams to clarify the developments and connections he saw – evidence that conceptual rigor continued to underlie a kind of discourse that could be dense and mystifying (GA 65: 130, 138, 308, 310).

The major impetus for Heidegger's mature philosophy, as the *Contributions* show, is twofold: intense distress at the character of modern culture and affection for the rural culture of his native region. *Distress (die Not)* is one of the key words of the *Contributions* and more especially the distress at the general incapacity for the recognition of how distressing times really were. In a section titled "Machination and Experience," Heidegger says this about these two phenomena:

> It lies in the nature of both of these not to know any limits and above all no embarrassment and finally no shyness. Most remote to them is the strength of safekeeping. Instead there is exaggeration and excessive shouting and blind mere shouting-at in which shouting one shouts at oneself and diverts oneself from how reality is being hollowed out. (GA 65: 131)

Needless to say, this was not the picture of the world that the Nazis promoted in the mid-1930s, but neither is Heidegger's distress aimed squarely at the tightening grip of fascism and anti-Semitism.

Just as the Heidegger of the *Contributions* is more openly anguished about the rise of the technological culture than in the philosophical writings he published, so he is less guarded in acknowledging the inspiration of rural life for his thought. Thus he likens his work to that of a farmer:

> How then does the thinker save the truth of beyng [*des Seyns*, Heidegger's archaic spelling of *being*] if not in the heavy slowness of the walk of his questioning steps and their fixed sequence? Inconspicuously, as on the lonely field under the big sky, the sower with his heavy, halting, ever composed step walks along the furrows and with the cast of his arm measures and shapes the space of all growth and ripening. (GA 65: 19)

Even poetry and philosophy attain their force under the aegis of country and nature. At least in part, Hölderlin became such a crucial inspiration and confirmation for Heidegger because he was born in the same region as Heidegger and drew on some of the same local sources. This is how Heidegger sees the significance of Hölderlin for his work: "What supports in all this unsupported questioning after the truth of beyng the

425

conjecture that the thrust of beyng may have cast a first tremor into our history? Once more just one thing: that Hölderlin had to become the sayer that he is" (GA 65: 485).

The interpretations, too, of the great figures and themes of philosophy are assimilated to natural landmarks. Heidegger titles one of the sections of *Contributions* "The Great Philosophies" and says they:

> are soaring mountains, unclimbed and unclimable. But they lend the land its highest points and point to its bedrock. They stand as markers and constitute the circle of visibility; they yield vision and concealment. When are mountains what they are to be? Certainly not when supposedly we have hiked and climbed all over them. Only when they truly stand there for us and for the land. (GA 65: 187)

We get further insight into the emergence of technology at the center of Heidegger's thought in the "Conversations on a Country Road" of 1944–5, unpublished during Heidegger's lifetime. It is a conversation of a Researcher (a physicist), a Scholar (a traditional philosopher), and a Sage (the voice of Heidegger; Heidegger mitigates the implied presumption by pointing out that, in German, "sage" and "one who points, a pointer" are homonyms: *ein Weiser*; GA 77: 84–5). It is a highly stylized dialogue, and whether any of it stemmed from actual exchanges we will not know until we have an exhaustive biography of Heidegger.

As in other writings of the period, there is an eerie silence about the persecutions by the Nazis and the destruction and despair of the concluding war. Heidegger is concerned with what he must have considered more profound problems. The ostensible issue is the resumption of a discussion that revolved about Kant's distinction between intuition and thought. The Researcher assimilates thought to theory and intuition to experiment, and he gives primacy to theory, whereupon the Sage stresses the crucial role of the technology of experiments, and within four pages the dispute is about whether technology is applied science or science is applied technology.

What may surprise one who has only read the writings Heidegger published himself is the frank and direct way in which the Researcher raises, against the Sage, the questions and objections that would leap to the mind of an analytic philosopher sitting still for Heidegger's sort of discourse, such as when the Researcher says: "And so, generally speaking, technology is a particular kind of thinking, namely the sort of thinking that concerns itself with the practical application of the theoretical sciences for the purpose of dominating and exploiting nature. Hence we physicists commonly say that technology is nothing but applied physics" (GA 77: 6). For the Sage and for Heidegger technology is prior to science in the sense that the objectifying spirit of technology, understood as the temperament of the modern era, underlies both science and technology, the latter taken in the specific sense of the Researcher. Here too the Researcher replies in just the way a scientific realist would:

> But you do not mean to say that nature is violated in physics? Nature, and only nature as it manifests itself to us, has the last word in physics. It is among the overwhelming experiences of a scientist that nature often answers in a way that is different from what the questions that the researcher addresses to it would have us expect. (GA 77: 17)

426

This is a plausible answer and suggests that the problem with the scientific picture of nature is not that it violates or manipulates nature – in fact it depicts nature as nature reveals itself. The problem instead is that the scientific view, due to its prominence, obscures the moral and poetical force of nature. It follows that technology in its broad epochal sense is the temperament of an era that enables humans to grasp the lawful mathematical structure of nature and that gives that structure a prominent, perhaps an unduly important, place in its culture. That view is surely compatible with the scientific realism we find in contemporary mainstream philosophy.

In his later writings on technology, Heidegger draws a distinction that roughly parallels the senses of technology that divide the Sage from the Researcher. Heidegger calls the broader and epochal sense "the essence of technology" and keeps "technology" for the narrower industrial and mechanical sense. However, while the way he characterizes the essence of technology illuminates well what we mean by technology in the narrow sense, it obscures, if it does not distort, the realist sense of science and comes closer to the instrumentalist conception the Researcher complains about.

Finally, the *Conversations on a Country Road* reveal Heidegger's misgivings about the attitude of patience and gratitude that later become a canonical part of his thinking and a necessary condition for the advent of the power that can save us from the devastations of technology. Notably, these reservations surface in the *Conversations* before the "thinking is thanking" (GA 77: 100) suggestion was published and became subject to public criticism. Consider this exchange:

Researcher: What in the world am I supposed to do?
Scholar: That's my question as well.
Sage: We are not supposed to do anything but wait.
Scholar: That's poor consolation.
Sage: Poor or not, we are not to expect solace either, which is what we do even when we merely slip into despair.
Researcher: What then are we supposed to wait for? And where should we wait? I hardly know any more where I am and who I am. (GA 77: 110)

Outwardly Heidegger's lectures between 1935 and 1944 do not seem different from those between 1928 and 1933. They too are devoted to the great topics and thinkers of Greek and German philosophy. But they show a renewed sense of purpose and direction, and technology is increasingly, if always briefly, the target on which the reflections converge.

The end of the war brought Heidegger personal distress and disgrace, and his career as a philosopher might have come to an inglorious end had it not been for French philosophers who sought Heidegger's acquaintance and conversation. One of them, Jean Beaufret, provoked Heidegger's first postwar publication, the *Letter on Humanism*, written in the autumn of 1946 and published in 1947 (GA 9). Heidegger's concern was to regain philosophical standing, to disavow nationalism, to recognize humanism, and to acknowledge ethics, and yet to insist on the tentative and superficial character of these conventional worries. Beneath them all he saw a profound and pervasive homelessness that was to be traced to technology, traced in turn to "the history of metaphysics" (GA 9: 88).

Heidegger made his first public appearance on December 1, 1949, at the unlikely venue of a gentlemen's club in Bremen, founded in 1783. Under the overall title of *Insight into What Is* (GA 79), he presented the fruits of his thinking since 1935 in four lectures:

1   The Thing (*Das Ding*).
2   The Framework (*Das Ge-stell*).
3   The Danger (*Die Gefahr*).
4   The Turning (*Die Kehre*).

These presentations contained the substance of Heidegger's mature philosophy, and although Heidegger continued to think, write, and speak for another twenty-seven years, little regarding technology was added. As before, his writings on being, thinking, language, poetry, and some of his great predecessors by far outweighed in quantity what he said and published on technology after the war, and it is this massive material that has chiefly concerned the Heideggerians and postmodernists. But his enduring legacy may well be his insights into the framework of technology and his reminders of the fourfold nature of the thing.

Remarkably, Heidegger seems to have been unsure of the cohesiveness and persuasiveness of the Bremen lectures, for he never had them published as a whole during his lifetime. In 1954, he published the second lecture under the title "The Question Concerning Technology" and the first under the same title, "The Thing," in a collection of essays (GA 7: 9–40, 157–79). However, these two Bremen lectures were grouped in different parts of the anthology and out of sequence, and without any indication of their original connection. "The Question Concerning Technology" was rendered in English in 1977 in an unfortunate translation that has given us the neologisms of "enframing" (*das Gestell*, better the framework) and "standing-reserve" (*der Bestand*, better resources) (Heidegger 1977: 3–35).

The essay falls into roughly eight parts, or perhaps we should say *steps*, for Heidegger begins by portraying his investigation of technology as the building of a path. Next he turns to the common understanding of technology as a neutral instrument under the control of humans. The neutral sense is both instrumental and anthropological. It is correct, but not true, i.e. not revealing. He proposes to get to the true sense via the correct sense.

The third part, then, analyses the notion of instrumentality to reach the truth or the essence of technology. Instrumentality is traced to causality; causality is explicated in its fourfold Aristotelian mode – the material cause in Heidegger's example is silver, the formal cause is the shape of a sacrificial bowl, the final form or purpose is worship, and the efficient cause is the silversmith. Heidegger describes the process of making the bowl to have us realize that the silversmith does not so much produce the bowl as he brings it forward into the open. His work is a disclosure or revelation.

Having argued that revelation underlies production, Heidegger, in his fourth step, invites us to think of technology as a kind of revealing as well. He describes the particular mode of disclosure that is technology and, very importantly, the revealing that *modern* technology constitutes. The description articulates the five key terms of his philosophy of technology. Modern technology *challenges* (*herausfordern*) nature to yield its treasures to humans. Next, technology *positions* (*stellen*) and *orders* (*bestellen*) the yields of nature so that they are available and disposable to humans. Whatever is so positioned and ordered becomes a *resource* (*der Bestand*). Finally, Heidegger gathers this entire way of treating and disclosing nature under the title of *the framework* (*das Gestell*) – the essence of technology.

Heidegger's fifth part discusses the relation of modern science to the essence of technology. He restates the point made in the *Conversations* that (the essence of) technology is prior to science, and he does so without the earlier scruples about the strictly disclosive character of science. Instead he claims for the sciences the aggressive approach to nature that goes well with technology, but poorly with science.

The sixth step takes Heidegger to the framework of technology as destiny and to the question of how humans are involved in the dispensation of that framework. Destiny is neither an inevitable fate that descends on humanity, Heidegger claims, nor the result of human willing. Disclosure of destiny and human freedom are one and the same.

There is, however, a twofold danger to destiny – the concern of the seventh step. One is the danger that human being reduces itself to a resource and in so appearing to have taken total control encounters nothing any more but itself. The other is the danger that the disclosure of the framework forecloses every other dispensation and conceals that it too is a disclosure.

Still, the framework *is* a disclosure. It involves human being. And it therefore harbors the possibility of a saving power. This is the eighth and concluding step of the essay. But given the possibility of saving, Heidegger asks more directly: "How can this happen?" (GA 7: 37). In the reply, there is a scarcely recognizable reference to "The Thing": "Here and now and in what is inconspicuous" (*im Geringen*) (GA 7: 37). The inconspicuous presence of the thing is the concluding point of the essay on "The Thing." But this trace of the thing in the technology essay is all but obscured by the discussion of art that Heidegger thinks is our best hope, since art is both akin to the essence of technology and "fundamentally different" from it (GA 7: 39).

In 1962, Heidegger once more published "The Question Concerning Technology," this time under separate cover along with the fourth Bremen lecture, "The Turn." In the prefatory remark he acknowledges their origin in the Bremen lectures. Of "The Question" he says that it is an enlarged version of the second lecture. The fourth lecture, "The Turn," is unchanged, he says further. We can now see that his last remark is accurate. "The Question," however, though enlarged in some parts (parts one and two, for example), is quite different from "The Framework" (*das Ge-Stell*) in the Bremen version.

"The Question" is entirely rewritten. There are only a few verbatim sentences left from "The Framework." Compared with "The Framework," "The Question" is less immediate, less impassioned, less involved in its terminology, and innocent of all the direct references to "The Thing." Heidegger must have been concerned to publish a measured and simplified analysis of technology that was not susceptible to easy dismissal on the grounds that his presentation of technology was hopelessly mixed up with a nostalgic invocation of a thing and a world that were irrevocably past. Nor did he want to be accused of cultural prejudice and partisanship.

To speak in more detail, Heidegger added the notion of the path of thinking and of ancient making as revealing to disarm the reader of what Heidegger took to be unhelpful beliefs in cogent argument and in making as manufacturing. In the analysis

429

of technology he dropped terms such as *circulation* and *rotation*, which had been parts of the framework in the Bremen lecture, and *machination* and *machinery*, which were remnants of the older terminology in *Contributions* (GA 79: 29, 34, 35, 38). Distrusting his description of "The Thing," he turned instead to art as a possible turning point, although he had, in the postscript to "The Origin of the Work of Art," agreed with Hegel that the vigor of art had passed and was lost (GA 5: 67–70).

In the prefatory remark to the 1962 edition, Heidegger claimed that the Bremen lecture "The Danger" "remains unpublished" (Heidegger 1962: 3). But the crucial part was in fact incorporated in "The Question." What Heidegger tellingly omitted was the danger that lay in the "refusal of world" that comes to pass "as the neglect of the thing" (GA 79: 51). It is not only the unwelcome mention of the thing that made Heidegger think better of including this part. The German for "neglect," *die Verwahrlosung*, derives from a verb that means "to run down," "to mistreat," "to make shabby." This was the kind of anger and distress that Heidegger wanted to avoid (although here, as in *Being and Time*, Heidegger, having introduced a damning vocable, immediately denies that it carries a "value judgment") (GA 79: 47).

The same concern to move away from involvement in the issues of the day and the promptings of the heart governed the transition from "The Framework" to "The Question." Compare these two passages, both at the conclusion of a paragraph, the first from *The Bremen Lectures*, the second from "The Question." "Agriculture is now mechanized food industry, essentially the same thing as the production of corpses in gas chambers and annihilation camps, the same thing as the blockade and intentional starvation of countries, the same thing as the production of hydrogen bombs" (GA 79: 27). "Agriculture is now a mechanized food industry. Air is positioned to yield nitrogen, the ground to yield ore, the ore to yield, for example, uranium, this to yield nuclear energy that can be released for destruction or peaceful use" (GA 7: 18–19).

One has to respect Heidegger's decision to make his case for the essence of technology in the kind of judicious and even-minded manner that was least likely to be rejected because of incidental and subsidiary issues. But even in its more orderly version, the analysis of technology digresses and wanders. By the standards of reasoning that proceeds from premises and evidence via rigorous inferences to clear conclusions, "The Question" does not score very well (Feenberg forthcoming). To be told that his essay wanders might not have troubled Heidegger. He begins, after all, by characterizing the piece as a path rather than an argument.

The objection that "The Question" concludes with an unsatisfactory answer and that the thing in his eminent sense rather than art should be the reply to the danger of technology might have mattered more to Heidegger. In fact, eight years after the first publication of "The Question," he added the concluding Bremen lecture, "The Turn," to the reprinting of "The Question." The last Bremen lecture asserts a close connection between the framework of technology and the fourfold of the thing (and Heidegger inserted a direct reference to "The Thing" in "The Turn"; Heidegger 1962: 42).

But that connection raises a problem that goes deeper than the economy of presentation and pedagogy. In *The Bremen Lectures*, "The Thing" comes first, and "The Framework" follows as the subversion of the thing and its world. The proposition that the thing in turn follows the framework as the response to the danger of technology is asserted but not credibly disclosed (Feenberg forthcoming). Whether the case can be made is a question that the philosophy of technology, inspired by Heidegger, has paid little attention to. To the contrary, the passionate engagement and the attention to topical issues that the older Heidegger had abandoned have in fact been embraced at least by much of American philosophy of technology – independently of Heidegger, perhaps, since the *Contributions* and *The Bremen Lectures* were not published until 1989 and 1994.

There are additional problems in "The Question." A second problem concerns the relation of the disclosure of the framework and the involvement of humanity. Were humans free to participate in this revelation or not? Clearly Heidegger intended a relation beyond the antinomy of libertarianism and determinism. But it is less than clear how an alternative position can be worked out on Heideggerian premises.

A third problem lies in the failure of the framework to shed any light on the attractiveness of technology. It is not enough to say it is the encompassing and pervasive culture and sweeps everything before it. Epochal changes come in different flavors, as curses and as blessings, as oppressions and as liberations. Heidegger, when talking about technology, addresses its aggressive and strenuous side. He says nothing about the pleasures of consumption, though, when talking about contemporary culture more generally, he does, and did so rather early, score the slackness and languor that are consequences of consumption (GA 29/30: 7, 32, 238, 240–1, 245, 426; GA 65: 61–2).

The fourth and final problem revolves about the technology – society relation. Even if the thing and its fourfold world turned out to be the fruitful counter and turning point for the problem of technology, we would still be left with the question of how this solution can be made socially and politically fruitful. There is a large gap between the profundity of Heidegger's thoughts on the thing and technology and the ailments that trouble us in the broad daylight of contemporary politics and culture.

The importance of Heidegger's philosophy of technology is threefold. Most importantly, he shows that technology is a phenomenon of deep roots, wide sweep, and radical effects. Thus he has inspired serious and painstaking work in the philosophy of technology. Second is his apt choice of examples. They are concrete, varied, and provocative and suggest investigations and arguments that Heidegger himself never took the time to pursue. Finally there is Heidegger's practice of capturing his insights in a firm and distinctive terminology. Good terminology prevents insights from evaporating and lends guidance to further exploration.

How influential has Heidegger's philosophy of technology been? The scholarly reception in the Anglo-American world has been slow and awkward at first and limited to this day (Borgmann and Mitcham 1987). As a cursory look at the *Philosopher's Index* or at cyberspace via a search engine shows, Heidegger is widely discussed today. But attention to his philosophy of technology has remained a small part of the overall interest in his work. However, his influence on American philosophy of technology, among the most vigorous schools in the world, has been significant. In a collection of essays on *American Philosophy of Technology* (Achterhuis 2001), Heidegger is easily the most frequently mentioned figure.

In the culture at large, Heidegger's involvement with the Nazis has been much more thoroughly discussed than his philosophy of technology. Thus Heidegger's attempt to protect the thrust of his thought by playing down and misrepresenting his participation in the Nazi movement proved counter-productive. Has there been any detectable

Heideggerian influence in the wider cultural conversation? Consider the work of Bill McKibben (2003). His work is widely known and his critique of technology as a pervasive and perilous force and his devotion to a grounded sort of life as an antidote is clearly congenial with Heidegger's thought. But McKibben never mentions Heidegger, and whether there is some indirect influence of Heidegger's is hard to say.

References and further reading

Achterhuis, H. (ed.) (2001) *American Philosophy of Technology* (trans. R. P. Crease). Indianapolis: Indiana University Press.

Blackburn, S. (2000) Enquivering. *New Republic*, October 30, 43–8.

Borgmann, A., with Mitcham, C. (1987) The question of Heidegger and technology: a critical review of the literature. *Philosophy Today*, 33, 97–194.

Dreyfus, H. and Wrathall, M. (eds.) (2002) *Heidegger Reexamined: Art, Poetry, and Technology*. New York: Routledge.

Feenberg, A. (forthcoming) *Heidegger and Marcuse: The Catastrophe and Redemption of Technology*. New York: Routledge.

Heidegger, M. (1947) *Platons Lehre von der Wahrheit mit einem Brief über den Humanismus*. Berne: Francke.

Heidegger, M. (1954) *Vorträge und Aufsätze*. Pfullingen: Neske.

Heidegger, M. (1962) *Die Technik und die Kehre*. Pfullingen: Neske.

Heidegger, M. (1977) *The Question Concerning Technology and Other Essays* (trans. W. Lovitt). New York: Harper.

Heidegger, M. (1979) *Sein und Zeit*. Tübingen: Niemeyer.

Heidegger, M. (1999) *Contributions to Philosophy (from Enowning)* (trans. P. Emad and K. Maly). Bloomington: Indiana University Press.

McKibben, B. (2003) *Enough: Staying Human in an Engineered Age*. New York: Times Books.

Ott, H. (1988) *Martin Heidegger* (trans. A. Blunden). New York: Basic Books.

27

Heidegger on Language

CHARLES TAYLOR

I want to offer a reading of Heidegger's views on language which places him within the context of the revolutionary change in the understanding of language and art that took place in the late eighteenth century in Germany. I believe this is the most fruitful context in which to set his writings on this topic.

I

The late Heidegger's doctrine of language is strongly anti-subjectivist. He even inverts the usual relation in which language is seen as our tool, and speaks of language speaking, rather than human beings ("denn eigentlich spricht die Sprache"; GA 7: 194). This formulation is hardly transparent on first reading. But I think we can understand it if we first place Heidegger against the background of the tradition of thought about language which I have just invoked, and then try to define his originality in relation to this tradition.

I want to call this line of thinking "expressive-constitutive." It arises in the late eighteenth century in reaction to the mainline doctrine about language which develops within the confines of modern epistemology, the philosophy articulated in different ways by Hobbes, Locke, and Condillac. On this view, language is conceived as an instrument. The constitutive theory reacts against this, and Heidegger's image of language speaking can be seen as a development out of this original reaction.

The issue between the two views could perhaps be understood in this way. The mainline, instrumental view was an "enframing"[1] theory. I want to use this term to describe attempts to understand language within the framework of a picture of human life, behavior, purposes, or mental functioning, which is itself described and defined without reference to language. Language can be seen as arising within this framework, and fulfilling some function within it, but the framework itself precedes, or at least can be characterized independently of language. By contrast, a "constitutive" theory gives us

This chapter is a revised version of Taylor, Charles, "Heidegger, Language, and Ecology" from *Heidegger: A Critical Reader*, edited by Hubert L. Dreyfus and Harrison Hall. Oxford: Blackwell, 1992. Reprinted with permission.

a picture of language as making possible new purposes, new levels of behavior, new meanings, and hence as not explicable within a framework picture of human life conceived without language.

A good contemporary example of the enframing approach can be found in Steven Pinker. Language, Pinker says,

> does not call for sequestering the study of humans from the domain of biology, for a magnificent ability unique to a particular living species is far from unique in the animal kingdom. Some kinds of bats home in on flying insects using Doppler sonar. Some kinds of migratory birds navigate thousands of miles by calibrating the positions of the constellations against the time of day and year. In nature's talent show we are simply a species of primate with our own act, a knack for communicating information about who did what to whom by modulating the sounds we make when we exhale. (Pinker 1994: 19)

It is typical of Pinker's approach that he identifies the issue of whether the study of humanity "should be sequestered from the domain of biology" (which few in their right minds would propose) with the issue of whether a reductive, enframing theory of language is viable (which is highly dubious).

The classical case, and most influential first form of an enframing theory, was the set of ideas developed from Locke through Hobbes to Condillac. I have discussed this in "Language and Human Nature" (Taylor 1985). Briefly, the Hobbes–Locke–Condillac (HLC) form of theory tried to understand language within the confines of the modern representational epistemology made dominant by Descartes. In the mind, there are "ideas." These are bits of putative representation of reality, much of it "external." Knowledge consists in having the representation actually square with the reality. This we can only hope to achieve if we put together our ideas according to a responsible procedure. Our beliefs about things are constructed, they result from a synthesis. The issue is whether the construction will be reliable and responsible or indulgent, slapdash, and delusory.

Language plays an important role in this construction. Words are given meaning by being attached to the things represented via the "ideas" which represent them. The introduction of words greatly facilitates the combination of ideas into a responsible picture. This facilitation is understood in different ways. For Hobbes and Locke, they allow us to grasp things in classes, and hence make possible synthesis wholesale where non-linguistic intuition would be confined to the painstaking association of particulars (Hobbes 1947: 20; Locke 1975: section 3.3.2). Condillac thinks that the introduction of language gives us for the first time control over the whole process of association; it affords us "empire sur son imagination" (Condillac 1746: sections 1.2.4.45–6).

The constitutive theory finds its most energetic early expression in Herder, precisely in a criticism of Condillac. In a famous passage of the treatise on the "Ursprung der Sprache," Herder repeats Condillac's fable – one might say "just so" story – of how language might have arisen between two children in a desert (Herder 1975: 12–14). But he professes to find something missing in this account. It seems to him to presuppose what it is meant to explain. What it is meant to explain is language, the passage from a condition in which the children emit just animal cries to the stage where they use words with meaning. The association between sign and some mental content is already there with the animal cry (what Condillac calls the "natural sign"). What is new with the "instituted sign" is that the children can now use it to focus on and manipulate the associated idea, and hence direct the whole play of their imagination. The transition just amounts to their tumbling to the notion that the association can be used in this way.

This is the classic case of an enframing theory. Language is understood in terms of certain elements: ideas, signs, and their association, which precede its arising. Before and after, the imagination is at work and association takes place. What is new is that now the mind is in control. This itself is, of course, something that didn't exist before. But the theory establishes the maximal possible continuity between before and after. The elements are the same, combination continues, only the direction changes. We can surmise that it is precisely this continuity which gives the theory its seeming clarity and explanatory power: language is robbed of its mysterious character, is related to elements that seem unproblematic.

Herder starts from the intuition that language makes possible a different kind of consciousness, which he calls "reflective" (*besonnen*). That is why he finds a continuity explanation like Condillac's so frustrating and unsatisfying. The issue of what this new consciousness consists in and how it arises is not addressed, as far as Herder is concerned, by an account in terms of pre-existing elements. That is why he accuses Condillac of begging the question. "Der Abt Condillac . . . hat das ganze Ding Sprache schon vor der ersten Seite seines Buchs erfunden vorausgesetzt" (Herder 1975: 12).

What did Herder mean by "reflection" (*Besonnenheit*)? This is harder to explain. We might try to formulate it this way: pre-linguistic beings can react to the things which surround them. But language enables us to grasp something *as* what it is. This explanation is hardly transparent, but it puts us on the track. Herder's basic idea seems to be that while a pre-linguistic animal can learn to respond to some object appropriately in the light of its purposes, only the being with language can identify the object as of a certain kind, can, as we might put it, attribute such and such a property to it. An animal, in other terms, can learn to give the right response to an object – fleeing a predator, say, or going after food – where "rightness" means "appropriate to its (non-linguistic) purposes." But language use involves another kind of rightness. Using the right word involves identifying an object as having the properties which justify using that word. We can't give an account of this rightness in terms of extralinguistic purposes. Rightness here is irreducible to success in some extralinguistic task.[2]

Now to be sensitive to the issue of non-reductive rightness is to be operating, as it were, in another dimension. Let me call this the "semantic dimension." Then we can say that properly linguistic beings are functioning in the semantic dimension. And that can be our way of formulating Herder's point about "reflection." To be reflective is to operate in this dimension, which means acting out of sensitivity to issues of irreducible rightness.

But we need to extend somewhat our notion of the semantic dimension. My remarks above seemed to concern purely descriptive rightness. But we do more things in language than describe. There are other ways in which a word can be "le mot juste." For instance, I come up with a word to articulate my feelings, and thus at the same time shape them in a certain manner. This is a function of language which cannot be

435

reduced to simple description, at least not description of an independent object. Or else I say something which re-establishes the contact between us, puts us once again on a close and intimate footing. We need a broader concept of irreducible rightness than just that involved in aligning words with objects.

Thus when I hit on the right word to articulate my feelings, and acknowledge that I am motivated by envy, say, the term does its work because it is the right term. In other words, we can't explain the rightness of the word "envy" here simply in terms of the condition that using it produces; rather we have to account for its producing this condition – here, a successful articulation – in terms of its being the right word. A contrast case should make this clearer. Say that every time I get stressed out, tense, and cross-pressured, I take a deep breath, and blow it explosively out of my mouth, "how!" I immediately feel calmer and more serene. This is plainly the "right sound" to make, as defined by this desirable goal of restored equilibrium. The rightness of "how!" admits of a simple task account. That is because we can explain the rightness simply in terms of its bringing about calm, and don't need to explain its bringing about calm in terms of rightness.

This last clause points up the contrast with "envy" as the term which articulates/clarifies my feelings. It brings about this clarification, to be sure, and that is essential to its being the right word here. But central to its clarifying is its being the right word. So we can't just explain its rightness by its *de facto* clarifying. You can't define its rightness by the *de facto* causal consequence of clarifying, in other words, you can't make this outcome criterial for its rightness, because you don't know whether it is clarifying unless you know that it is the right term; whereas in the case of "how!" all there was to its rightness was its having the desired outcome; the bare *de facto* consequence is criterial. That is why normally we wouldn't be tempted to treat this expletive as though it had a meaning.

Something similar can be said about my restoring the intimacy between us by saying "I'm sorry." This was "the right thing to say," because it restored contact. But at the same time, we can say that these words are efficacious in restoring contact because of what they mean. Irreducible rightness enters into the account here, because what the words mean can't be defined by what they bring about. Again, we might imagine that I could also set off a loud explosion in the neighborhood, which would so alarm you that you would forget about our tiff and welcome my presence. This would then be, from a rather cold-blooded, strategic perspective, the "right move." But the explosion "means" nothing.

What this discussion is moving us toward is a definition of the semantic dimension in terms of the possibility of a reductive account of rightness. A simple task account of rightness for some sign reduces it to a matter of efficacy for some non-semantic purpose. We are in the semantic dimension when this kind of reduction cannot work, when a kind of rightness is at issue which cannot be cashed out in this way. That is why the image of a new "dimension" seems to me apposite. To move from non-linguistic to linguistic agency is to move to a world in which a new kind of issue is at play, a right use of signs which is not reducible to task-rightness. The world of the agent has a new axis on which to respond; its behavior can no longer be understood just as the purposive seeking of ends on the old plane. It is now responding to a new set of demands. Hence the image of a new dimension.

436

If we interpret him in this way, we can understand Herder's impatience with Condillac. The latter's "natural signs" were things like cries of pain or distress. Their right use in communication could only be construed on the simple task model. Language arose supposedly when people learned to use the connection already established by the natural sign, between, say, the cry and what caused the distress, in a controlled way. The "instituted sign" is born, an element of language properly speaking. Herder cannot accept that the transition from pre-language to language consists simply in a taking control of a pre-existing process. What this leaves out is precisely that a new dimension of issues becomes relevant, that the agent is operating on a new plane. Hence in the same passage in which he declares Condillac's account circular, Herder reaches for a definition of this new dimension, with his term "reflection."

On my reconstruction, Herder's "reflection" is to be glossed as the semantic dimension, and his importance is that he made this central to any account of language. Moreover, Herder's conception of the semantic dimension was multifaceted, along the lines of the broad conception of rightness above. It didn't just involve description. Herder saw that opening this dimension has to transform all aspects of the agent's life. It will also be the seat of new emotions. Linguistic beings are capable of new feelings which affectively reflect their richer sense of their world: not just anger, but indignation; not just desire, but love and admiration.

The semantic dimension also made the agent capable of new kinds of relations, new sorts of footings that agents can stand on with each other, of intimacy and distance, hierarchy and equality. Gragarious apes may have (what we call) a "dominant male," but only language beings can distinguish between leader, king, president, and the like. Animals mate and have offspring, but only language beings define kinship.

Underlying both emotions and relations is another crucial feature of the linguistic dimension, that it makes possible value in the strong sense. Pre-linguistic animals treat something as desirable or repugnant by going after it or avoiding it. But only language beings can identify things as *worthy* of desire or aversion. For such identifications raise issues of intrinsic rightness. They involve a characterization of things which is not reducible simply to the ways we treat them as objects of desire or aversion. They involve a recognition beyond that, that they *ought* to be treated in one or another way.

II

Now this theory of language which gives a privileged place to the semantic dimension deserves the appellation "constitutive" in an obvious sense, in that language enters into or makes possible a whole range of crucially human feelings, activities, relations. It bursts the framework of pre-linguistic life forms, and therefore renders any enframing account inadequate. But the constitutive theory which Herder's critique inaugurates has another central feature, that it gives a creative role to expression.

Views of the HLC type related linguistic expression to some pre-existing content. A word is introduced by being linked with an idea, and henceforth becomes capable of expressing it, for Locke (1975, section 3.2.2). The content precedes its external means of expression. Condillac develops a more sophisticated conception. He argues that introducing words ("instituted signs"), because it gives us greater control over the train of thoughts, allows us to discriminate more finely the nuances of our ideas. This means that we identify finer distinctions, which we in turn can name, which will again allow us to make still more subtle discriminations, and so on. In this way, language makes possible science and enlightenment. But at each stage of this process, the idea precedes its naming, albeit that its discriminability results from a previous act of naming.

Condillac also gave emotional expression an important role in the genesis of language. His view was that the first instituted signs were framed from natural ones. But natural signs were just the in-built expressions of our emotional states, animal cries of joy or fear. That language originated from the expressive cry became the consensus in the learned world of the eighteenth century. But the conception of expression here was quite inert. What the expression conveyed was thought to exist independently of its utterance. Cries made fear or joy evident to others, but they didn't help to constitute these feelings themselves.

Herder develops a quite different notion of expression. This is in the logic of a constitutive theory, as I have just described it. This tells us that language constitutes the semantic dimension, that is, that possessing language enables us to relate to things in new ways, e.g. as loci of features, and to have new emotions, goals, and relationships, as well as being responsive to issues of strong value. We might say: language transforms our world, using this last word in a clearly Heidegger-derived sense. That is, we are talking not of the cosmos out there, which preceded us and is indifferent to us, but of the world of our involvements, including all the things they incorporate in their meaning for us.

Then we can rephrase the constitutive view by saying that language introduces new meanings in our world: the things which surround us become potential bearers of properties; they can have new emotional significance for us, e.g. as objects of admiration or indignation; our links with others can count for us in new ways, as "lovers," "spouses," or "fellow citizens"; and they can have strong value.

But then this involves attributing a creative role to expression. Bringing things to speech can't mean just making externally available what is already there. There are many banal speech acts where this seems to be all that is involved. But language as a whole must involve more than this, because it is also opening possibilities for us which wouldn't be there in its absence.

The constitutive theory turns our attention toward the creative dimension of expression, in which, to speak paradoxically, it makes possible its own content. We can actually see this in familiar, everyday realities, but it tends to be screened out from the enframing perspective, and it took the development of constitutive theories to bring it to light.

A good example is the "body language" of personal style. We see the leather-jacketed motorbike rider step away from his machine and swagger toward us with an exaggeratedly leisurely pace. This person is "saying something" in his way of moving, acting, speaking. He may have no words for it, though we might want to apply the hispanic word "macho" as at least a partial description. Here is an elaborate way of being in the world, of feeling and desiring and reacting, which involves great sensitivity to certain things (like slights to one's honor: we are now the object of his attention, because we unwittingly cut him off at the last intersection), and cultivated-but-supposedly-spontaneous insensitivity to others (like the feelings of dudes and females); which involves certain prized pleasures (riding around at high speed with the gang) and others which are despised (listening to sentimental songs); and this way of being is coded as strongly valuable; that is, being this way is admired, and failing to be earns contempt.

But how coded? Not, presumably, in descriptive terms, or at least not adequately. The person may not have a term like "macho" which articulates the value involved. What terms he does have may be woefully inadequate to capture what is specific to this way of being; the epithets of praise or opprobrium may only be revelatory in the whole context of this style of action; by themselves they may be too general. Knowing that X is "one of the boys" and Y is a "dude" may tell us little. The crucial coding is in the body expressive language.

The bike rider's world incorporates the strong value of this way of being. Let's call it (somewhat inadequately, but we need a word) "machismo." But how does this meaning exist for him? Only through the expressive gesture and stance. It is not just that an outside observer would have no call to attribute machismo to him without this behavior. It is more radically that a strong value like this can only exist for him articulated in some form. It is this expressive style that enables machismo to exist for him, and more widely this domain of expressive body language is the locus of a whole host of different value-coded ways of being for humans in general. The expression makes possible its content; the language opens us out to the domain of meaning it encodes. Expression is no longer simply inert.

But when we turn back from this rather obvious case to the original description case, which was central to HLC theories, we see it in a new light. Here too expression must be seen as creative, language opens us to the domain it encodes. What descriptive speech encodes is our attribution of properties to things. But possessing this descriptive language is the condition of our being sensitive to the issues of irreducible rightness which must be guiding us if we are really to be attributing properties, as we saw above. So seeing expression as creative generates Herder's constitutive theory as applied to descriptive language.

This illustrates the inner connections, both historical and logical, between the constitutive theory and a strong view of expression. Either the espousal of the first can lead one to look for places where expression obviously opens us to its own content, which we will find in this domain of body language, and with emotional expression generally. Or the sense that expression is creative, which will likely strike us if we are attending closely to the life of the emotions, will lead us to revise our understanding of the much-discussed case of description. In the case of Herder, the connections probably go in both directions, but if anything the second is more important than the first. The major proponents of the HLC were all rationalists in some sense; one of their central goals was to establish reason on a sound basis, and their scrutiny of language had largely this end in view. The proto-Romantic move to dethrone reason, and to locate the specifically human capacities in feeling, naturally led to a richer concept of expression than was allowed for in Condillac's natural cries, which were quite inert modes of utterance. From the standpoint of this richer notion, even the landscape of descriptive speech begins to look very different. But whatever the direction of travel, a road links the constitutive insight with the strong view of expression, so that the alternative to the enframing theory might with equal justice be called the constitutive-expressive.[3]

There are three further features of this view as it developed to its mature form which it would be useful to draw out here. The first is that attributing the central role to expression leads to a redefinition of what it is to acquire language. The crucial step is no longer seen as taking on board a *mental capacity* to link sign and idea, but as coming to engage in the *activity* of (overt) *speech*. In Humboldt's famous formulation, we have to think of language primarily as *energeia*, not just as *ergon* (Humboldt 1988: 49).

This speech activity has an inescapable expressive-projective dimension; even when we are engaged in disinterested description, we are as speakers projecting a certain stance to our interlocutors and to the matter at hand. But it has another feature as well, and this is the second that I want to touch on here. It is conversation. The first, and inescapable, locus of language is in exchange between interlocutors. Language involves certain kinds of links with others. In particular, it involves the link of being a conversational partner with somebody; let's call this an "interlocutor." Standing to someone as an interlocutor is fundamentally different from standing to him or her as an object of observation, or manipulative interaction. Language marks this most fundamental distinction in the difference of persons. I address someone as "you," speak of them as "him" or "her."

What this corresponds to is the way in which we create a common space by opening a conversation. A conversation has the status of a common action. When I open up about the weather to you over the back fence, what this does is make the weather an object for *us*. It is no longer just for you, and for me, with perhaps the addition that I know it is for you and you know it is for me. Conversation transposes it into an object which we are considering together. The considering is common, in that the background understanding established is that the agency which is doing the considering is us together, rather than each of us on our own managing to dovetail his or her action with the other.[4]

Third, implicit in this Herder–Humboldt understanding of language is the recognition that the constitutive forms of expression, those which open us to a new range of meanings, go beyond descriptive language, and even beyond speech of any form, to such things as gesture and stance.

This suggests that the phenomenon which needs to be carved out for explanation is the whole range of expressive-constitutive forms, that we are unlikely to understand descriptive language unless we can place it in a broader theory of such forms, which must hence be our prior target. This view is strengthened when we reflect how closely connected the different forms are. Our projections are carried at once in linguistic (speech style and rhetoric) and in extralinguistic (gesture, stance) form. Description is always embedded in acts which also projectively express. The idea that these could be treated as a single range was already pre-delineated in the definition I gave earlier of the semantic dimension. For even the projections of body language fit within its scope, as having their own kind of intrinsic rightness. The swagger of our bike rider is right in relation to the way of being he values, in a way which cannot be accounted for in terms of a simple task.

So constitutive theories go for the full range of expressive forms (what Cassirer 1953 called the "symbolic forms"). Now within these falls another sub-range not mentioned so far, the work of art, something which is neither expressive projection nor description. In a sense, the work of art played an even more important role in the development of expressivism than what I have been calling projection. We can see this in the conception of the symbol, as opposed to the allegory, which played an important role in the aesthetic of the Romantic period and, indeed, since. As described, for instance, by Goethe, the symbol was a paradigm of what I have been calling constitutive expression.

A work of art which was "allegorical" presented us with some insight or truth which we could also have access to more directly. An allegory of virtue and vice as two animals, say, will tell us something which could also be formulated in propositions about virtue and vice. By contrast, a work of art had the value of a symbol[5] when it manifested something which could not be thus "translated." It opens access to meanings which cannot be made available any other way. Each truly great work is in this way *sui generis*. It is untranslatable.

This notion, which has its roots in Kant's Third Critique, was immensely influential. It was taken up by Schopenhauer and all those he influenced, in their understanding of the work of art as manifesting what can't be said in assertions in ordinary speech. And its importance for Heidegger in his own variant needs no stressing. I return to this shortly.

The work of art as symbol was perhaps the paradigm on which the early constitutive theories of language were built. In its very definition, there is an assertion of the plurality of expressive forms, in the notion that it is untranslatable into prose. From this standpoint, the human expressive-constitutive power – or, alternatively, the semantic dimension – has to be seen as a complex and many-layered thing, in which the higher modes are embedded in the lower ones.

Outside of the attribution of properties, I mentioned above three other ranges of meanings which are opened to us by language: the properly human emotions, certain relations, and strong value. But each of these is carried on the three levels of expressive form that crystalized out of the above discussion: the projective, the symbolic (in works of art), and the descriptive. We express our emotions, and establish our relations, and body forth our values, in our body language, style, and rhetoric; but we can also articulate all of these in poetry, novels, dance, music; and we can also bring all of them to descriptive articulation, where we name the feelings, relations, and values, and describe and argue about them.

III

I have developed this portrait of the constitutive-expressive theory at length, because I think Heidegger's own views on language stand squarely within this tradition. Heidegger is a constitutive theorist. By this I mean not just that he happens to have such a theory of language, but also that it plays an essential role in his thinking.

There may be some question about this in relation to Heidegger's early writings, but his thinking after the "Kehre" seems to be articulating the central notions of the constitutive view. To describe language as the "house of being," for instance, is to give it a

441

more than instrumental status. Indeed, Heidegger repeatedly inveighs against those views of language which reduce it to a mere instrument of thought or communication. Language is essential to the "clearing."

Heidegger stands in the Herder tradition. But he transposes this mode of thinking in his own characteristic fashion. While Herder in inaugurating the constitutive view still speaks in terms of "reflection," which sounds like a form of consciousness, Heidegger clearly turns the issue around, and sees language as what opens access to meanings. Language discloses. The deeper and darker and more difficult and problematic thesis, that language speaks, is something I want to go into in a minute. But at least it is clear that language is seen as the condition of the human world being disclosed. The disclosure is not intrapsychic, but occurs in the space between humans; indeed, it helps to define the space that humans share.

This is already clear in "The Origin of the Work of Art," as is, incidentally, Heidegger's debt to the whole expressivist topos of the symbol. The work of art brings about the crucial constituting disclosure of a way of life, in a way that no set of mere descriptive propositions could. These could as descriptions be "correct"; that is, they could represent reality rightly. But the work of art isn't a representation, at least not primarily. "Ein Bauwerk, ein griechischer Tempel, bildet nichts ab" ("A building, a Greek temple, portrays nothing"; GA 5: 27/Heidegger 1971: 41). It defines the objects of strong value: "Das Tempelwerk fügt erst und sammelt zugleich um sich die Einheit jener Bahnen und Bezüge, in denen Geburt und Tod, Unheil und Segen, Sieg und Schmach, Ausharren und Verfall die Gestalt und den Lauf des Menschenwesens in seinem Geschick gewinnen" ("It is the temple-work that first fits together and at the same time gathers around itself the unity of those paths and relations in which birth and death, disaster and blessing, victory and disgrace, endurance and decline acquire the shape of destiny for human being"; GA 5: 27–8/Heidegger 1971: 42). It does this not for individuals, but for a people: "Die waltende Weite dieser offenen Bezüge ist die Welt dieses geschichtlichen Volkes" ("The all-governing expanse of this open relational context is the world of this historical people"; GA 5: 28/Heidegger 1971: 42).

These crucial theses of the expressive-constitutive view are clearly recaptured by Heidegger in his own fashion, no longer as truths about "consciousness," but as crucial conditions of Being, or the clearing.[6]

IV

But Heidegger is more than just a constitutive theorist. He also has his very original position within this camp, in particular in his late philosophy. Here we find dark sayings of the kind that I have just adverted to above, that it is not humans that speak, but language. I don't claim to understand these fully, but I think they can be made partly intelligible if we develop further certain potentialities which are implicit in any constitutive theory, but which were not fully explored by his predecessors.

This theory rests on the central intuition that it is through language that disclosure to humans takes place. Animals may have their own kind of clearing,[7] but ours is constituted by language. In particular, ours is a world in which things have worth, in which there are goods in the strong sense: things which are *worth* pursuing.

Goods show up through finding expression, paradigmatically "symbolic," in terms of Goethe's distinction; as the goods of the Greeks showed up in the temple. Human beings build the temple. So constitutive theory puts a new question on the agenda, i.e. what is the nature of this (in one obvious sense) human power of expression, which has such fateful consequences?

This is the basis for a massive parting of the ways. Different answers to this question are central to most traditions of "continental" philosophy, from the followers of Schopenhauer, through Heidegger and those he has influenced, to the deconstructionists and postmodernists. The issue has also been central to modernist poetics. Enframing theories, either in mainline semantics or in post-Fregean theories of language like Davidson's, are on a completely different wavelength, because for them the question doesn't even exist. How could it? Only a constitutive theory can put it on the agenda. This, I think, is one of the most important sources of that talking past each other which we see when these two modes of philosophizing meet.

This issue connects up in a certain way with the very beginning of our philosophical tradition. Aristotle defined the human being as "*zoon echon logon*." This was usually translated as "rational animal." But Heidegger suggested that one go back behind the traditional interpretation that this rendering enshrines, and simply say "animal possessing logos," with all the polysemy of that latter term, which centers, however, on language. Humans are language animals. They are beings who somehow possess, or are the locus of, this constitutive power of expression. In order to know the essence of human beings, you have to understand this power, i.e. language in the broad sense constitutivists use the term. This will give you the aret*ē* of human beings, what the life is proper for them. Aristotle can be read as proceeding in this way (*Ethics* I.7), and so can Heidegger, with all the massive differences.

So the task is: explain the constitutive dimension of language; explain the power of expression. Our temptation right off is to see it as *our* power, something we exercise; disclosure is what we bring about. For Heidegger this is a deeply erroneous view, i.e. not just a trivial mistake, but one that is generated out of the thrust of our culture and tradition. This reading can be called subjectivist. But in fact it can take a number of forms, and in order to understand them, we should examine what is at stake.

Language is essential to what we could argue is the central focus of Heidegger's philosophy, early and late, the fact/event that things show up at all. We can call this by one of Heidegger's terms, the "clearing" (*Lichtung*). Heidegger taught us to reorder the history of philosophy and culture in the light of how the clearing was understood.

One crucial point for Heidegger is that the clearing cannot be identified with any of the entities which show up in it. It is not to be explained by them as something they cause, or one of their properties, or as grounded in them. Later Heidegger thought that some pre-Socratics had a vision which avoided this identification. But with Plato, Western culture starts on a fatal course. Plato's notion of the Idea places the clearing among beings. An Idea is not just another entity waiting to be discovered. It is not like the things which participate in it. It can be understood as self-manifesting. It gives itself to be understood. That is what underlies the image of light in which Plato frequently expounds the Ideas, and particularly that of the Good. This latter is likened to the sun; turning from the changing things of this world to the Ideas is likened to leaving the dark cave. Plato speaks of the soul turning to the illuminated side. And so on.

Plato, it can be said, had an ontic account of the clearing. It is still in an obvious sense a non-subjectivist one. But Heidegger thinks that it somehow put us on a slide toward subjectivism, perhaps because the very act of ontically placing the clearing reflects a drive toward grasping it, exercising intellectual control over it; and this fully worked out will emerge in the Will to Power. But in any case, the Platonic understanding gets transformed after Aristotle through a series of intermediate steps, each one more subjectivist, into a modern mode of thinking which explains the clearing through a power of the subject, that of representation. The understanding of reality as disposed through the power of a subject is greatly furthered by the medieval view of the world as the creation of an omnipotent God. This at first coexists with Platonic and Aristotelian theories of the Ideas; it is the high noon of what Heidegger calls "ontotheology." But its inherent thrust pushes toward a definition of being as what it is through the disposition of subjective power.

In the modern age, this takes form at first in the idealism which emerges out of the central tradition of modern epistemology, and which Heidegger thinks is already implicit in its founding figures, in, for example, Descartes and Locke. The real is what can be represented by a subject. This view culminates in various forms of non-realism. But for Heidegger the same thrust leads to our conceiving reality itself as emanating from will. It is to be understood in relation not just to the knowing subject, but to a subjectivity of striving and purpose. Leibniz is obviously one of the key figures in this development. But it reaches its culmination on the Nietzschean claim that everything is Will to Power.

Modern subjectivism onticizes the clearing in the opposite way from Platonism. Now things appear because there are subjects which represent them, and take a stand on them. The clearing is the fact of representation; and this only takes place in minds, or in the striving of subjects, or in their use of various forms of depiction, including language.

But the real nature of the clearing is neither of the above. Plato on one side, and most moderns on the other, can be seen as making equal and opposite mistakes. Each misses something important about it. The Platonic mode can't acknowledge our role. The clearing in fact comes to be only around Dasein. It is our being there which allows it to happen. At least the representational theory grasps that. But it on its side cannot appreciate that the clearing doesn't just happen within us, and/or is not simply our doing. Any doing of ours, any play with representations, supposes as already there the disclosure of things in language. We can't see this as something that we control, or that simply happens within our ambit. The notion that it is simply in our heads already supposes in order to make sense that we understand our heads and ourselves as placed in a world, and this understanding doesn't happen just in our heads. This would be Heidegger's remake of Hegel's disproof of the Kantian thing in itself. The idea that this clearing is our doing collapses into incoherence as well; it is only through the clearing that we have any idea of doing at all, that action is in our repertory.

So the clearing is Dasein-related yet not Dasein-controlled. It is not Dasein's doing. Here we can see how for Heidegger enframing theories of language are redolent of modern subjectivism. They purport to understand language, i.e. that whereby the clearing comes to be, as a mode of representation which functions within a human life whose purposes are not themselves set by language. Language is enframed, and can be seen as performing a set of functions which can, except for representation itself, be defined non-linguistically. Language is something we can use; it is an instrument. This instrumentalization of the clearing is one of the furthest expressions of the Will to Power.

Heidegger's position can be seen from one point of view as utterly different from both Platonism and subjectivism, because it avoids onticizing altogether; from another point of view, it can be seen as passing between them to a third position which neither can imagine, one which is Dasein-related, but not Dasein-centered.[8]

Now it seems obvious that Heidegger found some of the background he needed to develop this position out of the constitutive-expressive tradition. Its understanding of expression, in particular of the symbol, begins to explore this middle ground. The symbol is both manifestation and creation, partakes of both finding and making. The philosophies which arose out of the Romantic turn (which can't necessarily themselves be called "Romantic"), e.g. those of Schelling and Hegel, begin to stake out a middle position. In a sense, they have something in common with Plato, and with the whole ancient and medieval conception of a cosmic order which embodies Ideas. For Hegel reality conforms to the Idea. But at the same time, they see the cosmos as crucially incomplete until brought to its adequate expression in human-sustained media, e.g. Hegel's Art, Religion, and Philosophy. The Idea isn't a reality quite independent from the being which can bring it to manifestation, i.e. human being. But this way of differing from the ancients doesn't take the standard modern form of locating the clearing in representation. The expression-articulation of the Idea is not a mere representation, but a kind of completing; at the same time, the completing is not itself just a human achievement. The human agent is here an emanation of cosmic spirit.

What we can see from this is that the idea of expression itself can nudge us toward a third way of locating the clearing. It gives us a notion of the clearing which is essentially Dasein-related; in this it is at one with the standard modern view. But it doesn't place the clearing simply inside us as a representation; it puts it instead in a new space constituted by expression. And in some versions it can acknowledge that the constituting of this space is not simply our doing.

It can acknowledge, but doesn't necessarily do so. There are two issues here which we can distinguish. The first concerns the ontic status of the clearing. The second is rather a clutch of issues, and touches the nature of the expressive power itself.

As to the first, the space of expression is not the same as, that is, it can't be reduced to either ordinary physical space or inner "psychic" space, the domain of the "mind" on the classic epsitemological construal. It is not the same as the first, because it only gets set up between speakers. (It is Dasein-related.) It is not the same as the second, because it can't be placed "within" minds, but is out between the interlocutors, as we saw in the previous section. In conversation, a public or common space gets set up, in which the interlocutors are together.

If we see the clearing as the space opened by expression, then the basis is there for a de-onticizing move, relative to the categories of our modern ontology, matter and mind. For this space is neither. The move is made possible, but it isn't taken right away. Hegel still draws heavily on the old ontotheology, and the Chain of Being, to ground the manifestations of spirit. Later with Schopenhauer a strange new twist is introduced.

445

The ontic basis of expression is Will. But this is no longer seen as the benign source of being and goodness, but as the source of endless, disordered striving and suffering. This reversal undoubtedly helped to prepare the way for the move which Heidegger is the first to make explicitly, though one can perhaps see forerunners among those who prepared the way to modernist poetics, such as Mallarmé. In declaring the ontological difference, Heidegger is realizing a potentiality opened by expressivism.

When we turn to the second gamut of issues, we can see that the expressivist turn didn't put an end to subjectivism. On the contrary, it opens up a whole new range of forms, some of them among the most virulent. Here again, there is a potentiality, which may remain unrealized. What expressivism does is open the issue of the nature of the expressive power. The options are many. We can perhaps single out three sub-issues, which open up as it were a three-dimensional problem space, in which different thinkers and writers have located themselves.

(a) First, if, like the earlier theorists, e.g. Hegel, you see expression as bringing something to manifestation, then you can think of this reality as the self; and the essential activity is self-expression. Or one can identify it as something beyond the self; in Hegel's case, with a cosmic spirit or process. This is one dimension in which one can move toward subjective or objective poles.

(b) But then, more radically, one can challenge the whole idea that expression manifests something; one can see it not as a bringing to light, but as a bringing about. The space is something we make. The potentiality for this more radical subjectivism is already there in the canonical notion of the symbol current in the Romantic era. The symbol manifests something; but this doesn't mean that it simply copies some model already in view. It instead creates the medium in which some hitherto hidden reality can be manifest. Prior to expression, this reality is not something which *can* be in view, and hence there can be no question of copying. Manifesting through the symbol therefore involves an element of creation, the making, one might say, of a medium in which the reality can for the first time *appear*. If we add, as did Hegel and others, that appearance was part of the potentiality of what comes to light, then this creation also counts as bringing this reality to completion.

Expression partakes of both finding and making. In the original variant, there is a balance between the two, but the second basically is in the service of the first. The radical step is to overturn this balance, and to see the clearing as something projected. Through the power of expression we make this space, and what appears in it shouldn't be seen as a manifestation of anything. What appears is a function of the space itself. Once again, Mallarmé might be seen as one of the pioneers of this view, with his image of *le néant*. Nietzsche could be read as teetering on a knife-edge between the two views, and a term like "transfiguration" remains ambivalent between them. But the major carriers of the radical, "creationist" view today are deconstructionists, particularly Derrida, with slogans like: "il n'y a pas de hors-texte."

(c) There is a third issue on which one can be more or less subjectivist, and that is on the question of the "who?" of expression. Is it the work of the individual agent? Or is it something which arises out of the conversation, so that its locus is the speech community? Or should we think of the locutors themselves purely as artifacts of the space of expression, so that there is no "who" of expression at all? The first answer has been more or less discredited in the constitutivist tradition, for reasons which were touched

446

on in the earlier sections. The second, Humboldtian one has been the most widespread. Each locutor, as he or she enters the conversation from infancy, finds their identity shaped by their relations within a pre-existing space of expression. In this sense, they are the creatures of this space. But as they become full members of the conversation, they can in turn contribute to shape it, and so no simple one-sided relation of dependence can capture the reality of speakers and language, as the third theory supposes.

The third theory is exemplified by Derrida. "Différance" is the non-agent setting up the space of expression. This might be thought to be on the far anti-subjectivist end of the spectrum of this third question. But I believe that one should instead see the second, Humboldtian solution as the truly non-subjectivist one. The Derridean one is in fact the mirror image of the subjectivist outlook. It gets its plausibility from the implausibility of this outlook, which Derrida parades before us in its more extreme forms as the only alternative. But I haven't got space to argue this here.

These two main questions, the latter divided into three sub-issues, set up a problem space with many possible positions, combining different options on the various dimensions. The Derridean philosophy combines a radical "creationist" position on sub-issue (b) (hence question (a), which asks what is manifested, doesn't arise), with a relegation of the locutor to purely derivative status when it comes to (c). This is what gives his philosophy its strongly anti-subjectivist appearance, which I suggested is mere appearance. The rhetoric of the end of the subject masks the option in favor of a highly subjectivist stance on (b). In fact, one might argue that the relegation of the locutor on (c) is just another consequence of the radical creationism on (b). It is a corollary of the idealist thesis that there is no "hors-texte."

Heidegger stands quite differently in this space, I want to argue, so that Derridean readings gravely misperceive him. He is a "manifestationist" on sub-issue (b); his strong anti-subjectivist stance is taken on sub-issue (a). Expression is not self-expression; creative language is a response to a call. On sub-issue (c), he is pretty close to the Humboldtian view. Statements like the famous one in "Dichterisch wohnet der Mensch": "Denn eigentlich spricht die Sprache" (GA 7: 194/Heidegger 1971: 216) I understand as conveying his anti-subjectivist stand on (a), rather than a proto-Derridean invocation of a super(non)agent.

This makes Heidegger come pretty close to a commonly held position in the constitutivist tradition on the second complex of issues, about the nature of the expressive power. Where he departs radically is on the first main issue, in his thoroughgoing insistance that the clearing is not to be ontically grounded. This might be confused with the creationist view of the expressive power on sub-issue (b). But these are quite different questions. To see the clearing as not ontically grounded, or locatable, is not to see it as self-enclosed, as related to nothing outside it. A self-enclosed picture of the clearing would run clean against Heidegger's brand of anti-subjectivism.

What emerges with Heidegger is thus a novel position, one which was hard to imagine before he began to pose the questions of philosophy in his own peculiar way. The confusion between a de-onticized view of the clearing and a creationist one is easy to make if we operate in familiar categories. For most manifestationist readings of the space of expression were based on some firm ontic posits, which were thought to be the essential underpinnings of this reading, like Hegel's Geist, or Schopenhauer's Will, or

447

Nietzsche's Will to Power, for that matter. Denying these seemed to mean opting for a view of the space of expression as purely made.

But Heidegger alters the whole philosophical landscape by introducing the issue of the clearing and its ontic placing. Once we disintricate this question from that of the nature of the expressive power, we can combine a manifestationist view on this latter with a rejection of all ontic grounding. But on what, then, do we base this manifestationist view, if we can no longer recur to some ontic underpinnings of the familiar kind? On a reading of the space of expression itself. Otherwise put, the clearing itself, or language itself, properly brought to light, will show us how to take it. Heidegger as always moves to retrieve what is hidden, not in some beyond, but in the event of disclosure itself.

That is why I believe that articulating the themes of the constitutivist view of language can help in explaining Heidegger. He in fact draws on these, because he formulates the clearing through describing the action/event which makes it possible, and these are crucially linguistic.

Let me try to reconstruct Heidegger's démarche drawing on what has been said in earlier sections about language in the broad sense of the constitutivist tradition, that is, about the expressive power. We can follow the Aristotle-derived thread I mentioned at the beginning of this section: read the expressive power to glean the excellence, the aretē, implicit in it.

Through language, a world is disclosed; a world in which features are located, which is also a locus of strong goods, of objects of the specifically human emotions, of human relations. So plainly one telos, or range of telē, that we can find in language prescribe that this disclosure be properly done: that the features be correctly located, that the goods be fully acknowledged, that our emotions and relations be undistortedly discerned. Some of this range of goals is carried out in what we define as science; other parts require other types of discourse, including in their own way, literature and philosophy, and the other arts also have their articulative role.

This range of goals gives a manifestationist cast to the clearing. In the case of natural science, one might define the end as more like depiction, the representation of an independent object, but in, for example, clarifying emotions, language also helps to constitute, or complete; the model of the symbol is here the appropriate one. Attributing this approach to language to Heidegger makes of him an uncompromising realist, and that is what I think he was.

But beyond these goals of first-order disclosure, there is a telos in the clearing to disclose itself, to bring itself undistortedly to light. If its goal is undistorted uncovering, then how can this uncovering itself be an exception? Showing up should itself show up. But this makes a problem, because Heidegger has argued that there is a tendency precisely to distort our understanding of the clearing. At least in the tradition determined by our Western "destining," we come to see language as our instrument, and the clearing as something which happens in us, and reflects our goals and purposes. At the end of this road is the reduction of everything to standing reserve in the service of a triumphant will to will. In the attempt to impose our light, we cover the sources of the clearing in darkness. We close ourselves off to them.

That this second-order disclosure is part of the telos of language comes clear in Heidegger's notion that the total mobilization of everything as standing reserve threatens the human essence ("Die Frage nach der Technik," in GA 7: 9–39/Heidegger 1977: 3–35). For this is just the next stage in a basically Aristotelian line of argument. The human is *zoon echon logon*, "das Menschliche [ist] ist in seinem Wesen sprachlich" ("the human is indeed in its nature given to speech," GA 12: 27). So what goes against the telos of language goes against the human essence.

But I can already sense that some readers may be uneasy at this Aristotelizing of Heidegger. So let me hasten to point out the difference. The human essence is not here derived from the ontic examination of a particular species of hairless ape who happens to use language. We aren't deriving this from the nature of the "rational animal." It is, on the contrary, purely derived from the way of being of the clearing, by being attentive to the way that language opens a clearing. When we can bring this undistortedly to light, we see that it is not something we accomplish. It is not an artifact of ours, our "Gemächte." It must be there as the necessary context for all our acting and making. We can only act insofar as we are already in the midst of it. It couldn't happen without us, but it isn't our doing. It is the basis for all the sense that our lives make; or that anything makes. Hence the sense of our lives must at least include as a central element the part we play in the clearing coming to be. This is not the major role that a creator would have, but a secondary one, helping it to happen, protecting and maintaining it. We have to "take care" of (*pflegen*) being, "spare" (*schonen*) it ("Bauen Wohnen Denken" in GA 7: 145–64/Heidegger 1971: 145–61). The human agent is "the shepherd of being" ("Brief über den Humanismus" in GA 9: 331/252, 342/260: "Der Mensch ist Hirt des Seins").

Denying this role, trying to transform it into something else, acting as though we were in control, is going against our essence, and cannot but be destructive. The parallel with Aristotle's line of reasoning is unmistakable. It has been transposed, however, into a new key. Our essence is derived not from any ontic description, but from our role in relation to the clearing. That is why Heidegger sees his philosophy as non-, even anti-, humanist, aligning "humanism" as he does with an anthropocentric doctrine of human control.

But how do you acknowledge the way of being of the clearing? How do you make showing up undistortively show up? Disclosure is not some extra entity over and above the ones which show up. So meta-disclosure occurs in the way that first-order entities show up. And for Heidegger this means that they, or an important subset of them, have to show up as "things," and not simply as objects, or even worse, as standing reserve.

The thing about a "thing" is that in being disclosed it co-discloses its place in the clearing. Later Heidegger introduces the notion of the "fourfold" to explain this: mortal and divine beings, earth and sky. Take a humble entity, like a jug. As it shows up in the world of a peasant, as yet unmobilized by modern technology, it is redolent of the human activities in which it plays a part, of the pouring of wine at the common table, for instance. The jug is a point at which this rich web of practices can be sensed, made visible in the very shape of the jug and its handle which offers itself for this use. So much for the human life which co-shows up in this thing.

At the same time this form of life is based on, and interwoven with, strong goods, matters of intrinsic worth. These are matters which make a claim on us. They can be called "divine." So these too are co-disclosed. Heidegger imagines this connection as arising from an actual ritual of pouring a libation from the jug. But I doubt if the

449

Christian, Black Forest peasantry of Swabia (as against ancient Greeks) actually did this kind of thing; and it is sufficient to point out that the human modes of conviviality that the jug co-discloses are shot through with religious and moral meaning. Perhaps the pastor said grace, but even if he didn't, this life together has central meaning in the participants' lives.

The jug is something shaped and fashioned for human use. It is one of those objects which is already clearly identified as a locus of features. As such it stands on and emerges out of a vast domain of as yet unformed and unidentified reality. This is a field of potential future forming, but it is limitless, inexhaustible. All forming is surrounded by, and draws on, this unformed. If we are not closed to it, the jug will also speak of its history as a formed entity, of its emergence from unformed matter, of its continuing dependency on the unformed, since it can only exist as an entity as long as it is supported by the whole surrounding reality. It rests ultimately on the earth, and that is the word Heidegger uses for this dimension of co-disclosure.

Finally, the jug and the whole round of activities it speaks of, and the earth, are open to greater cosmic forces which are beyond the domain of the formable, and which can either permit them to flourish or sweep them away. The alternation of day and night, storms, floods, earthquakes, or their benign absence; these are the things which Heidegger assembles under the title "sky." They provide the frame within which the earth can be partly shaped as our world.

All these are co-disclosed in the thing. Heidegger says that it "assembles" (*versammelt*) them and they "sojourn" (*verweilen*) in it (GA 7: 175). When this happens, then the clearing itself can be said to be undistortively disclosed. The undistorted meta-disclosure occurs through this manner of first-order showing up. Being among things in such a way that they show up thus is what Heidegger calls "dwelling." It involves our "taking care" of them.

> Der Aufenthalt bei den Dingen ist die einzige Weise, wie sich der vierfältige Aufenthalt im Geviert jeweils einheitlich vollbringt. Das Wohnen schont das Geviert, indem es dessen Wesen in die Dinge bringt. Allein die Dinge selbst bergen das Geviert *nur dann*, wenn sie selber *als* Dinge in ihrem Wesen gelassen werden. Wie geschieht das? Dadurch, daß die Sterblichen die wachstümlichen Dinge hegen und pflegen, daß sie Dinge, die nicht wachsen, eigens errichten. [Staying with things is the only way in which the fourfold stay within the fourfold is accomplished at any time in simple unity. Dwelling preserves the fourfold by bringing the essence of the fourfold into things. But things themselves secure the fourfold only when they themselves as things are let be in their essence. How does this happen? In this way, that mortals nurse and nurture the things that grow, and specially construct things that do not grow.] (GA 7: 153/Heidegger 1971: 151)

As is evident from this quote, "things" include more than made objects. They include living things. And they go beyond that: "Ding ist . . . auch nach seiner Weise der Baum und der Teich, der Bach und der Berg" ("tree and pond, brook and hill, are also things, each in its own way"; GA 7: 183–4/Heidegger 1971: 182). So that part of what is involved in preserving the fourfold is the "Retten der Erde" ("saving the earth"; GA 7: 152, 153/Heidegger 1971: 150, 151).

Living among things in this way allows the fourfold to be manifest in their everyday presence. This is already an effect of language, because the fourfold can be co-disclosed only to us, who have already identified the thing itself, and marked out the four dimensions in language. But there is a more concentrated mode of language, where we try to bring to its own proper expression what is co-disclosed in the thing. We try to capture this in a deliberate formulation through an expressive form. Heidegger's own form of philosophizing (properly, "thinking") is an attempt to do this. But it can also be done in works of art. So the peasant woman, as she puts on her shoes, experiences her life in the fields and the seasons and the ripening corn. She "knows all this without observation or consideration." But in van Gogh's painting of the peasant's shoes, their thingly nature is shown as something we can contemplate, in an express formulation which we can consider and observe (GA 5: 18–19).

But we close ourselves to all this when we turn away from living among things, and formulating what they co-disclose in art, and identify them as context-free objects, susceptible of scientific study; and even more so when we are swept up in the technological way of life and treat them as just standing reserve. If we make these our dominant stance to the world, then we abolish things, in a more fundamental sense than just smashing them to pieces, though that may follow. "Das in seinem Bezirk, dem der Gegenstände, zwingende Wissenschaft hat die Dinge als Dinge schon vernichtet, längst bevor die Atombombe explodierte" (GA 7: 172).

So what does this tell us about language? It has a telos, and that requires that entities show up in a certain way. This is already made possible through language. But more, when it is lost, an essential role in its retrieval devolves on certain uses of language in philosophy and art, or in Heideggerese "Denken" and "Dichten." And when we understand the potential role that these can have, we understand that the original way of dwelling which we have lost flowed itself from some founding acts of one or the other.

So language, through its telos, dictates a certain mode of expression, a way of formulating matters which can help to restore thingness. It tells us what to say, dictates the poetic, or thinkerly word, as we might put it. We can go on talking, mindful only of our purposes, unaware that there is anything else to take notice of. But if we stop to attend to language, it will dictate a certain way of talking. Or, otherwise put, the entities will demand that we use the language which can disclose them as things.

In other words, our use of language is no longer arbitrary, up for grabs, a matter of our own feelings and purposes. Even, indeed especially, in what subjectivism thinks is the domain of the most unbounded personal freedom and self-expression, that of art, it is not we but language which ought to be calling the shots.

This is how I think we have to understand Heidegger's slogan "Die Sprache spricht," rather than as a proto-Derridean invocation of a super(non)subject. That is why Heidegger speaks of our relation to this language in terms of a call (Ruf) which we are attentive to. "Die Sterblichen sprechen insofern sie hören." And he can speak of the call as emanating from a "silence" (Stille) (GA 12: 27–9). The silence is where there are not yet (the right) words, but where we are interpellated by entities to disclose them as things. Of course, this doesn't happen before language; it can only happen in its midst. But within language and because of its telos, we are pushed to find

451

unprecedented words, which we draw in this sense out of silence. This stillness contrasts with the noisy *Gerede* in which we fill the world with expressions of our selves and our purposes.

These unprecedented words (in fact, better "sayings," but "word" is pithier) are words of power; we might say: words of retrieval. They constitute authentic thinking and poetry.[9] They are on a different level from everyday speech; not because they are "heightened" speech, but because everyday speech is a kind of dulling, a falling off from, a forgetfulness of the more full-blooded disclosure they bring (GA 12: 28: "Eigentliche Dichtung ist niemals nur eine höhere Weise . . . der Alltagssprache. Vielmehr ist umgekehrt das alltägliche Reden ein vergessenes und darum vernütztes Gedicht, aus dem kaum noch ein Rufen erklingt"). That is why I want to speak of retrieval.

V

Heidegger is on to something very important, a power of words that enframing theories can make no sense of. It has tremendously positive uses, but also terrifyingly dangerous ones. Heidegger is characteristically only aware of the former. The danger comes from the fact that much can be retrieved from the gray zone of repression and forgetfulness. There are also resentments and hatreds and dreams of omnipotence and revenge, and they can be released by their own appropriate words of power. Hitler was a world-historical genius in only one respect, but that was in finding such dark words of power, sayings that could capture and elevate the fears, longings, and hatreds of a people into something demonic. Heidegger has no place for the retrieval of evil in his system, and that is part of the reason why Hitler could blindside him, and why he never thereafter could get a moral handle on the significance of what happened between 1933 and 1945.[10]

But those people are just as one-sided as Heidegger, but in another way, who refuse to see the positive insights in his vision of language, because they are too focused on his own blindness to its demonic potentialities. Heidegger's understanding of language, its telos, and the relevance for this to the human essence opens new avenues of understanding the human condition with potentially wide ramifications. As an example, and remaining on the same level as Heidegger's most passionate critics – that of politics – his view can be the basis of an ecological stance to the environment, founded on something deeper than an instrumental calculation of the conditions of our survival (though that itself ought to be enough to alarm us). It can be the basis of in one sense a "deep" ecology.

For as I put it above, we can think of the demands of language also as a demand that entities put on us to disclose them in a certain way. This amounts in fact to saying that they demand that we acknowledge them as having certain meanings. But this manner of disclosure can in crucial cases be quite incompatible with a stance of pure instrumentality toward them. Take wilderness, for instance. This demands to be disclosed as "earth," as the other to "world." This is compatible with a stance of exploration, whereby we identify the species and geological forms it contains, for instance, as long as we retain the sense of the inexhaustibility of their wilderness surroundings. But a purely technological stance, whereby we see the rain forests as simply standing reserve for timber production, leaves no room for this meaning. Taking this stance is "annihilating" wilderness in its proper meaning, even before we step in and chain-saw all the trees, to parallel Heidegger's remark about things and the atom bomb above.

This stance does violence to our essence as language beings. It is a destruction of us as well, even if we could substitute for the oxygen, and compensate for the greenhouse effect. This way of putting it might make it sound as though Heidegger's ecological philosophy were after all a "shallow" one, grounded ultimately on human purposes. But we have already seen how this misdescribes his view. For the purposes in question are not simply human. Our goals here are fixed by something which we should properly see ourselves as serving. So a proper understanding of our purposes has to take us beyond ourselves. Heidegger has perhaps in that sense bridged the difference between "shallow" and "deep" ecology, and come up with a genuine third position. As in a number of other areas (as, for instance, in the questions about expression discussed above), his position is in a sense unclassifiable in the terms the issue is generally debated in. It breaks genuinely new ground.

Properly understood, the "shepherd of being" can't be an adept of triumphalist instrumental reason. That is why learning to dwell among things may also amount to "rescuing the earth" (GA 7: 151–2). At this moment when we need all the insight we can muster into our relation to the cosmos in order to deflect our disastrous course, Heidegger may have opened a vitally important new line of thinking.

Notes

1 "Enframing" is not used here in the sense of efficient ordering, which is the meaning of Heidegger's term, *Gestell*, standardly translated "enframing," although there is obviously an affinity between the two.

2 I have argued for this reconstruction of Herder in terms of irreducible rightness at greater length in "The Importance of Herder" (in Taylor 1995), and in "Heidegger versus Davidson."

3 Charles Guignon has used the term "expressive" for this view on language, in specific application to Heidegger. See Guignon (1989).

4 I have discussed this phenomenon of common space in "Theories of Meaning" (in Taylor 1985).

5 "Symbol" is being used here in the way it is generally used by the tradition which starts in Goethe's time. But the opposed terms symbol/allegory are not always applied in the same sense. When, in "The Origin of the Work of Art," Heidegger says that the artwork is *not* a symbol, he is accepting a use of the term which is synonymous with "allegory" in the terminology I am using here, something which points beyond itself for its meaning. In the standard distinction, this kind of "symbol" is called allegory, and contrasted with what I am calling "symbol," something whose meaning cannot be made manifest by some other route.

6 This claim seems to me indisputable as far as late Heidegger is concerned. The question might arise about the author of *Sein und Zeit* as to what extent he was a constitutive theorist. I would like to argue that the Herder tradition was very much present in the earlier phase as well, although Heidegger had not yet drawn all the conclusions from it that shape his later philosophy. In particular, for instance, the discussions in *Sein und Zeit* about the

"apophantic as" have, I think, to be understood in the light of some doctrine of the semantic dimension (¶¶32–3).

7 This seems at least to be Heidegger's view. "Sichentbergen und Sichverbergen sind im Tier auf eine Art einig, daß unser menschliches Auslegen kaum Wege findet. . . . Weil das Tier nicht spricht, haben Sichentbergen und Sichverbergen samt ihrer Einheit bei den Tieren ein ganz anderes Lebe-Wesen" ("Self-revealing and self-concealing in the animal are one in such a way that human speculation practically runs out of alternatives. . . . Because the animal does not speak, self-revealing and self-concealing together with their unity, possess a wholly different life-essence with animals" (GA 7: 281–2/Heidegger 1984: 116–17).

8 In "Heraklit," Heidegger explains that mortal legein doesn't define the logos, but nor does it simply copy (*nachbilden*) it. We have to find a third way between these two extremes. "Gibt es dahin für sterbliches Denken einen Weg?" ("Is there a path for mortal thinking to that place?") (GA 7: 230/Heidegger 1984: 75).

9 Heidegger's placing of "Dichten" alongside "Denken" reflects the fact that his view is substantially anticipated not only in the practice, but also in the self-understanding of some twentieth-century poets, notably Rilke. In the ninth "Duino Elegy," Rilke offers his own understanding of the word of power. It is a word of praise: "Preise dem Engel die Welt . . . Sag ihm die Dinge . . . Zeig ihm, wie glücklich ein Ding sein kann, wie schuldlos und unser" (Praise the world to the angel . . . Tell him about the things . . . Show him how happy a thing can be, how blameless and ours). The word "thing" here is taking on a special force, closely related to Heidegger's. Our task is to *say* them. And the list of examples is very reminiscent of Heidegger's. "Sind wir vielleicht *hier*, um zu sagen: Haus / Brücke, Brunnen, Tor, Krug, Obstbaum, Fenster – / höchstens, Säule, Turm" (Are we *here* perhaps just to say: house, bridge, well, gate, jug, fruit tree, window – at most, column, tower). And this saying is a kind of rescue. "Und diese, von Hingang / lebenden Dinge verstehn, dass du sie rühmst: vergänglich, / traun sie ein Rettendes uns, den Vergänglichsten, zu" (And these things that live, slipping away, understand that you praise them; transitory themselves, they trust us for rescue, us, the most transient of all). This rescue is all the more necessary because of the rush of technological society to turn everything into a storehouse of power deprived of all form, as the sixth "Elegy" says. "Weite Speicher der Kraft schafft sich der Zeitgeist, gestaltlos / wie der Spannende Drang, den er aus allem gewinnt. / Tempel kennt er nicht mehr" (The spirit of the times makes vast storehouses of power, formless as the stretched tension it gathers from everything. Temples it knows no longer). The concept of "standing reserve" was originally a poetic image of Rilke.

10 The different uses of words of power is discussed with characteristic insight by Vaclav Havel in his "Words on Words," the speech (he would have) delivered on receiving the German Book Prize (Havel 1990). The Heideggerian provenance of some of his thinking on this score (partly via Patocka) is evident in the text.

References and further reading

Cassirer, E. (1953) *The Philosophy of Symbolic Forms*. New Haven, CT: Yale University Press.
Condillac, É. (1746) *Essai sur l'origine des connoissances humaines*. Amsterdam: P. Mortier.
Guignon, C. (1989) Truth as disclosure: art, language, history. *Southern Journal of Philosophy*, 28, 105–20.
Havel, V. (1990) Words on words. *New York Review of Books*, January 18, 5–8.
Heidegger, M. (1971) *Poetry, Language, Thought* (trans. A. Hofstadter). New York: Harper & Row.
Heidegger, M. (1977) *The Question Concerning Technology and Other Essays* (trans. W. Lovitt). New York: Harper & Row.

Heidegger, M. (1984) *Early Greek Thinking* (trans. D. F. Krell and F. A. Capuzzi). San Francisco: Harper & Row.

Herder, J. G. (1975) Abhandlung über den Ursprung der Sprache. In *Johann Gottfried Herder's Sprachphilosophie* (ed. E. Heintel). Hamburg: Felix Meiner.

Hobbes, T. (1947) *Leviathan* (ed. M. Oakeshott). Oxford: Basil Blackwell.

Humboldt, W. von (1988) *On Language* (trans. P. Heath). Cambridge: Cambridge University Press.

Locke, J. (1975) *An Essay Concerning Human Understanding* (ed. P. H. Nidditch). Oxford: Clarendon Press.

Pinker, S. (1994) *The Language Instinct*. New York: Morrow.

Taylor, C. (1985) *Human Agency and Language*. Cambridge: Cambridge University Press.

Taylor, C. (1995) *Philosophical Arguments*. Cambridge, MA: Harvard University Press.

28

The Thinging of the Thing: The Ethic of Conditionality in Heidegger's Later Work

JAMES C. EDWARDS

I

History washes some words clean, tumbling them along the bottom until all their edges have been smoothed and all their glitter ground to matte. So it has been with "thing," now surely among the most colorless of English substantives. Almost anything can be tagged with the word, a word that seems simultaneously essential and empty, and essential because of its very emptiness.[1] But even so dull a pebble, worn down by its ceaseless and indiscriminate employment, might yet with polishing become a brilliant gem; and it is the task of the philosopher – or of a certain kind of philosopher – to foster an unexpected word's capacity to shine and to cut.

In a remarkable series of lectures and essays beginning in 1949 Heidegger builds upon some of the themes broached in "The Origin of the Work of Art" to set out a comprehensive account of the thing (see Dreyfus, chapter 25 in this volume). The centerpiece of these reflections is, of course, "The Thing," originally a lecture delivered in 1951; but it can only be understood as part of a constellation comprising "Building Dwelling Thinking" (1951/1954; GA 7), "Language" (1950/1959; GA 12), ". . . Poetically Man Dwells . . ." (1951/1954; GA 7), and "The Question Concerning Technology" (1955/1954; GA 7).

Heidegger's reflections on the thing take place within an endeavor that can only be called (to use a word he would himself resist) *ethical*. In these essays a particular kind of human life, a life that he calls *poetic dwelling on the earth as a mortal*, is being explored and valorized; the thing, properly understood, is central to that life and can only be accounted for as part of its ethos (see GA 7: 192/Heidegger 1971: 214). In the final analysis, of course, every human life is a life of poetic dwelling, even if some are such only privatively. (One can dwell by explicitly refusing to dwell; one can also dwell in disabling ignorance of what one's proper dwelling is.) To be able to trace the contours of such a life, and especially to appreciate the life of poetic dwelling in its full flower, is the great ambition of much of Heidegger's later work. His project of overcoming metaphysics, and thus of recovering styles of thinking and living hidden by its triumph, is given its point by this ethical (one might even say religious) aim.[2] To preserve the force of Dasein's elemental words against the corrosive power of routine and of absent-mindedness is essential to philosophy only because these words – with "thing" taking its place among the most important of them – are our access to that life proper to us. "Naming calls," as he says in "Language," playing off the familiar German proverb; and to name the thing *as* the thing is to call near the kind of life in which human beings have a world that is truthfully their own (GA 12: 21/Heidegger 1971: 198).

The proper dwelling of human beings, the kind of life truly appropriate to us, is first of all *poetic*, according to Heidegger.[3] Nowadays the word is almost always misunderstood, since we immediately think of poetry as poesy, as the making of verse, and since we furthermore think of that activity as something essentially "aesthetic" or "artistic," divorced from the real business of living. As Heidegger puts it, we nowadays think of poetry as an "ornament," as a prettifying (and thus probably falsifying) elaboration of what is solid and real (GA 7: 193/Heidegger 1971: 215). But he hears sounding in the word its Greek root: poetry is *poiesis*, the making of things; and the making of verse, fashioning the carefully wrought speech that we normally use the word "poetry" to describe, is only one sort of such making (GA 7: 192/Heidegger 1971: 214). Who can deny that *Homo sapiens* is *Homo faber*?

But not every making of an entity is fully the making of a *thing*. If I sit on an assembly line putting the finishing touches on a plastic toothbrush, or if I spend countless hours in my cubicle coding the newest version of a spreadsheet, or if I interrupt my plowing to fashion in my workshop a new hitch for better attaching the harrow to the tractor, I am not, in Heidegger's sense, making things. And that is not because things (in his usage) cannot be of obvious and everyday use; a jug or a farmhouse can be just as much a thing, just as much the result of *poiesis*, as can be a sonnet or a painting.[4] So what is the difference? Why is a toothbrush or a tractor hitch or a piece of software not a thing, while a jug or a house or sonnet may be?

Heidegger's answer is not, to say the least, transparent at first glance.

> The jug's presencing is the pure, giving gathering of the onefold fourfold into a single time-space, a single stay. The jug presences as a thing. The jug is the jug as a thing. But how does the thing presence? The thing things. Thinging gathers. Appropriating the fourfold, it gathers the fourfold's stay, its while, into something that stays for a while: into this thing, that thing. (GA 7: 175/Heidegger 1971: 174)

A great deal here must be unpacked, especially and primarily the notion that the thing *gathers the fourfold*.

What is the fourfold (*das Geviert*) of which Heidegger so cryptically speaks? Visualize it as the intersection of two axes. At the head of each of the four semi-axes is one of "the four": *earth; sky; mortals; divinities*. One axis is formed at either end by earth and sky; the other is formed at either end by divinities and mortals. At the center, at the intersection of the axes, sits *the thing*. As that which sits at the center in this way, the thing, as Heidegger says, "gathers the fourfold."

What does Heidegger intend "the four" to be? His description of them is typically overblown and cryptic.

> Earth is the serving bearer, blossoming and fruiting, spreading out in rock and water, rising up into plant and animal. . . . The sky is the vaulting path of the sun, the course of the changing moon, the wandering glitter of the stars, the year's seasons and their changes,

457

the light and dusk of day, the gloom and glow of night, the clemency and inclemency of the weather, the drifting clouds and blue depth of the ether. . . . The divinities are the beckoning messengers of the godhead. Out of the holy sway of the godhead, the god appears in his presence or withdraws into his concealment. . . . The mortals are the human beings. They are called mortals because they can die. (GA 7: 151–2/Heidegger 1971: 149–50)

Each of the four is, I think, intended to put us in mind of some one of the particular *conditions* that make possible ("grant," one might say, or "give," as in *Es gibt*, "it gives"/"there is") the life that brought to presence the actual thing – jug, farmhouse, sonnet – before us; each of the four is what one might call a particular *dimension* of that indispensable conditionality.[5] Conditionality is indebtedness. The conditions of a life, and thus the conditions of the particular things that such a life brings forth, are what make that life (and those things) possible as such. Any actual and determinate life is possible only in virtue of something not itself, something "prior" (both temporally and logically), to which that life, along with all its goods and ills, is indebted. To live, therefore, is to owe one's life; to be human is always already to be in debt.

The point may seem banal, but only if we fail to pay attention to the ways in which our life is arranged so as to blind us to that indebtedness. The Heideggerian word that condenses his reflections on this point is *technology (die Technik)*. Technology is a way – according to Heidegger, it is now the *fundamental* way – in which the world of human beings is revealed, constituted, and populated; it is an over-arching set of linguistic and behavioral practices that allow our entities to appear around us in a particular way, that give to the entities that appear in our world a particular being, a particular significance, a particular sense. The machines and tools we think of as distinctively "technological," such as power plants and particle accelerators, are just the most obvious instances of the being of *all* – or at least *almost* all – our entities as they are constituted by our most basic social practices.

And what is that characteristically technological being of entities?

The revealing that rules throughout modern technology has the character of a setting-upon, in the sense of a challenging-forth. That challenging happens in that the energy concealed in nature is unlocked, what is unlocked is transformed, what is transformed is stored up, what is stored up is, in turn, distributed, and what is distributed is switched about ever anew. Unlocking, transforming, storing, distributing, and switching about are ways of revealing. . . . What kind of unconcealment is it, then, that is peculiar to that which results from this setting-upon that challenges? Everywhere everything is ordered to stand by, to be immediately on hand, indeed to stand there just so that it may be on call for a further ordering. Whatever is ordered about in this way has its own standing. We call it the standing-reserve [*Bestand*]. . . . [The word *Bestand*] designates nothing less than the way in which everything presences that is wrought upon by the challenging revealing. Whatever stands by in the sense of standing-reserve no longer stands over against us as object. (GA 7: 17/Heidegger 1977: 16–17)

The kind of entity brought to light by the practices of technology is *Bestand*, "standing-reserve," "stock": that which in an orderly way awaits our use of it for the further ordering of things. When I walk into my study in the morning and glance at the computer on the desk, the computer, as the entity it is, is *Bestand*. It reveals itself to me as waiting patiently for me to turn it on, to "get its things in order," so I can use it to order and re-order those things and others. The data stored there – words, sentences, bank balances – await my command so they can be transformed, distributed, and switched about: they too are *Bestand*. And it is not just the glass-and-plastic machines that reveal themselves to me as standing-reserve. As I glance out the window onto the leaves I have not yet raked, they too are *Bestand*: they patiently await my collection of them so they can be put on the compost heap ("stored up" so the energy in them can later be "unlocked") or bagged for the garbage collection ("switched about"). The very house I inhabit is, as we have famously been told, "a machine for living in," with the window out of which I gaze a device for the orderly collection of light (and the orderly retention of heat). The house patiently awaits its tenants – whoever they are – for their use of it in ordering their lives; the land on which the house sits reveals itself through the window as garden and as landscape, waiting for the orderly touch that shapes and preserves and culti-vates. The mugs on the kitchen shelf, the television in the loft, the cereal in the pantry, the toothbrush on the bathroom sink: all "stand by" in the manner of "stock," as resources awaiting their call to orderly use in the ordering of things.

And the entities just named wonderfully conspire in our treatment of them as *Bestand*. The deftly shaped buttons on the television's remote control are made to be punched again and again (by anyone) with no delicacy or attention, just as the white ceramic coffee mug is intended to offer to my hand (and to any hand) no resistance or interest. These entities, like the toothbrush and innumerable others, are supposed to disappear into our use of them; they are supposed to be there for us only insofar as they are useful without impediment and without our careful scrutiny. "In themselves" they are, one wants to say, *anonymous and interchangeable*; they have no reality for us as *particular* entities. My television set looks and performs much like every other one, and certainly my coffee mug and my toothbrush are virtually indistin-guishable from an indefinitely large number of similar objects that anyone might pur-chase and use. Today's breakfast Grape-Nuts taste exactly like yesterday's, and mine taste just like those sold in Seattle or in São Paulo – and (this is the crucial point) *that is what makes them what they are*. That anonymous interchangeability is what gives them their being as *Bestand*. They are no one's because they are everyone's. Their nature, one might say, is to have only a *general* nature, a nature exhausted by their impersonal usefulness to any one of us. Or, to put it more precisely, all these things are entities the being of which fails to gather the manifold conditions of their coming to presence.

Here it is useful to think a bit more about coffee mugs, toothbrushes, and Grape-Nuts. Specific instances of these entities are, as I put it above, largely anonymous and interchangeable. This coffee mug looks and feels no different from that one; this bowl of Grape-Nuts tastes just like the one I had yesterday; any Oral-B 60 is much the same as any other. (Of course there are differences at the margins. The point is that those dif-ferences, to the extent they can't be suppressed, are not taken to matter.) What is crucial to see is that this anonymity and this interchangeability are not just accidents, and not just unfortunate features of living in a society rich enough to mass-produce breakfast foods and implements of personal hygiene; they are essential to our need for these enti-ties readily to disappear into our use of them. In practices given over – as Heidegger thinks almost our whole life is – to ordering for the sake of ordering, the more easily and quickly an entity can be thoughtlessly taken up into its particular task of ordering, the better. Explicit attention to the tool one is using distracts one from the job the tool is being used to accomplish and in that way makes the successful completion of the job less likely. If I notice the texture of the handle of my coffee mug, and then begin to wonder how it was made, and maybe even to wonder who made it, and under what conditions, I may be led into a train of thought that disrupts my normal and efficient progress from breakfast to newspaper to car to classroom, thus introducing a bit of disorder into my quite ordinary life. The more "unconditional" and "smooth" the appearance of the thing, the more readily it disappears into our use of it. The less we pay attention to particular entities *qua* particular entities, the more efficiently we carry on with the tasks we have inherited from the social practices that have constituted us (and those entities). An impetus to ordering for the sake of ordering – Heidegger's characterization of the essence of technology – will seek to efface anything that impedes such ordering (GA 7: 16–20/Heidegger 1977: 16–19). Thus it will seek to produce things that efface their own conditions of production.

Caught up in our everyday world of technological practices, and availing ourselves of the "standing-reserve" of the entities we bring to presence and use within those practices, we proceed as if our lives were unconditional. Neither our practices nor our entities announce themselves as dependent for their being on the marriage of several contingencies, both material and conceptual. My successful employment of my toothbrush or my television set requires that – to some extent or other – I be able to forget about them and about the "frames" (*Ge-Stelle*) that make them what they are.[6] My ability to give myself over fully to the practices within which they function depends upon my being able to *see through* my implements, and therefore finally to *see through* the practices themselves. The implements and the practices must be both transparent and fully permeable. I must see through them without noticing them; they must not resist and obtrude upon my consciousness or my action. To be *in* the practices, not to reflect upon them: that is the mark of their full value for us. The good of our practices is their ability to consume us, to obliterate any hint of their conditionality, to take us up into them without remainder: to make *us* an orderly part of our ordering of what there is. The most successful technology, therefore, obliterates *even us* as a condition of what gets done. The doing is all.

II

In Heidegger the contrast between "thing" and "*Bestand*" is stark and fundamental, and their opposition lies in the way they acknowledge (or fail to acknowledge) the conditionality of entities and of their constitutive practices. The "standing-reserve" of technological production deliberately effaces its conditionality in just the way we have seen: a toothbrush successfully put to use offers no hint of the various contingencies necessary to its appearance on the sink top; it disappears completely into the activity of brushing, allowing itself (and thus the brusher) to be consumed in the action without explicit notice. A thing, on the other hand, resists this double obliteration. But how does a simple earthen jug found on a Black Forest farmstead of a couple of centuries ago

(Heidegger's example from "The Thing") escape the depredations of *die Technik?* How does the jug remain a thing while my plastic toothbrush devolves into mere *Bestand?*

As is typical for Heidegger, he looks for an answer in the history of the word. In his account, the Old High German word for *thing* (*dinc*) means a *gathering*, "and specifically a gathering to deliberate on a matter under discussion, a contested matter." From this (alleged) etymological insight he draws the conclusion that the thing is something that *gathers*: "This manifold-simple gathering is the jug's presencing. Our language denotes what a gathering is by an ancient word. That word is: thing" (GA 7: 175–6/Heidegger 1971: 174). At first glance, this emphasis on gathering might seem only a florid way of calling attention to the sort of meaning-holism one sees so clearly in *Being and Time.* Just as "there 'is' no such thing as *an* equipment," there "is" no such thing as *a* thing (SZ: 68). Just as any one piece of Dasein's gear necessarily "refers to" other pieces of that gear (a *pen* is to be filled with *ink* for writing on *paper*, etc.), so it is that any thing (such as a farmhouse jug) is the thing it is only insofar as it presences in a social practice alongside other things (such as wine, plates, bread, cups, and so forth). A thing always "gathers" the other things that belong together with it. Its being – its significance, its meaning, its sense – is always given in relation to those other things, just as their being is always given in relation to it.

But this sort of gathering would not distinguish the jug from the toothbrush, since the toothbrush too is what it is – a toothbrush – only in relation to entities such as toothpaste, dental floss, deodorant soap, sinks, faucets, and the like: all the "personal-grooming-gear" we turn-of-century consumers count on. That something is *Bestand* doesn't mean that meaning-holism doesn't apply to it. The "gathering" distinctive of the thing is, as we noted above, the gathering of the fourfold, and now we can see what that gathering comes to.

Each of "the four" calls our attention to a specific condition of the life that produced the jug presencing there before us. To call attention to the *earth*, to start with that dimension of the fourfold, is to call attention to the thing as conditioned by that which is ultimately "material," i.e. by that which is finally beyond our power to make or to name. (Here there is an obvious affinity with the way "earth" is used in "The Origin of the Work of Art.") Earth is not simply that which is (in our sense) "physical"; it is Heidegger's way of talking about what is *an sich.* Earth is the dark *physis*, that which rises up out of itself to confront us with its brute reality; it is that mystery which challenges us to respond to it by trying to draw it out into the light of our common understanding. Earth is that condition of human life that confronts us with the adamant "thereness" of certain unnamable but unignorable powers. It is a grasp out of the darkness; a seizing that shakes us into awareness of itself, demanding to be named. But earth has no final name. To speak of the earth is to be reminded of that always unilluminated darkness from which arises whatever we can see and thus learn to give words to. To speak of the earth, however, is also to speak of the "serving bearer." It is to recognize that the dark mystery of those powers that can never be finally named is also that out of which all that we make is made. If there were no darkness that surges and rises out of itself, no earth, then there would be nothing to emerge into the light of our conceptions, nothing to demand that light, however flickering. Our life of enlightened things is sheltered by that darkness.

Any life is a life lived "on the earth." Any life is, first of all, a life the illuminating conceptions of which are always conceptions of something that transcends those conceptions even as it makes them possible. The steady and reliable illuminations furnished by our constitutive linguistic and behavioral practices are always the lighting-up of something "in itself" dark, in the sense that in one way or another in its brute "materiality" it will challenge and defeat our attempts to constrain it only to our enlightened uses. Sooner or later the jug will decisively "assert its materiality"; sooner or later it will, perhaps through breakage or prolonged disuse, withdraw from the shadowless light of our use of it into the darkness of its brute "stuff." It will fall out of our practices and become nothing at all. And here the jug is just an image for a condition of *all* intelligibility: that which is now intelligible was, at some point, not so, and at some point will not be so again. Before there was this world of illuminated things, there was the earth; and after this (or any) world of particular things, particular practices, has passed away, the earth will remain. In Heidegger's idiom, *earth* is a metaphor for the dark and unnamable substance of all things. And that substance, dark as it is, is the necessary condition of any thing that is.

But a life lived "on the earth" is also a life lived "under the sky." In Heidegger's usage, the metaphor has two resonances. First, the sky is the source of light; it is only "under the sky" and its varying degrees of luminance that anything can be seen as the thing it is. In this way, to speak of the sky is to speak of those ongoing social practices – in full flower or in decline; bright as day or dim as dusk – within which things come to presence as the things they are. Out of the "darkness" of earth, something – some particular (kind of) thing – proceeds into the "light" of our common understanding and use.[7] In this way, a thing is the thing it is "under the sky" of those illuminating linguistic and behavioral practices that constitute us and our common world. Those practices, whatever they are, are the conditions for whatever presences within their shelter.

But to speak of the sky is to speak of more than just those practices that light up things. The sky is "the vaulting path of the sun, the course of the changing moon," and thus to speak of the sky is Heidegger's way of talking about the fit (or, more likely, the lack of fit) of the human and its purposes into the inhuman and its impersonal cycles and necessities. Our constitutive social practices – patterns of normalized and normalizing behaviors – are not the only regularities that appear to our reflection. Our projected rounds and congruencies are conditioned on patterns we can come to see are prior to them. Our lives, we might say (using an effective nominalization), always already answer (or fail to answer) to Nature. Under the spell of technology, human beings take themselves to be the center and the point of all things; there is little awareness, and even less overt acknowledgment, that our activities and projects are set within – and must ultimately accommodate themselves to – the inhuman, uncaring cycles of the "natural" world. The *Bestand* of technology appears to offer itself up to our use, and thus to offer *us* up to our technological practices, without reference to anything beyond ourselves. Our sky – our horizon – becomes *the* sky.

So the first axis on which the thing is situated is the axis formed by earth and sky: the thing is set "on the earth" and "under the sky." The second axis also reveals conditions of the life that produced the thing; it is the axis formed by the divinities and the mortals. The divinities, says Heidegger, are "the beckoning messengers of the godhead."

They are presences from another world, annunciators of a place of haleness and whole-ness. The divinities are the reality both of human need for such weal and of our hope that it will someday be vouchsafed to us. "Mortals dwell in that they await the divini-ties as divinities. In hope they hold up to the divinities what is unhoped for" (GA 7: 152/Heidegger 1971: 150). Need and eschatological hope are (according to Heidegger) *conditions* of human life as such. To recognize one's fundamental neediness; to acknowl-edge that one is not the healthy and complete being one can imagine – if only inchoately – oneself to be; to look to the future for the gift of one's completion brought on the wings of a presence from another world: these are not just psychological tics or cultural quirks. They are – according to Heidegger – part of the matter of what it is to be us.

Despite the trope of theological language, it is clear that Heidegger is not identifying the divinities with the personified supernatural presences of vulgar religious belief. His presences from another world may be poems, paintings, works of philosophy, revolu-tionary political practices, new vocabularies of self-description: in short, whatever holds the promise of our healing self-transformation. To "await the divinities" is to solicit from the future – presumably by living a certain way here and now – the advent of some new "god" and its dispensation. And to live with this sort of attitude toward the future is at the same time to live in past and present in a particular fashion. Present and past are both wrapped up in one's eschatological hope. The apocalyptic future, though impossible to force, must be prepared for; and present and past are the story in which the traces of the god – traces both of absence and of coming presence – must be discerned.

> The turning of the age does not take place by some new god, or the old one renewed, burst-ing into the world from ambush at some time or other. Where would he turn on his return if men had not first prepared an abode for him? How could there ever be for the god an abode fit for a god, if a divine radiance did not first begin to shine in everything that is? (GA 5: 270/Heidegger 1971: 92)

The second constituent of the second axis of the fourfold is the mortals. "The mortals are the human beings. They are called mortals because they can die. To die means to be capable of death *as* death" (GA 7: 152/Heidegger 1971: 150). Everything at some point ceases to exist, but only human beings die. Only human beings live in awareness of their inevitable end: that is to be capable of death *as* death. "Mortals dwell in that they initiate their own nature – their being capable of death as death – into the use and practice of this capacity, so that there may be a good death" (GA 7: 152/Heidegger 1971: 151). Death is not an accident of human life; it is its very condition. The pres-ence of death – of insuperable limitation, of our world's contingency, of inevitable failure at the last – is what makes a human life distinctively human: "Only man dies, and indeed continually, as long as he remains on earth, under the sky, before the divini-ties" (GA 7: 152/Heidegger 1971: 150). To be a human being is to be mortal and, in some way or another, to acknowledge (even if only by frantic denial) that mortality. Death is Heidegger's trope in this essay for conditionality itself. To know oneself to be mortal is not (merely) to know that one will oneself die; it is to know that all one knows and most cares about – *everything*: every thing – is contingent upon a constellation of

463

circumstances that will someday no longer hold together. To acknowledge one's mortality is to acknowledge that abyss over which everything precariously juts, which is the abyss of pure, pointless time: time that is not history.

Heidegger's fullest description of the thing gathering the fourfold is his famous account of the Black Forest farmhouse:

> Let us think for a while of a farmhouse in the Black Forest, which was built some two hundred years ago by the dwelling of peasants. Here the self-sufficiency of the power to let earth and heaven, divinities and mortals enter *in simple oneness* into things, ordered the house. It placed the farm on the wind-sheltered mountain slope looking south, among the meadows close to the spring. It gave it the wide overhanging shingle roof whose proper slope bears up under the burden of snow, and which, reaching deep down, shields the chambers against the storms of the long winter nights. It did not forget the altar corner behind the community table; it made room in its chamber for the hallowed places of childbed and the "tree of the dead" – for that is what they call a coffin there: the *Totenbaum* – and in this way it designed for the different generations under one roof the character of their journey through time. A craft which, itself sprung from dwelling, still uses its tools and frames as things, built the farmhouse. (GA 7: 162/Heidegger 1971: 160)

Notice how this house, as a thing, "gathers the fourfold," i.e. makes clear in the thing itself the conditions of the life out of which the thing comes.[8] The house is set "on the earth" and "under the sky." Its materials – wood and stone that will always bear the physical marks of their working – show the recalcitrance to human purpose of the dark *physis* from which they have been extricated by human labor and to which they will someday return; they also show how earth solicits and rewards the human working that it simultaneously resists. Its placement in relation to light, wind, and water acknowledges both the "bright sky" of the practices (of farming, of cooking, of child-rearing) within which it comes to presence and the priority of the inhuman cycles of the seasons and of pure bodily need to any plans and projects we may voluntarily undertake. The juxtaposed presence of childbed and coffin corner are reminders of the specifically temporal character of human existence, and in particular of the death that awaits us all. The altar with its crucifix is a way of showing the openness to the future as the site of apocalyptic transformation for which the family hungers; it symbolizes the way in which the divinities, as messengers from another world to come, are always already being made present in our waiting for them.

And notice how this house, as a thing, gathers all the conditions of its life "in simple oneness." No one of the features we have mentioned is an *ornament* (as they would be, if one were to imagine this house transported bodily to a turn-of-the-century American suburb). All these features of the thing play off one another in an organic whole. The life within which the house comes to presence contains all four dimensions of our common condition, and it acknowledges both them and their necessary interpenetration. The thing exists at the intersection of the two axes, and none of "the four" is separable from the others. "The united four are already strangled in their essential nature when we think of them only as separate realities, which are to be grounded in and explained by one another" (GA 7: 181/Heidegger 1971: 180). That is, these conditions – the conditions that make the thing the thing it is – are not themselves *entities*. They are not *super*-entities that "ground" the being of the things there are. In this way the fourfold is in no way *metaphysical*; it escapes the Platonic paradigm, in which the being of beings is itself identified as a being. The fourfold cannot be presenced as such. It is the "dimension" within which all presencing happens. The fourfold is visible only in the things that occur at the intersection of its axes.

<h1 style="text-align:center">III</h1>

"The thing things. Thinging gathers. Appropriating the fourfold, it gathers the fourfold's stay, its while, into something that stays for a while: into this thing, that thing." We now can see (at least part of) what these odd sentences mean. The plastic toothbrush, disappearing into its use without remainder, in no way "stays for a while." It in no way slows the rush of my life of orderly ordering; it in no way brings me "for a while" to a stand in which I become visible to myself as what I am. By presenting itself to me as unconditional, the toothbrush allows me, encourages me, perhaps even forces me, to think of myself in the same way. Thus, when I think at all, I come to think of myself as my own and only condition; no wonder the Cartesian ego-subject is so powerful and enduring a fantasy.

> If we let the thing be present from out of the worlding world, then we are thinking of the thing as thing. Taking thought in this way, we let ourselves be concerned by the thing's worlding being. Thinking in this way, we are called by the thing as the thing. In the strict sense of the German word *bedingt*, we are the be-thinged ones, the conditioned ones. We have left behind the presumption of all unconditionedness (GA 7: 182/Heidegger 1971: 181).

And when I conceive myself as unconditional, or as conditioned only by myself (ethically, they come to the same thing), I am cut free of everything that might actually matter to me, except myself. *Die Technik* thus produces a kind of radical egoism; one might even call it narcissism. If I am unconditional, or solely self-conditioning, nothing makes any essential demand on me except myself.[9] Since I am what I am only by reference to myself, there is nothing that I *must* care for – act so as to preserve and enhance – in order to live the life that is mine to live. (I don't even have to care for myself; self-disgust, even self-obliteration, is certainly not foreign to egoism of this sort.) And if there is nothing I must care for, nothing that is mine and only mine to do or foster, then how could I ever care for anything at all? To be free of all demands, to be loose of all the entanglements that (as we say) tie us down, is a common fantasy for us (Jung, I suppose, would call it the typical fantasy of the *puer aeternus*, the eternal youth who walks away when things get too heavy); but it is really a recipe for nihilism, since the unconditioned will – the will that must answer to nothing except the self whose will it is – is incapable of sustaining its attachments or of motivating itself past the superficial. If I love this child only because I want to (or choose to, or have decided to), then I don't love her at all. To love is always to find, somehow, that one *must* love; that this – this child, this man, this woman, this job, this book, this talent, this landscape – is mine and only mine to care for. Such demand cannot (*pace* Kant) come purely from inside.

Love – any passion capable of sustaining care in the face of time and its depredations – is always conditional on a requirement that is itself conditional. It always comes from outside, so to speak; and what is outside is the world, shot through at every point with conditionality.

So it is that the thing, gathering and making visible its conditions, and thus simultaneously making clear through that conditionality its proper relation to us, forces us to acknowledge our own conditionality. The thing is always, in some way or other, *our own*, and that means we are its as well. The ownership of a thing is always symmetrical: it owns me (brings me into my own) as much as I own it. My toothbrush is mine only in the barest legal sense. It makes no sense that I might care about it, or be responsible to or for it. If I want to microwave it just to see the handle melt, who could possibly object? But the Black Forest farmhouse, home to my family for six generations, let us say, is mine in a way that exerts a corresponding claim on me. Gathering the fourfold, it tells me who I am, rooting me in a life and in a place that is proper to me. In this case, since this farmstead is *my own* (which, of course, is to say *our* own), it is possible for me to care about, and to be responsible for, that building of wood and stone and thatch. In fact it is not just possible but necessary: to sell the farm to a developer in order to finance a vacation home on Sylt would be a betrayal.

By living lives in which we make things – jugs, houses, paintings, books, marriages, children, whatever – that in their simple oneness gather the fourfold, we abandon some of the presumption that, in this age of technology and its *Bestand*, blinds us to our proper selves and to our sheltering world. Attuned to the autochthony of our lives by attention to the autochthony of our things, we dwell poetically on the earth as mortals. To live in acknowledgment of our manifold conditions, to gather ourselves to ourselves and others through the gathering of things, is an ethical achievement; it restores us to a more truthful condition of life, a more proper being. "We have left behind the presumption of all unconditionedness."

Notes

1 Although I am making the point about "thing" in English, it holds true for *das Ding* in German as well (as well as for *la cosa* in Italian).

2 This sort of perspective on Heidegger is explored in Edwards (1997, especially chapter 4). I have used some of the ideas of that book in this chapter.

3 ". . . Poetically Man Dwells . . .", GA 7: 189–208/Heidegger 1971: 213–29 is the key text, of course. The phrase comes from Hölderlin.

4 The jug is an example in "The Thing." The house is an example in ". . . Poetically Man Dwells . . ."

5 For a more literal reading of "the four," see Wrathall (2003). Julian Young is also helpful on these matters. See "The Fourfold," to appear in the revised version of *The Cambridge Companion to Heidegger*.

6 For "Ge-Stell" see GA 7: 20/Heidegger 1977: 19. These frames are primarily "conceptual," of course. A philosopher like Rorty would call them *vocabularies*.

7 In a fuller treatment of these issues, one would need to talk about the role of *die Lichtung*, "the clearing," in Heidegger's thinking. For more on the topic, see Edwards (1997: chapter 4).

8   I leave aside here the interesting question of whether all things gather the fourfold to the same extent. For example, does the Black Forest farmhouse display (through its gathering) all the conditions of the life lived under its roof? Does it, for instance, tell us what kind of life the women of this farmstead had? In Edwards (1997: especially 186–8), I explore this question of the relative truthfulness of things. Heidegger himself never seems to raise the issue.

9   For the emphasis on demand in this paragraph and the next, I am indebted to Mark Wrathall's fine paper (Wrathall 2003).

References and further reading

Edwards, J. C. (1997) *The Plain Sense of Things: The Fate of Religion in an Age of Normal Nihilism.* University Park, PA: Penn State Press.

Heidegger, M. (1971) *Poetry, Language, Thought* (trans. A. Hofstadter). New York: Harper & Row.

Heidegger, M. (1977) *The Question Concerning Technology and Other Essays* (trans. W. Lovitt). New York: Harper & Row.

Wrathall, M. A. (2003) Between the earth and the sky: Heidegger on life after the death of God. In M. A. Wrathall (ed.), *Religion after Metaphysics.* Cambridge: Cambridge University Press.

29

The Truth of Being and the History of Philosophy

MARK B. OKRENT

Introduction

In a recent article, Richard Rorty has attempted to juxtapose Heidegger and Dewey. While finding significant points of agreement between the two, and by implication, praising much of Heidegger's work, Rorty also suggests a series of criticisms of Heidegger. The problems which Rorty finds with Heidegger can, I think, all be reduced to one basic criticism, which has two main sides. In Rorty's view Heidegger cannot really differentiate between Being and beings in the way that he wants, and thus can give no sense to the word "Being" other than the old metaphysical one. That is, Being and the ontological difference are metaphysical remnants, the last evaporating presence of the Platonic distinction of the real world and the apparent world. This is indicated in two ways. First, Rorty feels that Heidegger can make no real distinction between philosophy, which they both agree has ended, and "thinking" in the specifically Heideggerian sense. Second, Rorty claims that it is impossible to distinguish ontic from ontological becoming. That is, the various epochs of Being which Heidegger distinguishes are, for Rorty, parasitic upon and reducible to the ordinary history of man's activity in relation to things, material and social. As such Heidegger's account of ontological epochs is a species of idealistic reflection upon the history of man's activity upon things.

This chapter attempts to reflect upon the adequacy of both main parts of Rorty's criticism of Heidegger. Is it possible to differentiate Being and beings in such a way as to allow for epochs of Being which are not simply reducible to ordinary historical periods? If not, then we will have reason to accept Rorty's criticism of the ontological difference, and hence of Heidegger's formulation in regard to Being. If this distinction can be maintained then one major element of Rorty's pragmatist criticism of Heidegger will need to be abandoned. Is it possible to distinguish the matter of Heidegger's thought from the concerns of philosophy in such a way as to preserve this thought given the end of philosophy? If not, then Heidegger's thinking is just another attempt to keep alive a bankrupt tradition. If this distinction can be maintained, then the other major element of Rorty's criticism must be abandoned.

Okrent, Mark, "Truth of Being and History of Philosophy" from *Heidegger: A Critical Reader*, edited by Hubert L. Dreyfus and Harrison Hall. Oxford: Blackwell, 1992. Reprinted with permission.

Varieties of Difference

Rorty thinks that Heidegger is necessarily impaled on the horns of a dilemma in regard to the history and historicity of Being. *Either* Being is radically different and distinct from beings, in which case "Being" can be nothing other than the old Platonic "real" world, a "real" which is impossibly vague, abstract, and lacks content and historical determinacy, *or* in order to give the historical becoming of Being definiteness, the history of "Being" can be seen as utterly dependent on the history of beings. If Heidegger accepts the first alternative then he is committed to, in words Rorty quotes from Versenyi, "an all too empty and formal, though often emotionally charged and mystically-religious, thinking of absolute unity."[1] On the other hand, if Heidegger admitted that the history of Being must be seen in terms of the history of beings, then he would see that philosophy (or Heidegger's own alternative, "thought"), as a discipline or even a distinct activity, is obsolete. That is, his concern with Being would be replaced by concrete attention to beings. In fact Rorty feels that Heidegger wants it both ways. While maintaining that he is giving us a history of Being, Heidegger necessarily has recourse to the ordinary history of nations, persons, and their relation to beings in order to give concreteness and definiteness to his ontological history.

It seems clear that before we can evaluate this criticism we need a better notion of just what Heidegger means by "Being" and how it is supposed to be different from beings. Rorty, of course, denies that Heidegger can give any other than a negative account.

> All we are told about Being, Thought, and the ontological difference is by negation. . . . Heidegger thinks that the historical picture which has been sketched offers a glimpse of something else. Yet nothing further can be said about this something else, and so the negative way to Being, through the destruction of ontology, leaves us facing beings-without-Being, with no hint about what Thought might be of.[2]

But Rorty himself inadvertently indicates Heidegger's attempt to hint at the matter to be thought, although he doesn't discuss it. In the first quote from Heidegger in the paper, from the "Letter on Humanism," Heidegger clearly distinguishes the truth of Being from Being itself. "Ontology, whether transcendental or pre-critical, is subject to criticism not because it thinks the Being of beings and thereby subjugates Being to a concept, but because it does not think the truth of Being."[3] Often Heidegger commentary does not recognize that in *all* of his periods Heidegger focuses not so much upon Being as on the *sense* of Being, or the *truth* of Being, or the *place* of Being.[4] The distinction between Being and the truth of Being is swallowed, as it were, by the distinction between Being and beings. This failure to note the distinction between Being and the truth of Being is perhaps not surprising, given that Heidegger himself is often unclear in regard to it. In the *Introduction to Metaphysics*, for example, which Rorty cites extensively, this distinction barely makes an appearance as the distinction between the inquiry into Being as such and the inquiry into the Being of beings.[5] Nevertheless, this distinction is present in both Heidegger's texts and the hidden light which illuminates

469

those texts. Heidegger "knows with full clarity the difference between Being as the Being of beings and Being as "Being" in respect of its proper sense, that is, in respect of its truth (the clearing)."[6]

"Being" then is used by Heidegger in two different, indeed opposed, senses. First, "Being" is the Being of beings, what each being is thought to need so that it is, rather than nothing. That is, "Being" in this first sense refers to that which each being involves simply and solely insofar as it is at all. The science which studies Being in this sense is metaphysics, the science *of* Being *qua* Being Equally, metaphysics, as the science of Being *qua* Being, increasingly comes to see Being in this sense, i.e. the Being of beings, as the ground of beings and itself. "The Being of beings reveals itself as the ground that gives itself ground and accounts for itself."[7] Metaphysics thus comes to see Being in this first sense as both what is most general, that which every being possesses in that it is, and that which supplies the ground for all such beings. "Metaphysics thinks of the Being of beings both in the ground-giving unity of what is most general, what is indifferently valid everywhere, and also in the unity of the all that accounts for the general, that is, of the All-Highest."[8] As such, such views of Being as pure act, as absolute concept, or even Heidegger's own view of the Greek notion of Being as the presence of the presencing, all speak to this first sense of Being.

The question of Being also concerns the *aletheia* of Being that which allows for the possibility of *any* answer to the question of Being in the first sense.

> The question of Being, on the other hand, can also be understood in the following sense: Wherein is each answer to the question of Being based i.e., wherein, after all, is the unconcealment of Being grounded? For example: it is said that the Greeks defined Being as the presence of the presencing. In presence speaks the present, in the present is a moment of time; therefore, the manifestation of Being as presence is related to time.[9]

In this second sense "Being" is sometimes used, unfortunately, as a shorthand expression standing for the "sense of Being," or the unconcealment (truth) of Being, or, more simply, the clearing or opening in which Being, in the first sense as presence, occurs. This "Being," as the sense of Being, time, is the concern of Heidegger's thought from *Being and Time* onward.

What then does Heidegger mean by "the truth of Being?" (Although there are serious differences among Heidegger's successive formulations, the sense of Being, the truth of Being, and the place of Being, for the sake of brevity I will speak mainly of the truth of Being, the formulation from his "middle" period.) Abstractly, the truth of being is thought as the opening or clearing which allow Being as presencing to appear and manifest itself. In order to think this it is necessary to explicate the sense in which Heidegger uses the term "truth." Beginning with *Being and Time* and continuing until very late in his career Heidegger interprets "truth" with the aid of an idiosyncratic and etymological translation of the Greek *aletheia*. Etymologically "*aletheia*" is a privative of "*lethe*," it is the not-hidden, the uncovered. " 'Being-true' ('truth') means Being-uncovering."[10] Yet equally essential to Heidegger's thinking on truth is the claim that unconcealment also involves concealment, hiddenness.

470

The nature of truth, that is, of unconcealment, is dominated throughout by a denial. Yet this denial is not a defect or a fault, as though truth were an unalloyed unconcealment that has rid itself of everything concealed. If truth could accomplish this, it would no longer be itself. . . . Truth, in its nature, is untruth. We put the matter this way in order to serve notice . . . that denial in the manner of concealment belongs to unconcealedness as clearing.[11]

The initial motivation for this interpretation of truth is clear enough. In order for there to be truth in either of the traditional senses, as correspondence or coherence, there must be evidence. That is, the object referred to in the true statement must be manifest, must show itself, it must be uncovered. But that the being disclosed can be uncovered depends upon the possibility of such uncovering. In *Being and Time* this possibility is supplied by the being whose Being consists in Being-in-the-world, Dasein. Thus the early Heidegger distinguishes two senses of "true," the Being-uncovered of beings and the Being-uncovering of Dasein.

Circumspective concern, or even that concern in which we tarry and look at something, uncovers entities within-the-world. These entities become that which has been uncovered. They are "true" in a second sense. What is primarily "true" – that is, uncovering – is Dasein. "Truth" in the second sense does not mean Being-uncovering, but Being-uncovered.[12]

When the later Heidegger speaks of truth as unconcealedness he is speaking on analogy with the Being-uncovering of *Being and Time*, without the subjectivist bias of the latter. That is, "truth" is that which allows beings to show themselves through providing an area of showing. As such Heidegger's "truth" is analogous with the horizon of earlier phenomenology, but with Heidegger the horizon allows for the possibility of focus, or being manifest, and in that sense is primary truth. As such however it itself is that which is ordinarily *not* manifest, not present. "Only what *aletheia* as opening grants is experienced and thought, not what it is as such. This remains concealed."[13] The concealedness and hiddenness which is fundamental to truth is primarily the essential non-presence (in the sense of not being in the present) of the opening which allows beings to be present. Only secondarily is it the perspectival hiddenness native to those beings themselves.

After 1964 Heidegger gives up the translation of *aletheia* as truth, without giving up the matter thought by *aletheia*. This matter, the clearing or opening in which both beings and Being can appear, remains the primary "object" of Heidegger's thought. In *On Time and Being* Heidegger returns to his earliest treatment of the clearing, in terms of temporality. The ecstatic temporality which is the meaning of the Being of Dasein in *Being and Time* is now thought as "time-space." Time-space is introduced during a discussion of presence in terms of the present and absence. As opposed to the traditional understanding of the present as a now point in a sequence of now points, Heidegger interprets the present as that which concerns human being, the matter illuminated in concern. "What is present concerns us, the present, that is: what, lasting, comes toward us, us human beings." "Presence means: the constant abiding that approaches man, reaches him, is extended to him."[14] Presence, understood in this way as that which lasts in concern, involves more than the present ordinarily so called. It necessarily also involves absence, the absence of that which has been, and of that which is coming toward us. That which is "past" and "future" for Heidegger, is equally present, but *only* in the sense of being of concern, not in the sense of being in the temporal now. There is a presence of "past" and "future" precisely insofar as they are absent from the now, i.e. as having been and coming toward.

> But we have to do with absence just as often, that is, constantly. For one thing, there is much that is no longer present in the way we know presencing in the sense of the present. And yet, even that which is no longer present presences immediately in its absence – in the manner of what has been, and still concerns us . . . absence, as the presenting of what is not yet present, always in some way concerns us, is present no less immediately than what has been.[15]

Thus not every presencing involves the present. But the present too is itself a mode of presence.

Heidegger's concern, however, is not with that which is present, past, or future. Reverting to a distinction which is focal in *Kant and the Problem of Metaphysics*, he is rather interested in temporality itself or the opening in which that which is temporal can be so. "For time itself is nothing temporal, no more than it is something that is." "Time-space now is the name for the openness which opens up in the mutual self-extending of futural approach, past, and present."[16] Time-space supplies this openness in which present and absent beings can be, however, only in that the dimensions of time, past, present, and future, are both related to one another and distinct. Within this distinction lies a withholding of the present. The past and future are present *only* through their absence.

> we call the first, original, literally incipient extending in which the unity of true time consists "nearing nearness," "nearhood." . . . But it brings future, past, and present near to one another by distancing them. For it keeps what has been open by denying its advent as present. . . . Nearing nearness has the character of denial and withholding.[17]

It is both possible and helpful to distinguish Heidegger's truth of Being, as we have just interpreted it, from certain other contemporary notions which seem to be similar to it. First, the truth of Being should not be seen as analogous to a conceptual scheme. Aside from the obvious fact that Heidegger associates the truth of Being with temporality, rather than concepts, there is a deeper difference between these notions. As Donald Davidson pointed out in his paper "On the Very Idea of a Conceptual Scheme," the idea of a conceptual scheme depends ultimately upon something like the hard Kantian distinction between sensibility and understanding. But Heidegger rejects this distinction as fully as do Davidson, Sellars, and Rorty. As early as *Being and Time*, Heidegger held that we never have merely "raw feelings."[18] Rather, for Heidegger, all human "experience" is only possible within *a world*, a world which is always already linguistically articulated. But then, perhaps the truth of Being should be seen as similar to the analytic notion of a set of linguistic rules which allow for the possibility of language use? There is more to be said in favor of this analogy, as Heidegger frequently remarks on the connection between the truth of Being and the pre-thematic articulation of a world by language. We must be careful here with the concept of a rule. The word "rule" suggests a situation in which a person acting according to a rule must either be obeying the rule (i.e. the rule is a principle which is explicit *for* the agent) or merely acting in conformity to a rule (i.e. the agent's acts fall into a regular, perhaps causal, pattern, although the agent is not aware of this).[19] Heidegger wishes to avoid both of these alternatives, which he sees as metaphysical. In both cases we are seen as capable, in principle, of giving a single correct interpretation and explication of what is involved in acting according to any particular rule. That is, every rule can be made explicit and focal, either by the agent (in the case of obeying a rule) or by a scientist observing the behavior (in the case of conforming to a rule). For Heidegger, the necessity of the hermeneutic circle, which precludes the possibility of any fully grounded interpretation, points to the *necessarily* non-focal character of both language and the truth of Being. Thus Heidegger's truth of Being must also be distinguished from the notion of a set of linguistic rules. Put bluntly, Heidegger's position is that "rules" cannot be successfully used to account for the possibility and actuality of language use.

The matter of Heidegger's thought, then, is the truth of Being, the clearing in which beings can appear and in which Being, as the presencing of presence, can manifest itself. The clearing is analogous with the phenomenological horizon. As such it is the concealed possibility of unconcealment, the "truth" of Being. Further, the opening is temporality, the ecstatic extendedness and distinction of past, present, and future. All of this is different from Being, or presencing as such. But how is any of this relevant to Heidegger's insistence on the epochal history of Being, and his distinction of thought and philosophy, and Rorty's criticism of these?

The Truth of Being and the History of Philosophy

The thrust of Rorty's criticism of Heidegger is aimed at the supposed vacuity of Heidegger's thought of Being without beings. In order to overcome this vacuity, Rorty thinks that Heidegger has recourse to the history of beings. But the form ordinary history takes for Rorty's Heidegger is the alienated form of the history of philosophy. "If he [Heidegger] were true to his own dictum that we should 'cease all overcoming, and leave metaphysics to itself,' he would have nothing to say, nowhere to point. *The whole force of Heidegger's thought lies in his account of the history of philosophy.*"[20] For Rorty's Heidegger, therefore, the content of the history of Being arises out of the history of philosophy. But the history of Being can be subsumed under the history of philosophy, for Rorty, only if philosophy is *of* Being. Thus Rorty's Heidegger is necessarily committed to the view that metaphysics was always about Being, and that his own thought is tied to this tradition. "The only thing which links him with the tradition is his claim that the tradition, though persistently sidetracked onto beings, was really concerned with Being all the time – and, indeed, constituted the history of Being."[21]

But if Heidegger's "thought" is really different from the tradition as Heidegger claims, then he is committed to the odd view that his thought is essentially a continuation of the *same* thinking as metaphysics, although at the same time he utterly rejects everything in that tradition. The criticism thus has three steps. First, Being without being is a vacuous notion. Second, this vacuity is overcome through a consideration of the history of philosophy. This in turn commits Heidegger to the absurd position that his thought is both entirely different from the tradition and also a continuation of the tradition which is about the very same thing as that tradition. Heidegger needs the tradition in order to identify the matter of his thinking, but then turns around and denies that the tradition tells us anything about that matter.

The criticism is dominated throughout by the reading of Heidegger which sees his primary distinction in the difference between Being and beings. Rorty's initial claim, that Being without beings is a vacuous notion, is motivated by this reading. We have argued in the previous section that this understanding of Heidegger is inadequate. Nevertheless, this fact, by itself, is not sufficient to show that the criticism is not cogent. It still may be the case that this other matter of Heidegger's thought, the truth of Being, may also prove to be vacuous. That is, Heidegger might be equally unable to determine the truth of Being without recourse to his version of the history of philosophy. As Heidegger rejects that tradition as, at least, inadequate, he would once again be in the position of identifying the matter of his thinking through ontology, while denying that ontology has anything positive to say about that matter.

Although Heidegger's truth of Being is in no sense the same as is thought in Kant's thing in itself (the truth of Being is not a "real world" or beings as they are independent of experience), there does seem to be a certain formal analogy between them. The truth of Being cannot successfully be made into an object of experience. This is because it is not an object at all, whether of experience or to itself. It is not. Rather it is meant as the concealed space in which objects can be. But if the truth of Being can never be an object of experience, how can it be indicated, "pointed to"? It cannot be ostensively determined, it cannot be distinguished as this as opposed to that, and it cannot be defined in terms of some being. The reference to Kant, however, suggests a transcendental procedure for the determination of the truth of Being. But, even though Heidegger often uses transcendental sounding language, even in his late writings, he specifically precludes the option of considering the truth of Being as merely the necessary condition for the possibility of experience, as this would be overly subjectivistic. Nonetheless, Heidegger often *does use* quasi-transcendental arguments in order to identify the place and role of the truth of Being. Indeed, the characterizations we have already given to the truth of Being in the last section all arise out of such transcendental considerations. On the other hand, the base step for these procedures is not the certainty of experience. When the truth of Being is discussed as the clearing, that which it supplies the condition of the possibility of is not experience, but Being. Similarly, when *aletheia* or temporality are under consideration it is Being in the sense of present evidence or presencing as such which is the basis for the transcendental discussion.[22]

It is clear that Heidegger thinks there can be no direct access to the truth of Being, no uncovering of the truth of Being such as occurs in regard to beings. I am suggesting that Heidegger substitutes a quasi-transcendental approach. The foundation for this transcendental access is not experience, however, but rather Being. But how is Being itself to be determined and characterized? It seems that we are back to Rorty's problem. If the truth of Being can only be identified in and through Being, then Being itself must be available to us. But Being as presencing is not. It, Being, is not in the open to be viewed. Where then does Heidegger get the determination of Being as presencing? Heidegger explicitly addresses this question in "On Time and Being." He suggests two answers, one of which is a blatant statement of Rorty's contention that Heidegger can only determine Being from out of the tradition of ontology.

> But what gives us the right to characterize Being as presencing? This question comes too late. For this character of Being has long since been decided without our contribution. . . . Thus we are bound to the characterization of Being as presencing. It derives its binding force from the beginning of the unconcealment of Being as something that can be said. . . . Ever since the beginning of Western thinking with the Greeks, all saying of "Being" and "Is" is held in remembrance of the determination of Being as presencing which is binding for thinking.[23]

In this same passage Heidegger also suggests a second mode of access to Being or presencing. Harkening back to *Being and Time* he asserts that a phenomenological approach to *Zuhandenheit* and *Vorhandenheit* will also yield a characterization of Being as presencing. We will leave aside this second answer to the question concerning the determination of being as presencing and concentrate on the adequacy of the first answer, given Rorty's criticism of it.[24]

Heidegger explicitly asserts that Being has already been characterized as presencing, and that this has been done at the beginning of the Western philosophical tradition.[25] It would thus seem that Rorty is right in regard to the first two steps of his argument. Even though Heidegger is not primarily concerned with Being but rather with the truth of Being, the characterization of the truth of Being depends upon the determination of Being. Apart from the phenomenological arguments developed in *Being and Time* and then mostly ignored by Heidegger, there is no way to determine Being except through the supposedly already established determination given by the tradition. Rorty is thus apparently correct in his contention that Being is a vacuous notion which is only given content in and through the history of philosophy.

The third step in Rorty's argument is accomplished through the juxtaposition of Heidegger's dependence upon the tradition with his rejection of that tradition But Heidegger *never* simply rejects or refutes the tradition of Western thinking as wrong. In speaking specifically of Hegel, he makes the general point that it is impossible ever to give such a refutation or to hazard such a rejection. "Whatever stems from it [absolute metaphysics] cannot be countered or even cast aside by refutations. It can only be taken up in such a way that its truth is more primordial, sheltered in Being itself and removed from the domain of mere human opinion. All refutation in the field of essential thinking is foolish."[26] But if Heidegger does not see himself as refuting or rejecting the history of ontology as wrong, then what is the character of his rejection of the tradition? For reject it he does. The answer has already been given. The tradition is inadequate because it never thinks the truth of Being. This, necessarily, remains hidden from metaphysics: "the truth of Being as the lighting itself remains concealed from metaphysics. However, this concealment is not a defect of metaphysics but a treasure withheld from it yet held before it, the treasure of its own proper wealth."[27]

> In the history of Western thinking . . . what is, is thought, in reference to Being; yet the truth of Being remains unthought, and not only is that truth denied to thinking as a

possible experience, but Western thinking itself, and indeed in the form of metaphysics, expressly, but nevertheless unknowingly, veils the happening of that denial.[28]

The tradition of ontology, for Heidegger, is not wrong in regard to its continuous thinking of Being as presencing. It is inadequate and incomplete in that it fails to think the clearing, or truth of Being, in which there can be both present being, and presencing itself, Being.

Two crucial conclusions rest upon the character of Heidegger's rejection of the tradition. First, the fact that Heidegger rejects metaphysics in the way he does does not commit him to the position that metaphysics is wrong in regard to its characterization of Being. Quite the contrary appears to be the case. It is not ever possible for us to "give up" the content of Being as presencing, we necessarily live in terms of it. We can no longer *do* metaphysics not because it is wrong, but rather because it has ended in, and been continued by, technology and the positive sciences. Second, Heidegger's thinking is *not* about the very same thing metaphysics was about. Rorty is just wrong in his contention that it is. Rather Heidegger's thinking is distinguished from metaphysics precisely insofar as it is not concerned with Being, but is concerned with the truth of Being. It is in this sense that we must read his dictum that we need to leave metaphysics to itself. Heidegger would seem to agree with Rorty that the proper "end" to philosophy is in the sciences, natural and social, and in practical, technological activity. But there is something left unthought in philosophy, the clearing in which philosophy happens, the truth of Being.

Indicating the nature of Heidegger's rejection of metaphysics does not yet, however, decide the issue between him and Rorty. One additional step is necessary. We have already seen that there is a sense in which Heidegger cannot "leave metaphysics to itself." Even though he is not directly determining the matter of his thinking through the characterization of Being in the history of philosophy, Rorty is right in thinking that Heidegger does need the tradition in order to identify that matter. The truth of Being is identified by asking how Being as presencing is possible. Only through rethinking the tradition as the successive revelation of Being as presencing does it become possible to ask this question. But *this* relation between Heidegger and the tradition is not open to the criticism Rorty levels. There is nothing odd, contradictory, or impossible about rejecting ontology as incomplete because it does not think the truth of Being, which is necessary for its own possibility, and then determining the truth of Being through a quasi-transcendental discussion of the possibility of the ontological tradition. On the contrary, this is the "method" which is adequate and appropriate to the task.

The Truth of Being and Epochs of Being

Rorty's criticism of Heidegger in regard to the possibility for thinking at the end of philosophy is coordinated with a second criticism. This criticism concerns the relation among Heidegger's account of Being, the history of Being, and ordinary history. Heidegger's account of Being is, admittedly, dependent for its determination upon his understanding of the history of Being. Rorty claims that this history of Being is reducible to history in the usual sense. At best it is a history of ideas, which itself is parasitic upon the social, political, and economic history of peoples. At worst it is vacuous.

There are two distinct though related claims involved in Rorty's criticism of Heidegger on the history of Being. For most of his paper Rorty asserts that Heidegger's history of Being must be seen as simply a version of the history of philosophy. "Heidegger's sense of the vulgarity of the age . . . is strongest when what is trivialized is the history of metaphysics. For this history is the history of Being."[29] On this account, the history of Being is both constituted by and manifest in the writings of the great philosophers. As such, ordinary history is seen as secondary to metaphysical history – a period is characterized as a failure or a success in terms of its ability to actualize the thought of its philosophers. On the other hand, Rorty also claims that the history of Being must he seen in terms of, and gets its content from, the ordinary history of "ages, cultures," etc. "Unless Heidegger connected the history of Being with that of men and nations through such phrases as 'a nation's relation to Being' and thus connected the history of philosophy with just plain history, he would be able to say only what Kierkegaard said,"[30] i.e. his history of Being would be vacuous. These two claims do not, of course, contradict one another. Rather, together they amount to a single assertion concerning Heidegger's history of Being. For Rorty, Heidegger sees the history of Being as the history of philosophy. But, for Rorty, following Marx and Dewey, the history of philosophy itself is composed of a series of *Weltanschauung*, which in turn are determined in and through ordinary history. Rorty emphasizes those passages in Heidegger which connect the history of Being with ordinary history because for Rorty it is ultimately through this reference that the history of philosophy is made definite.

There are thus two relations in question in Rorty's discussion of Heidegger's history of Being – the relation between the history of Being and the history of philosophy, and the relation between the history of philosophy and ordinary history. We have already seen that there is a sense in which the history of metaphysics is a history of Being for Heidegger. The various metaphysical determinations of Being as presencing do constitute something like a history of Being. "The development of the abundance of transformations of Being [in metaphysics] looks at first like a history of Being."[31] It is also the case that whatever genuinely characterizes the history of Being for Heidegger, the indications for the concrete stages of this history are taken almost exclusively from the thinking of philosophers. But these metaphysical systems are not *themselves* the epochs of Being which compose the history of Being, for Heidegger. Rather, Heidegger attempts to differentiate the epochs of Being, which are tie stages of his history of Being, from the metaphysical systems, which are merely concrete indicators for discovering the content of this history. This differentiation can be seen clearly in Heidegger's use of the term "epoch" to stand for the stages of the history of Being. For the word "epoch" has a specific technical sense in Heidegger's thought which goes beyond and is different from its ordinary sense.

To hold back is, in Greek, *epoche*. Hence we speak of the epochs of the destiny of Being. Epoch does not mean here a span of time in occurrence, but rather the fundamental characteristic of sending, the actual holding back of itself in favor of the discernability of the gift, that is of Being with regard to the grounding of beings.[32]

An epoch of Being, then, is not characterized by what is positive in any metaphysical thesis in regard to Being. Rather, it is determined by what is absent, held back, in that position. The history of Being is a history of hiddenness, not of presence. It is a history of the specific ways in which the place and truth of Being have been forgotten, not of Being in the ontological sense, itself.

At this point an apparent, but only apparent, similarity between Heidegger and Hegel suggests itself and is instructive. Hegel's history of philosophy is also a history of absence, of holding back. For Hegel, each successive stage in philosophical development (corresponding roughly to moments in the Logic) is, as finite, determined by its limit. A philosophical system is as it is because it fails to incorporate within its own thought something which is nonetheless necessary for itself. This other, its limit, is both the determination of the philosophy, and, ultimately, its *Aufhebung*. But in Hegel's "history of Being" this holding back is itself limited. That is, thought progressively overcomes each of its successive limits until limitation itself is finally incorporated into philosophy in the *Science of Logic*. In this culmination the form of finitude, temporality, is also *Aufgehoben*. In Heidegger's history of Being, on the other hand, there is not and cannot be any such final reappropriation of the hidden. At best there can be only a simple recognition of the hidden, non-present limit of all philosophical discourse.

Returning to the main problem, however, how does the epochal character of Heidegger's history of Being affect the relation between that history and the history of philosophy? The history of Being is obviously dependent upon Heidegger's critical rethinking of the history of philosophy, but only in a negative way. The actual content that Heidegger gives to his history of Being is both discovered through and different from the actual content of the history of philosophy. It is discovered through the tradition in that it traces what is necessary for each specific moment in the history of philosophy. It is different from the content of the tradition in that no particular stage in the tradition, or even that tradition taken as a whole, thinks what is at issue in the history of Being. For what is at issue in the history of Being is *not* Being, but the truth of Being. The history of Being includes, for example, a history of the ways in which temporality functions but is passed over, and must be passed over, in ontology, but if this is the case then it is clear that the history of Being is not simply reducible to the history of metaphysics. Rorty's claim that "this history [the history of metaphysics] is the history of Being" is just false. As was the case in regard to the relation of thinking and philosophy, Rorty has confused an admitted *dependence* of Heidegger on the tradition with the false proposition that the matter of Heidegger's thinking must be *identical* with the content of the tradition.

If Heidegger is not committed to the view that the history of Being is reducible to the history of metaphysics, then what are we to make of the relation between the history of Being and ordinary history? A simple transitive relation like the one implied by Rorty will not do. That is, if the history of Being is *not* the history of philosophy, then the determination of the content of the history of philosophy by ordinary history does not necessitate, by itself, an equal determination of the content of the history of Being by ordinary history. But *we* can *discover* the actual content of the history of Being only through recourse to the actual content of philosophical thought. Doesn't this imply the dependence in question? Not really. As the history of philosophy and the history of Being are correlative, and the history of philosophy and ordinary history are also, at least, correlative, there must be some correlation between ordinary history and the history of Being. But this correlation would allow for a criticism of Heidegger only if it made it impossible to differentiate Being or (more accurately) the truth of Being, from beings. That is, if the history of Being were a function of ordinary history, and ordinary history was not reciprocally a function of the history of Being, then the truth of Being would also be a simple function of the actual history of beings. In that case the investigation of the history of Being, in Heidegger's sense, could only be an alienated and unselfconscious study of the ordinary history of beings. Being and the truth of Being would not be radically different from beings, but only abstract and alienated ways in which a tradition of scholars had indirectly encountered beings. Rorty accepts this inference because he thinks of the history of Being as identical with the history of metaphysics and further thinks of the history of metaphysics as a function of ordinary history. We have already seen, however, that the history of Being is *not* identical with the history of metaphysics, for Heidegger. Given this lack of identity, Rorty's argument could work only if he showed that the history of Being were a function of the history of metaphysics. This relationship between the history of Being and the history of metaphysics he does not show, and Heidegger would deny. Although there is a correlation between an epoch of Being and a positive metaphysical assertion in regard to Being itself, which allows for the possibility of discovering the content of an epoch of Being, a positive metaphysical assertion does not *determine*, causally or otherwise, the holding back which is definitive for an epoch. Rather, Heidegger suggests, the reverse is more likely. Thus, even if the history of philosophy is a function of ordinary history, it does not follow that the history of Being is a function of ordinary history. An epoch of Being is defined by the field of openness in which both beings and Being can be manifest in the particular way they are in that epoch. This "clearing," as the truth or place of Being, is itself hidden from the period. The correlation between ordinary history and the history of Being can he accounted for and is necessitated by the fact that the truth of Being opens a field or world of possibility in which the life of peoples, nations, etc., occurs. This implies no priority to either the ordinary historical events and structures or to the particular character of the open during a particular temporal period. Nor does this correlation make it impossible to distinguish and differentiate beings from the truth of Being.

The history of Being, although discoverable for Heidegger in and through the history of metaphysics, is not the history of metaphysics. Equally, the history of Being, although correlated with ordinary history, need not be for Heidegger simply a function of ordinary history. We then see that the second main aspect of Rorty's criticism of Heidegger fails to be conclusive. As was the case with the first main aspect of his criticism (in regard to the relation of thinking and philosophy), Rorty's failure to identify the difference between Being and the truth of Being in Heidegger's thought is crucial here. If this distinction is ignored, then the history of Being can only be identified with the history of metaphysics. If this were the case, Rorty's criticism would be correct and cogent. But as the history of Being is not simply a new version of the history of metaphysics, Rorty's criticism must be rejected.

Conclusion: Heidegger, Rorty, and Appropriation

Although the aims of this chapter have now been reached, there is still a matter involved in the chapter that needs further elucidation. I have somehow managed to write a chapter which is primarily concerned with Heidegger but which never once speaks of *Ereignis*, or "appropriation."

It has been suggested throughout this chapter that the real "matter" of Heidegger's thinking is not Being, but rather the truth of Being. This is not entirely accurate. The ultimate concern of Heidegger's thought is neither Being nor the truth of Being. It is appropriation. "What lets the two matters [Being and time] belong together, what brings the two into their own and, even more, maintains and holds them in their belonging together – the way the two matters stand, the matter at stake – is Appropriation."[33]

Why then have I intentionally suggested that the matter is temporality, or the truth of Being? This has been done for the sake of simplicity. Appropriation itself can only be grasped in terms of the relation between Being and the truth of Being. As such, it is almost totally incomprehensible without a prior thinking of the truth of Being, a thinking which Rorty's paper lacks. For appropriation operates for Heidegger precisely in the relation, the belonging together, of the two. "The matter at stake [appropriation] first appropriates Being and time into their own in virtue of their relation."[34] Heidegger often speaks of appropriation as the "It" which gives both time and Being. This suggests that appropriation is some third thing, a Being over and beyond Being and time. But this substantialization of appropriation is a mistake. "Appropriation neither is, nor is Appropriation there."[35] Rather, the mutual opening up and belonging together of Being and the truth of Being is at issue in appropriation, and only that. In appropriation Heidegger is suggesting an entirely "formal" feature of all historical worlds, the difference and relation of Being, as presenting and the truth of Being as temporality. A preliminary attention to the truth of Being is thus necessary to open the way to Heidegger's appropriation. Since Rorty's article fails to give this attention to the truth of Being, this chapter has attempted to remedy this lack. To have brought up *Ereignis* prematurely would only have muddied the waters.

Then does this chapter assert that Heidegger is right and Rorty is wrong, that "thinking" is possible at the end of philosophy, and that there is indeed a history of Being independent of ordinary history? No, it remains uncommitted in regard to these issues. Neither does it suggest that there is no significant difference between Rorty and Heidegger. There is indeed such a difference. But Rorty has misidentified it. Rorty thinks that the difference between Heidegger and himself lies in Heidegger's insistent consideration of "Being." This amounts, for Rorty, to the "hope" that even after the end of ontology there might still be philosophy, as thought, which searches for the "holy," which while rejecting the tradition, still looks for something analogous to the "real world." In an odd way Rorty's interpretation and criticism of Heidegger mirrors

Derrida's reading and criticism of Heidegger. For Derrida, "Being" is used by Heidegger as a "unique name," signifying a "transcendental signified." That is, the verb "to be" is thought of by Derrida's Heidegger as having a "lexical" as well as a grammatical function, a lexical use which signifies a transcendental "Being" in a unique way. This supposed Heideggerian meaning of "Being" amounts, for Derrida, to a certain "nostalgia" for presence. In fact, as we have seen, neither of these interpretations can be justified in Heidegger's texts. The truth of Being is not Being as presencing, and *Ereignis* is nothing outside of the open field in which beings and meanings occur. Heidegger does not "hope" for a "real world," nor is he nostalgic concerning presence. Dominique Janicaud has made this point persuasively in regard to Derrida's criticism.

> I do not think it right to claim that there is nostalgia in Heidegger's works. . . . The Heideggerian *Ereignis* does not mean any self-closure or self-achievement, but rather an *ek-statikon*. My last words on this point will be taken from "Time and Being": "*Zum Ereignis als solchem gehort die Enteignung*," which one might translate as follows: disappropriation belongs to appropriation as such. I thus do not see how one could assimilate the Heideggerian *Ereignis* to the appropriation of presence.[36]

But if "Being" in Heidegger is not a "transcendental signified," if Heidegger does not hold out any "hope" for a "holy" real world, what then does oppose Heidegger and Rorty? It is precisely the same thing which really distinguishes Rorty from Derrida. Both Heidegger and Derrida consider the field in which presencing can occur, in Heidegger's language the open and appropriation, in Derrida's language "*differance*," as worthy of thought. Heidegger is claiming that there is a "formal" necessity involved in any actual world of activity and meaning, the opposition and belonging together of Being and time. This clearing and belonging together is approachable for Heidegger through something like transcendental argumentation. These arguments do not get us outside of our world, however, only into it in a different way. It is this claim and this "hope" which Rorty is really denying. "Overcoming the Tradition: Heidegger and Dewey" unfortunately does not address this issue.

Notes

1 R. Rorty, "Overcoming the tradition: Heidegger and Dewey." *Review of Metaphysics*, 30(2), 297 (cited hereafter as OTT).

2 OTT, p. 297.

3 OTT, p. 280.

4 Otto Poeggeler and Thomas Sheehan are among those who *have* recognized the importance of the meaning or truth of Being in Heidegger's thought. For example, see Poeggeler's "Heidegger's topology of being," in J. J. Kockelmans (ed.), *On Heidegger and Language*. Evanston, IL: Northwestern University Press, 1972; and Sheehan's "Heidegger's interpretation of Aristotle: *Dynamic and Ereignis*." *Philosophy Research Archives*, 4 (1978), 1–33.

5 This distinction itself appears mostly in an interpolation into the text which was written after 1935. See Heidegger, *Introduction to Metaphysics*. Garden City, NY: Doubleday, 1961, pp. 14ff.

6 Heidegger, *On the Way to Language*. New York: Harper & Row, 1971, p. 20.

7   Heidegger, "The Onto-theo-logical constitution of metaphysics," in J. Stambaugh (ed.), *Identity and Difference*. New York: Harper & Row, 1969, p. 57.

8   Ibid., p. 58.

9   Heidegger, *Martin Heidegger in Conversation* (ed. R. Wisser). New Delhi: Arnold Hinneman Publishers, 1977, p. 45.

10 Heidegger, *Being and Time*. New York: Harper & Row, 1962, p. 262, H. 219.

11 Heidegger, "The origin of the work of art," in Hofstadter (ed.), *Poetry, Language, Thought*. New York: Harper & Row, 1971, p. 54.

12 Heidegger, *Being and Time*, p. 263, H. 220.

13 Heidegger, "The end of philosophy and the task of thinking," in J. Stambaugh (ed.), *On Time and Being*. New York: Harper & Row, 1972, p. 71.

14 Heidegger, "On time and being," in Stambaugh (ed.), *On Time and Being*, p. 12 (cited hereafter as OTB).

15 OTB, p. 13.

16 OTB, p. 14.

17 OTB, p. 15. At this point Heidegger's discussion of time bears a striking resemblance to Hegel's treatment of time in the *Philosophy of Nature*. What distinguishes Heidegger's treatment from Hegel's, however, is his insistence that temporality is irreducible to a mode of thought.

18 Cf. *Being and Time*, ¶34, etc.

19 This tendency can be seen in Sellars's article "Some reflections on language games," in *Science, Perception, and Reality*. London: Routledge and Kegan Paul, 1963, pp. 321–58. As I understand it, Sellars's own attempt to avoid these poles ultimately depends on a simple conformity, perhaps causal, to metarules.

20 OTT, pp. 302–3.

21 OTT, p. 303.

22 I describe Heidegger's procedure for identifying the truth of Being as "quasitranscendental." This term needs some explication. For Heidegger, there is a sense in which the truth of Being is phenomenal, roughly the same sense in which a phenomenological horizon is phenomenal. (As opposed to a Husserlian horizon, however, the truth of Being can *never* be made focal.) It is this that leads Heidegger to assert, in the Introduction to *Being and Time*, that both the sense of Being and the Kantian forms of intuition are "phenomena." So, if a transcendental argument is seen as one which necessarily argues to a conclusion which asserts the being of a non-phenomenal condition, Heidegger's procedure cannot be termed transcendental. Nevertheless, Heidegger's method for identifying and determining the truth of Being does have a transcendental form. That is, he moves from that which is admitted to be the case, beings and their Being, to the necessary condition for the possibility of beings, the truth of Being. For this reason I have called his procedure quasitranscendental. I have no objection, however, to calling this method "transcendental," as long as it is remembered that: (1) the argument does not start from experience and (2) the condition argued to is neither an existent nor non-phenomenal.

23 OTB, pp. 6–7.

24 But see the next section of this chapter.

25 OTB, p. 8.

26 Heidegger, "Letter on humanism," in *Basic Writings* (ed. D. Krell). New York: Harper & Row, 1977, pp. 215–16.

27 Heidegger, "Letter on humanism," p. 213.

28 Heidegger, "The word of Nietzsche," in Lovitt (ed.), *The Question Concerning Technology*. New York: Harper & Row, 1977, p. 56.

29 OTT, p. 299.

30 OTT, p. 296.
31 OTB, p. 8.
32 OTB, p. 9.
33 OTB, p. 19.
34 OTB, p. 19.
35 OTB, p. 24.
36 D. Janicaud, "Presence and appropriation." *Research in Phenomenology*, 8 (1978), 73.

30

Derrida and Heidegger:
Iterability and *Ereignis*

CHARLES SPINOSA

Followers of Heidegger are likely, when feeling tendentious, to find that Derrida's reading of Heidegger is self-aggrandizingly reductionist and that Derrida's work is simply a sophisticated version of what Heidegger diagnosed as nihilistic, Nietzschean, technological thinking.[1] Derrideans, with the encouragement of Derrida himself, read Heidegger as the forerunner Derrida has outstripped.[2] Derrida, it is said, learned from the failure of Heidegger's heroic attempt to overcome metaphysics and, in his bettering of Heidegger's deconstruction, has gone well beyond his teacher. Like compulsive shoppers, Richard Rorty and neo-pragmatists in his mold read both Heidegger and Derrida to see how much of each they can buy. It turns out that all of Heidegger, except early Heidegger's transcendental language and later Heidegger's nostalgia, can be bought by the pragmatists; and all of Derrida, except his transcendental language and his anti-metaphysical activism, can be bought as well. This state of affairs with its partisans and compulsive shoppers has stood in the way of getting a clear picture of how Derrida and Heidegger are really very close to each other and yet divided by fundamentally different intuitions about how human practices, and consequently human beings, work. The different intuitions show up in how each thinker understands language, in particular its moving force, and are focused in the difference between Heidegger's *Ereignis*[3] and Derrida's Iterability. Getting clear about what lies behind these terms, then, should give us a relatively clear and unmysterious picture of Heidegger's and Derrida's thought, show us that we should see them both as post-metaphysical and non-technological, and reveal that their unpragmatic content is large enough to make the price of assimilating them too exhorbitant for pragmatists.[4]

First, in order to develop a clear sense of what Heidegger and Derrida are claiming, we will need to lay out the meaning of a handful of roughly corresponding terms or notions. Ranging from the easy to the more difficult and giving Derrida's first, they are: system of differences and equipmental totality; trace and phenomenon; *difference* and the truth of being;[5] Derrida's version of Heidegger's ontological difference and the metaphysical version of the ontological difference; temporalization into present

Spinosa, Charles, "Derrida and Heidegger: Iterability and *Ereignis*" from *Heidegger: A Critical Reader*, edited by Hubert L. Dreyfus and Harrison Hall. Oxford: Blackwell, 1992. Reprinted with permission.

moments and pragmatic temporality; and, finally, temporalization and authentic temporalization. Then, in this context, the significance of Iterability and *Ereignis* can be worked out with particular reference to how both notions fit in with recognizable human behavior. Finally, showing how Heidegger and Derrida are neither metaphysical nor pragmatic will be a matter of drawing the consequences from the examples of Iterability and *Ereignis*.

Terms and Positions

The main point of this section will be to get beyond the polemics and misunderstandings to show just how close Heidegger's and Derrida's positions are. To do this, the first things to adapt to are the two different starting points for their thinking. Derrida typically focuses on language as the practice that reveals the most about how we are. Heidegger, instead, starts with simple (usually rural) activity such as a craftsman working on something in his shop. But this difference ought not come to much since Derrida says that the deep aspect of language – writing – structures any meaningful activity[6] and Heidegger thinks of language as a particularly revealing practice. They are both, then, starting with meaningful human activity. With no more preamble we may examine the first two sets of related distinctions.

Derrida takes over from Saussure the notion that language is a system of differences. By this, Derrida and Saussure mean that we do not respond to particular phonemes as such or to particular meanings as such but that we encounter word sounds or things (positivities) only in terms of the differences among the phonemes or meanings. Each phoneme or meaning is understood only in terms of its difference from the others. This notion is now fairly widely understood. Moreover, we encounter things in terms of a whole series of differences that are particularly charged for us; so we might say that if for us some of the particularly charged differences are true/false, real/imaginary, sensible/intelligible, discovered/invented, perceived/remembered, natural/cultural, masculine/feminine, then anything we encounter will show up in terms of these differences. But we might easily imagine that if at another time or in a different culture holy/profane, saint/sinner replaced the first two charged differences, then things would show up differently for us. In living within this alternative set of charged differences, we would pass over some things that seem important to us now (such as the discipline of science) and other (now trivial) things would show up for us as of fundamental importance (such as the purity of one's soul). Again, if we replaced holy/profane with warlike/pastoral and saint/sinner with hero/shepherd, then things would show up in yet another wholly different way. The point to get from this is that "in language there are only differences *without positive terms*."[7] This is to say, positive things like a saint or a sinner only show up, if they show up at all, as effects of the way a language's differences sort things out.

Heidegger's thinking is very close to this Saussurean/Derridean account. Indeed, when Heidegger says that there really is no such thing as "an equipment,"[8] he is making the same sort of point Derrida makes when he says that language has no positive terms. But Heidegger starts, as was said, with the situation of a craftsman at work in his shop. The craftsman shows up as involved in comporting himself in certain ways to make something. He shows up, that is, in terms of the skills and practices he embodies. And for the most part, these are skills and practices for dealing with equipment. But notice in terms of his involved activity, which Heidegger takes as basic, it does not make sense to say that the craftsman encounters a hammer or a nail alone. Rather, he encounters them as things *in order to* secure some planks of wood *towards* building a chest *for the sake of* enacting himself as, say, a cabinetmaker. The point is that he understands nothing, not even himself, independently of everything else in the shop that has some role in pursuing his occupation, his involved activity. A particular piece of string good, even exceptionally good, for tying together bamboo for making huts in the South Sea Islands would just not show up for him as such, even if it were hanging on his wall above his hammer. It would not show up as having such a use because he has no skills or practices for making such huts. He would pass over it or see it as waste material or as something to use in one of his normal activities. Thus, everything, even the craftsman himself, shows up in terms of a context of equipment, a world of involvement.

The differences between a system of differences and an equipmental context further narrow as we see how Derrida and Heidegger work with these notions. Because nothing can show up as wholly independent of either a system of differences or an equipmental context, Derrida becomes interested in traces and Heidegger in phenomena. These two, traces and phenomena, turn out to be roughly equivalent, though Derrida thinks that the trace goes beyond the phenomenon.[9] The trace is something that shows up in such a way that it is a ghost or sham of presence; its presence is shown as not really there; it is, as Derrida says, a "simulacrum" of its presence, it "dislocates itself, displaces itself, [and] refers itself."[10] The meaning of these claims comes out on two different levels. On the lower level, a word shows up as a trace when we respond to it with sensitivity to how its meaning is dependent on its context, how, that is, its meaning shifts as its context changes. We are alert to words in this way in reading works of literature where we expect that the meaning of its words will change as, say, more of a work is read and reread over the course of a life or lives. On the higher level, the trace refers to the way that no fixed or natural set of charged differences ever comes to hold sway over any system of differences. The "weave of differences" is always changing with history; so the trace also refers to this play (the changing of the charged differences) in the systems of difference. (This play, we shall come to see, is *differance*.)

Heidegger's phenomenon has precisely the same structure as the trace. It, like the trace, is not an appearance or just any old thing showing up, as common sense might suggest.[11] Rather, in Heidegger's terms, a phenomenon is "That which already shows itself in the appearance as prior to the 'phenomenon' as ordinarily understood and as accompanying it in every case."[12] Heidegger's point here is that the phenomenon he is interested in is, in effect, the way skillful coping in an equipmental totality allows any particular thing to show up. Like Derrida, Heidegger wants to see things in a way that is alert to the background understandings, activities, and structures that generate them. Both trace and phenomenon, then, are the aspect of anything that reveals how its particular context, linguistic and social, allows it to show up.

For Heidegger, the context that makes it possible for things to show up is usually understood not linguistically but rather as a particular way of being or revealing (a style of skillful coping) that is associated with a particular thing. This notion of particular ways of being (or revealing) is cashed out differently over the course of Heidegger's career. But even around the period of *Being and Time*, Heidegger already saw the history of the West – at least from Plato onwards – as the history of understanding being in terms of productivity.[13] This meant that the basic practice guiding our understanding of most other practices was the practice of a craftsman's productivity, his *techne*. So, for example, the power of Plato's ideas came from the sense that an idea preceded the way a craftsman formed his matter. Again, the notion of a Prime Mover or First Cause arose from fitting all beings into the mode of those made by a craftsman. This history of productivity took many different turns starting out with form/matter as the essential distinction, moving through essence/existence to subject/object.

Thus, phenomena show up not only in terms of a particular use (a hammer is in order to hammer, a car to transport oneself), but also in terms of a place in this history of being. They manifest a particular historical style of being. So, for example, one might find oneself engaged in a practice that reveals something of the pre-Platonic Greek way of being. We might suppose that a kind of training for, and taking part in, marathons might do this, especially if a particular harmony of thinking and acting is required.[14] If we think of early Greek culture as focused by competence, we might find its way of revealing things in certain academic practices where competence alone seems to count. Clearly, the sort of revealing in these practices is quite a bit different from the kind of revealing that goes on in, say, psychological testing or other subject/object, disciplinary practices. So phenomena that reveal that their showing up itself depends upon one particular historical way of making things show up are like the trace in that they reveal that revealing (another word for being)[15] in all its multiplicity could not ever be fully revealed unless history could be stopped. Here again, Derrida and Heidegger are on all fours.[16] Derrida even authorizes us to see an identity here, for he claims that the way Heidegger sees a usage (or a practice) is precisely as a trace in Derrida's sense. He only doubts that the being of usage or trace may be brought out in terms of a thinking dedicated to the essence of being.[17] Derrida has this doubt, as we shall see, because he does not read Heidegger intently enough.

In the course of giving an account of the terms, system of differences, equipmental context, trace, and phenomenon, Heidegger's "being" has come up and "*differance*" has been implicit. Can a clear sense now be given to these terms? Being amounts to revealing practices, which amount to "that on the basis of which beings are already understood."[18] But revealing always comes with one particular understanding or truth or essence.[19] The simplest way to make sense of this is to hear understanding, truth, or essence as style. Heidegger claims that, in the history of the West, we have had one style of revealing where things showed up as drawing humans to them, another where things showed up as signs telling human beings about creation, another where things showed up as objects organized for human intelligibility and control by necessary operations of the mind, and still others. These are all large-scale differences in the style of the revealing practices. To understand more fully what is meant here by "style," it will be easier to look more locally to those slightly different inflections of our general modern style in which things are revealed in different ways. We frequently see in our classes people whose style is rather careless and sloppy. They encounter chairs as things for resting the bodies they are forced to lug around. Work assignments are jobs to get done to please someone else. Reading, since it is boring, is best done when something else is going on for distraction's sake. This style pervades the lives of these people. The chairs are hard because they are not suited to relaxing. Sitting attentively erect is just not a way to encounter a chair in this style. Feeling a craftsman-like pride or concern about each sentence one is writing just does not fit with this relaxed way of approaching the world. And finally, poring over a text for hours, writing summaries of arguments and objections in the margins, is a skill that has no place within this general way of approaching things. For people with different styles, one will pass over some things that will show up as crucial for another. In the cross-cultural limit, one person will live in a very different world from another. Since a style of revealing is the source and ground of how things show up, Heidegger thinks of it as an understanding of the truth or the essence of being.

Differance comes very close to Heidegger's notion of revealing (being) once we make adjustments for seeing things in terms of systems of differences instead of practices or components. Derrida writes:

> we will designate as *differance* the movement according to which language, or any code, any system of referral in general, is constituted "historically" as a weave of differences.[20]

> Essentially and lawfully, every concept is inscribed in a chain or in a system within which it refers to the other, to other concepts, by means of the systematic play of differences. Such a play, *differance*, is thus no longer simply a concept, but rather the possibility of conceptuality, of a conceptual process and system in general.[21]

> *Differance* is the non-full, non-simple, structured and differentiating origin of differences.[22]

The point here is that *differance* is the movement that shifts the charges of particular differences (or re-constellates them) in any particular system of differences. As such, it is responsible for the particular set of important differences in any particular system at any time. This movement or play in any system of differences can be clarified in various ways. But for now, the way this *differance* works may be shown by looking at what is supposed to happen when Derrida shifts the charge in the speech/writing difference. Instead of seeing writing as different from and a deferred form of speech, Derrida wants, *in the first instance*,[23] writing to become the dominant term so that we see speech as an imitation of and as derived from writing.

Derrida is not trying to tell us that in the course of history, writing came first and then speech came as a representation of writing. Rather, he argues that the important feature of language is the way it bridges particular contexts, not the way it can be used as a tool to get someone nearby to do something. To put this as concretely as possible, Derrida claims that the request by the surgeon for a scalpel when he says, "Scalpel," and the response of the nurse of handing the surgeon a scalpel is *entirely* a derivative aspect of language. (And Derrida would argue this is no matter whether this use of language were glossed in terms of words indicating or pointing out things or as calling upon or activating particular skills for handling things.[24]) In fact, he would say any language use from the interior monologue to that of a close group of friends who are all sharing in a common project covers up the aspect of language that drives it. For in these situations, all the participants are already involved in the same practice. What is important about language, Derrida claims, is that it bridges different practices. The point of saying that an expression has meaning is to say that the expression retains that meaning from one context to the next. So, to go back to the surgeon example, saying "scalpel" does not get at what is linguistic in language, according to Derrida. For with a little more training and practice with the same nurse, this surgeon and nurse might, in the general course of things, work so well together that the surgeon need never say anything at all. The nurse might follow the procedure so well that when the surgeon holds out his hand, she finds herself already handing him the right scalpel. Handing the surgeon the scalpel could become as unarticulated as all the various ways of cutting the surgeon does in response to different textures of flesh and so on. What language does, the word "scalpel" in particular, is open the practice of surgical cutting to all sorts of other practices, like purchasing more scalpels from scalpel salesmen after the operation and allowing the surgeon to tell the hospital newspaper reporter that he saved the president's life by using a scalpel, and so on. This, Derrida thinks, is the defining aspect of language, and it is the aspect emphasized in writing, which is regularly used when two people are not working together in the same practice. Speech misses this point. Moreover, in having a culture where speech is understood as primary – a phonocentric culture – we are predisposed to think of ourselves as always involved in the same practice and to ignore all the different practices being bridged. By shifting the charge of the speech/writing distinction, speakers ought, in the first instance, to begin to see all the different practices being bridged. And, indeed, this seems to be happening. We speak now about mosaics and not melting pots. But, we want to object, Derrida did not get us to talk in terms of mosaics by reversing the charge of the speech/writing distinction. But this would be precisely Derrida's point. Of course, *he* did not do it. He, as Heidegger would also say, simply marked (or remarked upon) a shift that was taking place anyway. No person controls *differance*. That would be like thinking that someone controls language. We might as well say that a new way of revealing is happening – this amounts to putting Derrida's insight *about differance* into Heidegger's language. And so far, that is as far as Derrida's and Heidegger's intuitions have been worked out, nothing is left out by this translation.

Why then is Derrida not content to speak as Heidegger? There are two reasons that keep getting confused with one another. The first is that Derrida simply has a mistaken view of part of what Heidegger argues and the second is because of a profound difference. Before we get to the profound difference, the confusion must be cleared up. This can be done by getting straight about the ontological difference, or ontological differences, since, for Heidegger, there are really two. The metaphysical version of the ontological difference is the difference between being, as the most general quality of beings (which Heidegger sometimes calls beingness), and particular beings. Heidegger thinks that from Anaximander on, the West has understood this metaphysical difference as that between Presence (the most general quality of beings) and present things. Heidegger gives at least two different accounts of why this happened and of its necessity. The simplest account to understand, though it seems to have the least necessity about it, is the one, already mentioned, that Heidegger developed early in his career. Thinkers, he says, tended to understand things showing up in terms of the then-current practices of production. The paradigmatic being was the one produced by the craftsman, something that, once finished, could stand alone without needing any more work; consequently, all beings were understood in terms of coming to presence (being crafted) and presence (the quality of existing fully and independently of a creator-craftsman).

After all, in a tool-making, competence-centered culture, Heidegger would argue, presence, or the quality of being finished and ready for use, should seem the most general quality of anything at all. And just as Heidegger sees productive practices, in their various inflections, dominating the West, so presence shows up under various inflections as the most general quality of beings.

So far the account given of Heidegger's ontological difference concerns what Heidegger understands as the metaphysical version of the ontological difference. Focusing on this account, Derrida is led to think that Heidegger's contribution is almost entirely limited to thematizing explicitly for the first time that Western thought is constituted by thinking the presence of the present and then forgetting the distinction between presence and the present.[25] Derrida sets himself off from Heidegger by claiming that he is the one who first tries to understand the space within which the difference between presence and the present may be thought: "it is the determination of being as presence or as beingness that is interrogated by the thought of *difference*," he writes.[26] But Heidegger himself understood that he was attempting to think the disclosive space or clearing in which this metaphysical understanding of the difference between being and beings could show up. For Heidegger this space is the one opened up by the real ontological difference, the one between being as revealing and the revealed. Indeed, in his later works, Heidegger's thinking of this deeper ontological difference takes two tracks. He thinks through the history of the West as the history of being in order to see the different modes of revealing and to get a sense of how they happen, how, that is, they are "sent" by revealing or being itself. And, second, he looks at marginal practices in the West where things are revealed in ways that do not fit with the dominant understandings of being guided by productive practices.[27] Indeed, as a matter of terminology, when thinking about the way things show up in marginal practices, he does not speak in terms of presencing or productivity but rather in terms of bestowal and gathering. (The meanings of these two terms will be worked out in the discussion of temporality.)

Since Derrida mistakenly thinks that Heidegger merely thinks of being as presencing and the ontological difference as the difference between presence and the present, his distinction between his project and Heidegger's turns out to be no distinction at all. His project, in fact, agrees entirely with Heidegger's. This can be seen fairly clearly by looking at the contrast Derrida draws between himself and Heidegger: "the history of being, whose thought engages the Greco-Western *logos* such as it is produced via the ontological difference, is but an epoch of the *diapherein*."[28] If for *diapherein* we read Heidegger's *ontological* difference and not the *metaphysical* one, we have Derrida reproducing Heidegger. To get at their profound difference, we must develop an understanding of how Heidegger sees non-metaphysical revealing; that is, how he understands revealing from early to late in terms other than presencing. We must see, in other words, how Heidegger's understanding of human practices as temporal leads to things showing up in terms of bestowing and gathering. For this we must turn to Derrida's and Heidegger's sense of temporality.

Both Derrida and Heidegger think our everyday way of encountering time is misleading and consequently draws us to inadequate temporal understandings.[29] For Heidegger, our inadequate formulations of time come from our absorption in handling

490

things. In our involved comportment, we organize things according to what is appropriate when. "It is appropriate to put the handles on *after* we make the drawers," our cabinetmakers say. "The varnish takes as long to dry as it takes for me to build this rack for the top shelf," another cabinetmaker might add. Both these statements reveal an understanding of time in terms of a particular sense of what ultimately should get done (the cabinet should be made), what has already been done (supplies have been collected and the wood has been varnished), and what the ultimate goal and what has been done leave open for one's current occupation (building drawers or making the rack). As these statements show, in doing what is appropriate, we articulate our activity according to a temporality where the present is of first importance and where the future and past show up as a matter of taking stock of where we are in the process. Heidegger argues that the time of the philosophers, with its divisible nows and the rest, derives from this pragmatic time.[30]

Derrida describes a similar sense of normal time, only, as expected, his model is not based on artisans working but on a philosopher reading a text very closely. He writes:

> the movement of signification is possible only if each so-called "present" element, each element appearing on the scene of presence, is related to something other than itself, thereby keeping within itself the mark of the past element, and already letting itself be vitiated by the mark of its relation to the future element, this trace being related no less to what is called the future than to what is called the past, and constituting what is called the present by means of this very relation to what it is not: what it absolutely is not, not even a past or a future as a modified present.[31]

Heidegger would find this account too abstract; Derrida's present is exceedingly close to a now point. But Derrida saves his account, from a Heideggerian attack, first by thinking in terms of an actual activity – close reading – and, second, by realizing that the past and the future are not modified present moments but part of the structure of the activity of having any meaningful experience at all. For a meaningful experience cannot be a wholly unique (wow) moment but, for the sake of intelligibility, must always sort with other similar or identical experiences and become the ground for other meaningful experiences.[32]

That both Derrida and Heidegger think that these relatively pragmatic accounts of time are inadequate points to an important claim for both of them. As is well known, Heidegger holds that there is authentic and inauthentic temporalizing (and activity). For Derrida, likewise, human activity (writing) has in it something like a hierarchy. But Derrida has regularly been seen as someone who demolishes all hierarchical distinctions. Could he have one of his own? We need to see first what is at stake in higher-order kinds of temporalizing.

For Heidegger what makes human acitivity distinctive is not that it is so good at producing things or even that in any culture (or equipmental context) all the activity is coordinated. Rather, he is interested in two things. First, he notes that the coordinated activity of any culture (or equipmental context) has a particular style, which we describe in meaningful ways, and, second, that style can change. So, for example, productivity comes in various sorts of styles. Producing can occur in the style of subjects

491

and objects where things are accomplished by large organizations in which each member works on some little task. We have, then, individual subjects that need to be controlled and uninteresting interchangeable objects (neither things nor finished works). This description obviously amounts to production as Foucault describes it in a disciplinary society where each worker engages in part of the project and is watched by a mighty panoptic subject. Or producing could occur in the way of the small craftsman who gets drawn by a particular piece of material to work it in a certain way. He might very well see the chair as coming out of the wood. His skilled labor reveals what the wood can do. These different styles of production would show up, especially according to later Heidegger, as radically different ways of being or of revealing. The fact that there are such different styles in our history shows as well that these styles change. That there are styles of revealing and that they change is what Heidegger thinks is most important about revealing. Moreover, it is the activity of holding on to a style, including holding on to it in such a way that it changes, that provides the ground for authentic temporalizing.

The paradigmatic experience of this kind of temporalizing is, for Heidegger, receiving a new vision of how things are, finding a story that makes sense of your life, finding that your puttering around at something has finally clicked and now you can do it as you never could before. From early to late, Heidegger describes this kind of temporalizing as a receiving, a bestowal, or allotment, and with any bestowal or allotment goes a gathering together or a consolidating of the new sense of things.[33] Here we may see bestowal or allotment as a way of describing what we mean when we say, about some interpretation or some way of doing things that really works, "It just came to me" or "It just dawned on me that . . . "

Gathering is Heidegger's name for the way the new insight or the new way of doing something brings all the disparate aspects of the matter or activity together. When, for instance, we suddenly get a new reading of a text, part of getting the sense that our new reading is illuminating is the activity of collecting together in terms of the new reading all sorts of aspects of the text we had ignored or forced into shape before. This sort of activity is, at least, a good first approximation of this gathering.[34] This general activity of bestowal and gathering, though, has a particular temporal structure. A bestowal is a case where the future has opened up and bestowed or allotted some new way of dealing with all the things that we were *already* coping with. This opening up upon what is already, Heidegger thinks, is the structure of the authentic future and past. The present then shows up as the activity of coming alive to one's coping because of the new clarity that has been bestowed upon it. This present is a matter not of seeing what to do *now* but of sensing, perhaps even celebrating, how everything fits together. We get a rough sense of this difference between the pragmatic present and the authentic present by comparing the way things show up as present to be worked on when we are carrying out chores as opposed to the way things show up as present during a toast at a wedding feast when the entire life of the couple and ourselves are there in the articulation of the occasion. A more fully developed concrete example that shows how this bestowing/gathering temporalizing works and is related to the temporality of producing things should put these matters in order.

Many people, but men in particular, in my generation worked throughout college and professional school in order to establish lives with large amounts of personal ease and nonchalance. Our activity in the classroom, our jobs, our love lives were all held together by a general style of producing a freedom from the ties that would force us into compromises we did not want to make. This meant that we worked very hard to develop niches for ourselves in our public lives. In our private lives, we worked on the little things that we could control. We developed sophisticated cooking skills, gardening skills, home-repair skills, personal finance skills, athletic skills, skills for easy-going romances, and all the tastes that go along with all of these. But slowly life started to dull. And suddenly starting a family has come to many men my age to seem just the thing to do. But it is not the idea or concept of starting a family that comes to this group of men. Rather, suddenly, life is felt as something directed towards having a family. In the light of this future, everything takes on a new look. All the sophisticated skills now show up in an intensified, collected way as means of forming a family where the husband need not dominate his wife and where the father can nurture the baby. So having a family has come out of the future to make sense of the past and to redirect the current ways of coping with things, yielding an intense feeling of the connectedness or integrity of all the small skills. So, yes, it is still appropriate to boil the water before putting in the pasta, but before it was appropriate in order to produce (in terms of lived sentiments) pasta with precisely the right *al dente* texture. Now it is appropriate in order to produce (in terms of lived sentiments) the right family moment. So it is in this sense that authentic temporalizing – the temporality of receiving a particular general meaning or style – is the source of pragmatic temporalizing – the temporality of the way things show up in terms of coping with them.[35] Authentic temporalizing is the source of what makes pragmatic time count for something. Put another way, bestowing and gathering are the source of presencing.

Derrida's full account of temporalizing differs quite a bit, and even explicitly, from Heidegger's, and it is in terms of this difference that we may begin to see his profound disagreement with Heidegger. As we have seen, Derrida focuses on shifts in the charged differences in a system of differences. These shifts are the activity – though, Derrida insists, not activity in the regular ontic sense of the word – of *differance*. Moreover; he argues that these shifts cannot be directly experienced. This is what he means when he says that *differance* cannot be thought on the basis of the present. And so far he makes good sense. No one experiences the actual shift in vision and feeling entailed by falling in love. Though once we are in love, we realize that our way of dealing with things and people has changed (our world changed). In a like manner, once any one of Derrida's shifts has occurred, we find ourselves belatedly making sense of things according to the new ordering occasioned by the shift. This is what Derrida means when he talks about an essential belatedness in our lives. But, although we may reorder various projects of our lives around the shift in the play in the system of differences, we do not and cannot bring the shift itself into present direct experience in that reordering. For this reason, Derrida claims that Heidegger's gathering, collecting in a newly intensified way the meaning of the bestowal or shift, ought not to count as a genuine part of authentic temporalizing. For that gathering could only disguise the radical unexperienceable quality of the shift. Thus, thinking in terms of bestowal or allotment is a mistake because the inflection of both of those terms makes sense only if gathering or regathering is a genuine activity, rather than a cover-up of a radical shift. Take away the genuineness of gathering, and the change that the terms "bestowal" and "allotment" get at becomes better depicted as a relieving (as in one guard relieving another)[36] or as a displacing of one world with another. For Derrida, then, an adequate account of temporalizing sees it as a matter of constantly trying to make sense of, or take account of, some completely incomprehensible advent in our lives. Our present, then, is always belated, always following a past advent that we cannot comprehend. The future, on a first impression, bifurcates, either looking like more belated activity trying to clarify the past shift or looking totally incomprehensible and showing up as the possibility of an incomprehensible shift. But, on second thought, any account of a totally incomprehensible futural shift will be understood in the terms of the current belated activity, so the future will show up as an impure advent, indescribable and already falsely described.

Derrida says that a life temporalized this way would look like accounts of life given by Nietzsche and Freud. For simplicity's sake, the picture of one of Freud's compulsives will do here. The Ratman, for instance, finds himself moving about stones in the path of his girlfriend's carriage and each time justifying what he is doing in clever ways. But the point of Freud's account is that the Ratman is responding to something unconscious, as Derrida says, a shift in a system of differences that could never be conscious. It is wholly other.[37] So the poor Ratman's attempts at consolidation or gathering are wholly out of touch with what motivates them.

This sort of talk, and example, may seem unpersuasive to Heideggerians. And shifting from the Freudian model to the Nietzschean one is not likely to help very much. But Derrida's point becomes more trenchant if put in Heidegger's terms. An aspect of Heidegger's being (characterized here as human practices for revealing things and people) is that new understandings of being (new ways of revealing) are sent, but this sending cannot be responded to in the way we generally respond to a thing. In responding to a style of revealing in the practices, human beings can at best deal more consistently with things and people in a way more appropriate to the general style. Presumably this means dropping the old, worn-out ways of treating things and people and developing new ones. So men in my generation stop dealing with things in terms of personal growth and freedom and start dealing with them in terms of family and fatherhood. (The arugula, which made every salad a hit, now shows up as something the children have to be taught to like.) But all of this activity, Derrida objects, has to do with things. It is not aimed at the revealing practices or, even more important, at the way a particular way of revealing comes about. It wholly misses the shift. True temporalizing ought to get at the temporal structure of our activity when we are attending to revealing itself, and that occurs, he argues, strictly in terms of our experience of belatedness. Any other relation to revealing such as the gathering involved in reordering one's dealing with the old everyday matter of one's life is "forbidden":

> The structure of delay in effect forbids that one make of temporalization (*temporization*) a simple dialectical complication of the living present as an originary and unceasing synthesis – a synthesis constantly directed back on itself, gathered in on itself and gathering.[38]

Which view is right? Does it make sense to claim, as Heidegger does, that gathering is a genuine aspect of the human activity of responding to one's revealing practices? Or must we agree with Derrida that no way of dealing with things can put us into a special, authentic relation with the current way of revealing? The point here will not be to answer these questions, but rather to make them show up in very concrete ways as two very different pictures of how the revealing practices work. To see this difference concretely, we must turn to Iterability and *Ereignis*.

Iterability and *Ereignis*

The main points of this section will be to show (a) why Derrida sees revealing practices (the system of differences or writing) as only authentically revealing when the practices or system is changing its way of revealing (as it always is at one speed or another), and (b) why Heidegger thinks that authentic revealing occurs when one is simply in touch with the current *appropriate* way of revealing (and therefore implies that there is a certain deep stability in the revealing practices).

Iterability reveals best Derrida's sense of the constant change of charged differences. Put another way, Iterability shows that language or any meaningful practice can only manifest itself if structured by *difference*. How does this work? Derrida's argument begins rather simply. Repeating or recalling or reporting, he argues, is implicit in any human speech practice. In fact, some variant of repeating is implicit in any meaningful human practice whatsoever. For a meaningful event, either a speech act or a vision or a mood or whatever, could only be meaningful if we had some way of getting at it, of bringing it to our attention, independent of the original context in which it occurred. (This point was made before with the surgeon example.) If some event were so unique that it could not be prescinded from its context and did not show up for us with this potential already apparent, then we could not have any means of recalling it outside of that original context. And even if we were to return to its original context and the event were to recur, we could have no way of identifying it as the same event we experienced before. Without marking the experience in some way that is at least partly independent of the context of the experience, we would simply be awash in the experience each time it was repeated. Derrida wants us to think of language and meaningful experience as innately intertextual; this is just to say that we could have no way of identifying any experience at all even in the first instance, if it did not show up, somehow, already prescinded from its context. Without such abstracting, an experience would remain wholly embedded and unnoticed to begin with. In arguing this way Derrida is on all fours with at least one interpretation of Wittgenstein's private language argument. He simply tells us that signs, meanings, or experiences must be recognizable outside of their original context in order to be meaningful.

Derrida adds, though, that this feature of meaning practices, this Iterability, shows that the meaning of words or experiences cannot be controlled by the speaker. In the first instance all this means is that as soon as a speaker's words leave his mouth, others will determine them according to their own lights. But this claim does not seem to reveal very much. For most of human experience shows that this difference in understanding is relatively minimal, except when very complicated ideas are being expressed. So when someone says to another, removed from the original situation, that, for instance, he heard A make an ungenerous comment regarding B the day before, the identities of A and B and of ungenerous comments are altered only to the slightest degree as the context changes from A and his intimates on the first day to one of A's intimates and an outsider on the second day. The degree of A's ill-temper towards B may be understood to be slightly greater or less than in fact it was. But, for the most part, the identities remain fairly stable, or else change occurs in predictable ways as words are reported from context to context. Now if the report were of a very difficult text's meaning or the contexts crossed large historical or cultural distances, then the disparity of understanding from context to context might be greater but, generally speaking, different contexts are not all that different or are well coordinated with each other.

Derrida claims, however, that the changes in meaning attendant upon Iterability are more radical than our simple commonsensical account would suggest. He wants to exhibit from the phenomenon of Iterability not only that the receiver may misunderstand the speaker's meaning but also that the speaker never really controls his meaning even for himself at the very beginning. The meanings of his own words might change for him at the very instant he speaks them. This is quite a telling claim, if it can be justified, so, first, let us see that Derrida in fact makes it. Here Derrida starts with the normal view that a mark, a saying, will be less stable the greater the distance from its original utterance, but then he adds that he has merely put things this way for pedagogical reasons:

> What holds for the receiver holds also, *for the same reasons*, for the sender or the producer. To write is to produce a mark that will constitute a sort of machine which is productive in turn, and which my future disappearance will not, in principle, hinder in its functioning, offering things and itself to be read and to be rewritten. When I say "my future disappearance" . . . it is in order to render this proposition more immediately acceptable. I ought to be able to say [instead of] my disappearance, pure and simple, *my nonpresence in general*, for instance *the nonpresence of my intention of saying something meaningful*, of my wish to communicate, from the emission or production of the mark.[39]

To drive this slightly muddled point home, that in the general case, the speaker is not present to his own meaning and hence the subject is not the ground of his meanings, Derrida adds: "the situation of the writer . . . is, concerning the written text, basically the same as that of the reader."[40]

To develop an intuition of what Derrida thinks of as the general case of language use or of having meaningful experiences, a concrete example is needed. We need to see an example of a speaker's words *actually* changing the context that gives meanings to his words, pulling that context out from under him. To see this, suppose we have a newly arrived Easterner in California who finds that people seem to misunderstand his jokes, are rather numb to his ideas, seem to respond to the things he says with the wrong affects, and so on. His mood would be one of confusion, irritation, annoyance. He would feel, in general, out of sorts, and things would show up to him in this way, as either perpetuating his view that things are all slightly off in California or that Californians show signs here and there of getting with it. Everything he says or feels about himself he would understand in the context of this mood. But as he speaks more and more, he might very well find himself uttering words that before he had only used in a joking way back in the East, in imitation of, say, Woody Allen, and now too so far as he clearly intends them it is to repeat them in this same old way. "I guess I'm just not laid back," he says. But, suddenly, precisely as he utters these words, everything changes. He sees that, in actual living fact and not just as a matter of course, he is not laid back and that is why people have been misunderstanding him, his gestures, and his expressions generally. In uttering these words, he sees himself as transformed. He understands his being anew and with clarity. Moreover, the people who were numb, cold, and impossible to get through to now show up as laid back, as having a different but definable way of being. His mood suddenly shifts from being out of sorts to being focused and curious about the new world he is adventuring into. Indeed, in the course of uttering *ces mots justes*, the meaning of the very words has changed and so has the speaker's identity and his context.[41]

This, I think, is what we ought to take as the paradigmatic Derridean experience of language and other meaningful experiences. It is one where the meaning of our sentences, such as it is, transforms us. It does not get at something that we already are but transforms us in a way that just happens to fit with our circumstances. It is for this reason that Derrida can say that *differance* is not a word or a concept.[42] It is supposed to transform us and consequently itself when it is used. It is also for this reason that Derrida can claim that the human subject is a function of language.[43] A speaker is created and recreated in his or her speaking. But the speaker is never ultimately the center or meaning giver of his or her speech.

One small and one larger point now need to be made. First, if language transforms us in this way, then it may seem to do so because it is a resource rich with meanings. But to think this is precisely to miss Derrida's point. Meanings are not stable, but generate new meanings only loosely related to the old. This transformational working of language impoverishes any rich sense of meaning. Another way to put this is to say that meaning for Derrida ought to be experienced as wonder and not as something that coordinates our practices, that makes them resonate together. Meaning is wonder not resonance.

Second, we should like to see an argument for why an experience that most people would take to be marginal at best should be understood by Derrida to be the most deeply revealing and indeed, in some sense, the most typical case of language use.[44] Before presenting an argument we should see, again, that it is in fact the case that Derrida sees language or revealing practices as transformational. Here, in one of Derrida's most recent writings, he tells us that although the norms of minimal intelligibility change slowly, they are always in the process of changing and have only been slowed by unnatural cultural power formations such as, one may assume, logocentrism and phallocentrism:

> the norms of minimal intelligibility are not absolute and ahistorical, but merely more stable than others. They depend upon socio-institutional conditions, hence upon nonnatural relations of power that by essence are mobile and founded upon complex conventional structures that in principle may be analyzed, deconstructed, and transformed; and, in fact, these structures are in the process of transforming themselves profoundly and, above all, very rapidly . . . *"deconstruction" is firstly this destabilization on the move.*[45]

497

The picture that we see here is that the shared practices[46] that allow for things and people to show up (to become intelligible), if left to their own nature, would change in a more rapid and noticeable way than they do today. This is to say that Iterability as exemplified above would show itself in normal language use. But the workings of intelligibility are jelled or gummed up, and the culprit for gumming up the works is metaphysical practices, the hold of which deconstruction will weaken. (Here we glimpse the political side of deconstruction that neo-pragmatist commentators of Derrida such as Fish and Rorty slight.[47]) But this brings us back to our original question: why believe at all that our revealing practices are naturally in a state of flux?

The best place to turn for Derrida's reasons for this claim is his recent writing on the law.[48] His point in this legal writing is to clarify the indeterminancy in the meaning of judicial decisions. According to Derrida, as we might expect, this indeterminancy of meaning is due to the poverty of meaning that exists in any meaningful experience. (For meaningful experience is, as described, transformational, full of wonder, and not resonant.) So interpreting the law, on the level Derrida describes it, is much like any other form of interpretation. Following this line of thought, Derrida, first, makes the Wittgensteinian point[49] that laws (rules in general) cannot determine their own interpretation. They can only show up as determinate against a background of practices or form of life (system of differences) that determines them in one way or another. But the fact that we have a judicial system with lawyers and judges' rulings and the rest shows that our practices for revealing people and things do not fully determine any particular rule. And, indeed, no particular single set of practices could fully determine the meanings of any set of laws or rules, because meaningful words, signs, rules, etc., depend, as has been argued, on having implicitly a sort of impoverished generality that bridges (and generates new) contexts or sets of practices.[50] So far so good. But how is it that these revealing practices work at all, since they do not work according to any rational rules that could be set out?

Derrida sees the determination of a law in everyday life as occurring by means of a running together or competition of examples,[51] exemplary rulings situated in the past, each claiming priority and singularity, with one winning the day at a particular instant because of some contingent likeness to the present situation. "We are," Derrida says, noting our general condition, "in a realm where, in the end, there are only singular examples. Nothing is absolutely exemplary."[52] Roughly, the picture that Derrida sets up is one where in interpreting – that is, in the activity of giving meaning to particular things and people – human beings understand new things in terms of how close they come to one or another formerly experienced thing. Something shows up as a bird because it comes closer (for some wholly contingent, momentary reason) to examples of birds than examples of insects or man-made flying objects. One chess master might think that the feel and lay of pieces on the chess board require move A and another chess master might think the same situation requires move B, because one master has habituated himself to a slightly different set of examples from those that the other master has habituated himself to.[53]

This picture, sketchy as it is, should now give us clear grounds for seeing how Derrida's thought holds together. First, if the background practices for revealing work by using a loosely coordinated cache of examples (here Derrida has replaced sets of charged differences with caches of examples), then shifts in the relative exemplariness of various examples ought to happen frequently. Indeed, any particular interpreting, speaking, writing, whatever, would involve a complicated assignment of more weight to certain examples and less weight to others. Doing this would understandably produce a sense of wonder at the change in the way things and people show up. So the experience of transformation implied in seeing Iterability as the central feature of language ought to happen more regularly. We can also see now why it does not.

Under the delusive metaphysical regimen that tells us that we ought to have a secure, fundamental way of interpreting things, we have grown to ignore and repress experiences that would make us aware of this jostling around of examples. So, for instance, if experience in our culture is set up so that men normally take a firm judicial decision with clear winners and losers as the most exemplary kind of decision and women normally take as paradigmatic a tentative compromise that tries to accommodate the needs of all those involved, then we will determine that the way women understand decisions bespeaks infirmity and a weak will. A man who suddenly has a womanish response to a decision is clearly, at best, having a bad day. Social structures supporting this invidious distinction are the sort of non-natural, metaphysically inspired structures that Derrida claims we have set in place. It is clear as well that deconstruction, which makes us sensitive to small changes in what is exemplary and to how certain examples are unnaturally maintained, is a movement that will loosen the hold of the unnatural metaphysical, logocentric, phallocentric structures. Presumably, its goal is not to demolish these structures so much so as to weaken their hold and to put them in their place, to let them be employed only when properly solicited.

Finally, we may now see, too, how this view of the Iterability in the revealing practices fits with Derrida's view of temporality. Derrida, we remember, saw true temporalizing as an effect of belatedness. The notion was that understanding (in the normal sense) occurred as an after-effect of the wonder of a meaning-giving event. And consolidating the effects of a particular meaning-giving event was a privative kind of activity. Now we see that Derrida makes these claims because he understands these background revealing practices as working by means of loosely coordinated examples whose authority shifts to accord with the different sorts of situations in which people find themselves. These shifts in relative authority are experienced as the primary meaningful or wonderful event, and they are primary because they manifest most fully the unstable nature of the practices. The consolidating that does, in fact, take place covers up the looseness of the coordination of the practices and consequently does not constitute a deep response to the practices that reveal things and people.

In contrast, Heidegger considers the clearing or background practices that reveal people and things to be tightly coordinated, and finds that this coordination does not, in the richest instances, arise from the imposition of stabilizing metaphysical practices. Consequently, acting in accord with a mode of coordination of the revealing practices is a genuine response to the revealing itself. Working out the sense of *Ereignis*, Heidegger's rather mysterious word which means happening, appropriation, owning, will show how this according oneself with a style of revealing can be genuine. We shall also see (a) that Heidegger's "metaphorics of proximity," of "neighboring, shelter, house, service, guard, voice, and listening," is *not* associated with a "simple and imme-diate presence,"[54] and (b) that Heidegger's understanding of *Ereignis* does not show that he thinks the metaphysics of presence a necessary aspect of Western revealing as Derrida seems to think.

Ereignis is Heidegger's counterpart to Derrida's Iterability. Like Iterability for Derrida, *Ereignis* is the essential aspect of language. To see that Heidegger believes this, we have to keep in mind, as a rough first approximation, that language for Heidegger allows for the revealing of things in such a way that it is understood that they show up differently, under different aspects, in various modes of revealing. We need also to keep in mind that the essence of *Ereignis* is *Eignen* or owning. With just this much, we can at least see what Heidegger means when he claims *Ereignis* is the essential moving force of lan-guage and also says: "The ruling power [*Regende*] in [the] showing of saying is owning [*Eignen*]."[55] Explaining more precisely what this sentence means and how, in particu-lar, *Ereignis* moves Heidegger's thinking in the opposite direction from Derrida's will be the point of the rest of this section.

When thinking of language, Heidegger, as Derrida accuses,[56] focuses on speech. Indeed, in his first stab at language in *Being and Time* and even later, Heidegger focuses on people speaking to others who dwell with them and are concerned with the same things.[57] Nothing could start out further from Derrida's account. But what Heidegger wants us to notice is not the closed situation in which *speaking* occurs – which Derrida thinks language itself opposes – but rather that the situation and the people are given to each other by the speaking itself.[58] This sets up a sort of dilemma. For language, according to Heidegger, turns out to be something of a grab bag. It is "pervaded by all the modes of saying and of what is said, in which everything present or absent announces, grants or refuses itself, shows itself or withdraws."[59] So we move rather quickly from a closed, local setting to a language, which like Derrida's, constitutes many different contexts. To put this in the terms used earlier, language is constituted by a col-lection of ways of cutting up the world that go with various expressive styles of reveal-ing.[60] It might very well seem that in looking at language so generally, Heidegger has discovered babble and not language at all. The question, for Heidegger, is how some-thing so multifarious as language produces local situations at all.

In order to understand Heidegger's solution, two aspects of the way he sees linguis-tic practices must become clear. First, Heidegger thinks that speaking is a matter of lis-tening to what language is saying or showing. What he has in mind here is relatively plain. We can see it when we begin to take up any particular practice, like playing chess or discussing how Heidegger's thinking works. The practice, chess or Heidegger's think-ing, already has ready-made articulations suitable to the sorts of things the practice does. We hear instructors talk in terms of pawns and knights and queen's gambits or we hear them speak of Dasein and the truth of being, presencing, and so on. And when we speak, we use these terms as we have heard others use them in various contexts with the hope, each time, of coming to a better understanding of the phenomenon the words pick out and why it is an important one. What we want to have happen is what the Easterner had happen when he learned that he was not laid back. We want to understand more completely how the meaning of the words gets filled in. But this expe-rience, as Heidegger would have us see it, is not a transformation so much as a deep-ening. We develop a richer understanding of a practice we are already involved in. We are listening, we may say now, to hear the inner sense of our words in the way they articulate the practice in which we are engaged.

But a deep problem remains. For if language is as multifarious as Derrida argues and Heidegger begins by conceding, then how can anyone's listening strike just the right vein of articulations suited to a particular revealing practice? For in repeating the words of an instructor, these words might get filled in in a way that runs against the particular practice the student started out in. So, for instance, a student might very easily hear a philosopher's example about *les mots justes* as revealing a peculiar historical fact about the current philosophical moment, that philosophers at this particular time for particular historical reasons find *les mots justes* attractive for their examples. Confusion would *seem* to fall away as he progressed to think more and more about the history of philosophical examples. But the student would be led wholly out of the philosophic practice in which he began. And this could happen over and over again. What is to keep the student from doing this? On a Derridian account, nothing would prevent this, nothing, that is, but for the non-natural, metaphysical authority in our practices insisting on keeping disciplines completely distinct and ordered according to their supposed natural kinds. But Heidegger claims that there is another aspect of language, *Ereignis*, which is the tendency of the revealing of language to reveal particular things in the mode that is best suited to the kind of thing they are. Since this may be both hard to believe and to understand, let us show first that this is in fact what Heidegger thinks. Here Heidegger first says that it is *Ereignis* that allows people to speak and then claims that speaking by way of *Ereignis* means revealing beings in the way most suited to them:

> *Ereignis* grants to mortals their abode within their nature, so that they may be capable of being those who speak. If we understand "law" as the gathering that lays down that which causes all beings to be present *in their own*, in what is appropriate for them, then *Ereignis* is the plainest and most gentle of all laws.[61]

What does Heidegger mean by claiming that *Ereignis* tends to make sure that a thing is revealed in the mode of revealing best suited to it? Heidegger gets at this when he speaks of revealing a thing in its primordial being. In doing this, he frequently writes as though by primordial being he means revealing the thing in terms of the style of revealing predominant at its origin. One can see relatively easily what he means by this. It would not be unusual to think that, for instance, the richest way to understand technological equipment like data processors of various kinds would be in terms of the technological mode of revealing, where everything shows up as available for flexible use. To try to appreciate a computer printout the way one might appreciate a handwritten letter, noticing the care with which the letters were shaped and the boldness or elaborateness of the shaping of the letters, would surely be mistaken. A fountain pen, however, would best be understood according to the subject/object kind of revealing (prominent when it was invented) where people show up as complicated subjects trying to understand themselves and objects. In this mode of revealing, the fountain pen could be appreciated for the kinds of stroke one could make with it, the intricate ways that it would allow one to express his or her subjectivity. Likewise, a handwritten letter would obviously be best suited to being appreciated through this mode of revealing. The point is

501

that one kind of revealing will be best suited to bringing out the usable aspect of any piece of equipment most fully. As far as equipment is concerned, this account runs with common intuitions.

But what about natural objects? Should we regard them as flexible material to be used up or as producing the sublime effects to be cherished as the Romantic poets did? Should we regard them as having the kind of energy they had for the ancient Greeks or as signs from God that tell us of the order in His creation as the Medievals thought? Here the answer is not so obvious, for obviously here we cannot be expected to respond to natural things according to the revealing that was current when they were invented. But primordiality need not cause us to recur to actual originary moments. A primordial relation to natural objects would be the one that, like the relation to the computer printout or the fountain pen, gives us a way of dealing with the thing that resonates with the thing in such a way that we become more sensitive to our relation with the thing as one that focuses our shared revealing practices. Put a little more concretely, a primordial relation with a thing is one where the thing makes us sensitive (generally in the spirit of thanks or celebration) to the way of life we lead that makes us take cognizance of the thing in the first place. A couple of instances should show how this works. For many of us now who find that the conservation of natural things makes sense, the most primordial way of responding to them is in terms of practices attached to old pantheistic ways of seeing things. For under this view, all natural things seem worthy of celebration, and this yearning for celebration awakens us to our ecological way of life. Others, of course, may well find that, because such sanctifying practices too easily grant the worthiness of *every* natural thing, they empty out nature's vital energies. Those country people who hunt, let's say, to supplement their diet would live in such a way that natural things show up most richly – that is, resonate with their way of life – when understood as prizes to be taken in a genuine struggle.

If we allow, then, that this tendency named *Ereignis* could lead us to respond to things in the way that makes them resonate most intensely with our way of life, then speaking, which is where *Ereignis* occurs, would be a way of letting any particular thing show itself in its ownmost (most resonant) being. Moreover, *Ereignis* would be the tendency in language that counters the Derridian Iterability. But, we want to know, What is the evidence that such a thing as *Ereignis* goes on at all?

There are two ways to show *Ereignis* in our practices, *Ereignis*, that is, as distinguished from frantic, neurotic attempts at metaphysical closure. For the first, we can return to the story of the *mot just*, of the Easterner who discovers that he *is not laid back*. For Derrida this event would look like an event of transformation. For Heidegger, this event would be a matter of the Easterner owning up or coming into his own. (Here is the sense of owning in *Ereignis* that Heidegger is at some pains to bring out.[62]) We need not go so far as to say that the Easterner has found his single true identity but we may say that he has come upon a way of revealing (as positively not laid back) that reveals and unites many aspects of his style of daily life.

Perhaps, though, a better way to see this is to think in terms of sagas which, according to Heidegger, capture saying's natural essential sense.[63] We imagine that sagas held their high places in various cultures because they collected together various practices and showed, in a glamorizing way, how the practices were connected together. So we might easily imagine that a fishing culture might very well have in it a great flood saga where ship-building became an essential activity. Such a saga would reveal the essential place in the culture of people other than the fishermen by collecting the shipbuilders and paddle-makers and making them important too. Of course, this culture could as well have another saga about the lost founding figure who was nurtured by sea hawks, and this saga would collect, among other things, nurturing practices and, in collecting them, glamorize them and make them important. We see similar effects in our own culture now. Towards the end of the 1960s and beginning of the 1970s, films about con artists and small-time criminals seemed to give us a fix on the way we, Americans, felt that we were involved in revealing practices that were hypocritical. At the beginning of the 1980s popular films captured a sense of naive confidence, and this spoke to and of the way we were having things show up. In these cases, the films brought us in touch with our own ways of revealing things and people.

But how are these ways of collecting, the sagas or the films, different from the neurotic activity that Freud describes and that Derrida uses to characterize this collecting and gathering, this resonating kind of meaning? Is it not the case that becoming attached to these films, like the neurotic's attachment to his explanations, hides the changes in the revealing practices. It certainly seems to resemble what is going on in the neurotic's case. But neurotics' explanations seem neurotic precisely because they do not resonate with many of our shared social practices. These explanations always come short of what they need to explain, and, somehow sensing this, their authors add to these accounts solutions that try to bridge this gap in a too completely meticulous way. The neurotic account seeks a closure that makes us hear in it a flatness that fails to achieve the sort of reasonable but open and forthright explanation the neurotic himself seeks. This, however, is simply not the case with the way sagas or films work. They do allow us to get a fix on the way that we are revealing things. They do make us feel more at home with what we are doing. Furthermore, they open us up to further distinctions, so we do not find ourselves displacing one explanation with another or seeking closure. Rather the films, and our thinking about them, give us a general sense of what we are about and allow us to be at home with, and therefore open to, more and more of our own practices.

But does not all this seeking for a particular work of art, saga, or film to reveal our way of revealing to us constitute the motivation of metaphysics? Are we not seeking a foundation? And if we are not seeking a final foundation, are we not seeking some sort of second best thing to it? Are we not, then, as Derrida accuses, living beyond metaphysics but longing for proximity with some quieting location, some consolation, some truth of being?[64] The answer to these questions goes directly to how we understand revealing practices to be constituted. For Heidegger, they are made up, like language, of many styles of revealing, but the various styles are collected together as substyles of larger styles. This collecting does not produce a single style that coordinates all the other styles. But it does mean that various new ways of revealing, various changes, let us say, in the importance of various examples (various exemplary moves in chess, for example), generally remain within one particular general style of revealing. In fact, we could have no experience of deepening resonance unless *Ereignis*, as the tendency to give us things in their richest, most resonant manner, could bring these changes of paradigms into proximity with one of the appropriate styles of revealing. Without these general styles, one thing revealed in a particular way would not resonate with other things picked out in other particular ways.[65] Having noted this, we may see, finally, that the activity of *Ereignis*, as this collecting, is the source of all of Heidegger's metaphorics of proximity.

But, finally, we want to ask on Derrida's behalf, are not all of Heidegger's styles various aspects of the metaphysics of presence? For does not this metaphysics finally collect every way of revealing? On the one hand, we know that Heidegger cannot mean this because he does uncover non-metaphysical ways of revealing. He calls them by odd names such as things thinging, artworks working, language speaking. But, on the other hand, matters are not so certain, for what are we to make of the following quotation Derrida relies upon in his polemic?[66] Does not Heidegger here confess that all ways of revealing in the West understand being as presence?

> In the sending of the destiny of being, in the extending of time, there becomes manifest a dedication, a delivering over into what is their own, namely of being as presence and of time as the realm of the open. What determines both, time and being, in their own, that is, in their belonging together, we shall call *Ereignis*.[67]

Once we understand that, by "*Ereignis*," Heidegger means the tendency to make things show up in the most resonant way, we can see that Heidegger is simply saying here that some time around the fifth century BC, the style of revealing appropriate to craftsmen producing things urged itself upon the early philosophers as a sort of *mot juste* that they were lucky enough to receive as the most resonating (gathering) account of how things showed up in general. Focusing on terms that articulated this practice seemed to bring poeple and things into their own, and the West has thought out of this Greek understanding ever since. But all of this resonant collecting, this metaphysical talking, occurs strictly within a more general tendency of the revealing practices to deal with things in a way most suited to those things and to collect different styles of revealing together as substyles. Nothing in this quotation says that productivity exclusively determines thinking in the West. Nothing says that revealing or being must be exclusively thought in terms of presence. Heidegger simply says that the story of productivity, of presence, has the strongest hold upon us. Who would deny it? Thinking about *Ereignis*, though, ought to loosen that hold, yet not wed us to Derrida's notion of loosely stuctured practices.

Rorty's Neo-pramatist Reading

If the main point here has been to show that neither Derrida nor Heidegger is trapped within a thematics of presence and that, therefore, neither is metaphysical, then it may seem that this chapter comes to a conclusion similar to Rorty's general conclusions about Derrida and Heidegger. Rorty, after all, evaluates both thinkers according to their different, not necessarily metaphysical, magical words.[68] And it turns out that Heidegger's magical words work for deconstructing the closure of the tradition; Derrida's work for deconstructing Heidegger.[69] But what Rorty wants most is the Nietzschean gaiety of new beginnnings that Derrida gives us with his Iterability and *differance*. Rorty sees this in new vocabularies replacing old. Yet he also wants to retain the Heideggerian gratitude that makes sense only when a new understanding is focused by a gathering activity.[70] One ought not to feel gratitude for stark Derridean transformations, because those transformations are supposed not to enrich meaning but to impoverish it. Rorty, in short, wants both wonder and resonance. But what Derrida and Heidegger have shown is that these two ways of understanding linguistic practices depend upon radically different views about how revealing practices work. To have both wonder and resonance, Rorty should give a third, independent account of how the practices work. It seems that Rorty's adoption of the Kuhnian picture of revolutions in vocabulary followed by periods of normal science which builds connections among the new words is a start in this direction. But, to make sense of this, we need an account of what could impose this Kuhnian order on Iterability and *Ereignis*. And this sort of account is precisely what Rorty resists for being too philosophical. The account would necessarily focus on something cross-cultural and transhistorical, a condition for the possibility of things showing up, and the transcendental is a price Rorty will not pay.

Notes

1 Richard Rorty speaks in this Heideggerian voice – though not directly imagining a confrontation with Derrida – in his "Heidegger, contingency, and pragmatism," in this volume. In Charles Taylor's "Heidegger on language," also in this volume, we see him – speaking about Derrida in a Heideggerian voice – locate Derrida's position as a particularly extreme form of the subjectivist outlook. This is to say that Taylor locates Derrida's position where Heidegger rightly or wrongly located Nietzsche's.

2 Jacques Derrida, *Positions* (trans. Alan Bass), Chicago: University of Chicago Press, 1981, pp. 52, 54. See also Gayatri Chakravorty Spivak's Preface to Jacques Derrida's *Of Grammatology*, Baltimore: Johns Hopkins University Press, 1976, pp. xiv–xix, xxxviii, xlviii–l. Herman Rapaport's book *Heidegger and Derrida*, Lincoln: University of Nebraska Press, 1989, chronicles how close Rapaport thinks Heidegger came to doing Derridian deconstruction at various points in his career.

3 *Ereignis*, most literally translated as "enowning," is standardly glossed as an event of appropriation or more simply as appropriation. I am leaving the term in the German, not because I find the translations misleading in any particular way, but because "appropriation" or "event of appropriation," while good translations, already implicitly contain the sort of interpretation I plan to work out in detail. I would prefer not to help out my interpreation by a trick of translation.

4 It is especially important to make this point, at least for Derrida, since he has claimed that on occasion what he is doing could be construed as pragrammatology. (See Jacques Derrida, "Afterword: toward an ethic of discussion," *Limited Inc* (trans. Samuel Weber), Evanston, IL: Northwestern University Press, 1988, p. 151.) Unfortunately, on the occasion where he made this claim, Derrida did not take the time to separate his effort from that of the pragmatists and neo-pragmatists.

5 To be consistent and avoid confusion, I will always write the translation of "*Sein*" as "being" with a lower case "b" even in quotations, unless the grammar of the sentence requires otherwise.

6 Jacques Derrida, "Signature event context," *Limited Inc* (trans. Samuel Weber and Jeffrey Mehlman), Evanston, IL: Northwestern University Press, 1988, p. 9.

7   Jacques Derrida, *"Differance," Margins of Philosophy* (trans. Alan Bass), Chicago: University of Chicago Press, 1982, p. 11.

8   Martin Heidegger, *Being and Time*, trans. John Macquarrie and Edward Robinson, New York: Harper & Row, 1962, p. 97.

9   Derrida, *"Differance,"* p. 23.

10 Ibid., p. 24.

11 Heidegger, *Being and Time*, p. 54.

12 Ibid., pp. 54–5.

13 Martin Heidegger, *Basic Problems* (trans. Albert Hofstadter), Bloomington: Indiana University Press, 1982, pp. 106–12. For a later and similar account, see Martin Heidegger, "The question concerning technology," *The Question Concerning Technology* (trans. William Lovitt), New York: Harper Colophon, 1977, pp. 6–12.

14 I think that Albert Borgmann's claims about running are best understood in this way. See Albert Bormann, *Technology and the Character of Contemporary Life*, Chicago: University of Chicago Press, 1984, p. 207.

15 Martin Heidegger, *Nietzsche* (trans. Frank A. Capuzzi), 4 vols, New York: Harper & Row, 1982, volume 4, p. 212.

16 A significant difference between the two, however, could be shown to come out of their views of the history of the West. Derrida has a Nietzschean view, that history is the repetition of various systems of differences, which like so many perspectives or world pictures are ontologically fundamentally the same as far as none of them reveals the play in systems of difference any more than any other. At best, the play, the changing of the charged differences, can only be revealed, Derrida says, in a dissimulation. It is always a sort of mysterious other, like the unconscious (Derrida, *"Differance,"* p. 6). So Derrida sees historical change as a sort of zero-sum game, a general economy, as he calls it, a moving set of world pictures that always leave *differance* out or disguised. Heidegger, on the other hand, thinks that while revealing (or being) cannot be fully revealed within the world, it can be revealed mediately by works of art, thinker's words, the founding of states, and the founding of religions (Martin Heidegger, "The origin of the work of art," *Poetry, Language, Thought* (trans. Albert Hofstadter), New York: Perennial Library, 1971, p. 62). So cultures can have better and worse relations to "the source or their intelligibility." I use the phrase "source of their intelligibility" as a neutral term to get at the *determining* aspects of both *differance* and being; therefore "source" is not to be understood as a self-sufficient ground. The relation of *differance* to being will be developed later.

17 Here are Derrida's words: "it is at this moment when Heidegger recognizes *usage* as *trace* that the question must be asked: can we, and to what extent, think this trace and the *dis of differance* as *Wesen des Seins*? Does not the *dis of differance* refer us beyond the history of Being, and also beyond our language, and everything that can be named in it?" (Derrida, *"Differance,"* p. 25).

18 Heidegger, *Being and Time*, pp. 25–6.

19 Here I use the terms "truth and essence" in a Heideggerian way. So these terms do not get at any sort of conceptual definition but rather the "truth" or "essence" of something or of the revealing practices in the way that it or they work.

20 Derrida, *"Differance,"* p. 12.

21 Ibid., p. 11.

22 Ibid., p. 11.

23 I say "in the first instance" because Derrida has a grander design than just reversing the speech/writing difference. That grander design will come out in the discussion of Iterability.

24 These are two ways of taking Heidegger's early account of everyday language in *Being and Time*, pp. 195–210, 260–5. I add the adjective "everyday" here because it is evident that at

the same time as the writing of *Being and Time* or very shortly after it, Heidegger had a different way of describing artistic language. See Martin Heidegger, *Basic Problems*, pp. 171–3.

25   Derrida, *"Differance,"* pp. 21, 22, 23. See also Jacques Derrida, "The ends of man," *Margins of Philosophy*, p. 128; and *"Ousia* and *Gramme," Margins of Philosophy*, pp. 63–7.

26   Derrida, *"Differance,"* p. 21.

27   A good example of this marginal revealing is presented in Heidegger's essay on the thing. See Martin Heidegger, "The Thing," *Poetry, Language, Thought*, pp. 165–86.

28   Derrida, *"Differance,"* p. 22.

29   Derrida, however, is quite suspicious of any account that attempts to come up, as Heidegger does, with some sort of pure, originary time. He argues that all accounts of time must be infected with their inadequate, vulgar counterparts. See Derrida, *"Ousia* and *Gramme,"* pp. 45–6, 60, 63. Indeed, as we shall see, his more adequate conception of time is really based on the denial of any adequate conception of time at all.

30   Heidegger, *Being and Time*, pp. 458–72.

31   Derrida, *"Differance,"* p. 13.

32   This point will be developed more fully in discussing Iterability.

33   Heidegger, *Being and Time*, p. 463.

34   Heidegger in his later writings thinks that this gathering has a particular structure; it brings together mortals, earth, sky, and divinities. He also thinks the early Greeks understood language as ultiinately a kind of gathering. This he thinks is the sense of the verbal form of *logos, legein*. These sophisticated workings out of gathering need not be developed here.

35   Heidegger, *Basic Problems*, pp. 228, 268–9; and Heidegger *Being and Time*, pp. 377, 457, 472–80.

36   See Jacques Derrida, "From restricted to general economy: a Hegelianism without reserve," *Writing and Difference* (trans. Alan Bass), Chicago: University of Chicago Press, 1978, pp. 262–5, 271–2. I thank Steven Knapp for pointing out this aspect of Derrida's work to me. See also on this matter Alan Bass's footnote 23 in Derrida, *"Differance,"* pp. 19–20.

37   Derrida, *"Differance,"* pp. 19–21.

38   Ibid., p. 21.

39   Derrida, "Signature event context," p. 8.

40   Ibid., p. 8.

41   Both Charles Taylor and Richard Rorty have similar cases of *mots justes*, and I have benefited from their analyses, but the case here of *ces mots justes* differs in important ways from theirs. In Charles Taylor's case, it is important to see that the speaker's words get it right about some particular thing already implicit in his situation. This is not the point here. Presumably there are lots of different ways of getting at the differences of Californians and Easterners. An Easterner might as well say that Californians have lost all their European ethnicity or he might sense that Californians are deeply flaky or purists of a peculiar sort or any of dozens of other things. On the other hand, this example is meant to differ from Rorty's examples of new words in that in its use as *un mot juste* it is immediately fully meaningful. Rorty argues, for instance, that the first time Derrida used *differance*, "that collocation of letters, it was indeed, not a word, but only a misspelling. But around the third or fourth time he used it, it had *become* a word" ("Deconstruction and circumvention," p. 102). This is to say that, for Rorty, a new use of an expression remains at first something mostly meaningless and only gets its meaning as new practices gather around it. But this misses Derrida's point about *differance* and his other words. They are not words in any normal sense; they transform us in our use of them. They then have whatever meaning it is that gets the transformation going. But obviously this cannot be a deep resonating meaning. It is more the wonder of seeing a new vista. The relevant texts are: Charles Taylor, "Heidegger and language" in this volume; Richard Rorty, "Deconstruction and circumvention," *Essays on*

Heidegger and Others, Cambridge: Cambridge University Press, 1991, p. 102; and Richard Rorty, *Contingency, Irony, and Solidarity*, Cambridge: Cambridge University Press, 1989, p. 18.

42 Derrida, *"Differance,"* p. 11.

43 Ibid., p. 15.

44 In claiming that such transformational language use is typical, Derrida, at least, has not distanced himself very far from Heidegger who himself, in his later writings, claims that a particular kind of poetic language use, which will be described later, is the typical and most revealing language use. See Heidegger, "Language," *Poetry, Language, Thought*, p. 208.

45 Derrida, "Afterword," p. 147; emphasis mine.

46 Notice that with his use of the term "norms," Derrida reveals that he could acquiesce to the more Heideggerian "practices" or comportments.

47 See Stanley Fish, "With the compliments of the author," *Doing What Comes Naturally*, Durham, NC: Duke University Press, 1989, pp. 37–67, esp. 57; and Rorty, "Deconstruction and circumvention," pp. 98–101. Rorty develops the case he presented in "Deconstruction and circumvention" in his "Two meanings of 'logocentrism'"; and "Is Derrida a transcendental philosopher?" *Essays on Heidegger and Others*, pp. 107–18, 119–28.

48 Jacques Derrida, "Force of law: the mystical foundation of authority," *Cardozo Law Review*, 11 (1990), pp. 919–1037.

49 I follow roughly John Searle's reading of Wittgenstein here. See John R. Searle, "Skepticism about rules and intentionality," forthcoming.

50 Derrida, "Force of law," pp. 961–7.

51 Ibid., p. 967.

52 Ibid., p. 977.

53 Hubert and Stuart Dreyfus have elaborated a worked-out account of this in their book *Mind over Machine*, New York: The Free Press, 1986.

54 Derrida, "The ends of man," p. 130.

55 Martin Heidegger, "The way to language," *On the Way to Language* (trans. Peter D. Hertz), New York: Harper & Row, 1971, p. 127; and Martin Heidegger, "Der Weg zur Sprache," *Unterwegs zur Sprache*, 1959; Frankfurt-am-Main: Vittorio Klostermann, 1985, p. 246, volume 12 of *Gesamtausgabe* (the Hertz translation has been altered slightly). Heidegger makes the connection between *Ereignis* and *Eignen* explicit; see Heidegger, "The way to language," p. 128; and Heidegger, "Der Weg zur Sprache," p. 247.

56 Derrida, "The ends of man," p. 132, n. 36.

57 Heidegger, "The way to language," p. 120.

58 Ibid., p. 121.

59 Ibid., p. 122.

60 Since this is a surprising claim for Heidegger to make, I shall include this quotation here: "Speaking, *qua* saying something, belongs to the design of the being of language, the design which *is pervaded by all the modes of saying and of what is said*, in which everything present or absent announces, grants or refuses itself, shows itself or withdraws. *This multiform saying from many different sources is* the pervasive element in the design of the being of language. With regard to the manifold ties of saying, we shall call the being of language in its totality 'Saying' – and confess that even so we still have not caught sight of what unifies those ties" (Heidegger, "The way to language," pp. 122–3; emphases added). Although language looks like a hodgepodge here, Heidegger's last sentence should be noted. That unity is what he and this chapter go on to explore.

61 Ibid., p. 128; emphasis added.

62 Ibid., p. 128.

63 Ibid., p. 123. Heidegger adds, though, that the sense of Saying he is after is not precisely that of the saga.

64 Derrida, "The ends of man," pp. 135–6.

65 If we line up Heidegger's view of the revealing practices, or clearing as he calls it, with Derrida's view, we see something very interesting. Heidegger's view is that the clearing consists of various loosely connected sets of revealing practices each set tightly coordinated by its particular paradigms. For a time, Heidegger would say, a particular set can dominate a particular culture. And, over time too, new paradigms and new sets may establish themselves. Against this, Derrida's view is that the "clearing" (Heidegger's term) consists, in its natural state, of loosely coordinated practices. Paradigms come forth in a moment and then die off just as quickly. To common sense the Derridion view, with its constant change, will look like a prescription for constant breakdowns and confusion. So why does Derrida see the clearing this way? What motivates his view? It is well known that Derrida develops his position from the margins of texts and behavior. The reason for this should not seem obscure. For it is on the margins of texts and behavior that one can actually see the traces of revealing practices. Even when John Searle, Derrida's most notorious antagonist, teaches his students about the Background – Searle's term, roughly speaking, for the revealing practices – he himself retreats to the margins of our activity. He tells his students, for instance, a funny story of how it became clear to him that a mug of beer could only show up for him on the basis of many unthematized, non-intentional skills and capacities. For years he had known, Searle says, how to handle mugs of beer. But then at some point in the 1970s, he grabbed his mug and, because it was made of plastic and much lighter than he had expected, he ended up tossing his beer up in the air. The point of the story is that he had a skill for handling the weight of beer in mugs that he never really thought about, until the practices for making beer mugs changed. Then, the breakdown occurred and one aspect of the background skill became apparent. Stories such as these could be multiplied and must be in order to make people sensitive to the background revealing practices. Derrida, like John Searle, is quite good at making us see them, only Derrida calls them by various names indicating the situation in which the practices revealed themselves. The difference, however, between Derrida and Heidegger or Derrida and Searle is that Derrida seems to have read the state of the revealing practices when they became apparent back into their normal state. That is, Derrida seems to claim that it is a natural, normal feature for revealing practices to be constantly shifting. He then has to give an account of how this constant shifting is disguised and covered up by repressive social practices. Heidegger saw this kind of move as the traditional philosophers' mistake of reading breakdown phenomena back into the normal situation and then constructing an account of how the true state of the normal is hidden. So, for instance, in *Being and Time*, Heidegger suggests that philosophers developed the notion that people always act on the basis of beliefs and goals (either conscious or unconscious ones) because people normally only notice how they act in breakdown situations, and in breakdown situations, where they can no longer simply cope, they do indeed act deliberately on the basis of explicit beliefs and goals (Heidegger, *Being and Time*, pp. 102–7). Philosophers took aspects of the breakdown situation – explicit beliefs and goals – and assumed that these mental states underlay any directed action, just as Derrida takes another aspect of a different kind of breakdown situation – that the background becomes apparent when it is shifting – and generalizes that the background is continuously changing. Against the first, traditional generalization, Heidegger argued that most everyday behavior is transparent in the sense that, for instance, the activity of opening a door and taking a seat in a classroom is not accompanied by an experience of any beliefs and goals (Heidegger, *Basic Problems*, p. 163). Moreover, Heidegger claims, no one need have a theory of how door knobs

509

work and the beliefs that there is a relatively flat surface and no chasm on the other side of the door in order to stride into a classroom. Against Derrida's generalization, Heidegger would argue likewise that for the most part the background revealing practices are relatively stable and that is why our experience is characterized for the most part by resonance and not wonder. (For more on Heidegger's account of this traditional mistake, see Hubert L. Dreyfus, *Being-in-the-World*, Cambridge, MA: MIT Press, 1991, pp. 60–87. For more on John Searle's account of the Background, see his *Intentionality*, Cambridge: Cambridge University Press, 1983, pp. 141–59. The suspicions developed in this note were worked out in conversations with Hubert Dreyfus and John Searle.).

66 Derrida, "The ends of man," p. 132, n. 35. Derrida also suggests, without this quotation from "Time and being," that thinking the difference between being and beings even if this difference does not cash out presence and the present draws one to another kind of presence and a repetition of metaphysics. Metaphysics itself, he argues, is constituted on trying to think another kind of presence. See Derrida, "*Ousia* and *Gramme*," generally, but pp. 63–7 in particular.

67 Heidegger, "Time and being," p. 19.

68 Rorty, "Deconstruction and circumvention," p. 104.

69 Ibid., pp. 105–6.

70 Richard Rorty, "Heidegger, contingency, and pragmatism." Rorty ingeniously redescribes Heideggerian gratitude as Deweyan.

31

Heidegger, Contingency, and Pragmatism

RICHARD RORTY

One of the most intriguing features of Heidegger's later thought is his claim that if you begin with Plato's motives and assumptions you will end up with some form of pragmatism. I think that this claim is, when suitably interpreted, right. But, unlike Heidegger, I think pragmatism is *a good* place to end up. In this chapter, I shall try to say how far a pragmatist can play along with Heidegger, and then try to locate the point at which he or she must break off.

A suitable interpretation of Heidegger's claim requires defining Platonism as the claim that the point of inquiry is to get in touch with something like Being, or the Good, or Truth, or Reality – something large and powerful that we have the duty to apprehend correctly. By contrast, pragmatism must be defined as the claim that the function of inquiry is, in Bacon's word, to "relieve and benefit the condition of man" – to make us happier by enabling us to cope more successfully with the physical environment and with each other. Heidegger is arguing that if you start with Plato's account of inquiry you will eventually wind up with Bacon's.

The story Heidegger tells about the transition from the one set of goals to the other is summarized in his "Sketches for a History of Being as Metaphysics" in the second volume of his *Nietzsche*.[1] Here is one sketch, entitled "Being" (*Das Sein*).

Alethia (apeiron, logos, hen – arche).
Revealing as the order at the start.
Physis, emergence (going back to itself).
Idea, perceivability (*agathon*), causality.
Energeia, workness, assembly, *en-echesia* to *telos*.
Hypokeimenon, lie present (from *ousia, ergon*).
(presence – stability – constancy – *aei*).
Hyparchein, presencing that rules from what is already present.
Subiectum.

Rorty, Richard, "Heidegger, Contingency, and Pragmatism" from *Heidegger: A Critical Reader*, edited by Hubert L. Dreyfus and Harrison Hall. Oxford: Blackwell, 1992. Reprinted with permission.

Actualitas, beings – the real – reality
    Creator – ens creatum
    causa prima (ens a se).
Certituido-res cogitans.
Vis – monas (perceptio appetitus), exigentia essentiae.
Objectivity.
Freedom
    will-representation
    practical reason.
Will – as absolute knowledge: Hegel.
Will – as will of love: Schelling.
Will to power – eternal recurrence: Nietzsche.
Action and organization – pragmatism.
The will to will.
Machination (enfaming).[2]

This potted history of Western philosophy stretches from the Greek conviction that the point of inquiry is apprehension of *archai*, principles, things greater and more powerful that everyday human existence, to the American conviction that its point is technological contrivance, getting things under control. Heidegger sees this chronological list of abbreviations for philosophers' "understandings of Being" as a downward escalator. Once you have gotten on you cannot get off until you have reached the bottom. If you start off with Plato you will wind up with Nietzsche and, worse yet, Dewey.

Heidegger claims that to understand what is going on here at the bottom of the escalator, in the twentieth century, the age in which philosophy has exhausted its possibilities, "we must free ourselves from the technical interpretation of thinking." The beginnings of that interpretation, he says, "reach back to Plato and Aristotle."[3] As I read him, his point here is the same as Dewey's: that Plato and Aristotle built what Dewey called "the quest for certainty" into our sense of what thinking is for. They taught us that unless we can make the object of our inquiry *evident* – get it clear and distinct, directly present to the eye of the mind, and get agreement about it from all those qualified to discuss it – we are falling short of our goal.

As Heidegger says, "All metaphysics, icluding its opponent, positivism, speaks the language of Plato."[4] That is, ever since Plato we have been asking ouselves the question: what must we and the universe be like if we are going to get the sort of certainty, clarity, and evidence Plato told us we ought to have? Each stage in the history of metaphysics – and in particular the Cartesian turn toward subjectivity, from exterior to interior objects of inquiry – has been an attempt to redescribe things so that this certainty might become possible. But, after many fits and starts, it has turned out that the only thing we can be ceratin about is what we want. The only things that are really evident to us are our own desires.

This means that the only way we can press on with Plato's enterprise is to become pragmatists – to identify the meaning of life with getting what we want, and imposing our will.[5] The only cosmology we can affirm with the certainty Plato recommended is our own (communal or individual) world picture, our own way of setting things up for manipulation, the way dictated by our desires. As Heidegger says:

world picture, when understood essentially, does not mean a picture of the world but the world conceived and grasped as picture. What is, in its entirety, is now taken in such a way that it first is in being and only is in being to the extent that it is set up by man, who represents and sets forth.[6]

To see how the quest of certainty took us down this road, think of Plato as having built the need to overcome epistemological skepticism – the need to answer questions like "What is your evidence" "How do you know" "How can you be sure – into Western thinking. Then think of the skeptic as having pressed the philosopher back from a more ambitious notion of truth as accurate representation to the more modest notion of truth as coherence among our beliefs. Think od Spinoza and Leibniz as having elaborated proto-coherence theories of truth. Think of the coherence theory of truth becoming philosophical common sense after Kant explained why a "transcendental realist" account of knowledge would always succumb to skeptical attack. Think of Kant as completing the Cartesian turn toward interior objects by replacing the realist story about inner representaions of outer originals with a story about the relation between privileged representations (such as his twelve categories) and less privileged, more contingent representaions.

As soon as we adopt this Kantian story, however, we begin to drift toward Nietzsche's view that "the categories of reason" are just "means toward the adjustment of the world for utilitarian ends."[7] We begin to see the attractions of Deweyan redefinitions of terms like "truth" and "rationality" in terms of contributions to Satisfactions' and "growth." We move from Kant to pragmatism when we realize that a coherence theory of truth must be a theory about the harmony not just of beliefs, but rather of beliefs *and desires*. This realization leads us to the common element in Nietzsche's perspectivalism and C. I. Lewis's "conceptual pragmatism" – the doctrine that Kantian categories, the forms in which we think, the structures of our inquiries, are malleable. We change them (as, for example, we changed from an Aristotelian to a Newtonian understanding of space and time) whenever such a change enables us better to fulfill our desire by making things more readily manipulable.

Once we take this final step, once human desires are sdmitted into the criterion of "truth," the last remnants of the Platonic idea of knowledge as contact with an underlying non-human order disappear. We have become pragmatists. But we only took the path that leads to pragmatism because Plato told us that we had to take evidence and certainty, and therefore skepticism, seriously. We only became pragmatists because Plato and Aristotle already gave us a technical, instrumental account of what thinking was good for.

Heidegger thinks of himself as having tracked down the assumption common to Plato, the skeptic, and the pragmatists – the assumption that truth has something to do with evidence, with being clear and convincing, with being in possession of *powerful, penetrating, deep* insights or arguments – insights or arguments which will put you in a commanding position *vis-à-vis* something or somebody else (or *vis-à-vis* your own old, bad, false self). The West, Heidegger thinks, has been on a power trip ever since, with the Greeks, it invented itself. A metaphysics of the Will to Power (the metaphysics Heidegger ascribed to Nietzsche by taking some of Nietzsche's posthumous fragments to be the "real" Nietzsche) and an antimetaphysical technocratic pragmatism are the destined lost stages of Western thought. This is the ironic result of Plato's attempt to rise above the pragmatism of the marketplace, to find a world elsewhere.

A familiar way to see Plato as power freak – as an example of what Derrida calls "phallogocentrism" – is to emphasize his conviction that mathematical demonstration is the paradigm of inquiry, his awe at the geometers' ability to offer knockdown arguments. But another way is to think of him as convinced that all human beings have the truth within them, taht they are already in possession of the key to the ultimate secrets – that they merely need to know themsleves in order to attain their goal. This is the basic assumption of what Kierkegaard, in his *Philosophical Fragments*, called "Socratism." To make this assumption is to believe that we have a built-in affinity for the truth, a built-in way of tracking it once we glimpse it, a built-in tendency to get into the right relation to a more powerful Other. In Plato, this assumption was expressed as in the doctrine that the soul is itself a sort of *arche* because it is somehow connate with the Forms. Down here at the bottom of the escalator, it is expressed in the pragmatist's claim that to know your desires (not your deeply buried "inmost," "true" desires, but your ordinary everyday desires) is to know the criterion of truth, to understand what it would take for a belief to "work."

For Kierkegaard, the opposite of Socratism was Christianity – the claim that man is not complete, is not in the truth, but rather can attain truth only by being recreated, by being made into a New Being by Grace. Kierkegaard thought that Socratism was Sin, and that Sin was the attempt by Man to assume the role of God, an attempt which found its *reductio* in Hegel's System. A lot of Heidegger can profitably be read as a reflection on the possibility that Kerkegaard was right to reject Socratism but wrong to accept Christianity – or, more generally, on the possibility that humanism and Pauline Christianity are alternative forms of a single temptation. Suppose that both are expressions of the need to be overwhelmed by something, to have beliefs forced upon you (by conclusive evidence, rational conviction, in the one case, or by Omnipotence recreating you, in the other). Suppose that this desire to be overwhelmed is itself just a sublimated form of the urge to share in the power of anything strong enough to overwhelm you. On form such sharing might take would be to become identical with this power, through a purificatory askesis. Another would be to become the favored child of this power.

The result of thinking through these suppositions was Heidegger's attempt tp struggle free from what he came to think of as the underlying assumption of the West – the assumption that truth is somehow a matter of the stronger overcoming the weaker. This notion of overcoming is what is common to suggestions that intellect can overcome sensual desire, that Grace can overcome Sin, that rational evidence can overcome irrational prejudice, and that human will can overcome the nonhuman environment. This assumption that power relations are of the essence of human life is, Heidegger thinks, fundamental to what he sometimes call "the ontotheological tradition." I take Heidegger to be saying that if one is going to stay within this tradition, then one might as well be a pragmatist. One might as well be a self-conscious, rather than a repressed and self-deceived, power freak. Pragmatism has, so to speak, turned out to be all that the West could hope for, all we had a right to expect once we adopted a "technical" interpretation of thinking. Plato set things up so that epistemological skepticism would become the recurrent theme of philosophical reflection, and pragmatism is, in fact, the only way to answer the skeptic. So if the only choice is between Platonism and pragmatism, Heidegger would wryly and ironically opt for pragmatism.

This qualified sympathy for pragmatism is clearest in *Being and Time*, the book which Dewey described as "sounding like a description of 'the situation' in transcendental German." In Part I of his *Heidegger's Pragmatism*, Mark Okrent has shown, very carefully and lucidly, how to read *Being and Time* as a pragmatist treatise.[8] The crucial point is the one Okrent puts as follows: "it is built into Heidegger's view of understanding that beliefs and desires must be ascribed together."[9] Once understanding is de-intellectualized in the way in which both Dewey and Heidegger wanted to de-intellectualize it – by viewing the so-called "quest for disinterested theoretical truth" as a continuation of practice by other means – most of the standard pragmatist doctrines follow.[10] In particular, it follows that, as Heidegger puts it, Dasein's Being-in-the-world is "the *foundation* for the primordial phenomenon of truth."[11] It also follows that "Being (not entities) is something which 'there is' only in so far as truth is. And truth is only in so far and as long as Dasein is. Being and truth 'are' equiprimordially."[12] That is to say: Being, which Plato thought of as something larger and stronger than us, is there only as long as we are here. The relations between it and us are not power relations. Rather, they are relations of fragile and tentative codependence. The relation between *Sein* and *Dasein* is like the relation between hesitant lovers; questions of relative strength and weakness do not arise.[13]

With Okrent, I read Division I of *Being and Time* as a recapitulation of the standard pragmatist arguments against Plato and Descartes. I read Division II, and in particular the discussion of Hegelian historicism, as recapitulating Nietzsche's criticism of Hegel's attempt to escape finiyude by losing himself in the dramas of history. Hegel hoped to find in history the evidence and certainty that Plato hoped to find in a sort of super-mathematics called "dialectic," and that positivism hoped to find in a unified science. But from Heidegger's point of view, Plato, Descartes, Hegel, and positivism are just so many power plays. They are so many claims to have read the script of the drama we are acting out, thus relieving us of the need to make up this drama as we go along. Every such power play is, for Heidegger as for Dewey, an expression of the hope that truth may become *evident*, undeniable, clearly present to the mind. The result of such presence would be that we should no longer have to have projects, no longer have to create ourselves by inventing and carrying out these projects.

This quest for certainty, clarity, and direction from outside can also be viewed as an attempt to escape from time, to view *Sein* as something that has little to do with *Zeit*. Heidegger would like to recapture a sense of what time was like before it fell under the spell of eternity, what we were like before we became obsessed by the need for an overarching context which would subsume and explain us – before we came to think of our relation to Being in terms of power. To put it another way: he would like to recapture a sense of *contingency*, of the fragility and riskiness of any human project – a sense which the ontotheological tradition has made it hard to attain. For that tradition tends to identify the contingent with the merely apparent. By contrasting powerful reality with relatively impotent appearance, and claiming that it is all-important to make contact with the former, our tradition has suggested that the fragile and transitory can safely be neglected.

In particular, the tradition has suggested that the particular *words* we use are unimportant. Ever since philosophy won its quarrel with poetry, it has been the thought that counts – the proposition, something which many sentences in many languages express equally well. Whether a sentence is spoken or written, whether it contains Greek words or German words or English words, does not, on the traditional philosophical view, greatly matter. For the words are mere vehicles for something less fragile and transitory than marks and noises. Philosophers know that what matters is literal truth, not a choice of phonemes and certainly not metaphors. The literal lasts and empowers. The metaphorical – that which you can neither argue about nor justify, that for which you can find no uncontroversial paraphrase – is impotent. It passes and leaves no trace.

One way to describe what Heidegger does in his later work is to see him as defending the poets against the philosophers. More particularly, we should take him at his word when, in the middle of *Being and Time*, he says: "In the end, the business of philosophy is to preserve the *force of the most elemental words* in which Dasein expresses itself, and to keep the common understanding from levelling them off to that unintelligibility which functions as a source of pseudoproblems."[14] I think that we should read "unintelligibility" here as "the inability to attend to a word which is common currency."[15] When a word is used frequently and easily, when it is a familiar, ready-to-hand instrument for achieving our purpose, we can no longer *hear it*. Heidegger is saying that we need to be able to hear the "most elemental" words which we use – presumably the sort of words which make up the little "Sketch of the History of Being" I quoted above – rather than simply using these words as tools. We need to hear them in the way in which a poet hears them when deciding whether to put one of them at a certain place in a certain poem. By so hearing them we shall preserve what Heidegger calls their "force." We shall hear them in the way in which we hear a metaphor for the first time. Reversing Hobbes, Heidegger thinks that words are the counters of everyday existence, but the money of Thinkers.[16]

Another way of describing Heidegger's later work is to emphasize a line in his own quasi-poem, *Aus der Erfahrung des Denkens*: "Being's poem, just begun, is man."[17] Think of the list of words cited above as a sort of abstract of the first stanza of that poem. Then think of the stanza being abstracted as us, the dwellers in the West.[18] To think of that poem that way, we have to think of ourselves as, first and foremost, the people who used – who just happened to use – those words. This is hard for us to do, because our tradition keeps trying to tell us that it isn't the words that matter, but the realities which they signify. Heidegger, by contrast, is telling us that the words do matter: that we are, above all, the people who have used those words. We of the West are the people whose project consisted in running down that particular list, in riding that particular escalator. There was no more *necessity* about getting on that escalator than there is about a poet's use of a given metaphor. But once the metaphor is used, the fate of the poet's audience is, Heidegger, thinks, determined.

It is important to emphasize at this point that there is no hidden power called Being which designed or operated the escalator. Nobody whispered in the ears of the early Greeks, the poets of the West. There is just us, in the grip of no power save those of the words we happen to speak, the dead metaphors which we have internalized. There is no way, and no need, to tell the dancer from the dance, nor is there any point in looking around for a hidden choreographer. To see that there *is just us* would be simultaneously to see ourselves – to see the West – as a contingency and to see that there is no refuge from contingency. In particular, it would be to accept Heidegger's claim that "Only as long as Dasein (that is, only as long as an understanding of Being is ontically possible) 'is there' Being."[19] If we could only see *that* Heidegger thinks, then we might shake off the will to power which is implicit in Plato and Christianity and which becomes explicit in pragmatism.

But if Being is not a hidden choreographer, not a source of empowerment, what is it? So far I have tossed "Being" around insouciantly, spoken Heideggerese. Now, in a brief excursus from my main topic – the relation between Heidegger and pragmatism – I shall try to say something about why Heidegger uses this term, and to offer a quasi-definition of it.

I think that Heidegger goes on and on about "the question about Being" without ever answering it because Being is a good example of something we have no criteria for answering questions about. It is a good example of something we have no handle on, no tools for manipulating – something which resists "the technical interpretation of thinking." The reason Heidegger talks about Being is not that he wants to direct our attention to an unfortunately neglected topic of inquiry, but that he wants to direct our attention to the difference between inquiry and poetry, between struggling for power and accepting contingency. He wants to suggest what a culture might be like in which poetry rather than philosophy-cum-science was the paradigmatic human activity. The question "What is Being?" is no more to be *answered correctly* than the question "What is cherry blossom?" But the latter question is, nevertheless, one you might use to set the theme of a poetry competition. The former question is, so to speak, what the Greeks happened to come up with when they set the theme upon which the West has been a set of variations.

But doesn't Heidegger's use of "Being" immerse him in the tradition which he wants to wriggle free of: the ontotheological tradition, the history of metaphysics? Yes, but he wants to get free of that tradition not by turning his back on it but by attending to it and redescribing it.[20] The crucial move in this redescription, as I read Heidegger, is his suggestion that we see the metaphysician's will to truth as a self-concealing form of the poetic urge. He wants us to see metaphysics as an inauthentic form of poetry, poetry which thinks of itself as antipoetry, a sequence of metaphors whose authors thought of them as escapes from metaphoricity. He wants us to recapture the force of the most elementary words of Being – the words on the list above, the words of the various Thinkers who mark the stages of our descent from Plato – by ceasing to think of these words as the natural and obvious words to use. We should instead think of this list as contingent as the contours of an individual cherry blossom.

To do this, we have to think of the West not as the place where human beings finally got clear on what was really going on, but as just one cherry blossom alongside actual and possible others, one cluster of "understandings of Being" alongside other clusters. But we also have to think of it as the blossom which *we* are. We can neither leap out of our blossom into the next one down the bough, nor rise above the tree and look down at a cloud of blossoms (in the way in which we imagine God looking down on a cloud of galaxies). For Heidegger's purposes, we are nothing save the words we use, nothing but an (early) stanza of Being's poem. Only a metaphysician, a power freak, would think we were more.

So is Being the leaf, the blossom, the bole, or what? I think the best answer is that it is what elementary words of Being refer to. But since such words of Being – words like *physis* or *subiectum* or *Wille zur Macht* – are just abbreviations for whole vocabularies, whole chains of interlocked metaphors, it is better to say that *Being is what vocabularies are about*. Being's poem is the poem about Being, not the poem Being writes. For Being cannot move a finger unless Dasein does, even though there is nothing more to Dasein than Being's poem.

More precisely, Being is what *final* vocabularies are about. A final vocabulary is one which we cannot help using, for when we reach it our spade is turned. We cannot undercut it because we have no metavocabulary in which to phrase criticisms of it.[21] Nor can we compare it with what it is about, test it for "adequacy" – for there is no non-linguistic access to Being. To put the point in slightly more Heideggerian language: all we know of Beings is that it is what understandings of Being are understandings of. But that is also all we need to know. We do not need to ask which understandings of Being are better understandings. To ask that question would be to begin replacing love with power.

To see the point of this quasi-definition of "Being," it is essential to realize that Being is not the same thing under all descriptions, but is something different under each. That is why the line between Being and Language is so thin, and why Heidegger applies many of the same phrases to both. Heidegger insists that he is writing a History of *Being*, not just a History of Human Understandings of Being. An imperfect analogy is that every description of space given by the definitions and axioms of a geometry is a description of a different space (Euclidean space, Riemannian space, etc.), so there is no point in asking whether the space was there before the geometry, nor in asking which geometry gets space-in-itself right. A History of Geometry would also be a History of Space. The analogy is imperfect because we construct geometries for particular purposes, but we do not *construct* final vocabularies. They are always already there; we find ourselves thrown into them. Final vocabularies are not tools, for we cannot specify the *purpose* of a final vocabulary without futilely twisting around inside the circle of that very vocabulary. The metaphysical thinker thinks that if you can just get the right understanding of Being – the one that gets Being right – then you are home. Heidegger thinks that the notion of "the right understanding of Being" is a confusion of Being with beings. You can relate beings to other beings (e.g. points in space to other points in space) in more or less useful ways – indeed, such relating is what Being-in-the-world consists of. But you cannot relate some beings – and in particular, some words – to Being any more than they are already related by the wimpy, impotent relation of "aboutness." In particular, Being is not the sort of thing which one can master, or which masters one. It is not related by the power relationships, the means–end relationships, which relate *beings* to one another.

The metaphysician, as Heidegger tells us in "On the Essence of Truth," regularly confuse truth with correctness. He confuses the relation of a vocabulary to Being with the relation of a sentence like "the sky is blue" to the color of the sky. There are criteria of correctness for deciding when to use that sentence to make a statement, but there are no criteria of correctness for final vocabularies.[22] If I am right in interpreting *Seinsverständnis* as "final vocabulary" and *Sein* as what final vocabularies are about, then one would expect Heidegger to say that no understanding of Being is more or less an understanding of Being, more or less true (in the sense of truth-as-disclosedness – *aletheia, Erschlossenheit, Unverborgenheit, Ereignis*) than any other. No petal on a cherry blossom is more or less a petal than any other.

Sometimes Heidegger does say things like this. For example: "Each epoch of philosophy has its own necessity. We simply have yo acknowledge that philosophy is the way it is. It is not for us to prefer one to the other, as is the case with regard to various *Weltanschauungen*."[23] But often, as his use of the term "Forgetfulness of Being" suggests, he seems to be saying the opposite. For he makes all sorts of invidious comparisons between the less forgetful people at the top of the escalator – the Greeks – and the more forgetful ones at the bottom, us. The question of whether he has any business making such comparisons is the question of whether he has any business disliking pragmatism as much as he does. So now I return from my excursus on Being to the main topic of this paper.

The question of Heidegger's relation to pragmatism can be seen as the question: does Heidegger have any right to nostalgia? Any right to regret the golden time before Platonism turned out to be simply implicit pragmatism? Is there any room in his story for the notion of belatedness, for the notion of a downward escalator? To put it another way, should be read him as telling a story about the contingency of vocabularies or about the belatedness of our age? Or rather: since he is obviously telling both stories, can they be fitted together? I do not think they can.

To get this issue about contingency and belatedness in focus, consider the preliminary problem of whether Heidegger's early "ontological" enterprise can be fitted together with his later attempt to sketh the "history of Being." The reader of *Being and Time* is led to believe that the Greeks enjoyed a special relationship to Being which the moderns have lost, that they had less trouble being ontological than we do, whereas we moderns have a terrible time keeping the difference between the ontological and the ontic in mind. The reader of the later work, however, is often told that Descartes and Nietzsche were as adequate expressions of what Being was at their times as Parmenides was of Being at his time. This makes it hard to see what advantage the Greeks might have enjoyed over the moderns, nor how Parmenides and Nietzsche could be compared in respect of the "elementariness" of the "words of Being" with which they are associated. Since there is no more to Being than its understanding by Dasein, since Being is not a power over and against Dasein, it is not clear how there could be anything more authentic or primal about the top of the escalator than the bottom. So it is not clear why we should think in terms of an escalator rather than of a level moving walkway.

Although *Being and Time* starts off with what looks like a firm distinction between the ontological and the ontic, by the end of the book the analytic of Dasein has revealed Dasein's historicity. This historicity makes it hard to see how ontological knowledge can be more than knowledge of a particular historical position. In the later work, the term "ontology" drops out, and we are told that what the Greeks did was to invent something called "metaphysics" by construing Being as "presence." What *Being and Time* had called "ontological knowledge," and had made sound desirable, now looks very like the confusion between Being and beings which the later work says is at the heart of the metaphysical tradition. Something seems to have changed, and yet the more one rereads Heidegger's writings of the 1920s in the light of his later essays the more one realizes that the historical story which he told in the 1930s was already in his mind when he wrote *Being and Time*. One's view about what, if anything, has changed will determine what one makes of the idea that, for example, *logos* is *more* primordial than *Wille zur Macht* (in some honorific sense of "primordial").

Heidegger's own later glosses on *Being and Time* are of little help when it comes to the question of whether "the average vague understanding of Being" which is supposed to be the datum of the "analytic of Dasein" is itself an historical phenomenon, rather than something ahistorical which provides a neutral background against which to portray the differences between the Greeks and ourselves. My own guess is that in the 1920s Heidegger thought that it is a historical and that in the 1930s he came to think of it as historically situated.[24] If this guess is right, then the later Heidegger abjures the quest for ahistorical ontological knowledge and thinks that philosophical reflection is historical all the way down. But if it is, then we confront the problem of contingency and belatedness I sketched above. We face the question: is coming to an understanding of what Heidegger calls "what in the fullest sense of Being now is"[25] simply a matter of recapturing our historical contingency, of helping us see ourselves as contingent by seeing ourselves as historical, or is it, for example, learning that this is a particularly dark and dangerous time?[26]

The $32 question of whether the later Heidegger still believes there is an ahistorical discipline called "ontology" leads fairly quickly to the $64 question of whether he has a right to the nostalgia for which Derrida and others have criticized him, and to the hostility he displays towards pragmatism. Returning now to the former question, I would argue that the "analytic of Dasein" in *Being and Time* is most charitably and easily interpreted as an analytic of *Western* Dasein, rather than as an account of the ahistorical conditions for the occurrence of history.[27] There are passages in *Being and Time* itself, and especially in the roughly contemporary lecture course *The Basic Problems of Phenomenology*, which support this interpretation. These passages seem to make it clear that Heidegger comes down on the historicist side of the dilemma I have sketched. Thus towards the end of *Being and Time* he approvingly quotes Count von Yorck as saying: "it seems to me methodologically like a residue from metaphysiscs not to historicize one's philosophizing."[28] At the very end of that book he remind us that the analytic of Dasein was merely preparatory and that it may turn out not to have been the right way to go;[29] he hints that it might be what it later turned out to be; a disposable ladder.

In *Basic Problems of Phenomenology* he says that "even the ontological investigation that we are now conducting is determined by its historical situation." He goes on to say that

These three components of phenomenological method – reduction, construction, destruction – belong together in their content and must receive grounding in their mutual pertinence. Construction in philosophy is necessarily destruction, that is to say, a de-constructing [Abbau] of traditional concepts carried out in a historical recursion to the tradition. . . . Because destruction belongs to construction, philosophical cognition is essentially at the same time, historical cognition.[30]

This seems a proto-Derridean line of thought, in which philosophy becomes identical with historicist ironism, and in which there can be no room for nostalgia.

But there are plenty of passages in which the other horn of the dilemma, the onto-logical horn, seems to be grasped. In the "Introduction" to *Basic Problems*, from which I have just been quoting, Heidegger says that in our time, as perhaps never before, phi-losophizing has become "barbarous, like a St Vitus' dance." This has happened because contemporary philosophy is no longer ontology, but simply the quest for a "world-view." Heidegger defines the latter by contrast with "theoretical knowledge." The definition of "world-view" which he quotes from Jaspers sounds a good deal like my definition of "final vocabulary." Something is equally a world-view whether it is based on "supersti-tions snd prejudice" or on "scientific knowledge and experience.

However, after seeming to contrast ontology and world-view, Heidegger goes on to say the following:

> It is just because this positivity – that is, the relatedness to beings, to world that is, Dasein that is – belongs to the essence of the world-view, and thus in general to the formation of the world-view, that the formation of a world-view cannot be the task of philosophy. To say this is not to exclude but to include the idea that philosophy itself is a distinctive primal form [*eine ausgezeichnete Urform*] of world-view. Philosophy can and perhaps must show, among many other things, that something like a world-view belongs to the essential nature of Dasein. Philosophy can and must define what in general constitutes the structure of a world-view. But it can never develop and posit some specific world-view *qua* just this or that particular one.[31]

But there is an obvious tension in this passage between the claim that philosophy "is a distinctive primal form of world-view" and that "philosophy . . . can never develop and posit some specific world-view." Heidegger never tells us how we can be historical through and through and yet ahistorical enough to step outside our world-view and say something neutral about the "structure" of all actual and possible world-views. To put the point in my own jargon, he never explains how we could possibly do more than create a new, historically situated, final vocabulary in the course of reacting against the one we found in place. To do something more – something ontological – would be to find a vocabulary which would have what he calls "an elementary and fundamen-tal relation to all world-view formation" – the sort of relation which all the vocabular-ies of the metaphysical tradition have tried and failed to have. To possess such a vocabulary would, indeed, be to have a "distinctive primal form of world-view." Yet the very *attempt* at such a vocabulary looks like what Yorck called "a residue of metaphysics."

I read this confusing passage about philosophy and world-view as an early expres-sion of the tension between saying that each epoch in the "history of Being" – each stage in the transition from the Greeks to the moderns – is on an ontological par, and saying that the Greeks' relation to Being was omehow closer than ours, that our "for-getfulness of Being" and lack of "primordiality" is reponsible for the barbaric and

521

frenzied character of the modern world. In other words, I see the difficulty about the historicity of ontology as a manifestation of the more basic difficulty about whether it can make sense to *criticize* the "understanding of Being" characteristic of one's own age. The early work suggests that the present age can be criticized for its lack of ontological knowledge. The later work continues to criticize the present age but seems to offer no account of the standpoint from which the criticism is made.

In the later work, as I have said, the term "ontology" drops out, as does "Dasein." The pejorative work done by ontic–onotological distinction in *Being and Time* is now done by the distinction between the non-primordial and the primordial. Yet we are never told what makes for primordiality, any more than we were told how to step outside of our faciciti long enough to be ontological. "Primordial" (*ursprünglich*) in the later work has all the resonance and all the obscurity which "ontological" had in the earlier.

This point can be put in other words by saying that Heidegger has two quite different things to say about the way the West is now: that it is contingent and that it is belated. To say that it is contingent it is enough to show how self-deceptive it is to think that things *had* to be as they are, how provincial it is to think that the final vocabulary of the present day is "obvious" and "inescapable." But to say that this vocabulary is belated, to contrast it with something more primordial, one has to give "primordial" some kind of normative sense, so that it means something more than just "earlier."

The only candidate for this normative sense which I can find in Heidegger is the following: an understanding of Being is more primordial than another if it makes it easier to grasp its own contingency. So to say that we in the twentieth century are belated, by comparison with the Greeks, is to say that their understanding of Being in terms of notions like *arche* and *physis* was less self-certain, more hesitant, more fragile, than our own supreme confidence in our own ability to manipulate beings in order to satisfy our own desires. The Greek thinkers presumably did not think of their "most elementary words" as "simply common sense," but we do. As you go down the list of words for "Being" in the West, the people using those words become less and less able to hear their own words, more and more thoughtless – where "thoughtless" means something like "unable to imagine alternatives to themselves." Something in these words themselves makes it increasingly easy not to hear them.

The importance of appreciating contingency appears most clearly, I think, in a passage from "On the Essence of Truth" in which Heidegger seems to be saying that history, Being's poem, begins when the first ironist has doubts about the final vocabulary he finds in place. It begins when somebody says "maybe we don't have to talk the way we do," meaning not just "maybe we should call this Y rather than X" but "maybe the language-game in which 'X' and 'Y' occur is the wrong one to be playing – not for any particular reason, not because it fails to live up to some familiar criterion, but just because it is, after all, only one among others." Here is the passage:

> History only begins when beings themselves are expressly drawn up in their unconcealment and conversed in it, only when this conversation is conceived on the basis of questioning regarding beings as such. The primordial disclosure of being as a whole, the question concerning beings as such, and the beginning of Western history are the same.[32]

I interpret this as saying that prehistorical people living in the West may have played sophisticated language-games, written epics, built temples, and predicted planetary motions, but they didn't count either as "thinking" or as "historical" until somebody asked "Are we doing the right things?" "Are our social practices the right ones to engage in?"

Thought, in Heidegger's honorific sense of the term, begins with a willing suspension of varificationism. It begins when somebody starts asking questions such that nobody, including himself or herself, can verify the answers for correctness. These are questions like "What is Being?" or "What is a cherry blossom?" Only when we escape from the verificationist impulse to ask "How can we tell a right answer when we hear one?" are we asking questions which Heidegger thinks worth asking. Only then are we Dasein, because only then do we have the possibility of being *authentic* Dasein, Dasein which knows itself to be "thrown." For, at least in the West, "Dasein . . . is ontically distinguished by the fact that, in its very Being, that Being is an *issue* for it."[33] So only then is there a *Da*, a clearing, a lighting-up. Before that, we were just animals that had developed complicated practices, practices we explained and commended to one another in the words of a final vocabulary which nobody dreamt of questioning. Afterward, we are divided into inauthentic Dasein, which is still just a complexly behaving animal in so far as it hasn't yet realized that its Being is an issue for it, and authentic Dasein, made up of Thinkers and Poets who know that there is an open space surrounding present-day social practices.

In Heidegger's mind, the attitude of questioning which he thinks begins historical existence, and thus makes Dasein out of an animal, is associated with an ability to do what he calls "letting beings be." This, in turn, is associated with freedom. In "Letter on Humanism" he says that there is a kind of non-ontological thinking which is "more rigorous [*strenger*] than the conceptual"[34] – a phrase which I take to mean "more difficult to achieve than the kind of 'technical' verificationist thinking which submits to criteria implicit in social practices." "The material relevance [*sachhaltige Verbindlichkeit*]" of such thinking, Heidegger says, is "essentially higher than the validity of the sciences, because it is freer. For it lets Being – be."[35] In "On the Essence of Truth" he says "The essence of truth reveals itself as freedom. The latter is ek-sistent, disclosive letting beings be [*das ek-sistente, entbergende Seinlassen des Seienden*]."[36]

You let beings be when you disclose them, and you disclose them when you speak a language. So how can any language-user be less free, less open, less able to let Being and beings be, than any other? This is a reformulation of my previous question – how can any understanding of Being be preferable to any other, in the mysterious sense of being "more primordial"? The beginning of Heidegger's answer is that "because truth is in essence freedom, historical man can, in letting being be, also *not* let beings be the beings which they are and as they are. Then beings are covered up and distorted. Semblance [*der Schein*] comes to power." Further, Heidegger claims, this ability to *not* let beings be increases as technical mastery increases. As he says:

> where beings are not very familiar to man and are scarcely and only roughly known by science, the openedness of beings as a whole can prevail more essentially than it can where the familiar and well-known has become boundless, and nothing is any longer able to withstand the business of knowing, since technical mastery over things bears itself without

limit. Precisely in the leveling and planning of this omniscience, this mere knowing, the openedness of beings gets flattened out into the apparent nothingness of what is no longer even a matter of indifference but rather is simply forgotten.[37]

But *what is* forgotten when we forget the "openedness of beings"? Heidegger's familiar and unhelpful answer is "Being." A slightly more complex and helpful answer is: that it was Dasein using language which let being be in the first place. The greater the ease with which we use that language, the less able we are to *hear* the words of that language, and so the less able we are to think of language as such. To think of language as such, in this sense, is to think of the fact that no language is fated or necessitated. So to forget the openedness of beings is to forget about the possibility of alternative languages, and thus of alternative beings to those we know. It is, in the terms I was using before, to be so immersed in inquiry as to forget the possibility of poetry. This means forgetting that there have been other beings around, beings which are covering up by playing the language-games we do, having the practices we have. (The quarks were covered up by the Olympian deities, so to speak, and then later the quarks covered up the deities.) This forgetfulness is why we Westerners tend to think of poets referring to the same old beings under fuzzy new metaphorical descriptions, instead of thinking of poetic acts as the original openings up of the world, the acts which let new sorts of beings be.

In "On the Essence of Truth" the sections on freedom as the essence of truth are followed by a section called "untruth as concealing." This section is rather difficult to interpret, and I am by no means certain that I have caught Heidegger's intent. But I would suggest that the heart of Heidegger's claim that "Letting-be is intrinsically at the same time a concealing"[38] is just that you cannot let all possible beings be at once. That is, youcannot let all possible langauges be spoken at once. The quarks and the Olympians, for example, would get in each other's way. The result would be chaos. So the best you can do is to remember that you are not speaking the only possible language – that around the openness provided by your understandings of Being there is a larger openness of other understandings of Being as yet unhad. Beyond the world made available by *your* elementary words there is the silence of other, equally elementary, words, as yet unspoken.

If I understand him, Heidegger is saying that the ability to *hear* your own elementary words is the ability to hear them against the background of that silence, to be aware of that silence. To be primordial is thus to have the ability to know that when you seize upon an understanding of Being, when you build a house for Being by speaking a language, you are automatically giving up a lot of other possible understandings of Being, and leaving a lot of differently designed houses unbuilt.

Assuming this interpretation is on the right track, I return to the question of why the Greeks are supposed to have been so good at knowing this, and why we are supposed to be so bad. Heidegger says

However, in the same period in which the beginning of philosophy takes place, the *marked* domination of common sense (sophistry) [*Herrschaft des gemeinen Verstandes (die Sophistik)*] also begins.

> Sophistry appeals to the unquestionable character of the beings that are opened up and interprets all thoughtful questioning as an attack on, an unfortunate irritation of, common sense.[39]

I take this to say that right after we ceased to be animals, as a result of some Thinker having questioned whether the beings which our practices had opened up were the right beings, we divided up into sophistic and thoughtful Dasein. Sophistic, inauthentic Dasein could not see the point of questioning common sense, whereas thoughtful and authentic Dasein could. But, somehow, sophistry has become easier here in the twentieth century than it was back then. Somehow the beings that have been opened up by the languages *we* are speaking have become more questionable than those which the early Greeks opened up.

But is it in fact the case that we in the twentieth century are less able to question common sense than the Greeks were? Offhand, one can think of a lot of reasons why we might be *more* able to do so: we are constantly reminded of cultural diversity, constantly witnessing attempts at novelty in the arts, more and more aware of the possibility of scientific and political revolutions, and so on. If one wants complacent acceptance of common sense, one might think, the place to go is a fairly insular society, one which did not know much about what went on beyond its borders, one in which historiography had barely been invented and in which the arts were just getting started – some place like Greece in the fifth century BC.

Heidegger, of course, would dismiss this suggestion. For him, the very diversity and business of the modern world is proof that it is unable to sit still long enough to hear "elementary words." For Heidegger, cosmopolitanism, technology, and polymathy are enemies of Thinking. But why? Here we face the $64 question in all its starkness, a question which may be rephrased as follows: can we pragmatists appropriate all of Heidegger except his nostalgia, or is the nostalgia integral to the story he is telling? Can we agree with him both about the dialectical necessity of the transition from Plato to Dewey, and about the need to restore force to the most elementary words of Being, while nevertheless insisting that we in the twentieth century are in an exceptionally *good* position to do the latter? Can pragmatism do justice to poetry as well as to inquiry? Can it let us hear as well as use?

Predictably, my own answer to these last two questions is "yes indeed." I see Dewey's pragmatism – considered now not simply as an antirepresentationalist account of experience and an antiessentialist account of nature, but in its wholeness, as a project for a social democratic utopia – as putting technology in its proper place, as a way of making possible social practices (linguistic and other) which will form the next stanza of Being's poem. That utopia will come, as Dewey put it, when "philosophy shall have co-operated with the course of events and made clear and coherent the meaning of the daily detail, [and so] science and emotion will interpenetrate, practice and imagination will embrace. Poetry and religious feeling will be the unforced flowers of life."[40]

I cannot, without writing several more papers, back up this claim that Dewey was as aware as Heidegger of the danger that we might lose the ability to hear in the technological din, though more optimistic about avoiding that danger. But I think that anybody who reads, for example, the section of Dewey's *A Common Faith* called "The Human Abode," or the concluding chapter ("Art and Civilization") of *Art and Experience*, will see the sort of case that might be made for my claim.[41]

If one asks whst is so important about the ability to hear, the ability to have a sense of the contingency of one's words and practices, and thus of the possibility of alternatives to them, I think Dewey's and Heidegger's answers would overlap. They both might say that this ability, and only this ability, makes it possible to feel *gratitude* for and to those words, those practices, and the beings they disclose.

The gratitude in question is not the sort which the Christian has when he or she thanks Omnipotence for the stars and the trees. It is rather a matter of being grateful to the stars and trees themselves – to the beings that were disclosed by our linguistic practices. Or, if you prefer, it means being grateful for the existence of *ourselves*, for our ability to disclose the beings we have disclosed, for the embodied languages we are, but not grateful to anybody or anything. If you can see yourself-in-the-midst-of-beings as a *gift* rather than as an occasion for the exercise of power, then, in Heidegger's terms, you will cease to be "humanistic" and begin to "let beings be." You will combine the humility of the scientific realist with the spiritual freedom of the Romantic.

That combination was just what Dewey wanted to achieve. He wanted to combine the vision of a social democratic utopia with the knowledge that only a lot of hard work and blind luck, unaided by any large non-human power called Reason or History, could bring that utopia into existence. He combines reminders that only attention to the daily detail, to the obstinacy of particular circumstance, can create a utopia with reminders that all things are possible, that there are no *a priori* or destined limits to our imagination or our achievement. His "humanism" was not the power mania which Heiddeger thought to be the only remaining possibility open to the West. On the contrary, it put power in the service of love – technocratic manipulation in the service of a Whitmanesque sense that our democratic community is held together by nothing less fragile than social hope.

My preference for Dewey over Heidegger is based on the conviction that what Heidegger wanted – something that was not a calculation of means to ends, not power madness – was under his nose all the time. It was the new world which began to emerge with the French Revolution – a world in which future-oriented politics, romantic poetry, and irreligious art made social practices possible in which Heidegger never joined. he never joined them because he never really looked outside of philosophy books. His sense of the drama of European history was confined to the drama of his own "Sketches for a History of Being as Metaphysics." He was never able to see politics or art as more than epiphenomenal – never able to shake off the philosophy professor's conviction that everything else stands to philosophy as superstructure to base. Like Leo Strauss and Alexandre Kojeve, he thought that if you understood the history of Western philosophy you understood the history of the West.[42] Like Hegel and Marx, he thought of philosophy as somehow geared into something larger than philosophy. So when he decided that Western philosophy had exhausted its possibilities, he decided that the West had exhausted its. Dewey, by contrast, never lost the sense of contingency, and thus the sense of gratitude, which Heidegger thought only an unimaginably new sort of Thinking might reintroduce. Because he took pragmatism not as a switch from love to power, but as a switch from philosophy to politics as the appropriate vehicle for love, he was able to combine skill at manipulation and contrivance with a sense of the fragility of human hopes.

In this paper I have been reading Heidegger by my own, Deweyan lights. But to read Heidegger in this way is just to do to him what he did to everybody else, and to do what no reader of anybody can help doing. There is no point in feeling guilty or ungrateful about it. Heidegger cheerfully ignores, or violently reinterprets, lots of Plato and Nietzsche while presenting himself as respectfully listening to the voice of Being as it is heard in their words. But Heidegger knew what he wanted to hear in advance. he wanted to hear something which would make his own historical position decisive, by making his own historical epoch terminal.

As Derrida brilliantly put it, Heideggerian hope is the reverse side of Heideggerian nostalgia. Heideggerian hope is the hope that Heidegger himself, his Thinking, will be a decisive event in the History of Being.[43] Dewey had no similar hope for his own thought. The very idea of a "decisive event" is foreign to Dewey. Pragmatists like Dewey hope that things may turn out well in the end, but their sense of contingency does not permit them to write dramatic narratives about upward of downward escalators. They exemplify a virtue which Heidegger preached, but was not himself able to practice.

Notes

1 Martin Heidegger, "Entwurfe zur Geschichte des Seins als Metaphysik," *Nietzsche* II, Pfullingen: Neske, 1961, pp. 455ff. This and the preceding section, "Die Metaphysik als Geschichte des Seins," have been translated by Joan Stambaugh and appear in Heidegger, *The End of Philosophy*, New York: Harper & Row, 1973.

2 *The End of Philosophy*, pp. 65–6 (*Nietzsche* II, pp. 470–1). Stambaugh leaves words untranslated because, as I shall be saying later, Heidegger insists that the sounds of words matter, not just what they have in common with their translations in other languages. (In particular, he thinks that Cicero's translation into Latin of Plato's and Aristotle's Greek was a decisive turn in Western thought.) Nevertheless, I shall list the most common English translations of the Greek and Latin terms here. *Aletheia*, truth; *apeiron*, infinite; *logos*, word, reason, thought; *hen*, one; *arche*, principle; *physis*, nature (derived from *phyein*, to grow, to emerge); *idea*, idea in the Platonic sense of "Idea" of "Form," deriving from *idein*, to see, to perceive; *agathon*, the good; *energeia*, actuality (as opposed to potentiality) *en-echeta to telos*, having the end within it, having achieved its purpose (*entelechia* is a word sometimes used synonymously with *energeia* by Aristotle; it too is frequently translated as "actuality"); *hypokeimenon*, substrate (a term applied to matter when Aristotle is discussing metaphysics, and to the subject of predication when he is discussing logic), *ousia*, substance (but also a participle of the verb *einai*, "to be"); *ergon*, work, activity; *aet*, eternity; *hyperarchein*, to possess, or (in Aristotle's logic) to have as a property; *subiectum*, Latin translation of, and etymologically equivalent to, *hypokeimenon*, "substrate," but also, after Descartes, a word for "subject" in both senses, the subject of a sentence and the ego as subject of experience; *actualitas*, Latin translation of *energeia*, "actuality"; *creator*, creator; *ens creatum*, created being; *causa prima*, first cause; *ens a se*, being capable of existing by itself (i.e. God); *certitudo*, certitude; *res cogitans*, thinking thing (Descartes's term for the mind); *vis*, force, power; *monas*, monad (Leibniz's term for the ultimate components of the universe, non-spatiotemporal loci

of force, of perception (*perceptio*), of appetite (*appetitus*), and of a need to exist in order to express themselves (*exigentia essentiae*)). Heidegger offers, in one place or another in his writings, alternative translations of each of these terms, designed to restore their force by stripping them of their familiar connotations.

3 Heidegger, "Letter on humanism," in *Basic Writings* (hereafter abbreviated as *BW*), ed. David Krell, New York: Harper & Row, 1977, p. 194. The original is at Heidegger, *Wegmarken* (hereafter *WM*) 2nd edn, Frankfurt: Klostermann, 1978, p. 312.

4 Heidegger, "The end of philosophy and the task of thinking," *BW*, p. 386. The original is at Heidegger, *Zur Sache des Denkens*, Tübingen: Niemeyer, 1976, p. 74. See also Heidegger, *Nietzsche, Volume 4*, trans. Frank Capuzzi, New York: Harper & Row, 1982, p. 205; "*Metaphysics as metaphysics is nihilism proper*. The essence of nihilism is historically as metaphysics, and the metaphysics of Plato is no less nihilistic than that of Nietzsche." The original is at *Nietzsche* II, Pfullingen: Neske, 1961, p. 343.

5 "In the subjectness of the subject, will comes to appearance as the essence of subjectness. Modern metaphysics, as the metaphysics of subjectness, thinks the Being of that which is in the sense of will." Heidegger, "The word of Nietzsche," in *The Question Concerning Technology and Other Essays* (hereafter *QT*), trans. William Lovitt, New York: Harper & Row, 1977, p. 88. The original is at Heidegger, *Holzwege*, Frankfurt: Klostermann, 1972, p. 225. This quotation summarizes the transition, on the list above, from Being as Cartesian *subiectum* to Being as the Leibnizian *exigentia essentiae* within the monad, and thence to the Kantian conception of the non-phenomenal self as will under the aspect of practical reason. The notion of "will" is then reinterpreted by Hegel and Schelling in a way which quickly brings one to Nietzsche and Dewey. The same transition is formulated at *QT*, p. 128, by saying that with "man becoming subject," gradually "man becomes the relational center of all that is."

6 *QT*, pp. 129–30. *Holzwege*, p. 81.

7 Nietzsche, *The Will to Power*, trans. W. Kaufmann, New York: Random House, 1967, s. 584, p. 314.

8 I first learned how much of *Being and Time* can be read as a pragmatist tract from Robert Brandom's seminal "Heidegger's Categories in *Being and Time*," *Monist*, 66 (1983), 387–409.

9 Mark Okrent, *Heidegger's Pragmatism*, Ithaca, NY: Cornell University Press, 1988, p. 64. See also p. 123: "Husserl conceives of the fundamental form of intentionality as cognitive; Heidegger conceives of it as practical. As a result, Husserl thinks of the horizons in which beings are presented on the model of sensuous fields in which objects are placed before us for our intuitive apprehension, whereas Heidegger thinks of these horizons as fields of activity." One can substitute "the early Russell" or "the early Wittgenstein" for "Husserl," and "Dewey" or "the later Wittgenstein" for "Heidegger," in these sentences *salva veritate*. On Heidegger's conception of the relation between cognition and action, see Brandom, "Heidegger's Categories," pp. 405–6. Brandom notes that on the traditional, Platonic account "the only appropriate response to something present-at-hand is an assertion, the only use which can be made of assertion is inference, and inference is restricted to theoretical inference" whereas on the Heideggerian and pragmatist accounts "the only way in which the present-at-hand can affect Dasein's projects is by being the subject of an assertion which ultimately plays some role in practical inference."

10 The difference between pragmatists and non-pragmatists on this point comes out very clearly in an early criticism of Bradley by Dewey ("The Intellectualist Criterion for Truth," in *Middle Works*, Volume 4, pp. 50–75; the quotations that follow are from pp. 58–9). After quoting Bradley as saying "You may call the intellect, if you like, a mere tendency to a movement, but you must remember that it is a movement of a very special kind. . . . Thinking is

the attempt to satisfy a special impulse." Dewey comments: "The unquestioned presupposition of Mr Bradley is that thinking is such a wholly separate activity . . . that to give it autonomy is to say that it, and its criterion, having nothing to do with other activities . . ." Dewey argues that "intellectual discontent is the practical conflict becoming deliberately aware of itself as the most effective means of its own rectification." Compare Heidegger, *Being and Time* (hereafter *BT*), trans, Macquarrie and Robinson, New York: Harper & Row, 1962, p. 95: "The kind of dealing which is closest to us is . . . not a bare perceptual cognition, but rather that kind of concern which manipulates things and puts them to use" (the original is at *Sein und Zeit* (hereafter *SZ*), Tübingen: Niemeyer, 1963, p. 67). In Part I of the first volume of these papers, I criticize Bernard Williams for agreeing with Bradley about the autonomy of truth-seeking, about the distinction between theoretical inquiry and practical deliberation. The assumption of such autonomy is, I think essential to the intelligibility of Williams's notion of "the absolute conception of reality." The Heideggerian–Deweyan reply to Descartes and Williams on this topic is put by Brandom ("Heidegger's Categories," p. 403) as follows: "the move from equipment, ready-to-hand, fraught with socially instituted significances, to objective things present-at-hand, is not one of decontextualization but of recontextualization."

11 Heidegger, *BT*, p. 261, *SZ*, p. 219.
12 *BT*, p. 272, *SZ*, p. 230.
13 To be fair to Kierkegaard, he too realized that something other than power relations was needed to make sense of Christianity. See his claim that "the form of the servant was not something put on" in his discussion of the Incarnation as a solution to a loving God's need not to overwhelm the beloved sinner. *Philosophical Fragments*, trans. Howard and Edna Hong, Princeton, NJ: Princeton University Press, 1985, p. 32.
14 *BT*, p. 262, *SZ*, p. 220. Emphasis in the original.
15 This interpretation cheres with Heidegger's remark at *BT*, p. 23, (*SZ*, p. 41) about the easy intelligibility of "is" in "the sky is blue." He says that "here we have an average kind of intelligibility, which merely demonstrates that this is unintelligible."
16 On hearing, see *BT*, p. 228, (*SZ*, p. 183): "But Being 'is' only in the understanding of those entities to whose Being something like an understanding of Being belongs." Heidegger added a marginal note here which reads, "Understanding is to be taken here in the sense of 'hearing.' That does not mean that 'Being' is only 'subjective' but that Being (as the Being of beings) is 'in' Dasein as the trown in the throwing" (*SZ*, 15th edn, p. 443). I construe this passage in the light of the passage I quoted earlier about "the force of the most elementary words." See also *BT*, p. 209, (*SZ*, p. 163): "Hearing constitutes the primary and authentic way in which Dasein is open for its ownmost potentiality-for-Being – as in hearing the voice of the friend whom every Dasein carries with it."
17 Heidegger, *Poetry, Language, Thought*, trans. Albert Hofstadter, New York: Harper & Row, 1971, p. 4. The original is "*Wir kommen fü die Gotter zu Spät und zu früh für das Seyn. Dessen angefangenes Gedicht ist der Mensch.* Heidegger, *Aus der Erfahrung des Denkens*, Pfullingen: Neske, 1954, p. 7.
18 Heidegger often refuse to make a distinction between Dasein, the "Da" of Dasein, and the lighting-up of beings by Dasein's use of language to describe beings. See *BT*, p. 171 (*SZ*, p. 133); "To say that it [Dasein] is illuminated [*erleuchtet*] means that *as* Being-in-the-world it is cleared [*gelichtet*] in itself, not through any other entity, but in such a way that it is itself the clearing [*die Lichtung*]." But he also, especially in the later works, refuses to make a distinction between Dasein and Sein. Note the use of *Lichtung* in "Letter on Humanism" (*BW*, p. 216; *WM*, p. 333), where Heidegger says that "Being is essentially broader than *all* beings because it is the lighting [*Lichtung*] itself." When

Heidegger says, at the beginning of "Letter on Humanism," that "Language is the house of Being. In its home man dwells" (*BW*, p. 193; *WM*, p. 145), the suggestion that the two dwellers cannot be distinguished from one another is deliberate. The more you read later Heidegger, the more you realize that the distinctions between language, human beings, and Being are being deliberately and systematically blurred. I read this blurring as a warning, analogous to Wittgenstein's, against trying to get between language and its object, plus a further warning against trying to get between language and its user. In Heidegger's version, the warning says: if you try to come between them – if you try to make the user more than his or her words, and the object described more than its description in words, you risk winding up with some version of the Subject–Object or Human–Superhuman dualisms, and thus being condemned to think in terms of power relations between the terms of these dualisms. Though for purposes of *manipulating* them you may *have* to separate subject and object from each other, remember that there are other purposes than manipulation.

19 *BT*, p. 255.

20 In 1962 Heidegger suggests that he may have done too much redescribing, and needs to start ignoring: "a regard for metaphysics still prevails even in the intending to overcome metaphysics. Therefore our task is to cease all overcoming, and leave metaphysics to itself." *Of Time and Being*, trans. Joan Stambaugh, New York: Harper & Row, 1972, p. 24; *Zur Sache des Denkens*, p. 25. But by 1962 he had put in thirty years struggling to overcome – the years in which he wrote his most intriguing and provocative works.

21 For a fuller explicit definition of "final vocabulary" see my *Contingency, Irony, and Solidarity*, Cambridge: Cambridge University Press, 1989, p. 73. Chapter 4 of that book is a sort of long contextual definition of this term.

22 See Okrent, *Heidegger's Pragmatism*, p. 286: "It seems possible to raise the question of which language, which vocabulary, which intentional horizon is the right or correct one. In fact, this is the very question that metaphysics in Heidegger's sense was designed to raise and answer. . . . But according to both American neopragmatism and Heidegger as we have interpreted him, there is no determinate answer to this question, because being cannot be seen as grounding and justifying a particular intentional horizon." I agree with what Okrent says in this passage, but disagree with much of what he goes on to say at pp. 289–97 about the status of pragmatism as a doctrine. Okrent thinks that one should avoid "Heidegger's own desperate recourse to the view rhar assertions concerning the truth of being are not really assertions at all" (p. 292). I am not sure one should; if pragmatism is to be viewed as saying something about the "truth of Being" (a phrase which Okrent finds more intelligible than I do) then I should like it to take the form of a proposal ("Let's try it this way, and see what happens") rather than an assetion. My disagreement with Okrent here is connected with my doubts about Okrent's claim that "all pragmatism either must be based on a transcendental semantics or be self-contradictory" (p. 280). See Okrent's "The metaphilosophical consequences of pragmatism," in *The Institution of Philosophy*, ed. Avner Cohen and Marcello Dascal, Totowa, NJ: Rowman & Littlefield, 1988, for his defense of this latter claim and for criticism of some of my own views.

23 *BW*, p. 375; *Zur Sache des Denkens*, pp. 62–3.

24 Heidegger would of course deny this. But, as Okrent (*Heidegger's Pragmatism*, p. 223) notes, Heidegger "stubbornly refused to admit that he had changed his mind, made any crucial mistakes in earlier works, or significantly altered terminology over time."

25 "Letter on Humanism," *BW*, p. 221. The original is just as obscure as the English: "*was in einem erfüllten Sinn von Sein fetzt is* (*WM*, p. 338).

26 One should be clear that for Heidegger things like the danger of a nuclear holocaust, mass starvation because of overpopulation, and the like, are not indications that the time is par-

ticularly dark and dangerous. These merely ontic matters are not the sort of thing Heidegger has in mind when he say that "the wasteland spreads."

27 The ambiguity between these two alternatives is nicely expressed by a note which Heidegger inserted in the margin at *BT*, p. 28 (*SZ*, p. 8). Having said "This guiding activity of taking a look at Being arises from the average understanding of Being in which we always operate and *which in the end belongs to the essential constitution of Dasein itself* [*und das am Ende zur Wesensverfassung des Daseins selbst gehort*]," he glosses "in the end [*am Ende*]" with "that is, from the beginning [*d.h. von Anfangan*]." "*Am Ende*" would naturally have been read as meaning "in the nature of Dasein," but "*von Anfangan*" can be read as reminding us that Dasein does not have a nature, but only an historical existence. The question remains whether Heidegger earlier, at the time of writing *Being and Time*, did think that Dasein – not just Western Dasein – had a nature which Daseinsanalytik could expose, or whether he meant the indexical "Da" to express historicity even back then.

28 *BT*, p. 453; *SZ*, p. 402.

29 *BT*, p. 487; *SZ*, pp. 436–7.

30 Heidegger, *The Basic Problems of Phenomenology* (hereafter *BP*), trans. Albert Hofstadter, Bloomington: Indiana University Press, 1982, p. 23. The original is at Heidegger, *Gesamtausgabe*, Vol. 24: *Die Grundprobleme der Phäomenologie*, Frankfurt: Klostermann, 1975, p. 31.

31 *BP*, p. 10; *Die Grundprobleme*, pp. 12–13.

32 *BW*, p. 129; *WM*, p. 187.

33 See *BW*, p. 32; *WM*, p. 12. I take it that for *das Man*, for the ordinary person-in-the-street, for inauthentic Dasein, Being is *not* an issue. If Heidegger means that it is an issue even for inauthentic Dasein, then I have no grasp of what "being an issue" is, what it is *um dieses Sein selbst gehen*.

34 *BW*, p. 235; *WM*, p. 353.

35 *BW*, p. 236; *WM*, p. 354.

36 *BW*, p. 130; *WM*, p. 189.

37 *BW*, p. 131; *WM*, p. 190.

38 *BW*, p. 132; *WM*, p. 190.

39 *BW*, p. 138; *WM*, p. 196.

40 Dewey, *Reconstruction in Phikosophy*, Boston: Beacon Press, 1957, pp. 212–13.

41 The latter book is full of the kinds of criticisms of aestheticism which Heidegger himself makes. Heidegger would heartily agree with Dewey that "As long as art is the beauty parlor of civilization neither art nor civilization is secure," *Art as Experience*, New York: Putnam, 1958, p. 344. But Heidegger would not agree "that there is nothing in the nature of machine production *per se* that it is an insuperable obstacle in the way of worker consciousness of the meaning of what they do and work well done" (p. 343). Heidegger thought it in principle impossible that assembly line workers could have what Schwarzwald peasants had. Dewey had some ideas for arranging things so that they might. In *A Common Faith*, New Haven, CT: Yale University Press, 1934, Dewey praises "natural piety" for much the same reasons as Heidegger criticizes "humanism." See, for example, p. 53, in which both "supernaturalism" and "militant atheism" are condemned for lack of such piety, and for conceiving of "this earth as the moral center of the universe and of man as the apex of the whole scheme of things."

42 This preoccupation with philosophy made Heidegger ungrateful to the time in which he lived, unable to realize that it was thanks to living at a certain historical moment (after Wordsworth, Marx, Delacroix, and Rodin) – living in what he sneeringly called the age of the world picture – that he could paint his own picture, and find an appreciative audience for it.

43 See Derrida, "Differance," in *Margins of Philosophy*, trans. Alan Bass, Chicago: University of Chicago Press, 1982, p. 27. "From the vantage of this laughter and this dance, from the vantage of the affirmation foreign to all dialectics, the other side of nostalgia [cette autre face de la nostalgia], what I will call Heideggerian hope [esperance], comes into question."

Index